POSTCOLONIAL STUDIES

Now in its fourth edition, this popular A-Z guide provides a comprehensive overview of the issues which characterize postcolonialism: explaining what it is, where it is encountered and the crucial part it plays in debates about race, gender, politics, language and identity.

Fully revised and updated, the fourth edition contains more than 30 new entries, including:

- Anthropocene
- Biopolitics
- Decoloniality
- Ecocriticism
- Global South
- Postcolonial sciences
- Transnationalism.

With substantial updates to the further reading, *Postcolonial Studies: The Key Concepts* remains an essential guide for anyone studying this vibrant field.

Bill Ashcroft is Emeritus Professor at the University of New South Wales, Australia. He is a renowned critic and theorist, founding exponent of postcolonial theory, and author of 21 books and over 200 articles and chapters. He is co-editor of *The Postcolonial Studies Reader* (with Gareth Griffiths and Helen Tiffin); he is also co-author of *The Empire Writes Back* (also with Gareth Griffiths and Helen Tiffin), the first text to offer a systematic examination of the field of postcolonial studies.

Gareth Griffiths is Emeritus Professor and Honorary Senior Research Fellow at the University of Western Australia. He is a pioneer in the field of postcolonial studies. He has also written extensively on African literatures and theatre. He has authored and edited 15 books and more than a hundred articles and chapters.

Helen Tiffin is Adjunct Professor at the University of Wollongong, Australia. She has authored or edited 8 books and over 80 articles and chapters on postcolonial literatures, literary theory and animal and environmental subjects.

ROUTLEDGE KEY GUIDES

International Relations
The Key Concepts
Steven C. Roach and Alexander D. Barder

Fifty Key Theatre Designers
Arnold Aronson

Listening
The Key Concepts
Elizabeth S. Parks, Meara H. Faw and Laura R. Lane

Secular Religions
The Key Concepts
Tamás Nyirkos

Fifty Key Improv Performers
Actors, Troupes, and Schools from Theatre, Film, and TV
Matt Fotis

Fifty Key Scholars in Black Social Thought
Edited by Marie-Claude Jipguep-Akhtar and Nazneen M. Khan

Applied Theatre
The Key Concepts
Kay Hepplewhite

Music Business
The Key Concepts
Richard Strasser

Postcolonial Studies
The Key Concepts
Bill Ashcroft, Gareth Griffiths and Helen Tiffin

For a full list of titles in this series, please visit: https://www.routledge.com/
Routledge-Key-Guides/book-series/RKG

POSTCOLONIAL STUDIES

The Key Concepts

Fourth Edition

Bill Ashcroft, Gareth Griffiths and Helen Tiffin

Routledge
Taylor & Francis Group

LONDON AND NEW YORK

Designed cover image: Anna Pismenskova, Getty

Fourth edition published 2025
by Routledge
4 Park Square, Milton Park, Abingdon, Oxon, OX14 4RN

and by Routledge
605 Third Avenue, New York, NY 10158

Routledge is an imprint of the Taylor & Francis Group, an informa business

First edition published by Routledge 2000
Third edition published by Routledge 2013

British Library Cataloguing-in-Publication Data
A catalogue record for this book is available from the British Library

Library of Congress Cataloging-in-Publication Data
Names: Ashcroft, Bill, 1946– author. | Griffiths, Gareth, 1943– author. |
Tiffin, Helen, author.
Title: Postcolonial studies: the key concepts / Bill Ashcroft, Gareth Griffiths, and
Helen Tiffin.
Description: Fourth edition. | Abingdon, Oxon; New York, NY: Routledge, 2025. |
Series: Routledge key guides | First edition published by Routledge 2000; Third
edition published by Routledge 2013 — Title page verso. | Includes bibliographical
references and index. |
Identifiers: LCCN 2024033872 (print) | LCCN 2024033873 (ebook) |
ISBN 9781032805948 (hardback) | ISBN 9781032805917 (paperback) |
ISBN 9781003497561 (ebook)
Subjects: LCSH: Colonies—Dictionaries. | Decolonization—Dictionaries. |
Postcolonialism—Dictionaries. | Ethnic attitudes—Dictionaries. |
Race relations—Dictionaries.
Classification: LCC JV22 .A84 2025 (print) | LCC JV22 (ebook) |
DDC 325/.303—dc23/eng/20240724
LC record available at https://lccn.loc.gov/2024033872
LC ebook record available at https://lccn.loc.gov/2024033873

ISBN: 978-1-032-80594-8 (hbk)
ISBN: 978-1-032-80591-7 (pbk)
ISBN: 978-1-003-49756-1 (ebk)

DOI: 10.4324/9781003497561

Typeset in Bembo
by codeMantra

CONTENTS

Introduction to the Fourth Edition   vii
List of Key Concepts   ix

THE KEY CONCEPTS   1

Bibliography   363
Name Index   435
Subject Index   440

INTRODUCTION TO THE FOURTH EDITION

In the nearly three decades since *Key Concepts in Postcolonial Studies* was first published, the field has remained remarkably relevant within the moving landscape of cultural politics and power relations. As we noted in previous editions, political questions usually approached from the stand-points of nation-state relations, race, class, economics and gender are made clearer when we consider them in the context of their relations with the colonialist past. This is because the structures of power established by the colonizing process remain pervasive, though often hidden in cultural relations throughout the world. The prevalence of neo-liberalism and the significance of globalization reaffirm the importance of concepts that demonstrate the persistence of neo-colonial power.

This edition has included some classic terms that could have been included before, such as civilizing mission, East India Company, Charter Companies, Colonial Governance, the Scramble for Africa and Transnationalism, and several terms have been updated. But many new terms have entered the postcolonial vocabulary because of the historical significance and repercussions of European imperialism. This expansion of the number of terms relevant to the field indicates the continuing importance of a postcolonial perspective on global power relations and a reminder of the extent to which so much of the present world's reality has a prehistory in imperial intervention and control. The concept of postcolonial science, digital colonialism, patriarchy, precarity and postnationalism are just some of the 38 new terms included in this edition. The developments in climate science, indigenous identity and of course the radical increase in global mobility and xenophobia are reminders of the disruption that imperialism caused over the five centuries since the Spanish invasion of America.

LIST OF KEY CONCEPTS

Aboriginal/Indigenous Peoples 3
Abrogation   3
Affect   4
African American and
Postcolonial Studies   8
Agency   10
Allegory   10
Alterity   12
Ambivalence   13
Anthropocene   15
Anthropocentrism   18
Anti-Colonialism   19
Apartheid   21
Appropriation   23
Assimilation   24
Atavism   26
Authentic/Authenticity   27
Axial and Deontic   28
Bandung Conference   29
Binarism   32
Biocolonialism/Biopiracy   35
Biopolitics/Biopower   37
Black Atlantic   39
Bollywood   41
Black Studies/Black
Consciousness   44
Borderlands   46
Cannibal   47
Caribbean/West Indian   48
Cartography (Maps and
Mapping)   49

Catachresis   51
Catalysis   51
Centre/Margin (Periphery)   53
Charter Companies   54
Chimerican Age   59
Chromatism   60
Civilizing Mission   61
Clash of Civilizations   63
Class and Postcolonialism   66
Colonial Desire   70
Colonial Discourse   71
Colonial Governance   73
Colonial Patronage   77
Colonialism   78
Commodification   83
Commonwealth   85
Commonwealth Literature   85
Comprador   88
Contact Zone   89
Contrapuntal Reading   90
Conversion and the
Postcolonial   90
Cosmopolitanism   92
Counter Discourse   95
Creole (See Pidgins/
Creoles)   96
Creolization   97
Cultural Difference/Cultural
Diversity   98
Cultural Tourism   100
Decoloniality   102

Decolonization	106	Green Postcolonialism	177
Dependency Theory	109	Hegemony	178
Deracinate	110	Hybridity	179
Development/Development		Hyphenated Identity	183
Studies	111	Imperialism	184
Diaspora	114	Indentured Labour	188
Digital Colonialism	115	Independence	188
Discourse	118	Indigenous Mapping	190
Dislocation	120	Indigenous Sovereignty	191
Displacement	122	Interpellation	194
Double Colonization	124	Liminality	194
East India Company	124	Local	195
Ecocriticism	128	Lusotropicalism	197
Ecofeminism	128	Mabo Turn	199
Ecological Imperialism	131	Magic Realism	200
Empire	132	Manicheanism	201
Environmentalism	133	Mapping and the	
Epistemic Violence	135	Postcolonial	203
Essentialism/Strategic		Marginality	205
Essentialism	136	Mestizo/Mestizaje/	
Ethnicity	138	Mesticos/Metisse	206
Ethnography	142	Metonymic Gap	207
Ethno-Psychiatry/		Metropolis/Metropolitan	207
Ethno-Psychology	146	Middle Passage	209
Ethnoscapes	148	Migrants/Refugees/Asylum	
Ethnosymbolism	148	Seekers	209
Eurocentrism	149	Mimicry	211
Exile	151	Miscegenation	214
Exotic/Exoticism	153	Missions and Colonialism	215
Exploration and Travel	154	Modernism and	
Fanonism	157	Postcolonialism	216
Feminism and		Modernity	217
Postcolonialism	159	Mulatto	220
Filiation/Affiliation	162	Multiculturalism	220
First Nations	164	Multitude	222
Frontier	164	Nation Language	222
Fundamentalism	166	Nation/Nationalism	223
Global South	169	National Allegory	229
Globalization	170	National Liberation	
Glocalization	174	Movements	230
'Going Native'	176	Native	231

Nativism	232	Speciesism	313
Necropolitics	233	Subaltern	314
Négritude	235	Subject/Subjectivity	318
Neo-Colonialism/		Sustainability	323
Neo-Imperialism	236	Surveillance	324
Neo-Europes	239	Syncretism	326
Neo-Liberalism	239	Synergy	326
New Literatures	241	*Terra Nullius*	327
Orality	242	Testimonio	329
Orientalism	244	Third World (First, Second,	
Other	246	Fourth)	331
Othering	248	Trafficking	332
Palimpsest	249	Transculturation	335
Partition	251	Translects	336
Pastoralism	255	Translocal	336
Patriarchy	255	Transnation	338
Pidgins/Creoles	257	Transnational Literatures	340
Place	258	Translation	341
Postcolonial Body	263	Trauma	343
Postcolonialism	265	Universalism/Universality	344
Postcolonial Reading	270	Washington Consensus	346
Postcolonial Science	271	Whiteness	347
Postcolonial State	274	World Bank	350
Postcolony	275	World Englishes	352
Postnationalism	279	World Literature	355
Precarity/Precariat	282	World System Theory	356
Primitivism	284	Worlding	359
Race	285	Zoocriticism	360
Rastafarianism	292	Notes	361
Religion and the			
Postcolonial	293		
Resistance	296		
Rhizome	300		
Sacred/Sacral	301		
Savage/Civilized	302		
Scramble for Africa	304		
Settler	305		
Settler Colony	305		
Slave/Slavery	307		
Slow Violence	309		
Social Darwinism	311		

THE KEY CONCEPTS

ABORIGINAL/INDIGENOUS PEOPLES

Indigenous peoples are those 'born in a place or region' (OED). The term 'aboriginal' was coined as early as 1667 to describe the indigenous inhabitants of places encountered by European explorers, adventurers or seamen. While the terms 'aboriginal' and 'aborigine' have been used from time to time to describe the indigenous inhabitants of many **settler colonies**, they are now most frequently used as a shortened form of 'Australian Aborigine' to describe the indigenous inhabitants of Australia. The adjective 'aboriginal' has been more frequently used as the generic noun in recent times, the term 'aborigine' being considered by many to be too burdened with derogatory associations. Furthermore, the feeling that the term fails to distinguish and discriminate among the great variety of peoples who were lumped together generically as 'aborigines' by the colonial white settlers has been resisted with the assertion of special, local terms for different peoples and/or language groups such as the use of South-Eastern Australian terms like Koori, Queensland terms such as Murri and Western Australian terms such as Nyoongah. So far, though, no single term has been accepted as a general term by all the various peoples concerned, and the generic term most frequently used for the descendants of all precolonial indigenes is 'Australian Aboriginal peoples'.

In the Americas, the term 'aborigines' gained currency as a generic term for indigenous peoples as it did in Australia. Terms such as 'Indian' and later 'Amerindian', which, like Aboriginal in Australia, accrued derogatory connotations, were employed by settler-invaders (and their descendants). In the twentieth century, terms generated by indigenous peoples themselves, such as 'First Nations' and 'Native Americans', have replaced the older settler-invader nomenclatures. The term has also been, and is still used to describe the descendants of the earliest inhabitants of other regions, such as the 'orang asli' of Malaysia and Indonesian Borneo (Kalimantan) or the original inhabitants of the Indian sub-continent now referred to as the 'scheduled tribes' and Andaman Islanders (see **First Nations, Settler Colony, Third World**.)

ABROGATION

Abrogation refers to the rejection by postcolonial writers of a normative concept of 'correct' or 'standard' English used by certain classes or groups, and of the corresponding concepts of inferior 'dialects' or 'marginal variants'. The concept is usually employed in conjunction with the term **appropriation**, which describes the processes of English adaptation itself, and is an important component of the postcolonial assumption that all language use is a 'variant' of one kind or another (and is in that sense 'marginal' to some illusory standard). Thus abrogation is an important political stance, whether articulated or not, and even whether conscious or not, from which the actual appropriation of language can take place.

In arguing for the parity of all forms of English, abrogation offers a counter to the theory that use of the colonialist's language inescapably imprisons the colonized within the colonizer's conceptual paradigms – the view that 'you can't dismantle the master's house with the master's tools'. Abrogation implies rather that the master's house is always adaptable and that the same tools offer a means of conceptual transformation and liberation.

Although abrogation has been used to describe the rejection of a standard language in the writing of postcolonial literatures, it can, like **appropriation**, be used to describe a great range of cultural and political activities – film, theatre, the writing of history, political organization and modes of thought and argument. Individuals who are involved in these things may abrogate any centralizing notion of the 'correct', or standard, way of doing things and re-define the practice in a different setting.

Further Reading: Ashcroft et al. 2002; Ziff and Rao 1997.

AFFECT

Affect is one of the three divisions described in modern psychology: the cognitive, the conative and the affective, and refers to the domain of non-cognitive experience that includes feelings, emotions and other autonomic responses to stimuli. It is useful for describing a dimension of human response existing below or beyond the level of representation, yet deeply operative in people's experience of the world. The field of Affect Studies has grown rapidly in the humanities and social sciences because many theorists believe that philosophers and critics have historically overvalued the role of reason in politics, ethics and aesthetics. Consequently 'they have given too flat or "unlayered" or disembodied an account of the ways in which people actually form their political opinions and judgments' (Leys 2011: 436). The result has been a growing awareness of the role of the non-rational and non-cognitive in human attitudes, responses and decision-making. For instance, Nigel Thrift states that:

> The envelope of what we call the political must increasingly expand to take note of 'the way that political attitudes and statements are partly conditioned by intense autonomic bodily reactions that do not simply reproduce the trace of a political intention and cannot be wholly recuperated within an ideological regime of truth'.
>
> (Thrift 2004: 64)

There is, however, no stable definition of affect and most commentators insist that the term is not synonymous with emotion. The term 'affect' can be taken to indicate an instinctual reaction to stimulation occurring before the typical cognitive processes considered necessary for the formation of a more complex emotion. Massumi, widely credited with emphasizing the distinction between affect and emotion, defines affect as 'a nonsignifying, nonconscious "intensity" disconnected from the subjective, signifying, functional-meaning axis to which the more familiar categories of emotion belong. Affect is most often used loosely as a synonym for emotion. But... emotion and affect—if affect is intensity—follow different logics and pertain to different orders' (Massumi 2002: 27).

Shouse follows Massumi by remarking that

> it is important not to confuse affect with feelings and emotions.... Affect is not a personal feeling. Feelings are personal and biographical, emotions are social,... and affects are pre-personal.... An affect is a nonconscious experience of intensity; it is a moment of unformed and unstructured potential.... Affect cannot be fully realised in language... because affect is always prior to and/or outside consciousness.... Affect is the body's way of preparing itself for action in a given circumstance by adding a quantitative dimension of intensity to the quality of an experience. The body has a grammar of its own that cannot be fully captured in language.
>
> (Shouse 2005: 5)

Zajonc suggests affective reactions can occur without extensive perceptual and cognitive encoding, and can be made sooner and with greater confidence than cognitive judgements (Zajonc 1980). In short 'affects are biologically located and experienced, but socially responsive and culturally modulated' (Sharrad 2012: 56). In her analysis of affect, Ruth Leys asserts that

> what fundamentally binds together the new affect theorists and the neuroscientists is their shared anti-intentionalism. My claim is that whatever differences of philosophical-intellectual orientation there may be among the new affect theorists themselves, and between them and the neuroscientists whose findings they wish to appropriate (differences do of course exist), the important point to recognize is that they all share a single belief: the belief that affect is independent of signification and meaning.
>
> (Leys 2011: 443)

The realm of the political may be the first way in which affect becomes useful for postcolonial studies.

Affect has always been a key element of politics and the subject of numerous powerful political technologies which have knotted thinking, technique and affect together in various potent combinations. One example is the marshalling of aggression through various forms of military trainings such as drill... In the neo-Darwinian universe, affect is a deep-seated physiological change written involuntarily on the face. How might we think of the politics of affect, given that these different notions would seem to imply different cues and even ontologies? (Thrift 2004: 64).

Affect studies, and particularly the technologies used in directing various affective responses may be useful in understanding the ways in which cultural hegemony works in imperial dominance. In many respects, the operation of cultural hegemony, much like Althusser's explanation of ideology, depends to a large extent on the non-rational and non-cognitive. For Thrift, this is

> part and parcel of why it is so crucial to address affect now: in at least one guise the discovery of new means of practicing affect is also the discovery of a whole new means of manipulation by the powerful.
>
> (58)

This means may not be so new when we consider the long-standing operation of imperial cultural hegemony – certainly in the British

Empire and particularly through literature (Viswanathan). But it may well offer a new way of approaching the issue. Identification with a dominant and oppressive force remains to some extent a mystery in that it appears, in general, to conflict with the colonized subject's best interests. This may also offer a useful direction of study for the function of affect in postcolonial literatures in particular.

On the other hand, affect may provide a useful category for considering forms of resistance, particularly those examples that Bhabha refers to as 'sly civility'. He takes the term from an 1818 sermon by Archdeacon Potts:

> If you urge them with their gross and unworthy misconceptions of the nature and the will of God, or the monstrous follies of their fabulous theology, they will turn it off with a sly civility perhaps, or with a popular and careless proverb.
>
> (1994: 99)

Bhabha describes this 'off-turning' response as 'the native refusal to satisfy the colonizer's narrative demand', a frustration of the imperial strategy of surveillance. But 'sly civility' may be regarded as a sophisticated affective response that in its ambivalence – outward compliance and inner resistance – may be far more effective in its evasion than overt resistance.

A significant feature of Affect studies has been the question of the cultural basis of affect. The postcolonial approach to affect asks 'to what extent we can think meaningfully about affect outside the concepts and terms of European psychoanalysis'? (Gunew 2009: 15) In an examination of praise in Hindu culture Appadurai argues that the Western 'topography of the self' with its distinction of 'inner states' and 'outer forms' is specifically Western, and room needs to be made for alternative topographies of the self (1990: 93). Appadurai suggests that engagement with creative works occurs within affective communities. However, understood as a pre-conscious intensity, in Massumi's terms, affect may be significant in cross-cultural aesthetic engagements of the kind generated by postcolonial creative production, where affective response to the phenomenon of the visual or aural text occurs prior to 'understanding'.

Further Reading: Angel 2005; Appadurai 1990; Ashcroft et al. 2012; Brennan 2004a, 2004b; Clough and Halley 2007; Gunew 2009;

Leys 2011; Massumi 2002; McCormack 2007; Reddy 2001; Shouse 2005; Sharrad 2012; Solomon 1995; Thrift 2004; Wilson 2004; Zajonc 1980.

AFRICAN AMERICAN AND POSTCOLONIAL STUDIES

Recent work in postcolonial studies by U.S. scholars has stressed the relationship between postcolonial theory and the analysis of African American culture (DuCille 1996). In practice, the exponents of African American culture have often engaged with classic postcolonial theorists such as Fanon, though not always in an uncritical way. African American studies has been one of the most influential of recent intellectual, social and political movements, not only affecting the United States but also influencing many people who have suffered oppression from racial discrimination in other parts of the world. It has had a widespread and often quite separate development from postcolonial studies, to which it is related only in a complex and ambiguous way.

Most postcolonial theorists who have engaged with the issue have seen the study of black culture in the Americas as, in part, the study of one of the world's major **diasporas**. In this respect, the history of African Americans has some features in common with other movements of oppressed diasporic peoples. Many groups were moved against their will from their homelands to serve the economic needs of empire in the societies that evolved from the wave of European expansion from the sixteenth century onwards. Comparative studies of these movements are a productive development in recent postcolonial theory, not least in the consideration of the different effects of these large-scale events on individual groups that such studies reveal.

Early formulations of African American studies in the United States and elsewhere reflected the complex relationship between the African source cultures and their adopted societies, as they interacted with other influences in the new regions to which Africans were taken (see **négritude**). The fact that the bulk of African peoples were shipped under conditions of **slavery** makes the relationship between that institution and the wider practices of imperialism central to an understanding of the origins of African American culture. It also sheds light on the violence that was often hidden beneath the civilizing rhetoric of imperialism (DuCille 1996). Beyond this prime fact of oppression and violence, however, the relationships between the newly independent American societies, the wider diasporic black movement and the modern independence movements in Africa itself, remain complex.

The history of the struggle for self-determination by African Americans is historically intertwined with wider movements of diasporic African struggles for independence. For example, figures like Jamaican-born Marcus Garvey assumed a central role in the American struggle for self-determination. The 'Back to Africa' movement that he initiated, and which has affinities with the modern West Indian movement of **Rastafarianism**, supported the various movements to return African Americans to Africa. The national flag of Liberia, which was founded specifically to facilitate the return of freed black slaves to their 'native' continent, still bears the single star of Garvey's Black Star Shipping Company. In addition, many of the dominant figures in early African nationalism, such as Alexander Crummell, were ex-slaves or the children of slaves who had their ideas formed in the struggle for African American freedom (see de Moraes-Farias and Barber 1990; Appiah 1992).

Of course, African American studies are also concerned much more directly with the history and continuing effects of specific processes of race-based discrimination within US society. In this regard, African American studies investigates issues that share certain features with other US groups affected by racial discrimination, such as the Chicano community. These studies have relevance to movements for the freedom of **indigenous** peoples, such as Native American Indians or Inuit peoples, despite their very different historical backgrounds (one group being victims of invasive settlement and the other of slavery and exile). Distinctions also need to be made between these various groups and linguistically and racially discriminated groups such as Chicanos, a great many of whom are part of a more recent wave of immigration, though some, of course, are the descendants of peoples who lived in parts of the United States long before the current dominant Anglo-Saxon peoples. Other groups, such as the descendants of French Creoles, also occupy places contiguous in some respects to these latter Spanish-speaking peoples, though their history and their treatment within US society may have been very different. For this, and other reasons, critics have often hesitated to conflate African American studies or the study of any of these other groups with postcolonial theory in any simple way. The latter may offer useful insights, but it does not subsume the specific and distinctive goals and history of African American studies or Native American studies or Chicano studies as distinctive academic disciplines with specific political and social struggle in their own right.

Further Reading: DuCille 1996; Flint 2006; Gòkè-Paríolá 1996; Gruesser 2005; Hanchard 1997; McInturff 2000; Mostern 2000; Olson and Worsham 1999; Schueller 2003; Singh and Schmidt 2000; Wise 1995; Zeigler 1996; Zeigler and Osinubi 2012.

AGENCY

Agency refers to the ability to act or perform an action. In contemporary theory, it hinges on the question of whether individuals can freely and autonomously initiate action, or whether the things they do are in some sense determined by the ways in which their identity has been constructed. Agency is particularly important in postcolonial theory because it refers to the ability of postcolonial subjects to initiate action in engaging or resisting imperial power. The term has become an issue in recent times as a consequence of post-structuralist theories of **subjectivity**. Since human subjectivity is constructed by ideology (Althusser), language (Lacan) or discourse (Foucault), the corollary is that any action performed by that subject must also be to some extent a consequence of those things. For the colonial discourse theory of Bhabha and Spivak, which concurs with much of the post-structuralist position on subjectivity, the question of agency has been a troublesome one. However, many theories in which the importance of political action is paramount take agency for granted.

Theorists such as Said suggest that although it may be difficult for subjects to escape the effects of those forces that 'construct' them, it is not impossible. While *Orientalism* owes a debt to Foucault's concept of a discourse, Said is clear about the capacity of the colonized to resist (see **counter discourse**).

The very fact that such forces may be recognized suggests that they may also be countermanded.

Further Reading: Ashcroft 1994; Bhabha 1994; Fanon 1952; Parry 1987, 1994; Slemon 1994; Leonard 2005; Werbner and Stoller 2002.

ALLEGORY

The simplest definition of allegory is a 'symbolic narrative' in which the major features of the movement of the narrative are all held to refer symbolically to some action or situation. Allegory has long been a prominent feature of literary and mythic writing throughout the world, but it becomes particularly significant for postcolonial writers for the way in which it disrupts notions of orthodox history, classical realism and imperial representation in general. Allegory has assumed an important function in imperial discourse, in which paintings and statues have often been created as allegories of imperial power. Consequently, one form of postcolonial response to this has been to **appropriate** allegory and use it to respond to the allegorical representation of imperial dominance.

Fredric Jameson made a controversial suggestion, in 'Third World Literature in the era of multi-national capitalism' (1986), that all Third World literatures, indeed all Third World cultural constructions, are 'necessarily' **national allegories**. Aijaz Ahmad vigorously criticized the homogenizing nature of this statement (Ahmad 1992). But Stephen Slemon suggested that what is really wrong with the suggestion is that it simply takes a Eurocentric literary notion of allegory and applies it to colonized societies. Slemon suggests that we might rather see allegory as a function of the 'conditions of postcoloniality'. This is because allegory has always been a dominant mode of colonial representation and therefore becomes a particularly valuable form in which postcolonial literature may conduct forms of counter discourse.

This means, firstly, that postcolonial cultures may use allegory to 'read' the text of colonialism (Slemon 1987a: 11). So much of the life of the colonized subject has been constructed by, that is, metaphorically 'written' by, colonialism that allegory becomes a way in which such writing may be contested. But there are many other ways in which allegory has been used by postcolonial writers. One group of postcolonial allegories, such as Ayi Kwei Armah's 'An African fable', for example, seeks to contest colonialist or Eurocentric notions of history. In other texts, such as Lamming's *Natives of My Person*, or Coetzee's *Waiting for the Barbarians*, allegory is employed to expose the ways in which the allegorical form is used in the colonizing process. Thus, in the Coetzee text, for example, the life of a magistrate isolated on the boundaries of an unnamed empire, and his peaceful relations with the people beyond the boundary, is disrupted when they are reclassified as 'barbarians' by the visit of an egregious secret policeman. This causes the magistrate to realize for the first time the full truth about the society in which he lives. Although such texts do not deal directly with specific colonial situations, they present a powerful allegory of underlying colonial ideology.

In other texts again, such as Randolph Stow's *Tourmaline* or Kofi Awoonor's *This Earth My Brother*, the use of the allegorical form seeks to replace monolithic traditions with a cross-cultural pluralism. In Stow's novel, for example, the small Western Australian mining town of Tourmaline is opened up to a perspective that places it in an older landscape of the Dreaming traditions of Australian Aboriginal cultures. The limited world of the small white town is framed by the huge forces of desert and sky, not merely as back-drops, but as symbols of a different and more integrated way of conceiving of the human relationship with nature and the natural world. In these latter cases, a 'postcolonial' allegory contests and disrupts the narrative assumptions of colonialism, such as the inevitability of 'development', of 'progress', of 'civilization', the dominance of the chronological view of history, the Eurocentric view of 'the real'. By reinforcing the fact that 'real' events occupy various horizons of meaning, postcolonial allegory becomes a common strategy of resistance in postcolonial texts.

Further Reading: Ahmad 1992, 1995a; Buchanan 2003; Franco 1997; Hulme 2005; Jameson 1986; San Juan 1996; Schmidt 2000; Slemon 1987a; Szeman 2006.

ALTERITY

Alterity is derived from the Latin *alteritas*, meaning 'the state of being other or different; diversity, otherness'. Its English derivatives are alternate, alternative, alternation and alter ego. The term alterité is more common in French and has the antonym identité (Johnson and Smith 1990: xviii).

The term was adopted by philosophers as an alternative to 'otherness' to register a change in the Western perceptions of the relationship between consciousness and the world. Since Descartes, individual consciousness had been taken as the privileged starting point for consciousness, and 'the "other" appears in these [post-Enlightenment] philosophies as a reduced "other", as an epistemological question' (xix). That is, in a concept of the human in which everything stems from the notion that 'I think, therefore I am', the chief concern with the other is to be able to answer questions, such as 'How can I know the other'? and 'How can other minds be known'? The term 'alterity' shifts the focus of analysis away from these philosophic concerns with other-ness – the 'epistemic other', the other that is only important to the extent to which it can be known – to the more concrete 'moral other'– the other who is actually located in a political, cultural, linguistic or religious context (xix). This is a key feature of changes in the concept of **subjectivity**, because, whether seen in the context of ideology, psychoanalysis or discourse, the 'construction' of the subject itself can be seen to be inseparable from the construction of its others.

Literary theorists commonly see the most influential use of alterity in Mikhail Bakhtin's description of the way in which an author moves away from identification with a character (Todorov 1984). The novelist must understand his or her character from within, as it were, but must also perceive it as other, as apart from its creator in its distinct alterity. Importantly, dialogue is only possible with an 'other', so alterity, in Bakhtin's formulation, is not simply 'exclusion', but an apartness that stands as a precondition of dialogue, where dialogue implies a transference across and between differences of culture, gender, class and other social categories. This is related to his concept of 'exotopy' or 'outsideness', which is not simply alienness, but a precondition for the author's ability to understand and formulate a character, a precondition for dialogue itself.

In postcolonial theory, the term has often been used interchangeably with otherness and difference. However, the distinction that initially held between otherness and alterity – that between otherness as a philosophic problem and otherness as a feature of a material and discursive location – is peculiarly applicable to postcolonial discourse. The self-identity of the colonizing subject, indeed the identity of imperial culture, is inextricable from the alterity of colonized others, an alterity determined, according to Spivak, by a process of othering. The possibility for potential dialogue between racial and cultural others has also remained an important aspect of the use of the word, which distinguishes it from its synonyms.

Further Reading: Bhabha 1984b; Fazzini 2004; Harris 2004; Johnson and Smith 1990; Slemon 1987b; Taussig 1993; Todorov 1984.

AMBIVALENCE

A term first developed in psychoanalysis to describe a continual fluctuation between wanting one thing and wanting its opposite. It also refers to a simultaneous attraction towards and repulsion from an object, person or action (Young 1995: 161). Adapted into colonial discourse theory by Homi Bhabha, it describes the complex mix of attraction and repulsion that characterizes the relationship between colonizer and colonized. The relationship is ambivalent because the colonized subject is never simply and completely opposed to the colonizer. Rather than assuming that some colonized subjects are 'complicit' and some 'resistant', ambivalence suggests that complicity and resistance exist in a fluctuating relation within the colonial subject. Ambivalence also characterizes the way in which colonial discourse relates to the colonized subject, for it may be both exploitative and nurturing, or represent itself as nurturing, at the same time.

Most importantly in Bhabha's theory, however, ambivalence disrupts the clear-cut authority of colonial domination because it disturbs the simple relationship between colonizer and colonized. Ambivalence is therefore an unwelcome aspect of colonial discourse for the colonizer. The problem for colonial discourse is that it wants to produce compliant subjects who reproduce its assumptions, habits and values – that is, 'mimic' the colonizer. But instead, it produces ambivalent subjects whose **mimicry** is never very far from mockery. Ambivalence describes this fluctuating relationship between mimicry and mockery, an ambivalence that is fundamentally unsettling to colonial dominance. In this respect, it is not necessarily disempowering for the colonial subject but rather can be seen to be ambi/valent or 'two-powered'. The effect of this ambivalence (the simultaneous attraction and repulsion) is to produce a profound disturbance of the authority of colonial discourse.

Ambivalence therefore gives rise to a controversial proposition in Bhabha's theory, that because the colonial relationship is always ambivalent, it generates the seeds of its own destruction. This is controversial because it implies that the colonial relationship is going to be disrupted, regardless of any resistance or rebellion on the part of the colonized. Bhabha's argument is that colonial discourse is compelled to be ambivalent because it never really wants colonial subjects to be exact replicas of the colonizers – this would be too threatening. For instance, he gives the example of Charles Grant, who, in 1792, desired to inculcate the Christian religion in Indians, but worried that this might make them 'turbulent for liberty' (Bhabha 1994: 87). Grant's solution was to mix Christian doctrines with divisive caste practices to produce a 'partial reform' that would induce an empty imitation of English manners. Bhabha suggests that this demonstrates the conflict within imperialism itself that will inevitably cause its own downfall: it is compelled to create an ambivalent situation that will disrupt its assumption of monolithic power.

Robert Young has suggested that the theory of ambivalence is Bhabha's way of turning the tables on imperial discourse. The periphery, which is regarded as 'the borderline, the marginal, the unclassifiable, the doubtful' by the centre, responds by constituting the centre as an 'equivocal, indefinite, indeterminate ambivalence' (1995: 161). But this is not a simple reversal of a binary, for Bhabha shows that both colonizing and colonized subjects are implicated in the ambivalence of colonial discourse. The concept is related to **hybridity** because, just as ambivalence 'decentres' authority from its position of power, so that authority may also become hybridized when placed in a colonial context in which it finds itself dealing with, and often inflected by, other cultures. The hybridity of Charles Grant's suggestion above, for instance, can be seen as a feature of its ambivalence. In this respect, the very engagement of colonial discourse with those colonized cultures over which it has domination, inevitably leads to an ambivalence that disables its monolithic dominance.

Further Reading: Bhabha 1984a, 1985, 1996; Burton 2004; Papastergiadis 1996; Young 1995.

ANTHROPOCENE

The term Anthropocene is used to describe the period when human activity became the dominant influence on climate and environment. Although increasingly accepted by scientists as an effective if still unofficial unit of time, there is still considerable disagreement as to when it began and what its defining moments were. Some would place it back many thousands of years and relate it to the development of agriculture, making it a new way of conceiving and defining the official geological era known as the Holocene, so dating it to the time of the last ice age. Others place it much more recently and link it to the rise of the industrial revolution (Crutzen and Stoermer 2000). The reason for doing this is the evidence for dramatic changes to the atmosphere and to global temperatures linked to the increase of polluting agents resulting from the development of machinery and machine-driven industrial processes. The rise of the use of fossil fuels to power industry and the massive increase in transportation of both people and goods is also a feature of this period and increasingly recognized as one of the causes for these changes.

As well as the effect on climate, the development of larger urban conglomerations, as human populations increased exponentially after industrialization, had a deleterious effect on biodiversity, with massive shrinkage in population numbers in the non-human species and increasing numbers of animal species extinctions. Plant life too has seen similar extinctions of specific plants, as well as the loss of old growth forests worldwide. Much of this is the result of massive tree clearance to allow large-scale single-crop planting on an industrial scale (monoculture farming). Some scientists have suggested that we are now experiencing what they call the sixth great extinction in the planet's history, and the first one caused not by natural processes, or events such as asteroid strikes, but by the behaviour of a single species, human beings. (Barnosky 2011) Attempts to further define the changes have led to the suggestion that in the period following the Second World War (1939–1945), there was what has been called a Great Acceleration of such change. This is characterized by rapid population growth, much greater exploitation of natural resources and much increased pollution.

For some commentators, the initiation of the Anthropocene followed directly from the colonial enterprise, which is a central feature of the era:

> Colonialism and capitalism have remade the planet drastically and pushed us towards the crises we are beset with today. Instead, of an undifferentiated *anthropos*, a particular section of the human species that benefited historically from colonialism and capitalism are at the root of the Anthropocene crisis.
>
> (Baishya and Kumar 2022)

Colonial enterprises 'placed tremendous pressures on long-standing anthropogenic landscapes leading to significant modifications with the invasion of foreign species, the disruption of native habitats, the extermination of keystone species and in some cases the loss of biodiversity' (Lightfoot et al. 2013: 1). For these commentators, the stress on the industrial revolution as the start of the Anthropocene era neglects the fact that that revolution was preceded by and stimulated by colonization. Modern globalization, they argue, has its roots in the global exploitation of resources that colonization brought into being (see **globalization**). It was this exploitive pressure on poorer countries that exacerbated their environmental decay and 'transformed existing anthropogenic landscapes created by indigenous peoples' (Lightfoot et al. 2013: 1–2). Climate change and the decline in biodiversity, the destruction of natural habitats, the loss of diverse agricultural cropping to accommodate large-scale monoculture and the disruptive activities of mining and resource extraction has had an especially deleterious effect on the poorer communities of the world, most of whom had been colonized when these destructive processes were initiated. For this reason, the term has been seen as increasingly influential in postcolonial studies which examine the uneven effect of these changes to climate, biodiversity etc. on these postcolonial communities (Nixon 2011; see **slow violence**).

But the concept of the Anthropocene has also been subject to more radical negative criticism by postcolonial scholars and theorists of decoloniality such as Sylvia Wynter. Wynter does not dispute that human activities have had a major effect on the planet, especially since the mid-eighteenth century when industrialization began, but she too draws attention to the fact that this period coincides with the development of colonization. She notes too that the period of the Great Acceleration coincides with the period of decolonization. The danger she sees in the concept is that just as colonized peoples were becoming politically independent, the Anthropocene concept threatens to

> *reincorporate* us neo colonially, and thereby mimetically, by telling us that the problem with us *wasn't* that we'd been imperially subordinated, *wasn't* that we'd been both socioculturally dominated and economically exploited, but that we were *underdeveloped*. The West said: 'Oh, well, no longer be a *native* but come and be Man like us! Become *homo oeconomicus!*'
>
> (Wynter 2015)

For Wynter, the unproblematic assertion of the idea of the human as universally defined by the European scientific definitions of the nineteenth century as a secular concept (*homo oeconomicus*) excludes the many other models by which different cultures have conceived of the human. So, for some postcolonial critics, the idea of the Anthropocene erases the crucial feature of postcolonial differences (see **difference**).

These negative postcolonial critiques draw attention to the historical antecedents of the recent theories of the Anthropocene and argue that they 'unwittingly [reproduce] centuries-old Eurocentric assumptions but also that [the Anthropocene's] onto-epistemological underpinnings serve to discredit and delegitimize ways of understanding contemporary conditions that are less thoroughly grounded in the narratives of Western modernity' (Simpson 2020) (see **Eurocentrism**). Similar issues are raised by recent postcolonial critiques of the claims of science and technology to be value-free and not constructed within the specific cultural and political formations of colonization (see **postcolonial science**).

Thus, the Anthropocene is not simply about climate and environmental change but is deeply imbricated with the historical force of colonialism. Recognizing this allows us, these critics of the concept argue, to see beyond it as a deterministic theory of the future and opens the possibilities of multiple and diverse human responses to the challenges it raises for the future/futures of different human societies. These critics have suggested that the term should be seen not as closing but as opening a debate on the causes of the changes it defines and suggest that there may be more ways of defining and even of naming these significant events (Haraway 2015).

Further Reading: Crutzen and Stoermer 2000; Barnosky 2011; Nixon 2011; Wynter 2015; Baishya and Kumar 2022; Simpson 2020; Haraway 2015.

ANTHROPOCENTRISM

Anthropocentrism (not to be confused with anthropomorphism) literally means 'regarding man as the central fact of the universe' (OED), including the interpretation of reality exclusively in terms of human values, and most human societies, particularly monotheistic societies, it may be argued, have done so. The attitude is summed up in the words of the Greek philosopher Protagoras: 'Man is the measure of all things'. Some societies, such as North American and Australian Aboriginal cultures, while still prioritizing human interests have nevertheless regarded themselves as existing not just within, but through the extra-human biosphere of animals, plants and the earth itself. For many, a human being is solely constituted by such relationships.

A key period in the emerging dominance of anthropocentrism was the Enlightenment, when the universe was seen to be human rather than theocentric. This focus has constituted a primary moral perspective of **Western modernity**. In the consequent Western colonization of the globe, as Val Plumwood has argued, anthropocentrism and Eurocentrism were so closely aligned as to be at times almost inseparable. Europeanization occasionally imposed, was, much more significantly, hegemonic, its influence persisting from colonial to post-independence eras. The 'dualistic thinking' that provides much of the foundation for anthropocentrism still informs attitudes to the environment as it once helped to secure and sustain European imperial dominance. This, Plumwood shows, now proves ruinous in the face of mass extinctions and fast approaching 'biophysical limits of the planet' (Plumwood 2001: 5). For cultures whose foundational ontology was bioshpheric, the result has unsurprisingly been anomie and annihilation.

Further Reading: Huggan and Tiffin 2010; Plumwood 2001.

ANTI-COLONIALISM

The political struggle of colonized peoples against the specific ideology and practice of colonialism (see **colonization**). Anti-colonialism signifies the point at which the various forms of opposition become articulated as a resistance to the operations of colonialism in political, economic and cultural institutions. It emphasizes the need to reject colonial power and restore local control. Paradoxically, anti-colonialist movements often expressed themselves in the appropriation and subversion of forms borrowed from the institutions of the colonizer and turned back on them. Thus the struggle was often articulated in terms of a discourse of anti-colonial 'nationalism' in which the form of the modern European nation-state was taken over and employed as a sign of resistance (see **nation/nationalism**). The sometimes arbitrary arrangements of colonial governance – such as the structures of public administration and forums for local political representation – became the spaces within which a discourse of anti-colonial nationalism was focused and a demand for an independent postcolonial nation-state was formed (see Anderson 1983; Chatterjee 1986, 1993).

Anti-colonialism has taken many forms in different colonial situations; it is sometimes associated with an ideology of racial liberation, as in the case of nineteenth-century West African nationalists such as Edward Wilmot Blyden and James Africanus Horton (ideologies that might be seen as the precursors of twentieth-century movements such as **négritude**). Conversely, it may accompany a demand for a recognition of cultural differences on a broad and diverse front, as in the Indian National Congress which sought to unite a variety of ethnic groups with different religious and racial identities in a single, national independence movement.

In the second-half of the twentieth century, anti-colonialism was often articulated in terms of a radical, Marxist discourse of liberation, and in constructions that sought to reconcile the internationalist and anti-élitist demands of Marxism with the nationalist sentiments of the period (National Liberation Fronts), in the work and theory of early national liberationist thinkers, such as C.L.R. James, Amilcar Cabral and Frantz Fanon, (see **Fanonism, national liberation**). Such anti-colonial, national liberation movements developed the Marxist idea of a revolutionary cadre to explain the crucial role of the European (colonial) educated intelligentsia in the anti-colonial struggle. These movements argued that the peasant/proletarian needed to be led to a practice of liberation – through various stages of local and national affiliation – by a bourgeois élite who would eventually, in Cabral's dramatic formulation, 'commit suicide' by developing a popular and local social practice in which they would be assimilated.

Cabral, in particular, developed this idea of the need to empower and recognize the local as a specific and distinct feature of postcolonial politics in ways that radicalized the more rigid and orthodox practices of post-Stalinist Marxist thought. Unlike later nationalist formulations of the new bourgeois post-independence élites, however, there is here no sentimental or mythologized attachment to an idealized precolonial condition. The local is perceived to be fully corrigible and involved in an inevitable process of historical change:

> the working masses and in particular the peasants, who are usually illiterate and have never moved beyond the boundaries of their village or their region, come into contact with other groups and lose those complexes of their own that constricted them in their relationships with other ethnic and social groups. They realise their crucial role in the struggle. They break the bonds of the village universe. They integrate progressively into their country and the world.... The armed liberation struggle implies, therefore, a veritable forced march along the road to cultural progress.
>
> (Cabral, January 1969)

(See also the account offered by Edward Said [1993: 264] of the contrastive and more progressive discourse of nationalism employed by these early anti-colonialist figures compared with the regressive discourse of some modern postcolonial nationalists.)

Cabral's contribution has received less recognition than that of Fanon, whose political practice was arguably less developed, though his theories of the formation of colonial consciousness were among the most powerful contributions to the creation of an effective anti-colonial discourse. Anti-colonialism frequently perceived resistance to be the product of a fixed and definitive relationship in which colonizer and colonized were in absolute and implacable opposition. As such, it was less a feature of **settler colonies**, where a more obvious form of complicity occurred between the colonial power and the settler in, for example, their suppression of the **indigenous peoples**. Settler colonies illustrate the power of filiative modes of cultural representation to effect a stronger and more complete **hegemony** of the colonial culture. In settler colonies, the struggle to articulate the underlying economic and political discriminations of a colonial relationship, that is to move to an awareness of the limited and affiliative connections of the colony and the colonial power, is central to any anti-colonial impulse. In settler colony situations, resistance at the level of cultural practice may occur before the political importance of such resistance is articulated or perceived. Although more nuanced than overt anti-colonialism, Decoloniality sees opposition and dismantling of colonialism as a key function of post-colonial analysis.

Further Reading: Cabral 1973; Davidson 1994; Fanon 1961; Gandhi 2006; Goswami 2005; Hawes 2003; Ngugi 1981a; Pratt 2004; Simpson 2004; Slemon 1990.

APARTHEID

An Afrikaans term meaning 'separation', used in South Africa for the policy initiated by the nationalist government after 1948 and usually rendered into English in the innocuous sounding phrase, 'policy of separate development'. Apartheid had been preceded in 1913 and 1936 by the Land Acts which restricted the amount of land available to black farmers to 13%. But in 1948, the apartheid laws were enacted, including the Population Registration Act, which registered all people by racial group; the Mixed Amenities Act, which codified racial segregation in public facilities; the Group Areas Act, which segregated suburbs; the Immorality Act, which illegalized white–black marriages; and the establishment of the so-called Bantustans, or native homelands, to which a large proportion of the black population was restricted.

Theoretically, the establishment of the Bantustans was supposed to provide a solution to the racial tension of South Africa by providing a series of designated territories or homelands in which the different races could develop separately within the state. But since the white minority retained for themselves the bulk of the land, and virtually all of the economically viable territory, including the agriculturally rich areas and the areas with mining potential, it was, in practice, a means of institutionalizing and preserving white supremacy. Since the economy required a large body of non-white workers to live in close proximity to white areas, for which they provided cheap labour, the Group Areas Act led to the development of specific racially segregated townships, using low-cost housing, such as the notorious Soweto area (South-West Townships) south of Johannesburg. Under the same Act, people of African, Cape, Coloured or Indian descent were forcibly removed from urban areas where they had lived for generations. The notorious and still unreconstructed District Six in central Cape Town, bulldozed and cleared of its mixed-race inhabitants under the Act, is an often-cited example of this aspect of apartheid policy.

The policy of segregation extended to every aspect of society, with separate sections in public transport, public seats, beaches and many other facilities. Further segregation was maintained by the use of Pass Laws which required non-whites to carry a pass that identified them, and which, unless it was stamped with a work permit, restricted their access to white areas. The racist basis of the policy was nowhere more apparent, and nowhere more bizarre in its application, than in the frequent re-designations of races conducted by the government, in which individuals were reclassified as Black, Coloured, Indian or White. Most of these rectifications were, predictably, downwards within the white-imposed hierarchy of race. The process demonstrated the sheer fictionality of suggesting that these racial divisions were either fixed or absolute, as did the necessity of passing a law against miscegenation between the races. The so-called Immorality Act, designed to preserve 'racial purity', indicated the desire to rewrite the fact that the societies of Southern Africa had for centuries intermingled culturally and racially.

The term apartheid acquired very widespread resonance, and it became commonly used outside the South African situation to designate a variety of situations in which racial discrimination was institutionalized by law. An extreme instance of this is when the post-structuralist philosopher and cultural critic Jacques Derrida employed the term in an influential essay, suggesting that it had acquired a resonance as a symbol that made it an archetypal term of discrimination and prejudice for later twentieth-century global culture (Derrida 1986).

In recent times, various and often contentious attempts have been made to apply the term to more recent conflicts, notably the Israeli-Palestinian conflict (Makdisi 2018, Ellis 2019). In addition, there has been attempts to argue that the policies of separating peoples on the basis of race to zones of containment allowing the use of some regions of the world to exploit the labour of others is part of a new form of global apartheid (see Global South; Besteman 2020).

Further Reading: Alexander 1996; Besteman 2020; Collett 2002; Coombes 2003; Ellis 2019; Jacobs 2004; Lapping 1987; Makdisi 2018; Pechey 1994; Price and Rosberg 1980; Richmond 1994; Sono 1999; Woods 1986.

APPROPRIATION

A term used to describe the ways in which postcolonial societies take over those aspects of the imperial culture – language, forms of writing, film, theatre and even modes of thought and argument, such as rationalism, logic and analysis – that may be of use to them in articulating their own social and cultural identities. This process is sometimes used to describe the strategy by which the dominant imperial power incorporates as its own the territory or culture that it surveys and invades (Spurr 1993: 28). However, postcolonial theory focuses instead on an exploration of the ways in which the dominated or colonized culture can use the tools of the dominant discourse to resist its political or cultural control.

Appropriation may describe acts of usurpation in various cultural domains, but the most potent are the domains of language and textuality. In these areas, the dominant language and its discursive forms are appropriated to express widely differing cultural experiences, and to interpolate these experiences into the dominant modes of representation to reach the widest possible audience. Chinua Achebe (quoting James Baldwin), noted that the language so used can 'bear the burden of another experience', and this has become one of the most famous declarations of the power of appropriation in postcolonial discourse. However, the very use of the colonial language has been opposed by writers such as Ngugi wa Thiong'o (Ngugi 1981a), who, after a successful career as a writer in English, has renounced the language of the former colonizer to write his novel and plays in Gikuyu. Nevertheless, Ngugi continues to appropriate the novel form itself, and it has been argued that the very success of his political tactic of renouncing English has relied on his reputation as a writer in that tongue.

Many other non-English speaking writers who have chosen to write in English do so not because their mother tongue is regarded by them as inadequate, but because the colonial language has become a useful means of expression, and one that reaches the widest possible audience. On the other hand, writers such as Ngugi argue that since access to English in the postcolonial societies themselves is often restricted to an educated élite, this 'wider' audience is largely outside the country, or restricted to the **comprador** class within the society. The debate has been a persistent and unresolved one.

These arguments based on the political effect of choosing English as a medium of expression are frequently contested by the alternative claim that language itself somehow embodies a culture in a way that is inaccessible to speakers of another language. Those critics and writers who appropriate ex-colonial languages to their own use argue that although language may create powerful emotive contexts through which local identities are formed, and while the use of non-indigenous languages may, as a result, appear to such communities to be less **authentic** than texts in indigenous languages, such languages do not, in themselves, constitute an irrecoverably alien form, and they may be appropriated to render views that are just as powerful in constructing anti-colonial texts. They may also effect further results that texts in the indigenous languages cannot do so easily, offering a different mode of postcolonial resistance to cultural hegemony.

By appropriating the imperial language, its discursive forms and its modes of representation, postcolonial societies are able, as things stand, to intervene more readily in the dominant discourse, to interpolate their own cultural realities, or use that dominant language to describe those realities to a wide audience of readers. Many writers feel, however, that as well as encouraging translation between all the languages used in the various postcolonial societies (including translations of indigenous languages into English and into other indigenous languages), it is equally important to insist on the need for metropolitan institutions and cultural practices to open themselves up to indigenous texts by encouraging the learning and use of these languages by metropolitan scholars.

Further Reading: Ashcroft et al. 2002; Butler 1997; Fuchs 2000; Hart 1997; Pennycook 2002; Ziff and Rao 1997.

ASSIMILATION

This refers to the process of becoming a part, or making someone become a part of a group country or society. In the postcolonial context, it refers to the process whereby individuals or groups in the colonized society, almost always of a different ethnic heritage, are absorbed into the dominant colonizing culture either by force or choice. The process of assimilating involves adopting the traits of the dominant culture without necessarily adapting them to features of the original culture. As such, assimilation is the most extreme form of acculturation, and often occurs as a function of the **civilizing mission**. Although assimilation may be compelled through force or undertaken voluntarily, it is rare for a minority to replace its previous cultural practices completely; religion, food preferences and aesthetic values are among the characteristics that tend to be most resistant to change. Assimilation does not usually denote 'racial' or biological fusion, though such fusion may occur.

Attempts to compel minority groups to assimilate occurred frequently in colonial history. The forced assimilation of indigenous peoples was particularly common in the European empires of the eighteenth, nineteenth and twentieth centuries and remains one of the most contentious aspects of postcolonial relations. In North and South America, Australia, Africa and Asia, colonial policies towards indigenous peoples frequently compelled their religious conversion, the removal of children from their families, the division of community property into individually owned parcels of land, the undermining of local economies and gender roles by shifting responsibility for farming or other forms of production from women to men and the elimination of access to indigenous foodstuffs.

In 1937, the Australian government held a national conference on Aboriginal affairs which agreed that Aboriginal people 'not of full blood' should be absorbed or 'assimilated' into the wider population. The aim of assimilation was to make the 'Aboriginal problem' gradually disappear so that Aboriginal people would lose their identity in the wider community. Protection and assimilation policies which impacted harshly on Indigenous people included separate education for Aboriginal children, town curfews, alcohol bans, no social security, lower wages and State guardianship of all Aboriginal children and laws that segregated Indigenous people into separate living areas, mainly on special reserves outside towns or in remote areas. The most tragic and contentious feature of the Australian assimilation policy was the forcible removal of Indigenous children from their families and their placement in white institutions or foster homes leading to their identification as the 'stolen generations'.

However, forced assimilation is rarely successful, and it generally has enduring negative social and psychological consequences for the recipient culture. This is a political landscape in which the precarious members of society have learned to navigate the structures of power. For indigenous societies and immigrants, compelled assimilation can lead to a loss of identity, a distancing between generations. In a mobile world in which the movement of people as **migrants and refugees** and the proliferation of social mores is increasing in variety, the question remains: 'assimilation to what'. The issue of assimilation is not improved by less contentious terms such as 'integration'. Salman Rushdie demonstrates the ways in which societies continue to discriminate against newcomers.

At first, we are told, the goal was 'integration'. Now this word rapidly came to mean 'assimilation': a black man could only become integrated when he started behaving like a white one. After 'integration' came the concept of 'racial harmony'. Now once again, this sounded virtuous and desirable, but what it meant in practice was that blacks should be persuaded to live peaceably with whites, in spite of all the injustices done to them every day. The call for 'racial harmony' was simply an invitation to shut up and smile while nothing was done about our grievances. And now, there's a new catchword: 'multiculturalism'... Multiculturalism is the latest token gesture towards Britain's blacks, and it ought to be exposed, like 'integration' and 'racial harmony', for the shame it is (1991: 137).

In theory 'integration' implies the capacity to maintain original cultural practices, particularly those relating to language, religion, food and social mores while adhering to the social, economic, legal and political aspects of the host society. However, as Rushdie demonstrates, the ultimate goal is that **cultural difference** should be eliminated.

Further Reading: Alcala 2022; Armitage 1995; Rowse and Nile 2005.

ATAVISM

Derived from the Latin ativus, meaning ancestor, atavism refers to the process of reversion to an earlier type or form and was originally used in nineteenth- and twentieth-century scientific discourse. Biologists (after Darwin's 1856 *Origin of Species*) formulated the once generally accepted biogenetic law that 'Ontogeny recapitulates phylogeny', that is, that the developmental stages of animals' embryos repeat the evolutionary steps undergone by the species as a whole. The occasional appearance of so-called 'throwback' features and vestigial organs or limbs in fully grown individuals also seemed to support this.

Although the 'biogenetic law' was increasingly questioned, and is now virtually discredited in scientific circles, its social, racial and philosophical implications seized upon in the climate of the late nineteenth century persist today. The tendencies referred to as **Social Darwinism** encouraged the promulgation of social and racial hierarchization; and bolstered by Cesare Lambroso's contention that criminality was genetically determined and could be identified in 'throw-back' physical features – long arms, low brows, reminiscent of ape ancestry – supported theories of atavism. Certain races and/or classes were deemed more backward and less evolved than others. Moreover, that individual human ontogenesis apparently reprised the evolutionary stages of the species itself suggested that although the 'primitive' or 'savage' races were well behind the evolutionary development of the more 'civilized', their recapitulation in utero meant that such savagery might still lurk – literally or metaphorically – within the more evolved, civilized European. Reversion to this earlier evolutionary state might, it was speculated, be catalysed by contact with 'savage' or 'primitive' peoples, the very ones Europeans necessarily encountered at the periphery of empire, breeding a perpetual feat of **going native**. Joseph Conrad's 1901 novel, *Heart of Darkness* offers the most striking and well-known example of a narrative expression of European fears of atavistic reversion.

AUTHENTIC/AUTHENTICITY

The idea of an authentic culture is one that has been present in many debates about postcolonial cultural production. In particular, the demand for a rejection of the influence of the colonial period in programmes of **decolonization** has invoked the idea that certain forms and practices are 'inauthentic', some decolonizing states arguing for a recuperation of authentic precolonial traditions and customs. The problem with such claims to cultural authenticity is that they often become entangled in an **essentialist** cultural position in which fixed practices become iconized as authentically indigenous and others are excluded as hybridized or contaminated. This has as its corollary the danger of ignoring the possibility that cultures may develop and change as their conditions change.

Significantly, this was not as common a feature of the work of the early anti-colonialist writers working with a Marxist model of culture (see **anti-colonialism**). Later post-structuralist models have found the issue much more difficult to resolve, reflecting, perhaps, the political problem of discovering a firm ground for material practice in an analysis that emphasizes the radical instability of signs and the fundamental and persistent difficulty of 'grounding' systems in an objective, material, extra-discursive 'space'. In some respects, cultural **essentialism**, which is theoretically questionable, may be adopted as a strategic political position in the struggle against imperial power. Clearly, certain kinds of practices are peculiar to one culture and not to others, and these may serve as important identifiers and become the means by which those cultures can resist oppression and oppose homogenization by global forces.

However, the emergence of certain fixed, stereotypical representations of culture remains a danger. The tendency to employ generic signifiers for cultures that may have many variations within them may override the real differences that exist within such cultures. Markers of cultural difference may well be perceived as authentic cultural signifiers, but that claim to authenticity can imply that these cultures are not subject to change. The use of signifiers of authenticity may be a vital part of the attempt by many subordinated societies to argue for their continued and valid existence as they become inevitably hybridized and influenced by various social and cultural changes. But too rigid a definition can militate against such resistance if they are used to police and license the determining boundaries of the culture by the dominant group (Griffiths 1994: 6).

Further Reading: D'Cruz 2001; Fee 1989; Fenwick 2000; Ganguly 2002; Griffiths 1994.

AXIAL AND DEONTIC

Axial ethics are premised on the 'assumption that empathy (and hence compassion) is the basis for ethics' (Mathews 2012: 122). The axial age and axial consciousness refer to the period when Western philosophic traditions developed and when the major religions of the world today were formed (Armstrong 2006). The term 'axial age' was developed by the philosopher Karl Jaspers (1953) which he defined as the period from 900 to 200 BCE. Axial consciousness is the core of ethics that insists on reciprocity of compassion and care between humans, and which insists on the central notion that we should do to others what we would have done to ourselves. Recent commentators on animal rights and on the theory of speciesism have pointed out that this principle should be applied not just to human interactions but to the interactions of 'all sentient beings' (Mathews 2012: 124).

Axial ethics are not the only means of rethinking and realigning contemporary ways of dealing with interspecies interaction. Axial ethics are associated with the formation of certain forms of social organization, namely 'sedentary, stratified, agrarian societies' (Mathew 2012: 124). Axial societies were preceded by non-axial societies, and these are associated with earlier social organizations such as hunter/gatherer societies, who illustrate 'a distinctive alternative conception of the normative root of society' (Mathews 2012: 125). Mathews uses Australian indigenous societies to illustrate a pre-axial or deontic concept. In this, concepts such as the Law or Dreaming Law replace the post-axial idea of ethics. This deontic order 'emphasizes that it is the living cosmos that has given people existence, and it details what people *owe* the cosmos in return, what they need to do-*ought* to do-to ensure that this generative order is perpetuated' (Mathews 2012: 125). In this deontic order, a notion of ongoing complementarity replaces compassion as the core. Contradictory and yet complementary oppositions define the generative force of the cosmos: 'night and day, wet and dry, drought and flood, life and death, eating and being eaten, flourishing and affliction, abundance and decline' (Mathews 2012: 125). This implies that restoring or regenerating the natural world needs a more complex response than the simplistic 'compassionate' ethic of the axial order.

These alternative ways of structuring how species interact are key elements in seeking to address the complexities that arise when animal rights and ecological conservation interact in complex post-agricultural societies such as ours. Matthews and others imply that the reintroduction of traditional features of the ecological order, e.g. introducing natural predators to reduce numbers of species rather than culling, require the more holistic thinking characteristic of older orders of consciousness of the deontic kind, illustrated by indigenous societies such as those of the Australian Aboriginal. Mathews contends that even though these two orders axial and deontic appear to pull in different directions 'at this particular historical junction it seems crucial to reconcile them' (Mathews 2012: 123). Discussions of these concepts underline the increasing use of traditional indigenous practices in dealing with ecological recovery.

Further Reading: Armstrong 2006; Mathews 2012; Callicott 1980; Callicott 1989; Jaspers 1953; Rose 1992.

BANDUNG CONFERENCE

The Asian-African Conference, which took place in Bandung from 18 to 24 April 1955, was a crucial event that has come to symbolize anti-colonial solidarity. Twenty-nine formerly colonized nations met at Bandung in Java for a groundbreaking meeting, organized by Indonesia, Burma, Pakistan and Ceylon, that represented 1.5 billion people. The African contingent was quite small: despite having the largest number of colonies, only Egypt, Libya, Ethiopia and Liberia were independent, since most African colonies didn't receive independence until the 1960s.

The stated aims of the conference were to promote Afro-Asian economic and cultural cooperation and to resist the control increasingly being exercised by the post-war, dominant world powers of the United States and Soviet Russia, powers that offered a new threat to the newly independent nations and their rights to self-determination and economic and political freedom. The conference was an important step towards the crystallization of the Non-Aligned Movement and the way their unity might assist them in resisting the emerging challenge characterized by the term **neo-colonialism**. Despite its call for **national liberation**, some delegates considered that Soviet Russia offered as much a threat of such control as the capitalist West. As a result, much of the discussion of the conference revolved around the question of whether the Soviet Union should be censured as neo-colonial. The meeting unanimously adopted a ten-point 'declaration on promotion of world peace and cooperation':

1. Respect for fundamental human rights and for the purposes and principles of the charter of the United Nations
2. Respect for the sovereignty and territorial integrity of all nations
3. Recognition of the equality of all races and of the equality of all nations large and small
4. Abstention from intervention or interference in the internal affairs of another country
5. Respect for the right of each nation to defend itself, singly or collectively, in conformity with the charter of the United Nations
6. (a) Abstention from the use of arrangements of collective defence to serve any particular interests of the big powers; (b) Abstention by any country from exerting pressures on other countries
7. Refraining from acts or threats of aggression or the use of force against the territorial integrity or political independence of any country
8. Settlement of all international disputes by peaceful means, such as negotiation, conciliation, arbitration or judicial settlement as well as other peaceful means of the parties own choice, in conformity with the charter of the United Nations

9. Promotion of mutual interests and cooperation
10. Respect for justice and international obligations (Jayaprakash 2005).

Despite the political euphoria generated by the conference, Richard Wright in his 1956 account of the occasion, *The Color Curtain*, portrayed it as a missed opportunity. Excited at reading about the conference and recognizing the unique moment, one that seemed to promise a vision beyond left and right, he attended the conference with high hopes for a change in global power relations. But, according to Ahmad, his report 'depicts the moment of transition from anti-colonial dream to postcolonial reality as one already rife with failure' (Ahmad 2009: 179).

In his words, all the men at the Bandung conference 'represented governments that had already seized power and they did not know what to do with it' (Wright 1994 [1956]: 207). Despite its historic importance, the conference showed 'how the newly independent nations have lost the energy of resistance and gained an unwelcome accountability without achieving anything resembling the motivating utopia' (Ahmad 2009: 180). This betrayal of nationalist hope provided the themes for much postcolonial writing in the years to come.

Despite Wright's gloom and the appearance of Cold War rhetoric in the meeting, the conference can be regarded as the symbolic birth of a new a vigorous assertiveness by decolonizing nations. The waning of the British Empire proceeded with the seizing of the Suez Canal in 1956 and the eventual independence of African states by the early 1960s. Thus, while the conference achieved little, the mere fact of the occasion represented a moment of historic change. Recently, there has been a revival of interest in the importance of Bandung, and it is increasingly seen by recent critics of the 'New World order' led by the United States as the first attempt by the non-aligned nations to address the forces of **globalization** vested in the institutions and system of international money management that had developed after the Bretton Woods Conference (1944) a few years before. These institutions included the World Bank and the International Monetary Fund (see **World Bank**). Recently forces strongly present in the undeveloped nations and opposed to the practices of these institutions have formed resistant groups such as the World Social Forum. The debate over these issues sharpened on both sides of the question after the global financial crisis of 2008 caused many people to ask if the entire system that Bretton Woods had initiated needed to be either overhauled or discarded. In light of these recent developments, many commentators now look back to the meeting at Bandung as the crucial moment when the need for opposition to these new forms of global control was first articulated (Benjamin 2007).

Further Reading: Jayaprakash 2005; Ahmad 2009; Wright 1994.

BINARISM

From 'binary', meaning a combination of two things, a pair, 'two' or duality (OED), this is a widely used term with distinctive meanings in several fields and one that has had particular sets of meanings in post-colonial theory.

The concern with binarism was first established by the French structural linguist Ferdinand de Saussure, who held that signs have meaning not by a simple reference to real objects, but by their opposition to other signs. Each sign is itself the function of a binary between the signifier, the 'signal' or sound image of the word and the signified, the significance of the signal, the concept or mental image that it evokes. Saussure held that although the connection between the signifier and signified is arbitrary (that is, there is no necessity in nature for the link between the word 'dog' and the signified dog), once the link is established, it is fixed for everyone who speaks that language.

While signs mean by their difference from other signs, the binary opposition is the most extreme form of difference possible – sun/moon; man/woman; birth/death; black/white. Such oppositions, each of which represents a binary system, are very common in the cultural construction of reality. The problem with such binary systems is that they suppress ambiguous or interstitial spaces between the opposed categories, so that any overlapping region that may appear, say, between the categories man/woman, child/adult or friend/alien, becomes impossible according to binary logic and a region of taboo in social experience. The extent to which moral panics have developed around LGBTQA+ and transgender identities demonstrates the deep hold maintained by binarism in social thinking and the taboos generated by interstitial categories.

Contemporary post-structuralist and **feminist** theories have demonstrated the extent to which such binaries entail a violent hierarchy, in which one term of the opposition is always dominant (man over woman, birth over death, white over black), and that, in fact, the binary opposition itself exists to confirm that dominance. This means that any activity or state that does not fit the binary opposition will become subject to repression or ritual. For instance, the interstitial stage between child and adult – 'youth' – is treated as a scandalous category, a rite of passage subject to considerable suspicion and anxiety. Subsequently, the state between the binarism, such as the binary colonizer/colonized, will evidence the signs of extreme ambivalence manifested in **mimicry**, cultural schizophrenia or various kinds of obsession with identity, or will put energy into confirming one or other side of the binarism, e.g. Anglocentrism or nationalism.

The binary logic of **imperialism** is a development of that tendency of Western thought in general to see the world in terms of binary oppositions that establish a relation of dominance. A simple distinction between centre/margin; colonizer/colonized; metropolis/empire; civilized/primitive represents very efficiently the violent hierarchy on which imperialism is based and which it actively perpetuates. Binary oppositions are structurally related to one another, and in colonial discourse, there may be a variation of the one underlying binary – colonizer/colonized – that becomes rearticulated in any particular text in a number of ways, e.g.

> colonizer : colonized
> white : black
> civilized : primitive
> advanced : backward
> good : evil
> beautiful : ugly
> human : bestial
> teacher : pupil
> doctor : patient

The binary constructs a scandalous category between the two terms that will be the domain of taboo, but, equally importantly, the structure can be read downwards as well as across, so that colonizer, white, human and beautiful are collectively opposed to colonized, black, bestial and ugly. Clearly, the binary is very important in constructing ideological meanings in general, and extremely useful in imperial ideology. The binary structure, with its various articulations of the underlying binary, accommodates such fundamental binary impulses within imperialism as the impulse to 'exploit' and the impulse to 'civilize'. Thus, we may also find that colonizer, civilized, teacher and doctor may be opposed to colonized, primitive, pupil and patient, as a comparatively effortless extension of the binary structure of domination. In fact, of course, as we are increasingly aware, the one depends on the other in a much more complex way than this simplistic binary structure suggests, with the 'civilizing mission' of the former categories acting as the cloak for the naked exploitation of those consigned to their binary opposites, and the former category all too often acting to conceal and justify the latter, as Conrad showed so graphically in the *Heart of Darkness*.

Binary distinctions are not necessarily motivated by a desire to dominate. David Spurr (1993: 103) discusses the ways in which Rousseau, in the *Essay on the Origin of Languages*, attempts to validate the 'life and warmth' of Oriental languages such as Arabic and Persian. But in employing the 'logic and precision' of Western writing to do so, Rousseau effectively negates these languages because they become characterized by a primitive lack of rational order and culture. Although setting out to applaud such languages, he succeeds in confirming the binary between European science, understanding, industry and writing on the one hand, and Oriental primitivism and irrationality on the other.

It may be argued that the very domain of postcolonial theory is the region of 'taboo' – the domain of overlap between these imperial binary oppositions, the area in which ambivalence, hybridity and complexity continually disrupt the certainties of imperial logic. Apart from illuminating the interstitial spaces, postcolonial theory also disrupts the structural relations of the binary system itself, revealing the fundamental contradictions of a system that can include, for instance, the binaries civilized/primitive or human/bestial along with doctor/patient or enlightener/enlightened. In this way, it uncovers the deep ambivalence of a structure of economic, cultural and political relations that can both debase and idealize, demonize and eroticize its subjects.

Perhaps one of the most catastrophic binary systems perpetuated by imperialism is the invention of the concept of **race**. The reduction of complex physical and cultural differences within and between colonized societies to the simple opposition of black/brown/yellow/white is in fact a strategy to establish a binarism of white/non-white, which asserts a relation of dominance. By thus occluding the vast continuum of ethnic variation, relegating the whole region of ethnicity, racial mixture and cultural specificity to one of taboo or otherness, imperialism draws the concept of race into a simple binary that reflects its own logic of power. The danger for anti-colonial resistance comes when the binary opposition is simply reversed, so that 'black', for instance, or 'the colonized' become the dominant term. This simply locks the project of resistance into the semiotic opposition set up by imperial discourse.

Much contemporary postcolonial theory has been directed at breaking down various kinds of binary separation in the analysis of colonialism and imperialism. For instance, Guyanese novelist and critic Wilson Harris' attempt to break down the binaristic structuration of language precedes the poststructuralists' efforts in European theory. Thus in a novel such as *Ascent to Omai*, for example, this process is continually foregrounded, as the following extract makes clear:

> 'Do you remember?' the judge addressed the hidden personae in his pack, blurred masks or readers looking over his shoulder backwards into the future: flicked the pages of his book like an expert gambler with currencies of time obverse and reverse. On the one side judge on the other judged. On one side again father on the other son. On one side still again ancient on the other modern.
>
> (Harris 1970: 86)

An important consequence of this disruption of imperial binary systems is a particular emphasis on the interactive and dialectical effects of the colonial encounter. Imperial binarisms always assume a movement in one direction – a movement from the colonizer to the colonized, from the explorer to the explored, from the surveyor to the surveyed. But just as postcolonial identity emerges in the ambivalent spaces of the colonial encounter, so the dynamic of change is not all in one direction; it is in fact transcultural, with a significant circulation of effects back and forth between the two, for the engagement with the colonies became an increasingly important factor in the imperial society's constitution and understanding of itself.

Further Reading: Russell 2006.

BIOCOLONIALISM/BIOPIRACY

Although the term 'biocolonialism' has only recently been broadly adopted, biocolonialist practices have had a long history. Since the inception of European exploration, conquest and colonization, animals, plants, (and humans) were transported from their areas of origin to Europe for imperial interest, knowledge and profit. Botanical resources in particular were shipped to Europe (and re-distributed to other colonies) as commercial crops or as raw materials, particularly after the industrial revolution.

Such earlier practices have their modern equivalents in Western and international attempts to acquire and patent plants and animals and human genes as profitable sources of medical, pharmaceutical and nutraceutical (plants that provide health benefits) products or as 'raw materials' for the multi-billion dollar industries of the twenty-first-century biotechnology revolution.

Two aspects of this new biocolonization are of particular note. The first is that three quarters of the materials sought by bioprospectors are to be found in the remaining rainforest areas of the world, ones still largely occupied by so-called 'underdeveloped' indigenous peoples. The second is that, in spite of assurances by the multinational companies that profits will be shared with local people, 'first world' patenting of plants and genes has rendered such assurances meaningless. The ability of companies to patent live material goes back to a landmark 1971 case in the US Supreme Court in relation to a bacterium. This provided legal precedent for subsequent attempts to patent human genes, a move that has been strongly resisted.

As a consequence, the term **biopiracy** has been increasingly preferred to the apparently less potent 'biocolonialism', as indigenous peoples attempt to retain control of their own genetic material and environmental resources. 'Biopiracy' was first coined by an activist of the Canada-based RAFI (Rural Advancement Foundation) in the 1990s because of 'growing frustrations about the appropriation and monopolisation of long-held medicinal and agricultural knowledge about nature, as well as the related physical resources (plants, animals and their components)' (Robinson 2010: 40).

The term 'bioprospecting' was coined in response to a work entitled Biodiversity Prospecting (Reid 1993). This work, as D.F. Robinson notes,

> Championed a 'win-win' scenario of 'benefit sharing' and respect for indigenous and traditional knowledge and also a boon for humanity through scientific research.
>
> (2010: 40)

Socioeconomic factors have generally rendered such sharing impossible. The term 'biopiracy' has definite negative connotations and was intended (again by Mooney and RAFI) as a critique of the positive promises of Biodiversity Prospecting.

Further Reading: Gollin 2008; Harry 2001; Reid 1993; Robinson 2010; Robinson 2010a.

BIOPOLITICS/BIOPOWER

Near the end of *The Will to Knowledge*, Foucault used the term 'biopolitics' to denote how social and political power is used to structure and control human life, and although it was not fully worked out in the lectures comprising that volume, his concept and method of analysing political structures is currently used widely across disciplines. It broadly refers to the administration of life and populations: 'to ensure, sustain, and multiply life, to put this life in order'. Biopower thus names the way in which biopolitics is put to work in society, and involves what Foucault describes as 'a very profound transformation of [the] mechanisms of power' of the Western classic age. In *The Will to Knowledge*, he writes of

> [A] power that exerts a positive influence on life, that endeavours to administer, optimize, and multiply it, subjecting it to precise controls and comprehensive regulations.
>
> (11)

Biopower's *positive* influence on life doesn't replace the repressive and carceral functions of power, what Foucault calls its 'juridico-discursive' character, but rather works with them. This is related to his concept of the capillary operation of power, which holds that power operates within society from many directions rather than downwards. Thus, as Foucault notes, sovereign juridical power was in fact only a power to '*take* life or *let* live', whereas biopower constituted 'a power to foster life or disallow it to the point of death'. As he puts it

> Power would no longer be dealing simply with legal subjects over whom the ultimate domination was death, but with *living beings*, and the mastery it would be able to exercise over them would have to be applied at the level of life itself.
>
> (1978: 142–143)

One the one hand, 'life' in its fullest sense, is that which exceeds attempts to order and control it. On the other hand, life is that which is made productive through techniques of intervention. Those techniques constitute the work of biopower.

This is relevant to postcolonial studies because while colonization and the subjugation of the invaded society is a clear example of the control of human life through the introduction of laws and regimes of punishment, biopower is required 'foster life', to maintain the society in a way that benefits the colonizing forces. Biopower enables the colonizer to propose the benefits of the **civilizing mission** and the controls and regulations that attend the maintenance of health, education, and the political economic order of the capitalist system. Thus, the repressive reality of colonial power is buttressed by the productive functions of biopower.

Each of these aspects of the civilizing mission requires its own technology, but a specific and critical example of biopolitics is the maintenance of the health of the colonized population. There is a dark paradox in this, because introduction of new diseases in the colonized world was part of a wider pattern of plant, animal and microbial transfers between Europe and its colonies, one that environmental historian Alfred W. Crosby dubbed the Columbian Exchange (2003). That exchange was profoundly unequal, and continued to be so as colonization advanced. But disease had a particular function in the colonial enterprise related to this unequal exchange, for it simultaneously removed the threat of indigenous resistance, while paving the way for the myth of colonial philanthropy that functions in the civilizing mission.

The catastrophic effect of disease on indigenous populations has led Crosby to argue that Old World pathogens were the most potent weapon of colonial invasion whether intentional or not

> ...their success provides the most spectacular example of the power of the biogeographical realities that underlay the success of European imperialists overseas. It was their germs, not these imperialists themselves, for all their brutality and callousness, that were chiefly responsible for sweeping aside the indigenes and opening the Neo-Europes to demographic takeover.
>
> (1986, 196)

Australian Aboriginal people, for instance, had their own diseases, particularly trachoma, but colonization unleashed a virtual tsunami of maladies to which they had no resistance, such as smallpox, measles, diphtheria, whooping cough, chicken pox, bubonic plague, malaria, typhoid fever, cholera, yellow fever, dengue fever, scarlet fever, amoebic dysentery, influenza and a number of parasitic infestations (Crosby 1986, 198).

The operation of biopolitics can be seen in the impact of smallpox on colonized people. John Winthrop, first governor of Massachusetts Bay Colony and a lawyer by training, noted on 22 May 1634, 'For the natives, they are neere all dead of small Poxe, so as the Lord hathe cleared our title to what we possess' (Crosby 1986: 20). In many cases, the devastation was so great that colonial invasion could proceed with little opposition. When the French penetrated the hinterlands of the Gulf of Mexico where the Spanish had already introduced smallpox, one of the French wrote 'Touching these savages, there is a thing that I cannot omit to remark to you, it is that it appears visibly that God wishes that they yield their place to new peoples' (Crosby 1986: 215). There is evidence that early settlers in Australia distributed infected blankets along with poisoned flour to attempt to eradicate the Aboriginal population. This more sinister aspect of biopolitics is also thought to explain how a marine detachment under attacks from Aboriginal parties and exposed by depleted arms and ammunition could have adopted a well-tried tactic and released smallpox material intentionally.

Clearly, the power of colonizing forces in the area of health, hygiene and medicine constituted 'a power to foster life or disallow it to the point of death'. The depredations of diseases such as smallpox were so catastrophic that the colonizers were obliged to combat a disease that put both indigenous and colonizers at risk. The intervention into the state of health of colonial subjects is only one mechanism of biopower, but it demonstrates more starkly than any other the ways in which biopower is manifested in colonial society.

Further Reading: Foucault 2008; Crosby 1986; Mills 2018; Feher 1994; Griffiths 2016.

BLACK ATLANTIC

The term Black Atlantic was employed first by the black British critic Paul Gilroy (Gilroy 1993). In that study, he addressed the cultural and historical linkages, which unified the peoples of African descent on both sides of the ocean that had been the scene of the diaspora of black Africans resulting from the Atlantic slave trade across the infamous Middle Passage and the so-called 'triangular trade' which flowed from it between Africa, the Americas and Europe, a trade which had a powerful effect on modern economies. For Gilroy, the important point is not just to register this linkage as an historical event, but to show how the ongoing effects of that exchange remain the constituting factor in a discursive economy that continues to dominate the social and political practices of the modern world in societies as diverse as the United States, Brazil, Britain and in the independent colonies of Africa, the Caribbean and the Americas. His contention is that all those societies, and indeed the economic and political framework of the Atlantic region as a whole, have been determined in large part by the linkages formed in that first era of mercantilism and expansion when the principal cargo was the bodies of black Africans. In this foundational work, Gilroy stresses the interdependence of all the cultures which depended on this exchange of enslaved bodies across the Black Atlantic. Thus, he analyses the cross-influence of black intellectuals, who worked not within specific and isolated nations or states but within a transnational framework in which their work flourished and cross-fertilized.

It is Gilroy's contention therefore that far from being a limited or marginalized experience, the black experience prefigured many of the problems and issues which were faced later by all peoples dealing with the emerging transnational and globalized conditions of the modern world. Recently, the term has been recruited in the concept of a Black Atlantic Literature, which traces the interconnections and influences which have occurred between writers and artists across the region. It has also been extended back into studies of earlier periods of black cultural exchange into the mediaeval period (Campbell 2006) and into many discussions of music and popular culture which take up the issues raised in the final chapter of Gilroy's 1993 book which deals with these cultural forms. In fact, as a brief online search will show, the term has now become a shorthand reference to any and all projects which have a transcultural dimension across one or more sections of the black African **diasporic** cultures of the region.

In the work that has followed, Gilroy himself has produced a series of studies of the effects of this historical process on contemporary social interaction in societies such as Britain (Gilroy 2002, 2004). Although critical of the failure of **neo-liberalism** to address the racism endemic in these cultures, he has not turned away from an attempt to discuss how the descendants of these intersecting cultures can forge effective means of working within a single polity. The deeply ironic turn of his earlier study of racism in British life *Ain't No Black in the Union Jack!* (1987) has yielded more recently to the more hopefully titled *After Empire: Melancholia or Convivial Culture?* (2004) in the introduction to which he argues that for all its limitations 'beleaguered multiculture [needs to be defended] against the accusations of failure' (2004: xi). In part, this has been a response to the conservative attacks on the idea of multiculture which have erupted in many societies across the region and elsewhere since the 9/11 attacks on the World Trade Centre and the Pentagon in 2001. Gilroy argues that, instead of the failed discourse of official multiculturalism, which has done little to address real, ongoing and indeed increasing cultural and racial prejudices, he suggests that we might develop the idea of 'conviviality'. He uses this term

> to refer to the processes of cohabitation and interaction that have made multiculture an ordinary feature of social life in Britain's urban areas and in postcolonial cities elsewhere. I hope an interest in the workings of conviviality will take off from the point where "multiculturalism" broke down.
>
> (2004: xi)

Gilroy is careful to note that he does not mean that racism has disappeared. But the term which stresses shifts in interpersonal relations

> introduces a measure of distance from the pivotal term "identity," which has proved to be such an ambiguous resource in the analysis of **race, ethnicity**, and politics. The radical openness that brings conviviality alive makes a nonsense of closed, fixed, reified identity and turns attention towards the always-unpredictable mechanisms of identification.
>
> (2004: xi)

Gilroy's later work, though far less sombre in tone, has some elements in common with Mbembe's work on the postcolony, at least in its stress on the analysis of actual daily practices and the interactive processes of social production. It is also interesting to compare its critique of sim-plistic models of identity with some of the recent accounts of identity politics in texts on **whiteness** such as Hill 2004.

Further Reading: Campbell 2006; Gilroy 1987, 1993, 2004.

BOLLYWOOD

A portmanteau term from 'Bombay' and 'Hollywood' referring to the Hindi language film industry centred in Mumbai, Bollywood has come to describe a particular highly coloured, musical and romantic film genre popular throughout India and now throughout the world. Mihir Bose claims that every year the Indian film industry produces more than 1000 feature films, every day fourteen million people see a movie in the country, a billion more people a year buy tickets to Indian movies than they do to Hollywood ones. What is more, while Hollywood is no longer growing, the Indian numbers are likely to grow.

(Bose 2006: 26)

The story of India's very early love affair with film is, in an indirect way, a story of its relationship to the British Empire and of the contingent moments by which modernity develops. Cinema was born in Paris with the Lumière show that opened on 28 December 1885. Maurice Sestiere, the Lumière man was on his way to Australia, but owing to shipping routes between the colonies had to stop over in Bombay where he decided screen the Lumière film. It was first shown to whites only in Watson's hotel but was soon screened to the general public so that on 7 July 1896 – the same day as the Tsar of Russia was seeing the film – it was being shown to Indian audiences. Thus, virtually by an accident of history and imperial geography, the Indian film industry was born, and from this moment, a culturally situated film industry arose. Obviously, it is a very long way from the Lumière screening to the largest film industry in the world but this demonstrates how protracted and how internal the process of postcolonial transformation of imperial technologies can be.

India's first silent film *Raja Harishchandra* was produced in 1913, and by the 1930s, over 200 films a year were being produced. The period from independence to the 1980s is regarded as the 'golden age' of Indian cinema (Gokulsing et al. 2004; Sharpe 2005; Sharmistha 2002), but the industry was pivotal in the project of national construction. In 1949, the Film Enquiry Committee commissioned by the Ministry of Information and Broadcasting appealed to Indian producers and directors to co-operate with the government, and share the responsibility of nation building. Indian cinema should serve as an 'effective instrument' for 'national culture, education and healthy entertainment' to promote and further induce 'a national character with its multifaceted aspects' (Government of India 1951: 46). Mehboob Khan, under his studio's banner of hammer and sickle, completed this monumental saga eight years later. Indian cinema became a protector of the official culture and the history of the nation, and gained the status of the generally accepted social and ethical consciousness of India.

Mehboob reproduced 'the Indian woman' as an icon of national martyrdom, and submission to the nation-state, although for one critic, 'It is neither in touch with the reality of the largely economic, social and political exploitation of Indian women, nor does it sympathise in any way with the real plights of peasants' (Schulze 2002: 75). Ever since Mother India filmmakers have been adapting and reproducing its national iconic imagery and emotional set-up albeit as the same scenario of the individual sacrificing for the collective. Mother India had a profound impact on the postcolonial world.

Despite its central function in the Nehruvian project of national modernization, the influence of Mother India was indicated by Shyam Benegal, who recalled the response of the Ethiopian filmmaker Haile Gerima.

> ... if there was one film that influenced him to the extent that he wanted to become a film maker it was the film Mother India. In Ethiopia, he said they would view films every month; his grandmother would gather her whole group, children and grandchildren, and they would all go to see Mother India. The story... which somehow expressed the deepest needs and aspirations of the Indian people, had a message not only for the Indian people but for people from outside India like Haile and his fellow Ethiopians.
> (Bose 2006: 20)

Quite apart from its nationalist function, the simple fact that the film had been made, and made outside Hollywood, inspired Gerima and postcolonial filmmakers throughout the world.

In 1976, the Committee on Public Undertakings, after investigating the film industry, accused the Film Finance Corporation of being too committed to artistic films and not doing enough to promote commercial cinema. By the 1980s, commercial cinema had developed considerably, leading to the Palm D'or winner, Salaam Bombay. The late 1980s and 1990s saw the proliferation of the type of film now identified with Bollywood: family-centric romantic musical comedies. The opening up of an overseas market and an increase in Bollywood releases abroad led to wider box office successes in India and the world, such as Lagaan (2001), the story of a group of villagers in colonial India who teach themselves cricket to challenge the British officers to a game in order to reduce punitive village taxes.

The 2000s saw the growth and world popularity of Bollywood cinema and a wide range of non-Hindi speaking fans. One of the most interesting characteristics of Indian film concerns the audience. Rather than the intense focus required by Western films, Bollywood has a different impact, in a sense they are constructed for a different audience.

Hindi films are constructed around a set of easily recognizable conventions... There is, in other words, a strong ritualistic element in the viewing of Indian films, a light-heartedness, a tongue-in-cheek mimetic relationship to all kinds of styles and genres derived from western cinema... Knowledge of these genre conventions and the ability to appreciate films in this relaxed, repetitive, intensely social form is crucial to the larger 'reading competence' that characterizes the average, often extremely film-literate spectator in India (Hansen in Kaur and Sinha 2005: 241).

In the Bollywood film, there is a high degree of pre-knowledge and expectation occasioned by the conventions of the form. Bollywood generates a massive insider group of knowledgeable viewers, but this knowledge has not been confined to Indian viewers. The distribution of Bollywood films to diasporic audiences in Africa, Asia, Caribbean Europe and America led to exposure within those societies simply by the principle of proximity. Proximity may be augmented by exoticism in Europe and America, but in Africa, distribution has led to a form of filtration, producing generations of Bollywood fans who do not speak Indian languages but for whom the visual language of the films has been captivating (Larkin 1997). Bollywood films have generated considerable identification in audiences in the Third World, and in Asia and Africa, in particular, it has confirmed the liberating possibility of a film industry outside Hollywood or Europe.

Further Reading: Bose 2006; Gooptu 2002; Gokulsinf et al. 2004; Kaur and Sinha 2005; Sharpe 2005.

BLACK STUDIES/BLACK CONSCIOUSNESS

This was one of the earliest models for cross-cultural studies of peoples affected by colonization, and centred on African peoples who had been transported, enslaved or otherwise made **diasporic** by colonialism and by slavery. It developed mainly in the United States. In the nineteenth century, black American intellectuals, such as Frederic Douglas (circa 1817–1895), Booker T. Washington (1856–1901) and W.E.B. Du Bois (1868–1963), men who had either been born slaves or were the children of slaves, as well as others like Marcus Garvey (1887–1940), a Jamaican who settled in the United States, had developed a body of texts and institutions dedicated to black education and black development. Many colleges were founded, through their inspiration, to educate black Americans. These included Wilberforce College, Lincoln College, Howard University, Tuskegee Institute and Fisk University. These intellectuals advocated an investigation of the distinctiveness of the African cultural elements in black American and Caribbean societies. Cultural historians such as Paul Gilroy have argued that these links across and between the various regions where black diasporic intellectuals had emerged formed a crucial part of the emergence of a distinctive and transnational movement, which he has dubbed the Black Atlantic.

The widespread growth of Black (variantly African American or African Caribbean) Studies followed the Civil Rights activism of the 1960s. Black Studies rapidly established itself in US institutions as a powerful model to investigate any and all aspects of the African negro **diaspora**. It encouraged investigations of African origins for American and Caribbean language usage and cultural practices (see **creole**), and examined the cross-cultural influence on Africa itself of American and Caribbean intellectuals such as Alexander Crummell (1819–1898) and Edward Wilmot Blyden (1832–1912), who had been so influential there in the nineteenth century with the founding of colonies of freed slaves in Liberia and Sierra Leone. Influenced in part by the example of the francophone movement of **négritude**, Black Studies both predated and outlasted that movement. In the 1960s, it embraced many of the ideas developed by **Fanonist** thinkers and, in the form of the black consciousness movement, sought to redress the negative self-image created in many black people by their long history of enslavement and discriminatory treatment, treatment made inescapable, as Fanon had noted, by the visibility of their perceived 'difference' (*The Fact of Blackness* in Fanon 1952: 109–140).

Various movements in different parts of the world have embraced elements of the black consciousness programme, for example in Australia and New Zealand, where Australian Aboriginal and Maori groups have used the concept of 'blackness' as an ethnic signifier, and among the many diasporic 'peoples of colour' who now make up an increasing proportion of the people of the old European metropolitan centre where the term 'black' has been employed to identify a new **ethnicity** (Hall 1989).

Further Reading: Appiah and Gates 1995; Baker and Diawara 1996; Blassingame 1971; Bracey 2003; Butler 1981; Chrisman 2000, 2005; Joyce 2005; Mercer 1994; Moikabu 1981; White 1985.

BORDERLANDS

The idea of the border is clearly crucial to **postcolonial** studies and manifests itself in concerns with the constructed boundaries between peoples, nations and individuals. The idea of the border is implicit in the outreach of European cultures in the colonial period. The region which this aggressive **diasporic** movement of European settlers reached at any point became defined as the frontier. The settled area adjacent to this was also known sometimes as the borderlands. Contemporary transcultural studies have suggested that such borderland spaces can be spaces of energy, when they question fixities and release the potential for change and revision (Anzaldua 1987; Glissant 1989; Harris 1983). This is because these **liminal** spaces act to problematize and so dismantle the binary systems which bring them into being. It is this idea of the deconstructive potential of the space where two cultures encounter one another which also underlies the idea of the transformative energy of the **contact zone** (Pratt 1992).

The term has been especially important in studies of the United States–Mexican borderlands, spaces which have been occupied at various periods by the two **nation** states of Mexico and the United States and which remain profoundly **hybridized** in many aspects of their culture. The so-called **mestizo** (literally mixed) cultures of this region resulting from a long period of **transcultural** exchange between the various ethnic populations, extends to the cultural expression of the region e.g. musical forms, food (Tex-Mex cuisine), etc. But this admixture has had only the most superficial effect on the underlying power differences, which the border enforces. The borderland of the South-West remains the space where the United States most actively polices its difference from the rest of the Americas, differences rooted in racial, linguistic and economic factors which feed the idea of this as a region of threat and potential dissolution. The principal stress is on the exclusion of so-called illegals, Mexicans seeking to cross into the United States for economic reasons. But since the attacks on the World Trade Centre and the Pentagon in 2001, the South-West border region has been seen as a potential threat to national security. As a result, a physical barrier has been constructed along most of its length. The long border with Canada to the north, although also subject to more stringent regulations since 2001 has been seen as less dangerous, emphasizing the fact that the South-West is a borderland where more threatening forms of difference, racial and economic, are rendered visible.

Further Reading: Anzaldua 1987; Ashcroft 2001a; Ebner 2023; Hennessy 2007.

CANNIBAL

This term for an eater of human flesh is of particular interest to post-colonial studies for its demonstration of the process by which an imperial Europe distinguishes itself from the subjects of its colonial expansion, while providing a moral justification for that expansion. The OED definition of 'cannibal' reads: 'A man (esp. a savage) that eats human flesh; a man-eater, an anthropophagite. Originally proper name of the man-eating Caribs of the Antilles' (Hulme 1986: 16). This definition is itself a very good demonstration of two related features of colonial discourse: the separation of the 'civilized' and the 'savage', and the importance of the concept of cannibalism in cementing this distinction. To this day, cannibalism has remained the West's key representation of primitivism, even though its first recording, and indeed most subsequent examples, have been evidence of a rhetorical strategy rather than evidence of an objective 'fact'.

According to Peter Hulme, the first recording of the term 'canibales' is found in Columbus' journal, where he writes that the local Arawaks regarded a particular island with great trepidation saying:

> that this land was very extensive and that in it were people who had one eye in the forehead, and others whom they called 'canibales'. Of these last they showed great fear, and when they saw that this course was being taken, they were speechless, he says, because these people ate them and because they were very warlike.
>
> (Hulme 1986: 16–17)

Quite apart from the questions surrounding the validity of this journal – 'a transcription of an abstract of a copy of a lost original' – Columbus' 'record' is far from being an observation that those people called 'canibales' ate other people. It is a report of other people's words, spoken in a language of which he had no prior knowledge, and associated with the obviously dubious report of people with one eye in their forehead.

Why was it that the canibales were so readily accepted as man-eaters? Why was it that the term 'cannibal' so readily displaced 'anthropophagite' as a description of those who ate human flesh? In essence, Peter Hulme's explanation is that there was an implicit struggle occurring within Columbus' journal, as there was in European consciousness generally, over how the New World was to be depicted: a struggle between the rhetorical tropes of idealization and debasement, between Oriental civilization and savagery. With the report of the canibales, the discourse of savagery triumphs in Columbus' writing as the journal writer declares 'the Caniba are nothing else than the people of the Grand Khan' – the idealized Oriental civilization is displaced by the definitive primitivism of man-eating cannibals, and the demonization of the 'primitive' **other** in imperial discourse becomes (almost from this moment it seems) increasingly naturalized. The merging of 'cannibal' and 'primitive' into a virtually synonymous relationship extends to the present day as the pre-eminent sign of the power of 'othering' maintained by imperial discourse.

The eating of human flesh on occasions of extremity or transgression, or in ritual, has been recorded from time to time as a feature of many societies, but the emergence of the word 'cannibal' was an especially powerful and distinctive feature of the rhetoric of empire. The superseding of 'anthropophagy' by 'cannibalism' was not a simple change in the description of the practice of eating human flesh, it was the replacement of a descriptive term with an ontological category. From the time of Columbus, 'cannibal' became synonymous with the savage, the primitive, the 'other' of Europe, its use a signification of an abased state of being. In this sense, the term came to play an important part in the moral justification for the imperial rule.

Further Reading: Berglund 2006; Colás 2001; Hulme 1986; Kilgour 1993; Motohashi 1999; Obeyesekere 1992; Sanborn 1998; Sanday 1986; Shaw 2001; Slemon 1992.

CARIBBEAN/WEST INDIAN

The terms 'Caribbean' and 'West Indian' are often used interchangeably to refer to the island nations of the Caribbean Sea and territories on the surrounding South and Central American mainland (such as Guyana and Belize). More accurately, however, the term 'Caribbean' refers to all island nations located in the area (and mainland Guyana and Belize), while 'West Indian' refers only to those nations that were formerly British colonies, e.g. Jamaica, Trinidad, Barbados, St Lucia, St Vincent, Antigua, Dominica, Guyana (and sometimes Belize).

The origins of the two terms also differ, with 'Caribbean' deriving from a corruption of the Spanish 'caribal', itself generally considered to be a 'mishearing' of an Amerindian word. 'West Indies' arose in contrast to the designation 'East Indies', the 'spice islands' of Asia and Columbus' intended destination when he 'discovered' the Caribbean in 1492 (see **cannibal**).

Further Reading: Baugh 2000; Childs, Weber et al. 2006; Chin 2006; Dash 2003; Döring 2002; Hogan 2000; Murdoch 1999; Murray 2000; Puri 2004; Taylor 1995.

CARTOGRAPHY (MAPS AND MAPPING)

Both literally and metaphorically, maps and mapping are dominant practices of colonial and postcolonial cultures. Colonization itself is often consequent on a voyage of 'discovery', a bringing into being of 'undiscovered' lands. The process of discovery is reinforced by the construction of maps, whose existence is a means of textualizing the spatial reality of the other, naming or, in almost all cases, renaming spaces in a symbolic and literal act of mastery and control. In all cases, the lands so colonized are literally reinscribed, written over, as the names and languages of the indigenes are replaced by new names, or are corrupted into new and Europeanized forms by the cartographer and explorer. This was a long-standing feature of colonialism and not restricted to distant unknown lands. Irish playwright Brian Friel graphically illustrates this in *Translations*, which deals with the mapping and renaming of the West of Ireland by the English army in the nineteenth century, a process in which the native Irish (Gaelic) culture is literally overwritten by English imperialism.

Maps also inscribe their ideology on territory in numerous ways other than place names. The blank spaces of early maps signify a literal terra nullius, an open and inviting (virginal) space into which the European imagination can project itself and into which the European (usually male) explorer must penetrate. Such blank spaces invite other cultural superscriptions, such as the elaborately drawn monsters and sub-human wild-men (savages) of most early maps. Imaginative transferences are frequent. Thus, early maps of Australia (Terra Incognita or Terra Incognita Australis as it was known in the seventeenth century when the first European maps of the northern coast-line were drawn) show an interior populated by elephants and pygmies. Similarly, the so-called **cannibals** of the Indies (a term derived from the corruption of the Spanish name for the Carib peoples) appear frequently on maps of the interior of Africa. Indeed, by the early twentieth century, the term is almost synonymous with Africans in popular literature and humour, as witness the numerous cartoons that represent cannibals as black people with bones through their noses roasting missionaries in a pot.

The fictionality of the narratives of such processes of 'discovery', which the process of mapping objectifies, is emphasized by the role of the native guide in such explorations, who leads the explorer to the interior. The prior knowledge of the land that this dramatizes, and which cannot be wholly silenced in the written accounts of these explorations, is ignored, and literally silenced by the act of mapping, since the **indigenous people** have no voice or even presence that can be heard in the new discourse of scientific measurement and written texts that cartography implies. They figure, if at all, only as illustration – savages, cannibals or monsters. The allegorization of space (and its hierarchization) is also defined by maps, first by the decision as to which projection to favour, since this privileges some land spaces over others; or by the decision to orient all maps on a North–South axis; or by the creation of a body of special maps that divide the land into such 'objective' categories as climatic regions, population densities and, not least, natural resources.

Maps can also serve as (allegorical) tools of exploitation. In his analysis of *Mercator's Atlas,* José Rabasa (1993) demonstrates how the projection map became a major tool of **Eurocentrism**, defining European latitudes as pivotal reference points for the conception of a world hierarchy, and embodying as geographical fact European attitudes about the nature of the world. In effect, the European map created what has remained the contemporary geographical world reality. The definition of cultures as tropical in a world where temperate is the norm, or as densely populated or thinly populated, or as resource-rich or poor, are essential discriminations upon which a practice of exploitation or control can be erected. That these techniques also feature in such modern controlling discourses as 'development' studies illustrates how persistently the sciences of cartography and mapping have contributed to the establishment and reestablishment of the various world orders of the last few centuries.

Although **ethnography** (the supposedly objective scientific description of 'primitive' peoples and cultures) has frequently borne the brunt of anti-colonial attacks as being the principal intellectual discourse of colonization, it is worth noting that geography and geographers, and the science of cartography, played at least as important a role in underpinning the objects and values of the colonial enterprise. The Royal Geographical Society was a prime mover in the imperial conquests of the 'undiscovered' regions of the world, and it is significant that as Kipling's Kim illustrates (the cover of the Head of the Secret Service in that text, Creighton Sahib, is that of the Director of the General Survey of India), the colonial mapper and surveyor was frequently the most ubiquitous figure of imperial control.

Further Reading: Caquard 2013; Carter 1987; Clifford 1997; Hiatt 2005; Huggan 1995; Mignolo 1995a; Rabasa 1993; Ryan 1994.

CATACHRESIS

The application of a term to a thing that it does not properly denote (OED). Originally referring to grammatical 'misuse', this term is used by Gayatri Spivak in a way that is close to the meaning of **appropriation**. Catachresis is the process by which the colonized take and reinscribe something that exists traditionally as a feature of imperial culture, such as parliamentary democracy. When Spivak speaks, for instance, of the ability of the subaltern 'to catachretize parliamentary democracy' (1991: 70), she means 'the insertion and the reinscription of something which does not refer literally to the correct narrative of the emergence of parliamentary democracy' (70). That is, while parliamentary democracy emerges from a specific European history and culture, its adoption into, and adaptation by, the culture of the postcolonial society, including the assertion, for instance, that there exists a precolonial native tradition of parliamentary democracy, may offer an empowering avenue of self-determination to the subaltern subject. Another common and empowering catachresis is the application of the term 'nation' to a social group in existence before colonization, such as the 'Zulu nation', the 'Aboriginal nation' and the 'Sioux nation'.

Further Reading: Prakash 1997; Spivak 1991, 2000.

CATALYSIS

A term adopted by Guyanese novelist and critic Denis Williams to describe processes of racial change and racial intermixing in New World societies, a formulation that deliberately challenges the 'melting-pot' model. A catalyst, as Williams notes, is 'a body which changes its surrounding substance without itself undergoing any change' (1969: 10). For Williams, American societies are 'crucibles in which catalysts of greater or lesser potency operate'. The process of catalysis in such New World societies challenges the very concepts of race purity and its obverse, 'miscegenation', since it is what both makes the societies unique and gives them a potency lacking in Old World cultures that fetishize pure-race ancestry.

Arguing that this process is 'more dramatically marked' in Guyanese society than among any other New World peoples, Williams notes that in catalysis:

> the sperm is continually invested with a new skin, a new mask. There is no warrant from one generation to another as to the form in which this sperm will be handed on; unlike in [sic] the Old World Societies our culture inherently lacks those restraining institutions which act as checks and safeguards for the continued purity of the sperm, tribal, religious, social or psychic taboos which secure and protect the continuity of the line. No New World individual might pronounce with absolute certainty on what his grandchildren are racially likely to be.... There are no Africans in the New World; there is only the African sperm in various states of catalysis, and it is this fact of catalysis which constitutes our difference from all other peoples of the world.
>
> (1969: 11–12)

According to Williams, this process of catalysis becomes a distinguishing feature of the reality of 'the New World man' and also becomes the focus for 'the release of his original energies' (14). For him, New World philosophy must arise out of this energizing tension. It is generated out of the mutual insecurities created by the pressure of several racial groups qualifying and diminishing the self-image of the other. Although, on the face of it, this might seem to be a negative thing, the energy produced is the source of great creative potential. 'The resulting uneasiness, the sense of psychic erosion, the self-questioning' causes a catalytic reaction that leads to a new totality.

This qualifying process is also associated in Williams' view with a 'lack of union with the ancestral gods of the soil', another feature distinguishing New World from Old World cultures. Williams also draws a distinction between the New World societies of the Americas and those of, for instance, Australia and New Zealand, which he regards as filiative cultures on the Old World model.

Williams concludes that since 'reality' for Guyanese and other New World societies 'hinges on the fact of the human in infinite process of catalysis', the emphasis is necessarily on the present. 'It is the minute nature and definition of this present viewed in the fluctuating individual consciousness that seems to me crucial in assessing our cultural situation and in realising this situation in our works of art' (35). Catalysis is thus different from **creolization**, **hybridization** or **transculturation** even though it involves historically determined colonial racial and cultural 'mixing' and the creative products of these 'exchanges'.

Further Reading: Williams 1969.

CENTRE/MARGIN (PERIPHERY)

This has been one of the most contentious ideas in postcolonial discourse, and yet it is at the heart of any attempt at defining what occurred in the representation and relationship of peoples as a result of the colonial period. Colonialism could only exist at all by postulating that there existed a **binary** opposition into which the world was divided. The gradual establishment of an empire depended upon a stable hierarchical relationship in which the colonized existed as the **other** of the colonizing culture. Thus, the idea of the savage could occur only if there was a concept of the civilized to oppose it. In this way, a geography of difference was constructed, in which differences were mapped (**cartography**) and laid out in a metaphorical landscape that represented not geographical fixity, but the fixity of power.

Imperial Europe became defined as the 'centre' in a geography at least as metaphysical as physical. Everything that lay outside that centre was by definition at the margin or the periphery of culture, power and civilization. The colonial mission, to bring the margin into the sphere of influence of the enlightened centre, became the principal justification for the economic and political exploitation of colonialism, especially after the middle of the nineteenth century.

The idea is contentious because it has been supposed that attempts to define the centre/margin model function to perpetuate it. In fact, postcolonial theorists have usually used the model to suggest that dismantling such binaries does more than merely assert the independence of the marginal, it also radically undermines the very idea of such a centre, deconstructing the claims of the European colonizers to a unity and a fixity of a different order from that of others. In this sense, the dismantling of centre/margin (periphery) models of culture calls into question the claims of any culture to possess a fixed, pure and homogeneous body of values, and exposes them all as historically constructed, and thus corrigible formations.

Further Reading: Brah 1996; Brennan 2005; Castillo 1999; Clifford 1997; Harding and Narayan 2000; Huggan 2001; Marriott 2000; Mignolo 2000a; Sarkowsky 2002; Smyth 2000.

CHARTER COMPANIES

At the heart of most imperial action and the resulting colonization of countries and regions was economic advantage and the interests of trade. When European nations started to colonize other places and peoples, it was the desire to find and import valuables that drove the enterprises. The first great imperial powers Spain and Portugal were primarily interested in obtaining the gold and silver which they found in the New World. These ventures were undertaken by individuals given the right to exercise power in the name of the Crown, as its local representatives. Although they also sought to trade in regions such as the East Indies (which they dominated until the late sixteenth century) and the Indian sub-continent, and Portuguese traders contested the other nations in those regions until the so-called Amboina massacre of 1623, their impact there was smaller than in the Americas. By the early seventeenth century, other national ventures centred on the valuable trade in spices from the East Indies were emerging. Their formation reflected wider changes to the ways many European countries were developing as a power in the seventeenth century, increasingly moving from landed aristocracies to urban-based traders from the emerging middle classes. These people were banding together to form groups (joint-stock companies) which invested in the trading exchanges which also developed in this period. The earliest of these, from which the modern stock exchange arose was formed in the Netherlands in 1602 and its first shares were issued by a company given a 21-year charter (in effect a monopoly) to trade to the Dutch East Indies called the VOC (*Vereenigde Oost-Indische Compagnie*).

The VOC became the model for many other rival companies in the next century, including the most famous and long-lasting of all, the English East India Company, the earliest charter for which had in fact been issued by Elizabeth I two years before that of the VOC in 1600. By the early eighteenth century, the French had also established a charter company for Indian trade called the *Compagnie Français pour le commerce des Indes orientales*. These commercial companies, through their charters, were granted the right to negotiate with and sign treaties with local rulers. This provided the basis for what would become the company's effective governance over large swathes of territory. At first, limited to trading from small, fixed enclaves on the coasts of India granted by local rulers the representatives of both the English and French companies began involving themselves directly in the political and military struggles between local rulers, especially in the early eighteenth century when the power of the Mughal Empire was increasingly challenged from within. This military involvement increased rapidly with the outbreak of the Seven Years War (1756–1763) between Britain and France, sometimes referred to as the first truly world war as the conflict was fought outside Europe from North America and the Caribbean to the Far East, notably in India.

Although Louis XIV and his finance minister Colbert actively tried to engage French merchants in the French Company, it never succeeded in attracting the kind of support the emerging middle-class traders in Britain and the Netherlands gave to their respective companies, with the French king always being its largest investor. This, of course, reflects the different political regimes in the countries of the respective national charter companies. Nevertheless, by 1740, the annual trade of the French Company was almost half as much as that of the East India Company, making it a threatening rival. Under its active local governor Dupleix, an attempt began to enlist local allies, training their troops and even participating directly in their contests with rivals. This process, under the pressure of the war that followed, meant that both companies were increasingly involved in local conflicts and in direct conflict between themselves as rivals not only for trade but also for the political dominance of the sub-continent. The East India Company now began to maintain its independent armies under the leadership of Company officers, often men who had begun as 'writers' (clerks) but who had shown an aptitude for military command. The most notable of these was Robert Clive, better known to history as Clive of India. After participating in several struggles with the French in the region adjoining Madras, Clive recognized that the policy of indirect rule via compliant local regimes they had established there was the key to success. In 1757, he oversaw the Company's troops at the battle of Plassey that established their rule in Bengal, the richest of the provinces of the failing Mughal Empire which they ruled through their puppet Nawab Mir Jafar.

'John Company' as it was known colloquially, raised independent armies that were drawn from the native Indian populations, though usually officered by Europeans and strengthened by a few regiments of European troops. These native soldiers, known as sepoys, remained the main source of military power in the sub-continent, and even after the disbanding of the Company's own troops after the so-called Indian

Mutiny (Indian War of Independence) of 1856, native troops formed the basis of British power in India until independence in 1947. This is an extreme example of how a small group could rule a native population that always greatly outnumbered them by a process of manipulation and propaganda (see **hegemony**). In most short accounts of the East India Company, it is assumed that it remained the accepted and undisputed ruler of India until the British government took direct control after 1856. In fact, despite its success and the eventual defeat of the French as a political force in India, the Company was always seen by the British government either as a source of financial loss or of corrupt power that needed to be contained. After rival groups in England unsuccessfully sought to limit its monopoly, the Company, now officially known as The United Company of Merchants of England trading to the East Indies, continued to be directed by its shareholders at meetings where shares were purchasable on the open market, including shareholders from other countries, notably the Netherlands. After the decisive shift in 1757 when Bengal became a fiefdom of the Company, this situation was clearly a worry to governments.

Attempts at reforming the way the Company was governed resulted from the failure of the Company to pay its debts to the government and from what was perceived as the tendency of Company officers to enrich themselves. The real cause for reform was the sense that the Company had ceased to be an economic benefit to the country and that its operation had become one that prevented an efficient exploitation of the ruled peoples and their resources. Much of this reform was announced by oppositional forces in the governments of the time as a moral attack on corruption. Reform began with the Regulating Act of 1773, which took away the right of Company employees to trade on their own behalf, and was followed by Pitt's India Act of 1784, which strengthened government control by appointing a Board that included government ministers. In the years between and afterwards, there had been numerous claims of corruption by Company officials, including Clive, and culminating in the later (though finally unsuccessful) impeachment of Warwick Hastings, the first Governor-General of Bengal, in 1795. These reforms culminated with the Charter Act of 1813, which ended the Company's trade monopoly with India. Although these reforms did not address the deep-seated problems arising from a division of power between an elected government and a company finally responsible only to its shareholders, they suggest that the idea of a simple break in power after 1856 is oversimplistic. In fact, the Company had divested itself of its trading assets in 1833 when the government assumed the Company's debts to be serviced from taxes raised in India. The shareholders were guaranteed a fixed dividend for 40 years, also to be serviced from taxes raised in India. Thus, before and after the government took final control in 1857, after the traumatic events of the previous year, India remained the source of the funds raised by the Company and by the government of Britain to pay for British presence in India and to fund the profits that they derived from its peoples and its resources. This remains perhaps the central fact about companies like the East India Company. They were initiated to derive profit from the exploitation of colonized peoples, and when they were dissolved, it was to ensure the successful continuation of this exploitation by the imperial power which had initially called them into being. The East India Company is the archetypal example of the indissoluble bond between imperialism and the economic exploitative forces it serves.

Although the East India Company was the greatest example of this mode of conducting imperial trade and governance, the use of charter companies, especially by the British, continued into the late nineteenth century, particularly in African colonies. The Imperial British East Africa Company (IBEAC) was granted a charter in 1888. It was formed because of the reluctance of the British government to take direct control of the regions that were under British influence, including what is now Kenya and Uganda, partly because of a fear of costs. The Germans who had taken what became Tanganyika to form German East Africa had established a similar use of a charter company (German East Africa Company) in their region of influence. Neither Company survived long, and arguably mainly served to foster the rivalries between the competing nations in the region. Before the IBEAC was dissolved in 1895 to be replaced by direct government control of their areas of interest by the formation of an East African Protectorate with an appointed commissioner, it played a lasting role in encouraging the development in Africa of the form of indirect rule that had been the model in India for the princely states. The young Indian-born employee of the IBEAC Captain Frederic (later Lord) Lugard succeeded in creating a successful cooperative governance with the aristocratic ruler (Kabaka) of the Bugandan people to create what he later termed a dual mandate that remained in fact an imperial annexation of the territory. This method of ruling indirectly through local traditional rulers was later to be employed by Lugard in Nigeria where it operated in direct contrast to the French system of direct rule in their adjacent territories (see **colonial governance**). Developed in areas where a traditional ruler existed, it was extended to other regions (such as Iboland in Nigeria) by colonial officials designating a person to act as chief where no traditional hier-archical structure existed.

As in India, the charter companies became the means of developing indirect imperial rule in many parts of the British Empire, for example, in Malaya where the native sultans were used in a similar way to mask imperial control. Some elements of this system were also present in the way Dutch authorities in the region of modern Indonesia used traditional rulers until the VOC was replaced with direct government control.

Charter companies in British African colonies were not a success as their history in West and South Africa illustrates. In both regions, an entrepreneur used the model of the charter company to advance the interests of their commercial companies. In Nigeria, George Dashwood Taubman Goldie, an adventurer who had inherited small commercial interests in the lower Niger region, succeeded in com-bining a number of companies there to form the National African Company. After the Berlin Conference 1885-5 that resulted in the so-called Scramble for Africa, Goldie was given a royal charter to form the Royal Niger Company. Like other such companies, he had thus obtained a monopoly of trade in the region, and the right to make treaties with local rulers to annex their territories and exercise authority over them. Here, as elsewhere, the use of such companies to annex territory at little or no direct cost to the government overrode any concerns of their treatment of the local peoples. However, in 1895, after the Colonial Office investigated allegations of corruption and abuse, the company was dissolved and a protectorate declared over its territories on the Upper Niger.

In Southern Africa, the even more successful entrepreneur, Cecil Rhodes, persuaded the British government to grant his companies a royal charter founding the British South Africa Company (BSAC) in 1889. Rhodes had a wide vision of uniting territories that would link South Africa to Sudan and Egypt, establishing the 'Cape to Cairo' railway. This project was beyond the scope of even the ambitious Rhodes and despite his linking his newly acquired territories in what is now Zimbabwe (then Rhodesia) through Bechuanaland (modern Botswana), this was never a feasible goal. But after Rhodes' death in 1902, the BSAC continued to operate in the areas north of the Zambezi. After 1924, it became financially viable as some of its ter-ritories became the source for minerals, especially in the copper belt of modern Zambia, to whose government it finally surrendered the rights only in 1964. In fact, the company still exists, if only as a paper, non-trading entity.

The most complex attempt to wed the idea of a royal company to imperial annexation was the so-called Belgian Free State, formed at the Berlin Conference by the then King of the Belgians Leopold II. Although established by the king, it was never a charter company in the same sense, being in fact a private state owned by the king. As what has sometimes been seen as the most vicious and brutal of all colonial states, Leopold's ironically entitled Free State shows how complex the relationship between commercial enterprises and imperial possessions had become by the end of the nineteenth century.

It is even arguable that the bond between the two survived the collapse of the colonial rule, and that the inheritors of the monopoly charter companies are the modern multinational companies, owned by both corporations and individuals, which often act against the interests of people in resource-rich postcolonial countries with weak or corrupt governments that lend themselves to such exploitation for personal power or enrichment (see **Neo-colonialism** and **Decolonization**).

Further Reading: Lawson 2013; Van Meersbergen 2017; Sivramkrishna 2014; Robins 2012; Schleck 2017; Keay 1991; Mostert and Clulow 2018; Gaastra and Daniels 2003; Gelderblom et al. 2013; Lucassen 2004; De Zwart 2017; Baker 1996; Muffett 1978; McCracken 2008; Rotberg and Shore 1998; Hochschild 1988; Phillips and Sharman 2020.

CHIMERICAN AGE

This term was coined by Rob Nixon in his very influential book *Slow Violence and the Environmentalism of the Poor* (see **slow violence**). He noted that

> the full-blown ascent of Chinese authoritarian capitalism, [ushered] in the Chimerican age, as through entangled rivalry, mutual dependence, and mutual mistrust, an emboldened China has joined an over-stretched America as a global force in annexing-and carting off-the very conditions of life.
>
> (Nixon 2011: 43)

The specific example he gives is of the Chinese acquiring three million acres of rainforest in the Democratic Republic of Congo and converting it to a monoculture to produce palm oil, effectively displacing the people of that area who had relied on subsistence farming to survive.

The term suggests that in the twenty-first century, the effective annexation of many of the poorer regions of the world by economic means has involved the effective colonization of these regions by powers that have long represented themselves, although from different ideological positions, as the opponents of classic imperialism. Indeed, he asserts that in the list of countries he characterizes as involved in a new Scramble for Africa,

> the continent's resource maps are redrawn and its riches carved up among Chinese, American, European, Australian and South African corporations typically working in cahoots with unelected officials or regional brigands... [all engaged in a] rampant disregard for socioenvironmental survival in the Chimerican age.
>
> (Nixon 43) (See Neo-colonialism/imperialism)

As this list of countries engaged in this suggests and as he also suggests, Africa is not alone in being subjected to this process of economic annexation involving widespread destruction of natural environments and of the lives and cultures of the peoples and societies the process displaces. Nor is it only China and America that engage in this. As commercial enterprises spring up in areas that Nixon in 2011 does not notice even countries that were themselves once subject to colonization such as Indonesia are engaged in destructive monoculture projects of this kind in its annexed territories, notably Irian Jaya (West Papua) where a huge 18,999 hectare palm oil plantation has caused devastation for the local Marind people, destroying not only their food crops but undermining the traditional relationship between humans and the native jungle plants that have disappeared, an essential feature of the local cultural identity (Chao 2022).

Further Reading: Nixon 2011; Chao 2022.

CHROMATISM

From 'chromatic' (1603) meaning 'of or belonging to colour or colours' (OED), this term is used to refer to the essentialist distinction between people on the basis of colour. It is sometimes used in conjunction with the term 'genitalism', a distinction between men and women based on the obvious biological difference between male and female. Both terms are employed to indicate the fallacy of making simplistic and stereotypical distinctions of **race** and gender and to suggest that the range of difference within these categories is a matter of representation and discursive construction.

CIVILIZING MISSION

The civilizing mission, or *mission civilisatrice*, represents the fundamental contradiction of empire between geographical expansion and invasion designed to increase the prestige, economic or political power of the imperial nation, and its professed moral justification, its mission to bring order and civilization to the barbarous hordes. This is a contradiction which also continues in subtler forms in the present-day exercise of global power under the guise of 'development' and 'modernization'. Underlying all colonial discourse is a binary of colonizer/colonized, civilized/uncivilized, white/black which works to justify the civilizing mission and perpetuate a cultural distinction which is essential to the 'business' of economic and political exploitation. This is a form of **epistemic violence** that has a lasting impact on the colonized culture.

One of the clearest expressions of this mission can be found in Lord Macauley's 1834 Minute to Parliament. Intervening in an argument between Anglicists and Orientalists as to the best way to educate the Indian population, Macaulay claimed that English was the unparalleled medium of instruction for its capacity to bring enlightenment. With breathtaking arrogance, he claims that 'whoever knows [the English language] has ready access to all the vast intellectual wealth, which all the wisest nations of the earth have created and hoarded in the course of ninety generations' (1835: 350). The method chosen to inculcate civilized Christian values in the Indian population was English literature which not only provided a means of cultural indoctrination but offered a heightened vision of English civilization. The purpose of such education was 'to form a class who may be interpreters between us and the millions whom we govern; a class of persons, Indian in blood and colour, but English in taste, in opinions, in morals, and in intellect'.

According to Gauri Viswanathan,

> The strategy of locating authority in these texts all but effaced the sordid history of colonialist expropriation, material exploitation, and class and race oppression behind European world dominance... the English literary text functioned as a surrogate Englishman in his highest and most perfect state.
>
> (1987: 23)

This Englishman was at the same time the embodiment of universal human values. This strategy proved a particularly effective one because the discourse of English literature was disseminated with its attendant spiritual values, cultural assumptions, social discriminations, racial prejudices and humanistic values more or less intact.

The idea of an obligation to disseminate the wealth of the language also has deep roots in a heroic view of the discipline of history; of the special calling of 'civilised' nations and their special relevance to the task of history. Bishop Stubbs, in his lecture on the purposes and methods of historical study in Oxford on May 1877 says:

> I will say that the true field of Historic Study is the history of those nations and institutions in which the real growth of humanity is to be traced: in which we can follow the developments, the retardations and perturbations, the ebb and flow of human progress, the education of the world...
>
> (cited in Williams 1972: 42)

Though it has the special flavour of British imperial history, such a concept is strongly reminiscent of Hegel's notorious statement that 'Africa has remained – for all purposes of connection with the rest of the World – shut up; it is the Gold-land compressed within itself' (1899: 91). It must be disregarded because 'Africa forms no historical part of the World' (99).

The belief in a mission to civilize the primitive cultures colonized by empire is present in all imperial ventures. Although French colonialism did not have a document that stated its aim as clearly as Macaulay did in British India, in French imperial possessions, especially in Africa and the Caribbean, the idea of colonialism as a mission to turn barbarous natives into civilized Frenchmen (*mission civilisatrice*) was equally central to the way in which their colonies were organized (see **colonial governance**). The idea that colonized peoples could be evolved from their native uncivilized state into 'civilized' by being deculturated from their own practices and recultured into those of their French colonizers was also designed to create a class (the evolved or évolué) who could bridge the gap between the two. The emphasis in the French model, as in the English, also stressed the need for this new class to become fluent in French and educated in French culture. In some ways, the French model went even further since it envisaged this class being educated in French metropolitan institutions and those who were so educated would then become indistinguishable from their colonizers. In practice, of course, this pious claim did not result.

Alongside this secular concept, the missionary claim that if the native could be converted s/he would be elevated morally and could then be **assimilated** into a society where all were equal. Again, in practice, this ideal never became realized in practice. In all these cases, the prejudices of racism undermined these spurious claims that colonialism had a noble aim to create equality between the rulers and the subject peoples of the imperial enterprise (see **missions** and **conversion** and the **postcolonial**).

Further Reading: Freeman 1898; Seeley 1890; Viswanathan 1987.

CLASH OF CIVILIZATIONS

The concept of the 'clash of civilizations' was coined by Samuel Huntington in 1993 article 'The Clash of Civilizations?' (*Foreign Affairs 1992–1993*) in which he suggested that the world was entering a new phase and that its various interpretations: 'the end of history, the return of traditional rivalries between nation states, and the decline of the nation state from the conflicting pulls of tribalism and globalism' (1992–1993: 22) all missed the point. The fundamental source of conflict in the New World would not be ideological or economic but cultural. He goes on to say that

> Nation states will remain the most powerful actors in world affairs, but the principal conflicts of global politics will occur between nations and groups of different civilizations. The clash of civilizations will dominate global politics. The fault lines between civilizations will be the battle lines of the future.
>
> (22)

Huntington developed this thesis in *The Clash of Civilizations and the Remaking of World Order* (1996). Whereas the article had included a question mark, he set out in the book to provide a comprehensive answer to the question. He posits the existence of eight major civilizations among which certain dividing lines exist, which help people to identify themselves as a member of a particular civilization. Huntington argues that different civilizations keep different views about the world and life in the world. These views are the product of history and transferred from generation to generation. Therefore, it is quite difficult to reject outright the importance of such metaphysical differences in the life of people. These kinds of differences develop the notions of 'us' and 'others'. He stresses the role of globalization as a chief cause of developing such consciousness.

Despite the immediate celebrity and widespread commentary that surrounded the concept, critics believed that the underlying ideas of the book depended on an overgeneral and even simplistic view of 'civilizations'. 'Civilizations and culture both refer to the overall way of life of a people', says Huntington, 'and a civilization is a culture writ large' (1996: 41)... Civilizations are the biggest 'we' within which we feel culturally at home as distinguished from all the other 'thems' out there (43). Furthermore, 'Civilizations have no clear-cut boundaries and not precise beginnings and endings' (43) which would appear to militate against their clear opposition as entities. Huntington did not come to terms with the possibility that civilizations, like cultures, have porous borders and flow into one another, affecting and transforming one another. If Islam represents a 'civilization', which in Huntington's terms is 'culture writ large', how would we account for the vast cultural differences between, say, Saudi, Turkish and Indonesian Islamic practices and cultures? Furthermore, the concept pays no attention to the extent to which behaviour can be a function of either class or social and economic disadvantage, causes that operate in all cultures.

In geopolitical terms, the capacity for 'civilizations' to operate as political entities is remote. One commentator makes the point that we might possibly say that China is a civilization very roughly approximating a political entity. But we could not say the same about other civilizations identified by Huntington because they lack the shared political and economic institutions to shape the behaviour of their constituent units. 'For instance, Pakistan, Iran and Afghanistan are part of the Islamic civilization, if we believe that Islamic civilization is a political entity then these three countries must complement each other's foreign policies. In reality, this is not the case' (Salman 2011: 3).

According to Edward Said, perhaps Huntington's strongest critic, 'the clash of civilizations relied on the vague notion of 'civilizational identity' and the interactions among seven or eight major civilizations', of which the conflict between two of them, Islam and the West, gets the lion's share of his attention (Said 2001: 1). Said claims that Huntington relies heavily on a 1990 article by Bernard Lewis' 'The Roots of Muslim Rage': 'in both articles the personification of enormous entities called "the West" and "Islam" is recklessly affirmed as if hugely complicated matters like identity and culture existed in a cartoonlike world where Popeye and Bluto bash each other mercilessly' (2001: 1).

The interest of this term for postcolonial studies lies in its demonstration of a contemporary form of orientalist stereotyping in which 'Muslim' replaces 'Oriental' and 'the internal dynamics, plurality and complexity of whole regions and civilizations are overlooked in favour of a typology that sets up one "civilization" as the binary opposite of the West'. Orientalism, for Said, was a way of defining and locating Europe's others, and in Huntington's theory, this becomes a way of defining the others of the West. Huntington could be seen to extend the field of Orientalism, 'which no single scholar can create but which each scholar receives and in which he then finds a place for himself, the individual researcher makes his contribution' (Said 1978: 272–273). While nineteenth-century Orientalism stereotyped the Middle East as the 'Orient', for Huntington, 'Islam' becomes the equivalent generalization.

The effect of Huntington's contribution, according to Said, is to make

> 'civilizations' and 'identities' into what they are not: shut-down, sealed-off entities that have been purged of the myriad currents and countercurrents that animate human history, and that over centuries have made it possible for that history not only to contain wars of religion and imperial conquest but also to be one of exchange, cross-fertilization and sharing.
>
> (Said 2001: 3)

Said's critique was significant because it came just after the events of September 11, 2001 when 'The carefully planned and horrendous, pathologically motivated suicide attack and mass slaughter by a small group of deranged militants has been turned into proof of Huntington's thesis' (2001: 2). The events of September 11 became a classic demonstration of how a particular event could become the signature of a whole civilization, largely due to the response of the United States. Despite the arguments against Huntington's theory, the phrase 'The Clash of Civilizations' took on a life of its own after 9/11, catching the popular imagination in the West and becoming widely used in the media by people who had never read the book.

The effect of the events of September 11 was to send the United States to war under the pretext of defending democracy. Terrorism was linked to Afghanistan, Iraq and Pakistan, all of which are Muslim countries. Despite what has been repeated by George W. Bush, and later by

Barack Obama, that the West was not at war against Islam, the Muslim world felt so, and the wars in Afghanistan and Iraq appeared to confirm this belief.

Further Reading: Huntington 1992, 1996; Salman 2011; Said 1978, 2001.

CLASS AND POSTCOLONIALISM

Like 'gender' and **race**, the concept of class intersects in important ways with the cultural implications of colonial domination. It is clear that economic control was significant, if not of primary importance in imperialism, and that economic control involved a reconstruction of the economic and social resources of colonized societies. Consequently, class was an important factor in colonialism, firstly in constructing the attitudes of the colonizers towards different groups and categories of the colonized (natives), and increasingly amongst the colonized peoples themselves as they began to employ colonial cultural discourse to describe the changing nature of their own societies. However, it is less clear to what degree categories like class were able to be employed as descriptors of colonized societies without undergoing profound modifications to accommodate their cultural differences from Europe.

The first contention to be answered is the notion that the kinds of inequity and injustice and exclusion and oppression found in post-colonial societies is simply explicable in terms of class. Is the condition of the colonized themselves simply referable to universal notions of class identification, so that they can be absorbed into some general category such as the international proletariat without a need for further cultur-ally discrete distinctions? The **Eurocentric** and **universalist** bias of such a contention is obvious. Nevertheless, it is clear that in many ways, the idea of a **binarism** between a proletarian and an owning class was a model for the **centre's** perception and treatment of the **margin**, and a model for the way in which imperial authority exercised its power within the colonies.

This conjunction is hardly surprising given the fact that ideas of class and race were deeply intertwined in nineteenth-century European thought, with figures like Gobineau, sometimes called 'the father of modern racism', motivated in his production of a theory of race and degeneration by his own aristocratic fear of the degeneracy produced by the emerging power of the new urban bourgeoisie (Biddiss 1970). The legitimization of sociopolitical (class group) interests by appeals to racial origins was a strong feature of nineteenth-century French thought, as myths of origin, Germanic and Gallic, were employed to legitimate different positions in the class struggles of the time. A similar association can be found in much nineteenth-century English thought, with appeals by literary texts to ideas of Norman and Saxon blood as features of a similar if less violent debate between the aristocracy and the new bourgeoisie.

The concentration of manufacturing in England and the use of colonies as sources of raw materials meant that colonial societies exercised no control over the 'means of production'. At the same time, a modern class analysis involves more than simply identifying the owners of the means of production and the wage-slaves of classic Marxism. It involves identifying the specific and complex array of class interests and affiliations that are established in the wake of capital investment in the colonies. It also involves an analysis of the ways in which the colonized themselves replicate the groupings of the capitalist system, with the emergence of distinctive forms of 'native' capitalists and workers whose social role will often be the result of an intersection of their place in the new social and economic structures with their own, older social and economic formations.

The question of class in colonial societies is further complicated by the kinds of cultural particularities that intersect with general economic categories. For Marx, as for Engels, the universal grouping of all pre-capitalist societies as either feudal or 'Asiatic' meant in effect that any detailed analysis of sociopolitical groups in non-European societies was effectively precluded. Thus one thing Marx himself did not account for, indeed perhaps could not account for, given the resolutely Eurocentric orientation of his models of society, was the fact that class does not transfer across cultures in a simple way, even when those cultures are deeply reconstructed along lines of capital accumulation.

For example, any analysis of ideas of 'class' in societies such as India, in which traditional caste divisions, replicating economic and social disadvantages from generation to generation, may be overlaid by modern, post-industrial forces, needs to take into account the ways in which models of class-divided groups, such as workers or capitalists, often cross and conflict with the older caste boundaries. Where these identities and differences coincide, they may reinforce the kinds of privileges or oppressions that a classic Marxist class analysis would emphasize. More recently, there has been a strong revival of Marxist critiques of postcolonial theory's emphasis on the discursive rather than materialist bases for colonial affect. These argue the need to place class and the class struggle more centrally in the postcolonial project and accuse postcolonial discourse theorists of seeking to replace Marxism as the most effective way of analysing the radical political drive to resistance in the anti-colonial movements. These include the work of Arif Dirlik (Dirlik 1996) and Benita Parry (Parry 2004). These critiques have been extended by the work of Vivak Chibber (Chibber 2013). Chibber targets the work of the influential **Subaltern** studies group in India and by the work of those he argues are the critics influenced by their pioneering work, such as Gayatri Spivak, Partha Chatterjee and Dipesh Chakrabarty. These critics, notably Chakrabarty, argue that although Marx provides a great inspiration for resistance in the postcolonial world, his work operates on universalist assumptions that undermine the claims of the postcolonies to their essential difference from a universal European norm. As Neil Lazarus (himself a strong, early exponent of a more materialist reading of the postcolonial) has argued Chibber's work is often mainly designed to attack these critics in a broadly polemic way but fails to

> identify its object precisely enough. In conflating the historiographic project of 'Subaltern Studies' with 'postcolonial theory', Chibber misrepresents the histories of each of these formations and also the institutional relationship between them. He is at his most compelling in his commentary on capital's 'universalising tendency', in which he demonstrates that arguments about capitalist globalisation do not require one to anticipate an increased homogenisation of the world or, more narrowly still, the progressive universalisation of 'western' norms, values and modes of social life. His critique of the deep-set postcolonialist conviction as to the radical difference and incommensurability between 'western' and 'non-western' worlds is also very valuable. But because he does not utilise the full resources of Marxist and anti-imperialist theory – above all, the theory of uneven and combined development – Chibber fails to diagnose 'postcolonial theory' for what it is: a conjuncturally distinct version of 'Third Worldism'. He wrongly accuses it, instead, of 'Eurocentrism'.
>
> (Lazarus 2016: Abstract)

Further, Lazarus shows that Chibber gets the chronology wrong by assuming that the Subaltern studies group (led by Ranajit Guha) initiated the work of postcolonial scholars. But as Lazarus shows

The truth is just the reverse: it was the consecration of the Subaltern Studies historians by the most prominent postcolonial theorists that brought recognition to them, not only in the fields of literary and cultural studies, but even in their own discipline of history. The key event in this respect, as has often been pointed out, was Oxford University Press's publication in 1988 of a selection of readings from Subaltern Studies, co-edited by Guha and Spivak, and containing a 'Foreword' by Edward W. Said, whose book Orientalism, published ten years earlier in 1978, is routinely taken to represent the inaugural text of postcolonial studies. Said's commentary makes clear that what was at stake in the publication of Selected Subaltern Studies was to bring the work of the Subaltern Studies group to the attention of what he calls 'the Western reader' and also to propose their project overall as ancillary to the established postcolonialist commitment to criticising or 'unthinking' Eurocentrism: '[T]he work of the Subaltern scholars', he wrote, 'can be seen as an analogue of all those recent attempts in the West and throughout the rest of the world to articulate the hidden or suppressed accounts of numerous groups – women, minorities, disadvantaged or dispossessed groups, **refugees**, exiles, etc.

(Lazarus 2016)

Footnoting this reference, Lazarus further argues (incorrectly, by identifying the colonial discourse theorists with postcolonial theory as a whole) that 'The supplementarity of "postcolonial studies" to post-structuralist studies is, of course, well attested; and in his Foreword, Said suggests that Derrida, Foucault, Barthes and Althusser are central to the formation of Subaltern Studies also, "along with the influence of British and American thinkers, like Thompson, E.P. Hobsbawn, Eric and others"' (Guha et al. 1988: x).

But of course, there remains a substantial and important element in the body of Marxist critiques emphasizing class and its existence as a decisive factor across the different societies that constitute the world. They do not necessarily imply that the world is integrated in an even way or developed uniformly. What they argue is that as Lazarus defines it 'the world as a whole must be taken as the appropriate unit of analysis' as is suggested by terms such as world system, **under-development**, **neo-colonialism**, **globalism** and **imperialism** (Lazarus 2016) The debate as to whether and how colonial difference can be sustained and whether or not dominant forms may lead to epistemic violence that silences the colonized and the postcolony is at the heart of the complex and heated exchanges that Chibber's work has provoked.

Even those **settler** societies, such as Australia, that would seem to reproduce the existing class structure of Britain more exactly than any other kind of colony, clearly do not do so in any unproblematic way. Thus, though they may reproduce many aspects of the imperial centre and may even perceive themselves to be filiatively related to it, they often construct opposing myths of their democratic or classless nature, or operate along the lines of internal division based on perceived racial or religious differences ('Irish Catholic convictism' for example) that have completely different orientations from that of the officially acknowledged 'Mother Country'. Such myths of egalitarianism or democracy clearly do not reflect economic truths since inequalities of wealth prevail in all these colonial situations, but they may well reflect self-perceptions that are important aspects of the construction of a new national mythology and identity.

Since recent postcolonial theory has tended to concentrate on the issues of **race**, **ethnicity** and, to a lesser extent, **gender** in the colonialist definitions and opposing self-definitions of colonized peoples, the importance of class has been downplayed. Fewer, if any, attempts have been made to see how the formation of categories, such as race, gender and class, both historically and in modern practice, intersect and coexist. The need to find ways of articulating the importance of economic structures to the formation of these categories of analysis is increasingly clear. An analysis of class has a crucial, if complex, role to play in emphasizing the link between representation and material practice in postcolonial discourse. This revision is necessary because in the final analysis, the means of representation and the means of production act together reflexively to create the complex conditions of the various colonial and postcolonial societies.

Further Reading: Ahmad 1992; Dirlik 1996; Parry 2004; Lazarus 2016.

COLONIAL DESIRE

This term, employed by Robert Young in a 1995 study, indicates the extent to which colonialist discourse was pervaded by sexuality. The idea of colonization itself is grounded in a sexualized discourse of rape, penetration and impregnation, while the subsequent relationship between the colonizer and colonized is often presented in a discourse that is redolent of a sexualized exoticism. Thus, even the positive features of colonial attitudes in discourses such as **Orientalism**, reflect an eroticized vision that is fundamentally reductive. Ideas of the seductive but enervating world of the 'native', to which the colonizer yields at his (or even more her) peril, lead to formulations such as **going native**, which embody the simultaneous lure and threat of the **other**. As Young has shown, the discourse of colonialism is pervaded by images of transgressive sexuality, of an obsession with the idea of the hybrid and miscegenated, and with persistent fantasies of interracial sex. He concludes that sexuality is the direct and congruent legacy of the commercial discourse of early colonial encounters, the traffic of commerce and the traffic of sexuality being complementary and intertwined:

> as in that paradigm of respectability, marriage, economic and sexual exchange were intimately bound up, coupled with each other, from the very first. The history of the meanings of the word 'commerce' includes the exchange both of merchandise and of bodies in sexual intercourse. It was therefore wholly appropriate that sexual exchange and its miscegenated product, which captures the violent antagonistic power relations of sexual and cultural diffusion, should become the dominant paradigm through which the passionate economic and political trafficking of colonialism was conceived.
>
> (Young 1995: 181–182)

Further Reading: Dissanayake and Wickramagamage 1993; Docker 1992; McClintock 1995; Young 1995.

COLONIAL DISCOURSE

This is a term brought into currency by Edward Said who saw Foucault's notion of a **discourse** as valuable for describing that system within which that range of practices termed 'colonial' come into being. Said's Orientalism, which examined the ways in which colonial discourse operated as an instrument of power, initiated what came to be known as colonial discourse theory, that theory which, in the 1980s, saw colonial discourse as its field of study. The best-known colonial discourse theorist, apart from Said, is Homi Bhabha, whose analysis posited certain disabling contradictions within colonial relationships, such as **hybridity**, **ambivalence** and **mimicry**, which revealed the inherent vulnerability of colonial discourse.

Discourse, as Foucault theorizes it, is a system of statements within which the world can be known. It is the system by which dominant groups in society constitute the field of truth by imposing specific knowledges, disciplines and values upon dominated groups. As a social formation, it works to constitute reality not only for the objects it appears to represent, but also for the subjects who form the community on which it depends. Consequently, colonial discourse is the complex of signs and practices that organize social existence and social reproduction within colonial relationships.

Colonial discourse is greatly implicated in ideas of the centrality of Europe, and thus in assumptions that have become characteristic of **modernity**: assumptions about history, language, literature and 'technology'. Colonial discourse is thus a system of statements that can be made about colonies and colonial peoples, about colonizing powers and about the relationship between these two. It is the system of knowledge and beliefs about the world within which acts of colonization take place. Although it is generated within the society and cultures of the colonizers, it becomes that discourse within which the colonized may also come to see themselves. At the very least, it creates a deep conflict in the consciousness of the colonized because of its clash with other knowledges (and kinds of knowledge) about the world. Rules of inclusion and exclusion operate on the assumption of the superiority of the colonizer's culture, history, language, art, political structures, social conventions and the assertion of the need for the colonized to be 'raised up' through colonial contact. In particular, colonial discourse hinges on notions of race that begin to emerge at the very advent of European imperialism. Through such distinctions, it comes to represent the colonized, whatever the nature of their social structures and cultural histories, as 'primitive' and the colonizers as 'civilized'.

Colonial discourse tends to exclude, of course, statements about the exploitation of the resources of the colonized, the political status accruing to colonizing powers, the importance to domestic politics of the development of an empire, all of which may be compelling reasons for maintaining colonial ties. Rather it conceals these benefits in statements about the inferiority of the colonized, the primitive nature of other **races**, the barbaric depravity of colonized societies, and therefore the duty of the imperial power to reproduce itself in the colonial society, and to advance the civilization of the colony through trade, administration, cultural and moral improvement. Such is the power of colonial discourse that individual colonizing subjects are not often consciously aware of the duplicity of their position, for colonial discourse constructs the colonizing subject as much as the colonized. Statements that contradict the discourse cannot be made either without incurring punishment, or without making the individuals who make those statements appear eccentric and abnormal.

Further Reading: Ashcroft 2001b; Barker et al. 1994; Bhabha 1983, 1984a, 1994, 1996; Chrisman and Williams 1993; Hulme 1989; Lazarus 1993; Mohanty 1995; Parry 1995; Pennycook 1998; Said 1978; Spivak 1987.

COLONIAL GOVERNANCE

As the various European nations developed their empires different models of colonial governance emerged. The earliest empires such as those of Spain and Portugal ruled their subject peoples through officials and institutions appointed directly on behalf of the crown and for much of their history provided no means for the participation of the people, even those who were from the metropoles and had settled in their colonies. Independence resulted from the disaffection of these settlers, allied with their descendants resulting from miscegenation with the indigenous peoples (see **mestizo/mestizaje**). Portuguese settlers claimed that this interbreeding had resulted in a more benign form of governance that obviated direct racism (see **luso-tropicalism**). Although this claim is now largely seen to be false, it is still occasionally invoked as a positive difference by the peoples of now independent ex-Portuguese colonies, such as Brazil, Mozambique and even Goa, though that is now a part of the Indian Republic.

Some Dutch colonies, notably those in the area that is now modern Indonesia, initially governed their territories through royal charter companies, granted the right to monopoly trading. These companies often governed some areas directly and others through alliances with local rulers. This pattern was established in many areas where these monopoly trading companies existed, notably India, where both the French and British operated such companies (see **charter companies**).

In the nineteenth century and especially after the surge of rivalry to gain further overseas territory as colonies that characterized the last half of the century, the French and the British developed distinctive forms of colonial governance that have left their mark on these countries to the present day.

The French form is usually referred to as direct rule, meaning that the institutions of the colonies were seen as coterminous with those of the French state itself. The French saw their rule as one designed to raise the 'savage' indigenes to the same level of 'civilisation' they claimed to embody (see **civilizing mission**). Other French-speaking colonies such as the Belgian Congo followed the same path. In this model, the aim was to make the colonized into Frenchmen (or Belgians), though as the underlying racism of the colonizer implied these brown, black or yellow Frenchmen would not be fully assimilated until they had evolved into a higher state. These few were known as the evolved (évolués). They were never more than a minority and usually held low-level white-collar jobs in urban areas. The evolved were described as having 'broken social ties with [their] group' and as having adopted 'another system of values' (Gillet and Cornet 2010: 19). A small but significant minority though were able to go to France and receive a tertiary education, and these produced some of the earliest intellectuals who became the leaders of the emerging nationalist movements, for example the poet and first president of independent Senegal, Leopold Sédar Senghor, who was also, along with other Africans educated in France, the founder of the négritude movement. The same policy was applied in other colonies such as those of the French Caribbean and saw the emergence of such figures as the Martinican writer and activist Aimé Césaire and his countryman Frantz Fanon (see **négritude**, **Fanonism**). Thus the policy which was clearly designed to mollify the colonized and provide an excuse for colonial exploitation paradoxically led to the emergence of a class of people who went on to lead the anti-colonial movements. This is similar to the role that missions unconsciously played in developing proto-nationalists and suggests the power of colonized people to subvert and adopt oppressive forces to their own distinct ends (see **missions and colonization**).

British colonial governance took a different path, though as in the case of India, as we have seen, governance could take multiple forms, including direct rule of the territory conquered or purchased by the great charter company, the East India Company. The influence of Macaulay's Minute of 1834 which sought to supplant the highly evolved cultures of India by what he declared was the infinitely superior culture represented by the literature and history of the English language was meant to educate a body of Indians who could act as 'interpreters between us and the millions whom we govern: a class of persons, Indian in blood and colour, but English in taste, in opinions, in morals, and in intellect' (see **civilizing mission**). A body of such men were recruited to the middle range of administrations in the law and eventually in the governance of the powerful Indian Civil Service. Though they never constituted more than a minority in these institutions, this group also included the native ruling class who usually received an English education. So much of India remained nominally under the rule of these assimilated and nominally 'independent' native princes, though indirectly controlled by the presence of a colonial advisory official who in practice dictated much of the policy. Such states also had no control over their foreign policy towards other states and, as was demonstrated in the 1914–1918 World War, these 'independent' rulers were often eager to provide their troops for imperial purposes. They could also be and were overthrown if, in the judgement of the Company or later of the government of the Raj, their personal or governmental practices were deemed to be improper or unfit. Nevertheless, they provided a model for governance that the British exported to other of their dependencies, as the model that came to be known as indirect rule, that is rule through or by local native authorities. Of course, as in the case of the French model of direct rule, the indirect rule through local leaders was never more than a cover for the actual control exercised by the colonial authorities: the governor, the courts and the district officers on the ground who, like the advisors to the Indian princes, were the final authority and power.

The Indian model was exported to Africa when Frederick Lugard, born in India and with an early career as a soldier involved in the administration of India, left India for a post with the recently formed Imperial British East African Company. Lugard, using the Indian princely model, ruled the newly annexed territory that became Uganda in what he termed a dual mandate with the then king (Kabaka) of the Bugandans, one of the several ethnic groups in the region. Having been moved to what was then the territory of the Upper Niger in what became modern Nigeria, Lugard ruled through the traditional leaders. A similar practice was followed in the Malay States where local sultans were so coopted. This system worked best when a ruling class already existed whose power could be annexed. But where no such class existed, the colonizers brought one into existence by selecting appointed chiefs, as in the case of the Ibo peoples of Eastern Nigeria.

In practice, both systems of direct and indirect rule effectively brought the colonized peoples under colonial governance. But the different effects can still be seen. For example, in the earlier establishment in British colonies of local institutions of tertiary education, whereas French colonies tended to send their 'evolved' citizens to metropolitan institutions. French colonies also tended to form more cross colony institutions, such as the shared monetary system of the CFA franc, or the shared server for digital platforms across French West Africa, reflecting the impulse to centralization implicit in the French model. Even now, the few colonial leftovers of the French colonial system (e.g. Martinique, New Caledonia and Réunion) are designated as *Départements d'Outre Mer* (Overseas Departments) sharing the same rights as Metropolitan Departments, including seats in the French National Assembly. Nevertheless, many of these cross nation institutions have been criticized as helping to maintain a high level of ongoing control and intervention by the ex-colonial power.

Beyond these specific direct forms of governing the colonized lies a vast body of practices by which control was exercised over the colonized:

> colonial and postcolonial forms of governmentality, … are annexed to a wide panoply of powers, techniques, and apparatuses for intervention into populations, and regulative forms of intervention into life, death, and the body, as such intervention is constituted at the intersection(s) of race, gender, class, sexuality, and species.
>
> (Griffiths 2016: 2)

Drawing on the ideas of theorists such as Foucault, the idea of power as defined by sovereign institutions and practices of the kind discussed above has been extended to what he terms the practice of **biopower**.

> 'Colonial governmentality has most generally been a species of power designed for the purposes of, in Scott's terms, 'disabling old forms of life' in order 'to oblige new forms of life to come into being' (Scott 1995: 193). Yet, for Foucault, governmentality in the form he would subsequently elaborate—biopolitics—concerns not only this government of the disposition of forms of life but also the modes by which forms of life can be permitted, or indeed, obliged to live according to a prescribed mode or, alternately, compelled to pass away. The wider implications of control over the bodies and living practices of the colonized subject'. (Griffiths 2016: 5).

Achille Mbembe's concept of **necropolitics** has provided the 'most explicit and extensive development of this logic of race and sovereignty's immanent relation to governmentality in biopolitical times' (Griffiths 2016: 6).

Further Reading: Gerring 2011; Gillet and Cornet 2010; Lugard F.D. [1922] 1965; Perham 1956; Scott 1995; Griffiths 2016.

COLONIAL PATRONAGE

Patronage is a term that refers to the economic or social power that allows cultural institutions and cultural forms to come into existence and be valued and promoted. Patronage can take the form of a simple and direct transaction, such as the purchase or commissioning of works of art by wealthy people, or it can take the form of the support and recognition of social institutions that influence the production of culture. The patronage system may even, in one sense, be said to be the whole society, in so far as a specific society may recognize and endorse some kinds of cultural activities and not others. This is especially true in colonial situations where the great differences between the colonizing and colonized societies means that some forms of cultural activity crucial to the cultural identity of the colonized, and so highly valued by them, may simply be unrecognizable or, if recognized at all, grossly undervalued by the dominant colonial system.

The dominance of certain ethno-centric ideas from European culture at the time of the colonization of other cultures, such as nineteenth-century romantic, liberal-humanist assumptions, concealed such communal cultural systems by promoting the idea that the only significant cultural product is that concerned with and produced by individuals. Postcolonial cultures resist such a concealment because it is impossible to discuss the culture of such societies without recognizing the power of colonial institutions, ideologies and patronage systems in validating some forms of culture and denying the validity of others. The privileging of writing and other inscriptive arts over the **oral** and the performative arts, as well as over other kinds of signifying practices such as sculpture, painting, carving, weaving, ceramics – the whole body of material inscription beyond the written – offers a classic example of such privileging.

Colonial powers instituted these privileges through patronage systems that preferred and encouraged written forms over orality. In the hands of the early missionary patrons, the acquisition of literacy was seen as the mark of civilization, and being raised to a 'civilized' state was a concomitant of, if not an absolutely necessary precondition for, salvation. This cultural hierarchy was reinforced by Colonial Educational Systems and Colonial Literature Bureaux, whose task was to develop certain forms of communication, such as written texts in the indigenous and colonial languages – newspapers, journals and various kinds of fiction – to encourage the development of a class of colonials willing to participate in colonial modes of social and artistic production (see **hegemony**).

Literature was given support, while oral practices were seen as primitive and were thus neglected or actively discouraged. Although some colonial administrations recognized and even encouraged writing in the indigenous languages, they often did so in ways that transformed local forms of cultural production and encouraged the colonized to accept the superiority of European practices over the local. Thus, for example, in Northern Nigeria, Hausa was encouraged by the Colonial Literature Bureau in the region as a language of expression, in accordance with the policies of 'indirect rule' that the British administration in West Africa favoured. But traditional, religious forms were discouraged, while modern forms such as the short fictional narrative were actively promoted. This was seen as consistent with the colonial policy of 'modernization' which resulted in the supplanting of local cultural practices by imported European ones.

Patronage systems continued to influence the development of postcolonial cultures into and beyond the period of independence, as publishers actively promoted some forms of expression over others (see Lefevere 1983; Griffiths 1996). The control exercised by missionary presses and Colonial Literature Bureaux is obvious, but it may be just as powerfully exercised by the more hidden forces of patronage operated by foreign-owned publishing companies or other media outlets and by the location of the prominent journals of critical assessment in the erstwhile metropolitan centres (Mitchell 1992). The dispute about language choice often intermeshes with these issues of patronage and control, as does the issue of the control of the ownership of the copyright to editions of texts in various designated worlds or local 'markets'. As culture is increasingly commodified, the ownership of these agencies for commissioning, licensing and distribution can have profound effects, not only on the pricing and availability of material, but on the selection of the art forms and genres and themes and styles of products that are actively promoted (see **commodification**).

Further Reading: Altbach 1975; Barringer and Flynn 1998; Griffiths 1997; Griffiths 2000; Lefevere 1983; Viswanathan 1989; Shepherd 2002; Krishna 2009.

COLONIALISM

The term colonialism is important in defining the specific form of cultural exploitation that developed with the expansion of Europe over the last 400 years. Although many earlier civilizations had colonies, and although they perceived their relations with them to be one of a central imperium in relation to a periphery of provincial, marginal and barbarian cultures, a number of crucial factors entered into the construction of the post-Renaissance practices of **imperialism**. Edward Said offers the following distinction: "'imperialism" means the practice, the theory, and the attitudes of a dominating metropolitan centre ruling a distant territory; "colonialism", which is almost always a consequence of imperialism, is the implanting of settlements on distant territory' (Said 1993: 8).

The scale and variety of colonial settlements generated by the expansion of European society after the Renaissance shows why the term colonialism has been seen to be a distinctive form of the more general ideology of imperialism. Although Said's formula, which uses 'imperialism' for the ideological force and 'colonialism' for the practice, is a generally useful distinction, European colonialism in the post-Renaissance world became a sufficiently specialized and historically specific form of imperial expansion to justify its current general usage as a distinctive kind of political ideology. This is encapsulated in the active concept of **coloniality** suggested by critics such as Quijano.

The fact that European post-Renaissance colonial expansion was coterminous with the development of a modern capitalist system of economic exchange (see **world system theory**) meant that the perception of the colonies as primarily established to provide raw materials for the burgeoning economies of the colonial powers was greatly strengthened and institutionalized. It also meant that the relation between the colonizer and colonized was locked into a rigid hierarchy of difference deeply resistant to fair and equitable exchanges, whether economic, cultural or social.

In colonies where the subject people were of a different race, or where minority indigenous peoples existed, the ideology of race was also a crucial part of the construction and naturalization of an unequal form of intercultural relations. **Race** itself, with its accompanying racism and racial prejudice, was largely a product of the same post-Renaissance period, and a justification for the treatment of enslaved peoples after the development of the **slave** trade of the Atlantic Middle Passage from the late sixteenth century onwards. In such situations, the idea of the colonial world became one of a people intrinsically inferior, not just outside history and civilization, but genetically pre-determined to inferiority. Their subjection was not just a matter of profit and convenience but also could be constructed as a natural state. The idea of the 'evolution of mankind' and the survival of the fittest 'race', in the crude application of social Darwinism, went hand in hand with the doctrines of imperialism that evolved at the end of the nineteenth century.

The sexist exclusivity of these discourses (man, mankind, etc.) demonstrated their ideological alliance with patriarchal practices, as numerous commentators have noted (see **feminism** and **postcolonialism**). As a result of these new formulations, colonization could be (re)presented as a virtuous and necessary 'civilizing' task involving education and paternalistic nurture. An example of this is Kipling's famous admonition of America in 1899 to 'Take up the White Man's Burden' after their war against Spain in the Philippines rather than follow their own anti-colonial model and offer the Filipinos independence and nationhood (Kipling 1899: 323–324). In this period, and for these reasons, colonialism developed an ideology rooted in obfuscatory justification, and its violent and essentially unjust processes became increasingly difficult to perceive behind a liberal smoke-screen of civilizing 'task', paternalistic 'development' and 'aid'. The development of such territorial designators as 'Protectorates', 'Trust Territories', 'Condominiums', etc. served to justify the continuing process of colonialism as well as to hide the fact that these territories were the displaced sites of increasingly violent struggles for markets and raw materials by the industrialized nations of the West.

In the case of the non-indigenous inhabitants of **settler colonies**, the idea of a cultural inferiority exceeded that of mere provincial gaucherie as race permeated even the construction of 'white' settlers. These were frequently characterized as having wholly degenerated (**gone native**) from contact with other races, as in the case of white Creoles in the West Indies (Brathwaite 1971), or, in the case of settler colonies such as Canada or Australia, as having developed specific limited colonial characteristics (physical prowess, sporting ability) but not others (cultural and social sophistication). The same practice of characterizing 'colonial' peoples by signifiers of naivety, of social and cultural provinciality and of originary taint ('Irishness', for example, was imported from the internal discriminations of Britain in the Victorian period to its colonialist constructions of both America and Australia) was a feature of English texts even as late as the early twentieth century.

This was so even for Americans, despite independence and the radical shift in their own power position in the world at large after American industrialization in the late nineteenth century (see, for example, the presentation of Americans in such late nineteenth-century and early twentieth-century texts as Conan Doyle's Sherlock Holmes stories, or Shaw's *Man and Superman*). Thus, the negative construction of self was as important a feature of self-representation for settler colonies as for colonies of occupation where race and the idea of an alien or decayed civilization were a feature of colonial discrimination. (Although Canada had achieved independent status in the 1870s and Australia became an independent Federation in 1900, the people of both these settler colonies retained many symbolic links that emphasized their continuing dependence on the imperial centre; thus, for example, Australians did not carry separate and distinctive national passports until 1946). By the end of the nineteenth century, colonialism had developed into a system of ahistorical categorization in which certain societies and cultures were perceived as intrinsically inferior.

In Britain, at least, and arguably elsewhere too, by the end of the nineteenth century, a domestic programme for the function of empire could be clearly discerned, as Victorian society faced increasing internal dissension and division (Disraeli's *Two Nations*). The doctrine of the New Imperialism was in many ways Disraeli's response to his perception that Britain was divided into two nations of rich and poor, industrial and non-industrial. Empire became the principal ideological unifier across class and other social divisions in Britain. It was to be the principal icon of national unity in the face of the widely perceived social threat of class unrest and revolution that had arisen in post-industrial British society. An **other** (the colonized) existed as a primary means of defining the colonizer and of creating a sense of unity beneath such differences as class and wealth and between the increasingly polarized life of the industrialized cities that developed the wealth and that of the traditional countryside to which its beneficiaries retreated or retired. The colonialist system permitted a notional idea of improvement for the colonized, via such metaphors as parent/child, tree/branch, etc., which in theory allowed that at some future time the inferior colonials might be raised to the status of the colonizer. But, in practice, this future was always endlessly deferred.

It is significant that no society ever attained full freedom from the colonial system by the involuntary, active disengagement of the colonial power until it was provoked by a considerable internal struggle for self-determination or, most usually, by extended and active violent opposition by the colonized. It is one of the great myths of recent British colonial history in particular that the granting of independence to its colonies was the result of a proactive and deliberate policy of enlightenment on the part of the British people, a policy that distinguished British colonialism from the inferior and more rapacious European brands. Such readings are, of course, part of the construction of the ideology of late-nineteenth-century imperialism in which literary representation played a vigorous part, whether actively, as in the work of Kipling, or in a more ambivalent way in the works of Conrad. Despite the anti-imperial strain in some of his writing, Conrad continues to actively distinguish between the English model of colonialism, which has 'an ideal at the back of it', and the mere rapacity of the imperialism of 'lesser breeds' of imperialists. These specious distinctions are projected back into the narratives of the rapacious Spanish conquistadores, though the British treatment of the Indians in Virginia differed from that of the Spanish only in quantity not in the degree of its brutality (Hulme 1986). Even the granting of dominion status or limited independence to white settler cultures was the result of long constitutional and political struggles and was made dependent on the retention of legal and constitutional links with the Crown that limited the right of those societies to conduct their own affairs and to develop their own systems of justice or governance. In such societies, of course, the indigenous peoples were not granted even the most limited form of citizenship under these new constitutional models. In Western Australia, for example, even in the 1920s, the Government Department that had charge of Aboriginal affairs was called the Department of Fisheries, Forests, Wildlife and Aborigines. Recent attempts to 'offload' the guilt of colonial policies onto the colonial 'settlers' as a convenient scapegoat emphasize the periods when metropolitan, government policy was more enlightened than that of the local settlers. But in general, such ideological discriminations were in no sense alien to the spirit of the metropolitan, colonial powers that had set up these colonies, nor did this essentially discriminatory attitude on the part of the 'home' country change after the granting of federal or dominion status. Racial discrimination was, in the majority of cases, a direct extension of colonial policy and continued to receive both overt and covert support from the ex-colonial powers as well as from the newly emerging power of America throughout the period up to and even after the Second World War.

Such policies of racial discrimination reached their nadir in South African apartheid, which had its roots in earlier colonial discriminatory policies (Davidson 1994). In the case of societies where the factor of race was less easily resolved by such internal discriminatory categorizations, the importance of racial discrimination was even more obvious. British India and European African colonies, for example, had to engage in a long and frequently bloody process of dissent, protest and rebellion to secure their independence. It is also significant that in those cases where European colonial powers held on longest, for example the Portuguese colonies, they were often able to do so and indeed were encouraged to do so by the degree to which their colonial governments were really only a front for a 'broader imperialism', as Amilcar Cabral himself noted (see **anti-colonialism**). Similarly, the nationalist government in South Africa was able to survive only because it was supported by the investment of those very countries who were supposedly opposed to the regime. Thus **colonialism**, far from disappearing as the century goes on, too often merely modified and developed into the **neo-colonialism** of the post-independence period.

Further Reading: Croizier et al. 2002; Dirlik 2005; Dixon and Heffernan 1991; Eagleton 1990; Easton 1964; Ferro 1997; Fieldhouse 1981; Hart 2003; Havinden and Meredith 1993; Hogan 2000; Kent 1992; Loomba 2005; Prakash 1995; Reiss 2004; Ukai and Harrington 2005; Wesseling 1997.

COMMODIFICATION

Commodification is the process of transforming something that had not been seen previously as a commodity into a marketable product. Commodification of culture is the process by which cultural traditions or objects are turned into marketable commodities. It reflects the way in which our increasingly globalized world allows cultures and cultural products to be circulated across wider areas (see **globalization**). Thus, commodifying culture may have positive aspects as cultures are exposed to a broader realm of cultural differences, but since market forces frequently demand the modification of cultural forms to make them more accessible or appealing to buyers beyond their own societies, it can also, paradoxically, be the source of a loss of cultural diversity. Helen Gilbert explains how artistic festivals centred on performance have featured in the emergence and consolidation of the new nations of the Pacific region and elsewhere. While these festivals can be part of a tourist vision of such cultures or can be employed by governments to publicize their self-interested programmes and aims, they can also be employed to ensure the survival and revaluation of traditional forms neglected or disparaged in the colonial period (Gilbert 2020).

With sensitive and independent control, commodification can be a source of empowerment for communities, opening their artistic and craft practices to allow them to generate economic power by opening their sales up to a global marketplace. But it can also be a source of loss of traditional forms as market demands enforce stereotypical practices that cease to represent the culture as it was. This process may undermine authentic cultural forms as recognized by the cultures before commodity marketing forced change, though the idea of an authentic cultural form is itself open to dispute (see **authentic/authenticity**).

Despite these complex issues which make the concept a problematic and divisive one, cultural commodification is usually seen as one of the many ways colonizing forces have appropriated and exploited the cultures of colonized peoples. This can be the case both in invaded cultures and in settler cultures, as in the exploitation of indigenous art from indigenous cultures: from First Nations people in the United States and Canada, to the indigenous peoples of Australia and New Zealand, to Pacific Island peoples and many more. Even where these cultures may have become independent, as is the case of Pacific communities or have achieved varying degrees of recognition within their erstwhile settler colonies (Australia, Canada, New Zealand, etc.), they are often dependent on tourism for the economic survival of their communities (Shepherd 2002). This leads to a rapid commodification of many aspects of their tradition and art. It can also mean that their traditional sacred sites, or symbols may be exploited and changed in culturally unacceptable ways. In some cases, the value generated by this commodification is not even directed back to the communities themselves but is diverted to the profits of the companies who have appropriated the cultural artefacts or practices (see **appropriation**).

An even more disturbing aspect of the effect of thinking of cultures as commodities occurs when the practice is extended to people. Obviously, this occurs at its most obvious in practices such as slavery other oppressive forms of recruitment to provide labour forces for colonies (see **slave/slavery**; **indentured labour**). But, as Ashis Nandy has argued (Nandy 1983), in its pursuit of modernity and in the name of development, many people in the postcolonial world were commodified and this practice continues under the force of neoliberal globalization as the new aspiring middle classes who rule in the independent ex-colonies continue to be driven by the idea of developing their societies through industrialization and modernization and create through 'the commodification of man and nature... unprecedented levels of inequality and violence besides rendering the poor expendable or redundant' (Krishna 2009: 168).

Further Reading: Gilbert 2020; Shepherd 2002; Krishna 2008; Appadurai 1986; Appadurai 1996; Nandy 1983.

COMMONWEALTH

This is the common name for what was called the British Commonwealth of Nations, i.e. the political community constituted by the former British Empire and consisting of the United Kingdom, its dependencies and certain former colonies that are now sovereign nations.

COMMONWEALTH LITERATURE

Broadly, the literatures of the former British Empire and the Commonwealth, including that of Britain. In practice, however, the term has generally been used to refer to the literatures (written in English) of colonies, former colonies (including India) and dependencies of Britain, excluding the literature of England. (The term has sometimes included literatures written in 'local' languages and oral performance, and it has been used to include the literatures of Wales, Scotland and Ireland.)

The rise of the study of national literatures written in English (outside Britain) begins with the study of 'American' literature (i.e. the literature of the United States). But those literatures that came to be collectively studied as literatures of the Commonwealth were beginning to be considered within their own national contexts from the late 1940s onwards. However, the concept of 'Commonwealth Literature' as a separate disciplinary area within English studies began in the early 1960s in both the United States and England. In the United States, it was formulated as the study of literatures written in a 'world' language in Joseph Jones' *Terranglia: The Case for English as a World Literature (1965)*, and as Commonwealth Literature in A.L. McLeod's *The Commonwealth Pen* (1961), a work dedicated to R.G. Howarth whose comparative grounding in South African and Australian literatures had proved inspirational for a number of early Commonwealth Literature scholars. The journal *World Literature Written in English* began in 1966 and had been appearing regularly by 1971; its precursor, the *CBC Newsletter*, was published from 1962 to 1966; a division of the MLA (ethno-centrically entitled 'World Literatures in English outside the United States and Britain') was constituted in the early 1960s. In England, the first international Commonwealth Literature Conference was held in Leeds in 1964 and the Association for Commonwealth Literature and Language Studies formed. (The Leeds meeting followed conferences held at Makerere, Uganda, on the role of English as an overseas language, and at Cambridge, England, on the teaching of English literature overseas). The *Journal of Commonwealth Literature* began in 1965 and the third major journal devoted exclusively to theory and criticism of commonwealth literatures (Kunapipi) was published in 1979 (the journal subsequently became a leading journal in establishing the shift to the use of the term postcolonial literatures).

Contemporary postcolonial studies represent the intersection of Commonwealth literary studies and what is usually now referred to as 'colonial discourse theory'. As Peter Hulme notes in his essay Subversive Archipelagoes (1989), colonial discourse is 'a formulation of recent currency which can perhaps be best understood as designating a conceptual area first marked out by Edward Said's Orientalism' although, as Hulme notes, 'much of the work in the area published after Orientalism obviously had its genesis long before'.

Like Orientalism, which established future developmental lines for colonial discourse theory, the papers delivered at the 1964 Leeds Conference, in particular D.E.S. Maxwell's Landscape and Theme, set some of the terms that dominated Commonwealth postcolonial criticism and theory for the next decade. But much that happened at Leeds had already been determined by the growth of nationalist (literary) movements and traditions of cultural critique in Commonwealth countries, a growth based on an understanding of both the deliberate and adventitious uses of English literature as a means of colonialist control throughout Britain's former empire. In the 1960s, the initiation of American literature courses in a number of Commonwealth universities, together with the rise of nationalist cultural sentiment, destabilized both the hitherto unquestioned centrality of British literature in English Department curricula and the grounds on which much of that study was based, particularly the notion of 'literary universality'. The Leeds Conference and the 1960s questioning of such Anglo-centric assumptions could themselves also be traced to a history of colonial (and racial) resistance and critique, of which the négritude movement of the 1930s and 1940s is a prominent example.

Commonwealth postcolonial critics, less engaged by Continental philosophies than colonial discourse theorists, initially concentrated their energies on rendering creative writing in English in Commonwealth countries visible within a discipline of literary studies whose assumptions, bases and power were deeply and almost exclusively invested in the literatures of England (or at best the United Kingdom). In fighting for the recognition of postcolonial Commonwealth writing within academies whose roots and continuing power depended on the persisting cultural and/or political centrality of the imperium, and in a discipline whose manner and subject matter were the focal signs and symbols of that power – British literature and its teaching constantly reified, replayed and reinvested the colonial relation – nationalist critics were forced to conduct their guerrilla war within the terms and framework of an English literary critical practice. In so doing, they initially adopted the tenets of Leavisite and/or New Criticism, reading postcolonial texts within a broadly Euro-modernist tradition, but one whose increasing and inevitable erosion was ensured by the anti-colonial pressures of the literary texts themselves. Forced from this New Critical hermeticism into a socio-cultural specificity by such local anti-colonial pressures, Commonwealth postcolonialism increasingly took on a localized orientation and a more generally theoretical one, bringing it closer to the concerns of what would become its developing 'sister' stream, colonial discourse theory.

Commonwealth postcolonialism remains primarily committed to the literary text, even though it has increasingly turned as well to imperial documents and the discourse of empire, and it has remained, following the Leeds Conference, both predominantly nation-based and determinedly comparative in its practice. Tending increasingly during the 1970s to the anti-colonial, it challenged the centrality of English values and the English canon, and raised the important issue of the continuing interpellative effects of English literary education. Such anti-colonialist arguments were necessarily accompanied by calls for the institutional introduction of national or regional literatures. Most significantly, in terms of future debate within the field, it retained its historical basis in the institutions and practices of British colonialism (and in resistance to these), continuing to include the study of the settler colonies as being crucial for the understanding of imperialism, resistance and the postcolonial.

The more broadly post-structuralist or colonial discourse theory stream, by contrast, with its basis in European philosophy and politics has generally been less interested in contemporary writing by the formerly colonized and the politics of anti-colonial pedagogy within the academies. It has been considerably less focused on creative writing (with the exception of British imperial works). Above all, perhaps, on the basis of its philosophical groundings, it has rejected the national as a kind of 'false consciousness', thereby bringing it into conflict with the Commonwealth Literature stream, much of whose important early anti-colonial work was necessarily grounded in the national as a decolonizing counter to both pre- and post-independence Anglo-interpellation.

Further Reading: Amur et al. 1985; Ashcroft et al. 1989; Bennett 2003; Boehmer 1995, 1998; Brahms 1995; Goodwin 1992; Head 2006; Hulme 1989; Jones 1965; King 1974, 1983, 1996; Mohanram and Rajan 1996; New 1975; Riemenschneider 1983; Rutherford et al. 1992; Spivak 2005; Talib 2002; Thieme 1996; Tiffin 1983, 1984.

COMPRADOR

A Portuguese word meaning 'purchaser', comprador was originally used to refer to a local merchant acting as a middleman between foreign producers and a local market. Marxists have used it to refer specifically to those local bourgeoisie who owe their privileged position to foreign monopolies and hence maintain a vested interest in colonial occupation. In postcolonial theory, the term has evolved a broader use, to include the intelligentsia – academics, creative writers and artists – whose independence may be compromised by a reliance on, and identification with, colonial power.

The notion of a comprador class, whether of capitalists or intellectuals, assumes the existence of a clear hierarchical structure of cultural and material relations, for it is arguable that nobody in a colonized society can ever fully avoid the effects of colonial and neo-colonial cultural power. In postcolonial societies, it is by no means the bourgeoisie alone who have gained 'access to' popular cultural media such as television or consumables such as Coca-Cola. The assumption that a comprador class is necessarily and identifiably distinct from the rest of the society is therefore somewhat questionable. The word continues to be used to describe a relatively privileged, wealthy and educated élite who maintain a more highly developed capacity to engage in the international communicative practices introduced by colonial domination, and who may therefore be less inclined to struggle for local cultural and political independence.

CONTACT ZONE

The term was first used by Mary Louise Pratt as part of a **transcultural** pedagogic exercise to try and involve students in understanding their own subject position in transcultural negotiation and confrontation.

> The lecturer's traditional (imagined) task – unifying the world in the class eyes by means of a monologue that rings equally coherent, revealing, and true for all, forging an ad hoc community, homogeneous with respect to ones own words – this task became not only impossible but anomalous and unimaginable. Instead, one had to work in the knowledge that whatever one said was going to be systematically received in radically heterogeneous ways that we were neither able nor entitled to prescribe.
>
> (Pratt 1991)

The term was then developed by Pratt to describe social spaces where 'disparate cultures meet, clash and grapple with each other, often in highly asymmetrical relations of dominance and subordination – like colonialism, slavery, or their aftermaths as they are lived out across the globe today' (Pratt 1992: 4). Since then, the term has proliferated. As the advertisement for a notable conference held at the University of Wisconsin-Madison in 2001 expressed it:

> In the past ten years, the explosion of work across the disciplines on contact zones, **borderlands**, **transculturation**, migrations, cultural and commercial traffic, and the various forms of resulting **hybridity**, **métissage**, **mestizaje**, and **créolité** has developed the term far beyond her original formulation. Interactions between global and local, transnational and national, identity and **difference**, conjuncturalism and identity politics, space and time have become important areas of research as the study of culture, society, and power has become increasingly comparative, historical, and global in scope' (http://btcs.wisc.edu/contactzone.htm).

What this suggests is that the contact zone is an extremely useful and flexible term for the many complex engagements which characterize the postcolonial space and its encounters. The term has had considerable usage in recent studies of settler/indigene relations in societies such as Australia (see Carter 1992; Somerville and Perkins 2003). Studies like the last which are produced by non-indigenous and indigenous collaborators seek to make the contact zone a space of engagement where the inequalities of the relations between the parties engaged can be confronted if not resolved. This is very much in the spirit of Pratt's initial exercise.

Further Reading: Pratt 1992.

CONTRAPUNTAL READING

A term coined by Edward Said to describe a way of reading the texts of English literature so as to reveal their deep implication in imperialism and the colonial process. Borrowed from music, the term suggests a responsive reading that provides a counterpoint to the text, thus enabling the emergence of colonial implications that might otherwise remain hidden. Thus, a reading of Jane Austen's *Mansfield Park*, for instance, can reveal the extent to which the privileged life of the English upper classes is established upon the profits made from West Indian plantations, and, by implication, from the exploitation of the colonized. By thus stressing the affiliations of the text, its origin in social and cultural reality rather than its filiative connections with English literature and canonical criteria, the critic can uncover cultural and political implications that may seem only fleetingly addressed in the text itself. 'As we look back at the cultural archive', says Said, 'we begin to reread it not univocally but contrapuntally' (1993: 59). The overarching implication is the extent to which English society and culture was grounded on the ideology and practices of imperialism.

Further Reading: Said 1993.

CONVERSION AND THE POSTCOLONIAL

Missions and religious conversion were central aspects of the colonial process (see **missions and colonialism**). In her groundbreaking study of conversion, Gauri Viswanathan has claimed that

> religious conversion is arguably one of the most unsettling political events in the life of a society. This is irrespective of whether

conversion involves a single individual or an entire community....
With the departure of members from the fold, the cohesion of a
community is under threat.

(Viswanathan 1998: xi)

But when colonized subjects were converted to Christianity, the
assumption that they were also decultured is far from true. Viswanathan
illustrates this with the case of Narayan Viman Tilak, a Maharashtrian
Brahmin converted to Christianity in late nineteenth-century western
India. She argues that

Although he assimilated norms of Christian belief and conduct,
Tilak also sought to indigenize Christianity and make it compat-
ible with Hinduism. His syncretic project contained an implicit
critique of the alienating effects of British colonialism. His subsequent use of Christianity to enunciate an anticolonial vision of
Indian nationalism was far more damaging to British imperial
ambitions that if he were to have remained a Hindu.

(Viswanathan 1998: 39–40)

This process occurred in other colonial settings, as Viswanathan acknowledges when she references the work of Robin Horton and his assertion
that 'African conversions were not so much a tribute to missionary
success as expressions of African nationalism, through which the colonial ruler's religion was given a strong indigenist bent' (Viswanathan
1998: 41). For Horton, as she says, 'conversion is a sign of acceptance of
modernity not of capitulation to colonial power' (Viswanathan 1998:
41). Conversions were not made in any great numbers until a body of
indigenous converts became the main force for the evangelization of
their communities. These early converts became the living proof that
it was possible to reconcile conversion with a continuing attachment to
their natal culture (see **Appropriation)**. Of course, certain practices
might be discarded, but others were affirmed, and these early indigenous
evangelists, often among the first to be educated in their communities
were also the earliest proto-nationalists. The case of the Rev. Tiya Soga,
the first black Presbyterian minister in South Africa illustrates this. As
an active Christian evangelizer, he nevertheless collected and recorded
many of his Xhosa cultural practices, and towards the end of his life in
the 1860s insisted that 'both Christian European and Xhosa cultures had
to be "sifted" for those elements that were beneficial' suggesting a syncretic model like the one Tilak later advocated in India (Brock et al.: 48).

As we now realize

> Early post-colonial accounts of missions and conversion simplistically assumed that conversion for colonized peoples inevitably meant deculturation from one's own culture and enculturation into the invasive power and so implied an inevitable collusion with the colonizing power... [more] recently post-colonial accounts of religious conversion increasingly stress that a simple binary of resistance or collusion does not adequately represent the complex practices of the transcultural engagement between colonized and colonizer, including those who converted to Christianity.
>
> (Griffiths 2015)

Further Reading: Viswanathan 1998; Brock et al. 2015; Horton 1971; Griffiths 2015.

COSMOPOLITANISM

The word 'cosmopolitan', which derives from the Greek word kosmopolitês (citizen of the world), continues to grow in popularity in postcolonial theory. Its rise to prominence in the 1990s came about in recognition of the diasporic mobility that had been set in motion by colonialism and greatly accelerated in the post-imperial twentieth century. The sense of the term that all human beings, regardless of their political affiliation, belong to a single community, while ultimately utopian, concurs with the postcolonial critique of nationalism and the nation-state. While there is some gesture towards cosmopolitanism in Plato, e.g. 'I regard you all as kinsmen, familiars, and fellow-citizens' (Protagoras [337c7–d3]), it was the Cynic Diogenes in the fourth century BC, who, when asked where he came from, replied 'I am a citizen of the world [kosmopolitês]' (Diogenes Laertius VI: 63). Stoic cosmopolitanism became enormously influential in the Greco-Roman world, partly because the world was so cosmopolitan at the time and it became most influential in early Christianity.

A resurgence of cosmopolitanism occurred during the Enlightenment, no doubt caused by the rise of capitalism and world-wide trade, by the expansion of European empires across the globe, voyages of exploration and anthropological 'discoveries', but also, ironically, by the emergence of a notion of human rights and a philosophical focus on human reason. But it was Immanuel Kant's ideas in *Perpetual Peace* that seem to have had the most lasting effect. For Kant, cosmopolitanism is a 'universally philanthropic' policy that would ensure peace among nations and grant individuals the right to international hospitality or 'the right of a stranger not to be treated with hostility when he arrives on someone else's territory' (Perpetual Peace 1795: 105). He proposed a form of international legal order in a 'league of nations', organized internally according to 'republican' principles and with no coercive military powers. The reflection of these ideas in the establishment of the League of Nations and present-day United Nations is clear. Kant also introduced the concept of 'cosmopolitan law', suggesting a third sphere of public law – in addition to constitutional law and international law – in which both states and individuals have rights, and where individuals have these rights as 'citizens of the earth' rather than as citizens of particular states.

If Kant proposed a form of political cosmopolitanism, the relationship between cosmopolitanism and capitalism, and the subsequent debate between its ethical and economic implications was set in motion by Marx and Engels and continues to the present day. They regarded cosmopolitanism as an ideological reflection of capitalism, and for them, the word 'cosmopolitan' is tied to the effects of capitalist globalization, including especially the bourgeois ideology which legitimatizes 'free' trade in terms of the freedom of individuals and mutual benefit, although this very capitalist order is the cause of the misery of millions, indeed the cause of the very existence of the proletariat. At the same time, however, Marx and Engels also hold that the proletariat in every country shares essential features and has common interests, thus implying a form of cosmopolitanism of their own.

Today, this argument continues between those, like Mignolo, who argue that cosmopolitanism is tied to neoliberal globalization, those like Cheah and Robbins' *Cosmopolitics: Thinking and Feeling Beyond the Nation* who see cosmopolitanism as evidence of a general movement beyond identification with 'nation', and Appiah, whose book *Cosmopolitanism: Ethics in a World of Strangers* dwells on the importance of the ethical dimension of cosmopolitanism to postcolonial theory. Since the scope of cosmopolitanism covers nothing less than relations between all humans, it is deeply embedded in ethical considerations of acceptance of the other. Ulf Hannerz suggests that: 'A more genuine cosmopolitanism is first of all an orientation, a willingness to engage with the Other. It entails an intellectual and aesthetic openness toward divergent cultural experiences, a search for contrasts rather than uniformity' (103). This is directly reminiscent of Levinas in *Totality and Infinity* when he suggests that 'to receive from the Other beyond the capacity of the I' is 'to have the idea of infinity'. Levinas' definition of ethics as a relation to the Other has become the cornerstone of most discussions of ethics in literature and this dimension of human relations is critically important to postcolonial studies (although Levinas' own paradoxical refusal to extend this ethical relation to Palestinians has not gone unremarked by postcolonial critics).

Apart from an ethical orientation to the Other, cosmopolitanism has been defined as a way of being in the world beyond the confines of nation and nationality. Jeremy Waldron, in 'What Is Cosmopolitan?' *Journal of Political Philosophy* 8, no. 2 (2000): 227–243; pp. 227, 228, defines it as 'a way of being in the world, a way of constructing an identity for oneself that is different from... the idea of belonging to or devotion to or immersion in a particular culture', or, 'the substantive utopian ideal of a polis or polity constructed on a world scale, rather than on the basis of regional, territorially limited states' (2000: 227–228). The title of Cheah's and Robbins' *Cosmopolitics: Thinking and Feeling Beyond the Nation* convey this dimension of the term as self-apprehension, an attitude of mind rather than a subject position. Hannerz regards it as 'a perspective, a state of mind... a mode of managing meaning' (Hannerz 102).

This sense of the word as a 'way of being in the world' suggests that it may operate better as an adjective than a noun. Hong Kong and Shanghai may be described as 'cosmopolitan spaces', but who is 'the cosmopolitan'? Within the cultural space of the 'cosmopolitan city' which category of its citizens may be constituted cosmopolitan subjects: expatriates, multi-lingual locals? Which narrative of identity in the transitional, open and exogenous space of the world city frames a cosmopolitan subject? Clearly cosmopolitanism operates at its most theoretically useful when it is seen as a strategy for subjects to locate themselves in the world rather than to define subjectivity itself.

Many other 'cosmopolitanisms', such as approaches to 'cosmopolitan pedagogy' may be instrumental in creating cultural openness in readers, but these 'strategies to manage meaning' do not necessarily create cosmopolitan subjects. Most theorists have decried the lingering connotation of urbanity, sophistication and wealth that the term carries with it (symbolized by the magazine *Cosmopolitan*) although Appiah believes the term can be 'rescued' (xiv). But none of the many attempts to define the term has managed to entirely rid itself of the fact that the person who is able to travel freely, experience and participate in other cultures for long periods, who has the time to engage with the Other in a 'cosmopolitan' way, must almost inevitably be a person with considerable material resources.

When Breckenridge et al. propose in the *Introduction to Cosmopolitanism* that 'cosmopolitanism be considered in the plural as cosmopolitanisms', (8) they mean that cosmopolitanism should not be identified with 'the singular, privileged location of European thought' (9). This attempts to shake off the baggage carried by the concept, such as John Stuart Mill's contention in *Political Economy* that 'capital is becoming more and more cosmopolitan' (cited Robbins 1992: 171). It is an attempt to exorcise the ghost of the *flaneur*, to open cosmopolitanism itself to plurality. Yet they also declare that '[r]efugees, peoples of the diaspora and migrants and exiles represent the spirit of the cosmopolitical community' (6). This runs the risk of implying that cosmopolitans have one spirit and one community, one apparently not represented by those who do not cross borders of one kind or another. Yet we do well to remember that distances and differences exist within localities.

This fact may be better apprehended by the term 'vernacular cosmopolitanism' coined by Homi Bhabha in *The Location of Culture* when he states that 'Vernacular cosmopolitanism represents a political process that works towards the shared goals of democratic rule rather than simply acknowledging already constituted "marginal" political entities or identities' (1996: xviii) or in Sheldon Pollock's analysis of 'cosmopolitan vernaculars' in India. In both cases, the apparent oxymoron of 'vernacular / cosmopolitanism' works to cross various kinds of boundaries: the boundary of political entity or identity and the boundary of location.

Further Reading: Appiah 2007; Bhaha 1996; Breckenridge, Bhabha and Pollock 2002; Hannerz 1996; Kant 1795; Levinas 1969; Peah and Robbins 1998; Robbins 1992; Waldron 2001; Fine 2007; Ostby 2018; Werbner 2008.

COUNTER DISCOURSE

A term coined by Richard Terdiman to characterize the theory and practice of symbolic resistance. Terdiman examines the means of producing genuine change against the 'capacity of established discourses to ignore or absorb would-be subversion' (1985: 13) by analysing nineteenth-century French writing. He identifies the 'confrontation between constituted reality and its subversion' as 'the very locus at which cultural and historical change occurred' (13).

Terdiman's work focused exclusively on French literature, but his term has been adopted by postcolonial critics to describe the complex ways in which challenges to a dominant or established discourse (specifically those of the imperial centre) might be mounted from the periphery, always recognizing the powerful 'absorptive capacity' of imperial and neo-imperial discourses. As a practice within postcolonialism, counter discourse has been theorized less in terms of historical processes and literary movements than through challenges posed to particular texts, and thus to imperial ideologies inculcated, stabilized and specifically maintained through texts employed in colonialist education systems.

The concept of counter discourse within postcolonialism thus also raises the issue of the subversion of canonical texts and their inevitable reinscription in this process of subversion. But Terdiman's general address to this problem is also useful here, in that an examination of the ways in which these operate as naturalized controls exposes their 'contingency and permeability'. Thus, such challenges are not simply mounted against the texts as such but address the whole of that discursive colonialist field within which imperial texts – whether anthropological, historical, literary or legal – function in colonized contexts.

Further Reading: Slemon 1987a; Terdiman 1985; Tiffin 1987, 1995.

CREOLE (SEE PIDGINS/CREOLES)

The English term 'creole' is derived from the Portuguese Criolulu (Spanish *criollo*) meaning 'native', via the French *créole*, meaning indigenous. 'Creole' originally referred to a white (man) of European descent, born and raised in a tropical colony. The meaning was later extended to include indigenous natives and others of non-European origin. The term was subsequently applied to certain languages spoken by Creoles in and around the Caribbean and in West Africa, and then more generally to other languages of similar type that had arisen in similar circumstances (see Romaine 1988: 38).

From the seventeenth century to the nineteenth, however, the most common use of the term in English was to mean 'born in the West Indies', whether white or negro. Although, therefore, the term had 'no connotation of colour' (OED), it increasingly conjured, in European eyes, the 'threat' of colonial miscegenation. Historically, and today, the word has been used in quite different ways by different societies. As the Caribbean historian Edward Brathwaite notes,

> in Peru the word was used to refer to people of Spanish descent who were born in the New World. In Brazil, the term was applied to Negro slaves born locally. In Louisiana, the term was applied to the white francophone population, while in New Orleans it applied to mulattoes. In Sierra Leone, 'creole' refers to descendants of former New World slaves, Maroons and 'Black Poor' from Britain who were resettled along the coast and especially in Freetown, and who form a social élite distinct from the African population. In Trinidad, it refers principally to the black descendants of slaves to distinguish them from East Indian immigrants. When used with reference to other native groups, an adjectival prefix – French creole, Spanish creole – is used. In Jamaica, and the old settled English colonies, the word was used in its original Spanish sense of criollo: born into, native, committed to the area of living, and it was used in relation to both white and black, free and slave.
>
> (Brathwaite 1974: 10)

CREOLIZATION

The process of intermixing and cultural change that produces a creole society. While the creolization processes might be argued to be going on throughout the world, the term has usually been applied to 'new world' societies (particularly the Caribbean and South America) and more loosely to those postcolonial societies whose present ethnically or racially mixed populations are a product of European colonization. According to Edward Brathwaite, creolization 'is a cultural process' – 'material, psychological and spiritual – based upon the stimulus/response of individuals within the society to their [new] environment and to each other'. Although 'the scope and quality of this response and interaction' are 'dictated by the circumstances of society's foundation and composition', they produce a totally 'new construct' (1971: 11).

Brathwaite stresses that creolization is not a product but a process incorporating aspects of both acculturation and interculturation, the 'former referring... to the process of absorption of one culture by another; the latter to a more reciprocal activity, a process of intermixture and enrichment, each to each'. In his Jamaican case study, Brathwaite

97

traces the ways in which the processes of creolization began as a result of slavery:

> and therefore in the first instance involving black and white, European and African, in a fixed superiority/inferiority relationship, tended first to the culturation of white and black to the new Caribbean environments; and, at the same time, because of the terms and the conditions of slavery, to the acculturation of black to white norms. There was at the same time, however, significant interculturation going on between these two elements.
>
> (Braithwaite 1971: 11)

Creolization, as described by Brathwaite, is specific to, and is best understood in the context of, Caribbean history and societies. But Brathwaite's model of creolization can be compared with, and be seen to be doing some of the same work discussed under the rubric of 'hybridization', though creolization has generally received a more historically specific discussion. Robert Young terms an 'unconscious **hybridity**, whose pregnancy gives birth to new forms of amalgamation rather than contestation' or 'the French métissage, the imperceptible process whereby two or more cultures merge into a new mode' as creolization, in contrast to a Bakhtinian hybridity which he regards as more 'contestatory' (1995: 21).

Further Reading: Berman 2006; Bongie 1998; Brathwaite 1971, 1981, 1995, 1995a; Colás 1995; Gates 1991; Lang 2000; Memmi 1965; Simmons-McDonald 2003; Young 1995; Werbner 2006; Price 2017; Tate 2023, Colwill 2023.

CULTURAL DIFFERENCE/CULTURAL DIVERSITY

The concept of cultural difference as opposed to cultural diversity was proposed by Homi Bhabha in 'The Commitment to Theory' (1994). Cultural diversity is an assumption of culture as an 'object of empirical knowledge' a stable repository of cultural contents, whereas cultural difference is the process of the enunciation of culture in its various dimensions. Cultural diversity concerns the recognition of multiple cultures, often within a multicultural framework, while cultural difference refers to the ways in which cultures articulate – enunciate – their difference. While cultural diversity acknowledges the variety of cultures in a particular setting, cultural difference refers to the many ways in which cultures may express their distinctiveness. Cultural difference suggests that cultural authority resides not in a fixed diversity of objects but in the process of how these objects come to be known and so come into being. By stressing the process by which we know and can know cultures as totalities, the term 'cultural difference' emphasizes our awareness of the 'homogenising effects of cultural symbols and icons' and places the emphasis on a questioning attitude towards 'the authority of cultural synthesis in general'.

The concept of difference inherits the sense of Derrida's *différance* which means to both differ and defer. In simple terms, there is always 'something more' in the description of a culture's difference. The enunciation of cultural contents is thus **ambivalent** since it occurs in a Third Space – the third space of enunciation – which exists between colonizer and colonized, but also between cultures that are different in various ways. This same ambivalence is implicit in the act of cultural interpretation itself since the production of meaning in the relations of two systems requires a Third Space. While Saussure suggested that signs acquire meaning through their difference from other signs (and thus a culture may be identified by its difference from other cultures), Derrida suggested that the 'difference' is also 'deferred'. Bhabha's Third Space can be compared to this space of deferral and possibility (thus a culture's difference is never simple and static but ambivalent, changing and always open to further possible interpretation). In short, this is the space of **hybridity** itself, the space in which cultural meanings and identities always contain the traces of other meanings and identities. Therefore, Bhabha argues, 'claims to inherent originality or purity of cultures are untenable, even before we resort to empirical historical instances that demonstrate their hybridity'.

Colonized societies described as diverse are vulnerable to descriptions that emphasize their 'pre-modernity' describing a pastness that is not a sign of the culture's historical memory, but of a reputed archaism or even primitiveness. Cultural difference on the other hand 'problematizes the division of past and present, tradition and modernity, at the level of cultural representation and its authoritative address'. Bhabha argues that it is insufficient to record signifiers of cultural diversity which merely acknowledge a range of separate and distinct systems of behaviour, attitudes and values. Such a framework may even continue to suggest that such differences are merely aberrant or **exotic**, as was implicit in imperialistic ethnographies. References to cultural diversity based on an assumption of 'pre-given cultural "contents" and customs' give rise to anodyne liberal notions of multiculturalism, cultural exchange or the culture of humanity (1994: 20).

Bhabha invokes Fanon's evocative description of culture as 'the zone of occult instability where the people dwell' which defines culture not as an epistemological object but as a site of struggle, change and transformation. Cultures are 'never unitary in themselves' but in a constant relationship with others, a difference that is constantly subject to self-enunciation. Fanon's idea of the development of a radical and revolutionary native intelligentsia is specifically invoked as the defining condition for such a radical native intelligentsia as opposed to a **comprador** class or **neo-colonialist** native élite, which merely positions itself within a totalized and controlled metaphor of cultural diversity. Such an élite, which invokes unchanging and fixed **nativist** forms, can never fully oppose the control of the dominant culture, since they define culture as fixed and unprogressive. Yet, ironically, it may be their very in-betweenness that allows a revolutionary potential for embracing change in members of the same native intelligentsia as **Fanonist** thought acknowledges. Bhabha suggests that

> for Fanon the liberatory "people" who initiate the productive instability of revolutionary cultural exchange are themselves the bearers of a hybrid identity... and they construct their culture from the national text translated into modern Western forms of information technology, language, dress... [transforming] the meaning of the colonial inheritance into the liberatory signs of a free people of the future.
>
> (38)

Despite Bhabha's intervention in many postcolonial discussions, the terms continue to be used interchangeably in the way defined at the beginning of this entry.

Further Reading: Bhabha 1994.

CULTURAL TOURISM

After independence, many colonized cultures sought various ways to preserve their traditional practices. One of the most controversial and disputed methods has been the establishment of cultural tourism, that is, the use of culture as an attraction for foreign tourists. Such tourism has also become an increasingly important part of the economy for many postcolonial states. Of course, the use of cultural practices to attract visitors is part of the tourist industry in most countries, e.g. the use of Britain's castles and stately homes, or the use of the American West and its traditions in so-called 'dude ranches'. But in postcolonial cultures, it is especially problematic since it engages with the broader issue of the **exoticization** of such cultures. The issue revolves around the control of the process. Who controls the process and who benefits from it? These are crucial questions. In some parts of the world, they are tied into issues related to the preservation of specific art forms. Elsewhere they are related to issues of land ownership and control. For example, in the Kimberley region of Western Australia, the local Mowanjum community has engaged in a process of renewing the sacred wanjina images originally painted on rock faces. They have used these images to create artwork, which has been sold to raise money for education and health facilities. But they also see the process as one which keeps the traditional culture alive and passes it on to the new generation (see Blundell and Woolagoodja 2005). In South Africa and in parts of Australia, the local communities have regained control of sacred areas that had been incorporated in National Parks. They have continued to allow access to these areas under their control to encourage tourism, which creates wealth for the community. Notable examples include the Uluru region (the erstwhile Ayer's Rock) in central Australia and the Gemsbok National Park in the Kalahari region of Southern Africa. These have become sites in which traditional cultural practices are displayed as part of a cultural tourism controlled by the local communities (see Carruthers 2006).

Although such examples show cultural tourism in a positive light, it is also clear that it has considerable potential for the further exploitation of postcolonial peoples and may be recruited to **neo-colonial** agendas. This more exploitative form of tourism has a long history, and has a clear link with the process of **exoticizing** the 'native', which underlay the display of living peoples in the colonial period. This process continues in the more frankly commercial ventures, such as the 'cultural villages' which can be found in locations as far apart as the West Indies, South Africa and South-East Asia. But it may also be seen to be extended by some of the ways in which postcolonial cultures continue to be represented within discourses such as development and heritage studies. Even projects such as the UNESCO Cultural Heritage programmes, are in danger of exploiting the very material and people they seek to 'preserve'. There is also the danger of regarding such 'preserved' cultures as fixed and unchanging, as embodying some **essential** and **authentic** tradition, which is rendered inflexible. This has consequences for the politics of such communities and their ability to appropriate and adapt the practices of their invaders to resist them. (see Griffiths 1994.) Some might argue that cultural tourism is a case of just this process of **appropriation** in action, as in the Mowanjum instance cited above. Nevertheless, even the most liberal of such ventures are potentially engaged in a commodification of the culture and even of the bodies of the colonized and this has been recognized. The UNESCO website on cultural heritage quotes its own Universal Declaration on Cultural Diversity 2001 which 'seeks to address this concern by emphasizing the Organization's commitment to the "fruitful diversity of... cultures" in a spirit of dialogue and openness, taking into account the risks of identity-based isolationism and standardization associated with globalization' (www.unesco.org/culture/heritage/). But it is significant that it recognizes the very real nature of those risks in an increasingly globalized world.

Further Reading: Appadurai 1986; Blundell 2000; Carruthers 2006; Griffiths 2007; Huggan 2001; Hulme 2000.

DECOLONIALITY

This term emerged from the specific conditions of Latin American colonialism, its proponents arguing that coloniality has existed since the Spanish invasion of the Americas in the fifteenth century. The origin of the term is credited to Anibal Quijano (2007: 168–178) and prominent in the development of decolonial theory are Quijano, María Lugones, Ramon Grosfoguel and Walter D. Mignolo. Quijano observed that the process involved 'a violent concentration of the world's resources under the control and for the benefit of a small European minority'. While Eurocentred colonialism seems to have been defeated, its successor, Western imperialism, maintains power through economic domination and the inculcation of 'cultural Europeanization'.

Decoloniality is more oriented to social science than cultural studies and as Gurminder Bhambra suggests 'It was strongly linked to **world system theory** from the outset as well as to scholarly work in development and underdevelopment theory and the Frankfurt School critical social theory tradition' (2014: 2). While postcolonial studies focus heavily on British imperialism – because postcolonial theory arose from literatures written in the colonizers language – Latin American scholars have responded with the observation that coloniality has existed for five centuries and continues in the present. Wallerstein's **world system theory** holds that capitalism has been the world system since at least the sixteenth century and decolonial theorists claim that coloniality has been an integral part of this system and continues in the present. This view of the *continued* operation of imperial power is a position maintained by postcolonial theory since the work of Nkrumah and the concept of **neo-colonialism**. Like postcolonial theory, decoloniality refers to 'a family of diverse positions that share a view of coloniality as a fundamental problem in the modern (as well as postmodern and information) age, and of decolonization or decoloniality as a necessary task that remains unfinished' (Maldonado-Torres 2011: 1).

The connection between **imperialism** and **modernity** has been asserted for some time (Ashcroft 1998); however, the connection between modernity and coloniality is central to decolonial theory. Anibal Quijano is credited with initiating this aspect of the decolonial movement, expounding the idea that coloniality, modernity and rationality are tightly implicated. He argues that, with the conquest of the lands that we now call Latin America, there arose 'a new world order, culminating, five hundred years later, in a global power covering the whole planet' (Quijano 2007: 168). Decoloniality pulls the discussion of **modernity** back to the fifteenth century, and extends it to take into account both the activities of southern European countries, such as Spain and Portugal, but also the southern half of the continent to be named the Americas.

María Lugones builds on Quijano's thesis of the coloniality of power by arguing that modernity/coloniality to be understood as shaped through specific articulations of race, gender and sexuality. She argues that not only did colonization invent the colonized, it also disrupted the social patterns, gender relations and cosmological understandings of the communities and societies it invaded. In doing so, it rearticulated particular European understandings of gender and sex from a bifurcation between male and female to a racialized understanding of the same embedded within a logic of colonial difference.

Mignolo developed Quijano's earlier theoretical work and, in elaborating his conception of modernity/coloniality highlights the epistemic decolonization necessary to undo the damage wrought by modernity and to demonstrate its embedding in coloniality. The **decolonization** of knowledge, he suggests, occurs in acknowledging the sources and geo-political locations of knowledge while affirming those modes and practices of knowledge that have been denied by the dominance of particular forms. He is not arguing simply for a geopolitics of location as central to any academic endeavour, but rather a consideration of *what* that geopolitics enables to be known and *how* it is to be known. The key issue for Mignolo is not only that epistemology is not ahistorical, but also, and perhaps more importantly, that epistemology 'has to be geographical in its historicity' (2000: 64). The concept has also gathered widespread recognition beyond Latin America. Ndhlovu-Gatseni relates this ostensibly Latin American movement to African subjectivity outlining the various ways in which Africa was incorporated into the Euro-North American-centric world.

The connection between decoloniality and Wallerstein's **World System Theory** gained currency from the early stages of decolonial theory. Grosfuguel characterizes Euro-North American-centric modernity as racially hierarchized, patriarchal, sexist, Christian-centric, hetero-normative, capitalist, military, colonial, imperial and modern form of civilization (2007: 216). He proposes that the coloniality of power has become the matrix of the modern colonial world (2007: 2011) and that what arrived in the Americas was a more complex world system than world-system analysis usually portrays. He outlines the interweaving elements of this system in *The Epistemic Decolonial Turn* (2007: 216–217)

1. a particular global class formation where a diversity of forms of labour (slavery, semi-serfdom, wage labour, petty-commodity production, etc.) are going to co-exist and be organized by capital as a source of production of surplus value through the selling of commodities for a profit in the world market;

2. an international division of labour of core and periphery where capital organized labour in the periphery around coerced and authoritarian forms (Wallerstein 1974);

3. an inter-state system of politico-military organizations controlled by European males and institutionalized in colonial administrations (Wallerstein 1979);

4. an international division of labour of core and periphery where capital organized labour in the periphery around coerced and authoritarian forms (Wallerstein 1974);

5. an inter-state system of politico-military organizations controlled by European males and institutionalized in colonial administrations (Wallerstein 1979);

6. a global racial/ethnic hierarchy that privileges European people over non-European people (Quijano 1993, 2000);

7. a global gender hierarchy that privileges males over females and European patriarchy over other forms of gender relations (Spivak 1988; Enloe 1990);

8. a sexual hierarchy that privileges heterosexuals over homosexuals and lesbians (it is important to remember that most indigenous peoples in the Americas did not consider sexuality among males a pathological behaviour and has no homophobic ideology);

9. a spiritual hierarchy that privileges Christians over non-Christian/non-Western spiritualities institutionalized in the globalization of the Christian (Catholic and later Protestant) church;

10. an epistemic hierarchy that privileges Western knowledge and cosmology over non-Western knowledge and cosmologies, and institutionalized in the global university system (Mignolo 1995, 2000; Quijano 1991);

11. a linguistic hierarchy between European languages and non-European languages that privileges communication and knowledge/theoretical production in the former and subalternize the latter as sole producers of folklore or culture but not of knowledge/theory (Mignolo 2000).

Walter Mignolo has become perhaps the best-known exponent of decoloniality and he declares that since coloniality is far from over, so should decoloniality be understood as continuing. Catherine Walsh elaborates the geopolitics of thought in modernity/coloniality and suggests a form of 'Other' thinking 'a collective mode of thinking that is produced and thought from difference, towards liberation'.

Whether, as decolonial theorists claim, there has been a 'decolonial turn' in contemporary theory, it is certain that decolonization is an unfinished process. Despite its assertion of the five-century long existence of coloniality, decolonial *analysis* does not differ much, if at all, from postcolonial analysis. It has the advantage of dispensing with the problems of the 'post' and of situating itself in a very different geo-political context. But in the main, the decolonial heralds the robust intervention of Latin American theorists into the postcolonial scene.

Further Reading: Bhambra (2014), Grosfoguel (2007), Maldonado-Torres (2011), Mignolo (2017), Ndhlovu-Gatseni (2013), Quijano 1991, Quijano (2007), Walsh (2012), Wynter (2003)

DECOLONIZATION

Decolonization is the process of revealing and dismantling colonialist power in all its forms. This includes dismantling the hidden aspects of those institutional and cultural forces that had maintained the colonialist power and that remain even after political independence is achieved. Initially, in many places in the colonized world, the process of resistance was conducted in terms or institutions appropriated from the colonizing culture itself. This was only to be expected, since early nationalists had been educated to perceive themselves as potential heirs to European political systems and models of culture. This occurred not only in **settler colonies** where the white colonial élite was a direct product of the system but even in colonies of occupation. Macaulay's infamous 1835 Minute on Indian Education had proposed the deliberate creation in India of just such a class of 'brown white men', educated to value European culture above their own. This is the locus classicus of this **hegemonic** process of control, but there are numerous other examples in the practices of other colonies.

Whether in India, Africa or the West Indies in the nineteenth and early twentieth centuries, the first nationalists were also modernizers, whose programme was less to effect a rejection of colonialist culture than to adopt its practices. This process of political and cultural 'broker-age', as some historians have called it, involved these early decolonizers in a profound complicity with the imperial powers from which they sought to emerge as free agents. Their general attitudes and practices were necessarily imbued with the cultural and social values they had been taught to regard as those of a modern, civilized state (de Moraes-Farias and Barber 1990). Consequently, political independence did not necessarily mean a wholesale freeing of the colonized from colonialist values, for these, along with political, economic and cultural models, persisted in many cases after independence.

In colonies where a majority culture or cultures had been invaded and suppressed or denigrated by colonialist practices, the process of resisting and overthrowing these assumptions has been more obviously active. The powerful designation of **neo-colonialism** to denote the new force of global control operating through a local élite or **comprador** class was coined by the Ghanaian independence leader Kwame Nkrumah (1965). As a socialist, Nkrumah restricted his concept of the neo-colonial operations of imperialism to the operation of the global capitalism of the West.

The **globalization** of the modern world economy has meant that political independence has not effected the kinds of changes in economic and cultural control that the early nationalists might have expected. It has even been argued by some recent commentators that the colonial powers deliberately avoided granting independence until they had, through internal discriminations and hegemonic educational practices, created an élite (**comprador**) class to maintain aspects of colonial control on their behalf but without the cost or the opprobrium associated with the classic colonial models.

As well as direct and indirect economic control, the continuing influence of **Eurocentric** cultural models privileged the imported over the indigenous: colonial languages over local languages; writing over orality and linguistic culture over inscriptive cultures of other kinds (dance, graphic arts, which had often been designated 'folk culture'). Against all these occlusions and overwritings of precolonial cultural practices, a number of programmes of decolonization have been attempted. Notable among these have been those that seek to revive and revalue local languages. The pressure of the global economy means that élite communication is dominated by the use of the ex-colonial languages, notably the new 'world language' of English, whose power derives from its historical use across the largest of the modern empires and from its use by the United States.

In postcolonial societies in which alternatives exist, it has been suggested that a return to indigenous languages can restructure attitudes to the local and the indigenous cultures, and can also form a more effective bridge to the bulk of the population whose lives have continued to be conducted largely in their mother tongues. Thus, decolonizing processes that have advocated a return to indigenous language use have involved both a social programme to democratize culture and a programme of cultural recuperation and re-evaluation. In Africa, the work of Ngugi wa Thiong'o has been at the forefront of this decolonizing model (Ngugi 1981a, 1986, 1993). But it has also had considerable advocacy in India where, due to the unbroken power of local languages and their literary traditions throughout the colonial period, a strong drive to revalue the literatures and other arts employing Indian languages has occurred in recent times (Ahmad 1992; Devy 1992). It is important, though, not to assume that these cultures remained untouched, and indeed the forms they often now employ, such as the novel, prose fiction, drama, magazines and television soap-opera, reflect an energetic engagement with dominant practices.

Only the most extreme forms of decolonization would suggest that precolonial cultures can be recovered in a pristine form by programmes of decolonization (see **nativism**). More recently, for example, some postcolonial African critics (Appiah 1992; Gikandi 1992; Mudimbe 1994) have questioned the bases on which such extreme decolonizing projects have been erected, arguing from a variety of different perspectives that the systems by which, to use Mudimbe's phrase, 'African worlds have been established as realities for knowledge' are always multiple and diverse, and are implicated in colonial and European orders of knowledge as much as in local ones. For example, Kenyan critic Simon Gikandi has argued that many decolonizing practices

> were predicated on the assumption that African cultures and selves were natural and holistic entities which colonialism had repressed, and which it was the duty of the African writer, in the period of decolonization to recover (if only the right linguistic and narrative tools could be developed), there is now an urgent need to question the ideological foundations on which the narratives of decolonization were constructed.
>
> (Gikandi 1992: 378)

Gikandi's analyses critique the simple equation of national narratives and decolonizing processes and argue that discourses of **nationalism** and national liberation (or, in some later texts, of the disillusioning failure of such narratives and such nationalist discourses) are increasingly inadequate ways of analysing and correcting the problems and conflicts of the post-independence condition. For Gikandi, the task faced by African writers now, and by implication by writers in many postcolonial societies, is 'to theorise adequately . . . the problematic of power and the state' (see **postcolonial state**). Thus Gikandi argues that formulations of decolonization, such as Ngugi's in novels like Matigari, are 'both a symptom of the problems which arise when the narrative of decolonization is evoked in a transformed postcolonial era and a commentary on the problematics of a belated national narrative' (Gikandi 1992: 379).

The projects of other writers, such as Salman Rushdie, who embrace a 'transnational' identity and seek to critique the contemporary postcolonial state, are often dismissed as not contributing to a decolonizing process. But this is to assume an absolute contiguity between decolonization and narratives of nation and nationalism, which arguments like Gikandi's seriously call into question. In fact, the borders and images of the postcolonial nation may be fictions that allow free passage to the continuing control of the **neo-colonialism** of multinational companies and global monetary institutions. Decolonization, whatever else it may be, is a complex and continuing process rather than something achieved automatically at the moment of **independence**.

In the **settler colonies**, this process can also be seen to occur in a different form. Although they were permitted political independence on the inherited British model at a relatively early stage, they often continued to suffer what the noted Australian commentator A.A. Phillips wittily characterized as 'a cultural cringe' from which they were not released by their nominal political 'independence' (Phillips 1958, 1979). Similarly, they have frequently been far less successful than other kinds of colonies in dismantling the colonialist elements in their social institutions and cultural attitudes. This is to some extent because of the peculiar hegemonic strength exerted by notions of a **filiative** connection with the imperial centre, reiterated in phrases such as 'sons and daughters of Empire'. Such connections tended to keep the settler colonies more dependent on the apron strings of their colonial masters (Docker 1978), usually at the expense of the recognition of the rights of their indigenous peoples.

Further Reading: Ahmad 1992; Appiah 1992; Betts 2004; Brydon and Tiffin 1993; Chamberlain 1999; Coutinho 1992; Crawford 2002; Devy 1992; Docker 1978; Duara 2003; Gikandi 1992; de Moraes-Farias and Barber 1990; Moreiras 2004; Mudimbe 1994; Nederveen Pieterse and Parekh 1995; Newsom 2001; Ngugi 1981a, 1986, 1993; Nkrumah 1965; Okonkwo 1999; Phillips 1979; Rothermund 2006; Shi-xu and Servaes 2005; Spivak 1993; Springhall 2001; Young 1998; Schayegh, Cyrus and Yoav Di-Capua 2020.

DEPENDENCY THEORY

Dependency theory offers an explanation for the continued impoverishment of colonized 'Third World' countries on the grounds that underdevelopment is not internally generated but a structural condition of global capitalism itself. It thus presents a similar argument to **world system theory** in that it explains underdevelopment as consequent of the global structure of domination, rather than an early stage in a process of development. Such 'underdeveloped' countries are usually formerly colonized states that are actually prevented, by the forces of global capitalism, from independent development. The economic rationale of colonization, by establishing colonies as producers of raw materials and foodstuffs for the industrialized metropolitan centres, played a major part in retarding the industrialization and development of those regions.

In drawing attention to this history, dependency theory thus challenges the hypotheses of modernization theory which explains underdevelopment in terms of the lack of certain qualities in 'under-developed' societies such as drive, entrepreneurial spirit, creativity and problem-solving ability. Writers such as André Gunder Frank (1979) dismiss modernization theory's argument that underdevelopment is a natural state caused by internal forces and show that it is the form of capitalist development of the West that is responsible for the continued underdevelopment of the 'Third World'.

However, dependency theory has been criticized for a tendency to offer a static analysis of the relation between developed and under-developed states and is thus unable to provide a convincing explanation of such phenomena as the 'Tiger' economies of South-East Asia. Nevertheless, it has been valuable for revealing the ethno-centric bias of modernization theory and for showing that the global system of capital prevents peripheral economies from developing in a manner more appropriate to their cultures and values.

Further Reading: Blomstrom and Hettne 1984; Darby 1997; Franco 1975; Frank 1979; Ghosh 2000; Pidd 2004; Seers 1981; B. C. Smith 2003; Wallerstein 1980.

DERACINATE

Literally, to pluck or tear up by the roots; to eradicate or exterminate. The root of the word thus has no direct relation to 'race', but as its emphasis in both English and French has shifted to 'uprooted from one's national or social environment' (as in the French déraciné), it has increasingly been associated with racial identity. The European slave trade and plantation slavery not only uprooted Africans from their home environments, but, through centuries of system-atic racial denigration, alienated enslaved Africans from their own racial characteristics. (The 'Black is Beautiful' movement of the mid-twentieth century in both the United States and the Caribbean represents systematic attempts by blacks to counter the deracination consequent of plantation slavery.)

DEVELOPMENT/DEVELOPMENT STUDIES

The 'development' of postcolonial states emerged in the post-war period of reconstruction and became a mantra of modernization theory. The successful colonial struggle for independence after WWII meant that economic stagnation and poverty could no longer be accepted as the 'normal' state of affairs. Postcolonial nations were hungry for economic growth and the Western powers became sensitive to this in the context of the Cold War. Former colonies engaged in the process of 'nation building' committed themselves to a developmental model of rapid economic growth through state intervention and they received material support from a variety of international institutions that emerged after WWII as machineries of decolonization were set in motion by colonial states, the United Nations and the industrialized countries of the West. During his 1949 inaugural speech President Harry Truman envisaged a programme of "development based on the concepts of democratic fair dealing' and assistance to developing countries became a feature of post-war US foreign policy.

For economists, decolonization was an unproblematic economic matter of taking up industrial development; classical Marxists and liberal economists alike shared this premise. But the inevitable consequence of seeing development as following the Western model meant that it became equated with a particular variety of Western capitalism, a process of change that would bring 'traditional' societies up to the 'standard' of Western societies. The underlying assumption of this modernization theory was that all societies go through the same stages of development. Consequently, modernization economists produced a schema based on European development that would provide a model for the 'Third World'. Nation-states could be lined up along a continuum of more or less evolved in terms of economy, society, politics and culture, and that a society could move from one rung of the ladder to the next. However, this theory did not take into account the fact that industrial development in newly postcolonial countries would have to compete with well-established industrialism in the West. European countries had had the considerable and unfair benefit of imperialism, which had protected their industries from competition from the colonies, which were used as producers of resources. Nor did it take into account the considerable social and political transformations necessary for economic modernization, nor the considerable cultural variations that would need to be pressed into one economic mould. Furthermore, the idea of development as based on the model of Western modernity overlooked the rise of multiple 'alternative' modernities in non-Western societies, modernities that might bear no relation to the linear historical model espoused by development theorists.

Critics of modernization theory claim that not only is postcolonial development unable or not obliged to follow the model of the West but that the 'Third World' is itself a product of Western industrialization. **Dependency theory** claimed that by using colonies as resource producers for Western industrial growth, and suppressing local industries to facilitate the importation of goods from the West, European industrialization actually *underdeveloped* the colonial world. The banning of the manufacture of cotton goods in India is perhaps the most notorious example of this – the destruction of an existing Indian industry to benefit the cotton mills of Manchester. Gandhi's famous response to this was to promote the production of Kadi or home spun cloth. The suppression of industry at the margin for the benefit of the centre is the core principle of dependency theories such as Wallerstein's **World System Theory**. From this perspective, the development of the non-Western world requires the elimination of the structures of dependency imposed upon it by a Western-dominated world system.

Analysts working in **Development Studies** soon realized that economic growth was an inadequate measure of development. Postcolonial development implies a process of social transformation rather than quantitative change alone. Such transformation may involve the appropriation and transformation of imperial technologies to make them fit local cultural needs, a process comprehensively demonstrated by postcolonial literatures in English. In Europe, capitalist development did not simply mean economic growth but a change in social relations, leading to the establishment of new classes, a different relation between town and country and the invention of civil society itself. By the 1970s, modernization theory came under sustained attack as it became clear that development could not be limited to economic growth. Such development necessitates a general improvement of human capital, and the development of infrastructure, competitiveness, environmental sustainability, social inclusion, health, safety and literacy. The obvious lack of these in post-independence societies has provoked the criticism that figures for economic growth have obscured the actual failure of development as an improvement of the well-being of the people. In the worst cases, such as Nigeria, a flood of oil money has not prevented most of the population remaining destitute. Despite the national project of development in which India has engaged since the 1950s its unevenness is demonstrated by the fact that only 16% of the 100 million people in the state of Bihar have access to the power grid (Guardian 2012).

The confusion of development with economic growth obscures the obvious fact that development only makes sense as a general improvement of the well-being of individuals in a society. Development, therefore, implies changes in technology and an increase in useful material resources. Without some such increase, there can be no improvement in the quality of life, which is the basic precondition for individual men and women to have more freedom to choose the way they live. In contrast, lack of development means that most people have insufficient material resources and are obliged to struggle even to survive. Development, or a general improvement in the quality of life, both depends on and stimulates social transformation. Such social changes involve a shift in the location of power in society and policies that ensure the redistribution of wealth. When productivity does grow without sufficient social change, its benefits are unequally distributed and do not generally improve the quality of life.

Most commentators agree that a rise in labour productivity is a necessary condition for development, since it ensures a shift from a life dominated by survival to one allowing greater leisure and self-expression. But rising labour productivity does not necessarily result in development. In countries, such as India or Brazil, the promotion of some industrial activities has created sectors of the economy where labour is highly productive but productivity in the rest of the economy remains low, in particular because agriculture remains stagnant. A rise in agricultural productivity is essential to development since this is the sector in which most people work. A transfer of workers to industry while agriculture is left to stagnate cannot lead to development and agricultural productivity requires social change rather than technological improvements.

This suggests that development can have no simple indicators. It cannot be reduced to the level of material productivity but depends in part on how the potential benefits of that productivity are used and distributed. Nor can it be regarded as a merely economic phenomenon since its economic elements are impossible without social preconditions. Ultimately development, as the word implies, is a process and not a state. But to succeed, it is a process that must account for social transformation rather than economic growth alone.

Further Reading: Alkire 2010; Power 2003; Sylvester 1999; Todaro and Smith 2009; Strongman 2014; Sondarjee and Andrews 2022.

DIASPORA

From the Greek meaning 'to disperse' (OED). Diasporas, the voluntary or forcible movement of peoples from their homelands into new regions, is a central historical fact of colonization. Colonialism itself was a radically diasporic movement, involving the temporary or permanent dispersion and settlement of millions of Europeans over the entire world. The widespread effects of these migrations (such as that which has been termed **ecological imperialism**) continue on a global scale. Many such 'settled' regions were developed historically as plantations or agricultural colonies to grow foodstuffs for the metropolitan populations, and thus a large-scale demand for labour was created in many regions where the local population could not supply the need.

The result of this was the development, principally in the Americas, but also in other places such as South Africa, of an economy based on **slavery**. Virtually all the slaves shipped to the plantation colonies in the Americas were taken from West Africa through the various European coastal trading enclaves. The widespread slaving practised by Arabs in East Africa also saw some slaves sold into British colonies, such as India and Mauritius, while some enslaving of Melanesian and Polynesian peoples also occurred in parts of the South Pacific to serve the sugarcane industry in places like Queensland, where it was known colloquially as 'blackbirding'.

After the slave trade, and when slavery was outlawed by the European powers in the first decades of the nineteenth century, the demand for cheap agricultural labour in colonial plantation economies was met by the development of a system of indentured labour. This involved transporting, under indenture agreements, large populations of poor agricultural labourers from population rich areas, such as India and China, to areas where they were needed to service plantations. The practices of slavery and indenture thus resulted in worldwide colonial diasporas. Indian populations formed (and form) substantial minorities or majorities in colonies as diverse as the West Indies, Malaya, Fiji, Mauritius and the colonies of Eastern and Southern Africa. Chinese minorities found their way under similar circumstances to all these regions too, as well as to areas across most of South-East Asia (including the Dutch East Indian colonies, in what is now Indonesia) and the Spanish- and later American-dominated Philippines.

Diasporas now exist throughout the world both in metropolitan centres and regions of conflict and their number is growing through voluntary **migration, asylum seeking** and other reasons for global movement.

The descendants of the diasporic movements generated by colonialism have developed their own distinctive cultures which both preserve and often extend and develop their originary cultures. Creolized versions of their own practices evolved, modifying (and being modified by) indigenous cultures with which they thus came into contact. The development of diasporic cultures necessarily questions **essentialist** models, interrogating the ideology of a unified, 'natural' cultural norm, one that underpins the **centre/margin** model of colonialist discourse. It also questions the simpler kinds of theories of **nativism** which suggest that **decolonization** can be effected by a recovery or reconstruction of precolonial societies. The most recent and most socially significant diasporic movements have been those of colonized peoples back to the metropolitan centres. In countries such as Britain and France, the population now has substantial minorities of diasporic ex-colonial peoples. In recent times, the notion of a 'diasporic identity' has been adopted by many writers as a positive affirmation of their hybridity.

Recently, the idea of diaspora has been complicated by the way in which the problems of forced migration and the complex status of refugees has made the status and nature of diasporic communities more problematic:

migration is not only made multi-directional but stories of origin and destination also lose conviction. This multiplicity of movements and of complex belongings gains analytical recognition in stories of multisitedness and hybridity, these are increasingly being evoked in a landscape where singular belonging is also being emphasized. People are increasingly required to choose between here and there.

(Mains 2013)

Further Reading: Brah 1996; Braziel and Mannur 2003; Brown and Coelho 1987; Carter 1996; Chow 1993; Gellner 2006; Gunew 2004; Hall 1996; Hayes Edwards 2003; Institute of Commonwealth Studies 1982; Mishra 1996a, 1996b; S. Mishra 2006; Nelson 1993; Rajan and Mohanram 1995; Ramraj 1996; Rath 2000; Roy 1995; Thompson 1987; West-Pavlov 2005; Mains et al. 2013; Ashcroft et al. 2024.

DIGITAL COLONIALISM

Digital colonialism refers to the capacity of global technology companies to exert unprecedented control over the cultural, economic and political domains of less powerful nations. The excessive power and market share of companies such as Google, Apple, Microsoft, Meta, Amazon and Nvidia has led to a form of imperialism that far exceeds the reach of classic empires. Digital colonialism involves four fundamental actors: (1) Western tech companies who harvest data; (2) advertising and consulting firms who use the data to target consumers; (3) local companies, political parties and organizations who use the data to help impose their various agendas; and (4) the citizens who knowingly or unknowingly act as data sources. The capacity of these companies to harvest the data of all individuals who have access to the internet means that digital colonialism is a potential colonization of the entire world. However, while extensive data protection laws and regulations emerged in developed countries to ensure ethical use of that data, the power of these companies over the data of poorer countries amounts to a new **Scramble for Africa** (Coleman 2019). For tech companies, the treasure trove of citizens' data that lies in Africa is a natural resource. The data may be extracted and sold as a commodity to corporations and political interests who base their revenue model on knowing their target groups so that they are able to push political messages and agendas or sell targeted products to citizens, thereby increasing their bottom-line (Coleman 422).

An earlier term, electronic colonialism or 'ecolonialism' was coined by Herbert Schiller in his *Communication and Cultural Domination* (1975). This advanced the proposition that mass media are leading to a new imperialism, not one based on military invasion but on mental and psychological control. However, since the explosive growth of tech companies in this century, digital colonialism has come to refer to the wholesale harvesting of data from poorly protected countries to enable the advertising and sale of goods produced in the West. This has arguably amounted to a more insidious and widespread form of psychological manipulation, because there is no need for geographical occupation, and it has led to a virtually unfettered access to the consumer data of poorer nations. Digital colonialism has more or less demolished the belief prevalent in the 1990s that the internet would lead to an age of social liberation, global communication and a breakdown of cultural barriers. Instead, the internet has become the means of the technical control of global communication, the increase in state surveillance and the uncontrolled harvesting of data. Data is the new currency, and access to data – rather than money, natural resources or advanced weaponry – is now the most valuable asset available to nation-states and corporations (ctd Coleman 2019: 424). Consumerism has 'now shifted from a story of mass consumption to a "story of one'" (425). In addition, the capacity of these companies to unleash – intentionally or not – the circulation of falsehoods and conspiracy theories far exceeds the control exerted by classic imperial actors over information and knowledge.

Like much commentary on **globalization**, this growing power of technology companies has often been characterized as the continued evolution of the US empire (Kwet 2021). However, while these companies are almost all based in the United States, they operate as a global force in their own right, often unfettered by state control. The results are increased inequality, the rise of state-corporate surveillance and sophisticated police and military technologies that have destabilized democratic governance in the **Global South**. The concept endorses Kwame Nkrumah's thesis of the danger of **neo-colonialism.** But digital colonialism goes further than Nkumah could have imagined because it affects much more than the control of commodities and trade, it involves the virtual harvesting of data from the entire globe. Like neo-colonialism, digital colonialism is geared to the unequal division of labour where the ownership of digital infrastructure, knowledge and their control of the means of computation keep the colonized world in a situation of permanent dependency.

Where sea routes once enabled the domination of maritime empires, the 'open veins' of the Global South, according to Eduardo Galeano, are the 'digital veins' crossing the oceans, wiring up a tech ecosystem owned and controlled by a handful of mostly US-based corporations (Kwet). Some of the transoceanic fibre-optic cables are fitted with strands owned or leased by companies, such as Google and Facebook, to further their data extraction. 'Today's heavy machinery are the cloud server farms dominated by Amazon and Microsoft that are used to store, pool and process big data, proliferating like military bases for US empire' (Kwet 2021). The new colonizers are armies of programmers, and the colonized are labourers co-opted to survey and cleanse social media platforms of disturbing content.

Some sophisticated consumers in the West have attempted to delete any online presence to try to defeat the data harvesting capacities of tech giants but have discovered how difficult, if not impossible, it has become. If this is the case in the West, it is clear how much more difficult it will continue to be in the Global South.

Further Reading: Coleman 2019, Galeano 1997, Kwet 2021, Rikap 2021, Schiller 1975.

DISCOURSE

This is a much-used word in contemporary theory and in postcolonial criticism, it is mostly employed in such terms as **colonial discourse**, which is specifically derived from Foucault's use of the concept. Discourse was originally used from about the sixteenth century to describe any kind of speaking, talk or conversation, but became increasingly used to describe a more formal speech, a narration or a treatment of any subject at length, a treatise, dissertation or sermon. More recently, discourse has been used in a technical sense by linguists to describe any unit of speech longer than a sentence.

However, the Foucauldian sense of the term has little to do with the act of speaking in its traditional sense. For Foucault, a discourse is a strongly bounded area of social knowledge, a system of statements within which the world can be known. The key feature of this is that the world is not simply 'there' to be talked about, rather, it is through discourse itself that the world is brought into being. It is also in such a discourse that speakers and hearers, writers and readers come to an understanding about themselves, their relationship to each other and their place in the world (the construction of **subjectivity**). It is the 'complex of signs and practices which organises social existence and social reproduction'.

There are certain unspoken rules controlling which statements can be made and which cannot within the discourse, and these rules determine the nature of that discourse. Since a virtually limitless number of statements can be made within the rules of the system, it is these rules that characterize the discourse and that interest analysts such as Foucault. What are the rules that allow certain statements to be made and not others? Which rules order these statements? Which rules allow the development of a classificatory system? Which rules allow us to identify certain individuals as authors? These rules concern such things as the classification, the ordering and the distribution of that knowledge of the world that the discourse both enables and delimits.

A good example of a discourse is medicine; in mundane terms, we simply think of medicine as healing sick bodies. But medicine represents a system of statements that can be made about bodies, about sickness and about the world. The rules of this system determine how we view the process of healing, the identity of the sick, and, in fact, encompass the ordering of our physical relationship with the world. There are certain principles of exclusion and inclusion that operate within this system; some things can be said and some things cannot. Indeed we cannot talk about medicine without making a distinction between different kinds, such as 'Western' and 'Chinese' medicine. For these are two discourses in which the body and its relationship to the world are not only different but virtually incompatible. This explains the very great resistance in Western medicine to forms of healing that do not accord with its positivistic idea of the body. Until such practices as acupuncture or herbal remedies could be incorporated into the positivistic framework of Western medicine, by being incorporated into other 'scientific' statements, they were rejected as charlatanism or superstition (they did not concur with 'truth'). It is only very gradually that such rules of exclusion, which keep a discourse intact, can be modified, because the discourse maintains not just an understanding of the world, but in a real sense the world itself. Such incursions, when not controlled, may represent a very great threat to the authority of the discourse.

Discourse is important, therefore, because it joins power and knowledge together. Those who have power have control of what is known and the way it is known, and those who have such knowledge have power over those who do not. This link between knowledge and power is particularly important in the relationships between colonizers and colonized and has been extensively elaborated by Edward Said in his discussion of **Orientalism**, in which he points out that this discourse, this way of knowing the 'Orient', is a way of maintaining power over it. Said's work lays more stress on the importance of writing and literary texts in the process of constructing representations of the other than does Foucault's, whose concern is more widely distributed across a variety of social institutions. Said's insistence on the central role of literature in promoting colonialist discourse is elaborated in his later work (Said 1993), where he argues that the nineteenth-century novel comes into being as part of the formation of Empire, and acts reflexively with the forces of imperial control to establish imperialism as the dominant ideology in the period. This emphasis has made Said's work to be of special interest to those concerned with postcolonial literatures and literary theory.

Foucault's view of the role of discourse though is even wider, and more pervasive, since he argues that discourse is the crucial feature of **modernity** itself. For the discourse of modernity occurs when what is said, the 'enunciated', becomes more important than the saying, the 'enunciation'. In classical times, intellectual power could be maintained by rhetoric, by the persuasiveness of the speaker 'discoursing' to a body of listeners. But gradually, the 'will to truth' came to dominate discourse and statements were required to be either true or false. When this occurred, it was no longer the act of discourse but the subject of discourse that became important. The crucial fact for postcolonial theory is that the 'will to truth' is linked to the 'will to power' in the same way that power and knowledge are linked. The will of European nations to exercise dominant control over the world, which led to the growth of empires, was accompanied by the capacity to confirm European notions of utility, rationality and discipline as truth.

We can extend our example, therefore, to talk about 'Eurocentric discourse', or the 'discourse of modernity', that is, a system of statements that can be made about the world that involve certain assumptions, prejudices, blindnesses and insights, all of which have a historical provenance, but exclude other, possibly equally valid, statements. All these statements and all that can be included within the discourse thus become protected by the assertion of 'truth'.

Further Reading: Ashcroft 1999; Bauman 1998; Bhabha 1994; Chrisman and Williams 1993; Ezzaher 2003; Foucault 1971; Gikandi 2004; Harrison 2003; Hulme 1989; Lazarus 1993, 1994; McHoul and Grace 1993; Said 1978, 1983; Tiffin 1995.

DISLOCATION

A term for both the occasion of displacement that occurs as a result of imperial occupation and the experiences associated with this event. The phenomenon may be a result of transportation from one country to another by slavery or imprisonment, by invasion and settlement, a consequence of willing or unwilling movement from a known to an unknown location. The term is used to describe the experience of those who have willingly moved from the imperial 'Home' to the colonial margin, but it affects all those who, as a result of colonialism, have been placed in a location that, because of colonial **hegemonic** practices, needs, in a sense, to be 'reinvented' in language, in narrative and in myth. A term often used to describe the experience of dislocation is Heidegger's term unheimlich or unheimlichkeit – literally 'unhousedness' or 'not-at-home-ness' – which is also sometimes translated as 'uncanny' or 'uncanniness'.

Nineteenth-century Australian writers show this process of dislocation in action: for example, novelist Marcus Clark, who speaks of the 'uncanny nature' of the Australian landscape's 'funereal gloom', or the poet Barron Field who declared that

All the dearest allegories of human life are bound up with the infant and slender green of spring, the dark redundance of summer,

and the sere and yellow leaf of Autumn . . . I can therefore hold no
fellowship with Australian foliage.

(Carter 1987: 43)

The implication of Field's remarks is that Australia exists outside of 'real'
or 'normal' experience, and in terms of the assumptions of imperial
discourse is unknowable until the place is brought under control by language. But it is here, in the attempt to convert the uncolonized 'space'
into colonized 'place', that dislocation becomes most obvious. Because
the words to describe the new place adequately cannot be found in the
language brought with the early settlers, new terms must necessarily be
invented. The necessity of dislocation does indeed become the mother
of invention. Hence, the disruptive and 'disorienting' experience of dislocation becomes a primary influence on the regenerative energies in a
postcolonial culture.

In a similar way, the extreme form of physical, social and individual
dislocation involved in the institution of slavery has led some Caribbean
critics, such as Dennis Williams, Wilson Harris and Edouard Glissant,
to suggest that dislocation is the key to a release of a distinctive form of
cultural energy. Harris employs the sign of the Caribbean limbo dance
or 'gateway', the dance that some speculate may reproduce the forced
and literal dislocation of the slave's body in the cramped conditions of
the slaver's holds, to signify the process of dismantling and rebirth that
generated the distinctive **catalytic** cultures of the New World. The
resulting restructuring generates new and powerful forms of culture
which, while having their roots in an African origin, are able to bring
forth a new 'Adamic' possibility of renewal and regeneration (Walcott
1974). **Diasporic** communities formed by forced or voluntary **migration** may all be affected by this process of dislocation and regeneration
too, and this has certainly been argued by some critics of the diasporic
and migrant experience (see essays in Rajan and Mohanram 1995).

Finally, dislocation in a different sense is also a feature of all invaded
colonies where indigenous or original cultures are, if not annihilated,
often literally dislocated, i.e. moved off what was their territory. At
best, they are metaphorically dislocated, placed into a hierarchy that sets
their culture aside and ignores its institutions and values in favour of the
values and practices of the colonizing culture. Many postcolonial texts
acknowledge the psychological and personal dislocations that result
from this cultural denigration, and it is against this dislocating process
that many modern **decolonizing** struggles are instituted.

See also **Fanonism**.

121

Further Reading: Bery et al. 2000; Glissant 1989; Harris 1981; Huggan 2000; Rajan and Mohanram 1995; Williams 1969

DISPLACEMENT

Since the beginning of European colonization, indigenous peoples have been dispossessed of their land and usually displaced to less arable land, to native reserves or government missions. While the experience of psychological and cultural displacement may affect those European peoples brought either freely or by coercion to settled colonies, this form of displacement occurs at the cost of intensely disruptive dispossession of indigenous peoples. Thus, the term is more often used today in conjunction with dispossession to describe the lot of those (usually hunter-gatherer) indigenous peoples displaced by the encroachment of colonizing and invading agricultural societies. The displacement, removal from traditional lands, relocation in reserves or missions and consequent familial, social and cultural fracturing of indigenous peoples has become the major cause of indigenous pathology.

Displacement and dispossession are by no means limited to the history of colonialism, as large populations of indigenous peoples continue to be disrupted and displaced by war, natural disasters and hazards, and perhaps most commonly by infrastructure and agricultural projects. Internally displaced people (IDPs)

> are persons or groups of persons who have been forced or obliged to flee or to leave their homes or places of habitual residence, in particular as a result of or in order to avoid the effects of armed conflict, situations of generalized violence, violations of human rights or natural or human-made disasters, and who have not crossed an internationally recognized state border.
> (1998, Guiding Principles on Internal Displacement).

An Amnesty International report on the displacement of indigenous people in Columbia revealed the disastrous effects of military conflict.

> Thousands of Indigenous Peoples have been forced off their land because they often live in areas of intense military conflict and rich in biodiversity, minerals and oil. Many other Indigenous communities have been unable to leave their territories because armed groups have laid landmines in surrounding areas.

While an estimated 25 million people are displaced worldwide by conflict, the number of people uprooted by **development** projects is thought to be much higher. Indigenous and other peoples have been displaced by the building of dams, the establishment of agricultural complexes, and even by misguided plans to build 'modern' urban centres.

In 1994, a study of all **World Bank**-assisted development projects from 1986 to 1993 that entailed population displacement found that just over half were in the transportation, water supply and urban infrastructure sectors. Extrapolating from World Bank data to derive estimates of global figures, the study concluded that, in the early 1990s, the construction of 300 high dams (above 15 metres) each year had displaced four million people. Urban and transportation infrastructure projects accounted for six million more displaced each year. India has constructed 3,000 dams since independence, displacing 60 million people, 55% of whom have been low-caste Adivasis, who constitute just 8% of India's population (Thakar 2009). Arundhati Roy has been prominent in the fight against the displacement of communities by modernization, particularly the building of the Narmada Dam in West India. It is estimated that 200 villages were submerged and a million people displaced by the construction of the dam.

The argument that the social consequences of displacement are a market problem, manageable by the economic advantages of infrastructure development is refuted by scholars (Bartolome et al. 2000) who point out that such an assumption rests on the idea that resettlement and compensation are adequate measures to address the issue of displacement. Displacement, they argue, is not simply a one-time experience but a 'multi-dimensional problem' that affects the lives of millions of people in different ways. Neither is it just about numbers, but involves various factors, such as violation of rights; self-determination; participation in decision-making; laws and policies.

The Internal Displacement Monitoring Centre of the Norwegian Refugee Council isolated eight effects of displacement caused by modernization projects: Landlessness; Joblessness; Homelessness; Marginalization; Food Insecurity; Increased Morbidity and Mortality; Loss of Access to Common Property; and Social Disintegration (iDMC 2003).

Further Reading: Amnesty International 2010; Bartolome et al. 2000; de Wet 2010; IDMC 2003; McDowell 1996; Thakkar 2009; Vandergeest 2003

One of the richest resources for the monitoring of all forms of internal displacement is the iDMC, the Internal Displacement Monitoring Centre at www.internal-displacement.org.

DOUBLE COLONIZATION

A term coined in the mid-1980s and usually identified with Holst-Petersen and Rutherford's *A Double Colonization: Colonial and Post-Colonial Women's Writing* published in 1985. The term refers to the observation that women are subjected to both the colonial domination of the empire and the male domination of patriarchy. In this respect, the empire and patriarchy act as analogous to each other, and both exert control over female colonial subjects, who are, thus, doubly colonized by imperial/patriarchal power. Feminist theory has propounded that women have been marginalized by patriarchal society and, consequently, the history and concerns of feminist theory have paralleled developments in postcolonial theory which foregrounds the marginalization of the colonial subject.

However, postcolonial nationalisms do not necessarily alleviate this situation but may entrench rather than dismantle the power of patriarchy, so that women's struggle against 'colonial' domination often continues after national independence. Postcolonial feminism continues to analyse the perpetuation of gender bias and 'double colonization' even in post-independence states, seeing the persistence of 'neo-colonial' domination of women in national patriarchies. There is considerable disagreement, however, among postcolonial feminists about whether imperialism or patriarchy is the force most urgently in need of contesting. One, perhaps most celebrated example is Hazel Carby's White Woman Listen (1982), but similar issues are addressed by Mohanty (1984), Suleri (1992) and others.

Further Reading: Carby (1982), Holst-Petersen and Rutherford (1985), Mohanty (1984), Suleri (1992).

EAST INDIA COMPANY

At the heart of most imperial action and the resulting colonization of countries and regions was economic advantage and the interests of trade. When European nations started to colonize other places and peoples, it was the desire to find and import valuables that drove the enterprises. The first great imperial powers Spain and Portugal were primarily interested in obtaining the gold and silver which they found in the New World. These ventures were undertaken by individuals given the right to exercise power in the name of the Crown, as its local representatives. Although they also sought to trade in regions such as the East Indies (which they dominated until the late sixteenth century) and the Indian sub-continent, and Portuguese traders contested the other nations in those regions until the so-called Amboina massacre of 1623, their impact there was smaller than in the Americas.

By the early seventeenth century, other national ventures centred on the valuable trade in spices from the East Indies were emerging. Their formation reflected wider changes to the ways many European countries were developing as power in the seventeenth century increasingly moved from landed aristocracies to urban-based traders from the emerging middle classes. These people were banding together to form groups (joint-stock companies) which invested in the trading exchanges which were also emerging in this period. The earliest of these from which the modern stock exchange has developed was formed in the Netherlands in 1602, and its first shares were issued by a company given a 21-year charter (in effect a monopoly) to trade to the Dutch East Indies called the VOC (Vereenigde Oost-Indische Compagnie). The VOC became the model for many other rival companies in the next century, including the most famous and long-lasting of all, the English East India Company, the earliest charter for which had in fact been issued by Elizabeth I two years before that of the VOC in 1600.

By the early eighteenth century, the French had also established a charter company for Indian trade called the Compagnie Français pour le commerce des Indes orientales. At first, limited to trading from small, fixed enclaves on the coasts of India granted by local rulers, the representatives of both the English and French companies began involving themselves directly in the political and military struggles between local rulers, especially in the early eighteenth century when the power of the Mughal Empire was increasingly challenged from within. This military involvement increased rapidly with the outbreak of the Seven Years War (1756–1763) between Britain and France, sometimes referred to as the first truly world war as the conflict was fought outside Europe from North America and the Caribbean to the Far East, notably in India. Although Louis XIV and his finance minister Colbert actively tried to engage French merchants in the French Company, it never succeeded in attracting the kind of support the emerging middle-class traders in Britain and the Netherlands gave to their respective companies, with the French king always being its largest investor.

This, of course, reflects the different political regimes in the countries of the respective national companies. Nevertheless, by 1740, the annual trade of the French Company was almost half as much as that of the East India Company, making it a threatening rival. Under its active local governor Dupleix, an attempt began to enlist local allies, training their troops and even participating directly in their contests with rivals. This process, under the pressure of the war that followed, meant that both companies were increasingly involved in local conflicts and in direct conflict between themselves as rivals not only for trade but also for the political dominance of the sub-continent. The East India Company now began to maintain its independent armies under the leadership of Company officers, often men who had begun as 'writers' (clerks) but who had shown an aptitude for military command. The most notable of these was Robert Clive, better known to history as Clive of India. After participating in several struggles with the French in the region adjoining Madras, Clive recognized that the policy of indirect rule via compliant local regimes they had established there was the key to success. In 1757, he oversaw the Company's troops at the battle of Plassey that established their rule in Bengal, the richest of the provinces of the failing Mughal Empire, which they ruled through their puppet Nawab Mir Jafar.

'John Company' as it was known colloquially, raised independent armies that were drawn from the native Indian populations, though usually officered by Europeans and strengthened by a few regiments of European troops. These native soldiers, known as sepoys, remained the main source of military power in the sub-continent, and even after the disbanding of the Companies own troops after the so-called Indian Mutiny (War of Independence) of 1856, native troops formed the basis of British power in India until independence in 1947. This is an extreme example of how a small group could rule a native population that always greatly outnumbered them by a process of manipulation and propaganda (see **Hegemony**). In most short accounts of the East India Company, it is assumed that it remained the accepted and undisputed ruler of India until the British government took direct control after 1856. In fact, despite its success and the eventual defeat of the French as a political force in India, the Company was always seen by the British government either as a source of financial loss or of corrupt power that needed to be contained. After rival groups in England unsuccessfully sought to limit its monopoly, the company, now officially known as The United Company of Merchants of England trading to the East Indies, continued to be directed by its shareholders at meetings where shares were purchasable on the open market, including shareholders from other countries, notably the Netherlands. After the decisive shift in 1757, when Bengal became a fiefdom of the Company this situation was clearly a worry to governments. Attempts at reforming the way the Company was governed resulted from the failure of the Company to paying its debts to the government and from what was perceived as the tendency of Company officers to enrich themselves. The real cause for reform was the sense that the company had ceased to be an economic benefit to the country and that its operation had become one that prevented an efficient exploitation of the ruled peoples and their resources. Much of this reform was announced by oppositional forces in the governments of the time as a moral attack on corruption.

Reform began with the Regulating Act of 1773, which took away the right of Company employees to trade on their own behalf, and was followed by Pitt's India Act of 1784, which strengthened government control by appointing a Board that included government ministers. In the years between and afterwards, there had been numerous claims of corruption by Company officials, including Clive, and culminating in the later (though finally unsuccessful) impeachment of Warwick Hastings, the first Governor-General of Bengal, in 1795. These reforms culminated with the Charter Act of 1813, which ended the company's trade monopoly with India. Although these reforms did not address the deep-seated problems arising from a division of power between an elected government and a company finally responsible only to its shareholders, they suggest that the idea of a simple break in power after 1856 is oversimplistic. In fact, the company had divested itself of its trading assets in 1833 when the government assumed the companies' debts to be serviced from taxes raised in India. The shareholders were guaranteed a fixed dividend for 40 years, also to be serviced from taxes raised in India. Thus, before and after the government took final control in 1857, after the traumatic events of the previous year, India remained the source of the funds raised by the company and by the government of Britain to pay for the British presence in India and to fund the profits that they derived from its peoples, its resources. This remains perhaps the central fact about companies like the East India Company. They were initiated to derive profit from the exploitation of colonized peoples, and when they were dissolved, it was to ensure the successful continuation of this exploitation by the imperial power which had initially called them into being. The East India Company is the archetypal example of the indissoluble bond between imperialism and the economic exploitative forces it serves. It is even arguable that the bond survived the collapse of colonial rule, and that the inheritors of the monopoly companies are the modern global companies which act against the interests of people in resource-rich countries with weak or corrupt governments that lend themselves to such exploitation for personal power or enrichment (see **Neo-colonialism** and **Decolonization**).

ECOCRITICISM

The term 'ecocriticism' was coined in 1978 by William Rueckert in his essay 'Literature and Ecology: An Experiment in Ecocriticism'. At its simplest, it is the interdisciplinary study of the connection between literature and the environment. It analyses the works of authors, researchers and poets in the context of environmental issues and nature. In postcolonial studies, it focuses on the ways in which literary and other creative works address the human relationship to the environment, in particular, the damaging effect of coloniality on the environment, on indigenous people and on animals. Deforestation, air pollution, endangered species, wetland loss, animal rights, and rampant consumerism have all been appearing as controversial issues in Western literature for hundreds of years. All of these subjects have a particular relevance to the postcolonial concern with colonized and formerly colonized peoples.

There is a considerable overlap between **environmentalism** and ecocriticism in postcolonial studies. There is also a significant overlap between ecocriticism and postcolonial studies as discourses, both being concerned with the intersection between the humanities and political activism. Postcolonial ecocriticism combines the critique of colonial regimes and transnational capitalism with ecocriticism's attention to the lands that have been exploited and damaged. By implication, the discipline attends to the rootedness of people in **place** and this leads to particular approaches to questions such as the origin of the **Anthropocene.**

Further Reading: Buell (1995), Clark (2011), Garrard (2023), Meeker (1972), Phillips (2003), Rueckert (1996)

ECOFEMINISM

Ecofeminism has become an increasingly important field in both contemporary feminist and environmental studies. Although, as Diamond and Orenstein note, ecofeminism is really 'a new term for an ancient wisdom' (Mies and Shiva 1993: 13), it first came to prominence in the early 1980s, with its bases in feminist philosophy, environmental activism and the European and American peace movements of the late 1970s. The term itself was first used by Françoise d'Eauborne in 1980 (Mies and Siva 1993: 13) and was increasingly adopted by both scholars and environmental activists. Organized in response to the Three Mile Island nuclear disaster, the 1980 'Women and Life on Earth: A Conference on Eco-Feminism' focused on 'the connections between feminism, militarization, healing and ecology' (Mies and Shiva 1993: 14). The adoption of the term had also been preceded by much of women's poetry and fiction in the 1960s and 1970s, and has gained increasing prominence through the work of philosophers Val Plumwood and Karen Warren. It has also been adopted by other disciplines through the writing and activism of Arundhati Roy and Vandara Shiva.

Ecofeminism stresses the indissoluble connectedness – both physical and conceptual – of the earth itself, and all life on it. Humans, as a part of this community depend on earth and sea, and the life this generates for survival, but they are even more fundamentally of it, one component part of the living whole. As Val Plumwood notes, the basic interconnectedness of all matter and psyche is such a 'truism' that it is puzzling that it should need to be remarked at all.

> But the reason why this message of continuity and dependency is so revolutionary in the context of the modern world is that the dominant strands of Western culture have for so long denied it, and have given us a model of human identity as only minimally and accidentally connected to the earth.
>
> (Plumwood 1993: 6)

Even though we all have a 'formal knowledge of evolutionary biology', this disconnection 'remains deeply and fatally entrenched in modern conceptions of the human and of nature', continuing to 'naturalize domination in both human and non-human spheres' (1993: 6).

Ecofeminists, however, reject the notion that 'man's freedom and happiness depend on an ongoing process of emancipation from nature, and an independence from and dominance over natural processes by the power of reason and rationality' (Mies and Shiva 1993: 6). The tenets of Enlightenment reason rely for their continuing power on a number of linked and hierarchized **binarisms**: nature and culture; black and white; civilization and savagery; the human and the animal. As Mies and Shiva argue, 'wherever women acted against ecological destruction or/and the threat of atomic annihilation, they immediately became aware of the connection between patriarchal violence against women, other people and nature' (14). The 'corporate and military warriors' aggression against the environment was perceived almost physically as an aggression against our female body' (14).

To stop the exploitation and despoliation of, in Plumwood's phrase, the 'more than human' world, radical changes in Western and Western-derived capitalist thinking are required. Central to such rethinking is the dismantling of those dangerous and divisive dualisms of patriarchal economies whose modern roots in Western cultures are traceable to the dictates of reason. Reason is interrogated not, as Plumwood stresses, to instantiate the unreasonable, but to understand the historically and philosophically contingent bases of the subjugation of women, non-Western people and the natural world.

Western rationality, which still assumes that the basis of human civilization consists in a progressive detachment from 'nature', also dominated the colonial period. The more closely associated with nature non-European peoples and women were considered to be, the more 'inherently' inferior they were; inferiority ensured and justified patriarchal/Western civilization's destruction and domination of other lands and peoples. Land itself, cast as a female and 'new' to Europeans, was 'ripe' for conquering and taming.

The legacy of the dominant discourse, as ecofeminists recognize, is environmental devastation and ongoing destruction of plants, animals and other subject peoples in the name of capitalist 'progress' identified as 'civilization'. Ecofeminism thus seeks to establish – or in the case of some colonized cultures, to re-establish, a sense of interconnectedness of being, through ontological change and political activism replicating the philosophy of connectedness in an amalgam of theory and practice. As its affirmation of the shared ground of all being suggests, ecofeminism (especially in the United States) has strong spiritual as well as political and scholarly dimensions; modern retrieval of the traditional confluence of material and spiritual being intimately connected to place and the earth in many precolonized cultures.

Further Reading: Mies and Shiva 1993; Plumwood 1993; Warren 2000; Gaard 2010, 2017; Phillips and Rumens 2015; Di Chiro 2021.

ECOLOGICAL IMPERIALISM

A term coined by Alfred W. Crosby (1986) to describe the ways in which the environments of colonized societies have been physically transformed by the experience of colonial occupation. According to this thesis, imperialism not only altered the cultural, political and social structures of colonized societies, but also devastated colonial ecologies and traditional subsistence patterns.

Crosby makes a convincing case for the success of European imperialism as having a primarily 'biological and ecological component'. European diseases were unwittingly (and more rarely deliberately) introduced to other parts of the globe, where they decimated indigenous populations and thus facilitated European military and technological conquest. More importantly, introduced crops and livestock not only supported conquering armies and colonizing populations but, in what Crosby calls 'the Neo-Europes' (**settler colonies**), radically altered the entire ecology of the invaded lands in ways that necessarily disadvantaged indigenous peoples and annihilated or endangered native flora and fauna on which their cultures (and sometimes their very lives) depended. The 'Neo-Europes' located in those temperate zones of the northern and southern hemispheres (e.g. Canada, the United States, Australia, New Zealand and Argentina) that most closely approximated the climate of Europe quickly became the major exporters of European food crops, even though their native biotas were considerably different and varied. 'The regions that today export more foodstuffs of European provenance – grains and meats – than any other lands on earth had no wheat, barley, rye, cattle, pigs, sheep, or goats whatsoever five hundred years ago' (Crosby 1986: 7). Arguably, this has led to one of the most profound ecological changes the world has seen.

The current famines in sub-Saharan Africa can be directly related to the European insistence on the repetitive cultivation of cash crops for export to the metropolitan centres in place of the traditional crop rotation that had kept the desert at bay. As a major form of Euro-spatialization, and as the most effective means of social and territorial control, ecological imperialism cannot be underestimated. Its range of meaning can be extended into the neo-colonial arena in the current Western (or 'multinational') patenting of '**third world**' plant and animal species and in the global destruction (sponsored by both Western and Asian companies) of, for instance, rain-forests.

Recently, it has been argued that current Western ecological awareness also has its roots in Empire (Grove 1994). In India and the Caribbean, Europeans encountered attitudes to the natural world that differed radically from their own and were more generally 'conservationist', respectful or animistic. European policies in the colonies frequently had to reach compromises with these differing attitudes.

Further Reading: Crosby 1986; Grove 1994; Verdesio 2002; Clark and Foster 2009; Griffiths and Robin 2011; Frame 2023.

EMPIRE

This term outlined by Hardt and Negri in the book of that name refers to a phenomenon arising from the increasing globalization of the world, transcending the power of even the strongest sovereign nations. Empire refers to something very different from those empires that have been the traditional consequence of imperialism: the extra-territorial extensions of sovereign nations beyond their own boundaries. For Hardt and Negri, Empire now 'establishes no territorial centre of power and does not rely on fixed boundaries or barriers. It is a decentred and deterritorializing apparatus of rule that progressively incorporates the entire global realm within its open, expanding frontiers' (2001: xii). Empire is thus a liminal and decentred principle of power underlying the operation of global capital. The emergence of Empire has many consequences, one of which is to scramble the distinction between the First, Second and Third worlds, as the relationship between capital, labour and markets transcends both national and regional distinctions.

Hardt and Negri reject the simplistic equation of US economic power and Empire. The United States does have a privileged position in Empire, but not because of its extension of traditional imperialism, nor its similarities to European empires, but because of its differences. 'Imperialism is over. No nation will be world leader in the way modern European nations were' (2001: xiv). Empire has no geographical limits, but effectively encompasses the spatial totality of the world; it has no historical limits, but 'suspends history' and fixes the present state of affairs forever; it has no class limits but operates at all registers of the social order. While the operation of Empire is 'bathed in blood', the concept of empire is always dedicated to peace. However, according to them, this new order of global control, despite its enormous powers of oppression and destruction, leads to new possibilities for the forces of liberation.

These forces they conceptualize as originating in the **multitude** – a collectivity that is naturally and inevitably disposed towards liberation. Rather than simply resisting Empire, the **multitude** will reorganize these new processes and put them towards new ends.

Further Reading: Hardt and Negri (2001)

ENVIRONMENTALISM

Perhaps the most significant change in the orientation of the human-ities in the second-half of the twentieth century has been the questioning of a once taken-for-granted anthropocentrism. Since the Enlightenment, Western epistemology has relegated the extra-human world to the sciences, while the study of the human became the prov-ince of the humanities. It is only relatively recently that the discip-lines of, for instance, history, anthropology, philosophy, literature and cultural studies have begun to reclaim the 'natural' environment as crucial to the understanding of a human 'being' (both past and pre-sent) and as of intrinsic worth. The enigma of place, the nature of indigeneity, the relationship between landscape and language, settler incursions with the consequent destruction of integrated biotas, colo-nial exploitation of resources and enforced cash-cropping (some-times leading to desertification) have all been subjects of postcolonial study, especially in relation to genocide and the wholesale disposses-sion of indigenous peoples. But it is only recently that the influences and impacts on the extra-human environment have been studied, both for their own importance and because of the increasing recog-nition that the more-than-human is indissolubly interwoven with the human past, present and now future. This increasing emphasis on the 'more-than-human' is environmentalism.

Environmentalism in postcolonial discourse has its beginnings in Alfred Crosby's account of the impact of European incursions into the Americas and the Pacific (see **ecological imperialism**). The conquest and colonization of so many extra-European environments produced irreversible changes in land use, in flora and fauna and frequently damaged beyond repair trad-itionally balanced relations between indigenous communities and their environments, a relationship – unlike that of their conquerors – crucial to their understanding of their 'being' as of the land rather than merely on it. These very different ontologies are particularly evident in the land claim disputes between Aboriginal and settler-descent peoples which continue today in what Alfred Crosby termed the 'Neo-Europes'. Europeans see land in terms of individual ownership, while many native traditions regarded it as the essential part of a communal (w)holism.

Imperial incursions and colonization have been regarded as environmentally destructive, yet as Richard Grove argues, the perception of what had already been lost in Europe – the sense of intrinsic connection between the 'more-than-human' and the human, and thus the urgency of environmental preservation – became strikingly evident in Europe's colonies, particularly in the late nineteenth century when the world's first National Parks were consequently established in the United States and New Zealand.

The legacies of that colonial past, together with neo-colonial environmental exploitation and outright destruction have energized environmental activism worldwide, from the tragic case of Ken Saro Wiwa to Arundhati Roy's protest against the Narmada dam project, to the desert walk for food in south-western United States. Much environmentalism in theory and practice has emanated from former imperial centres, such as Europe and the United States. While belated recognition of the crucial importance of other forms of life on earth is both welcome and necessary, its export and sometimes imposition on postcolonized cultures invites the obvious charge of hypocrisy and generates resentment against former imperial states, which, having degraded their own and their colonies' environments in the 'interests' of progress and 'development', now encourage (or impose) the theory and practices of environmental preservation on other peoples. This also frequently creates division within postcolonized cultures themselves, where, for instance, peoples are moved off their traditional lands to make way for game parks, essentially for the benefit of wealthy tourists (see Wolch, Elder and Emmel). Demands for the 'global' preservation of endangered species frequently clash with the policies of postcolonized governments eager to use their regained environmental sovereignty in the interests of a modern capitalism from which it is difficult for them to escape. Clashes between 'local' and 'global' environmental interests are explored in Amitav Ghosh's *The Hungry Tide* (2004).

The British eco-critic Dominic Head has prioritized the 'fundamental social restructuring associated with deep ecology' over the 'provisional management strategies' of environmentalism (Head 1999: 27). For Head, as for Lawrence Buell, environmental crises and Western thought are intrinsically interwoven. 'Western metaphysics and ethics need revision before we can address today's environmental problems' (Buell 1995: 2). We need, argues Buell, 'better ways of imagining nature and humanity's relation to it' (Buell 1995: 2). Ironically, some of the cultures destroyed by colonization had existed for centuries in such better ways.

Further Reading: Adams and Mulligan 2003; Buell 1995, 2005; Ghosh 2004; Guha and Martinez 1997; Head 1999; Plumwood 1993, 2002; Milbourne and Mason 2017; Mcleod 2016; Ashcroft 2017

EPISTEMIC VIOLENCE

Epistemic violence, that is, violence exerted against or through knowledge, is one of the key elements in any process of colonial domination. It is not only through economic exploitation or military control but also through epistemic frameworks that legitimize the process of domination that such domination becomes normalized. In this respect, the **civilizing mission** can be said to be a process of epistemic violence because its ultimate aim is to encourage the colonized to know themselves as other, inferior, in need of improvement, and conversely to recognize the dominant culture as normal, civilized and advanced. The civilizing mission would usually be thought of as benign rather than violent but the violence occurs in its destruction and replacement of existing epistemic frameworks, whether forced or not, thus causing great violence to the integrity of colonized culture.

Perhaps the most prominent postcolonial exponent of this concept is Gayatri Spivak who says that the 'clearest available example of such epistemic violence is the remotely orchestrated, far-flung, and heterogeneous project to constitute the colonial subject as Other'. She traces the concept back to Foucault who locates epistemic violence, a complete overhaul of the episteme, in the redefinition of sanity at the end of the European eighteenth century. Pierre Bourdieu's study of symbolic violence also led to the study of epistemic violence, but it has become a significant explanatory feature of colonial control. The process of 'civilizing' the other requires the acceptance by the colonial Other of its own primitiveness. Kristie Dotson (2011) regards it as 'the failure, owing to pernicious ignorance, of hearers to meet the vulnerabilities of speakers in linguistic exchanges'.

One prominent feature of epistemic violence is the colonial suppression of indigenous knowledge. A significant example of this is the complete blindness in Australia to the sophistication of Aboriginal land management. Bruce Pasco's *Dark Emu,* Rupert Gerritsen's *Australia and the*

Origins of Agriculture and Bill Gammage's *The Biggest Estate on Earth: How Aborigines made Australia* demonstrate that despite the colonial obsession with the connection between farming and property, Aboriginal land management represented a form of environmental knowledge that the depredations of European farming may have done well to copy (see **Environmentalism**). This knowledge was subjected to the violence of European ideas of the proper development of agriculture.

Further Reading: Brunner (2021), Dotson (2011), Spivak (1987), Pasco (2018)

ESSENTIALISM/STRATEGIC ESSENTIALISM

Essentialism is the assumption that groups, categories or classes of objects have one or several defining features exclusive to all members of that category. Some studies of race or gender, for instance, assume the presence of essential characteristics distinguishing one race from another or the feminine from the masculine. In analyses of culture, it is a (generally implicit) assumption that individuals share an essential cultural identity, and it has been a topic of vigorous debate within postcolonial theory. The Cartesian claim *Cogito ergo sum* (*I think therefore I am*) was the basis for the stress on the individual consciousness and the centrality of the idea of the human subject in the dominant intellectual discourse of the eighteenth and nineteenth centuries. The displacement of this Enlightenment concern for the individual by post-structuralist views of **subjectivity** put considerable pressure on contemporary cultural theory to revise this dominant way of conceiving of human behaviour.

Colonial discourse theory stressed this also when it drew attention to the ways of speaking and thinking that **colonialism** employed to create the idea of the inferiority of the colonial subject and to exercise **hegemonic** control over them through control of the dominant modes of public and private representation. Drawing on the critiques of language by post-structuralist theorists, such as Jacques Derrida, Jacques Lacan and Michel Foucault, colonial discourse theory contended that essentialist cultural categories were flawed. This criticism was extended by various writers to the institutions through which individual subjectivity achieved a sense of identity, for example, ideas of **race** or **nation**.

The political purpose of this critique was, in part, to expose the falsity of this mode of representing the colonial subject as **other** to the self of the dominant colonial culture.

Ironically, then, the very process of displacing the essentialist modes of identity ran counter to the pragmatic use of such concepts in various local agendas designed to recover a sense of self-worth and difference. The basis of the **National Liberation Movements** of the 1960s and 1970s was a recognition of the need to recover or develop a local identity and a sense of distinction damaged by imperial and colonizing discourses. At the same time, theorists warned of the dangers of simply reversing the categories of oppressed and oppressor without critiquing the process by which such simple binaries had come into being in the first place. They also warned of the dangers of creating a new indigenous élite who would act merely as **neo-colonial** puppets for the old forces of the colonizing powers.

Theorists such as Gayatri Spivak drew attention to the dangers of assuming that it was a simple matter of allowing the subaltern (oppressed) forces to speak, without recognizing that their essential subjectivity had been and still was constrained by the discourses within which they were constructed as **subaltern**. Her controversial question 'Can the Subaltern Speak?' (Spivak 1985b), was frequently misinterpreted to mean that there was no way in which subaltern peoples could ever attain a voice (see **agency**). Such negative misreadings of Spivak's position inevitably produced counter-claims from critics such as Benita Parry who asserted the political necessity of maintaining the idea of oppositionality between the binary divisions, such as black–white, colonizer–colonized and oppressed-oppressor (Parry 1987). In fact, Spivak's essay is not an assertion of the inability of the subaltern voice to be accessed or given agency, but only a warning to avoid the idea that the subaltern can ever be isolated in some absolute, essentialist way from the play of discourses and institutional practices that give it its voice.

In response to this negative interpretation of her earlier work, perhaps, and in an attempt to reassert the political force resident in her theory, Spivak spoke of the need to embrace a strategic essentialism, in an interview in which she acknowledged the usefulness of essentialist formulations in many struggles for liberation from the effects of colonial and neo-colonial oppression. She remarked, 'I think we have to choose again strategically, not universal discourse but essentialist discourse. I think that since as a deconstructivist . . . I cannot in fact clean my hands and say I'm specific. In fact I must say I am an essentialist from time to time' (Spivak 1984–1985: 183). And, again in the same interview, she remarked, 'I think it's absolutely on target . . . to stand against the discourses of essentialism, . . . [but] strategically we cannot' (184).

The argument suggests that in different periods, the employment of essentialist ideas may be a necessary part of the process by which the colonized achieve a renewed sense of the value and dignity of their precolonial cultures, and through which the newly emergent post-colonial **nation** asserts itself. However, as critics such as Edward Said have argued (Said 1993), the early National Liberation theorists, such as Fanon, Cabral and James, were always fully aware of the dangers of essentialism, and were always critical of the application of such essentialist discourses as nationalism and race in the construction of the modern **postcolonial state**.

Further Reading: Parry 1987; Said 1993; Spivak 1984–1985, 1985b, 1990.

ETHNICITY

Ethnicity is a term that has been used increasingly since the 1960s to account for human variation in terms of culture, tradition, language, social patterns and ancestry, rather than the discredited generalizations of **race** with its assumption of a humanity divided into fixed, genetically determined biological types. Ethnicity refers to the fusion of many traits that belong to the nature of any ethnic group: a composite of shared values, beliefs, norms, tastes, behaviours, experiences, consciousness of kind, memories and loyalties (Schermerhorn 1974: 2). A person's ethnic group is such a powerful identifier because while he or she chooses to remain in it, it is an identity that cannot be denied, rejected or taken away by others. Whereas race emerged as a way of establishing a hierarchical division between Europe and its 'others', identifying people according to fixed genetic criteria, ethnicity is usually deployed as an expression of a positive self-perception that offers certain advantages to its members. Membership of an ethnic group is shared according to certain agreed criteria, even though the nature, the combination and the importance of those criteria may be debated or may change over time.

Indeed, few terms are used in such a variety of ways or with such a variety of definitions – Isajaw (1974) deals with 27 definitions of ethnicity in the United States alone. This is possibly because ethnic groups, although they may seem to be socially defined, are distinguished both from inside and outside the group on the basis of cultural criteria, so that the defining characteristics of a particular 'ethnicity' have usually depended upon the various purposes for which the group has been identified. Not every ethnic group will possess the totality of possible defining traits, but all will display various combinations to varying degrees. Furthermore, both ethnicity and its components are relative to time and place, and, like any social phenomenon, they are dynamic and prone to change.

The simplest, and perhaps narrowest, definition of an ethnic group therefore might be

> A group that is socially distinguished or set apart, by others and/or by itself, primarily on the basis of cultural or national characteristics.

Indeed the word ethnic comes from the Greek ethnos, meaning 'nation'. In its earliest English use, the word 'ethnic' referred to culturally different 'heathen' nations, a sense that has lingered as a connotation. Some contemporary uses of the term identify ethnicity with national groups in Europe, where, with some exceptions, such as the Basques, the link between ethnicity and nationality has appeared justified. The first use of ethnic group in terms of national origin developed in the period of heavy migration from Southern and Eastern European nations to the United States in the early twentieth century. The name by which an ethnic group understands itself is still most often the name of an originating nation, whether that nation still exists or not (e.g. Armenia). The term 'ethnicity' however, really only achieves wide currency when these 'national' groups find themselves as minorities within a larger national grouping, as occurs in the aftermath of colonization, either through immigration to settled colonies such as the United States, Canada, Australia, New Zealand or by the migration of colonized peoples to the colonizing centre. One further consequence of this movement is that older European nations can no longer claim to be coterminous with a particular ethnic group but are themselves the heterogeneous and, in time, hybridized, mixture of immigrant groups.

A feature of the use of the term is that the element of marginalization evident in the earliest uses of 'ethnic' often seems to remain implied in contemporary usage. Where it originally referred to heathen nations, it now suggests groups that are not the mainstream, groups that are not traditionally identified with the dominant national mythology. Thus in **settler colonies** of the British Empire, the dominant Anglo-Saxon group is usually not seen as an ethnic group because its ethnicity has constructed the mythology of national identity. Such an identification is not limited to colonial experience, but does reveal the 'imperialistic' nature of national mythology, and the political implications of any link between ethnicity and nation.

Given the fact that 'ethnicity' comes into greatest contemporary currency in the context of immigration, we might therefore further define ethnicity in its contemporary uses as:

> a group or category of persons who have a common ancestral origin and the same cultural traits, who have a sense of peoplehood and of group belonging, who are of immigrant background and have either minority or majority status within a larger society.
> (Isajaw 1974: 118)

The perception of common ancestry, both real and mythical, has been important both to outsiders' definitions and to ethnic groups' self-definitions. Max Weber saw ethnic groups broadly as 'human groups that entertain a subjective belief in their common descent – because of similarities of physical type or of customs or both, or because of memories of colonization or migration – in such a way that this belief is important for the continuation of the nonkinship communal relationships' (1968a: 389).

In a 1974 study of 27 definitions of ethnicity, only 1 included the trait 'immigrant group', while 12 included 'common national or geographic origin', 11 included 'same culture or customs', 10 included 'religion' and 9 included 'race or physical characteristics'. However, the intervening decades have seen a great change in the ways in which the term 'ethnicity' is used: there are fewer ethnic groups in which religion has the greatest influence in the way its members see its character; the concept of race – with some notable exceptions, such as African Americans – has become more and more distinct from ethnicity because of the greater specificity of the latter (a 'racial' group may subsume several ethnic groups); in the societies in which ethnicity is most discussed, the practical and social implications of the group's status as an immigrant group have often outweighed memories of a common national origin. Recent studies have revealed that ethnic groups are not necessarily marginalized cultural groups, but that all ethnic groupings, and indeed the concept of ethnicity itself, have come to exert a powerful political function. Regardless of the status of a particular group, its ethnicity is a key strategy in the furtherance of group political interests and political advancement.

Inasmuch as group power is always a favoured solution to individual powerlessness, the ethnic group is a salient formation in the bid for political power within a society. However, the impermeability of an ethnic group's borders, the difficulty of moving in, and indeed out, of the group, along with its tendency to cut across class divisions, set it apart from other political groupings such as trade unions and political parties and suggests that its political nature is often largely unconscious. Nevertheless, the 'ethnic revolution', as Fishman (1985) calls it, was a direct consequence of the use, from the 1960s, of cultural identity and the assertion of ethnicity in political struggle.

To encompass the variety and complexity of social and cultural features constituting ethnicity, a more elaborate definition might be developed from Schermerhorn (1970: 12):

> A collectivity within a larger society having real or putative common ancestry (that is, memories of a shared historical past whether of origins or of historical experiences such as colonization, immigration, invasion or slavery); a shared consciousness of a separate, named, group identity; and a cultural focus on one or more symbolic elements defined as the epitome of their peoplehood. These features will always be in dynamic combination, relative to the particular time and place in which they are experienced and operate consciously or unconsciously A significant feature of this definition is the function of those 'symbolic elements' that may provide a sense of ethnic belonging. Examples of such symbolic elements are: kinship patterns, physical contiguity, religious affiliation, language or dialect forms, tribal affiliation, nationality, physical features, cultural values, and cultural practices such as art, literature and music. Various combinations of these elements ('one or more') may be privileged at different times and places to provide a sense of ethnicity.

This definition accommodates the complex status of groups, such as black Americans or black British, whose identity may be putatively constructed along racial as well as ethnic lines. The 'ethnic revolution' of the 1960s saw the construction of various such new ethnicities (ethnogenesis) which were much more consciously political in origin than other, increasingly attenuated ethnic connections in contemporary society. Indeed, black ethnicity in America and Britain becomes more intricately dependent upon politics in the process of ethnic legitimation than is evident with white ethnic groups.

Ethnic identities thus persist beyond cultural assimilation into the wider society and the persistence of ethnic identity is not necessarily related to the perpetuation of traditional cultures. In most cases, a very few features of traditional culture need to be selected as 'symbolic elements' around which ethnic identity revolves, and individuals need experience very few of the defining criteria (e.g. common ancestry) to consider themselves members of the group. No ethnic group is completely unified or in complete agreement about its own ethnicity and no one essential feature can ever be found in every member of the group. Nevertheless, this dynamic interweaving of identifying features has come to function as an increasingly potent locus of identity in an increasingly migratory, globalized and hybridized world.

In recent times, the growing body of people falling into the related categories of **Diaspora, Migrant, Refugee** has been increasingly the concern of those seeking to define terms such as ethnicity in a rapidly changing world. These new forces have led to increasing xenophobia in communities, often articulated in terms of the need to protect what is perceived as essential features of their 'core' identity. As Segal has argued, 'Migrants not only affect the receiving nation's culture, they alter the racial/phenotypic profile of a nation through entry and inter-marriage, often disturbing the native population. However, it is ethni-city, regardless of phenotype, which is associated with common ancestry and culture, including language, religion, traditions and behavioural norms that can contribute to, and challenge, a receiving nation's world view. When traditions clash, are devalued or interfere with established patterns of interaction and behaviour, fear and discrimination escalate, resulting in barriers that seem impossible to navigate' (Segal 2019).

Where once ethnicity might have seemed to be a less threatening and divisive way of conceiving identity than race, these new forces are causing a reexamination of how defining ethnicity works in the actual politics of a globalized world.

Further Reading: Darias 2000; Drew 1999; Fishman 1985; Gunew 1997; Hall 1989; Isajaw 1974; Olson and Worsham 1999; Schermerhorn 1970, 1974; Singh and Schmidt 2000; Sollors 1986, 1996; Weber 1968 a and Weber 1968ba; Desmet, Ortuño-Ortín and Wacziarg 2017; Segal 2019.

ETHNOGRAPHY

Ethnography is that field of anthropological research based on direct obser-vation of and reporting on a people's way of life. It is the basic methodology employed by cultural anthropologists and consists of two stages: fieldwork, which is the term used for the process of observing and recording data; and reportage, the production of a written description and analysis of the subject under study. Historically, ethnography concerned itself principally with recording the life and habits of peoples from societies not the observer's own – usually distant locales, distant, that is, geographically or culturally from the West, and seen as different from the normative European cultures. Anthropology began as a kind of natural history, a study of the peoples encountered along the frontiers of European expansion.

Anthropology is thus the term for the broad discipline in which ethnography is located. When the discipline began, these alternative cultures were constructed through a notion of the **exotic**, which differentiated them from the European, or of the primitive, which saw them in a Darwinian way as stages in the 'development' of man, ideas that were clearly useful to **colonial discourse** in constructing a hierarchy of cultures. For this reason, anthropology and ethnographic discourse have often been critiqued in postcolonial texts as classic examples of the power of Western discourse to construct its primitive **others**.

To its proponents, on the other hand, ethnography is simply a social research method whereby the ethnographer 'participates, overtly or covertly, in people's daily lives for an extended period of time, watching what happens, listening to what is said, asking questions; in fact collecting whatever data are available to throw light on the issues with which he or she is concerned' (Hammersley and Atkinson 1983: 2). Thus, it is a form of participant observation which attempts to gather data, 'on location', that will lead to an understanding of a particular social or cultural group.

However, criticism of ethnography argues that none of these activities – watching, listening, asking or collecting – is a neutral, value free act, nor does it exist beyond the assumptions and prescriptions of the **discourse** of the participant's own culture. Not even the concept of knowledge itself can be value free, because what is known depends upon how it is known, that is, cultural knowledge is 'constructed' rather than 'discovered' by ethnography. Indeed, the most vigorous criticism suggests that ethnography itself, as a 'science', has historically existed precisely to locate the observed subjects in a particular way, to **interpellate** them as Europe's others. Some of the more critical accounts (e.g. Asad 1973) have argued that anthropology itself was not simply a child of colonialism, in that colonization opened up areas of research and ethnographers provided information to colonial administrations, but rather that it was 'colonialism's twin' (Fardon 1990: 6). Anthropology reproduced versions of the colonized subject that both were motivated by and rationalized the exclusion and exploitation of those subjects by imperial discourse itself. This critical account of the role of anthropology and ethnography is put strongly by Richard Fardon:

> Anthropology necessarily reproduced versions of assumptions deeply embedded in a predatory European culture . . . the inversion of a self-image was generalized to some fictive collectivity based on geography, skin colour, tribe or whatever. To counterpose to an enlightened Europe we produced an African heart of darkness; to our rational, controlled west corresponded an irrational and sensuous Orient; our progressive civilization differed from the historical cul-de-sacs into which Oriental despots led their subjects; our maturity might be contrasted with the childhood of a darker humanity, but our youth and vigour distinguished us from the aged civilizations of the east whose splendour was past. . . .
>
> Subtly, not so subtly, and downright crassly, we produced our exemplar others; now, we pride ourselves that we see through the mirrors we set up, no longer dazzled by the pleasing images of ourselves they reflected. The temporal transpositions have been rendered transparent for what they were: artifices of imagination in the service of power.
>
> (Fardon 1990: 6)

More recently, ethnography itself has experienced vigorous debates about its methodology; between the claims of 'positivism' and 'naturalism', for instance, and about the status of reflexivity, the extent to which the ethnographer is conscious of his or her own **subject** position. There has been considerable debate between structuralists and ethnographers adopting a phenomenological or ethno-methodological approach. Since the advent of contemporary revelations of its own provisional textuality, ethnography has had increasingly to address the issue of whether there is an underlying conflict between the earlier claims about its ability to make objective representative statements about the conditions of human life in the world. This is necessarily associated with arguments that assert that human life can be known only through specific and therefore limited representations which inevitably reflect the power relations between those who represent and those who are represented.

One influential response to this question of representation and power has been James Clifford's insistence that ethnography is itself a form of writing and should be approached from the point of view of its textuality.

Clifford's argument is that, with the demise of colonialism, 'the West can no longer present itself as the unique purveyor of anthropological knowledge about others' (1988: 22). In Writing Culture, he takes up Clifford Geertz's suggestion that it is anthropologists' practice, especially their writing that should be examined. He distinguishes four main areas governing the reading and writing of ethnography: 'language, rhetoric, power and history' (Clifford 1986: 25), with his own emphasis being on the first two. Clifford demonstrates that ethnography, like any discourse, operates with its own set of rules, proscriptions and assumptions; it is a form of writing that may be examined using the techniques of reading more familiar to literary criticism.

Ultimately, Clifford is optimistic about ethnography's ability to shake off its Western epistemological legacy, and in *The Predicament of Culture* (1988), he surveys several modes of ethnographic writing that may do so. While ethnographic writing 'cannot entirely escape the reductionist use of dichotomies and essences, it can at least struggle self-consciously to avoid portraying abstract ahistorical "others"' (1988: 23). Despite the earlier role of ethnography in the colonial enterprise, Clifford propounds the need for a decentred ethnographic practice, a form of ethnographic writing that takes into account, and overcomes, its colonial history and the difficulties concerning the subject position of the ethnographer: 'It is more than ever crucial for different peoples to form complex concrete images of one another, as well as of the relationships of knowledge and power that connect them' (23). One consequence of such a position has been a form of localized ethnography that interrupts the **surveillance** of the process and produces knowledge from the point of view of the local subject (Fardon 1990).

Contemporary ethnography vigorously asserts its ability to produce useful, complex, 'thick' descriptions that seek to take the position of the observer and the problem of surveillance into account. Taking the dispute to the opposing camp, some anthropologists have gone further and argued that they, in fact, take far more account of the 'differences' between cultures than their critics. For example, they have drawn attention to the fact that they acknowledge the material inscriptive elements of cultures far more effectively than more textually oriented disciplines such as cultural studies, which, despite its claims to study a wide variety of social practices, has still largely concentrated on forms similar to or analogous in their significatory structures to Western cultural ideas of inscription and communication.

Anthropology has also tried to overcome the paralysis that extreme forms of post-structuralist critique would impose on all 'fieldwork' by engaging constructively with the issues of representation and discrimination in anthropological definitions of its subject's goals and range. In particular, anthropology has tried to reorientate itself towards the study of groups or sections of the cultures within the metropolitan spheres, breaking down the idea that sociology deals with 'us' and anthropology with 'them'. Forming links with other disciplines, with which in the past it had tended to compete, such as sociology, psychology and linguistics, contemporary cultural anthropology seeks to take its core practice of 'fieldwork' and ethnographic description into societies and sub-groups much closer to the observer's own culture. Ethnographic studies in the past few decades – studies of youth gangs in North American cities, gender in British rural villages, working-class youths in English schools – are offered as examples that suggest that it is in fact possible to reach some effective and meaningful descriptions that help us to understand social and cultural phenomena.

Contemporary ethnography, then, is concerned with describing and differentiating cultures in ways that acknowledge its own perspectives and roles. A recent development has been the increasing internationalization of the discipline with major studies by, amongst many others, Kenyan, Nigerian, South African, Indian, Brazilian, Indonesian and Mexican anthropologists. Although in itself this is no answer to critiques of the substantive, philosophical basis of ethnography, the fact that in recent times substantial contributions to the discipline have been made by people in the erstwhile 'target' communities themselves has helped to focus attention on the possibility of a more 'self-ascriptive' mode of social and cultural analysis, employing modern ethnographic methodologies.

Further Reading: Appadurai 1991; Asad 1973; Boon 1982; Clifford 1986, 1988; Fardon 1990; Ingold 1996; Mignolo and Shiwy 2003; Nederveen Pieterse 1992; Raheja 2002; Stocking 1983; Thomas 1994; Thobani 2015

ETHNO-PSYCHIATRY/ETHNO-PSYCHOLOGY

A particularly significant development in classic **ethnography** in colonial situations occurred from the 1920s onwards and had a negative influence on the representation of colonized peoples. This was the application of psychiatric and psychological theories to the construction of models of the so-called 'native mind' or 'native personality'.

Just as ethnography could be employed to control the colonized by creating scientific models of their culture that stressed those features that suited the colonial purposes, so ethno-psychiatry could suggest that there were certain ineradicable mental 'sets' that prevented 'natives' from exercising the same degree of control or responsibility as the colonial settlers. This form of pseudo-scientific construction was deeply embedded in the assumptions underlying the notion of race itself – that physical characteristics indicated deeply embedded psychological, intellectual and behavioural differences between racial groups.

The combining of race models with fashionable discourses such as psychiatry proved particularly powerful and useful in colonies with a large indigenous majority, such as Kenya or Rhodesia (Zimbabwe), as settlers came into conflict with their home governments over the long-term goals of colonization. Such disputes centred on whether the natives could be 'made ready' for self-government (the official British and European government policies on most colonies in the period), or would always remain dependent on white expertise and white support (the preferred settler position).

Ironically, the ideas of the proponents of this kind of psychiatric model were used by later anti-colonialist theorists, such as Fanon, who took the idea of a 'native mind' and employed it to suggest that certain colonial disorders were the direct result of the construction of the native as inferior and as deformed. Of course, Fanon did not accept the **essentialist** ideas that underlay colonial ethnopsychiatric models and critiqued the idea that the 'native' was a natural category, demonstrating how the mental deformations of the patients in Algerian psychiatric wards were the direct result of the racist policies of the colonial administration.

But far from being only a concept of interest to the practice of the colonial period, the concepts of Fanon and others, such as the Haitian psychiatrist Louis Mars, who first coined the term, have been shown to be of direct use in the modern attempts to define the specific psychiatric needs and treatments of those groups who through physical displacement or through being in other ways part of the contemporary **precariat** have experienced psychological trauma, for example, groups such as migrants or refugees or oppressed internal minorities such as Afro-Americans (Caroppo et al 2009, Turner and Neville 2020).

Further Reading: Carothers 1953; D'Andrade 1995; Fanon 1961; Caroppo et al. 2009; Turner and Neville 2020; Auguste et al. 2023.

ETHNOSCAPES

Arjun Appadurai outlines five specific scapes or flows as features of globalization: technoscapes, the flow of technology (such as the iPhone); ideoscapes, the flow of ideas; financescapes, the flow of money across political borders; and mediascapes, the flow of media. Of the many different forms of globalization, ethnoscape refers to the flow of people across boundaries, something that has grown in importance in an increasingly mobile world (see **Diaspora**). Examples of such individuals include tourists, exiles, **refugees**, **immigrants**, students studying abroad and temporary workers abroad. As people move around for any reason, so do ideas and information. The flow of people also includes tourists, who are generally from developed countries who come into contact with people in the developing world. While there is the potential for tourists to be positively affected by their experiences with 'the Other' while travelling, tourists are often regarded unfavourably for a tendency to ignore social mores and for their inadvertent display of wealth.

Further Reading: Appadurai (1991), Appadurai (1996)

ETHNOSYMBOLISM

This is a school of thought in the study of nationalism that stresses the importance of symbols, myths, values and traditions in the formation and persistence of the modern **nation-state**. It argues that modern national movements arise from older or ancient ethnic cores called *ethnies*. Its principal exponent is Anthony Smith whose *Ethosymbolism and Nationalism* argues against Hobsbawm's contention that it was nationalism and the state that engendered nations rather than the other way round. Smith labelled this the modernist explanation of nations, which asserted that nationalism, the ideology and the movement is both recent and novel; that nations are also recent and novel; both are a product of modernity. The modernist explanation is the one most widely accepted today and the postcolonial approach endorses the concept of emergent nationalisms inventing the concept of the primordial existence of the nation.

Ethno-symbolists agree with modernists on the importance of conceiving of nations as 'real' sociological communities. Given the continuing and severe conceptual difficulties raised by terms such as 'nation', 'national identity' and 'nationalism', it is tempting to treat nations as purely 'discursive formations', created and manipulated by states and their élites. But legal social and geographical features of the state, not the least of which is the reality of borders, conceive the modern nation as a real, albeit imagined community as Benedict Anderson proposes. However, ethnosymbolism remains an outlier in studies of nationalism which tend to produce copious evidence of the contemporary invention of national mythology.

Discussion of the issue fails to take into account the emergence of colonial nationalisms, which tend to adopt the architecture of the colonial state but often have a rich history of myths and traditions that may support the idea of the postcolonial nation-state. It also fails to take into account the emergence of settler colony nations for which the national mythology may be entirely invented or heavily dependent on the imperial centre for its symbols, myths and traditions. Notwithstanding this reliance on imperial mythology, the myths and symbols of the invaded indigenous people may have some presence in the settler colony but these are usually of minimum impact alongside the construction of a national mythology from recent postcolonial history.

Further Reading: Smith (2009), Leoussi and Grosby (1988)

EUROCENTRISM

The conscious or unconscious process by which Europe and European cultural assumptions are constructed as, or assumed to be, the normal, the natural or the universal. The first, and possibly most potent sign of Eurocentrism, as José Rabasa explains (1993), was the specific projection employed to construct the Mercator Atlas itself, a projection that favoured the European temperate zones in its distribution of size. This map of the world is not merely an objective outline of discovered continents, but an 'ideological or mythological reification of space' which opens up the territories of the world to domination and appropriation. 'The world' only acquired spatial meaning after different regions had been inscribed by Europeans, and this inscription, apart from locating Europe at the top of the globe or map, established an ideological figuration, through the accompanying text and illustrations, which firmly centralized Europe as the source and arbiter of spatial and cultural meaning.

By the eighteenth century, this conception of a collective 'Europe' constructed as a sign of superiority and in opposition to the rest of the world's cultures had become firmly consolidated. Then, as now, such collective constructions existed in a troubled or ambivalent relationship with an alternative stress on the nationalism of emerging individual European nation-states and their particular cultures. European colonization of the rest of the globe, which accelerated in the eighteenth century and reached its apogee in the nineteenth, actively promoted or facilitated Eurocentrism through exploration, conquest and trade. Imperial displays of power, both in the metropolitan centres and at the colonial peripheries, and assertions of intellectual authority in colonialist institutions, such as schools and universities, and through the civil service and legal codes, established European systems and values as inherently superior to indigenous ones.

Edward Said's Orientalism examines the ways in which Eurocentrism not only influences and alters, but actually produces other cultures. **Orientalism** is 'a way of coming to terms with the orient that is based on the orient's special place in European western experience' (1978: 1) or 'the western style for dominating, restructuring and having authority over the orient' (3). This authority is, in Said's view, a product of a systematic 'discipline' by which European culture was able to construct and manage the Orient during the post-Enlightenment period.

Eurocentrism is masked in literary study by concepts such as literary universality, in history by authoritative interpretations written from the point of view of the victors, and in early anthropology by the unconscious assumptions involved in the idea that its data were those societies defined as 'primitive' and so opposed to a European norm of development and civilization. Some cultural critics have argued that anthropology as a discipline in its classic, unrevised form came into being in such a close relationship with colonization that it could not have existed at all without the prior existence of Eurocentric concepts of knowledge and civilization. Eurocentrism is also present in the assumptions and practices of Christianity through education and mission activity, as well as in in the assumed superiority of Western mathematics, cartography, art and numerous other cultural and social practices which have been claimed, or assumed, to be based on a universal, objective set of values.

Further Reading: Blaut 1993; Chakrabarty 2000; Dirlik 1999; Dussel 1993; Dussel and Mendieta 1998; Ferro 1997; Kanth 2005; Lazarus 2002; Rabasa 1993; Shohat 1994.

EXILE

The condition of exile involves the idea of a separation and distancing from either a literal homeland or from a cultural and ethnic origin. Critics such as Andrew Gurr (1981) have suggested that a distinction should be drawn between the idea of exile, which implies involuntary constraint, and that of expatriation, which implies a voluntary act or state. In a sense, only the first generation of free settlers (of all the many peoples of the varied colonial societies) could be regarded as expatriates rather than exiles. For those born in the colonies, the idea of expatriation (defined as a state voluntarily entered into) needs to be revised. However, if the term is restricted, as Gurr suggests, to refer to those who cannot return to the 'place of origin', even if they wish to do so, then exile becomes a characteristic of a number of different colonial conditions. For example, it helps to account for the tension involved in constructing a distant place as 'home' by native-born descendants of the colonizers.

The degree and tenacity with which such native-born colonizers perceive the metropolitan colony as 'home' differs, of course, between 'settler-invader' colonies and colonies of occupation. Discourses of **race** and **ethnicity** were, however, in both a feature that conflicted with desires to claim a special status for the 'native-born' colonizer. In settler colonies, the 'native-born' colonial wished to claim an insider knowledge but wished to retain a 'racial' distinction from the 'native', for example Kipling's character Kim. In settler colonies, the settler also often wished to preserve a racial distinction from the 'natives' that depended on retaining a linkage with the absent homeland. As they formed specific attachments to the new space, tensions arose that were central to the continued pre-occupation with issues of 'identity' in settler colony discourses. A classic text illustrating this process is that by the Australian woman writer Henry Handel Richardson, whose hero in *The Fortunes of Richard Mahony* (1917) shuttles to and fro between Australia and Europe, unable to find a sense of wholly belonging in either space, so ambivalent is his identity. The situation of the increasingly large number of **diasporic** peoples throughout the world further problematizes the idea of 'exile'. Where is the place of 'home' to be located for such groups? In the place of birth (nateo), in the displaced cultural community into which the person is born, or in the nation-state in which this diasporic community is located? The emergence of new ethnicities that cross the boundaries of the diasporic groups' different cultural, geographical and linguistic origins also acts to problematize these categories further (e.g. Black British; see Hall 1989).

Exile was also produced by colonialism in another way, as pressure was exerted on many colonized peoples to exile themselves from their own cultures, languages and traditions. The production of this 'in-between' class, 'white but not quite', was often a deliberate feature of colonial practice. As Gauri Viswanathan (1989) has shown, it was the basis for the development of the education system in India following Macaulay's notorious Minute on Indian Education. It was also the condition of many of the creolized intellectuals of West Africa (de Moraes-Farias and Barber 1990). The possibilities shown by this class of colonially educated 'natives' to broker their position into a radical and nationalist political strategy does not mean that they did not suffer a form of profound exile. Such conditions of localized alienation or exile could sometimes contribute to the generation of new social and cultural practices and the questioning of old traditions.

Exile continues to be an ambivalent state in postcolonial studies, particularly in the work of Edward Said. While for him it is an almost necessary condition for true critical worldliness, 'the achievements of any exile are permanently undermined by his or her sense of loss' (1984: 49). While it is 'the unhealable rift forced between a human being and a native place' (49), nevertheless, the canon of modern Western culture 'is in large part the work of exiles' (49). This tension between personal desolation and cultural empowerment is the tension of exile in Said's own work, a tension which helps explain his own deep investment in the link between the text and the world. Consequently, Said's view of the intellectual is of a person whose detachment from the centres of power, whose ability to 'speak truth to power' is deeply enhanced by the experience of exile despite the debilitating sense of loss it engenders (Said 1994: 47–64).

The vastly increased number of people displaced in recent decades now exceeds the previous greatest number, i.e. the massive displacement of people at the end of the Second World War. Wars, civil conflicts, climate change and re-emergent exclusive nationalism and religious extremism have seen a massive increase in people fleeing their homelands to escape intolerable conditions of violence and discrimination or the economic consequences of the growing gap between the rich and poor regions of the world. These conditions have made the definition of where one 'belongs' increasingly fraught and politically sensitive. Traditional diasporic communities offer a relatively simple mode of definition compared with the complex issues of identity posed by the migrants and refugees that these recent global forces have brought into being (Gamal 2013; Mains 2013; Huggan 2017).

Further Reading: Barkan 1998; Chambers and Curti 1996; Gunew 2004; Gurr 1981; Said 1984, 1994, 1999; Ward 2002; Gamal 2013; Mains 2013; Huggan 2017.

EXOTIC/EXOTICISM

The word exotic was first used in 1599 to mean 'alien, introduced from abroad, not indigenous'. By 1651, its meaning had been extended to include 'an exotic and foreign territory', 'an exotic habit and demeanour' (OED). As a noun, the term meant 'a foreigner' or 'a foreign plant not acclimatized'.

During the nineteenth century, however, the exotic, the foreign, increasingly gained, throughout the British Empire, the connotations of a stimulating or exciting difference, something with which the domestic could be (safely) spiced. The key conception here is the introduction of the exotic from abroad into a domestic economy. From the earliest days of European voyages, exotic minerals, artefacts, plants and animals were brought back for display in private collections and museums and live specimens were cultivated, in Kew Gardens, for example, or in the many private and public zoos established in the period. Peoples of other cultures were also brought back to the European metropoles and were introduced in fashionable salons or travelled as popular entertainment. Omai from the Society Islands, Bennelong from Australia and later the 'Hottentot Venus' from South Africa, were displayed in European capitals as exotics. Not only indigenes from the colonies but those Europeans deemed to have had exotic experiences could also be exhibited or exhibit themselves, e.g. Eliza Fraser, who had been shipwrecked and survived among Australian aborigines, was displayed as a woman who had lived amongst savages.

The key point here, however, is made by Renate Wasserman that, 'Indians exhibited at Royal courts or turkeys and parrots in cages' could be seen as 'innocent signifiers' of an exotic other, one that could titillate the European public imagination while offering no threat since such exotics were, in her terms, 'non-systematic' (1984: 132). Isolated from their own geographical and cultural contexts, they represented whatever was projected onto them by the societies into which they were introduced. Exotics in the metropoles were a significant part of imperial displays of power and the plenitude of empires.

When the English language and the concepts it signified in the imperial culture were carried to colonized sites, through, for instance,

English education, the attribution of exoticism as it applied to those places, peoples or natural phenomena usually remained unchanged. Thus schoolchildren in, for instance, the Caribbean and North Queensland could regard and describe their own vegetation as 'exotic' rather than trees like the oak or yew that were 'naturalized' for them as domestic by the English texts they read.

Further Reading: Appadurai 1986; Arnold 2003; Célestin 1996; Forsdick 2001; Gualtieri 1996; Huggan 2001; Nederveen Pieterse 1992; Thomas 1994; Wasserman 1984, 1994; Yee 2016; Huggan 2020.

EXPLORATION AND TRAVEL

European exploration of other parts of the globe began with the actual movements out of Europe by land routes to the 'East', and by sea across the Mediterranean and into the Atlantic. Although there are many legendary accounts of early voyages, and considerable historical evidence of extensive, even intercontinental, travel by peoples such as the Vikings in the Dark and Middle Ages, European travel beyond the traditional fringes of the Mediterranean appears to have taken a giant leap forward in the early Renaissance. This was partly due to the decline of the Muslim control of the so-called Middle and Far East, which allowed travellers to proceed under the Pax Mongolica as far as China (Marco Polo), and partly due to the development of effective navigational aids and the advances in mapping (see **cartography**). Such advances meant that early sea-going explorers such as the Portuguese and the Spanish could venture further afield and risk leaving the coast-hugging voyages of the fifteenth century to start voyaging out into the Atlantic itself to discover the off-shore islands of the Canaries and the Azores, perhaps the earliest of all European 'colonies', which they occupied in the early sixteenth century.

In addition to such physical explorations, however, 'travel' also began as the imaginative construction of other people and places. This intermixing of actual exploratory voyages with fictive representations of otherness rooted in the imaginative practice of the Middle Ages persists through and beyond the actual eighteenth-century circumnavigation of the globe and the extensive travels in the land-mass interiors that followed in the nineteenth century. Of course, the idea of exploration and discovery in such travelling is profoundly Eurocentric, since what explorers purportedly discovered was invariably already known to local indigenous peoples, many of whom led white explorers to local land-marks, rivers and sources of food that enabled them to survive. Yet these discoveries were credited to the European explorers as though such places had not existed beforehand.

Renaissance sea voyages led to the widespread seizure of the goods of indigenous peoples as loot. Travel and exploration in the period was seen as strictly and unashamedly commercial and exploitative in purpose. During the eighteenth century, however, new kinds of travellers began to emerge, especially the scientific travellers in search of new geographical and biological information, and the missionaries who began increasingly to travel to spread the Christian religion and who, like the scientific explorers, saw their interaction with the people of the worlds they entered as essentially benign. Initially, these new kinds of travellers were often sponsored by trading companies or were attached to government expeditions. But they rapidly developed independent scientific and religious institutions to support their work, such as The Royal Geographical Society or the various Missionary Societies, a development that allowed them ostensibly to distance themselves from commercial and military expeditions and to portray themselves as harmless knowledge seekers in contrast to rapacious traders and military expeditionary forces of conquest. However, their travels and their accounts of these travels, whether ostensibly factual or fictionally embellished, were as effectively 'capturing' as commercial exploitation or conquest. Such knowledge also directly facilitated exploitation and intervention, processes whose real effects are reflected in phrases like 'the opening up of Africa'. Such a phrase also suggests the gendering of landscape and the associations between sexuality and exploration and conquest. 'Virgin territories' (never virgin, but the inhabitants were considered to be uncivilized and thus having no legal rights of ownership) were opened up by exploration to trade and settlement, their original inhabitants killed, displaced or marginalized within European settler communities. In extreme cases where peoples were seen to be without organizational forms recognizable as such to European eyes, as in Australia, the land was declared literally empty, a *terra nullius*.

Accounts of European travel and reports of explorations to the Royal Society helped produce and maintain ideas of Europe itself, ideas framed by Europe's sense of its difference from the places and cultures that were being explored and reported on. The knowledge produced by exploratory travel of these various groups is at the heart of the control of the new possessions. Once 'explored' and so 'known', these territories were possessed and able to be catalogued as under the control or influence of one or the other of the colonizing powers. Such travel accounts were quickly appropriated to fictional forms in works as diverse as *The Tempest*, *Gulliver's Travels* and *Robinson Crusoe*. In fact, the latter has been seen by many critics as the first modern novel, suggesting that the development of this powerful new genre and the discovery of new lands and their imaginative transformation are closely aligned (see Watt 1957 and Said 1993). Since then, travel literature has emerged as a distinctive genre of postcolonial representation. The travel account continues to be one of the most powerful tools through which the postcolonial world is shaped and controlled. But like all such representations, it has been appropriated by those it was used to define and control, and travel accounts of the colonized cultures by the colonized people who visited them entered the genre from the nineteenth century onwards (see Griffiths 2012b).

Contemporary tourism is in many ways the modern extension of colonial possession by exploration. The tourist enters the territory of the 'other' in search of an exotic experience. Early tourism parodied the exploration of earlier exploratory periods, with bands of Victorian gentlemen and ladies roped together to explore the lower Alps or the slopes of Vesuvius. Modern tourism divides between the contemporary form of this in the adventure or safari tour, and the mass form of modern comfort tourism in which the experience is typically stereotyped, packaged and reduced to an easily consumed product. In effect, the tourist, ostensibly in search of the new, is actually seeking the already known. In the same way that early travellers' experience was coloured by expectations formed over centuries of superstitious imagining, so the modern tourist travels to discover those stereotypical experiences already presented as **exotic**. Where signifiers of stereotyped exotic difference are absent (such as palm trees, white sand beaches, etc.), they are constructed as part of so-called resort developments. The idea of the tropical ceases to refer to an actual geographical reality that may involve such discomforting actualities as mosquitoes, mangrove swamps and poisonous fauna, as well as human poverty and exploitation, instead it becomes an imaginative construct that says more about the European fantasy than the actual location in which it finds its setting. Tourism also functions, therefore, as part of the process of cultural and economic control whereby economies of underdeveloped countries are constructed by and made dependent on external institutions and multinational companies (see **neo-colonialism**).

Further Reading: Abernethy 2000; Armstrong and Hestertun 2006; Arnold 2003; Blunt and McEwan 2002; Clark 1999; Clifford 1997;

Griffiths 2012b; Hall and Tucker 2004; Huggan 1989; Huggan 2000; Kincaid 1988; Korte 2001; Korte and Matthias 2000; Leer 1992; Mignolo 1995a; Mills 1991; Pratt 1992; Ryan 1994; Scott 2001.

FANONISM

A term for the anti-colonial liberationist critique formulated by the Martiniquan psychiatrist Frantz Fanon (1925–1961). Fanon's work in Algeria led him to become actively involved in the Algerian liberation movement and to publish a number of foundational works on racism and colonialism. These include *Black Skin, White Masks* (1952, translated 1968), a study of the psychology of racism and colonial domination. Just before his death, he published *The Wretched of the Earth* (1961), a broader study of how **anti-colonial** sentiment might address the task of **decolonization**. In these texts, Fanon brought together the insights he derived from his clinical study of the effects of colonial domination on the psyche of the colonized and his Marxist-derived analysis of social and economic control. From this conjunction, he developed his idea of a **comprador** class, or élite, who exchanged roles with the white colonial dominating class without engaging in any radical restructuring of society. The black skin of these compradors was 'masked' by their complicity with the values of the white colonial powers. Fanon argued that the native intelligentsia must radically restructure the society on the firm foundation of the people and their values.

However, Fanon, like other early National Liberationist figures such as the Trinidadian C.L.R. James and the Cape Verdean Amilcar Cabral, did not advocate a naive view of the precolonial. Fanon's nationalism was always what Edward Said in Culture and Imperialism has defined as 'critical nationalism', that is, formed in an awareness that precolonial societies were never simple or homogeneous and that they contained socially prejudicial class and gender formations that stood in need of reform by a radical force. As Said has noted '[Fanon's] notion was that unless national consciousness at its moment of success was somehow changed into social consciousness, the future would not hold liberation but an extension of imperialism' (1993: 323). For Fanon, the task of the national liberator, often drawn as he himself was from a colonially educated élite, was to 'join the people in that fluctuating movement which they are just giving a shape to . . . which will be the signal for everything to be called into question' (1952: 168) (see **cultural diversity/cultural difference**).

157

Although Fanon is sometimes recruited to the banner of a naive form of **nativism**, he took a more complicated view of tradition and the precolonial as well as of its role in the construction of the modern **post-colonial state**. Fanon, of course, recognized and gave a powerful voice to the fact that for the new national leaders 'the passionate search for a national culture which existed before the colonial era finds its legitimate reason in the anxiety shared by many indigenous intellectuals to shrink away from that western culture in which they all risk being swamped' and to 'renew contact once more with the oldest and most pre-colonial springs of their people' (1961: 153–154). But he also recognized the danger that such pasts could be easily mythologized and used to create the new élite power groups, masquerading as the liberators of whom he had warned.

> A national culture is not a folklore, nor an abstract populism that believes it can discover the people's true nature. It is not made up of the inert dregs of gratuitous actions, that is to say actions which are less and less attached to the ever present reality of the people. A national culture is the whole body of efforts made by a people in the sphere of thought to describe, justify and praise the action through which that people has created itself and keeps itself in existence.
>
> (1961: 154–155)

Throughout his historical analysis, Fanon never lost sight of the importance of the subjective consciousness and its role in creating the possibilities for the **hegemonic** control of the colonized subject, and of the **neo-colonial** society that followed political independence. In studies such as *The Fact of Blackness* (1952) he addressed the importance of the visible signs of racial difference in constructing a discourse of prejudice, and the powerful and defining psychological effects of this on the self-construction of black peoples. Much of Fanon's work gives definition to the radical attempt to oppose this in the discourses of the **black consciousness** movement that emerged in America and Britain in the 1960s and which drew much of its inspiration from Fanon's work. Although it might be argued that later theorists such as Amilcar Cabral presented a more effective political programme for implementing the radical transformation of the native colonial intelligentsia in what Cabral called, in a memorable phrase, 'a veritable forced march along the road to cultural progress' (Cabral 1973), it was in the interweaving of the specific and personal with the general and social that Fanon's distinctive and profoundly influential contribution was made.

Further Reading: Fanon 1952, 1959, 1961.

FEMINISM AND POSTCOLONIALISM

Feminism is of crucial interest to postcolonial discourse for two major reasons. First, both patriarchy and imperialism can be seen to exert analogous forms of domination over those they render subordinate. Hence the experiences of women in patriarchy and those of colonized subjects can be paralleled in a number of respects, and both feminist and postcolonial politics oppose such dominance. Second, there have been vigorous debates in a number of colonized societies over whether gender or colonial oppression is the more important political factor in women's lives. This has sometimes led to division between Western feminists and political activists from impoverished and oppressed countries, or, alternatively, the two are inextricably entwined, in which case, the condition of colonial dominance affects, in material ways, the position of women within their societies. This has led to calls for a greater consideration of the construction and employment of gender in the practices of imperialism and colonialism.

Feminism, like postcolonialism, has often been concerned with the ways and extent to which representation and language are crucial to identity formation and to the construction of **subjectivity**. For both groups, language has been a vehicle for subverting patriarchal and imperial power, and both discourses have invoked essentialist arguments in positing more authentic forms of language against those imposed on them. Both discourses share a sense of disarticulation from an inherited language and have thus attempted to recover a linguistic authenticity via a precolonial language or a primal feminine tongue. However, both feminists and colonized peoples, like other subordinate groups, have also used **appropriation** to subvert and adapt dominant languages and signifying practices.

The texts of feminist theory and those of postcolonialism concur on many aspects of the theory of identity, of difference and of the inter-pellation of the subject by a dominant discourse, as well as offering to each other various strategies of resistance to such controls.

Similarities between 'writing the body' in feminism and 'writing place' in postcolonialism; similarities between the strategies of bisexuality and cultural syncreticity; and similar appeals to nationalism may be detected (Ashcroft 1989).

In the 1980s, many feminist critics (Carby 1982; Mohanty 1984; Suleri 1992) began to argue that Western feminism, which had assumed that gender overrode cultural differences to create a universal category of the womanly or the feminine, was operating from hidden, universalist assumptions with a middle-class, Eurocentric bias. Feminism was therefore charged with failing to account for or deal adequately with the experiences of Third World women. In this respect, the issues concerning gender face similar problems to those concerned with **class**. Mohanty, for instance, criticizes

> the assumption that all of us of the same gender, across classes and cultures, are somehow socially constituted as a homogeneous group identified prior to the process of analysis. . . . Thus, the discursively consensual homogeneity of 'women' as a group is mistaken for the historically specific material reality of groups of women.
>
> (Mohanty 1984: 338)

Domatila Barrios de Chungara's *Let Me Speak* demonstrates how the material reality of different groups of women can lead to very different perceptions of the nature of political struggle. When she was invited to the International Women's Year Tribunal in Mexico City in 1974, the difference between the feminist agenda of the tribunal and her own political struggle against oppression in the Bolivian tin mines became very clear. In her view, the meeting's World Plan of Action 'didn't touch on the problems that are basic for Latin American women' (Barrios de Chungara 1977: 201). The overlap between patriarchal, economic and racial oppression has always been difficult to negotiate, and the differences between the political priorities of First and Third World women have persisted to the present. Such differences appear to be those of emphasis and strategy rather than those of principle, since the interconnection of various forms of social oppression materially affects the lives of all women.

More recently, feminism has been concerned that categories like gender may sometimes be ignored within the larger formation of the colonial, and that postcolonial theory has tended to elide gender differences in constructing a single category of the colonized. These critics argue that colonialism operated very differently for women and for men, and the 'double colonization' that resulted when women were subject both to general discrimination as colonial subjects and specific discrimination as women needs to be taken into account in any analysis of colonial oppression (Spivak 1985a, 1985b, 1985c, 1986; Mohanty 1984; Suleri 1992). Even post-independence practices of anti-colonial nationalism are not free from this kind of gender bias, and constructions of the traditional or precolonial are often heavily inflected by a contemporary masculinist bias that falsely represents 'native' women as quietist and subordinate.

One illuminating account of the connections between race and gender as a consequence of imperial expansion is Sander L. Gilman's *Black bodies, white bodies* (1985), which shows how the representation of the African in nineteenth-century European art, medicine and literature reinforced the construction of the sexualized female body. The presence of male or female black servants was regularly included in paintings, plays and operas as a sign of illicit sexual activity.

'By the nineteenth century the sexuality of the black, both male and female, becomes an icon for deviant sexuality in general' (228). Furthermore, the 'relationship between the sexuality of the black woman and that of the sexualized white woman enters a new dimension when contemporary scientific discourse concerning the nature of black female sexuality is examined' (231). Notorious examples of prurient exoticism, such as the Hottentot Venus displayed on tour in England, provide material examples of the ways in which signs of racial otherness became instrumental in the construction of a (transgressive) female sexuality.

In settler colonies, although women's bodies were not directly constructed as part of a transgressive sexuality, their bodies were frequently the site of a power discourse of a different kind. As critics like Whitlock have argued, they were perceived reductively not as sexual but as reproductive subjects, as literal 'wombs of empire' whose function was limited to the population of the new colonies with white settlers.

Further Reading: Alexander and Mohanty 1977; Bahri 2004; Boehmer 2005; Bulbeck 1998; Chang 2001; Donaldson 1993; Emberley 1993; Frankenberg 2001; Gandhi 1998; Harding 2000; Holst-Petersen and Rutherford 1985; hooks 1997; Hyam 1990; Jarratt 2000; Katrak 1996; Lionnet 1995; Loomba 2005; McClintock 1995; Mann 1995; Meyer 1996; Mills 2003; Minh-ha 1995; Mohanram 1999; Mongia 1996; Morgan 2006; Rajan 1993; Ray 2000; Spivak 1999; Suleri 1992; Weedon 1999; Whitlock 1995; Wisker 2000; Wynter 1990.

FILIATION/AFFILIATION

This pair of terms was brought to prominence by Edward Said, who suggested that patterns of 'filiation' (heritage or descent) that had acted as a cohering force in traditional society were becoming increasingly difficult to maintain in the complexity of contemporary civilization and were being replaced by patterns of 'affiliation'. While filiation refers to lines of descent in nature, affiliation refers to a process of identification through culture.

Said promotes affiliation as a general critical principle because it frees the critic from a narrow view of texts connected in a filiative relationship to other texts, with very little attention paid to the 'world' in which they come into being. For instance, his initial use of the terms suggested that canonical English literature tended to be approached filiatively, the literature being regarded as self-perpetuating and literary works having their most important hermeneutic relationships to the literature that had gone before. By contrast, an affiliative reading allows the critic to see the literary work as a phenomenon in the world, located in a network of non-literary, non-canonical and non-traditional affiliations. In this sense, affiliation is seen positively as the basis of a new kind of criticism in which a recognition of the affiliative process within texts may free criticism from its narrow basis in the European canon.

While filiation suggests a Utopian domain of texts connected serially, homologously and seamlessly with other texts, affiliation is that which enables a text to maintain itself as a text, the 'status of the author, historical moment, conditions of publication, diffusion and reception, values drawn upon, values and ideas assumed, a framework of consensually held tacit assumptions, presumed background, and so on' (Said 1983: 174–175). Affiliation sends the critical gaze beyond the narrow confines of the European and canonically literary into this cultural texture. 'To recreate the affiliative network is therefore to make visible, to give materiality back to the strands holding the text to society, author and culture' (175). This concern with the materiality of the text also allows him to read the texts of English literature 'contrapuntally' to see the extent to which they are implicated in the broad political project of **imperialism**. The political and social world becomes available to the scrutiny of the critic, specifically the non-literary, the non-European and above all, the political dimension in which all literature, all texts can be found (21). Traditionally assumed to be connected filiatively to the discourse of 'English literature', the text can now be seen to be affiliated with the network of history, culture and society within which it comes into being and is read.

Said has also used the concept to describe the way in which the network of affiliation links colonized societies to imperial culture. Cultural identities are understood as 'contrapuntal ensembles' (1993: 60), and the often hidden affiliations of both imperial and colonial cultures are amenable to a **contrapuntal reading**. Clearly, the concept of affiliation is useful for describing the ways in which colonized societies replace filiative connections to indigenous cultural traditions with affiliations to the social, political and cultural institutions of empire. Affiliation refers to 'that implicit network of peculiarly cultural associations between forms, statements and other aesthetic elaborations on the one hand and, on the other, institutions, agencies, classes, and amorphous social forces' (174). Said links the concept to Gramsci's notion of **hegemony** by suggesting that the affiliative network itself is the field of operation of hegemonic control, and this may be particularly evident in the case of the control of imperial culture.

The tendency for affiliation to reproduce filiation has implications far beyond the activity of the critic. For there is an affiliative process constantly at work in colonized societies: an implicit network of assumptions, values and expectations that continually places and replaces the colonized subject in a filiative relation with the colonizer. This indicates one way in which the affiliative process maintains its obdurate strength in colonial societies. Affiliation invokes an image of the imperial culture as a parent, linked in a filiative relationship with the colonized 'child'. Thus, while filiation gives birth to affiliation, in colonized societies, the reverse is also true.

Clearly, this move from filiation to affiliation specifically invokes the hegemonic power of a dominant imperial culture. Filiation is not limited to racial or genealogical ancestry; its real force comes from its suggestion of a cultural and psychological inheritance. Filiation is a powerful ideological consequence of the capacity of imperialist discourse to control representation and invoke networks of affiliation. It becomes a fundamental way of structuring relationships between empires and colonies, since it is by this process that the cultural power of the imperial centre and the sustainable rule of the mechanisms of state are maintained.

Further Reading: Said 1983.

FIRST NATIONS

This is a term originally referring to Native American peoples, originating, and used mainly in Canada, to refer to an indigenous American
Indian community officially recognized as an administrative unit by the
federal government or functioning as such without official status (OED).
Originally, it referred to the indigenous peoples located in the region
of North America that is now Canada who are not Inuit or Métis. The
term was coined in 1980 to replace 'Indian band' which has legal recognition in Canadian Law. Although referred to in the past as Aboriginal
peoples, (a term increasingly used to refer only to Australian Aboriginal
peoples), the indigenous people of North America are variously referred
to as Native Americans or 'Indians' (United States). The concept, if
not the term 'First nation' is growing in frequency in the United States
with terms such as the 'Six Nations' referring to the peoples of the
Iroquois confederacy. Over the last decade, the term has become used
more widely and is now used to refer to Australian Aboriginal peoples
as well as other indigenous communities.

The concept of 'Nation' in reference to indigenous peoples is a
recently developed **catachresis** that emphasizes their historical, ancestral and communal relationship with the land. Whereas 'nation' refers
to a large body of people united by common descent, history, culture
or language, inhabiting a particular state or territory (OED), this term
is now recognized as referring to both nation-states and First Nations as
a recognition of the latter's special claim to a communal identification
within the context of national law. This has allowed bodies such as The
First Nations Development Institute to work to restore Native control
over cultural assets, such as land, human potential, cultural heritage or
natural resources. In general, members of First Nations make no claim
to nation-state status but to a communal identity that in fact precedes
the nation-state, and in particular the colonial nations of Canada
and the United States.

Further Reading: Battiste and Barman (1995), Muckle (1998)

FRONTIER

The idea of a frontier, a boundary or a limiting zone to distinguish
one space or people from another, is clearly much older and used more
widely than in colonial and postcolonial theory. There is, for example, a

broad study of frontier history in American Studies, beginning with the so-called 'Turner thesis' advanced by Frederick Jackson Turner in 1893 (see Taylor 1971; Philp and West 1976). Turner theorized that American development could be explained by the existence of a vast area of free land into which American settlement advanced westward. Turner saw the frontier as the essential guarantor of American democratic freedoms, because whenever social conditions put pressure on employment or when political restraints tended to impede freedom, individuals could escape to the free conditions of the frontier. Men would not accept inferior wages and a permanent position of social insubordination, he believed, when a promised land of freedom and equality was open to everyone for the taking. Significantly, Turner also observed that the open frontier was already an environment of the past and that Americans should of necessity move on to another chapter of history.

Regardless of the validity of his thesis as a whole (and it has been severely critiqued as largely unproven by empirical evidence), few will quarrel with his assertion that the American frontier experience has been central to self-perceptions of identity in the United States as a result of its ubiquity in mass culture. It is, of course, significant that the frontier is perceived by Turner primarily as a shaping force on the westward expanding settler population, and little interest is shown in the perception of this expansion by the indigenous populations of the so-called frontier. Thus recent accounts by historians and others of Native American reactions to the westward expansion are a necessary corrective to this dominant myth of the West as a land of freedom and escape. For the Indians, the frontier experience was very different (Berkhofer 1978). The centrality of the idea to settler American self-perceptions may have had a great deal to do with the popularity of the term, and frontier studies have always been a major component of American studies ever since. The term has also been internationalized by modern American historians such as McNeill who took the idea of the frontier and argued that it should be seen as one of the most dominant tropes of recent world history (McNeill 1983).

Nevertheless, in its more recent use within postcolonial cultures, it has taken on a particular local significance. Colonial frontiers were created as imperial discourse sought to define and invent the entities it shaped from its conquests. The numerous ruler-straight frontiers of imperial maps indicate how colonial **cartography** existed as much to invent as to record actual features and distinctions between various places and peoples. The frontier or boundary that limited the space so defined was a crucial feature in imagining the imperial self, and in creating and defining (**othering**) those others by which that 'self' could achieve definition and value. That which lies 'beyond the pale' (itself a metaphor invoking one of the earliest delimiting frontiers of colonial Ireland, the fence between the Protestant enclave of Dublin and the wild, Catholic lands beyond) is often defined literally as the other, the dark, the savage and the wild.

As well as literal frontiers, the discourse of empire was metaphorically concerned to delineate boundaries and frontiers, inventing categories for which the spatial was always and only a loose image for a perceived or desired racial, cultural or gendered divide. 'East is East and West is West, and never the twain shall meet' wrote Kipling (1889), suggesting that the idea of a West and East had less physical than metaphysical boundaries. Even the creation of some literal juncture, 'East of Suez', seems less than physically specific, since Egypt, the land of the joining frontier, has been at different times defined both as the cradle of European civilization and the heart of the exotic and dangerous Orient, as discourses shift and meet on a terrain of abstraction to which frontiers and spatial categories refer only as metonyms.

The idea of a frontier civilization implies a civilization where rules of law and social graces wither as man reverts to a state of nature. The frontier then becomes a place of **savagery**. But it is also frequently imagined as a place where men (the pronoun is deliberate) can test themselves and where the effete weakness of the civilized can be bred into a renewed strength (Low 1996). This ambivalence is always present in the construction of settler frontier narratives, as the idea of civilization is both upheld and critiqued from the rude but vigorous perspective of the frontier world. Significantly, frontier narratives by women are far less romantic and more often emphasize the harsh daily realities of survival (Moodie 1852).

Further Reading: Billington 1966; Janiewski 1998; McNeill 1983; Philp 1986; Taylor 1971; Thorpe 1996; Turner 1961, 1962; Weber and Rausch 1994.

FUNDAMENTALISM

The term fundamentalism strictly means an adherence to fundamental principles in any field of human endeavour or belief, but in practice, it has usually been applied to ideological adherence, especially an adherence to religious dogma. The term was first widely employed in this sense in the 1920s in the United States, where it emerged during the religious backlash against Darwinism amongst Protestant sects in the Bible Belt of the mid-West and the South (Marsden 2022). It took the form of a literal interpretation of the sacred text of the Bible, insisting that the world was made by God in six days and that every moral issue could be resolved by reference to the authority of the Bible. The view of course is predicated on the idea that reading a text such as the Bible does not involve interpretation and dismisses the long history of Biblical exegesis and critical scholarship that had been underway for centuries, and especially since the mid-nineteenth century when Biblical scholarship became the source for the modern practice of hermeneutics. In other religions which have a central sacred text, this limited perception of what is involved in the act of reading and interpretation has also come to replace more subtle and full attempts at exegesis. Thus in extreme forms of fundamental Judaism, a similar uncompromising act of reading of the Torah occurs. The emphasis in recent years of the practice of this kind of fundamentalist interpretation has focused almost exclusively on Islamic practices and on the fundamentalist interpretation of the Quran. Although, as many authorities have shown, similar reading practices have occurred in virtually all religions that depend on the readings of a sacred text. Thus, even polytheistic religions such as Hinduism have also been increasingly influenced by this practice; although scholars such as Richard King have argued that Hinduism as it is now conceived was largely constructed through a series of unifying reforms in the nineteenth century, reforms that sought to unify a body of divergent practices that were far more loosely associated in earlier periods (King 1999). King also suggests that this shift was achieved by the elevation of a series of loosely related texts into a coherent body of scripture that could be understood by the kind of rigid interpretative practices that fundamentalists of all religions espouse.

Alongside these rigid forms of interpreting texts, fundamentalist thinking also often postulates a pure form of the religion that existed in the past and from which adherents have since fallen away. Just as fundamentalist interpretation of texts depends on the idea of a single indisputable reading, so this construction of the past of religions depends upon the contention that there was once a single, indisputable set of practices that must be recovered unchanged for believers to attain truth.

Each of the major monotheistic religions (Judaism, Christianity and Islam) developed through a series of extensive commentaries and interpretations of the historical facts and the core sacred text(s): Judaism has the commentaries of the Talmudic tradition, Christianity the tradition of Biblical scholarship and commentary, and Islam the interpretations of the Sayings and Acts of the Prophet contained in the Hadith. Other major religions such as Hinduism also have a long tradition of relating the various texts to each other and of seeking to discuss and refine these within the broad lines of the belief systems. In practice, each of the major religions of the world have developed various sects that interpret the core ideas and texts differently. In this respect, fundamentalists are no different to other such wielders of new interpretation. Where they differ is in the degree to which they have insisted on the right to impose these views on others by force rather than persuasion. Once again, all the major world religions have had periods when they have advocated the forcible conversion or exclusion of those who do not share their particular interpretation. The late twentieth century has seen a re-emergence of these kinds of coercive forms of belief. Historically, some religions have been more evangelistic than others (notably Christianity and Islam) whose adherents believe that they are called to convert others to the true faith. This process led to the historic persecution of heretics within both faiths, and to the use of a concept of holy war (crusade or jihad) at various points in the history of both major religions. But extreme orthodox beliefs that refuse to accommodate differences and refuse tolerance to those who practice other religions have also emerged in religions that have not actively practised evangelistic conversion such as Judaism and Hinduism.

A further and disturbing element in these modern fundamentalist movements has been the way they have sought increasingly to intervene directly or indirectly into the political process. The emergence of movements such as the Moral Majority in the United States, the role played by orthodox settlers in the Israeli–Palestinian conflict, the aggressive pursuit of religious politics by the Hindutva movements in India as well as the emergence of aggressive Islamic fundamentalist movements across the world all challenge the post-Enlightenment belief that the secular and sacred realms could and should be kept apart. The climate these shifts have created is arguably one of the most important changes of the late twentieth and early twenty-first centuries. For this reason, fundamentalism has been of increasing concern as one of the many **post-national** forces that have impacted on postcolonies as they struggle to define themselves in relation to wider emerging **global** movements. The emergence of violent struggles based on fundamentalist versions of religious identity and the demands for compliance with the social views and institutions they espouse, such as Sharia Law has been a feature of many postcolonial societies in recent times, including

Pakistan, India, Nigeria, other West African nations, Somalia, Kenya and the Philippines. The most recent (2012) example of the impact of fundamentalist ideas on postcolonial national identity occurred in Tanzania, where a resurgent movement to separate the two component regions of erstwhile Tanganyika and Zanzibar has emerged, claiming to defend the idea of Zanzibari identity as essentially Arab and Muslim, an identity that the leaders of the separatist movement claim is threatened by unity with the mainland. This is a classic example of the way fundamentalism bases its claims on a rigid and very partial history of a country or region (see Griffiths 2007, 2011). Although the separatist claims involved (as also, for example, in Northern Nigeria or in Somalia in recent times) sections of the independent postcolonies that often seem to have been provoked by local Islamic parties who have aligned themselves with international fundamentalist groupings such as the ubiquitous Al-Qaeda, they seem also to reflect older and longer divisions that resulted from the creation of arbitrary national formations in colonial times. In these circumstances, it is difficult to determine if fundamentalism is the root cause of these separatist movements, or whether it is only the latest manifestation of deeper schismatic tendencies rooted in the older problems that colonization created by constructing these arbitrary national entities (see Davidson 1992). At the beginning of the twentieth century, the great African-American activist and scholar W.E.B. Du Bois argued that 'the problem of the Twentieth Century is the problem of the color-line'. For some these recent events have suggested that for the twenty-first century the line along which identities may divide and over which struggles for tolerance and freedom will take place is the line of religious difference.

Further Reading: King 1999; Mezvinsky and Shahak 1999; Armstrong 2000; Kureishi 2005; Griffiths 2009; Stähler and Stierstorfer 2009; Marty and Appleby 1991–1995; Peel 2023; Marsden 2022.

GLOBAL SOUTH

This term was first used by Carl Oglesby in 1969 writing in the Catholic journal *Commonweal* in a special issue on the Vietnam War. This established the ambivalence of the term from the beginning since it does not refer to the geographical South but to countries and regions that are economically and politically less developed. In this respect, the term 'Global South' is best understood as a metaphor for underdeveloped countries in both hemispheres, a term used more widely to encompass the victims of colonialism and neoliberal capitalism wherever they live. The term has replaced other terms such as the **Third World** although it is equally unsatisfactory since much of the Global South is in the Northern Hemisphere, including Vietnam, the subject of Oglesby's analysis. Generally, it comprises Africa, Latin America, the Caribbean, Asia (excluding Japan and South Korea) and Oceania (excluding Australia and New Zealand). The phrase operates as a convenient shorthand for a broad swath of nations seeking to overhaul the unjust structures of the global economy and promote the emergence of a more multipolar system.

South Asia, in the Northern Hemisphere, represents a larger population than the rest of the Global South put together, which suggests that the term is a continuation of the historical denigration of the Southern Hemisphere as undeveloped and backward. The Southern Hemisphere was always a region of mystery and danger to European explorers before the discovery of longitude. Once the Empire reached into the Southern Hemisphere, the temperate regions of the South became the bread basket of Europe as settler colonies developed large-scale monocultural agriculture.

Despite the unsatisfactory nature of the term, the Southern Hemisphere does comprise a large proportion of formerly colonized nations. The South has been important to the Empire for the producer of commodities and even the prosperous areas of the hemisphere remained on what Wallerstein's **world system theory** called the periphery of the global economy, their exploitation being necessary for the enrichment of the imperial centres. Therefore, despite its geographical inaccuracy, the Global South remains a useful metaphor for global **postcolonies**.

Further Reading: Oglesby 1969; Stewart and Huggins 2023

GLOBALIZATION

Globalization is the process whereby individual lives and local communities are affected by economic and cultural forces that operate worldwide. In effect, it is the process of the world becoming a single place. Globalism is the perception of the world as a function or result of the processes of globalization upon local communities.

The term has had a meteoric rise since the mid-1980s, up until which time words such as 'international' and 'international relations' were preferred. The rise of the word 'international' itself in the eighteenth century indicated the growing importance of territorial states in organizing social relations, and is an early consequence of the global perspective of European **imperialism**. Similarly, the rapidly increasing interest in globalization reflects a changing organization of worldwide social relations in this century, one in which the 'nation' has begun to have a decreasing importance as individuals and communities gain access to globally disseminated knowledge and culture, and are affected by economic realities that bypass the boundaries of the state. The structural aspects of globalization are the nation-state system itself (on which the concepts of internationalism and international co-operation are based), global economy, the global communication system and world military order.

Part of the complexity of globalism comes from the different ways in which globalization is approached. Some analysts embrace it enthusiastically as a positive feature of a changing world in which access to technology, information services and markets will be of benefit to local communities, where dominant forms of social organization will lead to universal prosperity, peace and freedom, and in which a perception of a global environment will lead to global ecological concern. For this group, globalism is a term 'for values which treat global issues as a matter of personal and collective responsibility' (Albrow 1994: 4). Others reject it as a form of domination by 'First World' countries over 'Third World' ones, in which individual distinctions of culture and society become erased by an increasingly homogeneous global culture, and local economies are more firmly incorporated into a system of global capital. For this group, globalism 'is a teleological doctrine which provides, explains and justifies an interlocking system of world trade'. It has 'ideological overtones of historical inevitability', and 'its attendant myths function as a gospel of the global market' (Ferguson 1993a: 87). The chief argument against globalization is that global culture and global economy did not just spontaneously erupt but originated in and continue to be perpetuated from the centres of capitalist power. Neither does globalization impact in the same way, to the same degree, nor equally beneficially upon different communities. Proponents of 'critical globalism' take a neutral view of the process, simply examining its processes and effects. 'Critical globalism refers to the critical engagement with globalization processes, neither blocking them out nor celebrating globalization' (Nederveen Pieterse 1995: 13). Thus, while critical globalists see that globalization 'has often perpetuated poverty, widened material inequalities, increased ecological degradation, sustained militarism, fragmented communities, marginalized subordinated groups, fed intolerance and deepened crises of democracy', they also see that it has had a positive effect in 'trebling world per capita income since 1945, halving the proportion of the world living in abject poverty, increasing ecological consciousness, and possibly facilitating disarmament, while various subordinated groups have grasped opportunities for global organisation' (Scholte 1996: 53).

As a field of study, globalization covers such disciplines as international relations, political geography, economics, sociology, communication studies, agricultural, ecological and cultural studies. It addresses the decreasing agency (though not the status) of the nation-state in the world political order and the increasing influence of structures and movements of corporate capital. Globalization can also be 'a signifier of travel, of transnational company operations, of the changing pattern of world employment, or global environmental risk' (Albrow 1994: 13). Indeed, there are compelling reasons for thinking globally where the environment is concerned. As Stuart Hall puts it, 'When the ill winds of Chernobyl came our way, they did not pause at the frontier, produce their passports and say "Can I rain on your territory now?"' (1991: 25). The importance of globalization to postcolonial studies comes first from its demonstration of the structure of world power relations which stands firm in the twentieth century as a legacy of Western imperialism. Second, the ways in which local communities engage the forces of globalization bear some resemblance to the ways in which colonized societies have historically engaged and appropriated the forces of imperial dominance. In some respects, globalization, in the period of rapid **decolonization** after the Second World War, demonstrates the transmutation of imperialism into the supra-national operations of economics, communications and culture. This does not mean that globalization is a simple, unidirectional movement from the powerful to the weak, from the central to the peripheral, because globalism is **transcultural** in the same way that imperialism itself has been. But it does demonstrate that globalization did not simply erupt spontaneously around the world, but has a history embedded in the history of imperialism, in the structure of the **world system**, and in the origins of a global economy within the ideology of imperial rhetoric.

The key to the link between classical imperialism and contemporary globalization in the twentieth century has been the role of the United States. Despite its resolute refusal to perceive itself as 'imperial', and indeed its public stance against the older European doctrines of colonialism up to and after the Second World War, the United States had, in its international policies, eagerly espoused the political domination and economic and cultural control associated with imperialism. More importantly, US society during and after this early expansionist phase initiated those features of social life and social relations that today may be considered to characterize the global: mass production, mass communication and mass consumption. During the twentieth century, these have spread transnationally, 'drawing upon the increasingly integrated resources of the global economy' (Spybey 1996: 3).

Despite the balance between its good and bad effects, identified by critical globalists, globalization has not been a politically neutral activity. While access to global forms of communication, markets and culture may indeed be worldwide today, it has been argued by some critics that if one asks how that access is enabled and by what ideological machinery it is advanced, it can be seen that the operation of globalization cannot be separated from the structures of power perpetuated by European imperialism. Global culture is a continuation of an imperial dynamic of influence, control, dissemination and hegemony that operates according to an already initiated structure of power that emerged in the sixteenth century in the great confluence of **imperialism**, capitalism and **modernity**. This explains why the forces of globalization are still, in some senses, centred in the West (in terms of power and institutional organization), despite their global dissemination.

However, the second reason for the significance of globalization to postcolonial studies – how it is engaged by local communities – forms the focus of much recent discussion of the phenomenon. If globalism is not simply a result of top-down dominance but a transcultural process, a dialectic of dominant cultural forms and their appropriation, then the responses of local communities becomes critical. By appropriating strategies of representation, organization and social change through access to global systems, local communities and marginal interest groups can both empower themselves and influence those global systems. Although choice is always mediated by the conditions of subject formation, the belief that one has a choice in the processes of changing one's own life or society can indeed be empowering. In this sense, the appropriation of global forms of culture may free one from local forms of dominance and oppression or at least provide the tools for a different kind of identity formation.

The more recent directions of globalization studies concern the development of 'global culture', a process in which the strategies, techniques, assumptions and interactions of cultural representation become increasingly widespread and homogeneous. But, as Featherstone and Lash point out, 'only in the most minimalist sense can one speak of a "global society" or a "global culture", as our conceptions of both society and culture draw heavily on a tradition which was strongly influenced by the process of nation-state formation' (Featherstone et al. 1995: 2). However, global culture can be seen to be focused on mass culture, in what Stuart Hall calls a 'new globalization'. 'This new kind of globalization is not English, it is American. In cultural terms, the new kind of globalization has to do with a new form of global mass culture' (1991: 27). New globalization has two dominant features: one is that it is still centred in the West; the other is a peculiar form of homogenization, a form of cultural capital that does not attempt to produce mini versions of itself but operates through other economic and political élites (28).

The most active area of debate in globalization studies therefore appears to be the style and nature of the process by which external and internal forces interact to produce, reproduce and disseminate global culture within local communities. This is because one of the key questions at the centre of this interaction is the nature and survival of social and cultural identity. The interpenetration of global and local cultural forces is present in all forms of social life in the twentieth century. But the extent to which globalization exhibits the effects of domination by the powerful centres of global culture and the extent to which it offers itself to transformation by peripheral communities are still a matter of debate.

Further Reading: Albrow 1994; Albrow and King 1990; Behdad 2005; Brennan 2004; Brydon 2001a, 2001b; Cheah 1999; Dirlik 1999; Featherstone 1990; Featherstone, Lash and Robertson 1995; Gikandi 2001; Hoogvelt 2001; Huggan 2004; Hulme 2005; King 1991; Kofman and Youngs 1996; Koshy 2005; McCallum and Faith 2005; Mignolo 2000a; Robertson 1992; Spybey 1996; Isitt 2020.

GLOCALIZATION

First popularized in the English-speaking world by the British sociologist Roland Robertson in the 1990s, and later developed by Zygmunt Bauman, the term 'glocal' and the process noun 'glocalization' are formed by blending the words 'global' and 'local'. Both terms became aspects of business jargon during the 1980s, originating in Japan, but its use for postcolonial studies has been principally in its foregrounding of local agency against a seemingly relentless global culture. Globalization is itself always local and while globalization operates according to 'flows', the agency of the local ensures that the flow is very often recip-rocal. According to Robertson

> it makes no good sense to define the global as if the global excludes the local. In somewhat technical terms defining the global in such a way suggests that the global lies beyond all localities, as having systemic properties over and beyond the attributes of units within a global system.
>
> (1995: 34)

The concept is present in slogans such as 'think globally, act locally' but it has accompanied the greatly nuanced view of the relationship between the local and the global that has been introduced by post-colonial studies.

The concept is important to postcolonial studies because it can be understood in terms of the **transcultural** relationships pertaining between colony and imperial centre in imperialism. As with classical imperialism, the impact of colonial incursion was not simply one-way, oppressive and hierarchical but reciprocal, transcultural and eventually transformative. This is perhaps most clearly demonstrated in the cap-acity of postcolonial literatures to appropriate the language, forms and genres of English literature and transform the discipline. Both literary writing and its transcultural scenario emphasize the **agency** of the local and of individual subjects and colonial communities to interpolate the discourses of imperial power.

The relationship between the local and global has been of particular interest to postcolonial theorists such as Dirlik, Appadurai, Bhabha and Spivak. This involvement of postcolonial theorists in the discourse of cultural globalization has been so pronounced that Simon Gikandi has suggested that its 'cultural turn' has been entirely due to the interven-tion of postcolonial discourse over the last two decades. Globalization and postcolonialism

> have at least two important things in common: they are concerned with explaining forms of social and cultural organization whose ambition is to transcend the boundaries of the nation-state, and they seek to provide new vistas for understanding cultural flows that can no longer be explained by a homogenous Eurocentric narrative of development and social change.
>
> (Gikandi 2001: 627)

The language of postcolonialism provided a way of talking about the engagement of the global by the local, particularly local cultures, and, most importantly, provided a greatly nuanced view of globalization that developed from its understanding of the complexities of imperial relationships. This language needed to be adopted because by the 1990s, globalization could no longer be explained in terms of traditional social science models. Globalization constitutes what Appadurai calls 'a complex overlapping, disjunctive order that cannot any longer be understood in terms of existing centre-periphery models' (Appadurai 1996: 32).

Further Reading: Appadurai 1996; Bauman 1998; Gikandi 2002; Robertson 1995.

'GOING NATIVE'

The term indicates the colonizers' fear of contamination by absorption into native life and customs. The construction of **native** cultures as either primitive or degenerate in a binary discourse of colonizer/colonized led, especially at the turn of the century, to a widespread fear of 'going native' amongst the colonizers in many colonial societies. Variants occur such as 'going Fantee' (West Africa) and 'going troppo' (Australian), which suggest that both the associations with other races and even the mere climate of colonies in hot areas can lead to moral and even physical degeneracy. The threat is particularly associated with the temptation posed by inter-racial sex, where sexual liaisons with 'native' peoples were supposed to result in a contamination of the colonizers' pure stock and thus their degeneracy and demise as a vigorous and **civilized** (as opposed to **savage** or degenerate) **race**. But 'going native' could also encompass lapses from European behaviour, the participation in 'native' ceremonies, or the adoption and even enjoyment of local customs in terms of dress, food, recreation and entertainment. Perhaps the best-known canonical example of the perils of going native is Kurtz in Conrad's *Heart of Darkness*, a character who seems to embody the very complex sense of vulnerability, primitivism and horror of the process.

Further Reading: Torgovnick 1990.

GREEN POSTCOLONIALISM

Alfred Crosby was one of the first scholars to consider the pivotal role played by environmental change in the conquest and colonization of the New World. Since Crosby's pioneering account, a serious study of the impact of colonialist environmental damage – and where possible its attempted rectification –has been carried out in a number of different directions.

The specific impact of the introduction of exotics (both wild and domesticated, animal and plant) on previously pristine ecosystems and the repercussions of this on human history has been given detailed attention (Anderson 2004; Peirs 2003). Neocolonizing **development** in formerly colonized countries has also been examined (e.g. Anderson 2004; Huggan and Tiffin 2010; Roy 2002).

Conversely, Western attempts to restore precolonial ecosystems through the establishment of national parks and conservation areas has often been met with resistance and interpreted as a form of neo-colonialism. One obvious example, cited by Wolch and Emil are occasions when local people are forced off their land to accom- modate game parks for wealthy tourists, or where, as in Amitav Ghosh's *The Hungry Tide*, the national government is pressured by international NGOs to force human refugees out of a sanctuary for the endangered Bengal tiger, thus **displacing** large populations of local dwellers.

In terms of disciplinary approaches, disquiet has been expressed by environmental scholars over what they see as postcolonialism's rela- tive lack of attention to the extra-human sphere while postcolonialists have regarded environmentalists as ignoring the human cultural aspects of colonial history. The intractability of the argument is perhaps demonstrated by India's 'green revolution' of the 1950s, which included the building of major dams and widespread use of artificial fertilizers. This was not directed towards environmental enhancement but towards human sustainability – avoiding the boom/bust cycles responsible for India's previous devastating famines.

A third debate related to 'green postcolonialism' was initiated when Richard Grove claimed that the colonies (especially the settler colonies) where national parks were first established, were significant as the cradles of ecosystem preservation rather than environmental destruction.

Further Reading: Anderson 2004; Crosby 1986; Grove 1995; Menkhaus 2001; Huggan and Tiffin 2010; Peires 2003; Roy 2001; Wolch and Emel 1998

HEGEMONY

Hegemony, initially a term referring to the dominance of one state within a confederation, is now generally understood to mean domination by consent. This broader meaning was coined and popularized in the 1930s by Italian Marxist Antonio Gramsci, who investigated why the ruling class was so successful in promoting its own interests in society. Fundamentally, hegemony is the power of the ruling class to convince other classes that their interests are the interests of all. Domination is thus exerted not by force, nor even necessarily by active persuasion, but by a more subtle and inclusive power over the economy, and over state apparatuses such as education and the media, by which the ruling class's interest is presented as the common interest and thus comes to be taken for granted.

The term is useful for describing the success of imperial power over a colonized people who may far outnumber any occupying military force, but whose desire for self-determination has been suppressed by a hegemonic notion of the greater good, often couched in terms of social order, stability and advancement, all of which are defined by the colonizing power. Hegemony is important because the capacity to influence the thought of the colonized is by far the most sustained and potent operation of imperial power in colonized regions. Indeed, an 'empire' is distinct from a collection of subject states forcibly controlled by a central power by virtue of the effectiveness of its cultural hegemony. Consent is achieved by the **interpellation** of the colonized subject by **imperial** discourse so that **Eurocentric** values, assumptions, beliefs and attitudes are accepted as a matter of course as the most natural or valuable. The inevitable consequence of such interpellation is that the colonized subject understands itself as peripheral to those Eurocentric values, while accepting their centrality.

A classic example of the operation of hegemonic control is given by Gauri Viswanathan, who shows how 'the humanistic functions traditionally associated with the study of literature – for example, the shaping of character or the development of the aesthetic sense or the disciplines of ethical thinking – can be vital in the process of sociopolitical control' (1987: 2). Such control was maintained by the British government when it took responsibility for education in India after the Charter Act of 1813. Searching for a method of communicating the values of Western civilization to Indians which avoided offending their Hindu sensibilities, the administration discovered the power of English literature as a vehicle for imperial authority.

> The strategy of locating authority in these texts all but effaced the sordid history of colonialist expropriation, material exploitation, and class and race oppression behind European world dominance . . . the English literary text functioned as a surrogate Englishman in his highest and most perfect state.
>
> (Viswanathan 1987: 23)

This Englishman was, at the same time, the embodiment of universal human values. As Viswanathan puts it, the 'split between the material and the discursive practices of colonialism is nowhere sharper than in the progressive refraction of the rapacious, exploitative and ruthless actor of history into the reflective subject of literature' (22–23). This refraction is a precise demonstration of one mode of hegemonic control. It proved a particularly effective one because the discourse of English literature was disseminated with its attendant spiritual values, cultural assumptions, social discriminations, racial prejudices and humanistic values more or less intact.

Further Reading: Bharucha 1997; Gramsci 1988, 1991; Olson and Worsham 1999; San Juan 1995; Viswanathan 1989.

HYBRIDITY

One of the most widely employed and most disputed terms in post-colonial theory, hybridity commonly refers to the creation of new **transcultural** forms within the contact zone produced by colonization. As used in horticulture, the term refers to the cross-breeding of two species by grafting or cross-pollination to form a third, 'hybrid' species. Hybridization takes many forms: linguistic, cultural, political, racial, etc. Linguistic examples include **pidgin** and **creole** languages, and these echo the foundational use of the term by the linguist and cultural theorist Mikhail Bakhtin, who used it to suggest the disruptive and transfiguring power of multivocal language situations and, by extension, of multivocal narratives. The idea of a polyphony of voices in society is implied also in Bakhtin's idea of the carnivalesque, which emerged in the Middle Ages when 'a boundless world of humorous forms and manifestations opposed the official and serious tone of medieval ecclesiastical and feudal culture' (Holquist 1984: 4).

The term 'hybridity' has been most recently associated with the work of Homi K. Bhabha, whose analysis of colonizer/colonized relations stresses their interdependence and the mutual construction of their subjectivities (see **mimicry** and **ambivalence**). Bhabha contends that all cultural statements and systems are constructed in a space that he calls the 'Third Space of enunciation' (1994: 37). Cultural identity always emerges in this contradictory and ambivalent space, which for Bhabha makes the claim to a hierarchical 'purity' of cultures untenable. For him, the recognition of this ambivalent space of cultural identity may help us to overcome the **exoticism** of **cultural diversity** in favour of the recognition of an empowering hybridity within which cultural difference may operate.

> It is significant that the productive capacities of this Third Space have a colonial or postcolonial provenance. For a willing- ness to descend into that alien territory . . . may open the way to conceptualizing an international culture, based not on the exoticism of multiculturalism or the diversity of cultures, but on the inscription and articulation of culture's hybridity.
>
> (Bhabha 1994: 38)

It is the 'in-between' space that carries the burden and meaning of culture, and this is what makes the notion of hybridity so important.

Hybridity has frequently been used in postcolonial discourse to mean simply cross-cultural 'exchange'. This use of the term has been widely criticized, since it usually implies negating and neglecting the imbalance and inequality of the power relations it references. By stressing the transformative cultural, linguistic and political impacts on both the colonized and the colonizer, it has been regarded as replicating assimilationist policies by masking or 'whitewashing' cultural differences. The idea of hybridity also underlies other attempts to stress the mutuality of cultures in the colonial and postcolonial process in expressions of syncreticity, cultural **synergy** and **transculturation**. The criticism of the term referred to above stems from the perception that theories that stress mutuality necessarily downplay oppositionality, and increase continuing postcolonial dependence. There is, however, nothing in the

idea of hybridity as such that suggests that mutuality negates the hierarchical nature of the imperial process or that it involves the idea of an
equal exchange. This is, however, the way in which some proponents
of **decolonization** and **anti-colonialism** have interpreted its current
usage in **colonial discourse** theory. It has also been subject to critique as part of a general dissatisfaction with colonial discourse theory
on the part of critics, such as Chandra Talpade Mohanty, Benita Parry
and Aijaz Ahmad. These critiques stress the textualist and idealist basis
of such analysis and point to the fact that they neglect specific local
differences.

The assertion of a shared postcolonial condition such as hybridity has
been seen as part of the tendency of discourse analysis to de-historicize
and de-locate cultures from their temporal, spatial, geographical and
linguistic contexts, and to lead to an abstract, globalized concept of the
textual that obscures the specificities of particular cultural situations.
Pointing out that the investigation of the discursive construction of
colonialism does not seek to replace or exclude other forms, such as
historical, geographical, economic, military or political, Robert Young
suggests that the contribution of colonial discourse analysis, in which
concepts such as hybridity are couched,

> provides a significant framework for that other work by emphasising
> that all perspectives on colonialism share and have to deal with a
> common discursive medium which was also that of colonialism
> itself: . . . Colonial discourse analysis can therefore look at the wide
> variety of texts of colonialism as something more than mere docu-
> mentation or 'evidence'.
>
> (Young 1995: 163)

However, Young himself offers a number of objections to the indiscrim-
inate use of the term. He notes how influential the term 'hybridity' was
in **imperial** and colonial discourse in negative accounts of the union of
disparate races – accounts that implied that unless actively and persistently cultivated, such hybrids would inevitably revert to their 'primitive'
stock. Hybridity thus became, particularly at the turn of the century,
part of a colonialist discourse of racism. Young draws our attention to
the dangers of employing a term so rooted in a previous set of racist
assumptions, but he also notes that there is a difference between unconscious processes of hybrid mixture, or creolization, and a conscious and
politically motivated concern with the deliberate disruption of homogeneity. He notes that for Bakhtin, for example, hybridity is politicized,

made contestatory, so that it embraces the subversion and challenge of division and separation. Bakhtin's hybridity 'sets different points of view against each other in a conflictual structure, which retains "a certain elemental, organic energy and openendedness"' (Young 1995: 21–22). It is this potential of hybridity to reverse 'the structures of domination in the colonial situation' (23), which Young recognizes, that Bhabha also articulates.

> Bakhtin's intentional hybrid has been transformed by Bhabha into an active moment of challenge and resistance against a dominant colonial power . . . depriving the imposed imperialist culture, not only of the authority that it has for so long imposed politically, often through violence, but even of its own claims to **authenticity**.
>
> (23)

Young does, however, warn of the unconscious process of repetition involved in the contemporary use of the term. According to him, when talking about hybridity, contemporary cultural discourse cannot escape the connection with the racial categories of the past in which hybridity had such a clear racial meaning. Therefore 'deconstructing such essentialist notions of race today we may rather be repeating the [fixation on race in the] past than distancing ourselves from it, or providing a critique of it' (27). This is a subtle and persuasive objection to the concept. However, more positively, Young also notes that the term indicates a broader insistence in many twentieth-century disciplines, from physics to genetics, upon 'a double logic, which goes against the convention of rational either/or choices, but which is repeated in science in the split between the incompatible coexisting logics of classical and quantum physics' (26). In this sense, as in much else in the structuralist and post-structuralist legacy, the concept of hybridity emphasizes a typically twentieth-century concern with relations within a field rather than with an analysis of discrete objects, seeing meaning as the produce of such relations rather than as intrinsic to specific events or objects.

While assertions of national culture and of precolonial traditions have played an important role in creating **anti-colonial** discourse and in arguing for an active **decolonizing** project, theories of the hybrid nature of postcolonial culture assert a different model for resistance, locating this in the subversive **counter-discursive** practices implicit in the colonial ambivalence itself and so undermining the very basis on which imperialist and colonialist discourse raises its claims of superiority.

Further Reading: Bakhtin 1981, 1994; Bhabha 1994; Kraniauskas 2004; Puri 2004; Radhakrishnan 2000; Ramazani 2001; Smith 2004; Stoneham 2000; Young 1995; for opposing views see Ahmad 1992; S. Mishra 1996; Parry 1987; Smyth 2000.

HYPHENATED IDENTITY

A hyphenated identity (more often hyphenated ethnicity) is a reference to an ethnicity combined with the name of a country of citizenship, such as African American, British Asian or Chinese Australian. It implies belonging to more than one social group and in postcolonial terms is frequently a source of **ambivalence.** It is a consequence of global mobility and applies most often to **migrants, refugees** and other subjects born in another country.

There is a continuing controversy over the hyphenation of individuals who have migrated, fled persecution or sought asylum in another country. Many believe it is an inadequate response to **multiculturalism** and **cosmopolitanism** and serves to place such subjects in an invidious position since the hyphenation may be based on culture, nationality, religion, country of origin or skin colour. In a phrase coined by Homi Bhabha, it suggests the hyphenated subject is 'not quite. . . not quite white'. The hyphenation is discriminatory because the hyphenated identity does not seem to apply to white immigrants, while the hyphenated subject is a constant target of **assimilation** policies.

As one 'British Asian' put it, it evokes questions regarding which side of the hyphen the person belongs to, giving the impression that the person is oscillating between two cultures. I certainly have been asked 'So what are you, British or Asian'? I am aware that when I am in the United Kingdom, I am considered Asian, but when in India, I am referred to as British and even non-resident Indian (NRI). Thus, are these hyphenated identities based on culture, nationality, religion, country of origin or simply refer to skin colour?

The hyphenated subject is put in an invidious position, required to assimilate but permanently **othered** by the suggestion that he or she does not quite belong.

Further Reading: Habib (2021), Asher (2008), Bhabha (2004), Crenshaw (1991).

IMPERIALISM

In its most general sense, imperialism refers to the formation of an empire, and, as such, has been an aspect of all periods of history in which one nation has extended its domination over one or several neighbouring nations. Edward Said uses imperialism in this general sense to mean 'the practice, theory, and the attitudes of a dominating metropolitan centre ruling a distant territory', (Said 1993: 8), a process distinct from **colonialism**, which is 'the implanting of settlements on a distant territory'. However, there is general agreement that the word imperialism, as a conscious and openly advocated policy of acquiring colonies for economic, strategic and political advantage, did not emerge until around 1880. Before that date, the term 'empire' (particularly the British variety) conjured up an apparently benevolent process of European expansion whereby colonies accrued rather than were acquired. Around the mid-nineteenth century, the term 'imperialism' was used to describe the government and policies of Napoleon III, self-styled 'emperor', and, by 1870, was used disparagingly in disputes between the political parties in Britain. But from the 1880s, imperialism became a dominant and more transparently aggressive policy amongst European states for a variety of political, cultural and economic reasons.

The expansionist policies pursued by the modern industrial powers from 1880 have been described as 'classical imperialism' (Baumgart 1982: 5). The year 1885, when the Berlin Congo Conference ended and the 'scramble for Africa' got underway, has been regarded as the beginning of classical imperialism. But the 'scramble' itself really began earlier, in 1879, when the rivalry between Britain and France became intense in West Africa, and intensified further in 1882, when Egypt was occupied, and the Treaty of Brazza-Moroko initiated the struggle for the Congo. At the turn of the century, both European and American commentators enthusiastically advocated a policy of imperialism, because the idea of expansion could be seen, and was presented, in terms of the improvement of the lot of the 'barbaric nations'.

The significant feature of imperialism then is that, while as a term used to describe the late nineteenth-century policy of European expansion it is quite recent, its historical roots run deep, extending back to Roman times. Derived from the Latin word *imperium* to describe its sovereignty over the Mediterranean world, the term *Imperium populi Romani* was not merely rhetorical; it defined the sovereignty invested in the people and bestowed by the people on its magistrates abroad. It was this Republican use of the term that Cicero defended against the notion of the monarchical Imperium Romanum instituted by Caesar Augustus, a power invested in the imperator to whom all the people must show allegiance. However, the imperium was the creation and instrument of a self-perpetuating oligarchy, something that has remained relevant to modern imperialism. It is clear that the Roman empire has had more impact than any before it in modelling the strategies, techniques and rhetoric on which subsequent imperial practice has been based. Koebner claims that the modern concept of Empire 'unfailingly recalls the Roman Empires of the past' (Koebner 1961: 18).

Imperialism in its more recent sense – the acquisition of an empire of overseas colonies – is associated with the Europeanization of the globe which came in three major waves: the age of discovery during the fifteenth and sixteenth centuries; the age of mercantilism during the seventeenth and eighteenth centuries; and the age of imperialism in the nineteenth and early twentieth centuries. Europeanization was chiefly effected not by governments and states, but rather by those hundreds of thousands of colonists, merchants, missionaries and adventurers who permeated the non-European world. This general Europeanization of the globe is much harder to trace, but it is important to understand the extent to which European imperialism is grounded on this **diaspora** of ordinary travellers, explorers, missionaries, fortune hunters and settlers over many centuries.

Both the Roman internationalist and Carolingian dynastic senses of imperialism were very different from that which emerged as a consequence of the development of the nation-state. Hobson makes the point that colonialism 'is a natural overflow of nationality', its test being 'the power of colonists to transplant the civilization they represent to the new natural and social environment in which they find themselves' (1902: 7). But it is clear that mercantilism, or mercantile capitalism (that is, the 'merchant' capitalism that existed before the Industrial Revolution), was a significant feature of the European acquisition of colonies, and one tied up with national sentiment. During the mercantilist age, which began roughly with Cromwell's Navigation Act of 1651, rivalry between the European powers was based no longer on religion but on the competitive acquisition of wealth, particularly gold and silver, and its consolidation through the discouragement of imports by tariffs and the encouragement of exports through bounties and rebates. The principle was that one nation's gain was another's loss, since the world's wealth was thought to be a fixed quantity. (Adam Smith critiqued the mercantile system in the *Wealth of Nations* published in 1776, pointing out the absurdity of confusing material wealth with money.) But mercantilism was important to its supporters because 'its purpose was not to maximise welfare, but to promote the economic and political independence of the nation-state' (Lichteim 1971: 51). All European powers in the mercantalist age believed that the acquisition of colonies was beneficial, if only to deprive competitors of potential wealth.

Surprisingly, empire-building did not die out with the end of mercantilism and slavery but increased apace during the nineteenth century. Hobsbawm in *Industry and Empire* (1968) proposes that the earlier British empire was crucial in promoting the industrial transformation of 1750–1850 which in turn gave rise to the second British empire. His argument is that the Industrial Revolution could not have occurred in Britain but for the possession of a colonial empire that provided outlets far in excess of anything the home markets could offer. Industrialization entailed a sudden expansion of productive capacity possible only in a country that occupied a key position within the evolving world economy. Imperialism at this time was an unspoken assumption rather than a concrete doctrine.

After 1815, Britain ruled the seas and began to establish itself as the world's factory, so major colonial annexations were unnecessary. Economic penetration could take the place of military conquest, and this was facilitated by the doctrine of free trade that Britain preached because it could undersell the manufactures of its competitors. Robinson and Gallagher (1981) have called this a time of 'informal imperialism'. By the 1880s, capital was beginning to stagnate and so an openly imperialist movement, that is, one not content with the invisible 'imperialism of free trade', but one that called for a protective tariff wall to be built around the empire, rapidly rose to prominence. The debate over imperialism occupied an entire generation from 1880 to 1914, and its effect upon European public opinion has been seen by many historians as a factor in the outbreak of the First World War in 1914.

Although Lenin's analysis of imperialism in *Imperialism, The Highest Stage of* Capitalism (1916) has become perhaps the most influential in twentieth-century political economy, this specifically economic definition of the term was developed from J.A. Hobson, whose disgust with the war in South Africa led to his book *Imperialism* in 1902. Hobson asserted that as a nation enters the machine economy, it becomes more difficult for its manufacturers, merchants and financiers to dispose profitably of their economic resources, so they prevail upon government to acquire colonies in order to provide markets. As production at home exceeds the growth in consumption, and more goods are produced than can be sold at a profit, more capital exists than can be profitably invested. 'It is this economic condition of affairs that forms the taproot of imperialism' (1902: 71).

There are several arguments against purely economic views of European imperialism, not the least of which is the argument by historians such as Robinson and Gallagher that there was a continuation of imperial policy that became openly aggressive only in the 1880s. Empirical studies reveal that the flow of profit from colony to metropolis was not as great as had often been supposed during this period. Such was Prime Minister Disraeli's reluctance about maintaining costly colonies that Britain's involvement in the post-1880s scramble is better explained by political strategy and competitive nationalism than by economic considerations.

More importantly for postcolonial theory, there was a continuous development of imperial rhetoric and of imperial representation of the rest of the globe from at least the fifteenth century. As a continuous practice, this had much more to do with the desire for, and belief in, European cultural dominance – a belief in a superior right to exploit the world's resources – than pure profit. Said observes that the rhetoricians of imperialism after 1880 'deploy a language whose imagery of growth, fertility, and expansion, whose teleological structure of property and identity, whose ideological discrimination between "us" and "them" had already matured elsewhere – in fiction, political science, racial theory, travel writing' (Said 1993: 128). This is, of course, the most significant omission from accounts by economic theorists of imperialism: that the ideological grounding, the language of cultural dominance, the ideology of race and the **civilizing mission** of European cultural dominance had been accelerating since the eighteenth century.

The nineteenth-century growth in the activity of humanitarian organizations and missionary societies, which provided continuity between imperial policies before and after 1880, was a powerful impulse of classical imperialism. This, allied with the growth in **exploration and travel**, the perception of the new lands as regions of adventure and renewal where the Anglo-Saxon race could regenerate, or as 'el dorados', sites of fabulous wealth, provided very compelling motivation for the movement of European peoples to the colonial margins. Clearly, there is a case for arguing the existence of different kinds of imperialisms clustered around the philanthropic and exploitative, and indeed the worst colonialist scandals were exposed by humanitarian and missionary organizations. But the subtle way in which the two could become enmeshed can be seen in the work of David Livingston, whose claim was that 'Christianity, Commerce and Civilization' must go hand in hand. His aim was to promote legal trade and thus eradicate slavery and exploitation, to which end he encouraged the building of roads and railways and the establishing of steamship routes. But this very conjunction demonstrates the extent to which the European presence in Africa, whatever its purposes, involved a profound cultural imperialism which, along with the arbitrary geo-political division of the continent, proved ultimately disabling to African societies.

In the end, however, it was the control of the means of representation rather than the means of production that confirmed the hegemony of the European powers in their respective empires. Economic, political and military dominance enabled the dissemination of European ideas through the powerful agencies of education and publishing. But it was the power of imperial discourse rather than military or economic might that confirmed the **hegemony** of imperialism in the late nineteenth century. By 1914, the age of 'classical imperialism' had come to an end, but by this time, imperialism had demonstrated its protean nature, its ability to change centres, to adapt to the changing dynamic of world power and ultimately to develop into globalism, arguably its natural successor in the late twentieth century.

Further Reading: Abernethy 2000; Ansell-Pearson et al. 1997; Baumgart 1982; A. Burton 2003; Chrisman 2003; Darby 1998; Hobsbawm 1968; Hobson 1902; Koebner 1961; Koebner and Schmidt 1964; Lenin 1916; Lichteim 1971; Prakash 1995; Robinson and Gallagher 1981.

INDENTURED LABOUR

See **slave/slavery**

INDEPENDENCE

In postcolonial usage, this usually refers to the achievement by a colony of full self-government. Independence took a variety of forms and occurred at different times and in different guises, according to the diversity of colonialist practices. **Settler colonies** achieved political independence considerably earlier than others because, despite the degree to which they had also been constructed as marginal by **colonial discourse**, they were not identified by signs of difference such as race and religion. The period after the Second World War saw an upsurge of new independent states. India and Pakistan were 'granted' independence in 1947, as were the majority of African states in 1960. But it is worth noting how long the process of achieving independence took to complete. Some countries in the Caribbean, for instance, did not become independent until the 1980s. Nor did independence always occur in a simple and final form. Thus Malaya achieved its independence in 1957 but Singapore, never entirely and happily located in the newly formed Federation of Malaysia, became independent in its present form only after a further separation in 1965.

The forces of **neo-colonialism** and **globalization** are clearly part of the contentious problem of whether independence really meant the end of colonial control or merely its mutation. Disputes about the term 'independence' overlap those about the term **postcolonial** itself. For example, whether it is best employed only to designate the period after independence, on the grounds that this is essential to discriminate between the radical shifts in relationship at different historical periods (notably between the colonial and postcolonial – here meaning post-independence – periods). Others argue that **postcolonialism** is absolutely and only congruent with overt resistance and opposition (**anti-colonialism**) and that independence has often simply meant the installation of a neo-colonial form of government by local élites (a **comprador** class). Yet others have argued that the designation of the postcolonial as covering the whole period from the moment of colonization allows us to see such continuations of control even while we record the various moments of resistance, of which political independence is clearly the most crucial. The whole problem of defining and discriminating between the periods of the colonial/postcolonial is much more problematic than is often suggested, and the moment of independence, while a crucial signifier of a profound historical shift, is not in itself as definitive or absolute as has sometimes been implied. If the danger of one approach is to homogenize and eradicate historical difference, the danger of the other is to occlude the ongoing continuities and the elements of colonial influence that continue to mark postcolonial politics and the **postcolonial state**, even after it achieves political independence.

Further Reading: Barrington 2006; Ngugi 1986; Nkrumah 1965.

INDIGENOUS MAPPING

Mapping and cartography played a major role in imposing and maintaining colonial power by defining and naming the regions the colonizers sought to control. In response, the colonized sometimes sought to use the colonizers maps to help them in their claims for land rights (see **Mabo Turn**) or to assert their identities and histories (see **Mapping**). More radically, the indigenous peoples of colonized lands in recent times have developed their own mapping projects to assist them in these processes of land reclamation or identity assertion. "In general, indigenous mapping has shown itself to be a powerful tool and it has spread rapidly throughout the world" (Chapin et al. 2005: 619). As this pioneering article suggests, these projects include the participation in and adoption by indigenous peoples and organizations of developments in GIS (global information systems) technology, particularly to aid the mapping of remote regions. These projects were initiated in Canada and Alaska in the 1950s and developed strongly there from the 1970s onwards with the increasing claims to land and separate identity by First Nations and Inuit peoples in those regions. The use of mapping and GIS laboratory-based projects have more recently, since 2000 or so, also developed in poorer and less well-resourced groups of indigenous peoples in Africa, Asia and Latin America.

> In a very real sense, indigenous mapping represents a shift in the way cartography is both undertaken and used. Whereas those in power have employed maps over the centuries to mark off and control territories inhabited by indigenous peoples, indigenous peoples are now putting together their own maps and wielding them to defend their ancestral lands from encroachment by those in power.
>
> (Chapin et al. 2005: 620)

As well as putting power into the hands of indigenous peoples, the mapping that is undertaken often involves radically different priorities as to what is included and how it is recorded. One example is the use of digital cyber frameworks to empower indigenous groups to incorporate into this cyber mapping many traditional means of recording their cultures such as storytelling, visual representations and dance. This process is now sometimes referred to by the term cybercartography. Maps produced under this model have become the means of integrating visual and narrative (storytelling) aspects of the cultures being mapped (Fraser Taylor 2021). In this way, the story-telling aspect of the cybercartographic practices discussed above must be seen as part of an earlier way that illustrate how stories in themselves "must be thought of as 'material ordering practices'-that is . . . [a way to] structure our material and imaginative landscapes in a different way" (Hunt and Stevenson 2017: 378).

The production of indigenous maps discussed here has been referred to as counter-mapping or re-mapping. But important as these revisionary mapping projects are the history of indigenous mapping needs to be placed in a much longer time span. In Abenaki, scholar Lisa Brooks' *The Common Pot: The Recovery of Native Space in the Northeast*, Brooks outlines how pictographic 'message maps' were written on trees so Indigenous peoples could:

> inform each other of the location of game and the routes they would travel. . . rivers and streams appeared prominently on indigenous maps, and it was along these waterways that messages were carried from village to village . . . [mapping] conveyed knowledge from one person or place to another across the systems of waterways that connected them.
>
> (Brooks 2008: 9)

This longer perspective frees the notion of indigenous mapping from the ongoing dominance of the colonial narrative as the defining source which although countered by such practices nevertheless envelopes the indigenous response.

Further Reading: Chapin, Lamb and Threlkeld 2005; Fraser Taylor 2021; Bryan 2011, Brooks 2008; Cameron 2011; Hackett et al. 2020; Hunt and Stevenson 2017.

INDIGENOUS SOVEREIGNTY

Sovereignty derives from 'sovereign' meaning a supreme ruler or monarch, a person possessing supreme or ultimate power. The concept of national sovereignty is relatively recent, stemming from the Treaty of Westphalia in 1648, which can be said to herald the birth of the modern nation-state. Since the indigenous owners of settled colonies have been denied any kind of sovereign political power, the term 'indigenous sovereignty' – arising as late as the 1960s – refers to inherent and inalienable connections to land. This sovereign relationship to land, occupied, in the Australian case, for over 65,000 years relates to the longevity and widely experienced spiritual relationship of Aboriginal people to country. Aileen Moreton-Robinson writes that 'the first owners of the land were ancestral beings of Aboriginal peoples, and "since spiritual belief is completely integrated into human daily activity, the powers that guide and direct the earth are believed to exist with all human life"' (*Sydney Morning Herald* 9 February 2023). Unlike the political sovereignty of a nation-state, the Uluru *Statement from the Heart* defines indigenous sovereignty as a 'spiritual notion' that is 'the ancestral tie between the land, or "mother nature", and the Aboriginal and Torres Strait Islander peoples who were born therefrom remain attached thereto, and must one day return thither to be united with our ancestors'.

Indigenous sovereignty is a global issue and other Indigenous peoples such as the Inuit of the Arctic, the Yanomami of South America, the Saami of Scandinavia, the Shoshone and Cherokee of the United States, the Ojibwe and Mohawk of Canada, the Maori of New Zealand and the Jummas and Jarawa people of South Asia have gained some form of recognition of sovereignty. Indigenous sovereignty may not command attention as a world issue, but it continues in various forms throughout the global community, and is constantly debated in international forums such as the United Nations.

Indigenous sovereignty can be said to be a feature of a nation without a state, and the term **First Nations,** prevalent originally in North America, has been used increasingly to describe Australian Aboriginal and other indigenous groups. First Nations territory can include significant resources. As Carlson and Truscello point out, Canada includes 'more than 50 nations and 630 First Nation communities, controls the third largest oil reserve in the world, an amount of oil that approaches 10% of the known global reserve' (2003: 1). This gives the First Nations some leverage in dealing with governments and correspondingly, governments are loathe to cede ownership of resources to sovereign First Nations.

Indigenous sovereignty has not been recognized under Australian law, whether as sovereignty that existed before colonization or that still exists. However, the **Mabo** judgement of 1992 recognized the precolonial relationship to land and in the case of Eddie Mabo recognized a form of native title of the Torres Strait Islands. This has been taken to imply the existence of Aboriginal sovereignty prior to colonization. However, the issue of sovereignty has been problematic for colonial governments. The assumption of **terra nullius** was complicated by early legal judgements that implied a form of sovereignty. In 1835, Governor Bourke declared that indigenous Australians could not sell or assign land other than through distribution by the Crown, while apparently denying indigenous sovereignty the sense that land had been expropriated suggested the existence of Aboriginal sovereignty before colonization. However, subsequent legal judgements have declared that Aboriginal sovereignty was nullified by the assertion of sovereignty by the British Crown.

Until recently Australian Courts have asserted that they cannot recognize Aboriginal and Torres Strait Islander sovereignty. This is a form of **epistemic violence** but it declares that change must come through parliament, which theoretically represents the will of the Australian people. However, change is afoot. On 11 June 2024, the Australian federal court found the Kabi Kabi people are and always have been the traditional owners of what is now the Sunshine Coast and formally recognized them as native title holders. It is a groundbreaking determination in a number of ways, covering about 365,345 hectares of land and water. The declaration of precolonial sovereignty explains why the issue of a **treaty** is so prevalent in Aboriginal thinking. A treaty is a legally binding agreement between parties, usually state or sovereign powers. Therefore, a treaty *ipsi facto* recognizes the sovereignty of the treaty parties. While no treaty has been signed by the Australian federal government, some states and territories have begun to rethink the issue. For example, in the 2018 Barunga Agreement, signed by the Northern Territory government and the Territory's four Aboriginal Land Councils, both sides agreed that Aboriginal Territorians 'never ceded sovereignty of their lands, seas and waters'. In Western Australia, the 2016 Noongar Settlement was characterized by Deputy Opposition Leader Roger Cook as a process whereby the Noongar people and the Western Australian government 'recognis[e] each other's sovereignty'. At the federal level, the Uluru Statement from the Heart is a clear expression of Aboriginal and Torres Strait Islander sovereignty. It calls for a First Nations Voice to advise the government and parliament on laws that affect Aboriginal and Torres Strait Islanders peoples, and a Makarrata Commission to supervise a process of agreement-making and truth-telling. Although the referendum to implement these reforms was sadly lost some individual State governments are setting up these Voices to advise on legislation within their State parliaments. It is through these institutions that Aboriginal and Torres Strait Islander peoples can exercise their sovereignty within the Australian nation.

Further Reading: Carlson and Truscello (2023), Mead (2018), Moreton-Robinson (2007, 2015), Shrinkhal (2021)

INTERPELLATION

See **subject/subjectivity**

LIMINALITY

This term derives from the word 'limen', meaning threshold, a word particularly used in psychology to indicate the threshold between the sensate and the subliminal, the limit below which a certain sensation ceases to be perceptible. The sense of the liminal as an interstitial or in-between space, a threshold area, distinguishes the term from the more definite word 'limit' to which it is related.

The importance of the liminal for postcolonial theory is precisely its usefulness for describing an 'in-between' space in which cultural change may occur: the **transcultural** space in which strategies for personal or communal self-hood may be elaborated, a region in which there is a continual process of movement and interchange between different states. For instance, the colonized subject may dwell in the liminal space between **colonial discourse** and the assumption of a new 'non-colonial' identity. But such identification is never simply a movement from one identity to another, it is a constant process of engagement, contestation and **appropriation**.

Homi Bhabha quotes the art historian Renée Green's characterization of a stairwell as a 'liminal space, a pathway between upper and lower areas, each of which was annotated with plaques referring to blackness and whiteness' (Bhabha 1994: 4) to indicate how the liminal can become a space of symbolic interaction. That is, the stairwell, the liminal, prevents identities from polarizing between such arbitrary designations as 'upper' and 'lower', 'black' and 'white'. In a sense, one could say that postcolonial discourse itself consistently inhabits this liminal space, for the polarities of imperial rhetoric on one hand, and national or racial characterization on the other, are continually questioned and problematized.

For Bhabha, the liminal is important because liminality and **hybridity** go hand in hand. This 'interstitial passage between fixed identifications opens up the possibility of a cultural hybridity that entertains difference without an assumed or imposed hierarchy' (1994: 4). He further employs liminality to show that 'post-modernity, post-coloniality, post-feminism' are meaningless if the 'post' simply means 'after'. Each of these represents a liminal space of contestation and change, at the edges of the presumed monolithic, but never completely 'beyond'. The present can no longer be envisaged as a break or a bonding with the past or future; our presence comes to be revealed in its 'discontinuities, its inequalities, its minorities'.

Further Reading: Bhabha 1994.

LOCAL

In social and cultural terms, the "local" is usually employed in the distinction between local and global and may be defined as describing any group or community that operates from or identifies with as particular locality. The local is not only distinct from the global, it is also generally held to apply to a *sub-national* and sub-regional community. When we speak of the local, we speak of a community operating transversely to, or below the level of the state. It is a community small enough not to need to be 'imagined' as the nation, or region. It might be a spatial location, but it might also be an ethnic or cultural 'location'. Appadurai contends that localities are not simply there but are *produced* and that the "production of locality, as a dimension of social life, as a structure of feeling. . . challenges the order and orderliness of the nation-state".

> The work of producing localities, in the sense that localities are life-worlds constituted by relatively stable associations, relatively known and shared histories and collectively traversed and legible spaces and places, is often at odds with the projects of the nation-state.
>
> (Appadurai 2003: 338)

The reasons for theorizing the site of the local below the level of the nation are that nations have clearly and historically defined structures of relationships to an 'international' collectivity; that nations continue to exert a hegemonic pressure of their own upon the production of culture; and that nations have sometimes become locked within what Barber calls the axial principles of our time: 'tribalism' and 'globalism' – a 'McWorld' of homogenizing globalization *versus* a 'Jihad world' of 'lebanonization' (Barber 1992: 54). That is, many post-cold war national movements have generated a particularly bounded and xenophobic version of locality as a collection of coercive tribal pressures. This is only a more extreme version of the cultural homogenization of nationally constituted societies, which has been proceeding since the eighteenth century (coterminous with the rise of the concept of the 'international'). But it continues the general trend of the nation towards what we might call a suppression of locality.

The local is often theorized in terms of a binary relation with the global or the 'totalizing' force of hegemonic power. However, Foucault's theorizing of the operation of power suggests that this binary distinction may be too simplistic – the totalizing force, or the 'global', may be imbricated in the local rather than simply exerting a downward pressure on it. Power does not operate in a simple top-down way, percolating down through a hierarchy of institutions exerting and distributing itself through strata of dominated subjects. "Power is everywhere," says Foucault,

> not because it embraces everything but because it comes from everywhere. . . Power comes from below; that is, there is no binary and all-encompassing opposition between ruler and ruled at the root of power relations (1980: 93). Power is local because it is never global, but it is not local or localized because it is diffuse.
>
> (Foucault 1990: 26)

Imperial power, for instance, is *transcultural*, it circulates (through subjects as well as on them) and when it operates in postcolonial literatures such transculturality is demonstrated by the capacity of writers to transform the language by interpolating their own styles of usage into its wider circulation.

The **transcultural** relationship between colonizer and colonized in postcolonial studies offers an important model for understanding the complex relationship between local and global. In social science, this relationship was identified in the early 1990s by Robertson in the concept of **glocalization** in which the global is not only implicated in, or intrudes on the local but is transformed by the local. In postcolonial studies, particularly the study of postcolonial literatures, the relationship between local and global, like that between imperial discourse and colonized subject, is affected by the phenomenon of **agency** by which globalizing discourses, such as English literature, are actively transformed by the intervention of colonized subjects.

If we expand the postcolonial model to the local/global relationship, we find that the engagement of local communities with global *culture* is marked by a far greater degree of self-determination than that exists in global economic relationships. This is the same message delivered by colonial experience: no matter how oppressive the system, or how ubiquitous its effects, it is not immune to appropriation and adaptation by local communities for their own benefit. There is no question that the underlying pressure of the global economy, like the imperial economy before it, is to render the postcolonial world a mere instrument in the enrichment of the North. But this situation is neither inevitable nor irreversible. The experience of the postcolonial world shows that change is not going to occur by futile attempts to establish fortress societies or to abolish globalism, but rather by strategies to transform it as global *culture* has been transformed by appropriation and adaptation. Certainly defensive economic strategies, such as the control of speculative capital, will always be necessary. But the model of postcolonial societies reveals that local empowerment comes by means of the creative interpolation of the dominant, and increasingly a globally dominant, discourse (see **translocal**).

Further Reading: Appadurai 2003; Barber 1992; Foucault 1980, 1990

LUSOTROPICALISM

The conceptions underlying lusotropicalism were developed by the Brazilian sociologist Gilberto Freyre in a trilogy of books written between 1933 and 1959. The term itself was not used until the 1950s. Freyre's controversial assertion was that Portuguese colonization was intrinsically different to and in many ways superior to later colonizing practices. It was, he asserts, the oldest colonizing force reaching back more than 500 years in the colony of Brazil. He also asserted that Portugal itself was a much more diverse nation in the period before and during its colonial expansion, with influences from its diverse pre-modern roots in Celtic, Roman, Visigothic and Moorish cultures and from a large and better integrated body of enslaved and free black Africans in Portugal from the late sixteenth century onwards. As a result, Freyre suggests Portuguese colonizers were more humane and integrated other cultures more successfully than later European powers. Freyre controversially also claimed that Portuguese colonizers had become culturally hybridized (see **Hybridity**) by their more tolerant attitude to miscegenation.

This claim prevented the Portuguese authorities from endorsing his claims until the dictator Salazar employed the term and the theory in the 1950s to underpin his claim that since, as Freyre claimed, Portugal had always been a pluralist and multiracial society, its right to its overseas colonies was endorsed, as they were essentially part of the Portuguese nation.

> In its official discourse, Portugal was constituted by a multiracial community, composed by geographically distant territorial parts, inhabited by populations of various ethnic origins, united by the same sentiment and culture. As shown by Freyre's supposedly unsuspected studies, power as exercised in the Portuguese 'overseas provinces' was not of a colonial nature like in territories under the rule of other countries.
>
> (Castello 2015: n.a.)

Colonies were in this view simply a natural extension of the Portuguese nation, sharing its tolerance of different 'races'. In fact, of course, the territories that Portugal had obtained in the past and in more recent times in places such as Angola, Mozambique and Goa were obtained and sustained by the same processes of violent conquest and oppression that characterized all colonization. While it is true that a body of **mestiços** (the Portuguese term for the children of mixed-race relationships) existed in several Portuguese colonies, the implication drawn from Freyre's theorizing was that Portuguese colonies such as Brazil were far less marked by racial prejudice against marriages between different communities than other colonizing societies. Although in his later work Freyre sought to insist that he had never claimed that Portuguese colonization was free of racial prejudice, his concept of lusotropicalism as a form of colonization that was less oppressive and more inclusive than others was used by conservative forces to defend colonization. In the same way, his insistence on a positive cultural hybridization resulting from the tolerance of miscegenation allowed conservatives in Brazil to praise it as a racially integrated society much to the dismay of the victims of ongoing racism in that society (Fernandes 1970). His theory throughout is deeply marked by a discourse of race and racial definition that rests on notions of biological difference.

Further Reading: Castello 2015; da Silva and Villaverde Cabral 2020; Freyre 1946 [1933]; Freyre 1963 [1936]; Freyre 1970 [1959]; Fernandes 1970 [1965].

MABO TURN

This term describes the seismic shift in the representations of Australian culture that occurred as a result of the Eddie Mabo court case in the 1990s (Rodoreda 2018).

In *Mabo and Others v. Queensland (No. 2)*, [more commonly known as the "Mabo" judgement], handed down on 3 June 1992, Australia's highest court ruled in favour of Eddie Koiki Mabo (and his Torres Strait Islander co-plaintiffs) who had argued that the British annexation of their island in the Torres Strait in the nineteenth century had not lawfully extinguished their customary ownership of land. The court agreed that these litigants still had traditional, customary title to the land. The judgement determined that Indigenous Australians were entitled to the "possession, occupation, use and enjoyment" of those portions of the islands they had always considered their traditional home (*Mabo* 2). Australia's highest court thereby recognized, in the common law, a new form of customary land title for Indigenous Australians: "native title" (*Mabo* 2). Further, the court held that native title rights to land might still exist across the Australian continent where those rights had not been expressly extinguished by the Crown and where Indigenous people could still prove an attachment to land.

This led to a profound change in Australian law, politics and more widely, in the way the nation was imagined by writers, artists and cultural commentators. The 'Mabo Turn' refers to the realization by settler/immigrant Australians that the land was already known, named and owned by others – namely, Indigenous people – before they arrived. Although the effects of colonization on Aboriginal people had long been known Rodoreda (2018) argues that this 'seismic shift' affected Australian fiction, poetry film and theatre, drawing the reality of prior ownership of the land to centre stage. Mabo's re-assertion of an Indigenous presence in the Australian public and cultural sphere has been substantial, and it has been fiction writing that has been foremost in re-shaping and re-configuring imaginings and understandings of land and space, settlement and belonging, race and relationships and nation and history, both historically and contemporaneously. It is a post-Mabo *literary* imaginary that works to describe, articulate, reflect and ultimately represent post-Mabo discourse in Australia today.

The most recent effect of the Mabo Turn has been the proposal of an indigenous Voice to Parliament. This was a key recommendation of the Uluru Statement from the Heart, which was a 12-paragraph document written and endorsed by Aboriginal and Torres Strait Islander leaders in 2017 to change the Constitution to improve the representation of Indigenous Australians. The Voice to Parliament would have given Aboriginal people a say in any legislation pertaining to them through a group of elected Indigenous representatives who would advise the Australian parliament and government on matters relating to Aboriginal and Torres Strait Islander people such as employment, health, housing and justice. Despite the failure of this referendum the change in Australia public culture after the Mabo judgement can be seen to be irreversible.

Further Reading: Attwood (1996), Baker and Worby (2007), Collins and Davis (2004), Reynolds (2007), Rodoreda (2018), Rowse (1993), Strelein (2009)

MAGIC REALISM

This term, which has a long and quite distinctive history in Latin American criticism, was first used in a wider postcolonial context in the foundational essay by Jacques Stephen Alexis, 'Of the magical realism of the Haitians' (Alexis 1956). Alexis sought to reconcile the arguments of post-war, radical intellectuals in favour of social realism as a tool for revolutionary social representation, with a recognition that in many postcolonial societies a peasant, pre-industrial population had its imaginative life rooted in a living tradition of the mythic, the legendary and the magical. The term became popularized when it was employed to characterize the work of South American writers widely translated into English and other languages, such as Gabriel García Marquez. It tended to be used indiscriminately during the 'Boom' period of the 1960s and 1970s by some critics who saw it as a defining feature of all Latin American writing, in stark contrast to its older, more specific usage in Latin American criticism, a usage that differed in marked ways from the recent rather loose and generalized use of the term (Zamora and Faris 1995).

However, its origins in the 1950s lay in the specific need to wed Caribbean social revolution to local cultural tradition. Mythic and magical traditions, Alexis argued, far from being alienated from the people, or mere mystifications, were the distinctive feature of their local and national cultures, and were the collective forms by which they gave expression to their identity and articulated their difference from the dominant colonial and racial oppressors. They were, in other words, the modes of expression of that culture's reality. Radical social visions of art and culture thus regarded myth and magic as integral. For Alexis, 'The treasure of tales and legends, all the musical, choreographic and plastic symbolism, all the forms of Haitian popular art are there to help the nation in accomplishing the tasks before it'. More recently, the term has been used in a less specific way to refer to the inclusion of any mythic or legendary material from local written or oral cultural traditions in contemporary narrative.

The material so used is seen to interrogate the assumptions of Western, rational, linear narrative, and to enclose it within an indigenous metatext, a body of textual forms that recuperate the precolonial culture. In this way, it can be seen to be a structuring device in texts as varied as Salman Rushdie's *Midnight's Children*, Ben Okri's *The Famished Road*, Keri Hulme's *The Bone People* or Thomas King's *Green Grass, Running Water*. In texts like these and many others, the rational, linear world of Western realist fiction is placed against alter/native narrative modes that expose the hidden and naturalized cultural formations on which Western narratives are based. Although the term has been useful, its increasingly ubiquitous use for any text that has a fabulous or mythic dimension has tended to bring it into disrepute with some critics who suggest that it has become a catch-all for any narrative device that does not adhere to Western realist conventions.

Further Reading: Alexis 1956; S. Baker 1991; Durix 1998; Faris 2004; Molloy 2005; Parkinson and Faris 1995; Slemon 1988a, 1995.

MANICHEANISM

This term is adapted from the 'Manichaean heresy' of the third century AD which propounded a dualistic theology, according to which Satan was represented as coeternal with God. Matter was evil and God by His nature could not intervene in the world of evil matter. Thus Christ could not have been born into the flesh and had to be only spirit – a heresy against the doctrine of Christ's dual nature as both Man and God. The implication that the two realms of spirit and matter were always and eternally separate and could never be linked implies an extreme form of binary structure, and it is this to which contemporary postcolonial usage refers. The concept was popularized by Abdul JanMohammed (1983,

1985) who developed Frantz Fanon's identification of the Manichaean nature of the implacable opposition of colonizer and colonized.

In the field of postcolonial studies, Manicheanism is a term for the **binary** structure of **imperial** ideology. JanMohammed uses the uncompromisingly dualistic aspect of the concept to describe the process by which imperial discourse polarizes the society, culture and very being of the colonizer and colonized into the Manichean categories of good and evil. The world at the boundaries of civilization is perceived as uncontrollable, chaotic, unattainable and ultimately evil, while the civilized culture is the embodiment of good. The consequences of this for **colonial discourse** are that the colonizer's assumption of moral superiority means that 'he will not be inclined to expend any energy in understanding the worthless alterity of the colonized' (1985: 18). Much literature of cultural encounter,

> instead of being an exploration of the racial Other . . . affirms its own ethno-centric assumptions; instead of actually depicting the outer limits of 'civilization', it simply codifies and preserves the structures of its own mentality. While the surface of each colonialist text purports to represent specific encounters with specific varieties of the racial Other, the subtext valorizes the superiority of European cultures, of the collective process that has mediated that representation. Such literature is essentially specular: instead of seeing the native as a bridge toward syncretic possibility, it uses him as a mirror that reflects the colonialist's self image.
>
> (JanMohammed 1985: 19)

Borrowing from Lacan, JanMohammed claims that colonialist literature can be divided into 'imaginary' and 'symbolic' modes. The writer of the 'imaginary' text tends to 'fetishize a nondialectical, fixed opposition between the self and the native. Threatened by a metaphysical alterity that he has created, he quickly retreats to the homogeneity of his own group'. Writers of 'symbolic' texts tend to be more open to a modifying dialectic of self and Other, and it is this preparedness to consider the possibility of syncretism that is the most important factor distinguishing it from the 'imaginary' text. Ultimately, according to JanMohammed, it is the ability to bracket the values and bases of imperialist culture that determines the success of the symbolic text and its ability to subvert or avoid the economy of Manichean allegory.

Further Reading: JanMohammed 1983, 1985.

MAPPING AND THE POSTCOLONIAL

Cartography, the art and science of mapmaking, played a central role in constructing colonial discourse and enabling colonial power. Maps defined areas the colonizers sought to claim and control, allowing them to construct boundaries (lines on maps) where no such boundary had previously existed. Together with adding names, the colonizer could either redefine spaces or even bring into existence spaces where none had previously existed. Areas that had not been explored could be incorporated by enclosing them as empty spaces with no names or employing a designator such as *terra incognita*, literally unknown, territory, and thus defining them as spaces waiting to be named and so claimed by the colonizing European powers. (See **terra nullius**).

The map is the crucial signifier of control over place and thus of power over the inscription of being. Perhaps the most detailed discussion of this process is Paul Carter's *The Road to Botany Bay* (1987) which surveys at length the extent to which the language of travel, of exploration, of settlement, indeed naming itself, turned empty space into 'place' in Australia and has continued to re-write the text of that place. This was not a place which was 'simply there' but a place which is in a continual process of being 'written'. This is true of any place, but in postcolonial experience, the linkage between language, place and history is far more prominent because the interaction is so much more urgent and contestatory.

José Rabasa has shown the extent of the historical construction of a Eurocentric world in his analysis of the conception of the Mercator Atlas itself (Rabasa 1993). This early and massively influential early map of the world can be seen as a palimpsest on which Europe has written its own dominance through the agency of history:

> In Mercator's maps, previous names accompany contemporary usages. The different regions of the world carry a temporal disparity according to the periods when the sources of information were produced. Generally speaking, Mercator also displays a tendency to make space historical by incorporating legends into the empty areas in the maps. This practice ensures a centrifugal movement from the name-laden Europe to the periphery, where legends and drawings characterize vast territories without history. In the periphery itself, the concentration of names serves as an index of colonialization.

> (Rabasa 1993)

In addition, of course, the Mercator projection places emphasis on the accurate representation of the size of territories centred on the latitudes that encompass the dominant European powers and its New World extensions.

As a kind of counterpoint to Rabasa's critique of Mercator's Atlas, Graham Huggan demonstrates how maps are themselves decolonized in postcolonial constructions of place. Employing Deleuze and Guattari's idea that maps are experimental in orientation and susceptible to multiple deconstructions: ('The map is open and connectable in all its dimensions; it is detachable, reversible, susceptible to constant modification. It can be torn, reversed, adapted to any kind of mounting, reworked by an individual, group, or social formation' (Deleuze and Guattari 1987: 12) Huggan suggests that we can revision maps

> . . .to resist one form of cartographic discourse, whose patterns of coercion and containment are historically implicated in the colonial enterprise, but to advocate another, whose flexible cross-cultural patterns not only counteract the monolithic conventions of the West but revision the map itself as the expression of a shifting ground between alternative metaphors rather than as the approximate representation of a 'literal truth'.
>
> (Huggan 1989: 125)

He concludes:

> So, while the map continues to feature in one sense as a paradigm of colonial discourse, its deconstruction and/or revisualization permits a 'disidentification' from the procedures of colonialism (and other hegemonic discourses) and a (re) engagement in the ongoing process of cultural decolonization.
>
> (128)

Colonial maps have been employed directly to refute and contest the way colonial space has been designated and the oppressions or cultural erasures which have resulted from this. How this worked in practice is illustrated by the ways in which indigenous people in Australia have employed colonial maps 'to make claims on lands and rights or to help researchers develop family histories, trace trading paths and Songlines, investigate traditional fire management regimes, reconstruct land use patterns, and explore local languages' (Moylan 2019). Of course, indigenous peoples have also been actively engaged in producing their own maps employing radically different ways of representing spatial geographies and their cultural connections (see **Indigenous Mapping**).

Further Reading: Rabasa 1993; Huggan 1989, Deleuze and Guattari 1987; Moylan 2019; Ackerman 2017.

MARGINALITY

Being on the margin, marginal. The perception and description of experience as 'marginal' is a consequence of the binaristic structure of various kinds of dominant discourses, such as patriarchy, **imperialism** and **ethno-centrism**, which imply that certain forms of experience are peripheral. Although the term carries a misleading geometric implication, marginal groups do not necessarily endorse the notion of a fixed centre. Structures of power that are described in terms of 'centre' and 'margin' operate, in reality, in a complex, diffuse and multi-faceted way. The marginal therefore indicates a positionality that is best defined in terms of the limitations of a subject's access to power.

However, marginality as a noun is related to the verb 'to marginalize', and in this sense provides a trap for those involved in resistance by its assumption that power is a function of centrality. This means that such resistance can become a process of replacing the centre rather than deconstructing the binary structure of centre and margin, which is a primary feature of postcolonial discourse. Marginality unintentionally reifies centrality because it is the centre that creates the condition of marginality. In simple terms, we could ask, 'Who are the marginal?'

We might be tempted to reply spontaneously, 'imperialism marginalizes, the colonized people are marginalized'. But they are neither all marginalized nor always marginalized. Imperialism cannot be reduced to a structure, a geometry of power that leaves some particular races on the margin. It is continuous, processual, working through individuals as well as upon them. It reproduces itself within the very idea of the marginal. Therefore, despite its ubiquity as a term to indicate various forms of exclusion and oppression, the use of the term always involves the risk that it endorses the structure that established the marginality of certain groups in the first place.

Various group are marginal in postcolonial studies and such groups, e.g. women and the colonized in general, may demonstrate different forms of marginality that intersect (see **intersecting marginalities**). This is often described as a **double colonization**.

Further Reading: Gunew 1994; Jordan and Weedon 1995; Orgun 2000; Spivak 1996.

MESTIZO/MESTIZAJE/MESTICOS/MÉTISSE

These terms, respectively Spanish, Portuguese and French in origin, semantically register the idea of a mixing of races and/or cultures. Initially, they emerged from a **colonial discourse** that privileged the idea of racial purity and justified racial discrimination by employing the quasi-scientific precursors of physical anthropology to create a complex and largely fictional taxonomy of racial admixtures (mulatto, quadroon, octaroon, etc.).

Mestizo/mesticos differs from creole and from métisse in so far as its usage reflects the older, large-scale Spanish and Portuguese settlement of their South American and Meso-American possessions. This early settlement led to an intensive cultural and racial exchange between Spaniards and Portuguese settlers and the native Indians, in many cases prior to the influence of black African slaves upon this cultural mélange. The relatively early date of this colonizing process, and the equally early date at which Spanish and Portuguese colonies in the Americas achieved their independence, means that in Latin American cultural discourses, the idea of mestizo is much more developed as a positive 'national' cultural sign, as a sign of shared if disputed indigeneity.

Both terms have gradually moved from a pejorative to a positive usage, as they have begun to reflect a perception in these cultures that **miscegenation** and interchange between the different cultural **diasporas** had produced new and powerful **synergistic** cultural forms, and that these cultural and racial exchanges might be the place where the most energized aspects of the new cultures reside. These terms have not been used widely to describe aspects of cultures outside the Caribbean, the Americas and the Indian Ocean regions. The dominance of the use of **creole** as a generic term in linguistics and in wider cultural studies as well as in general discourse stems from its early adoption into English as the standard term, though English writers have occasionally used mestizo to indicate some of the special nuances discussed above. The use of the Spanish term **mestizaje** has also become prevalent, particularly in Latin American studies, and is used to describe the cultural processes attendant to a long history of **miscegenation** by emphasizing **heterogeneity** and **transculturation**. **Mestizaje** is employed most commonly in cultural and linguistic analyses to denote plurality and is a key feature of Latin American regionalist discourse.

Further Reading: Alonso 2004; Chanady 1995, 2003; Cornejo Polar 1997; Cornejo Polar and Dennis 2004a, 2004b; Echeverría 1998; Glissant 1981, 1989; Harris 1983; Hildebrant 1992; Klor de Alva 1995; Miller 2004; Moraña 2002; Pérez-Torres 2006; Vilanova 1977.

METONYMIC GAP

This is a term for what is arguably the most subtle form of abrogation. The metonymic gap is that cultural gap formed when appropriations of a colonial language insert unglossed words, phrases or passages from a first language, or concepts, allusions or references that may be unknown to the reader. Such words become synechdochic of the writer's culture – the part that stands for the whole – rather than representations of the world, as the colonial language might. Thus the inserted language 'stands for' the colonized culture in a metonymic way, and its very resistance to interpretation constructs a 'gap' between the writer's culture and the colonial culture. The local writer is thus able to represent his or her world to the colonizer (and others) in the metropolitan language, and at the same time to signal and emphasize a difference from it. In effect, the writer is saying 'I am using your language so that you will understand my world, but you will also know by the differences in the way I use it that you cannot share my experience'.

There are many ways in which the language can do this: syntactic fusion; neologisms; code-switching; untranslated words. An example of the latter occurs in Ngugi's *A Grain of Wheat*, in which Gikonyo sings a song to his future wife Mumbi in Gikuyu (W. D. Ashcroft 1989b: 61). The song itself is densely ironic and yet inaccessible to a non-Gikuyu reader. It reiterates that absence that lies at the point of interface between the two cultures. The insertion of a Gikuyu song in the text presents a cultural 'gap' that emphasizes difference yet situates it in a way that makes the piece accessible.

Further Reading: W. D. Ashcroft 1989b.

METROPOLIS/METROPOLITAN

'Metropolis' is a term used binaristically in colonial discourse to refer, metaphorically, to the 'centre' in relation to a colonial 'periphery'. In Greek history, a metropolis was the parent state of a colony. The first specific use of the term to cover the modern colonial situation, in which 'metro-politan' means 'belonging to or constituting the mother country', is listed in the OED as of 1806. The metropolis in European thought was always constituted as the seat of culture, and this meaning is readily transferred to the imperial/colonial relationship. There is frequent slippage in the use of the term to cover 'mother country' (England, France) or, metonymically, their chief cities, London and Paris. (Oswald Spengler claimed that at the turn of the century, the seat of world power was, in practical terms, focused in four cities.)

Since the binarism inherent in the concept connotes a **centre** and a **periphery**, colonies are by definition constructed as peripheral to the metropolitan 'centres'. Postcolonial writers such as V.S. Naipaul have attempted to question or dismantle/disrupt this hierarchized binary by exposing the idea of an imperial 'centre' as chimeric. Since the 'centre' can never be found, the distinction between metropolis and colony, centre and periphery necessarily collapses. In practical terms, however, control of publishing and distribution was (and in many cases still is) centred in the European (and, latterly, North American) metropoles, and, together with the migration of artists and intellectuals to Paris, London and Madrid, reinforced (and to some extent still reinforces) the cultural power of 'the metropolis'.

While there are obvious similarities here between the empires of England, France, Portugal and Spain, it should be noted that the ways in which their empires were administered and the attitudes of colonials to the different 'centres' varied significantly. As the concept of **decoloniality** maintains in the empire of France, cultural power was invested almost exclusively in a Parisian intellectual élitism that rendered the rest of France as culturally 'peripheral' as the African or Antillean colonies. Colonial intellectuals who migrated to Paris could share in that 'cultural capital'. By contrast, although the controlling cultural institutions of the British Empire were generally collected in London, significant cultural differences between colonies and 'the metropolitan' remained in a **binaristic** hierarchy more usually formulated as 'England and the colonies' or 'Britain and the colonies'. Colonial writers and artists could succeed in London, but their primary affiliation was usually regarded as being with their colonial homelands. As these writers became increasingly prominent, however, Britain has widened its metropolitan self-concept to include contemporary postcolonial writers originally from Australia, Africa, India and Pakistan under the label of 'British'.

Further Reading: Ball 2004; McLeod 2004; Spengler 1926; Stoneham 2000.

MIDDLE PASSAGE
(See **slave/slavery**)

MIGRANTS/REFUGEES/ASYLUM SEEKERS

In recent times, the effect of colonization on many regions of the world
has been further exacerbated by the increasing gap between wealthy
countries and those whose economies have continued to be impacted
negatively by unfair neo-colonial practices and the corrupt governments
these have supported, undermining the hopes of the independence
movements (see **Neo-Colonialism**, **Decolonization**). This wealth
inequality has been exacerbated by the impact of climate change on
the economies of many of the poorer regions of the world, as has been
described by Rob Nixon in his classic 2011 study *Slow Violence and the
Environmentalism of the Poor* (see **Slow Violence**). Referring to the effect
of climate change on the nations of the South Pacific and Indian Ocean,
Nixon comments:

> Here it's not brown immigrants threatening to "swamp" the
> neoliberal fortresses of the still predominantly white rich, but
> rather poor brown people confronting the threat of having their
> national territory swamped as a result of a 200-year experiment
> in hydrocarbon-fueled capitalism whose historic beneficiaries have
> been disproportionately rich and white.
>
> (Nixon 2011: 266)

In earlier periods, migrants to nations such as Britain (as well as other
European nations, the United States, Canada and Australia) were people
who undertook the journey voluntarily in search of resettlement in countries they felt would offer them a better future. Although the reception of
these peoples was often fraught with race prejudice and discrimination
and sometimes the call by some politicians to ban these immigrants,
these calls were not generally upheld nor consolidated in major changes
to immigration policies in most countries until fairly recently. But as
the flow of people seeking to resettle as migrants increased with the
growing economic and environmental pressures described above political and popular attitudes to these people hardened. The term migrant
was increasingly conflated with the term refugee, and the definition of
and requirement of proof as to so-called refugee status also hardened.
Refugees were ever more stringently divided into legal and illegal

categories, and the latter were also divided into sub-categories such as economic refugees (implying they were fleeing not because of political persecution but because the economies of their natal countries could no longer allow them to live), or climate refugees (whose countries were suffering climate caused famines, droughts or inundating floods or rising sea-levels). These refugees were regarded as not meeting the requirements that legal refugee status demanded, though their ability to live in the prevailing conditions of their homelands was as threatened as those directly in danger of political attack.

In the last decade or so the numbers of people who have been displaced, either by traditional causes of refugeeization such as polit-ical threats from the regimes of their countries, or by war and civil violence (some caused by the military intervention of the very coun-tries they sought to enter, as well as by the emergence of violent resist-ance to these by so-called terrorists) or by the other causes outlined above has reached astronomical numbers, now exceeding even the huge numbers of peoples displaced by the conflicts of the Second World War 1939–1945. Whether such interventions were justified is beyond the scope of this short article. Though one is perhaps reminded of the fact that, as was remarked about the ancient Pax Romana, often such peace was achieved by the destruction of those it had saved, suggesting that imperialism may change its face but often employs similar excuses and ends in similar tragic results.

Another common recent term, asylum seekers, also conflates sev-eral of the terms used to describe those who have not been accepted as possessing recognized legal refugee status. The current widespread policy of sealing off entry to most of those seeking asylum as "illegal" refugees does not address this growing crisis. The belief is that issues such as the dispersal of peoples under the economic pressures of unequal global wealth and rapid destructive climate change can be addressed by creating sealed boundaries flying in the face of the myriad examples of the failure of such sealed borders, policed by physical walls and rigid legal definitions of citizenship rights and human status, throughout human history.

Unfortunately, most of those people seeking refugee status or seeking permission to relocate in a more stable and economically viable region remain voiceless, represented if at all only by organizations that lack the political power to change the current situation and who are limited to ways of seeking to alleviate the suffering caused by this new radical wave of migrants/refugees. A ray of hope has emerged as a minority of those so displaced have found a way of recording their experiences, leading to the emergence of what has been termed refugee/migrant literature (Gallien 2018; Gamal 2013). As well as memoirs in traditional literary form, film and multi-media platforms have been employed to allow their voices to be heard (Khorana 2018). Critics like Sukhmani Khorana have shown that there had been a long-term tendency to 'dehumanize' so-called 'illegal' refugees and migrants by right-wing media in an attempt to manipulate public response by rendering them as other and distant groups who threaten national borders or cultural integrity. She shows that recently a more empathetic rendering of accounts of these groups in the wider public media has emerged. But as she and others have also argued while empathetically presenting specific cases, such as drowned children on Mediterranean beaches, may create a counter-balancing public discourse, such empathetic representations must move beyond empathy to embrace an activist response to the increasing crisis of displacement that threatens the world. Imaginative representations of these peoples must grapple "with the problem of invoking the compassion of their audiences, whilst also trying to ensure this affective response is not transient and/or de-politicized" (Khorana 2018: 302). The current crisis in this area shows no sign of decreasing and the solutions so far have failed to work.

Further Reading: Gallien 2018; Gamal 2013; Khorana 2018; Mains et al. 2013, Nixon 2011, Phillips 2016; Whitlock 2018.

MIMICRY

An increasingly important term in postcolonial theory, because it has come to describe the **ambivalent** relationship between colonizer and colonized. When colonial discourse encourages the colonized subject to 'mimic' the colonizer, by adopting the colonizer's cultural habits, assumptions, institutions and values, the result is never a simple reproduction of those traits. Rather, the result is a 'blurred copy' of the colonizer that can be quite threatening. This is because mimicry is never very far from mockery, since it can appear to parody whatever it mimics. Mimicry therefore locates a crack in the certainty of colonial dominance, an uncertainty in its control of the behaviour of the colonized.

Mimicry has often been an overt goal of imperial policy. For instance, Lord Macaulay's 1835 Minute to Parliament derided Oriental learning, and advocated the reproduction of English art and learning in India (most strategically through the teaching of English literature). However, the method by which this mimicry was to be achieved indicated the underlying weakness of imperialism. For Macaulay suggested that the riches of European learning should be imparted by 'a class of interpreters between us and the millions whom we govern – a class of persons Indian in blood and colour, but English in tastes, opinions, in morals, and in intellect' (Macaulay 1835). In other words, not only was the mimicry of European learning to be **hybridized** and therefore ambivalent, but Macaulay seems to suggest that imperial discourse is compelled to make it so in order for it to work.

The term mimicry has been crucial in Homi Bhabha's view of the ambivalence of colonial discourse. For him, the consequence of suggestions like Macaulay's is that mimicry is the process by which the colonized subject is reproduced as 'almost the same, but not quite' (Bhabha 1994: 86). The copying of the colonizing culture, behaviour, manners and values by the colonized contains both mockery and a certain 'menace', 'so that mimicry is at once resemblance and menace' (86). Mimicry reveals the limitation in the authority of colonial discourse, almost as though colonial authority inevitably embodies the seeds of its own destruction. The line of descent of the 'mimic man' that emerges in Macaulay's writing, claims Bhabha, can be traced through the works of Kipling, Forster, Orwell and Naipaul, and is the effect of 'a flawed colonial mimesis in which to be Anglicized is emphatically not to be English' (1994: 87).

The consequences of this for postcolonial studies are quite profound, for what emerges through this flaw in colonial power is writing, that is, postcolonial writing, the ambivalence of which is 'menacing' to colonial authority. The menace of mimicry does not lie in its concealment of some real identity behind its mask, but comes from its 'double vision which in disclosing the ambivalence of colonial discourse also disrupts its authority' (88). The 'menace' of postcolonial writing, then, does not necessarily emerge from some automatic opposition to colonial discourse, but comes from this disruption of colonial authority, from the fact that its mimicry is also potentially mockery. While Macaulay's interpreter, or Naipaul's 'mimic man' (discussed below), are appropriate objects of a colonial chain of command, they are also 'inappropriate' colonial subjects because what is being set in motion in their behaviour is something that may ultimately be beyond the control of colonial authority. This 'inappropriateness' disturbs the normality of the dominant discourse itself. The threat inherent in mimicry, then, comes not from an overt resistance but from the way in which it continually suggests an identity not quite like the colon-izer. This identity of the colonial subject – 'almost the same but not white' (89) – means that the colonial culture is always potentially and strategically insurgent.

Mimicry can be both ambivalent and multi-layered. In his novel *The Mimic Men*, V.S. Naipaul opens with a very subtle description of the complexity of mimicry when he describes his landlord:

> I paid Mr Shylock three guineas a week for a tall, multi-mirrored, book-shaped room with a coffin-like wardrobe. And for Mr Shylock, the recipient each week of fifteen times three guineas, the possessor of a mistress and of suits made of cloth so fine I felt I could eat it, I had nothing but admiration. . . . I thought Mr Shylock looked distinguished, like a lawyer or businessman or politician. He had the habit of stroking the fore of his ear inclining his head to listen. I thought the gesture was attractive; I copied it. I knew of recent events in Europe; they tormented me; and although I was trying to live on seven pounds a week I offered Mr Shylock my fullest, silent compassion.
>
> (Naipaul 1967: 7)

This deeply ironic passage uncovers the way in which both **hegemony** and mimicry work. Although the title suggests a disparagement of the tendency to emulate the colonizer, the complexity and potential insurgency of mimicry emerges in this passage. The narrator not only copies the habits of the landlord, but mimics the guilt of a post-war Europe concerning the Jews, a guilt that is embedded also in a cultural familiarity with the implications of the name 'Shylock' (the Jew who demanded repayment of a pound of flesh in Shakespeare's *Merchant of Venice*). He is encouraged to mimic a compassion for the one exploiting him. But the very irony of the passage suggests an inversion, a mockery just under the surface; not a mockery of Shylock but of the whole pro-cess of colonization that is being enacted in the narrator's mimicry and cultural understanding. The mimicry of the postcolonial subject is therefore always potentially destabilizing to colonial discourse, and locates an area of considerable political and cultural uncertainty in the structure of imperial dominance.

Further Reading: Bhabha 1984a, 1994; Castro-Klarén 1999; Huggan 1994, 1997; McQuillan 2002; Parry 1987.

MISCEGENATION

Miscegenation, the sexual union of different races, specifically whites with negroes (OED), has always haunted European colonizers and their settler descendants (see **apartheid**). Colonialist practice was obsessed with the products of such unions, particularly in those areas where black and white had also been further hierarchized as slave and free. Nineteenth-century slave-owners developed extensive codifications of the various divisions of admixture resulting from miscegenation. French colonizers, for example, developed no fewer than 128 differing degrees of pigmentation to distinguish between the children of mixed-race relations. Since the maintenance of absolute difference between Europeans and others, colonizers and colonized, was crucial to military and administrative control, miscegenation raised the constant spectre of ideological (and sometimes external) destabilization of imperial power. Yet, as theorists such as Bhabha have suggested, the very process of insisting on racial difference may mask a hidden and opposite fascination, as the colonizer sees a menacing **ambivalence** in the ways in which the colonized is both like and unlike. As some critics have argued, the fear of miscegenation thus stems from a desire to maintain the separation between **civilized** and **savage**, yet that binary masks a profound longing, occluding the idea of the inevitable dependence of one on the existence of the other.

One of the earliest theorists of **race**, Gobineau, expressed this ambivalence in his long and influential essay 'Essai sur l'inegalité des races humaines', emphasizing, as Robert Young notes, that there is a positive as well as a negative feature to racial admixture which 'accords with the consistent tendency for the positive to intermingle with the negative, growth with degeneration, life with death' (Young 1995: 115). Young also notes that in this respect, Gobineau looks forward to modern ideas concerning the tendency of the socially repressed to return symbolically, citing Stallybrass and White's argument that 'disgust always bears the imprint of desire'. These low domains, apparently expelled as 'Other' return as the objects of nostalgia, longing and fascination' (Stallybrass and White 1986: 191). Paradoxically, then, race is seen as the marker of civilization, and racial purity, its pre-eminent pre-condition. Yet, if civilization must be spread, then the road to the one must lead to the decline of the other. That is, as Gobineau expressed it,

> If mixtures of blood are, to a certain extent, beneficial to the mass of mankind, if they raise and ennoble it, this is merely at the

expense of mankind itself, which is stunted, abased, enervated, and humiliated in the persons of its noblest sons.

(Gobineau 1853–1855: 1, 410, translated by Young).

Further Reading: Anderson 1991; Fitz 2002; Gobineau 1853–1855, 1856; Lemire 2002; Moore 2000; J.D. Smith 1993 Young 1995.

MISSIONS AND COLONIALISM

The role of missions and missionaries in the development of colonization was crucial. In the words of one historian:

> The explosive expansion of Christianity in Africa and Asia during the last two centuries constitutes one of the most remarkable cultural transformations in the history of mankind. Because it coincided with the spread of European economic and cultural hegemony, it tends to be taken for granted as a reflex of imperialism.
>
> (Etherington 2005: 1).

As a result, for a long while, both imperial historians and radical revisers of their work either ignored altogether or radically simplified the complex role religion (see **religion and the postcolonial**) and their instrument, the Christian missions, played for good and bad in the spread of empire. In the last few years, we have seen a growth of studies of missions, which have treated the role they played with a new seriousness and which have detailed their importance in the story of colonization.

These new studies emphasized that although the story of Euro-American expansion and the story of missions are deeply intertwined, the relations between them are far more complex than has often been suggested. Radical critics of missions who argue that missions are the forerunners of more direct control ('First the missionary, then the Consul, and at last the invading army' [Hobson 1938: 204]) see **missionaries** as **conscious precursors** of **imperialism**. They forget the role missionaries also played in acting as a buffer between harsh government policy and indigenous peoples, and especially between settlers and indigenes in settler colonies. In fact, the role of missions in providing education, and so increasing literacy, was construed as a dangerous act by many traders and settlers. It is also certainly the case that many of the first generation of nationalist anti-colonial activists were mission educated. While their oppositional stance was certainly not a conscious product of mission intention, it was an undeniable offshoot of the mission emphasis on modernization. Apart from education, this included missionaries' involvement in medical and health issues and their broad concerns for the effects of practices such as slavery on the rights of individuals, especially groups such as women and children who were seen as particularly vulnerable (Scott and Griffiths 2005).

From a literary viewpoint, missions had a special role to play in many colonial situations. Of course, missions and their role have featured in many postcolonial literary accounts. For the most part, these accounts have emphasized the negative impact of missions, as might be expected. As with the general historical accounts, however, more complex readings of mission involvement in colonial texts are now emerging (see Griffiths 2005). Mission presses were often the first places in which colonized peoples were able to find a voice, even though they did so under conditions of patronage which were deeply constraining. Despite this, the degree to which they succeeded in speaking through these constraints is remarkable. Missions and their role exemplify once again how colonized peoples could appropriate and subvert colonial institutions and bend them to their own ends even under the most unpromising of conditions.

Further Reading: Dangaremba 1988; Etherington 2005; Griffiths 2005; Hobson 1902.

MODERNISM AND POSTCOLONIALISM

Modernism is a twentieth-century European movement in the creative arts that sought to break with the dominant conventions of nineteenth-century art, such as realism, linear narrativity, perspective and tonality. Although modernism is usually defined as a European movement, it has been argued that the encounter with African cultures in the so-called 'scramble for Africa' period of the 1880s and 1890s was crucial to the development of a modernist aesthetic. While the European powers were engaged in violently suppressing the 'savage' cultures of Africa, they were importing into Europe, as loot, the revelation of an alternative view of the world in the form of African masks, carvings and jewellery – artefacts that were often stored in museum basements until displayed in the early decades of the twentieth century. These African works, together with those from other so-called 'primitive' cultures, such as Papua New Guinea and the South Pacific,

North American Indian and Inuit, were seen as products of societies preserved in time, reflecting primitive and aboriginal impulses common to all people. Their art reflected a 'stage' in the development of 'civilized' art.

However, from its inception, this ethnographic view was accompanied by a more fearful and complex vision in which primitive art was seen as expressive of the other, darker side of European man, whose civilization might thus be considered merely a veneer. This fear is expressed in works such as Conrad's *Heart of Darkness* and Yeats' *Savage God*. But in the reaction of artists as diverse as Jarry, Rimbaud, Artaud, Lawrence and Picasso, a more radical critique was formulated in which the claims of European art to universal validity were questioned and in which the claims of Europe to being a unique civilization were exposed as a veneer on a deeper, 'universal' savagery. This view appears to have been vindicated when the claims of nineteenth-century Europe to be civilized collapsed in the horrors of the mass destruction of the First World War.

Further Reading: Bray and Middleton 1979; Esty 2004; Eysteinsson 1990; Fokkema 1984; Friedman 2006; Lazarus 2005; McDougall 1998; McGee 1992; Nunes 1994; Peretti 1995; Rajadhyaksha 1998; Ramazani 2006; Richards 2000; Ruthven 1968; Smith 1992; Weston 1996.

MODERNITY

The term 'modern' derives from the late fifth-century Latin term *modernus* which was used to distinguish an officially Christian present from a Roman, pagan past. 'Modern' was used in the mediaeval period to distinguish the contemporary from the 'ancient' past. But 'modernity' has come to mean more than 'the here and now': it refers to modes of social organization that emerged in Europe from about the sixteenth century and extended their influence throughout the world in the wake of European exploration and colonization. Three momentous cultural shifts around the year 1500 – the discovery of the 'new world', the Renaissance and the Reformation – had, by the eighteenth century, come to constitute 'the epochal threshold between modern times and the middle ages' (Habermas 1981: 5). The emergence of the French Enlightenment saw the development of the idea that modernity was a distinctive and superior period in the history of humanity, a notion that became habitual as successive generations saw their own 'present' as enjoying a prominent position within the modern. As European power expanded, this sense of the superiority of the present over the past became translated into a sense of superiority over those pre-modern societies and cultures that were 'locked' in the past – primitive and uncivilized peoples whose subjugation and 'introduction' into modernity became the right and obligation of European powers.

The concept of modernity is therefore significant in the emergence of **colonial discourse**. Modernity is fundamentally about conquest, 'the imperial regulation of land, the discipline of the soul, and the creation of truth' (Turner 1990: 4), a **discourse** that enabled the large-scale regulation of human identity both within Europe and its colonies. The emergence of modernity is co-terminous with the emergence of **Eurocentrism** and the European dominance of the world effected through imperial expansion. In other words, modernity emerged at about the same time that European nations began to conceive of their own dominant relationship to a non-European world and began to spread their rule through **exploration, cartography** and **colonization**. Europe constructed itself as 'modern' and constructed the non-European as 'traditional', 'static' and 'prehistorical'. The imposition of European models of historical change became the tool by which these societies were denied any internal dynamic or capacity for development.

Understanding modernity as a discourse rather than an epoch involves seeing it as characterized by major discontinuities separating modern social institutions from traditional social orders. Giddens identifies three: the pace of change, the scope of change and the nature of modern institutions. The advent of various technologies initiated an ever-accelerating pace of change, and the scope of this change came to affect the entire globe (Giddens 1990: 6). Many social forms and processes are not found in pre-modern societies: the nation-state, the dependence on inanimate power sources, the commodification of products and wage labour, formal schooling, the secularization of values and norms and the predominance of urban forms of life. These differences distinguish the modern from the pre-modern past, but also distinguish colonizing Europe from colonized cultures, thus becoming the source of profound misunderstanding and dislocation.

Apart from the distinctiveness of modern social institutions, and the many other reinforcing processes that accompany them, modernity can be characterized by developments in philosophical thought. The conception of modernity as a period that was superior to the past, buttressed as it was by the replacement of divine providence with the autonomous rational human mind, effectively ended the veneration of tradition and paved the way for the Enlightenment philosophical project of developing 'a rational organisation of everyday social life' (Habermas 1981: 9). In turn, of course, this characteristic of Enlightenment thought consolidated the assumption of European cultural authority as its influence spread throughout the world. Science and rationality were assumed to be the only possible course for modern consciousness, and modern (i.e. European) social institutions were then, and are still, regarded as creating 'vastly greater opportunities for human beings to enjoy a secure and rewarding existence than any type of pre-modern system' (Giddens 1990: 7).

Rationality became such a core feature of 'modern' thought that its origin as a specifically European mode of thinking was forgotten by the time Europe came to dominate the world in the nineteenth century. Modernity became synonymous with 'civilized' behaviour, and one more justification for the **civilizing mission** of European imperialism. Weber in particular regarded rationalization as a key component of modernization, but for him, it was also a key to its ambiguity. Modernization brings with it considerable possibilities: the erosion of univocal meaning, the endless conflict of polytheistic values, the threat of the confinement of bureaucracy. Rationalization makes the world orderly and reliable, but it cannot make the world meaningful. If Weber is correct, it would suggest that imperialism not only is a key aspect of the emergence of modernity and its connection with an aggressive European self-image, but also creates the cultural conditions for the (postcolonial) disruptions that modernity brings to European society.

Contemporary debate interrogates the relationship between modernity and post-modernity. Theorists such as Habermas see modernity as an unfinished project and the 'post-modern' as simply a stage of modernity, while others see the post-modern as a sign of the dissolution of modernity. Post-modernity may also be characterized as offering a different set of discontinuities from modernity. However, it would appear that the revolution in social organization and philosophical thought, and the geographical expansion that modernity entailed, still remains a fundamental constitutive feature of social life in contemporary times.

Further Reading: Ashcroft 2005; Barlow 2005; Bartolovich and Lazarus 2002; Burton 2003; Chakrabarty and Bhabha 2002; Comaroff and Comaroff 1993; J. Ferguson 2005; Friedman 2006; Gardiner 2001; George 2003; Giddens 1990; Gikandi 2000; Habermas 1981, 1987; Koundoura 2002; Lazarus 2002; Lloyd 2003; Mignolo 1995a, 1995b,

2001; Moore and Sanders 2001; Murray 1997a; Parry 2002, 2002a; Scott 1996; Turner 1990.

MULATTO

From the Spanish word for 'young mule' (1595), referring to the progeny of a European and a negro (OED). The term is sometimes used interchangeably with **mestizo/mestizaje/mesticos/métisse** to mean a mixed or miscegenated society and the culture it creates. However, its usage is usually confined to the classifications of miscegenation employed in **racist** slave discourse, specifically referring to a slave who is one-half white.

MULTICULTURALISM

This term refers to the characteristics of a society defined by cultural diversity rather than **cultural difference**, but it is more commonly used to refer to the policy or process whereby the distinctive identities of the cultural groups within such a society are maintained or supported. In a political context, the term has a wide variety of meanings, ranging from the advocacy of equal respect to the various cultures in a society, to a policy of promoting the maintenance of cultural diversity, to policies in which people of various ethnic and religious groups are addressed by the authorities as defined by the group to which they belong. A common aspect of many such policies is that they avoid presenting any specific ethnic, religious or cultural community values as central.

Multiculturalism has been a policy of most Western nations since the 1970s. While many states in Africa, Asia and the Americas are culturally diverse, multiculturalism as a government policy was initiated by those **settler colonies** whose populations have been largely composed of migrants. The Canadian government launched it as an official policy in 1971, followed by Australia in 1973. It was quickly adopted by most member states of the European Union and the United States in the 1980s, but criticisms of its effectiveness in integrating ethnically diverse peoples into the nation-state and open hostility to the policy in many right-wing politicians have seen a decline in its importance in Western governments.

While the policy has attracted strong criticism from conservatives, such as Australian historian Geoffrey Blainey, who asserted that it would transform Australia into a nation of tribes, the postcolonial critique of multiculturalism stems from its effects on the communal identity of diasporic and ethnically diverse peoples. As Rajeswari Mohan puts it in the case of the United States, 'Despite shifts in the ideological freight carried by the term, what remains constant is its connotation of "special interest" that supposedly weighs against an implied general interest' (Mohan 1995: 374). While the policy aims at a benign coexistence of cultures that interrelate with one another and yet remain distinct, in practice, it has effectively buttressed the dominant, mostly white, cultural group as the 'central' ethnicity of the multicultural mix, the norm against which other ethnicities are judged. The focus on ethnic 'minorities' operates as a *de facto* identification of the (white) 'majority' with the nation. For this reason, says Sneja Gunew, 'it has often been an embarrassing term to invoke partly because it is seen as automatically aligned with and hopelessly co-opted by the state in its role of certain kinds of conscious nation building'.

The postcolonial critique of multiculturalism coincides with that of **whiteness** studies. Henry Giroux (2002) argues that whiteness needs to be reinvented (once whites have begun to notice and take responsibility for their racial privilege). Otherwise, according to Giroux:

> whiteness as a marker of identity is confined within a notion of domination and racism that leaves white youth no social imaginary through which they can see themselves as actors in creating an oppositional space to fight for equality and social justice.
>
> (2002: 144)

The rise of Critical Whiteness Studies prompted the emergence of Critical Multiculturalism (McLaren 1994), which includes whiteness in the mix of ethnic diversity, alerts people to the inherent hybridity and diverse affiliations of all subjects and counters exclusionary hegemonic practices that stem from the implicit assumption of a white national ethnicity. Critical Multiculturalism therefore offers a more nuanced view of ethnic relations: 'references to "Anglo-Celts" in the work of multicultural theorists are not simply concerned with depicting historical continuities but are often attempts to highlight a language of representation dealing with inclusions and exclusion in the narratives of the nation' (Gunew 1997: 27).

The survival of the term multiculturalism depends therefore on a number of factors: the degree to which it incorporates the perspectives of **whiteness** studies, establishing whiteness as not only a visible factor in cultural diversity but also stressing the examination of issues of power relations between white and non-white ethnicities in a 'multicultural' society; the extent to which Critical Multiculturalism is developed, and, paradoxically, perhaps, the degree to which it fades as government policy.

Further Reading: Mohan 1995; Gunew 1997; Gunew 1994

MULTITUDE

This is the word used by Hardt and Negri to describe the location of the forces of liberation that are opposed to, but are themselves an integral part of **Empire**. The multitude, like Empire itself, is a concept that transcends geographical, historical and class boundaries, but in which the utopian hope of liberation is completely and optimistically focused. The reason for this is that the multitude is not simply an oppressed victim of Empire but is a part of Empire itself. The authors see Empire as composed of two phenomena, a juridical structure and 'the plural multitude of productive, creative subjectivities of globalization' (2001: 60). The significant thing about the multitude is that it is not merely negatively oppositional but is itself the source of new subjectivities that work towards the 'liberation of living labour'. The multitude exists in a constant ambivalent relationship with Empire. 'The de-territorializing power of the multitude is the productive force that sustains Empire and at the same time the force that calls for and makes necessary its destruction' (61). Another way of putting this is that the multitude, whose province is the local, is both the field of operation of globalization and the origin of its transformation and hence the agent of the potential destruction of Empire because Empire cannot exist without it.

Further Reading: Hardt and Negri (2001)

NATION LANGUAGE

Edward Kamau Brathwaite's term for culturally specific forms of Caribbean English. Brathwaite sees nation language as heavily influenced by the African heritage in Caribbean cultures, and contends that while the language used in, for instance, Jamaica, may be English in terms of its lexical features, 'in its contours, its rhythm and timbre, its sound explosions, it is not English, even though the words, as you hear them, might be English to a greater or lesser degree' (Brathwaite 1984: 311). Brathwaite suggests that this language is the result of a specific cultural experience when he says,

> it is an English which is not the standard, imported, educated English, but that of the submerged, surrealist experience and sensibility, which has always been there and which is now increasingly coming to the surface and influencing the perception of contemporary Caribbean people.
>
> (Brathwaite 1984: 311)

Brathwaite takes pains to distinguish nation language from 'dialect', which, he contends, is thought of as 'bad English', the kind of English used in caricature and parody. This is similar to the contention of a number of postcolonial linguists and theorists that all language is localized, heterogeneous and 'variant', and that the concept of a standard English is a construction of an imperial rhetoric that constantly separates 'centre' from 'margin'. Such a standard English is subverted by the nation language which 'is like a howl, or a shout or a machine-gun or the wind or a wave. It is also like the blues' (311). Nation language is first of all based on an **oral** tradition; the language is based as much on sound as it is on song, the noise it makes being part of the meaning. The communal nature of the language is thus important, 'the noise and sounds that the maker makes are responded to by the audience and are returned' (312). Nation language is thus a lived, dynamic and changing phenomenon, not merely a linguistic structure. It is something that people do, and the constitutive environment of language is as important as the utterance.

Further Reading: Brathwaite 1981, 1984.

NATION/NATIONALISM

The idea of the nation is now so firmly fixed in the general imagination, and the form of state it signifies so widely accepted, that it is hard to realize how recent its invention has been. In 1882, the French Orientalist Ernest Renan, addressing an audience at the Sorbonne in a lecture entitled 'What is a nation?', felt it necessary to remind his audience of the historical beginnings of the idea of a nation:

> Nations . . . are something fairly new in history. Antiquity was
> unfamiliar with them; Egypt, China and ancient Chaldea were in
> no way nations. They were flocks led by a Son of the Sun or by a
> Son of Heaven. Neither in Egypt nor in China were there citizens
> as such. Classical antiquity had republics, municipal kingdoms,
> confederations of local republics and empires, yet it can hardly be
> said to have had nations in our understanding of the term.
>
> (quoted in Bhabha 1990: 9)

Renan traces the emergence of the nation-state to the break-up of the
classic and mediaeval empires, locating its cultural provenance in a specifically European political and social environment. That nations were
and are profoundly unstable formations, always likely to collapse back
into sub-divisions of clan, 'tribe', language or religious group, is nothing
new, and the false tendency to assign this unstable condition to specific regions or conditions ('balkanization', 'the Third World', 'underdeveloped countries') is reflected in contemporary discussion of national
questions.

As thinkers as early as Renan were aware, nations are not 'natural'
entities, and the instability of the nation is the inevitable consequence
of its nature as a social construction. This myth of nationhood, masked
by ideology, perpetuates nationalism, in which specific identifiers are
employed to create exclusive and homogeneous conceptions of national
traditions. Such signifiers of homogeneity always fail to represent the
diversity of the actual 'national' community for which they purport to
speak, and, in practice, usually represent and consolidate the interests of
the dominant power groups within any national formation.

Constructions of the nation are thus potent sites of control and domination within modern society. This is further emphasized by the fact
that the myth of a 'national tradition' is employed not only to legitimize
a general idea of a social group ('a people') but also to construct a modern
idea of a nation-state, in which all the instrumentalities of state-power
(e.g. military and police agencies, judiciaries, religious hierarchies, educational systems and political assemblies or organizations) are subsumed
and legitimized as the 'natural' expressions of a unified national history
and culture (see **Ethnosymbolism**). Timothy Brennan comments on
this modern collapsing of the two concepts of nation and nation-state:

> As for the 'nation' it is both historically determined and general.
> As a term, it refers both to the modern nation-state and to some-
> thing more ancient and nebulous – the 'natio' – a local community,

domicile, family, condition of belonging. The distinction is often obscured by nationalists who seek to place their own country in an 'immemorial past' where its arbitrariness cannot be questioned.

(Bhabha 1990: 45)

The confusion of the idea of the nation with the practice and power of the nation-state makes nationalism one of the most powerful forces in contemporary society. It also makes it an extremely contentious site, on which ideas of self-determination and freedom, of identity and unity collide with ideas of suppression and force, of domination and exclusion. Yet for all its contentiousness, and the difficulty of theorizing it adequately, it remains the most implacably powerful force in twentieth-century politics. Its displacement has proved to be very difficult even within internationally oriented movements such as Marxism, at least in the Stalinist form in which it emerged in the Soviet Union and its client states. It is, perhaps, not insignificant that Stalin himself was an expert on the so-called Nationalities Question, and that he was one of the most ruthless advocates of the suppression of 'national differences', despite his own minority origins as a Georgian rather than a so-called Great Russian.

The complex and powerful operation of the idea of a nation can also be seen in the great twentieth-century phenomenon of global capitalism, where the 'free market' between nations, epitomized in the emergence of multinational companies, maintains a complex, problematic relationship with the idea of nations as natural and immutable formations based on shared collective values (see **globalization**). Modern nations such as the United States, with their multi-ethnic composition, require the acceptance of an overarching national ideology (*e* pluribus unum). But global capitalism also requires that the individual be free to act in an economic realm that crosses and nullifies these boundaries and identities. The tensions between these two impulses, increasing rapidly as modern communications make global contact a daily reality, are amongst the most important and as yet unresolved forces in the modern world.

Nations and nationalism are profoundly important in the formation of colonial practice. As Hobson puts it:

Colonialism, where it consists in the migration of part of a nation to vacant or sparsely peopled foreign lands, the emigrants carrying with them full rights of citizenship in the mother country . . . may be considered a genuine expansion of nationality.

(Hobson 1902: 6)

Hobson was explaining the economic emergence of late nineteenth-century **imperialism**, but the link between nation and expansion is much older – the emergence of the nation-state and the imperial-capitalist economies of post-Renaissance Europe being arguably inseparable. It is also arguable that without the provision of a greatly expanded source of supply for the dominant European standards of exchange (gold and silver) in the New World, the rapid development of long-distance trading ventures in the Renaissance period would not have occurred. Finally, this trade generated further demands for manufacture, and the raw materials for this expansion were supplied by the new economies of the colonized world, in the forms of plantations and mines which fuelled the industrialization of Europe.

This complex story which is here, of course, grossly simplified, became the basis for a narrative that acted to consolidate the interests of the new trading classes and which demanded new social formations that either integrated older forms (municipal kingdoms, city-states or city leagues) or developed new ones (oligarchic and radical republics) to represent the interests of the new trading classes whose wealth, derived from the distance trade with the colonies, replaced and challenged the power of the old feudal aristocracies. These new 'national' entities demanded a new national narrative, the 'Story of the Nation', which became disseminated through 'imagined communities' of speakers and listeners (or writers and readers) (Anderson 1983).

French Enlightenment thought heralded a shift in the theory of the 'nation', a shift that sought to relocate the legitimacy of the modern nation-state in a theory of the 'people' based on the idea of a universal set of principles (the 'Rights of Man') rather than on mythic and historical origins. In its strict form, the impulse to create such a universal vision is transnational and its revolutionary tendency to cross borders can be seen in the effects of Enlightenment thinking on many nations in Europe and in the Americas in the eighteenth century. Despite the conservative reaction that set in throughout Europe after Napoleon's defeat, and the various attempts to resurrect the traditional monarchies, the states that emerged were in various ways based upon a modern concept of 'state-power' rather than on the traditional ideas of inherited authority such as divine kingship. Even authoritarian regimes such as modern Prussia connected the idea of a dominant, traditional figure of authority ('king' or 'emperor') to a modern and highly efficient state bureaucracy and to the empowerment, through this bureaucracy, of the interests of the state conceived as an abstraction rather than as a personal fiefdom.

Conversely, in the France of the Second and Third Republics, the idea of a popular will was increasingly tied, not to a declaration of the struggle for universal human rights, but to a national vision of power and world expansion. Although, as Renan had noted, nations emerged only after the classical and mediaeval idea of an imperium (empire) had broken down, it was, ironically, the newly emergent nations of the post-Renaissance world that initiated the new, colonizing form of nineteenth-century imperialism. **Imperialism** now became an extension into the wider world of the ideology of a 'national' formation based on the unifying signifiers of language and race.

Significantly, the rump of the last of the mediaeval imperialisms, that of the Austro-Hungarian fragment of the erstwhile Holy Roman Empire, proceeded in the opposite direction, as it was increasingly assaulted from within by the demands of those who wished to develop political entities based upon racially and linguistically defined nationalities. On the other hand, the imperialisms of the second-half of the nineteenth century were expressions of the need to generate unifying cohesive myths within the complex and heterogeneous realities of the late nineteenth-century nation-states (such as England, France, Germany [Prussia], Russia, etc.) to prevent the re-emergence of older divisions based on earlier conceptions of the nation or to resist the emergence of new internal divisive forces based on theories of class. These were absolutely dependent on the expansionist vision which saw the home 'nation' as the centre of a larger formation and which defined itself specifically in opposition to the difference which that 'other' represented. In this sense, as Timothy Brennan has expressed it:

> Even though [nationalism] as an ideology . . . came out of the imperialist countries, these countries were not able to formulate their own national aspirations until the age of exploration. The markets made possible by European imperial penetration motivated the construction of the nation-state at home. European nationalism was motivated by what Europe was doing in its far-flung dominions. The 'national idea', in other words, flourished in the soil of foreign conquest.
>
> (Bhabha 1990: 59)

During the late imperial period, the dominance of the idea of the nation was such that it was largely in terms of a resistant nationalism that the anti-colonial movements of the late nineteenth and early twentieth centuries came into being, even though it was that force of nationalism that had fuelled the growth of **colonialism** in the first place. **Anti-colonial** movements employed the idea of a precolonial past to rally their opposition through a sense of difference, but they employed this past not to reconstruct the precolonial social state but to generate support for the construction of postcolonial nation-states based upon the European nationalist model. Just as the modern European nation-states had come into being in the wake of the break-up of the old imperial forms of the classical and mediaeval world, so the colonial empires these modern nations had constructed were now subject to a similar internal resistance and a demand for separation based on the construction of national entities and nationalist cultural constructions.

This is not just an ironic fact, it also suggests that the bases of the **postcolonial state** were themselves far less radical than their early exponents believed, and the degree to which they incorporated models and institutions based on the European concept of a nation created the continuing linkages that allowed the **neo-colonialist** control of these states to operate so effectively. Few commentators have been prepared to argue that this process was a mistake, though Basil Davidson has done so in the case of Africa (1992). However, the use of nationalist myths and sentiments to control, suppress and discriminate against minority groups within many postcolonial states has been the subject of much recent comment, as these groups claim their distinctive place and argue for a greater tolerance and acceptance of cultural diversity.

The role of limited and biased versions of the past masquerading as national tradition has been attacked by many groups, including those who see these 'national traditions' as limited in various ways by gender, religion or ethnicity. In practice, it is hard to see how the nation can cease to be employed as a definitive political entity within which these internal heterogeneities and differences can be resolved. Perhaps the issue is not whether we have nations but what kinds of nations we have, whether, that is, they insist on an exclusionary myth of national unity based in some abstraction such as race, religion or ethnic exclusivity, or they embrace plurality and multiculturalism.

Further Reading: Anderson 1983; Basch 1994; Bhabha 1990; Blaut 1987; Boehmer 1991; Brennan 1989; Burton 2003; Chatterjee 1986, 1993; Cheah 2003; Chrisman 2002, 2004; Cooppan 1999; Davidson 1992; Franco 1997; Gikandi 2006; Hawley 1996; Hobsbawm 1990; Lazarus 1994, 1999; Leonard 2005; McClintock et al. 1997; Murray 1997;

Paranjape 1998; Parker et al. 1992; Perera 1998; Puri 2004; Ray 2000; Reiss 2004; San Juan 1996; Sivanandan 2004; Szeman 2003; Young 1998.

NATIONAL ALLEGORY

A term given some notoriety by Frederic Jameson in his essay 'Third World literature in an era of multinational capitalism'. Jameson argued that:

> What all third-world cultural productions have in common, and what distinguishes them radically from analogous cultural forms in the first world [is that] all third-world texts are necessarily . . . allegorical, and in a very specific way: they are to be read as what I will call national allegories, even when, or I should say particularly when, their forms develop out of predominantly western machineries of representation, such as the novel.
>
> (Jameson 1986: 67)

The reason for this, according to Jameson, is that capitalism has not yet split the private experience from the public sphere as it has in developed countries. Consequently, the 'story of the private individual destiny is always an allegory of the embattled structure of the public . . . culture and society' (67).

The sweeping nature of this claim drew strong criticism from Aijaz Ahmad who saw in it a totalizing and universalizing tendency that failed to take into account the specificity of **Third World** cultures. But while Jameson admits this claim is sweeping, he denies that it is totalizing. Rather, he insists that his thesis is an attempt to intervene in the dominance of First World criticism, an attempt to take on board relational ways of thinking about global culture and to give some exposure to the culturally diverse ways in which literary and cultural forms have been appropriated. Whatever the merits of Jameson's claim that private experience is represented as allegorical of the public and national destiny, it has aroused considerable discussion regarding the nature of post-colonial allegory, the construction of three worlds and a questioning of the importance given to the nation over other social formations in the experience of Third World cultures.

Further Reading: Ahmad 1992, 1995a; Beverley 2003; Buchanan 2003; Jameson 1986; San Juan 1996; Schmidt 2000; Szeman 2001.

NATIONAL LIBERATION MOVEMENTS

A series of movements that emerged in **Third World** countries in the 1960s which put into practice the Leninist doctrine that nationalism could be a progressive force for revolutionary change within colonized or neo-colonized societies. Although nationalism had been exposed by Marxist theory as a bourgeois social formation that masked capitalism, its necessity as a stage in the freeing of the world's workers had been recognized by Lenin as early as the First Party Congress in 1919. By the time of the Second Party Congress in 1920, Lenin enjoined every Communist party to

> demand the expulsion of their own imperialists from these colonies, to inculcate among the workers of their country a genuinely fraternal attitude to the working people of the colonies and the oppressed nations, and to carry on a systematic agitation among the troops of their country against any oppression of the colonial peoples.
>
> (Connor 1984: 56).

As a specialist on the 'nationalities question', Stalin had initiated a policy of brutally suppressing similarly counter-revolutionary nationalist aspirations in the Soviet Union's own satellite territories. However, with the emergence of the external threat posed by fascism in the 1930s, he formulated a new ideological blend of the working class, the nation and the state in a call for a united national resistance to the threat of a fascist invasion. After the war, the Comintern continued to lend active support to a number of radical nationalist movements in locations across the world, ranging from Vietnam to Algeria. It distinguished these movements from classic bourgeois nationalism by the use of the term 'National Liberation Movements'. Led by local, Marxist-oriented intellectuals, these movements were epitomized by icons, such as Ché Guevara, the Argentinian revolutionary companion of Cuban revolutionary Fidel Castro. Elsewhere, a series of significant nationalist leaders publicly embraced the aspirations of the National Liberation Movements to create free but revolutionary societies in the postcolonial world, for example, Sekou Touré and Kwame Nkrumah in Africa and Ho Chi Minh in Vietnam. The movement also attracted some of the more significant intellectual figures to emerge in the **anti-colonial** struggles of the period, such as Frantz Fanon in Algeria, Amilcar Cabral in Guinea-Bissau and Agostino Nero in Mozambique (see **Fanonism**).

Further Reading: Alegría 1981; N. Alexander 1990; Amuta 1995; Balcárcel 1981; Blaut 1987; Connor 1984; Fanon 1959, 1964; Harlow 1987; Maolain 1985; Miller and Aya 1971; Moran 2006; Premnath 2002; San Juan 1991, 1991a; Sivanandan 2004; Thayer 1989.

NATIVE

The use of the term 'native' to describe the indigenous inhabitants of colonies has a long and chequered history. The root sense of the term as those who were 'born to the land' was, in colonialist contexts, over-taken by a pejorative usage in which the term 'native' was employed to categorize those who were regarded as inferior to the colonial settlers or the colonial administrators who ruled the colonies. 'Native' quickly became associated with such pejorative concepts as **savage**, uncivilized or child-like in class nouns such as 'the natives'.

The idea that 'the natives' were members of a less developed culture that required colonial nurture to bring it to modernity and/or civiliza-tion permeated **colonial discourse**. In cases where the 'native' cultures were based on entirely different models, such as the hunter-gatherer cultures of some **settler colonies**, or cultures that did not share the signifiers of the European model of civilization, such as writing, stone-buildings or industrial technology, the idea of the 'native' became part of a Darwinian characterization of the culture as 'primitive' or 'Stone Age'. Colonialist texts are replete with these kinds of characterizations of cultures as diverse as those of the Australian Aboriginal peoples, the New Zealand Maori, the Native American peoples of Canada and the many cultures of Africa or the South Pacific region whose complex and highly developed social and artistic forms were either not visible to the imperial gaze or were (and sometimes still are) deliberately obscured by such pejorative labelling.

Where cultures existed that clearly had, in European eyes, attained a high level of 'civilization', such as India and the South-East Asian region, the colonialist practice was to construe these as civilizations 'in decay', as manifestations of degenerate societies and races in need of rescue and rehabilitation by a 'civilized' Europe. Evidence of this social and moral degeneracy was perceived by the colonizers' obsessive focus on particular practices, such as sati or widow-burning, thuggee and ritual murder in India; or the supposedly characteristic forms of moral degeneracy on the part of specific races, evidenced in popular European representations of Malays 'running amok' in orgies of unmotivated violence.

The fear of contamination that is at the heart of colonialist discourse, and which results in the menacing ambivalence of **mimicry** or the obsessive colonialist fear of **miscegenation**, is often expressed through a fear amongst the colonizers of **going native**, that is, losing their distinctiveness and superior identity by contamination from native practices. The complexities of this can be seen in a text like Rudyard Kipling's 'Kim' where Kim, an Indian-born English boy, is clearly distinguished from the native-born Indians in a discourse of racial superiority even though the text claims that his indigenous status gives him a special and superior insight into the culture and attitudes of Indians. In fact, for Kipling, the combination of racial superiority and local knowledge constructs an image of the ideal ruling figure for the colonial world in which being native-born can be achieved without the fear of racial contamination.

Further Reading: Torgovnick 1990; Morgan 2016

NATIVISM

A term for the desire to return to indigenous practices and cultural forms as they existed in precolonial society. The term is most frequently encountered to refer to the rhetoric of **decolonization** which argues that **colonialism** needs to be replaced by the recovery and promotion of precolonial, indigenous ways. The debate as to how far such a return or reconstruction is possible (or even desirable) has been a very vigorous one. Colonial discourse theorists such as Spivak and Bhabha argue strongly that such nativist reconstructions are inevitably subject to the processes of cultural intermixing that colonialism promoted and from which no simple retreat is possible. Spivak has more recently defended the use by postcolonial societies of a 'strategic' essentialism whereby the signifiers of indigenous (native) cultures are privileged in a process of negative discrimination. Such a strategy may allow these societies to better resist the onslaught of global culture that threatens to negate **cultural difference** or consign it to an apolitical and exotic discourse of **cultural diversity**. An even more positive defence of the nativist position has been mounted recently by Benita Parry (1994).

On the other hand, the multicultural nature of most postcolonial societies makes the issue of what constitutes the precolonial 'native' culture obviously problematic, especially where the current postcolonial nation-state defines itself in terms that favour a single dominant cultural group. Minority voices from such societies have argued that 'nativist' projects can militate against the recognition that colonial policies of transplantation such as **slavery** and **indenture** have resulted in racially mixed diasporic societies, where only a multicultural model of the post-colonial state can avoid bias and injustice to the descendants of such groups. Minorities from these areas have thus argued against the idea that the postcolonial oppressed form a homogeneous group who can be decolonized and liberated by a nativist recovery of a precolonial culture.

The assumption of a homogeneous, unitary concept of the state is also challenged by the historical and cultural legacies of colonialism in the form of large and long-established **diasporic** communities in many multiracial postcolonial states, such as Malaysia, Singapore and Fiji, and in the Caribbean, where the present racial mixture is profound and virtually every group is in one sense or another the product of a cultural diaspora, rather than being native or **indigenous** in origin. Models of culture and nationality that privilege one geographical or racial originary sign (e.g. Africa or blackness) have similar problems in addressing the diverse and often **creolized** nature of the population.

Even within less diverse states, minority religious and linguistic groups have faced similar difficulties with the simpler nativist projects of recuperation. The reconstruction of traditions based on supposed nativist models that enshrine a male, patriarchal vision of the precolonial, indi-genous culture as **authentic** has necessarily aroused the resistance of women. For women, models of the traditional past have been seen as the product of present-day male practices which read the past through a biased sexist vision, and which are then used by a ruling élite to deny women their right to participate fully in the social model proposed (see Mba 1982; Stratton 1994) (see also **feminism and postcolonialism**). In practice, simple models of nativism, like simple models of **decolon-ization**, have raised as many issues as they have resolved.

Further Reading: Baber 2002; Mamdani 2001; Michaels 1995; Mosley 1995; Parry 1994; Rodrigues 2004; Singer 2002.

NECROPOLITICS

This term was developed by the Cameroonian theorist Achille Mbembe in his 2003 article Necropolitics in the journal *Public Culture* (Mbembe 2003) and expanded and further developed in the book of the same name published in 2019 (Mbembe 2019). Briefly, the term argues that the power to determine who will live and who will die is the basis of sovereignty. In his discussion of the term, Mbembe acknowledges its descent from the Foucaultian idea of **biopolitics.**

> To kill or to let live thus constitutes sovereignty's limits, its principal attribute. To be sovereign is to exert one's control over mortality and to define life as the deployment and manifestation of power. This sums up what Michel Foucault meant by **biopower**: that domain of life over which power has asserted its control.
>
> (Mbembe 2019: 66)

Mbembe also argues that in most societies past and present, certain people or groups of peoples exist in a state of exception. They are set aside from the idea of the accepted or normative, those who exercise sovereignty.

A similar idea can be seen in Ghassan Hage's idea of the governmentally empowered, referencing those who are seen to constitute the body of people whose cultural imaginary constitutes the normal and those who are set outside this, for example migrants or gender or religiously discriminated people (Hage 2002). But Mbembe's state of exception envisages a much more violent and radical displacement. Slavery, he speculates, may be a part of most societies, past and present, however reconfigured and disguised. Totalitarian regimes such as those of Nazi Germany and its death camps may stand as "the central metaphor for sovereign and destructive violence and as the ultimate sign of the absolute power of the negative" (Mbembe 2019: 67). But the exercise of violence and death as an instrument of power takes many forms and is especially prevalent in societies where colonization has created a ruling élite whose values replicate and maintain the inequalities and violence of the colonial period (see **Decoloniality; Slow Violence**).

Arguing that Western concepts of modernity that emphasize the basis of law and politics as founded on post-Enlightenment ideals of reason and democracy may have created a fixed idea of sovereignty as

> the production of general norms by a body (the demos) comprising free and equal individuals. These individuals are posited as full subjects capable of self-understanding, self-consciousness and self-representation . . . within this paradigm, reason is the truth of the subject and politics is the exercise of reason in the public sphere.
>
> (Mbembe 2019; 67)

But as Mbembe has argued throughout his body of work those who exercise sovereign power in the **postcolony** do so through the exercise of the power to determine who shall live or who shall die either directly by judicial and extra-judicial violence or through the limitation of the right to food, medicine and other life necessities (Mbembe 2001; Wilson et al. 2023).

In developing his idea of necropolitics "[Mbembe's] concern is those figures of sovereignty whose central project is not the struggle for autonomy but *the generalized instrumentalization of human existence and the material destruction of human bodies and populations*" (Original italics) (Mbembe 2019: 68).

Further Reading: Mbembe 2019, 2001, 2003; Hage 2000; Brennan 2024; Wilson et al. 2023.

NÉGRITUDE

A theory of the distinctiveness of African personality and culture. African Francophone writers such as Leopold Sédar Senghor and Birago Diop, and West Indian colleagues such as Aimé Césaire, developed the theory of négritude in Paris in the period immediately before and after the Second World War. These African and Caribbean intellectuals had been recruited under the French colonial policy of **assimilation** to study at the metropolitan French universities. The fact that they came from diverse colonies and that they were also exposed in Paris to influences from African American movements, such as the Harlem Renaissance, may have influenced them in developing a general theory of negro people that sought to extend the perception of a unified negro 'race' to a concept of a specifically 'African personality' (see **Black Atlantic**).

The négritudinist critics drew the attention of fashionable European intellectuals such as Jean Paul Sartre, who wrote an introduction, entitled 'Black Orpheus', to the first anthology of black African writing published in France, the *Anthologie de la nouvelle poésie négre et malgache de langue française* (1948). These critics insisted that African cultures and the literatures they produced had aesthetic and critical standards of their own, and needed to be judged in the light of their differences and their specific concerns rather than as a mere offspring of the parental European cultures.

The establishment of the critical magazine *Présence Africaine*, founded by Alioune Diop in Paris in 1947, had initiated a new critical interest in the French language writing of Africa and the Caribbean, and this important magazine became the vehicle for a number of crucial critical statements over the next 20 years or so, including Cheik Anta Diop's influential essay 'Nations, négres et culture' and Jacques Stephen Alexis 'Of the magical realism of the Haitians' (see **magic realism**). With the decision in 1957 that future publications would be in French and English, *Présence Africaine* also became an important location for critical consideration of African writing in English (Mudimbe 1994). Négritude, and the work it developed, took as its territory not only Africa but the whole of **diasporic** African culture, since, as Senghor defined it, négritude encompassed 'the sum total of the values of the civilization of the African world' (Reed and Wake 1965: 99). For this reason, it was the earliest and most important movement in establishing a wider awareness of Africa's claim to cultural distinctiveness.

The concept of 'négritude' implied that all people of negro descent shared certain inalienable essential characteristics. In this respect, the movement was, like those of earlier race-based assertions of African dignity by such negro activists as Edward Wilmot Blyden, Alexander Crummell, W.E.B. Du Bois and Marcus Garvey, both **essentialist** and **nativist**. What made the négritude movement distinct was its attempt to extend perceptions of the negro as possessing a distinctive 'personality' into all spheres of life, intellectual, emotional and physical.

Further Reading: Ahluwalia 2001; Bernasconi 2002; Haddour 2005; Irele 2003; Jack 1996; Kemedjio 1999; Kennedy 1975; Mosley 1995; Munro 2004; Nkosi 2005; Senghor 1964; Wise 1995.

NEO-COLONIALISM/NEO-IMPERIALISM

Neo-colonialism meaning 'new colonialism' was a term coined by Kwame Nkrumah, the first President of Ghana, and the leading exponent of pan-Africanism in his *Neo-Colonialism: The Last Stage of Imperialism* (1965). This title, which echoed Lenin's definition of **imperialism** as the last stage of capitalism, suggested that, although countries like Ghana had achieved political independence, the ex-colonial powers and the newly emerging superpowers such as the United States continued to play a decisive role in their cultures and economies through new instruments of indirect control, such as international monetary bodies, through the power of multinational corporations and cartels which artificially fixed prices in world markets, and through a variety of other educational and cultural non-governmental organizations (NGOs). In fact, Nkrumah argued that neo-colonialism was more insidious and more difficult to detect and resist than the direct control exercised by classic colonialism.

The term has since been widely used to refer to any and all forms of control of the ex-colonies after political independence. Thus, for example, it has been argued by some that the new élites brought to power by independence, and often educated and trained by the colonialist powers, were unrepresentative of the people and acted as unwitting or even willing agents (**compradors**) for the former colonial rulers. In a wider sense, the term has come to signify the inability of developing economies, the erstwhile so-called **Third World** economies to develop an independent economic and political identity under the pressures of **globalization**. Recently, the term has been associated less with the influence of the former colonial powers and more with the role of the new superpower of the United States, whose expansionist policy past and present, it is argued, constitutes a new form of imperialism. In the same immediate post-Second World War period and through the use of different institutions, such as Comintern and its economic wing, Comecon, as well as through loan organizations such as the International Bank for Economic Cooperation, it has been argued that the role of the erstwhile Soviet Union in the period of the 'Cold War' mirrored the role of the United States, with aid and development programmes from both sides having many political strings attached, despite the claims of the Soviet Union at the time to be the leading supporter of the many **National Liberation** movements as these contesting powers extended their struggle into the rest of the world. China also participated in this process, as witness its role in parts of Africa in the period from the 1960s onwards. In many ways, this process mirrored the way in which imperialist powers in the eighteenth and nineteenth centuries had also extended their struggle into the new regions opened up by colonial expansion.

Recently, with the demise of the Soviet Union and the rise of capitalism in China (see **Chimerican Age**), the United States (the nation-state most directly associated with **neo-liberal** capitalism) has become the primary concern of those who see globalization as continuing older forms of imperial control. Just as these theorists (Hardt and Negri 2001) have used the term **empire** to distinguish this new force from the classic **imperialism** of the era of direct colonization, so the term **neo-imperialism** has increasingly been used instead of **neo-colonialism** in a number of places, especially in material on the world wide web, to distinguish the ongoing control exercised over developing countries by a globalized capitalist economy often epitomized by the United States from earlier **neo-colonialism**. Although, of course, the main instruments of both were formed under the auspices of the United States after the end of the Second World War and in the aftermath of the Bretton Woods Conference in 1944 (see also **World System Theory**). The distinction draws attention to important shifts in the operation of global capital, but it should not be overlooked that many of the ways in which the new **empire** functions are directly analogous with operations in the era of classic imperialism, though the instruments may differ. Thus, for example, the role of modern NGOs, such as the World Bank, the International Monetary Fund, and especially non-governmental international aid and development organizations, such as UNESCO operate in areas of concern and through practices very analogous to organizations in the colonial period, such as missions. In fact, it is arguable that missions and missionaries were the NGOs of their time. In the case of cultural organizations, such as UNESCO, supporters have argued that the many benefits it brings may have been overlooked in the more radical objections to these global developments. In both cases, the story is probably more complex than is sometimes recognized, with such organizations having both positive and negative impacts (see **missions and colonialism**). Though it must be conceded that the claims of such NGOs then and now to be acting independently of the existing global superpowers may also seem increasingly naive. The negative view of these established international organizations has in recent times led to the setting up of counter organizations which have sought to speak for these more radical voices, notably the World Social Forum. Its charter claims that it represents

. . . an open meeting place for reflective thinking, democratic debate of ideas, formulation of proposals, free exchange of experiences and interlinking for effective action, by groups and movements of civil society that are opposed to **neo-liberalism** and to domination of the world by capital and any form of imperialism, and are committed to building a planetary society directed towards fruitful relationships among mankind and between it and the Earth.

Its emergence may be viewed as a reaction by radical forces to the collapse of the earlier formal opposition from anti-capitalist states, such as Russia and China in recent times, though it represents broader forces than the equivalent groups forged in the ideological conflicts of the post-war period, including environmentalists and human rights activists.

Further Reading: Benjamin 2007; Denning 2004; French 2005; Gowda 1983; Nkrumah 1965; Pomeroy 1970; Rajen 1997; Saini 1981; Sen and Marcuzzo 2018; Spivak 1999; B. Smith 1992; Ngugi 1983; Woddis 1967.

NEO-EUROPES

This term, which was used by Alfred W. Crosby in his pioneering study of imperial ecology, was the term he used for the settler colonies that were established in regions where settlers quickly outstripped in numbers the indigenous inhabitants (Crosby 1985). As he argued, that occurred as the result of what he termed the despoliation of the newly conquered lands through disease, the destruction of native flora and fauna, the felling of forests and land clearance and the introduction of grazing animals and 'pest' species that overwhelmed or even extinguished native animal and plant species.

For Crosby, what was notable about these neo-Europes was that they were scattered across the world, often many thousands of kilometres from Old Europe, though virtually all are located within the temperate zones north or south of the equator, such as Canada, the United States, Australia, Argentina, Uruguay and New Zealand. The climate in these regions, as Crosby notes, favoured the growth of European staples, such as grains, and the grazing necessary to raise cattle and sheep in large numbers. They are characterized too, he suggests, by the fact that they regularly produce food surpluses which they export. They are populated by between 80% and 90% European descended inhabitants, though that percentage is declining in the years since Crosby made this assertion in 1985. Their biogeographical advantages made them both wealthy and powerful. But erosion, over farming, and climate change may and have made these advantages diminish over recent decades, as witness the decline of nations in this category such as Argentina (see **Ecological Imperialism, Environmentalism**).

NEO-LIBERALISM

A term that refers to the theory and practice of an unfettered liberalization of market forces, sometimes regarded as synonymous with economic **globalization** or 'late capitalism'. Its major exponents over the last 50 years have been the International Monetary Fund (IMF) and World Bank, but it has deep philosophical roots in historical liberalism

and is a key feature of the **Washington Consensus**. It is significant for postcolonial studies because it has become the most obvious
medium of **neo-colonial/neo-imperial** domination and of economic
globalization.

Liberalism as a coherent social philosophy dates from the late
eighteenth century. At first, there was no distinction between political and economic liberalism, and classic liberal political philosophy
continued to develop after 1900 as pure conservative. Economic liberalization has always advocated the unrestrained operation of the market:
free trade, absence of state intervention, or of any outside interference,
and the reliance on the processes of the market to create profit. Maynard
Keynes' *General Theory*, published in the 1930s was revolutionary in its
advocacy of state intervention and served to better explain the economy
at that time, but philosophy of the totally free market reasserted itself
very quickly – in an extreme form – with Milton Friedman's monetarist
principles. This belief in the free operation of market forces has become,
in neo-liberalism, an end in itself, quite detached from the actual production of goods and services.

The term is of interest to postcolonial studies because economic liberalism has its origins in Adam Smith, whose view of the role of commodities in distinguishing the 'civilized' from the 'barbarous' is deeply
embedded in the ideology of empire. For him, the social body is a body
composed of things, a web of commodities circulating in an exchange
that connects people who do not see or know each other. These things
make it a 'civilized' body. Having an abundance of 'objects of comfort'
is the litmus test that distinguishes 'civilized and thriving nations' from
'savage' ones, 'so miserably poor' they are reduced to 'mere want' (1776:
lx). It is trade that has caused certain parts of the world to progress,
leaving others (such as Africa) in a 'barbarous and uncivilized state'. The
unfettered flow of goods, and the free operation of the market, is thus
attached, subtly but unshakably, to the idea of the '**civilizing mission**'
of empire.

This belief that the free market will lead to the greater happiness
of all remains the dominant myth of neo-liberal philosophy in the
'neo-colonial' operation of late capitalism. Free trade has been the economic policy of choice for the British and US empires because free
trade invariably favours the richest – those with most to trade. Arguably,
economic liberalization is a consequence of the rising dominance of the
British Empire, which went to war to maintain 'open markets'. Such
'open markets' had a catastrophic effect on the Indian textile industry
and led to the Opium Wars with China.

The major features of economic liberalism remain the foundations of neo-liberal economics, but the rapidity and scale of the intensification of these principles characterizes the contemporary version. In general, neo-liberal economic philosophy is to intensify and expand the market by increasing the number, frequency, repeatability and formalization of transactions. Clearly neo-liberal economic policies have become indistinguishable from economic globalization (which may nevertheless be distinguished from cultural, political and intellectual globalizations).

Ultimately, neo-liberalism is a philosophy in which the existence and operation of 'the market' are valued in themselves, quite apart from the production of goods and services. Consequently it can be seen, in its most extreme manifestations, to be a form of economic fundamentalism in which the operation of the market is an ethic in itself, capable of acting as a guide for all human action. Hence such statements as those of British Prime Minister Margaret Thatcher that 'there is no such thing as Society', and 'there is no alternative'. The market becomes the fundamental and universal truth in terms of which all human action – political, social, economic and ultimately ethical – may be viewed.

Further Reading: Harvey 2005; Scholte 2005; Hadiz 2006; Goodman and James 2007; Cahill 2017

NEW LITERATURES

A term used as an alternative to 'Commonwealth Literature' and later 'Postcolonial Literatures', especially during the late 1970s and 1980s.

'New Literatures' stressed the emergent nature of work from postcolonized societies and connoted freshness and difference. It also avoided problems with the term 'Commonwealth', which had been criticized as glossing historical and persisting power inequalities between colonizers and the colonized.

It is still sometimes used as a synonym for the term 'postcolonial', but has been employed much less frequently since the 1990s. This is in part because of a sense expressed by some critics that the term has paternalistic overtones and fails to ground cultural production in the history and legacies of the colonial encounter. Its major disadvantage, however, is that many of the cultures to which it refers (such as those in India) have literary traditions far older than British literature itself. To avoid this problem, the term is generally used in the phrase 'New Literatures in English'. This is to emphasize the fact that it refers only to writing produced in English and not to writing available in classical languages like Sanskrit or in any of India's other languages. Arguably, this itself is problematic since it suggests that such writing exists in isolation from contemporary writing in the indigenous languages, or from the ongoing influence of oral practices. Interestingly, despite such problems, the term continues to be used outside of Europe for a variety of different reasons. Some critics, for instance, regard it as an 'emancipatory concept', and the African writer Ben Okri, distancing himself from the implication of 'coming after' in postcolonialism, declares a preference for 'new' as 'literatures of the newly ascendant spirit' (Boehmer 1995: 4).

Further Reading: Boehmer 1995; Davis and Maes-Jelinek 1990; Gérard 1990; Gurnah 2000; Jurak 1992; King 1980, 1996; Lim 2002; McLaren 1993; Nasta 2000; Nightingale 1986; Rutherford, Holst Petersen and Maes-Jelinek 1992; Tiffin 1995; Walder 2000.

ORALITY

Postcolonial cultures have all, in various ways, been influenced by the interrelationship between orality and literacy. This is obvious, for example, in societies where oral culture predominated in the precolonial period, as in the case of some African societies, and in the indigenous cultures of all settler societies. In some parts of Africa, precolonial soci-eties also had highly developed literary cultures in Arabic or employed the imported Arabic script to create the so-called ajami literatures in their own languages, and these had already led to complex interactions between written and oral cultural forms in these areas.

In the case of India, for example, where many highly developed precolonial literary cultures flourished, there were also vibrant oral folk cultures that remained a vigorous part of popular culture and interacted with the literary traditions. Interactions between both literary sources and oral traditions are a marked feature of the so-called bhasa literatures of South Asia. (See Devy 1992). In the West Indies, the presence of the cultures of the **slaves** and indentured labourers, transported there in their millions throughout the eighteenth and nineteenth centuries, was preserved largely in oral form. It was to this popular oral tradition that West Indian intellectuals looked in seeking both to recover fragmented African heritages and to discover a **nation language** for their region.

Postcolonial cultural studies have led to a general re-evaluation of the importance of orality and oral cultures and a recognition that the dominance of the written in the construction of ideas of civilization is itself a partial view of more complex cultural practices. Even highly literate cultures have vigorous popular oral cultures, as the discipline of cultural studies has convincingly demonstrated. In postcolonial societies, the dominance of writing in perpetuating European cultural assumptions and Eurocentric notions of civilization, as well as the view of writing as the vehicle of authority and truth, led to an undervaluing of oral culture, and the assumption that orality was a precondition for postcolonial writing, which subsequently subsumed it. Both of these misperceptions are being rapidly redressed in postcolonial theory.

The dominance of anthropological texts in the recording of 'oral' forms was part of this process of undervaluing, helping to convey the impression that the oral was not as socially or aesthetically valuable as the literary. In classic anthropology, orality was often designated as 'traditional' in a discourse that opposed it to the **modern**, and it was assumed to be both of the past and immutable. The practice of transcription also involved fixing the forms of the oral in ways inimical to its essentially performative mode, although recent anthropological accounts have sought to address and redress both of these limitations. In an attempt to combat this limited perception of oral 'texts' as social documents rather than complex aesthetic constructs, alternative terms were coined, such as 'orature', which sought to suggest that verbal and performative arts were as aesthetically rich and complex as written literature. But of course it can be argued that this very binary failed to dismantle the dependency model involved in the relationship between the two terms. The result was to denigrate the continuation and validity of orality into the present time and to deny its continuing significance in contemporary postcolonial cultures.

Some studies (Barber and de Moraes-Farias 1989; Hofmeyer 1993) have stressed the fact that oral and literary cultures in colonial and postcolonial societies existed within unified social situations and were mutually interactive. Rather than being restricted to the past and therefore inferior to the written, oral forms in African societies, for instance, have a continuing and equal relationship with the written. This therefore challenges the simplistic and culture-specific assumption of post-structuralist critics such as Derrida that the written has precedence over the oral (logo-centrism).

The present continuity and vigour of orality in postcolonial societies is demonstrated in the example of the West Indies, where the emergence of a vigorous postcolonial culture is as much the result of figures like reggae performer Bob Marley, 'dub' street poet Michael Smith and the women storytellers and performers of the Sistren Collective, as of writers like Walcott, Harris, Brathwaite or Brodber. In South Africa, oral forms such as 'praise songs' have been adopted by such modern, European institutions as trade unions (for rallies) and have developed some of the formal and social aspects of literary texts and practices (see Gunner and Gwala 1991). In such cases, not only is the work of the written culture increasingly modified by the existence of popular oral forms, but the oral cultures are themselves transformed by their ongoing interaction with the written cultures of the modern period.

Further Reading: Adam 1996; Barber and de Moraes-Farias 1989; Casas 1998; Devy 1992; Gilroy 1993; Gunner and Gwala 1991; Gunner 1994; Gunner and Furniss 1995; Hofmeyer 1993; Hofmeyer 2004; Ong 1982; Swearingen 2004; Talib 2002; Zambare 2003; Leonie et al. 2022.

ORIENTALISM

This is the term popularized by Edward Said's *Orientalism*, in which he examines the processes by which the 'Orient' was, and continues to be, constructed in European thinking. Professional Orientalists included scholars in various disciplines, such as languages, history and philology, but for Said, the discourse of Orientalism was much more widespread and endemic in European thought. As well as a form of academic discourse, it was a style of thought based on 'the ontological and epistemological distinction between the "Orient" and the "Occident"' (Said 1978: 1). But, most broadly, Said discusses Orientalism as the corporate institution for dealing with the Orient 'dealing with it by making statements about it, authorizing views of it, describing it, by teaching it, settling it, ruling over it: in short, Orientalism as a Western style for dominating, restructuring, and having authority over the Orient' (3). In this sense, it is a classic example of Foucault's definition of a discourse.

The significance of Orientalism is that as a mode of knowing the other, it was a supreme example of power over the other. The Orient is not an inert fact of nature, but a phenomenon constructed by generations of intellectuals, artists, commentators, writers and politicians, and, more importantly, constructed by the naturalizing of a wide range of Orientalist assumptions and stereotypes. The relationship between the Occident and the Orient is a relationship of power, of domination, of varying degrees of a complex hegemony. Consequently, Orientalist discourse, for Said, is more valuable as a sign of the power exerted by the West over the Orient than a 'true' discourse about the Orient. Under the general heading of knowledge of the Orient, and within the umbrella of Western hegemony over the Orient from the eighteenth century onwards, there emerged 'a complex Orient suitable for study in the academy, for display in the museum, for reconstruction in the colonial office, for theoretical illustration in anthropological, biological, linguistic, racial, and historical theses about mankind and the universe' (7). Orientalism is not, however, a Western plot to hold down the 'Oriental' world. It is:

> a distribution of geopolitical awareness into aesthetic, scholarly, economic, sociological, historical and philological texts; it is an elaboration not only of a basic geographical distinction . . . but also of a whole series of 'interests' which . . . it not only creates but maintains. It is, rather than expresses, a certain will or intention to understand, in some cases to control, manipulate, even incorporate, what is a manifestly different world
>
> (Said 1978: 12).

Significantly, the discourse of Orientalism persists into the present, particularly in the West's relationship with 'Islam', as is evidenced in its study, its reporting in the media, its representation in general. But as a discursive mode, Orientalism models a wide range of institutional constructions of the colonial other, one example being the study, discussion and general representation of Africa in the West since the nineteenth century. In this sense, its practice remains pertinent to the operation of imperial power in whatever form it adopts; to know, to name, to fix the other in discourse is to maintain a far-reaching political control.

The generalized construction of regions by such discursive formations is also a feature of contemporary cultural life (See Griffiths 2003). Oddly enough, Orientalism spills over into the realm of self-construction, so that the idea of a set of generalized 'Asian' values (e.g. Asian democracy) is promoted by the institutions and governments of peoples who were themselves lumped together initially by Orientalist rubrics such as 'the East' (Far East, Middle East, etc.), the Orient or Asia. Employed as an unqualified adjective, a term like 'Asia' is in danger of eroding and dismantling profound cultural, religious and linguistic differences in the countries where it is applied self-ascriptively in ways not dissimilar to the Orientalist discourses of the colonial period.

Further Reading: Baber 2002; Ballantyne 2001; Boer 1994; Breckenridge and van der Veer 1993; Codell and Macleod 1998; Dallmayr 1996; Ezzaher 2003; Harlow and Carter 1999; R. King 1999; Lennon 2004; Lewis 1996; Lockman 2004; MacKenzie 1995; Moore-Gilbert 1996; Rotter 2000; Said 1978; Sardar 1999; Satchidanandan 2002; B.S. Turner 1994.

OTHER

In general terms, the 'other' is anyone who is separate from one's self. The existence of others is crucial in defining what is 'normal' and in locating one's own place in the world. The colonized subject is characterized as 'other' through discourses such as **primitivism** and **cannibalism**, as a means of establishing the **binary** separation of the colonizer and colonized and asserting the naturalness and primacy of the colonizing culture and world view.

Although the term is used extensively in existential philosophy, notably by Sartre in *Being and Nothingness* to define the relations between Self and Other in creating self-awareness and ideas of identity, the definition of the term as used in current postcolonial theory is rooted in the Freudian and post-Freudian analysis of the formation of **subjectivity**, most notably in the work of the psychoanalyst and cultural theorist Jacques Lacan. Lacan's use of the term involves a distinction between the 'Other' and the 'other', which can lead to some confusion, but it is a distinction that can be very useful in postcolonial theory.

In Lacan's theory, the other – with the small 'o' – designates the other who resembles the self, which the child discovers when it looks in the mirror and becomes aware of itself as a separate being. When the child, which is an uncoordinated mass of limbs and feelings sees its image in the mirror, that image must bear sufficient resemblance to the child to be recognized, but it must also be separate enough to ground the child's hope for an 'anticipated mastery'; this fiction of mastery will become the basis of the ego. This other is important in defining the identity of the subject. In postcolonial theory, it can refer to the colonized others who are marginalized by imperial discourse, identified by their difference from the centre and, perhaps crucially, become the focus of anticipated mastery by the imperial 'ego'.

The Other – with the capital 'O' – has been called the grand Autre by Lacan, the great Other, in whose gaze the subject gains identity. The Symbolic Other is not a real interlocutor but can be embodied in other subjects such as the mother or father that may represent it. The Symbolic Other is a 'transcendent or absolute pole of address, summoned each time that subject speaks to another subject' (Boons-Grafé 1992: 298). Thus, the Other can refer to the mother whose separation from the subject locates her as the first focus of desire; it can refer to the father whose Otherness locates the subject in the Symbolic order; it can refer to the unconscious itself because the unconscious is structured like a language that is separate from the language of the subject. Fundamentally, the Other is crucial to the subject because the subject exists in its gaze. Lacan says that 'all desire is the metonym of the desire to be' because the first desire of the subject is the desire to exist in the gaze of the Other.

This Other can be compared to the imperial centre, imperial discourse or the empire itself, in two ways: first, it provides the terms in which the colonized subject gains a sense of his or her identity as somehow 'other', dependent; second, it becomes the 'absolute pole of address', the ideological framework in which the colonized subject may come to understand the world. In colonial discourse, the subjectivity of the colonized is continually located in the gaze of the imperial Other, the 'grand-autre'. Subjects may be **interpellated** by the ideology of the maternal and nurturing function of the colonizing power, concurring with descriptions such as 'mother England' and 'Home'.

On the other hand, the Symbolic Other may be represented in the Father. The significance and enforced dominance of the imperial language into which colonial subjects are inducted may give them a clear sense of power being located in the colonizer, a situation corresponding metaphorically to the subject's entrance into the Symbolic order and the discovery of the Law of the Father. The ambivalence of colonial discourse lies in the fact that both these processes of 'othering' occur at the same time, the colonial subject being both a 'child' of empire and a primitive and degraded subject of imperial discourse. The construction of the dominant imperial Other occurs in the same process by which the colonial others come into being.

In contemporary postcolonial discussion, the Other and Othering, whether capitalized or not, generally refer to the marginalized, non-European and non-white subjects of colonial invasion. This sense of the term appeared in 1984 with the proceedings of the Essex conference of the sociology of literature titled *Europe and its Others* (1985). It has now become standard in the description of colonized people.

Further Reading: Barker 1985; Boons-Grafé 1992; Fuss 1994; Lacan 1968; Nederveen Pieterse 1992; Sartre 1957; Spivak 1985a.

OTHERING

Othering refers to the social and/or psychological ways in which one group excludes or marginalizes another group. The term was coined by Gayatri Spivak for the process by which imperial discourse creates its 'others'. Whereas the Other corresponds to the focus of desire or power (the M–Other or Father – or Empire) in relation to which the subject is produced, the other is the excluded or 'mastered' subject created by the discourse of power. Othering describes the various ways in which colonial discourse produces its subjects. In Spivak's explanation, othering is a dialectical process because the colonizing Other is established at the same time as its colonized others are produced as subjects.

It is important to note that while Spivak adheres faithfully to the Lacanian distinction between 'Other' and 'other', many critics use the spellings interchangeably, so that the Empire's construction of its 'others' is often referred to as the construction of 'the Other' (perhaps to connote an abstract and generalized but more symbolic representation of empire's 'others'). But in either case, the construction of the O/other is fundamental to the construction of the Self.

Spivak gives three examples of othering in a reading of colonial office dispatches between Captain Geoffrey Birch, his superior Major General Ochterlony and his superior the Marquess of Hastings, Lord Moira. The first is a process of **worlding** whereby Captain Birch, riding across the Indian countryside, can be seen to be 'consolidating the self of Europe', that is, representing Europe as the Other in terms of which colonial subjectivity of the inhabitants will be produced. The second is an example of debasement whereby the hill tribes are described by General Ochterlony in terms of 'depravity', 'treachery', 'brutality' and 'perfidy', and the surrender of their lands to the crown an 'obligation' (Spivak 1985a: 134). He can be observed, says Spivak, in the act of creating the colonized 'other(s)' by making them the 'object[s] of imperialism'. The third is an example of the separation of native states and 'our (colonial) governments' in the reprimand given the general by the Marquess of Hastings for allowing half-pay subalterns to serve with regular troops in Native governments. All three are engaged in producing an 'other' text – the 'true' history of the native hill states – at the same time that they are establishing the Otherness of Empire (135).

The process of othering can occur in all kinds of colonialist narrative. Mary Louise Pratt detects an example of othering in John Barrow's *Account of Travels in the Interior of Southern Africa in the Years 1797 and 1798* in which

The people to be othered are homogenized into a collective 'they,' which is distilled even further into an iconic 'he' (the standardized adult male specimen). This abstracted 'he'/'they' is the subject of verbs in a timeless present tense, which characterizes anything 'he' is or does not as a particular historical event but as an instance of a pregiven custom or trait.

(Pratt 1985: 139)

Apart from its almost inevitable presence in travel and ethnographic writing, othering can take on more material and violent forms. In *Waiting for the Barbarians* (1980), South African novelist J.M. Coetzee demonstrates the ways in which imperial discourse constructs its others in order to confirm its own reality. In this novel, the magistrate who tells the story is situated at the edge of the 'empire' conducting the humdrum business of the outpost town in relative tranquillity, until Colonel Joll, a functionary of the 'Third Bureau', the secret police, arrives to extract, by torture, any information about the 'barbarians' that can be gathered from a ragtag collection of old men, women and children who are 'captured' on a prisoner-gathering foray. The fact that the whole enterprise is manifestly absurd because there is no threat from the barbarians, a nomadic people who come to town from time to time to trade, and there were no 'border troubles' before the arrival of the 'Third Bureau' (114) does not deter Colonel Joll. For the Colonel is in the business of creating the enemy, of delineating that opposition that must exist, in order that the empire might define itself by its geographical and racial others. This is an example of Othering. The Colonel is engaged in a process by which the empire can define itself against those it colonizes, excludes and marginalizes. It locates its 'others' by this process in the pursuit of that power within which its own subjectivity is established.

Further Reading: Coetzee 1980; Olaniyan 1992; Pratt 1985; Spivak 1985a; Gaupp and Pelillo-Hestermeyer 2021.

PALIMPSEST

Originally, the term for a parchment on which several inscriptions had been made after earlier ones had been erased. The characteristic of the palimpsest is that, despite such erasures, there are always traces of previous inscriptions that have been 'overwritten'. Hence the term has become particularly valuable for suggesting the ways in which the traces of earlier 'inscriptions' remain as a continual feature of the 'text' of culture, giving it its particular density and character. Any cultural experience is itself an accretion of many layers, and the term is valuable because it illustrates the ways in which precolonial culture as well as the experience of colonization are continuing aspects of a postcolonial society's developing cultural identity. While the 'layering' effect of history has been mediated by each successive period, 'erasing' what has gone before, all present experience contains ineradicable traces of the past which remain part of the constitution of the present. Teasing out such vestigial features left over from the past is an important part of understanding the nature of the present.

An important use of the concept of the palimpsest has been made by Paul Carter in *The Road to Botany Bay* (1987) in which he demonstrates how 'empty' uncolonized space becomes **place** through the process of textuality. Mapping, naming, fictional and non-fictional narratives create multiple and sometimes conflicting accretions which become the dense text that constitutes place. In short, empty space becomes place through language, in the process of being written and named. Place itself, in the experience of the postcolonial subject, is a palimpsest of a process in language: the naming by which **imperial** discourse brings the colonized space 'into being', the subsequent rewritings and overwritings, the imaging of the place in the consciousness of its occupants, all of which constitute the contemporary place observed by the subject and contested among them. The most challenging aspect of this thesis is that the ordinary social subject, when looking at the surrounding environment, does not simply take in what is there as purely visual data, but is located with that place in a cultural horizon, that is, the simply observed place is a cultural palimpsest built up over centuries and retaining the traces of previous engagements and inscriptions, including the influence of the observer who is constructed in the act of 'observing'.

Guyanese novelist and critic, and erstwhile government surveyor and mapmaker, Wilson Harris also makes frequent use of this extended idea of the palimpsest in his critical writing, relating it through the metaphors of the layers of material that build up on the floor of a tropical rainforest and those of a fossil bed. Both are expressive of the engagement which occurs between subject and world, a process which engages what Harris has called the 'transformative imagination'. Thus, he regards the process of 'fossilization', not as a metaphor for dead forms but as a sign of the continuation of the forms of the past in the living present. No single feature of past or present can be singled out as an origin, since all are related to an endless and multiple set of processes, an 'infinite rehearsal' that never ends and in which 'history' is located as a transient structure. So, in Harris's vision of the Guyanese world, the palimpsestic metaphor is also applied to the many races whose traces are laid and overlaid in modern Caribbean societies, preventing the re-emergence of an oppressive single image of a 'pure' race or culture (see **catalysis**). Much postcolonial discourse constitutes a struggle for the restitution of 'writings' and 'readings' of the land expunged by colonialist texts (see **orality**). Colonial discourse erased prior constructions of the land, allowing it to be seen as an empty space, ready to receive their own inscriptions. This occurred even in 'spaces' such as India where a body of complex textualities already existed, as these were displaced or denigrated vis-à-vis the colonial values and modes of representation. That this was a widespread and long-standing colonial historical practice is illustrated by Brian Friel's play *Translations*, which shows the process of reinscription in nineteenth-century Ireland as British imperial power consolidated itself over Ireland's Gaelic-speaking west by renaming the Gaelic place names, thus suppressing the existence of a flourishing and highly literate Gaelic culture. In extreme cases where extensive colonial settlement required an even more radical **othering** of the existing indigenous cultures, the imperial doctrine of *terra nullius* invoked the complete erasure of the precolonial people and culture, a process that was helped by the dominance in imperial and colonial discourses of ideas of literacy over orality as a superior cultural mode.

The concept of the palimpsest is a useful way of understanding the developing complexity of a culture, as previous 'inscriptions' are erased and overwritten, yet remain as traces within present consciousness. This confirms the dynamic, contestatory and dialogic nature of linguistic, geographic and cultural space as it emerges in the postcolonial experience.

Further Reading: Carter 1987; Harris 1983.

PARTITION

Partition has occurred in many parts of the postcolonial world as postcolonial nations have divided along ethnic, religious or linguistic lines. But in the acknowledgement of one of the earliest such events, it is most often used to refer to the partition of British India on the basis of religious demography. The partition was declared in the Indian Independence

Act of 1947 and divided Hindu India from Muslim Pakistan (East and West). The division led to the **displacement** of 12.5 million people with estimates of loss of life of over a million people. The violent nature of the partition created an atmosphere of mutual hostility between India and Pakistan that continues to the present day.

While the partition is regarded as one of the most catastrophic consequences of British imperial decision-making, it had a long gestation. Muslims suspicious of the Hindu-majority Indian National Congress had formed the All India Muslim League in 1906. In his presidential address to the 1930 convention of the league, writer and philosopher Allama Iqbal asserted that a separate nation for Muslims was essential. A resolution to that effect was drafted in the 1935 convention, by Iqbal, Mahammad Ali Jinnah and others.

From this time, Jinnah led the way in calling for a separate Muslim state and he became the principal Muslim spokesman in the deliberations leading to the partition itself. At the time he called for a separate Muslim state in 1940, all Muslim political parties were opposed, as was the secularist Indian National Congress and Mohandas Gandhi who declared 'My whole soul rebels against the idea that Hinduism and Islam represent two antagonistic cultures and doctrines. To assent to such a doctrine is for me a denial of God' (Hanson 2006: 200).

The actual division of British India between the two new dominions was accomplished according to what has come to be known as the *3 June Plan* or Mountbatten Plan. Mountbatten announced it at a press conference on 4 June 1947, when the date of independence was also announced – 15 August 1947. The border between India and Pakistan (the Radcliffe Line) was determined by a British Government-commissioned report prepared under the chairmanship of a London barrister Sir Cyril Radcliffe. Pakistan came into being with two non-contiguous enclaves, East Pakistan (today Bangladesh) and West Pakistan, separated geographically by India. India was formed out of the majority Hindu regions of British India, and Pakistan from the majority Muslim areas.

The main points of the Mountbatten plan were:

1. Hindus and Muslims in Punjab and Bengal legislative assemblies would meet and vote for partition. If a simple majority of either group wanted partition, then these provinces would be divided.
2. Sindh was to take its own decision.
3. The fate of North-West Frontier Province and Sylhet district of Bengal was to be decided by a referendum.
4. India would be independent by 15 August 1947.

5. The separate independence of Bengal was also ruled out.
6. A boundary commission to be set up in case of partition.

The Indian political leaders accepted the plan on 2 June. It did not deal with the question of the princely states, but on 3 June, Mountbatten advised them against remaining independent and urged them to join one of the two new dominions. The Muslim League's demands for a separate state were thus conceded. The Congress position on unity was also taken into account while making Pakistan as small as possible. Mountbatten's formula was to divide India and at the same time retain maximum possible unity.

Given that the partition was a *fait accompli*, critics have blamed the consequent catastrophic loss of life upon the fact that the plan was not put into effect before independence, when British security was in place.

The importance of this event in the formation of identities in the nations of *Pakistan* and India is reflected in the many literary texts that have drawn on its events, for example, Sikh author Kushwant Singh's *Train to Pakistan* (1956), Parsi author Bapsi Sidhwa's *Cracking India*, originally titled *Ice Candy Man* (1988), and the basis for a collaboration with the expatriate Indian film-maker Deepa Mehta in the 'Earth' section of her recent notable trilogy on Indian history Earth, Fire and Water; and best-known of all the widely disseminated work of the Muslim author Salman Rushdie's *Midnight's Children* (1981). These works demonstrate that partition had effects on all the ethnic and religious groups that made up British India. The first two of these texts show the especially complex effects on those who were part of the substantial 'minority' groupings in the regions affected by the decisions of the Radcliffe Commission, such as Sikhs or Parsees. But as Rushdie's work demonstrates, members of the Hindu and Muslim majority groups often found themselves straddling these post-partition national formations, as was the case of Rushdie himself. Born in Bombay of Muslim parents, he fell foul of both sides at different times, regarded as having betrayed Pakistan when he criticized its rulers in his early novel *Shame* (1983) and then seeing his work criticized for its portrayal of post-independence Indian politics, notably the Emergency period of Indira Ghandi's Congress government.

The many postcolonial literary texts dealing with partition and its aftermath reflect the ongoing effect of this traumatic moment for the people of modern Pakistan and India and their descendants, who still live with the results. The fundamental unworkability of the rushed 1947 partition of British India led to the further partition of East Pakistan from Pakistan and the formation of the new nation of Bangladesh in 1971 after a devastating war. The two parts of what had been the Bangla-speaking peoples, split into two on the basis of religious differences at partition in 1947, now led, ironically enough, to Indian intervention to support the aspiration of the people of West Bengal to independence in one of the several wars that have resulted from the initial partition of British India. The 1971 war for the independence of Bangladesh resulted in a further influx of peoples across the new border, resulting in an even more complex form of splintered identities within this historic Bangla language group.

In Pakistan, whole communities descended from those Urdu-speaking Indian Muslims who emigrated from India to Pakistan (known as Muhajirs) are still being identified as a separate group even after more than half a century, though they were seeking to form a single national group with their co-religionists on the basis of the call for a separate Muslim nation. Similarly, many of the Hindus who fled from East Bengal across the border into India in 1947 are still waiting Indian citizenship, alongside their children in refugee camps first established in 1947. The refugees in these camps continued to be swollen by people fleeing what is now Bangladesh before and after the 1971 conflict that split Pakistan. Those of the opposed religious majorities, the partition defined (Muslim and Hindu) who did not flee to their supposed new national homelands also found that their condition remained difficult or sometimes impossible. The many Muslims who remained in India have since frequently complained of ongoing discrimination in employment and in general acceptance, particularly after the election of the Modi government, while most of the fewer Hindus who remained in Pakistan have since left, some suggesting that this was the result of a deliberate policy of forced expulsion through active government discrimination.

Whatever else this demonstrates, it is clear proof of the fact that partition did not produce the organized transition to stable separate nationhoods that its colonial architects claimed it was designed to ensure, and the people of both nations are still living with the conflicts that resulted from it, most notably in the ongoing and seemingly unresolvable issue of Kashmir, which remained part of India at partition despite having an overwhelmingly Muslim population.

Further Reading: Ansari 2005; Hanson 2006; Khan 2007; Wolpert 2006; Butali 2018

PASTORALISM

In postcolonial contexts, the term pastoralism has had and continues to have a number of provenances and continuing resonances. First, the Anglo-European tradition of the pastoral, with its bucolic associations of innocence, green downs, shepherds and shepherdesses has been radically transformed in settler colony situations and settler colony writing (see Huggan and Tiffin 2010). Challenged, undermined and ironized by historical circumstances, vastly more rugged topographies and the annihilation and/or displacement of indigenous peoples, 'pastoralism' undeniably lost its bucolic innocence in colonial contexts.

Second, 'pastoralism', meaning a system of crop cultivation or the local raising of a few livestock has become, in some postcolonized areas, synonymous with poverty. Pastoralism is not only a livestock-based livelihood strategy but also a way of life with sociocultural norms and values, and indigenous knowledge revolving around livestock. This has become the case in sub-Saharan Africa, India and South America, where rapidly industrializing and urbanizing societies have become dismissive of traditional modes of production. Pastoral systems in Africa are facing demographic, economic, socio-political and climatic pressures which are driving many pastoralists into non-livestock-based livelihood strategies. Such dismissal by urban élites not only reflects international neo-colonial '**development**' (often flawed) but a bias against nomadism inculcated in post-independence populations.

Third, pastoralism, in the settler colony context, where large fenced pastoral properties have been located on the traditional lands of indigenous peoples has meant the **displacement** of the traditional owners and the widespread degradation of fragile ecosystems.

Further Reading: Anderson and Broch-Due 1999; Huggan and Tiffin 2010.

PATRIARCHY

This widely used term, meaning 'the rule of the father', describes a social system in which positions of dominance and privilege are held by men. In practice, this is true of most societies except those specifically identified as matrilineal, which are often regarded as cultural outliers. Patriarchal ideology justifies this system by positing gender inequality between men and women, who are nominated the weaker sex and in need of protection. This gender difference is justified by biological, religious, social, legal, political and economic dictates but sociologists argue that gender roles and gender inequality are socially constructed and reinforced by **ideology**, which, in Althusser's formulation is not simply the enforcement of ideas by the powerful but a system of ideas that explains or makes sense of society.

The concept is of particular interest to postcolonial studies because imperialism and patriarchy are almost mirror images of one another. The rule of the father becomes the rule of the empire and its consequences are the subjugation of the colonized society in the way that patriarchy subjugates women. Imperialism is a patriarchal model in its structure, ideological assumptions and impact upon colonized society. And while imperialism modelled the ideology of patriarchy, it also had material effects on the lives of women (see **Double Colonization**). This can be described in terms of 'intersecting marginalities' (Ashcroft 1989) as the marginalizing power of imperial control works upon class, race and gender, often simultaneously.

The experiences of women in patriarchal societies and those of colonized subjects can be paralleled in a number of respects, and both feminist and postcolonial politics oppose such dominance. A continuing and vigorous debate rages over whether patriarchy or colonial oppression is the more important political factor in women's lives. This has sometimes led to division between Western feminists and political activists from impoverished and oppressed countries. Clearly the two are intertwined, and postcolonial women have initiated a mutual transformation of postcolonialism and feminism since the issues of subject formation, oppression and marginality can be seen to overlap. European patriarchy and European notions of sexuality, epistemology and spirituality were exported to the rest of the world through colonial expansion as the hegemonic criteria to racialize, classify and pathologize the rest of the world's population in a hierarchy of superior and inferior races. As Oyerónké Oyewùmí says,

> The imposition of the European state system, with its attendant legal and bureaucratic machinery, is the most enduring legacy of European colonial rule in Africa. . . One tradition that was exported to Africa during this period was the exclusion of women from the newly created colonial public sphere. In Britain, access to power was gender-based; therefore, politics was largely men's job; and colonization, which is fundamentally a political affair, was no

exception. . . . The emergence of women as an identifiable category, defined by their anatomy and subordinated to men in all situations, resulted, in part, from the imposition of a patriarchal colonial state.

(1997: 123–124)

The impact of both patriarchy and imperialism is much more subtle than the simple factor of male dominance or the imposition of ideas of racial or gender relations. In both cases, the ideology is hegemonic, that is, a view of social and gender relations that is accepted as natural and into which subjects are born, as Althusser says. This is where the **counter discourse** of postcolonial feminism has a particular and important function. As colonized societies have repeatedly demonstrated, ideology can be contested when it is exposed.

Further Reading: Oyewùmí (1997), Levy (2022)

PIDGINS/CREOLES

Pidgins are languages serving as lingua franca, that is, they are used as a medium of communication between groups who have no other language in common. (However, while English may serve as a lingua franca in, for instance, the Indian Parliament, it is not a pidgin or a creole.) When 'two or more people use a language in a variety whose grammar and vocabulary are very much reduced in extent and which is native to neither side' (Hall 1988: xii), they are using a pidgin. A creole 'arises when a pidgin becomes the native language of a speech community, as in the Caribbean' (xii). Pidgins typically develop out of trade languages and may evolve into creoles' (Seymour-Smith 1986: 223–224).

However, DeCamp (1977) draws attention to the continuing lack of agreement over precise definitions of pidgins and creoles, noting that

some definitions are based on function, the role these languages play in the community. . . . Some are based on historical origins and development. . . . Some definitions include formal characteristics: restricted vocabulary, absence of gender, true tenses. . . . Some linguists combine these different kinds of criteria and include additional restrictions in their definitions.

(DeCamp 1977: 3)

Most commentators agree that a creole is a more developed language than a pidgin and, as Muysken and Smith argue, one vital difference between pidgins and creoles is that 'pidgins do not have native speakers while Creoles do'. But they note that some extended pidgins are beginning to acquire native speakers, for example, Tok Pisin of Papua New Guinea, Nigerian Pidgin English and Sango (Central African Republic) (Muysken and Smith 1995: 3). Consequently, at this point in their development, they are increasingly considered as creoles.

Further Reading: Alleyne 1980; Blake 1996; Bongie 1998; Caldwell 2003; Colás 1995; Études Creóles; C. Gilman 1985; Hall 1988; Holm 1988, 1989; *Journal of Pidgin and* Creole Languages; Mulhausler 1986; Muysken and Smith 1995; Romain 1988; Seymour-Smith 1986; Simmons-McDonald 2003; Singh 2000; Singler 1990; Spears and Winford 1997; Todd 1984.

PLACE

The concepts of place and displacement demonstrate the very complex interaction of language, history and environment in the experience of colonized peoples and the importance of space and location in the process of identity formation. In many cases, 'place' does not become an issue in a society's cultural discourse until colonial intervention radically disrupts the primary modes of its representation by separating 'space' from 'place'. A sense of place may be embedded in cultural history, in legend and language, without becoming a concept of contention and struggle until the profound discursive interference of colonialism. Such intervention may disrupt a sense of place in several ways: by imposing a feeling of displacement in those who have moved to the colonies; by physically alienating large populations of colonized peoples through forced migration, slavery or indenture; by disturbing the representation of place in the colony by imposing the colonial language. Indeed, in all colonial experience, colonialism brings with it a sense of dislocation between the environment and the imported language now used to describe it, a gap between the 'experienced' place and the descriptions the language provides.

One of the deepest reasons for the significance of place in colonized societies lies in the disruptions caused by **modernity** itself in the links between time, space and place in European societies. In pre-modern or precolonial times, as Giddens (1990) explains, all cultures had ways of calculating the time, but before the invention of the mechanical clock, no one could tell the time without reference to other markers: 'when' was almost always connected to 'where'. The mechanical clock was instrumental in separating time from space, telling the time in a way that could allow the precise division of 'zones' of the day without reference to other markers. With the universalization of the calendar and the standardization of time across regions, the emptying of time (its severance from location) became complete and became the precondition for the 'emptying of space'. In pre-modern times, space and place are more or less synonymous with one another, but once relations with absent others were made possible by the invention of the clock, the calendar and the map, things changed radically. Locales became shaped by social influences quite distant from them, such as spatial technologies, colonizing languages or, indeed, the very conception of place that those languages came to transmit.

The movement of European society through the world, the 'discovery' and occupation of remote regions, was the necessary basis for the creation of what could be called 'empty space'. **Cartography** and the creation of universal maps established space as a measurable, abstract concept independent of any particular place or region. Significantly, the severing of time from space provides a basis for their recombination in relation to social activity. For instance, a train timetable appears to be a temporal chart, but it is in fact a time–space-ordering device. Consequently, while the separation of time and space allows social relations to be lifted out of their locale, 'place', which is in some senses left behind by modernity, becomes an anxious and contested site of the link between language and identity, a possible site of those local realities that the universal separation of time, space and place leaves virtually untouched.

In addition to the separation of space from place, brought about by European ways of measuring a 'universal' space and time that sever them from any particular location, place becomes an issue within language itself. A sense of displacement, of the lack of fit between language and place, may be experienced by those who possess English as a mother tongue or by those who speak it as a second language. In both cases, there appears to be a lack of fit between the place described in English and the place actually experienced by the colonized subject. This comes about firstly because the words developed to describe place originated in an alien European environment, and secondly because many of the words used by the colonizers described 'empty space' or 'empty time', and so had thrown off any connection to a particular locale. Place can thus be a constant trope of difference in postcolonial writing, a continual reminder of colonial ambivalence, of the separation yet continual mixing of the colonizer and colonized.

The concept of place itself may be very different in different societies and this can have quite specific political as well as literary effects in the extent of displacement. For instance, in Aboriginal societies, place is traditionally not a visual construct, a measurable space or even a topographical system but a tangible location of one's own dreaming, an extension of one's own being. A particular formation, like a stream or hill, for instance, may embody a particular dreaming figure, whose location on the dreaming track has a particular significance to a person's own life, 'totem', clan relationship and identity because that person may have been conceived near it. The idea of not owning the land but in some sense being 'owned by it' is a way of seeing the world that is so different from the materiality and commodification of a colonizing power, that effective protection of one's place is radically disabled when that new system becomes the dominant one.

This is perhaps the most extreme form of cultural disruption, but its general character is repeated throughout the colonial world because the colonizing powers brought with them a particular view of land that had a philosophical, legal and political provenance as well as an economic justification. The key to this attitude can be found in the idea of 'enclosure' that underlies the Western concept of property. John Locke's *Second Treatise of Government* (Book II Chapter 5 – 'Of Property') demonstrates the European rationale for the expropriation of lands by the 'advanced' agrarian communities from hunter-gatherer societies. For Locke, the very mark of property is the enclosure: the defining, or bounding, of a place that signals the perceived settling, or cultivation, of that place. Indeed, it is the figure of enclosure that marks the **frontier** between the **savage** and the civilized. Although nobody has an exclusive dominion over nature, says Locke, since the 'Fruits' of the earth and the 'Beasts' were given for the use of men, there must be a way to appropriate them before they can be of any use to a particular man, and this is the method of enclosure (Locke 1960: 330). Because it is man's labour that removes the products from nature and makes them his.

> As much Land as a Man Tills, Plants, Improves, Cultivates and can use the Product of, so much is his Property. He by his Labour does, as it were, inclose it from the Common . . . [For God] gave it to the use of the Industrious and Rational (and Labour was to be his Title to it).
>
> (Locke 1960: 333)

Quite apart from the ascription to God of the values of the European Enlightenment, the effect of this is to invalidate the claims over land of any people whose relationship with it does not involve agricultural 'improvement'. So powerful was the concept of property and its associated assumptions that the social reformer Thomas Fowell Buxton could say in the mid-nineteenth century that only the Bible and the plough could lead Africa on to a higher level of existence: for 'plough' meant agriculture, agriculture meant property and property meant civilization (Baumgart 1982: 14). Other colonists, of course, had a very different idea about the rights of African ownership of land, and the ideology of Social Darwinism as well as the long history of race thinking provided a justification for the long history of European land theft.

Superior military and economic strength enabled the colonizing power to establish its legal and economic perceptions of place as dominant, but it was the mode of representation, the language itself, that effected the most far-reaching pressure, which established the concept of place as a particularly complex site of colonial engagement. But at the same time, it was language that enabled colonized peoples to turn displacement into a creative resistance. In many respects, the political economy of property is a much less complicated aspect of imperial dominance than the discursive activity of language and writing and its involvement in the concept of place.

The most concerted discussion of place and its location in language has come from **settler colony** writers for whom the possession of English as a first language has produced a particularly subtle, complex and creatively empowering sense of the lack of fit between the language available and the place experienced. Canadian Robert Kroestch, in 'Unhiding the hidden', suggests that the particular predicament of the Canadian writer, and perhaps all settler colony writers, is that they work in a language that appears to be authentically their own, and yet is not quite. For another Canadian writer, Dennis Lee, this experience has had a profound effect on his writing, even drying up his writing altogether at one stage because he felt he could not find the words to express his experience authentically (1974).

What becomes apparent in these writers is that 'place' is much more than the land. The theory of place does not propose a simple separation between the 'place' named and described in language, and some 'real' place inaccessible to it, but rather indicates that in some sense, place is language, something in constant flux, a discourse in process. These writers become compelled to try to construct a new language that might fit the place they experience because the language does not simply report the visual or proximate experience but is implicated in its presence. Dennis Lee coins the term 'cadence' to describe this: 'a presence, both outside myself and inside my body opening out and trying to get into words' (1974: 397).

One of the most sustained discussions of the linguistic construction of place occurs in Paul Carter's *The Road to Botany Bay*, which proposes a concept he calls 'spatial history'. Such history examines place as a **palimpsest** on which the traces of successive inscriptions form the complex experience of place, which is itself historical. Imperial history, the teleological narrative of civilization and settlement, distinguishes itself by ignoring the place, the environment, as simply the empty stage on which the theatre of history is enacted. But if we see place as not simply a neutral location for the imperial project, we can see how intimately place is involved in the development of identity, how deeply it is involved in history, and how deeply implicated it is in the systems of representation – language, writing and the creative arts – that develop in any society but in colonized societies in particular.

Whatever the nature of the postcolonial society, language always negotiates a kind of gap between the word and its signification. In this sense, the dynamic of **naming** becomes a primary colonizing process because it appropriates, defines and captures the place in language. Perhaps the most comprehensive example of this is the drafting of the Mercator projection Atlas in 1636. The map demonstrates that geography, like place itself, 'is a series of erasures and overwritings which have transformed the world' (Rabasa 1993: 358). Our most profound, ubiquitous and unquestioned assumptions about the physical shape of the globe and its continents can thus be seen to be specific evidence of the power of European discourse to naturalize its construction of the world itself.

The provision of names to the non-European world through exploration and 'discovery' is thus an elaboration of the dynamic of control that the Atlas presupposes. To name a place is to announce discursive control over it by the very act of inscription, because through names, location becomes metonymic of those processes of travel, annexation and colonization that effect the dominance of imperial powers over the non-European world. The control over place that the act of naming performs extends even to an **ecological imperialism** in which the fauna, flora and the actual physical character of colonized lands changes under the pressure of the practical outworking of the European concern with property: enclosure, agriculture, importation of European plants and weeds; the destruction of indigenous species; possibly even the changing of weather patterns.

Further Reading: Ashcroft et al. 1995; Baucom 1999; Carter 1987; Carter et al. 1993; Chrisman 1998; Clayton and Gregory 1996; Crosby 1986; Darian-Smith et al. 1996; Harris 1983; Longley 1997; Mignolo 1995c; Mitchell 1994; Prentice 1991; Rice 2003; Sheridan 2001; Supriya 2004; van der Veer 1995; West-Pavlov 2010; Wright 2002.

POSTCOLONIAL BODY

While there is no such thing as 'the postcolonial body', the body has been central to colonialist and postcolonial discourses of various kinds. Much postcolonial writing in recent times has contended that the body is a crucial site for inscription. How people are perceived controls how they are treated, and physical differences are crucial in such constructions. This view of the body as a site for representation and control is central to many early analysts of postcolonial experience, notably Frantz Fanon (1961), but also to the arguments of Edouard Glissant (1989). These early concerns with the body centred on ideas of colour and race (see **chromatism**). They emphasized the visibility of signs of difference when manifested in skin colour, hair type and facial features, such as eye shape or nose shape. Although such 'differences' do not constitute any decisive genetic dissimilarity, and certainly do not indicate the existence of sub-groups within a single human species (as theories of race have often erroneously asserted), they nevertheless became prime means of developing and reinforcing prejudices against specific groups.

Such prejudices were generated either for economic reasons (see **slavery**) or to control indigenous populations in colonial possessions by emphasizing their difference and constructing them as inferior (see **hegemony**). More recently, there has been an increased concern with, and understanding of, the special role played by gender in constructing images of colonial inferiority (the emasculation or feminization of post-colonial cultural representation in image, word, etc.) and in constructing a special 'double' colonization for women within the general field of colonial oppression. This has led to a greater concern with the body as a site for gendered readings of postcolonial subjectivity.

The body, and its importance in postcolonial representation, emphasizes the very special nature of postcolonial discourses. For although the body is a text, that is, a space in which conflicting discourses can be written and read, it is an especially material text, one that demonstrates how **subjectivity**, however constructed it may in fact be, is 'felt' as inescapably material and permanent. This is important for postcolonial studies in that it reminds us that the discursive forces of imperial power operated on and through people, and it offers a ready corrective to the tendency to abstract ideas from their living context.

The location of the body as a site for discursive control has been examined in many ways in recent times. In museum studies and in fine arts, an interest in the representation and exhibition of people, their photographs and their preserved remains, is central to a radical rewriting of the history of ethnographic collections and public exhibitions (Coombes 1994; Maxwell 1998). The re-designing of exhibitions of such material to emphasize and deconstruct this bias is an important consequence of this kind of work; an example is the exhibition of Khoi-San bushmen and their preserved remnants in Cape Town in 1995 (See Skotnes 1996). The emphasis in both Native American and Australian Aboriginal communities upon the need to recover the bodies of ancestors converted by imperial museums into exotic 'exhibits', and their restoration to their proper place and role as revered human beings, is another example of this restitutive process in action.

But a recent critical discussion of the body in postcolonial spaces has also stressed the complexity of the ways in which the body can be constructed, and has elaborated its ambivalent role in the maintenance of, and resistance to, colonizing power. Thus, for example, Kadiatu Kanneh has spoken of the complexity of the idea of the 'veil' in the construction of discourses of the Muslim female, emphasizing that the motive for Western liberal 'unveiling' may itself be in some circumstances a form of imperial control (Kanneh 1995). In a different vein, Gillian Whitlock has stressed how habits of prudence and sexual restraint may interfere with and limit even the most liberal attempts to detail the reality of female abuse in institutions such as slavery, emphasizing physical brutality but unable to acknowledge sexual abuse (Whitlock 1995). Analyses such as these warn us of the danger of simply assuming that the body is neutral (natural) and not itself part of more widespread and contesting cultural institutions and practices.

Postcolonialism, for example, may offer us quite new ways of thinking about the implications of the centrality of nudity in artistic traditions in Western Europe. It may reveal the ways in which the discourse works not only to read the culture of the colonized, but also to deconstruct the hidden codes and assumptions of the colonial powers and their traditions. Even basic Western assumptions about the representation of sexuality itself may be opened up to be read in more complex ways, for example, if we observe the ways in which representations of the body in non-Western traditions, such as some West African carvings, frequently employ markers of both genders in a single image of the body. The relatively recent re-emergence in Western representations of the body of non-realistic codes such as Cubism may well be dependent on the discovery of these alternative traditions, and they may be the source for a renewed awareness of the limitations of the dominant 'naturalist' idea of the human body, its shape, its colour and its gender as fixed and determinate (see **modernism, primitivism**).

Further Reading: Ashcroft 1998; Coombes 1994; Crane and Mohanram 1996; Dale and Ryan 1998; R. Dixon 1997; Gilbert 1993; Handlarski 2010; Katrak 2006; Keown 2005; Low 1996; McClintock 1995; Massad 2000; Maxwell 1998; Mehan 2001; S. Mishra 1996; Mohanram 1999; Schoene-Harwood 1998; Thomas; 1995; Young 1995.

POSTCOLONIALISM

Postcolonialism (or sometimes post-colonialism) deals with the effects of colonization on cultures and societies. As originally used by historians after the Second World War in terms such as **the postcolonial state**, 'postcolonial' had a clearly chronological meaning, designating the post-independence period. However, from the late 1970s, the term has been used by literary critics to discuss the various cultural effects of colonization.

Postcolonial theory may be defined as that branch of contemporary theory that investigates, and develops propositions about, the cultural and political impact of European conquest upon colonized societies, and the nature of those societies' responses. The term refers to postcolonization and not post-independence, it identifies neither a chronology nor a specific ontology – it is not 'after colonialism' nor is it a way of being. 'Postcolonial' indicates a way of **reading**.

Although the study of the controlling power of representation in colonized societies had begun in the late 1970s with texts such as Said's **Orientalism**, and led to the development of what came to be called colonial discourse theory in the work of critics such as Spivak and Bhabha, the actual term 'postcolonial' was not employed in these early studies of the power of colonialist discourse to shape and form opinion and policy in the colonies and metropolis. Spivak, for example, first used the term 'postcolonial' in the collection of interviews and recollections published in 1990 called *The Postcolonial Critic*. Although the study of the effects of colonial representation were central to the work of these critics, the term 'postcolonial' per se was first used to refer to cultural interactions within colonial societies in literary circles (e.g. Ashcroft et al. 1977). This was part of an attempt to politicize and focus the concerns of fields such as Commonwealth literature and the study of the so-called New Literatures in English which had been initiated in the late 1960s. The term has subsequently been widely used to signify the political, linguistic and cultural experience of societies that were former European colonies.

Thus, the term was a potential site of disciplinary and interpretative contestation almost from the beginning, especially the implications involved in the signifying hyphen or its absence. The heavily post-structuralist influence of the major exponents of colonial discourse theory, Said (Foucault), Homi Bhabha (Althusser and Lacan) and Gayatri Spivak (Derrida), led many critics, concerned to focus on the material effects of the historical condition of colonialism, as well as on its discursive power, to insist on the hyphen to distinguish postcolonial studies as a field from colonial discourse theory per se, which formed only one aspect of the many approaches and interests that the term 'post-colonial' sought to embrace and discuss (Ashcroft 1996).

While this distinction in style still exists, the interweaving of the two approaches is considerable. 'Postcolonialism' is now used in wide and diverse ways to include the study and analysis of European territorial conquests, the various institutions of European colonialisms, the discursive operations of empire, the subtleties of subject construction in colonial discourse and the resistance of those subjects, and, most importantly perhaps, the differing responses to such incursions and their contemporary colonial legacies in both pre- and post-independence nations and communities. While its use has tended to focus on the cultural production of such communities, it is becoming widely used in historical, political, sociological and economic analyses, as these disciplines continue to engage with the impact of European imperialism upon world societies.

The prefix 'post' in the term also continues to be a source of vigorous debate amongst critics. The simpler sense of the 'post' as meaning 'after' colonialism has been contested by a more elaborate understanding of the working of postcolonial cultures which stresses the articulations between and across the politically defined historical periods, of precolonial, colonial and post-independence cultures. As a result, further questions have been asked about what limits, if any, should be set round the term. Aijaz Ahmad complains, for instance, that when the term 'colonialism' can be pushed back to the Incas (see

Decolonial) and forward to the Indonesian occupation of East Timor, then it becomes 'a transhistorical thing, always present and always in process of dissolution in one part of the world or another' (1995: 9). It is clear, however, that postcolonialism as it has been employed in most recent accounts has been primarily concerned to examine the processes and effects of, and reactions to, European colonialism from the sixteenth century up to and including the **neo-colonialism** of the present day.

No doubt the disputes will continue, since, as Stephen Slemon has argued, 'postcolonialism', is now used in its various fields, to describe a remarkably heterogeneous set of subject positions, professional fields and critical enterprises:

> It has been used as a way of ordering a critique of totalizing forms of Western historicism; as a portmanteau term for a retooled notion of 'class', as a subset of both postmodernism and post-structuralism (and conversely, as the condition from which those two structures of cultural logic and cultural critique themselves are seen to emerge); as the name for a condition of nativist longing in post-independence national groupings; as a cultural marker of non-residency for a Third World intellectual cadre; as the inevitable underside of a fractured and ambivalent discourse of colonialist power; as an oppositional form of 'reading practice'; and – and this was my first encounter with the term – as the name for a category of 'literary' activity which sprang from a new and welcome political energy going on within what used to be called 'Commonwealth' literary studies.
>
> (Slemon 1994: 16–17)

Yet the term still continues to be used from time to time to mean simply 'anti-colonial' and to be synonymous with 'post-independence', as in references to the **postcolonial state**. To further complicate the issue of how these overlapping projects continue to collide in recent discussions, Slemon notes also that the existence of the three overlapping fields has led to some

> confusion . . . in which the project . . . of identifying the scope and nature of anti-colonialist resistance in writing has been mistaken for the project . . . which concerns itself with articulating the literary nature of Third and Fourth-World cultural groups.
>
> (Slemon 1990: 31)

As he sees it, the second of these projects retains a concern with 'whole nations or cultures as [its] basic [unit]' and sets up comparisons or contrasts between these units, whereas the first project is concerned with 'identifying a social force, colonialism and with the attempt to understand the resistances to that force wherever they may lie' (31). Slemon is well aware that this raises its own problems, problems that have been part of the recent debate. As he notes,

> Colonialism, obviously, is an enormously problematic category: it is by definition transhistorical and unspecific, and it is used in relation to very different kinds of historical oppression and economic control. [Nevertheless] like the term 'patriarchy', which shares similar problems in definition, the concept of colonialism . . . remains crucial to a critique of past and present power relations in world affairs.
>
> (Slemon 1990: 31)

Slemon also makes the point in this same essay that an assumption that the reactions of oppressed peoples will always be resistant may actually remove agency from these people. Not only are they capable of producing 'reactionary' documents, but as Ahmad (1992) and others have insisted, postcolonial societies have their own internal agendas and forces that continue to interact with and modify the direct response to the colonial incursion. Clearly any definition of postcolonialism needs to include a consideration of this wider set of local and specific ongoing concerns and practices. It is unlikely that these debates will be easily resolved. At the present time, though, no matter how we conceive of 'the postcolonial', and whatever the debates around the use of the problematic prefix 'post', or the equally problematic hyphen, the grounding of the term in European colonialist histories and institutional practices, and the responses (resistant or otherwise) to these practices on the part of all colonized peoples, remain fundamental.

An equally fundamental constraint is attention to precise location. Every colonial encounter or 'contact zone' is different, and each 'post-colonial' occasion needs, against these general background principles, to be precisely located and analysed for its specific interplay. A vigorous debate has revolved around the potentially homogenizing effect of the term 'postcolonial' (Hodge and Mishra 1990; Chrisman and Williams 1993). The effect of describing the colonial experience of a great range of cultures by this term, it is argued, is to elide the differences between them. However, there is no inherent or inevitable reason for this to occur. The materiality and locality of various kinds of postcolonial experience are precisely what provide the richest potential for postcolonial studies, and they enable the specific analysis of the various effects of colonial discourse.

The theoretical issues latent in these two fundamentals – materiality and location – lie at the basis of much of the dispute over what the term references and what it should or should not include. Yet, despite these disputes and differences, signs of a fruitful and complementary relationship between various postcolonial approaches have emerged in recent work in the field. Whether beginning from a basis in discourse theory, or from a more materialist and historical reading, most recent discussions have stressed the need to retain and strengthen these fundamental parameters in defining the idea of the postcolonial/postcolonial. As critics like Young have indicated, the crucial task has been to avoid assuming that 'the reality of the historical conditions of colonialism can be safely discarded' in favour of 'the fantasmatics of colonial discourse' (Young 1995: 160). The most cogent criticism of discourse theory has been offered by materialist thinkers such as Mohanty, Parry and Ahmad who, as Young suggests, argue that it should not proceed 'at the expense of materialist historical enquiry' (161). On the other hand, as Young also warns, although the totalizing aspects of discourses of the postcolonial is of real concern, it is necessary to avoid a return to a simplified form of localized materialism that refuses entirely to recognize the existence and effect of general discourses of colonialism on individual instances of colonial practice.

The project of identifying the general discursive forces that held together the imperial enterprise and that operated wherever colonization occurred is often in conflict with the need to provide detailed accounts of the material effect of those discourses as they operated in different periods and different localities. To suggest that colonialism or imperialism were not themselves multivalent forces and operated differently according to the periods in which they occurred, the metropolitan cultures from which they proceeded, or the specific **'contact zones'** in which they took effect, is clearly to oversimplify. But to suggest that it is impossible to determine widespread common elements within these local particularities, especially at the level of ideology and discursive formation, seems equally inadequate as a basis for any but the most limited accounts.

Not every colony will share every aspect of colonialism, nor will it share some essential feature since, like any category, it is, to use Wittgenstein's metaphor, a rope with many overlapping strands (1958: 87). Nevertheless, it is likely that, as Robert Young has said, the particular historical moment can be seen to interact with the general discourse of colonialism so that:

> The contribution of colonial discourse analysis [for example] is that it provides a significant framework for that other work by emphasising that all perspectives on colonialism share, and have to deal with a common discursive medium which was also that of colonialism itself: the language used to enact, enforce, describe or analyse colonialism is not transparent, innocent, ahistorical or simply instrumental.
>
> (Young 1958: 163)

Young concludes a discussion of these recent disputational positions with a wise conclusion.

> Yet at this point in the postcolonial era, as we seek to understand the operation and effects of colonial history, the homogenization of colonialism does also need to be set against its historical and geographical particularities. The question is whether it can maintain, and do justice to, both levels.
>
> (165)

It is likely that the debate will not be resolved finally in favour of either extreme position, but that the increasingly detailed archival work done on all aspects of colonial/postcolonial culture will continue to correct the more simplistic generalizations that characterize early formulations of the field without overthrowing the validity of a general, comparative methodology in framing important questions that a strictly local materialist analysis alone could neither pose nor answer.

Further Reading: Ashcroft 2012; Ashcroft et al. 1989, 1995; Boehmer 1995; Brydon 2000; Castle 2001; Childs and Williams 1997; Chrisman 2003; Desai and Nair 2005; Gandhi 1998; Goldberg and Quayson 2002; Harrison 2003; Hawley 2001; Loomba 2005; Punter 2000; Quayson 2000; San Juan 1998; Spivak 1999; Venn 2006; Wisker 2007; Young 2001, 2003.

POSTCOLONIAL READING

A way of reading and rereading texts of both metropolitan and colonial cultures to draw deliberate attention to the profound and inescapable effects of colonization on literary production; anthropological accounts; historical records; administrative and scientific writing. It is a form of deconstructive reading most usually applied to works emanating from the colonizers (but may be applied to works by the colonized) which demonstrates the extent to which the text contradicts its underlying assumptions (civilization, justice, aesthetics, sensibility, race) and reveals its (often unwitting) colonialist ideologies and processes. Examples of postcolonial readings of particular texts include Eric Williams' interrogation of the formerly authoritative texts of Caribbean history in *British Historians and the West Indies* (1966); contemporary rereadings of the works of canonical European anthropologists such as Malinowski; numerous postcolonial rereadings (and rewritings) of Shakespeare's *The Tempest* in French, English and Spanish; rereadings of Jane Austen's *Mansfield Park* (see **contrapuntal reading**); Jean Rhys' rereadings (and thus rewriting, in *Wide Sargasso Sea*) of Charlotte Bronte's *Jane Eyre*.

The notion of a 'postcolonial reading' need not be restricted to interrogating a body of works (for example, documents dealing with the European history of an area) nor to rereading and rewriting individual texts. A postcolonial rereading of, for instance, English literary history would (hypothetically) involve far greater stress on colonial relations between England and Scotland, Ireland and Wales, and the historical and contemporary effects of these relations on literary production and representation. It would also involve reconsidering English literature and literary production as less a series of domestically inspired change and progressions than one emanating from and through the imperial process and/or colonial contacts. Thus, for instance, modernism can be argued to be the product of Europe's contact with the so-called 'savage' cultures of Africa and the South Pacific; while post-structuralist theories (such as that of Derrida) might be reread as less the products of the Parisian intellectual climate than inspired or significantly inflected by colonial experience.

Further Reading: Dimitriadis 2001; Kaul 1996; Said 1993; Tiffin 1987; Trees 1997.

POSTCOLONIAL SCIENCE

How science has travelled between different cultures and how this has transformed the science involved in this process has been one of the most important developments in the field of postcolonial studies. In their ground-breaking essay from 2007, Warwick Andersen and Vincanne Adams suggested that

> postcolonial studies might enable a . . . rephrasing of technoscience within the framework of globalization, allowing ample use of the analytical dynamics suited to a colonial era at a time when the political framework of such engagements lives on under other guises, other names.

(Anderson and Adams 2007: 183)

This and earlier work by others make the claim to a universal validity of science increasingly problematic (Bishop 1990). This should not be confused with a claim that science does not embody objective truths tested by experiment. But it does suggest that where this science is applied, and by whom it is employed will mean it is subject to transformative forces in how it is used and what effects it may have. In effect, technology and science needs to be 'defetishized', as Andersen and Adams suggest, and the social relations within which its operation is defined need to cease to be 'conveniently erased' (Anderson and Adams 2007: 182).

Readings of modernist science increasingly pay attention to alternative models with which such science may have interacted, creating the same idea of a localized modernity that has been for a long time a staple of anthropological thinking (see **Modernism, Anthropocentrism**). The resulting stress on how science interacts with local knowledge systems or beliefs that predate the colonial period makes clear that Western science needs to be evaluated in and alongside such local systems without being privileged epistemologically (see **Local**). As Andersen and Adams conclude,

> we need multi-sited histories of science which study the bounding of sites of knowledge production, the creation of value within such boundaries, the relations with other local social circumstances, and the traffic of objects and careers between these sites, and in and out of them. . . these histories will creatively complicate conventional distinctions between center and periphery, modern and traditional, dominant and subordinate, civilized and primitive, global and local.

(Anderson 2000: 736)

The work of feminist critics also highlights how both feminist and non-Western critiques of contemporary science studies formed a shared 'marker not of a set of theoretical perspectives but rather of the geographical and temporal positioning of standpoints often marginalized'. The consensus of both approaches stresses how one cannot oppose universalist science with localist belief but can only contrast one form of local knowledge with many other forms (Harding 2013; Seth 2017; Willey 2016).

Another and increasingly vital area is the development of psychopolitics. Building on the work of Fanon, and implicit in the activist resistance of postcolonial figures such as Steve Biko is a critique of the limitations of traditional European ideas of the psyche. The application of postcolonial ways of thinking to issues such as racism and alienation requires that we recognize it as insufficient to engage certain forms of power, like that of racism, without a consideration of their 'conditions of subjectivity'. . . . 'we need strong psychological accounts of racism if racism is to be adequately examined, confronted and hence contested' (Hook 2005: 487) The science of psychology is a crucial form of science that requires rethinking in light of recent reevaluations of the interaction of universal and local forms of knowledge.

Attempts have been made to embrace a more nuanced way of regarding science as neither simply another hegemonic master-narrative, nor merely a 'hybrid or pale copy valid only locally, in contrast to the universality of the European original' (Raj 2013: 341). These attempts emphasize how the recent hegemonic narratives of modern science were influenced by and functioned within the promulgation of the struggles of the Cold War period, and how contrastively some of the revisionary accounts 'in the hands of religious and political extremists, . . . led to a lot of chauvinistic gerrymandering, if not pure historical falsification' (Raj 2013: 340). In contrast is the argument for a focus on the circulatory as a 'site' of knowledge that is the possible way of opening a conversation between these two extreme views. This emphasis on the mutual circulation of knowledge between all parties involved serves as a 'strong counterpoint to the unidirectionality of "diffusion" or even of "dissemination" or "transmission"' (Raj 2013: 344).

This is part of the broader attempt within recent studies of postcolonial science to reengage with the agency of the colonized subject in the process of modernization. This reflects the influence of similar thinking in modern anthropology that has been a strong influence on the attempts to rethink how science needs to reevaluate its relations with local forms of modernity and the systems that existed to evaluate and measure the natural world before colonization and afterwards.

Further Readings: Anderson and Adams 2007; Bishop 1990; Seth 2017; Willey 2016; Hook 2005; Raj 2013.

POSTCOLONIAL STATE

The term 'post-colonial state' has often been used by historians, economists and political theorists as a synonym for 'post-independence state'. Its formation after independence is the clearest signal of the separation of the colonized from the imperial power. The independence of that newly formed state is the *sine qua non* of the claim to have left the power of the colonizer behind. However, in practice, such 'independence' may come to be seen as superficial, mainly because the dominance of the idea of the European concept of the **nation** in the minds of those who led the struggle for independence often meant that new postcolonial states were closely modelled on that of the former European powers. Postcolonial nation-states have usually (though not always) been coterminous with the boundaries of the colonial administrative units. Thus, in Africa, for example, the extent of independent countries, such as Nigeria and Ghana, broadly reflects the colonial enclaves carved out from the precolonial societies of West Africa. By contrast, in the Indian subcontinent, the apparent colonial unity of the Indian Raj was replaced by a partition into the separate states of India and Pakistan. The separately governed princely states of the Raj period were incorporated, often unwillingly, into the new postcolonial states so formed. In any case, the modern political entities bore only a notional relationship to the precolonial entities now incorporated as modern, postcolonial nation-states.

As in the case of the European nation-states on whose model they were created, the postcolonial nation-state was often created by a deliberate fusing or dividing of a number of already existing territories. In each case, the glue that held them together was a constructed national mythology in which unifying symbols such as flags, names and national symbols were vital elements. Thus, for example, postcolonial states like Ghana adopted the name of a mediaeval kingdom whose physical boundaries had no congruence with that of the colonial enclave of the Gold Coast protectorate. In the case of Zimbabwe (literally Stone Town), the country took its name from the local name for the many archaeological ruins of the precolonial cultures in the region. In the case of Pakistan, the name was invented as an anagram of the principal Muslim regions of the old North-West of colonized India.

More importantly, perhaps, postcolonial states were often tied to former colonial administrative, legal and economic systems that limited their independent action. This effectively allowed the continued control of many of these states in the period after independence (see **neo-colonialism**). The resulting back-lash in the form of an assertion of **native/nativist** practices was understandable, but posed new problems since no single, undisputed, national precolonial tradition could adequately represent the multiplicity of ethnicities and differences that made up most modern postcolonial states. In this, the postcolonial states were not different from those of their erstwhile colonizers, but the fact that these had succeeded in constructing relatively successful myths of national homogeneity (partly by contrasting themselves as unified against the differentness of the **other** represented by the colonized world) ironically meant that the newly formed postcolonial states were often compared with the European models in a very unfair and unfavourable way. The task facing contemporary postcolonial states, then, is to construct an effective unity while avoiding the oppression of minority groups whose practices clash with those of the dominant national mythology, whether over religion, language or cultural mores. Significantly, in this sense, the imperial nations also face the same problem as they are forced to redefine themselves in terms of the new **ethnicities** created by the influx of peoples from the erstwhile colonial **margins**.

Further Reading: Bhabha 1990; Chatterjee 1993; Davidson 1992; Premnath 2003; Stepputat and Hansen 2001.

POSTCOLONY

This term has been largely associated with the work of the Francophone Cameroonian critic Achille Mbembe who has written several influential accounts of how power and oppression actually work in the postcolonized states of Africa, the most influential of which has been the study translated into English as *On the Postcolony* (2001). Although the term has also been used by others in different ways, which do not necessarily concur with Mbembe's views (e.g. Comaroff 2006). The term has been used so far principally in studies of African states and in studies of the ongoing violence perpetrated in those states by those in power during and after colonization.

Mbembe suggests that although in Africa the postcolony is chaotically pluralistic; it has nonetheless an internal coherence. It is a specific system of signs, a particular way of fabricating simulacra or re-forming stereotypes. It is not the economy of signs in which the power is mirrored and imagined self-reflectively. The postcolony is characterized 'by a distinctive style of political improvisation, by a tendency to excess and lack of proportion, as well as by distinctive ways identities are multiplied transformed and put into circulation' (Mbembe 2001: 102). In response to this analysis, Mbembe emphasizes the need to address the fields of daily practice through which Africans in the postcolony

> exercise existence – that is, live their lives out and confront the very forms of their death. On this basis, I then asked what is the set of particular signs that confers on the current African age its character of urgency, its distinctive mark, its eccentricities, its vocabularies, and its magic, and make it both a source of terror, astonishment, and hilarity at once? What gives this set of things significations that all can share? In what languages are these significations expressed? How can these languages be deciphered?
>
> (15)

Mbembe's project is aimed towards a restorative goal, to restoring to Africans a sense of their wholeness, of their validity as 'autonomous African subject[s]'. As he suggests,

> On a sociological level attention must be given to the contemporary everyday practices through which Africans manage to recognise and to maintain with the world an unprecedented familiarity – practices through which they invent something that is their own and that beckons to the world in its generality.
>
> (258)

The African subject has been dismembered, fragmented and effectively rendered 'non-existent' by the physical and psychic violence of slavery and colonization. These violences have been projected forward into the ongoing representations of Africa and Africans in the **neo-colonial** discourses of the postcolonial world. Thus, Mbembe agrees with the emphasis in much **postcolonial** and **neo-colonial** theory on the ongoing effects of colonization but argues for a different emphasis in response, one which refocuses attention onto an analysis of the daily practices by which Africans have engaged with and negotiated the legacies of the processes of enslavement and colonization. In effect, he moves the attention away from the process of overcoming the violence and disruption to social and cultural forms, which is the legacy of this history and refocuses on the ways in which Africans have taken these things on board and survive within and even through them. For example, in his analysis of the operation of power in the postcolony, he argues that we need to move beyond the idea of a binary oppositional mode and embrace a more complex model in which the forces of oppressive power (the *commandemente* or the power elites, as he terms them) are revealed as symbolic languages, fetishized in a variety of daily rituals. Opposition to these modes of power may, often in startling ways, embrace these very rituals, engaging with them through laughter and mockery. Mbembe's analysis brings together the oppressor and the oppressed, the corrupt élite and their subjects in a process which he argues is continuous. Oppositionality is not an answer in itself since, he argues, the 'postcolonial relationship is not primarily a relationship of resistance or collaboration but can best be characterised as convivial, a relationship fraught by the fact of the *commandemente* and its "subjects" having to share the same living space' (104). Mbembe concludes:

> Hence, it would seem wrong to continue to interpret postcolonial relations in terms of absolute resistance or absolute domination, or, as a function of the binary oppositions usually adduced in conventional analyses of movements of indiscipline and revolt (e.g. counter-discourse, counter-society, counter-hegemony. . . .).

> (105)

Instead he argues that 'the [analytical] emphasis should be on the logic of 'conviviality', on the dynamics of domesticity and familiarity, inscribing the dominant and the dominated within the same episteme' (110) Direct or even indirect opposition is useless in the face of what Mbembe sees as a plurality which cannot be reduced to 'a single permanently stable system' (108), since the existence of such a stable system would be a prerequisite for successful formal opposition. Instead, the mockery which the subject conducts from inside the fetishized system of power is both a condition of that power and a prerequisite of its exposure. Both ruler and ruled in the postcolony are engaged in the production of a regime of unreality in which the subject who simulates the official rituals, e.g., hanging portraits of the ruler in their homes, wearing party uniforms, carrying party cards, etc. are '[saying] the unsayable and [recognising] the unrecognisable. . . . [Thus] . . . the fetish, seen for the sham it is, is made to lose its might and become a mere arte-fact'. (108) Mbembe clearly draws on the Bakhtinian idea of carnivale (see Bakhtin 1941) though his critique differs from that of Bakhtin, in that he argues that in the postcolony the public space is not singular as it is in the classic state but rather is constituted in many overlapping domains 'each having its own logic yet liable to be entangled with other logics' (104).

Mbembe's work has been criticized as not leading to an active policy, which might address the issues of violence and oppression within the postcolony, displacing political action into the realm of the personal and the libidinous. In response, Mbembe has argued that his analysis of the postcolony is apt since

> the usual categories of political economy are unable to highlight its complexities. In this kind of power formation, reality is each time erased, recreated, and duplicated. It is this power of proliferation (and its ability to obliterate the distinctions between truth and falsehood, the visible and the occult) that turns domination and subjection into a magical song, at that point where the originary arbitariness produces terror and hilarity.
>
> (Hoeller 2002)

Despite this defence, other commentators have suggested Mbembe's work is essentially pessimistic. For these critics, Mbembe's work 'places Africa's dire predicament in perspective. But it offers no solution (Jules-Rosette 2002; see also Janz 2002). Others, especially anthropologists and sociologists have been even more directly critical, suggesting that Mbembe's claim that Africa 'stands out as the supreme receptacle of the West's obsession with and circular discourse about the facts of "absence", "lack" and "non-being," of identity and difference, of negativeness – in short nothingness' (5) grossly misrepresents the more complex analysis of Africa which their disciplines have produced. In this respect, the debate about this text reflects the conflicting assessments of **ethnography** and of positivist scientific discourses over the effect of Eurocentric **surveillance** of the postcolonial subject (see Keita 2006). Mbembe analyses the role of the IMF, the World Bank and other non-government organizations in a controversially different way to many other postcolonial intellectuals (see **neo-colonialism/neo-imperialism**). Mbembe argues that despite their control by external powers and forces such as the United States, these institutions may act inadvertently to undermine power élites in the postcolony (the *commandemente*) because they encourage economic conditions which 'have created the conditions for a 'privatisation of sovereignty' through the decentralization of fiscal power and the emergence of self-administered social programmes not dependent on state patronage (78). (For a useful discussion of this view, see Adeeko 2002.) Mbembe's influential and controversial work has rekindled the debate on the nature and continuity of the African colonial legacy and the responses it has shaped in the region in a number of new ways.

Further Reading: Adeeko 2002; Janz 2002; Keita 2006; Jules-Rosette 2002; Hoeller 2002; Mbembe 2001, 2003.

POSTNATIONALISM

Postnationalism is a term used in two ways: to describe the shift of power from nation-states to supernational institutions; and to describe the decreasing function of the nation-state in the determination of social identity.

International Structures

Supernational institutions are the product of the changes associated with the globalization of contemporary political economies. These changes reflect new formations that have reduced the importance of national structures, for example political unions such as the European Union, trade associations, such as the North American Free Trade Association, or looser associations of nations across regions such as ASEAN. The role played by supranational economic powers such as the International Monetary Fund and the World Bank reflect the sense that nations have less control over their economies and over the political choices they can make than in the past. The problem some perceive is that existing organizations cannot any longer legislate effectively to control the way multi-national corporations act, leaving a power gap on issues, such as safety standards, wages and the transfer of profits. These matters arguably now lie beyond the effective control of either the traditional national authorities or the new international organizations.

On the positive side, the recent past has seen an attempt by postnational organizations such as the United Nations to develop universal codes of conduct on issues such as human rights (for example, the United Nations Universal Declaration of Human Rights), or the International Court of Justice based at the Hague that has sought to prosecute crimes against humanity wherever they occur. The problem again is that such institutions are subject to all the dangers that the idea of a universal standard continues to involve (see universalism). A further problem is that the institutions that seek to impose them are dependent upon the participation or at least acquiescence of the major world powers, some of whom have refused to participate in institutions such as the International Court of Justice (e.g. the United States), arguing that to do so would be to expose their citizens to laws not under the control of their own national authorities. In short, postnational organizations embody aspirations to a new and equal internationalism that so far has failed to satisfy either its advocates or its opponents.

Nevertheless, it seems inevitable that national forms will inevitably change radically in the future, not least because the means of communication have ceased to be controllable at a national level. The internet and the social media it has generated are increasingly difficult to police, as the recent Wikileaks example, or the failure of the People's Republic of China to shut down dissenting voices in the social media, has shown. As a result of these technologies, some have argued that the internet provides new ways for groups to identity that may be counter to or more important than the old bonds of national identity (See Sassen 1996; Bamya 2000).

Some of the more recent resurgences of extreme nationalism have been in reaction to these changes, reflecting the fact that post-nationalist institutions and ideas are seen by these groups as a threat to traditionally conceived national identities and rights. This has led to various forms of regressive nativism. Ironically enough, these have been a feature of many of the traditional European colonial powers, as they have responded to the increased migration of people from the ex-colonial countries. (See diaspora.) This has led to new ways of defining citizenship, either by legally restricting it only to certain groups or by emphasizing in more informal ways that only some categories of citizens have the power to define the national social imaginary while others are excluded from this "natural" right. (See Hage 1988, 2003.) For some, postnationalism is a way forward into ways of rethinking identity based on ways of defining common human values rather than on territorial identities that is a vital response to the changing conditions of the early twenty-first century; for others, it is a utopian idea that does not reflect political realities and threatens their traditional identities and self-images. Thus, like the term globalization itself, postnationalism reflects the contestatory nature of such theories and the ways they represent differing views of contemporary institutions and their practice in the world.

Beyond National Identity

As a feature of the discussions around cultural identity in an increasingly mobile world, the concept of the postnational has become the subject of vigorous argument (Pease 1997; Cheah 1999; Hansen 2009; Breen and O'Neill 2010). The term does not imply a denial of national identity or its endurance. Rather, the suggestion is that the nation-state and the forms of nationalism that underpinned it, are becoming less relevant in the determination of social being. This is particularly so in postcolonial theory. While nationalism, and the promise of an independent nation, was critical in decolonizing struggles, the increasing mobility of formally colonized populations has meant that the nation-state is no longer the overarching category of social formation. Furthermore, according to Peng Cheah, by the late twentieth century, nationalism had become

> probably one of the few phenomena we associate most closely with death. The end of this millennium is marked (and marred) by endless acts of fanaticist intolerance, ethnic violence, and even genocidal destruction that are widely regarded as extreme expressions of nationalism.
>
> (1999: 226)

Although some critics decry postnationalism's disregard for the nation's capacity to accord freedoms and rights to citizens (Hansen 2009), the erosion of the nation-state's centrality has been an inevitable response to global mobility.

While globalization and postcolonialism have both emerged at the site of the postnational, they differ radically in the significance they associate with the nation's change in status. While there is no question that transnational migration has weakened the mythology if not the power of citizenship, the postnational does not reject the nation, rather it attends to the structures of the state in order to define the ways in which ordinary subjects refuse its bordering practices. The idea of belonging in a postnational world seems contradictory, but that is only because we have become indoctrinated with the idea that national borders are the primary determinants of identity. Postnational experience echoes

Edward Said's testament to the power of exile, which consists not in rejecting ties to one's home but rather in "working through" them: "we achieve independence and detachment by working through attachments, not by rejecting them" (Said 2001: 185). In this way, the postnational is working through and around the borders of the nation.

Unlike the discourse of **globalization**, postnationalism emerged out of an implicit critique of state power. Like postcolonialism, postnationalism is not *after* nationalism but within its archive engaging with it contesting and transforming it. Breen and O'Neill ask four questions of the nation-state.

> First, how should we conceive of nationalism and the nation-state in a world in which there are many more nations than states? Second, can plural ethnic identities be accommodated within overarching national frameworks or do they pose a fundamental threat to such frameworks? Third, can conflicts generated by rival national projects find satisfactory institutional resolution? And, fourth, is nationalist politics of necessity a politics prone to violence and war?
>
> (2010: 7)

The question remains whether global egalitarianism or cosmopolitanism inimical to the national quest for sovereignty and self-determination. The connection made by theorists such as Mbembe and Cheah about the nation's connection with death add to the postcolonial suspicion of the nation and nationalism that we first find in Fanon.

Further Reading: J. Bhabha 1998; Sassen 1996; Smith and Eduardo 1998; Bamyah 2000; Cheah 1999; Breen and O'Neill 2010; Pease 1997

PRECARITY/PRECARIAT

The term precarity is used by sociologists to refer to the increasing spread of insecure labour in the employment market. According to Paret and Gleeson (2016), the term may be traced back, at least, to Pierre Bourdieu's study of Algeria, where he used it to differentiate casual workers from permanent workers (Waite 2009: 414). The term became popular in the 2000s, particularly in Europe, as a point of departure for May Day mobilizations and other protests against austerity and economic insecurity. Within academic circles, Guy Standing's (2011) *The Precariat: The New Dangerous Class*, asserted the 'precariat' as a new, global 'class in the making' and encouraged the wider use of the term beyond the European context.

The term has its roots in Marxist discourse and has sometimes been seen as a symptom of a development inherent in the neo-liberal, global stage of capitalism itself. (See **Globalization, Neo-liberalism**.) The theorists Hardt and Negri suggest that as modern labour has moved to a condition that embraces the notion of immaterial labour, that is when cognitive and intellectual labour is commodified and casualized, the precariat has become much more widespread. Feminists have suggested that this idea of immaterial labour includes domestic labour and caring roles, traditionally designated as feminine. The feminist critic Judith Butler suggests that precariousness is a condition shared by all humans as a condition of life itself but distinguishes precarity as a condition that is unevenly distributed between difference classes and groups in society. This is because some groups in society such as women, the poor and whole undeveloped societies in the world are more likely to experience precarity and the members of these groups have been termed the precariat. (See **Feminism and postcolonialism**.)

From this, we are led to the even more radical idea that societies which have been relegated to inferior economic status through exploitation are more likely to form a precariat. Precarity, it might be argued, is a norm in such societies, embracing the bulk of the population. It is this which makes the term of increasing significance in postcolonial studies. Societies which have experienced colonization were prevented from developing their own self-sufficient economies as they were exploited as a source of raw materials and a market for finished goods from the industrial metropoles. Even after independence, the direct exploitation of these countries through international cartels operating through a corrupt new ruling class saw this process continue. (See **Neo-colonialism, Neo-imperialism**.) This has been most obvious with the resulting growth of migrants from countries in the **Global South** which have suffered from these conditions to the rich Global North. The borders of these rich countries have hardened even as the free flow of global capital has increased, rendering the migrant as one of the fastest-growing elements of the precariat worldwide. (See **Migration/Refugees/Asylum Seekers**.) In the last 20 years, the term has been increasingly employed by movements which protest economic austerity measures and highlight the increasing spread of economic insecurity and unequal distribution of resources between the rich and the poor. In this sense, it is seen as a term which may be used positively to create and inspire people who share a common precariat identity, uniting the various groups who have been marginalized by modern neo-liberal capitalism and the forces of globalization.

Further Reading: Butler 2020; Castles 2011; Hardt and Negri 2004; Kasmir 2018; Paret and Gleeson 2016; Standing 2011

PRIMITIVISM

A term that has been widely used in art history and, to a lesser extent, in literary studies. It is used narrowly to identify a specific modern school of art and writing that emphasizes simplicity of form or theme. In this regard, in the history of modern European art, it is associated with the work of sculptors such as Brancusi and painters such as Miro. In this narrow sense, it is an ongoing and important influence on modern art. In modern writing, however, it is less frequently employed as a critical term, being associated with simplicity of style and a deliberate employment of simple themes and subjects (for example, the representation of peasant life). In some cases, notably in Latin American writing, it has had a radical association absent from most of its European uses. However, in many places, it has formed part of a more general movement of national self-assertion, for example, in Slavic countries, in the second-half of the nineteenth century, when it fostered the recovery and employment of motifs and themes from peasant and folk art as nationalist symbols.

Its broader use defines a form or style perceived to represent an early stage of human cultural endeavour. Thus, early human art is often described as primitive art. The problem with the term used in this way is that it assumes a linear, teleological unfolding of human history from simple to complex, where early or primitive art is seen as leading to a culmination and fulfilment in later sophisticated or civilized art. Even more dubiously, such criteria may lead to further categories. Thus uneducated, that is untrained and unschooled, artists whose work does not reflect the dominant artistic conventions, such as the Frenchman Henri Rousseau, or the American woman painter Granma Moses, or even trained artists who deliberately repudiate the conventions, such as the British painter Stanley Spencer, may be categorized as 'primitive'. Furthermore, whole alternative cultural and artistic traditions may be assigned to this category simply because their conventions do not match those of the dominant artistic codes of the West. This discrimination lends itself too easily to unfounded and often pejorative comparisons of the 'value' of different cultures. Thus African or Pacific Islander or Native American Indian or Australian Aboriginal art was often described as 'primitive' (implying a savage crudity and simplicity, if also a welcome freshness and a child-like vision) because its conventions did not match those of the dominant European tradition whose values were considered to establish the norms of civilized and mature art (see **universalism, savage**). Even the most positive descriptions based on the category of the primitive are in danger of exoticizing these cultures and **othering** them.

As these dominant European traditions associated with the **modernist** movement at the end of the nineteenth and early twentieth centuries became questioned and challenged, Western artists, such as Picasso, often deliberately sought to reproduce the innocence and 'child-like' qualities of primitive art. This was, in part, a repudiation of their own culture and did not necessarily involve an affirmation of the validity and difference of the cultures they employed as signifiers of the liberating force of the primitive. The signs of the primitive continued to be juxtaposed with icons of Western art, reinforcing the binary of primitive (savage) and modern (civilized), even as it sought to dismantle the claims of the latter. Thus, for example, in Picasso's famous and influential early painting *Les Demoiselles d'Avignon* (1907), the classical Greek icon of the three Graces in the grouping of the young women is juxtaposed against the image of an African mask which replaces the face of one of them. Such a juxtaposition may seek to dismantle the status of the classical tradition but does not necessarily affirm the value of the alter/native tradition it employs.

For these reasons, primitivism remains a problematic concept, and one that most postcolonial studies have treated with caution as a descriptive category, while recognizing that the artistic and social movements it describes have had powerful historical links with colonialist and postcolonialist discourses.

Further Reading: Arac and Ritvo 1995; Barkan and Bush 1995; Consentino 2000; During 1994; Harrison, Frascina, and Perry 1993; Hiller 1991; Lloyd 2023; Rhodes 1994; Rubin 1984; Torgovnick 1990.

RACE

'Race' is a term for the classification of human beings into physically, biologically and genetically distinct groups. The notion of race assumes, firstly, that humanity is divided into unchanging natural types, recognizable by physical features that are transmitted 'through the blood' and permit distinctions to be made between 'pure' and 'mixed' races. Furthermore, the term implies that the mental and moral behaviour of human beings, as well as individual personality, ideas and capacities, can be related to racial origin, and that knowledge of that origin provides a satisfactory account of the behaviour.

Race is particularly pertinent to the rise of colonialism, because the division of human society in this way is inextricable from the need of colonialist powers to establish a dominance over subject peoples and hence justify the imperial enterprise. Race thinking and colonialism are imbued with the same impetus to draw a **binary** distinction between '**civilized**' and 'primitive' and the same necessity for the hierarchization of human types. By translating the fact of colonial oppression into a justifying theory, however spurious, European race thinking initiated a hierarchy of human variation that has been difficult to dislodge. Although race is not specifically an invention of imperialism, it quickly became one of imperialism's most supportive ideas, because the idea of superiority that generated the emergence of race as a concept adapted easily to both impulses of the imperial mission: dominance and enlightenment.

In this respect, 'racism' is not so much a product of the concept of race as the very reason for its existence. Without the underlying desire for hierarchical categorization implicit in racism, 'race' would not exist. Racism can be defined as a way of thinking that considers a group's unchangeable physical characteristics to be linked in a direct, causal way to psychological or intellectual characteristics, and which on this basis distinguishes between 'superior' and 'inferior' racial groups. Physical differences did not always represent an inferiority of culture or even a radical difference in shared human characteristics. In the period of the Crusades, the racial difference of black African Coptic saint-warrior St Maurice is clearly recorded without prejudice in a statue in Magdeburg Cathedral which shows him to be a black African, even including his facial lineage cuts (Davidson 1994: 330). But with the rise of European imperialism and the growth of Orientalism in the nineteenth century, the need to establish such a distinction between superior and inferior finds its most 'scientific' confirmation in the dubious analysis and taxonomy of racial characteristics.

'Race' is first used in the English language in 1508 in a poem by William Dunbar, and through the seventeenth and eighteenth centuries, it remained essentially a literary word denoting a class of persons or things. It was only in the late eighteenth century that the term came to mean a distinct category of human beings with physical characteristics transmitted by descent. Humans had been categorized by Europeans on physical grounds from the late 1600s, when François Bernier postulated a number of distinctive categories, based largely on facial character and skin colour. Soon a hierarchy of groups (not yet termed races) came to be accepted, with white Europeans at the top. The Negro or black African category was usually relegated to the bottom, in part because of black Africans' colour and allegedly 'primitive' culture, but primarily because they were best known to Europeans as slaves.

Immanuel Kant's use of the German phrase for 'races of mankind' in his *Observations on the Feeling of the Beautiful and Sublime* (1764) was probably the first explicit use of the term in the sense of biologically or physically distinctive categories of human beings. Kant's stress on an intuitive, non-rational form of thought 'allowed the Romantics to posit the notion of an unchanging inner essence within human beings', an essence that 'found expression through the sense of "race"' (Malik 1996: 77). Debates about whether human variation was caused by descent or environment raged throughout the seventeenth and eighteenth centuries. But with the ascendancy of the biological sciences in the late nineteenth century, descent emerged as the predominant model. It was encapsulated in the transition of 'race' from signifying, in its literary sense, a line of descent that a group defined by historical continuity, to its scientific sense of 'race' as a zoologically or biologically defined group.

Despite its allegedly scientific grounding and application, the term 'race' has always provided an effective means of establishing the simplest model of human variation – colour difference. Colour became the means of distinguishing between groups of people and of identifying the behaviour to be expected of them. In 1805, the French anatomist Cuvier, who was particularly significant in the development of 'race' theory, postulated the existence of three major 'races': the white, the yellow and the black. The division of the whole of humanity into three such arbitrarily designated genetic groups seems so vague as to be entirely useless for any kind of analysis, but the concept has remained influential for the ideological reason that this typology rested upon a gradation from superior to inferior. Cuvier's typology of race influenced such works as Charles Hamilton Smith's (1848) *The Natural History of the Human Species;* Robert Knox's (1850) *The Races of Man;* Count de Gobineau's (1853) *Essai sur l'Inégalité des Races Humaines*; and Nott and Gliddon's (1854) *Types of Mankind*. The assumptions underlying this racial typology, though continually contradicted by actual observation, have remained stubbornly persistent to the present day, even when the categories are more elaborately defined as 'caucasoid', 'mongoloid' and 'negroid'. These assumptions are: first, that variations in the constitution and behaviour of individuals were to be explained as the expression of different biological types; second, that differences between these types explained variations in human cultures; third, that the distinctive nature of the types explained the superiority of Europeans and Aryans in particular; and fourth, that the friction between nations and individuals of different type emerged from innate characteristics.

The simple clarity of this view of race, more or less based on colour, was superseded by the implications of Darwin's *The Origin of Species* (1859). Natural selection now offered a mechanism for species alteration – either the superior races might be contaminated through contact with the inferior, or deliberate human intervention might maximize the benefits of selection and advance the emergence of pure races. In either case, the fundamental assumption of the hierarchy of races remained secure. Darwin's contribution was to provide the theory of race with a mechanism of change in the idea of natural selection, and consequently to offer the possibility for planned racial development (eugenics) – a central tenet of the school of thought that came to be known as Social Darwinism.

Social Darwinism, in both its positive and negative implications, concurred readily with imperial practice, particularly the paradoxical dualism that existed in imperialist thought between the debasement and the idealization of colonized subjects. On the one hand, the debasement of the primitive peoples could find in Social Darwinism a justification for the domination and at times extinction of inferior races as not only an inevitable but a desirable unfolding of natural law. On the other hand, the concept of racial improvement concurred with the 'civilizing mission' of imperial ideology, which encouraged colonial powers to take up the 'white man's burden' and raise up the condition of the inferior races who were idealized as child-like and malleable. The assumption of superiority thus supported by scientific racial theory could pursue its project of world domination with impunity.

The latter perception of blacks as helpless beings in need of care, protection and advancement was quickly overtaken in the nineteenth century by the former view of them as primitive and indolent savages, as colonial expansion found the need for increasing supplies of labour to service its enterprises. The evangelical anti-slavery impulse that had achieved the abolition of slavery in the 1830s began to give way to a virulent form of racial hostility. Thomas Carlyle's notorious *Occasional Discourse on the Nigger Question* (1849) vigorously propounded the right to coerce the 'indolent' black man into the service of colonial plantation agriculture, and by the 1870s, before the last phase of imperial expansion into Africa, such prejudice, supported as it was by Social Darwinism, had virtually overshadowed liberal brands of thought on issues of race.

The usefulness of the concept of race in both establishing the innate superiority of imperial culture as it approached its zenith, and at the same time lumping together the 'inferior' races under its control, can be seen in the example of English commentary on the 'races' of Britain itself – particularly the Irish. In early writings, although the Irish were initially seen to be physically much the same as the English, Irish culture was seen as alien and threatening. Rich (1986) traces the process from 1617 when Fynes Moryson found the language of the Irish crude, if indeed it was a language at all, their clothing almost animal-like and their behaviour shocking. Edmund Spenser refers to the 'bestial Irishmen', while William Camden in 1610 recounted the profanity, cannibalism, musicality, witchcraft, violence, incest and gluttony of the 'wilde and very uncivill' Irish. In this description, the Irish sound remarkably like Africans as described by nineteenth-century English commentators. Indeed, by 1885, John Beddoe, president of the Anthropological Institute, had developed an 'index of Nigrescence' that showed the people of Wales, Scotland, Cornwall and Ireland to be racially separate from the British. More specifically, he argued that those from Western Ireland and Wales were 'Africanoid' in their jutting jaws' and 'long slitty nostrils', and thus originally immigrants of Africa (Szwed 1975: 20–21). Bizarre though this might seem, it is a consumate demonstration of the exclusionary impetus of imperialism that operates so energetically in the concept of race.

The linking of the Irish and Welsh with Africa demonstrates remarkably clearly how imperial ideology operates to exclude and marginalize colonized peoples, whether in Britain or the Empire. Such a racial hierarchy was integral to the extension of the Empire. Kipling's notorious formulation, in the poem 'Recessional' (1897: 328–329), of the non-Caucasian races as 'lesser breeds without the law' may stand as a classic instance:

If, drunk with power we loose
Wild tongues that have not Thee in awe,
Such boastings as the Gentiles use,
Or lesser breeds without the Law –
Lord God of Hosts, be with us yet,
Lest we forget – lest we forget.

The most energetic period of imperial expansion in the last decades of the nineteenth century saw a rapid increase in anthropometric investigation of race differences. Disputes about the form of racial 'types' had raged throughout the century, but by 1886, anthropologists in Britain had reached a general consensus on the 'cephalic index': the discrimination of racial identity in terms of skull shape. Francis Galton, the founder of eugenics, measured 9,000 people at the International Health Exhibition in London in 1884, and the anthropological interest in race in the imperial context was reinforced at an Anthropological Conference on Native Races in British Possessions held in 1887 at the time of Queen Victoria's Golden Jubilee. By the late 1890s, many popular works began to appear, illustrating with lavish detail the nature and diversity of human races and the implicit superiority of the white Anglo-Saxon races and civilization. Despite the appearance of greater scientific rigour, the description of the negroid had not advanced much past the stereotype compounded by Carlyle.

The twentieth century has seen great swings in the theoretical attitude to race, but the term continues to hold a resilient sway in the ordinary thinking of people throughout the world. The 1911 Universal Races Congress held in London was a major demonstration of liberal thought and the promotion of 'monogenism' – the idea that there was 'only one species of man living on earth today'. But the universalist creed of the Victorian liberal tradition was considerably shaken by the First World War and the emergence of colonial nationalism which eroded confidence in the power of reason to ensure a growing unity between different races in a single world order (see Rich 1986: 49). In the early decades of the twentieth century, 'race' continued to acquire a legitimacy through the 'scientific' study of racial variation, but the horror of the Second World War and the slaughter of millions of Jews, Slavs, Poles and gypsies on racial grounds led to the 1951 UNESCO Statement of the Nature of Race and Racial Difference which pointed out that race, even from a strict biological standpoint, could at most refer to a group with certain distinctive gene concentrations. The statement asserts that mental characteristics should never be included in such classifications and that environment is far more important than inherited genetic factors in shaping behaviour.

However, in the 1960s, there was an upsurge in biological thinking about human behaviour once again, with writers, such as Lorenz, Ardry and Morris, asserting that individual behaviour was largely controlled by ancient instincts that could at best be modified by culture. This led the way for an upsurge in race thinking in popular science in the 1970s: Eysenck's Race, *Intelligence and Education* (1971), Richardson and Spears' *Race, Culture and Intelligence* (1972), Baxter and Sansom's *Race and Social Difference* (1972) indicate some of the wide range of popular books that maintained the centrality of 'race' in debates about human variation. At the same time, the neo-biologism of the 1960s led to a much more rigorous development in the 1970s with the emergence of sociobiology, which views all individual behaviour, and cultures themselves, as the end products of biological selection processes. These developments lent an air of legitimacy to race thinking, which also analyses behaviour and performance in biological terms, and the relation between sociobiology and modern racism has been examined by Barker (1981).

It is significant that academic debate during these decades sustained race rather than **ethnicity** as the centre of discussion. The sense of permanency that a dubious biological explanation offered, through an inexorable genetic determination and transmission, consolidated the concept of race at this time, rather than the more complex concept of ethnicity with its inherent plasticity and its basis in culture. Yet the 1970s and 1980s saw the gradual growth of interest and research into ethnicity, a growth that perhaps has not been reflected in popular thinking. In practice, 'race' may be a major constitutive factor in determining ethnic categories, but to revive the idea that it is somehow 'objective' and less socially constructed than ethnicities founded on religious, linguistic or other more obviously culturally determined factors is to fail to recognize that race is a cultural rather than a biological phenomenon, the product of historical processes not of genetically determined physical differences.

The most important fact about race was, as Fanon was the first to notice, that however lacking in objective reality, racist ideas such as 'black-ness' were, the psychological force of their construction of self, meant that they acquired an objective existence in and through the behaviour of people. The self-images and self-construction that such social pressure exerted might be transmitted from generation to generation, and thus the 'fact of blackness' came to have an objective determination not only in racist behaviour and institutional practices, but more insidiously in the psychological behaviour of the peoples so constructed. This **Fanonist** stress on the objective psychological fact of race as a determining part of the social process of constructing individuals' self-perceptions has been part of the response of many black commentators to the claims by critics such as Appiah that perceptions of race have acted only negatively in determining postcolonial responses to European domination. However fictional race may be shown to be as an objective category, its power as a discursive formation remains unabated.

Thus, a fraught and volatile term, 'race', continues to hold centre stage while the theories on which concepts of race were established have become more and more blurred. In this way, resistance becomes less and less able to dislodge the vague and untenable concept of race itself. Race in the time of neo-colonialism is just as vague and just as resilient as it was at the beginning of the history of European imperialism. It is perhaps up to the concept of ethnicity to change the direction of the debate.

Further Reading: Ashcroft 2003; Baxter and Sansom 1972; Bremen 1990; Chrisman 2003; Cooppan 1999; Fanon 1961; Frankenberg and Mani 1996; Gilroy 1996; Gunew 1997; Husband 1994; Malik 1996; McInturff 2000; Marriot 2000; S. Mishra 1993; Olson and Worsham 1999; Rich 1986; Ross 1982; H. Scott 2002; Sharpe 2000.

RASTAFARIANISM

A black nationalist religion that emerged in Jamaica in the 1930s. Its geneses are complex and include slave beliefs in the soul's return after death to Africa from exile in the Caribbean. Together with the visionary black restitutive politics of Marcus Garvey and the Ethiopianism of Leonard Percival Howell, Rastafarianism drew its inspiration from the Old Testament prophecy that 'Princes shall come out of Egypt; Ethiopia shall soon stretch forth her hands unto God' (Psalm 68: 31). In 1930, Ras Tafari, great grandson of King Saheka Selassie of Shoa, was crowned Negus of Ethiopia, taking the name Haile Selassie, meaning 'Mighty of the Trinity'. To this title was added 'King of Kings' and 'Lion of the Tribe of Judah', which placed him in the legendary line of King Solomon (Barrett 1988: 81). Celebrating the coronation of Ras Tafari as Haile Selassie, Jamaican Rastafarians initially looked forward to a literal repatriation to their African ancestral homelands through the agency of the Ethiopian Emperor.

This belief was supported by the fact that Ethiopia was one of the few countries not colonized in the **Scramble for Africa.** Increasingly, however, African repatriation was regarded less as a literal return than a figurative one: a reclaiming by Jamaicans of their African ancestry, a heritage systematically denigrated under slavery and in European colonialist ideologies. Initially a movement of the Jamaican under-class, Rastafarianism soon spread to sections of the middle class and to intellectuals, and across the Caribbean. It gained increasing popu-larity in other areas of the world, largely through the music and lyrics of Reggae star Bob Marley in the 1970s and 1980s, where its language and beliefs were co-opted in the fight against a wide variety of oppressions, both racial and economic. Rastafarians have always been acutely aware of the crucial connections between language and power, and in the cause of racial restitution have disrupted the rules of English grammar to refuse the 'objective case' (i.e. 'that which is acted upon') by eradi-cating the personal pronoun 'me' and insisting on 'I' no matter what the demands of conventional grammar.

Further Reading: Barrett 1977, 1988; Campbell 1985; Cashmore 1979, 1983; Chevannes 1997; Clarke 2000; Collins 2000; Gossai and Murell 2000; Hodges 2000; King and Jensen 1995; King et al. 2003; Miles 1978; Murrell and Spencer 1998; Oosthuizen 1993; Owens 1976; Pollard and Nettleford 2000; Savishinsky 1999; Somerson 1999.

RELIGION AND THE POSTCOLONIAL

There has been no more dramatic shift in recent times in postcolonial studies than the growing awareness of the role religion has played in both the practices of colonization and the developments which have occurred since political independence in the postcolonial world. This takes many forms. First, there is a growing awareness of the com-plex role religion played in the history of imperialism, both directly through the impact of missions (see **missions and colonialism**) and indirectly, as religion acted to shape the responses of both colonizer and colonized. The religious practices of colonized peoples were often denigrated as mere superstition or openly attacked as heathenism, and so used to justify the so-called '**civilizing mission**' (*mission civilatrice*) of the colonizer. This was particularly the case where these practices were not written down in forms (sacred texts), which Europeans could recognize. Even where their complexity and intellectual force was acknowledged (e.g. as in the case of cultures with written religious texts such as India), they were perceived to be decadent or decayed and in need of reform. So influential was this view that it even exerted force on the reformers sprung from within those cultures them-selves in the colonial period, e.g. Tilak and Vivekananda in India.

(See Viswanathan 1998; King 1999). Ironically, such reformers and the changes they effected went hand in hand with the development of secular anti-colonial resistances, which also borrowed forms from the practices of their colonizers, forms such as the European concept of the nation-state (See **nation/nationalism**), and broader discourses of reform, progress and modernization. Of course, as several commentators have already argued, colonized societies were always changing and modernizing in their own terms both before and after the impact of colonization (Ahmad 1992). But resistance after colonization often took the form of appropriation of institutions modelled on those of the colonizers. This was as true of religious institutions as of secular ones. Religion could therefore act either as a means of hegemonic control or could be employed by the colonized as a means of resistance. If this were true of the responses to and within the precolonial religious practices of colonized peoples, it was also true of the ways in which the Christian practices introduced under colonialism developed in postcolonized spaces. While for many, Christianity was a means by which their own cultures were being overwritten and ignored, for others, it became a vehicle for independent indigenous expression, at least when modified in an appropriated form. Christianity, which had been from its earliest years a religion of accretion and which thrived on the absorption of other practices and cultural modes, continued to change as it encountered the cultures of the colonized. In its most extreme form, notably in Africa, indigenous churches arose in which Christian and precolonial religions formed new synthesized forms. The leaders and 'prophets' of these new churches often played a vital role in the development of independence movements. This was aided by the fact that the rapid spread of Christianity in many areas of Latin America, Africa and Asia far outstripped the growth of these religions in Europe in the late nineteenth and twentieth centuries when religion in Europe was on the retreat (Van der Veer 2004). This rapid spread of Christianity beyond Europe was achieved not by the success of European proselytizers but by the work of indigenous evangelists. In fact, historians of religion now acknowledge that until indigenous evangelists emerged, Europeans had little or no success in converting large numbers of peoples in many of these regions (Etherington 2006). Many of these indigenous evangelists worked within existing religious forms and churches, though none of these forms and churches remained unchanged by the encounters. Such changes were clearly much more marked in the synthetized churches, which openly combined Christianity with elements of the precolonial religions.

If there is now a growing acknowledgement of the neglect of religion in the accounts of colonial times, then more recently, we have seen much more attention paid to the ongoing role of religion in the modern postcolony. Especially in North America and Canada, but increasingly elsewhere, indigenous scholars of religion have emphasized the role of religion in the modern era (Donaldson 2002; Treat 1996). As the balance of concern has begun to swing away from Europe and America, scholars and politicians alike have become increasingly aware that they are forced to engage with religious as well as other social and cultural practices within the framework of **globalization**. In fact, in the early twentieth century, it has become clear that religion has re-emerged as one of the key defining features of difference and that the role of religion has become central to the way in which Europeans and Americans think about identity with a force which it has not had for several centuries. This has resulted not from the growth of religious adherence in those areas (or at least not until very recently in the case of America) but in response to their awareness that for much of the world, the secular model of post-Enlightenment Europe was never dominant except for a small minority of Western educated intellectuals, and that it has increasingly been on the wane as the populations in many areas reassert their identity by a renewed adherence to their own traditions. In the resurgence of fundamentalist forces within many religions such as Islam, Hinduism and Christianity itself in recent times, especially in America and in areas such as Africa and Asia, we see the most obvious and, some would argue, the most negative effect of this renewed stress on religion as a component in social and national as well as personal identity. Islamic fundamentalism in particular has emerged in the public domain as a force that asserts a shared identity above and beyond other cultural allegiances, causing direct confrontation to emerge in many societies with earlier markers of identity based on secular formations such as nationality and citizenship. Though this is the most discussed example, religious leaders in many other societies such as those of America and Europe, as well as in many parts of the postcolonial world, e.g. India, assert their right to engage directly in secular politics and recruit adherents to social and political parties and causes. As a result, religious **fundamentalism** (a term whose origin, incidentally, is in the American Christian churches of the early twentieth century), that is religion offered as an alternative and indisputable form of personal and social identity and set over against ideas of secular reason and scientific evidence is likely to be an arena of confrontation in many of these societies for the foreseeable future. (See Pesso-Misquel and Stierstorfer 2006.) More positively though, we might see the questioning of the more simplistic formulations of the ideas of the

European Enlightenment (based on the idea that Western science and rational logic is the only meaningful way of organizing societies and the only way of guaranteeing human development and progress) may yield to an acknowledgement that Enlightenment reason too has had its dark side, not least in its embrace of a discourse of progress and science in forms inimical to older ideas of living in harmony with the environment rather than controlling and mastering it (See **ecological imperialism**). In this respect, the re-emergence of religious thought is part of a broader post-humanist critique which has taken many forms in recent times (See Wolfe 2003).

Further Reading: Ahmad 1992; Donaldson and Pui-Lan 2002; Etherington 2005, and Brock et al 2015 King 1999; Pesso-Miquel and Stierstorfer 2006; Sugirtharajah 2001; Treat 1996; Van der Veer 2005 Viswanathan 1998; Wolfe 2003.

RESISTANCE

Resistance movements arose within European empires as the demand for independence gathered force and the impetus for decolonization increased. Algerians, for instance, fought a sustained war against French conquest for two decades after 1830, led by Abd El-Khader. Although colonial wars were of shorter duration, such protracted hostilities were not uncommon, and often led to profound cultural consequences, such as the Treaty of Waitangi in 1840 in New Zealand which concluded the Maori wars, falsely ceding Maori *mana* to the crown. Armed rebellion began in the Caribbean as early as 1501, and, according to Julio le Riverend, the Governor of Cuba, Ovando, "asked for the complete prohibition of the [slave] trade, for, in previous years, the Negroes had shown an open tendency towards rebellion and conspiracy" (Riverend 1967: 82). The often unabashedly exploitative nature of colonial economic ventures, the actively racist attitudes of colonists – even those from France, which was determined to assimilate colonial societies into French political and administrative structures – and the overweening assumption of moral authority for colonial expansion, meant that political resentment, the motive for armed resistance, was constant. Indeed, such armed rebellion, from the "Indian Mutiny" to the resistance movements in Kenya, Zimbabwe and other African states, including the African National Congress (ANC) resistance to **apartheid** became the very focus of indigenous demands for self-determination.

Although resistance movements frequently engaged in armed struggle, postcolonial studies focus on the more ubiquitous and subtle effects of cultural resistance, with a particular focus on resistance literature. The concept of resistance literature (mugāwamah) was first applied in a description of Palestinian literature in 1966 by the Palestinian writer and critic Ghassan Kanafani in his study *Literature of Resistance in Occupied Palestine: 1948–1966*. For Kanafani, literature itself is an arena of struggle.

> The attempts at a history of the resistance literature of a given people are usually, for reasons that are self-evident', accomplished after liberation. With respect to the literature of resistance in occupied Palestine, however, it is necessary that the Arab reader in general and the Palestinian emigrant in particular study its persistent continuation, because it is fundamentally to be found in the language itself and speech of the Arabs of occupied Palestine. The resistance springs from these linguistic initiatives, working together with the rigidity of the conditions of the situation.
>
> (Kanafani 1966: 11)

Amilcar Cabral, the leader of the Guinea-Bissau liberation movement and a major theoretician of African resistance and liberation struggles, claimed in a speech delivered in 1970 in honour of the assassinated FRELIMO leader, Eduardo Mondlane, that "the armed struggle for liberation, in the concrete conditions of life of African peoples, confronted with the imperialist challenge, is an act of insemination upon history – the major expression of our culture and of our African essence". Ghassan Kanafani also asserts the integral relationship between armed resistance and culture, particularly through resistance literature.

Both thinkers locate the historical specificity of the resistance movement within a larger struggle against imperialism, and despite their promotion of armed struggle assert the significance of cultural resistance in determining the general strategies of the resistance organization. For Kanafani, the "extreme importance of the cultural form of resistance is no less valuable than armed resistance itself". Both Kanafani and Cabral were assassinated by the representatives of the imperialism they were resisting, perhaps signalling the effectiveness of cultural resistance. Kanafani's obituary in the Daily Star, a Beirut English-language newspaper, described him as the "commando who never fired a gun" and went on to say that "his weapon was a ballpoint pen and his arena newspaper pages. And he hurt the enemy more than a column of commandos".

For Selwyn Cudjoe, in *Resistance and Caribbean Literature*, resistance is "an act or complex of acts designed to rid people of its oppressors, be they slave masters or multi-national corporations" (1980: 19). It is something which so thoroughly infuses the experience of living under oppression that it becomes an almost autonomous "aesthetic-political" principle. Literary resistance, for Cudjoe, is a category of literary writing which emerges as an integral part of an organized struggle for national liberation. As such, its standard of value is entirely measured in terms of its social and political utility. He quotes Fidel Casto approvingly:

> Our evaluation is political. There can be no esthetic value where the human content is absent. There can be no esthetic value in opposition to man. Esthetic value cannot exist in opposition to justice, in opposition to the welfare or in opposition to the happiness of man. It cannot exist!
>
> (56)

The direct political function of resistance literature is emphasized by African poets such as Agostinho Neto, 'Angola's greatest poet and first president', or Marcelino do Santos, the president of Mozambique and 'one of Mozambique's finest poets' (Cudjoe 1980: 58). The concept of resistance literature arises from the central role of cultural expression in political struggle. Amilcar Cabral states that:

> The study of the history of national liberation struggles shows that generally those struggles are preceded by an increase in expression of culture, consolidated progressively into a successful or unsuccessful attempt to affirm the cultural personality of the dominated people, as a means of negating the oppressor culture.
>
> (1973: 69)

For Cudjoe, the relationship between literature and political struggle is much more specific, direct and functional:

> In literature, caught up in the struggle, words must be like bullets: sharp, straight-shooting and to the mark. To miss is literally to lose one's life in the process. With the crushing urgency of the revolution, literature becomes functional in that it has a very real task to perform.
>
> (Cudjoe 1980: 64)

According to this description, resistance literature, and hence, resistance *in* literature, must inevitably accompany the broader programme of political resistance, because it has a specific material function. Although it is clearly politically focused, it becomes an historically circumscribed, and an imaginatively limited aesthetic principle since it cannot account for the kind of subtle 'resistance' which may continue after the gaining of independence, that cultural resistance which is not accompanied by any clear political agenda.

The reason cultural resistance became more widespread and more prominent in postcolonial studies is suggested by J.M. Coetzee's observation in *Dusklands*

> The answer to a myth of force is not necessarily counterforce, for if the myth predicts counterforce, counterforce reinforces the myth. The science of mythography teaches us that a subtler counter is to subvert and revise the myth. The highest propaganda is the propagation of new mythology.
>
> (1974: 24–25)

The idea that 'counterforce' is the best response to the colonialist myth of force, or to the myth of nurture, both of which underly this civilizing mission, may serve to bind the colonized subject into the myth.

The effectiveness of a resistance which operates transformatively is demonstrated very well by the term '**counter-discourse**' coined by Richard Terdiman in 1985. Although Terdiman was talking about symbolic resistance in nineteenth-century France, the term has been eagerly embraced by postcolonial critics such as Slemon (1988) and Tiffin (1988). One common form of this is called 'canonical counter-discourse' or 'writing back', which operates within the discourse of literature itself. Canonical literary texts are 'consumed' in such a way that they become the basis for resistant, appropriated versions which subtly subvert the values and political assumptions of the originals.

Following from this concept of **appropriation**, the idea that anti-colonial resistance and collusion can be separated in an absolute way has been increasingly questioned. Appropriating power from the colonial power may have seemed to involve collusion, for example in adopting colonial ideas on Western education or by converting to the religious forms of the colonizer (two forms of collusion that often went hand in hand as **missions** actively proselytized in colonial spaces). But even where these collusions with the practices and beliefs of the colonizers occurred, it is clear that they did not involve a total deculturalization that aligned itself against all forms of resistance. The study of religious conversion in the colonies is a clear example of this, where converts and their descendants often continued to embody an active resistance and became the first generation of anti-colonial thinkers and activists.

Further Reading: Ashcroft 2001a; Cabral 1973; Coetzee 1974; Cudjoe 1980; Harlow 1987; Kanafani 1987; Viswanathan 1998.

RHIZOME

A botanical term for a root system that spreads across the ground (as in bamboo) rather than downwards and grows from several points rather than a single tap root. The metaphor was first popularized by Deleuze and Guattari in their critiques of psychoanalysis (Deleuze and Guattari 1972), but in postcolonial theory, it has been used to contest the binary, centre/margin view of reality that is maintained by **colonial discourse**.

The key value of the term is to demonstrate that the repressive structures of imperial power themselves operate rhizomatically rather than monolithically. The reason we do not normally think of power operating in this way is that structures of power characterize themselves in terms of unities, hierarchies, binaries and centres. Power does not, however, operate in a simple vertical way from the institutions in which it appears to be constituted: it operates dynamically, laterally and intermittently. There is no 'master-plan' of imperialism, and its advance is not necessarily secured through violence and oppression. Cultural hegemony operates through an invisible network of filiative connections, psychological internalizations and unconsciously complicit associations. This is why the term 'postcolonial' is best understood to cover 'all the culture from the moment of colonization to the present' (Ashcroft et al. 1989: 2), because the complex operations of imperialism problematize the existence of simple political categories of response or identification such as 'resistance' or 'minority', 'black' or 'white' and arguably even 'colonizer' and 'colonized'. These positions are constantly diffused and intersecting within the rhizome of imperial contact. For colonized cultures, the intermittent and rhizomatic nature of imperialism is the most difficult thing to combat because it operates alongside a mythology that asserts the presence of the tap root, the canon, the standard and the patented. It is this myth of monolithic power that the categories of marginality are addressing, not the intermittent, overlapping and intertwining nature of its actual operation. For this reason, however appealing certain **anti-colonialist** and **decolonizing** rhetorics may be in offering apparently powerful modes of resistance and opposition, they have sometimes been less than successful in combating older colonialist legacies and **neo-colonialism** whose practices inherit the rhizomic operations of imperialism itself.

Further Reading: Ashcroft 1999; Deleuze and Guattari 1972, 1980.

SACRED/SACRAL

The renewed interest in ideas of the sacred and of the sacral in recent postcolonial writing and criticism reflects the resistance that post-colonial spaces offered to Eurocentric ideas of the sacred. Colonialism and its project had a peculiar and paradoxical relationship with the sacred. Christianity was seen as very much part of the package of "civilisation" that colonialism would bring to the colonized peoples. Colonial **missions** expanded rapidly alongside the growth of colonies. The imperial project was often justified by the responsibility of the European nations to bring the benefits of the light of Christianity to the "dark places" of the Earth, where it was asserted only heathenism and superstition ruled. This characteristic dismissal of the indigenous sacred as mere superstition and idolatry was ubiquitous across the great variety of religious forms the colonizers encountered. Animist religions were characterized as mere paganism, while those religions which shared what were characterized as "advanced" forms such as written scriptures were dismissed like the ancient civilizations that had produced them as either false or as having fallen into decay. This applied to revealed religions such as Islam and Hinduism as well as to the sacral practices associated with religio-philosophical systems, such as Buddhism, Taoism and Confucianism.

The link between colonial attitudes to land possession and ideas of divine providential support for the colonizers' right to occupy and settle land was especially at variance with the idea held by many indigenous peoples that land was sacral, and not simply a utility or resource that could be possessed or traded (See **Settler colony**). For many indigenous peoples, in Australia, in the Americas, and elsewhere, cultural identity and sacredness were indivisible and came together in the sacral nature of their relationship with the land (See Jacobs and Gelder 1998). The post-colonial reassertion of these ideas of the sacral has, it has been argued, created the possibility of a new and renewing "theology of the earth"

(Ashcroft et al. 2009) that has influenced the settlers who occupied that space as well as uniting and focusing on the opposition of the indigenous peoples to their dispossession and **displacement**. These movements and ideas have received strong support from the growing awareness that environmental and ecological movements can learn a great deal from the older ways in which human beings related to the land and to the other species, plants and animals, with which they shared it (see **speciesism**).

Postcolonial studies of the sacred have also offered revisionary readings of the Christian Bible from the point of view of the post-colonial subject (See Sugirtharajah 2002, 2005). In fact, Christianity is growing faster in the postcolonies than in Europe and America, but in most cases, it is in ways that have developed a strong **local** form and, in many places, has evolved into synthetic forms that reflect an amalgam of Christian practices and the traditional sacred ideas of the precolonial cultures. What is also significant is that in many parts of the postcolonial world, people who may identify as a member of a non-indigenous religion such as Christianity or Islam continue to adhere to many traditional sacred beliefs. In some cases, these may have evolved into synthetic local forms of Christianity or Islam, but equally as current studies are increasingly acknowledging people can adhere to more than one belief system at a time and not regard them as incompatible (See Trigger and Asche 2010, Griffiths 2013).

Further Reading: Ashcroft et al. 2009; Jacobs and Gelder 1998 Scott and Simpson Housley 2001; Sugirtharajah 2002, 2005.

SAVAGE/CIVILIZED

The concept of a savage/civilized dichotomy is traceable at least as far back as Homer's *Odyssey*. In English, the OED defines 'uncivilized' as 'existing in the lowest stage of culture (1588)' and 'pertaining to or characteristic of savages' (1614). The notion of civilizing cultures (or persons) goes back at least to 1601: 'To make civil. To bring out of a state of barbarism; to instruct in the arts of life; to enlighten and refine'.

The term 'savage' has performed an important service in Eurocentric epistemologies and imperial/colonial ideologies. As Marianna Torgovniceable

As Marianna Torgovnick notes, terms like 'primitive, savage, pre-Colombian, tribal, third world, undeveloped, developing, archaic, traditional, exotic, "the anthropological record", non-Western and

Other . . . all take the West as norm and define the rest as inferior, different, deviant, subordinate, and sub-ordinateable' (1990: 21).

In 'An Image of Africa', Chinua Achebe, citing Joseph Conrad's *Heart of Darkness*, notes how Africa is used by the West to define and establish its own superiority as a 'civilized' culture against the 'darkness' of a 'primitive' Africa (Achebe 1988). But in the modern world, the West's construction of itself may be regarded as being dependent on the savage/civilized dichotomy in more complex ways. As Torgovnik (speaking from a Western perspective) puts it, our sense of the savage impinges on our sense of ourselves, and it is bound up with the selves who act in the 'real' political world. Freud's map of the psyche placed the ego at the point that mediates between the civilizing super-ego and the 'primitive' libido (or id) (Torgovnik 1990: 17). Whether his map was accurate or not is less important than its strength as a metaphor for the hierarchized relationship between Europe and its others. Contemporary Westerners thus understand themselves as poised between the 'civilized' and the 'savage', or as clinging to a veneer of civilization over a savage abyss. The Western conception of 'self' whether of 'itself' or of others, is thus forged within the dialectic of these terms.

Noble Savage

The best-known expression of the idea of the 'noble savage' is in Rousseau's *A Discourse on Inequality* (1755). The concept arises in the eighteenth century as a European nostalgia for a simple, pure, idyllic state of the natural, posed against rising industrialism and the notion of overcomplications and sophistications of European urban society. This nostalgia creates an image of other cultures as part of Rousseau's criticism of the failure, as he perceived it, of modern European societies to preserve and maintain the natural innocence, freedom and equality of man in a 'natural' state. It creates images of the savage that serve primarily to re-define the European. The crucial fact about the construction is that it produces an ostensibly positive oversimplification of the 'savage' figure, rendering it in this particular form as an idealized rather than a debased stereotype.

Further Reading: Barkan and Bush 1995; Jahoda 1999; Maes-Jelinek 1996; Mitchell and Hearn 1999; Nederveen Pieterse 1992; Sawyer 2003; Spurr 1993; Torgovnik 1990.

SCRAMBLE FOR AFRICA

The scramble for Africa was the carving up of Africa by seven European powers in the late nineteenth century. Although invasion and expropriation of African territory began before the Berlin Conference, this conference, held from November 15, 1884 to 26 February 28, 1885 is regarded as the focal point of the scramble because it regulated European colonization and trade on the continent. Although 14 countries attended the conference, only 7 gained colonial possessions. The period of the late nineteenth century, called the New Imperialism, was a period of rapid colonial incursion. In 1870, only 10% of the continent was controlled by European powers; by 1914, the figure had risen to almost 90%. England and France, the strongest powers at the time, held the lion's share of the continent but the rivalries exacerbated with other European powers by the scramble arguably contributed to the myriad causes of the First World War.

The scramble for Africa compressed into a period of twenty years most of the major forces driving classic imperialism. Industrialization meant there was a need for resources and people and in all imperial interventions, the search for resources and commodities remained paramount. A particularly egregious example is the resource-rich Belgian Congo, which King Leopold ruled over, with immense cruelty, as his own private possession and a means of amassing a fortune for himself.

While the colonization of Africa represented a concentration of the looting that underpinned European imperialism in general, it was also an occasion for the **civilizing mission** to enable the imperial powers to present themselves as saviours of the primitive tribes of the continent. The missionary activities of people such as David Livingstone were an important support to the purported moral justification of imperialism. Industrialization had provided the European powers with important aids to domination.

The European powers were aided by inventions such as the steam engine which led, with the steam boat and steam train to a revolution in transportation, allowing Europeans to trek further into the 'dark continent'. The invasion and dominance over the tribes of Africa was greatly enhanced by modern weapons systems such as the Maxim gun, invented by Hiram Maxim, which could fire up to 600 rounds per minute, making the colonial invasion of Africa irresistible.

The effects of the colonization of Africa remain observable to the present day as the borders of contemporary **postcolonial nation-states** are still largely those drawn during the period of the scramble. While

African colonies relied on **nationalism** to **decolonize,** they have been encumbered with the ambivalent reality of colonial boundaries some of which divide language groups. Perhaps even more significant is the lasting effects of a **world system** that depends on the poverty of the former colonies, such as those in Africa, to maintain the economic benefits of the centre. Indeed, in Wallerstein's view, capitalism must ensure that development remains a myth because Africa is not merely an early stage of development; its poverty is an inextricable feature of the capitalist world system.

SETTLER

The Shorter Oxford Dictionary defines 'settler' as 'one who settles in a new country; a colonist' (1695) and 'generally: one who settles in a place as a resident' (1815). Within colonial discourse, the settlers generally referred to are Europeans who moved from their countries of origin to European colonies with the intention of remaining. Increasingly, the term 'settler-invader' has been used to emphasize the less-than-benign repercussions of such 'settlement', particularly on indigenous peoples.

SETTLER COLONY

In postcolonial/colonial discourse, this term is often used to distinguish between two types of European colonies: settler (and increasingly settler-invader) colonies and colonies of occupation. Nigeria and India are examples of colonies of occupation, where indigenous people remained in the majority but were administered by a foreign power. Examples of settler colonies where, over time, the invading Europeans (or their descendants) annihilated, displaced and/or marginalized the indigenes to become a majority non-indigenous population include Argentina, Australia, Canada and the United States. Like all such designations, however, 'settler colonies' and 'colonies of occupation' provide the abstract poles of a continuum rather than precise descriptive categories or paradigms. The countries of the Caribbean, for example, are not usually considered 'settler colonies', even though the indigenous Caribs and Arawaks were virtually annihilated one hundred years after Columbus' entry into the area. Here the European 'settlers' comprised a relatively small but powerful group of white planters, while the majority of 'settlers' were Africans kidnapped as slaves and forcibly 'settled' in the region. Kenya, Ireland, South Africa, Mozambique and Algeria also provide examples of colonies whose patterns of settlement and cultural and racial legacies fall somewhere between the abstract paradigms of settler colony and colony of occupation.

Many critics and writers have commented on the ambivalent position of settlers in settler colonies, especially where they constitute a racially distinct majority with regard to the indigenous inhabitants or where they have imposed a dominance through force of arms and political institutions (see **apartheid**). Settlers are displaced from their own point of origin and may have difficulties in establishing their identity in the new place (see **exile**). They are frequently constructed within a discourse of difference and inferiority by the colonizing power ('colonials/colonial') and so suffer discrimination as colonial subjects themselves.

At the same time, they act as the agents of that power, and their own identity depends in part, at least initially, on retaining their sense of difference from the 'native' population. In this sense, they are simultaneously both colonized and colonizer. Settlers may seek to appropriate icons of the 'native' to their own self-representation, and this can, itself, be a form of oppression where such icons have sacred or social significance alienated by their new usages. On the positive side, as settlers themselves become indigenes in the literal sense, that is, born within the new space, they begin to forge a distinctive and unique culture that is neither that of the metropolitan culture from which they stem, nor that of the 'native' cultures they have displaced in their early colonizing phase. The new culture may, and indeed often does, involve borrowings from both of these prior social and cultural forms. Postcolonial theorists have responded to these new societies and cultures in a wide variety of ways, ranging from those who stress the complicit nature of these cultures and suggest that this is somehow absolute and inescapable (Hodge and Mishra 1990; Mukherjee 1990) to those who see them as defining examples of the rejection of a 'pure' model of culture, a model that is at the heart of the colonial process itself and its sustaining ideology (Brydon 1991; Slemon 1990; Lawson 1991).

Further Reading: Ahluwalia 2001; Brydon and Tiffin 1993; Dalziell 2004; Denoon 1979, 1983; Evans 2003; van Herk 1996; Lawson 1995; Lodge 1986; Matthews 1962; Maxwell 1994; Moses 2004; Pearson 2001; Prentice 1994; Russell 2001; Stasiulis and Yuval-Davis 1995; Wolfe 1999.

SLAVE/SLAVERY

Although the institution of slavery has existed since classical times and has occurred in many forms in different societies, it was of particular significance in the formation of many postcolonial societies in Africa and the Caribbean.

Columbus' arrival in the Caribbean in 1492 initiated a period of genocide and enslavement of the Native Amerindian peoples. But in 1503, Bishop Las Casas (protector of the Amerindians) proposed an alternative to indigenous labour in the form of systematic importation of blacks, initially to work in the mines. Building on an earlier Spanish and Portuguese practice of enslaving Africans along the Atlantic coast, Charles V granted a patent to a Flemish merchant in 1517 to import 4,000 black slaves per year into Hispaniola, Cuba and Jamaica. The organization of European slavery over the next three centuries has its genesis in this trading concession. It has been estimated that during 300 years of its operation, over 12 million blacks were forcibly shipped in chains across the infamous Atlantic 'Middle Passage' to Brazil, the Caribbean and the United States. Some historians estimate the figure to be much larger. The '**Middle Passage**' was so-called because it formed the central section of the euphemistically termed 'triangular trade', whereby goods were bought from Europe to exchange for people at 'factories' on the African coast. On arrival in the Americas, slaves were sold and products such as indigo and sugar were transported back to Europe, the 'hypotenuse' of this triangle.

The negro slave system that was employed and refined over this 300-year period was the extreme form known as commercial slavery, in which slaves were not just made to labour in domestic capacities or forced into concubinage but provided the dominant work-force of entire economies. Early forms of slavery (e.g. Greek and Roman) often granted slaves a much higher degree of freedom, and sometimes even permitted them to be integrated into the social or family group in ways that allowed them to be assimilated and even to acquire power and wealth. The European institutionalization of commercial slavery in the late sixteenth century offered colonizing powers a seemingly endless source of plantation labour, exploited by an ideology of absolute possession in which Africans became objects of European exchange. Commercial slavery was the logical extension both of the need to acquire a cheap labour force for burgeoning planter economies, and of the desire to construct Europe's cultures as 'civilized' in contrast to the **native**, the **cannibal** and the **savage**.

Although slavery existed in many periods and in many societies (e.g. many African societies had 'slaves'), they were not commercial slaves in this modern sense. Slavery was often associated with exogamous groups, captives or members of other groups outside the community, but the post-Renaissance development of an intense ideology of **racism** produced the peculiarly destructive modern form of commercial, chattel slavery in which all rights and all human values were set aside and from which only a few could ever hope to achieve full manumission (legal freedom). Many of the pseudo-objective, 'scientific' discourses by which colonialism justified its practices flowed from the need to rationalize such an indefensible commercial exploitation and oppression, on a mass scale, of millions of human beings. It has been suggested by some commentators that slavery gave birth to racism, at least in its modern form, just as racism became the excuse for slavery's excesses (Davidson 1994). **Race** and racial prejudice in their modern forms have thus been intimately bound up with the colonial form of the institution of slavery, to the degree that it seems almost impossible to disentangle them. The slave trade was abolished by most European parliaments in the early 1800s, but the European powers often found it difficult to enforce the new laws, and this was not very successful as each power had a different set of laws and ways of enforcing them. For example, a variety of national laws as to what constituted evidence of a ship engaging in slaving meant that in practice, it was hard to prove the offence. Without a ban on the institution of slavery, bans on its trade were unlikely to be successful. Yet, there were often long delays between these two bans on the trade and on the owning of slaves. Britain, for example, abolished the trade in 1807 but did not outlaw slavery in its possessions until 1833. As a result, the slave system (i.e. plantation slavery) persisted in the Caribbean and some South American areas until the 1830s. France had banned slavery early as a result of its revolutionary liberationist sentiment, but when the freed slaves asserted their independence from central control, as in the case of Toussaint L'Ouverture's revolt in Haiti, the retaliation from the government was swift. As South American countries became independent, they too banned slavery. By 1840, Spain and Portugal had also officially abolished traffic in slaves, but Portuguese ships continued their crossings, remaining a major source of smuggled slaves until late into the nineteenth century. In the newly independent United States, where slavery was a crucial element in the economy, especially of the South, although abolitionism began in the 1830s, the banning of slavery did not occur until after the outbreak of the American Civil War. The North proclaimed slaves free in 1861, but only ratified this formally by the 13th amendment to the Constitution in 1865. When slavery was finally outlawed in colonial systems such as Britain's, it was replaced by an extension of a system of employment called **indentured labour**. Although, as the term implies, indenture contracts were apparently voluntarily entered into, in practice, this operated as a system of forced labour, with many of the labourers impressed rather than recruited. Indenture became the main means of securing cheap labour after 1833, supplying the workers for British colonial plantations in locations as widespread as Fiji, Malaya, Northern Queensland and, of course, the Caribbean. Many **diasporic** groups, notably Indians and Chinese, were transported under this system. Consequently, even after the formal abolition of slavery, various forms of forced or contracted labour, such as indenture in English colonies, and debt peonage in Latin America, meant that oppressive labour habits died hard in these regions, where the forms of agriculture developed under the slave system required a continued supply of cheap and controlled labour.

Further Reading: Blackburn 1988; Berlin 2004; Berman 2006; Davidson 1994; Durrant 2003; Horton 2004; Klein and Miers 1999; Mackenthun 2000; Manning 1990; Mayer 2000; Plasa and Ring 1994; Sandiford 2000; Thompson 1987; Walvin 1992, 1996.

SLOW VIOLENCE

This term has its roots in earlier definitions of forms of structural violence, that is violence inherent in the structures and institutional practices of societies rather than violence caused by single distinctive acts. The term structural violence, indicating how forces such as poverty, racism, inequal wealth distribution or the effect on marginalized groups in society of a lack of health care or legal protection, was first developed in the work of the Norwegian sociologist Johan Galtung. (1969) It emphasized the broad social forces that adversely affected people rather than the violence caused by specific acts of oppression or abuse. For sociologists and medical anthropologists who developed the idea of structural violence (Farmer 2003), this form of violence, notably that produced by racism and sexism, is deeply embedded in the current world system, and so has become almost invisible. Structural violence is a feature affecting many people across all societies, but it is especially notable in poor and marginalized regions or amongst marginalized social groups in the rich nations.

The specific term **slow violence** was coined by the postcolonial theorist Rob Nixon in his 2011 book *Slow Violence and the Environmentalism of the Poor*. Like Galtung, Nixon describes a kind of violence that is structural but he was the first to draw attention to the fact that this violence can occur gradually over many years or even decades, hence his use of the word 'slow'. He focuses on concerns with the often silent and unnoticed violence that results from the long-term inequalities and entrenched destructive practices that exist in the poor regions often referred to as the Global South. (See **Global South**) Although this had featured in the earlier studies of structural violence discussed above the metaphor of this violence being 'slow' and so less noticeable than rapid one-off violent catastrophes made this formulation of the problem an especially powerful means of drawing attention to long-term issues such as climate change, the replacement of biodiversity by monocultural agriculture, the impact of resource extraction and mining, and other environmental catastrophes on the societies of the poor across the postcolonial world.

Nixon characterizes his work as driven by the need 'to engage the representational, narrative, and strategic challenges posed by the relative invisibility of slow violence' (Nixon 2011: 2). These include 'Climate change, the thawing cryosphere, toxic drift, biomagnification, deforestation, the radioactive aftermaths of wars, acidifying oceans, and a host of other slowly unfolding environmental catastrophes. . .' (Nixon 2011: 2). He also notes that 'Crucially, slow violence is often not just attritional but also exponential, operating as a major threat multiplier; it can fuel long-term, proliferating conflicts in situations where the conditions for sustaining life become increasingly but gradually degraded' (Nixon 2011: 3). A key feature of Nixon's work is to discuss how such violence can be represented in "stories dramatic enough to arouse public sentiment and warrant political intervention" (Nixon 2011: 3) in a world where 'media venerate the spectacular' (Nixon 2011: 3). Most of the book focuses on how writer/activists such as Arundhati Roy and Ken Saro-Wiwa have a vital role to play in alerting the world to the existence of and the dangers inherent in slow violence. These dangers Nixon argues include the way in which discourses of **transnationalism** and **globalization**, for all their usefulness, may need to be scrutinized to ensure they are not 'marred by political retreat, that **neo-liberal** acts of violence, for example-especially slow violence-are not hastily euphemized as "global flows"' (Nixon 2011: 38).

Further Reading: Nixon 2011; Galtung 1969; Farmer 2003; Davies 2019; Pain and Cahill 2021; Walzer 2023.

SOCIAL DARWINISM

This is a term used to extend Darwin's evolutionary theory of 'natural selection' to human societies, where 'inferior groups' make way for 'superior'. The term first appeared in Europe in 1877, in Joseph Fisher's article, "The History of Landholding in Ireland" which rejected the notion that a system of land tenure had existed in early Ireland. This use has little to do with the way in which the term came to be employed by critics of imperialism to describe the attitudes towards 'primitive' societies that were presumed to justify colonization and its attendant consequences of **displacement**, incarceration, 'civilizing' and (often) extermination.

Although the term is commonly used to describe the racist attitudes that attended European **imperialism,** it was not widely used until the American historian Richard Hofstadter popularized the term in the United States in 1944 in the ideological war effort against fascism. He used the term to denote a reactionary creed that promoted competitive strife, racism and nationalism, which, he asserted, showed the influence of Darwinism. Before Hofstadter's work, the term was used only rarely in English academic journals. In fact, says Riggenbach, '. . . there is considerable evidence that the entire concept of "social Darwinism" as we know it today was virtually invented by Richard Hofstadter' (2011). It had been used in the nineteenth century but 'before he wrote, it was used only on rare occasions; he made it a standard shorthand for a complex of late-nineteenth-century ideas, a familiar part of the lexicon of social thought'.

The term has rarely, if ever, been employed by proponents of imperial expansion and racial domination but is almost always used by opponents. Social Darwinism draws upon the theory of natural selection, which has been commonly, but inaccurately, described as the principle of 'survival of the fittest', a term actually coined by sociologist Herbert Spencer. While Social Darwinism has been applied to the claim that Darwin's theory of natural selection can be used to understand the social endurance of a nation or country, Social Darwinism commonly refers to ideas that predate Darwin's publication of *On the Origin of Species* such as those of Thomas Malthus and Francis Galton.

Although the term became a popular description of imperialist practices after 1944, it is now used to describe a range of nineteenth century movements and ideologies, such as eugenics, racialism and racism, imperialism and the civilizing mission. While the term may be applied generally to the attitudes underpinning European imperial expansion, it has been most harmful in the treatment of indigenous peoples of settler colonies. In Australia Social Darwinism became prominent in the early twentieth century, as Australian Aboriginal peoples were dismissed as a dying race. The missionary and author Daisy Bates described the function of social services to Aboriginal people as 'smoothing the dying pillow'. The assumption that the genetically weaker Aboriginal race was dying out led to draconian measures that led to what has been referred to as 'the stolen generations', whereby 'part-Aboriginal' children of one white parent were forcibly removed and placed in missions and foster homes.

At a Royal Commission in 1934, A.O. Neville, appointed Western Australia's Aboriginal Protector 1936–1940 expressed underlying Social Darwinist assumptions, stating that

> they have to be protected against themselves whether they like it or not. They cannot remain as they are. The sore spot requires the application of the surgeon's knife for the good of the patient, and probably against the patient's will.
>
> The children who have been removed as wards of the Chief Protector have been removed because I desired to be satisfied that the conditions surrounding their upbringing were satisfactory, which they certainly were not.
>
> (Zalums and Stafford 1980: 93)

The extent to which this misinterprets Darwin, while using similar imagery, can be seen by comparing Neville's statement with this extract from *The Descent of Man*.

> The aid which we feel impelled to give to the helpless is mainly an incidental result of the instinct of sympathy, which was originally acquired as part of the social instincts, but subsequently rendered, in the manner previously indicated, more tender and more widely diffused. Nor could we check our sympathy, even at the urging of hard reason, without deterioration in the noblest part of our nature. The surgeon may harden himself whilst performing an operation, for he knows that he is acting for the good of his patient; but if we were intentionally to neglect the weak and helpless, it could only be for a contingent benefit, with an overwhelming present evil. . . . We must therefore bear the undoubtedly bad effects of the weak surviving and propagating their kind; but there appears to be at least one check in steady action, namely that the weaker and

inferior members of society do not marry so freely as the sound; and this check might be indefinitely increased by the weak in body or mind refraining from marriage, though this is more to be hoped for than expected.

(1871: 169)

Neville has garnered considerable notoriety because of his outspoken views and the size of the Aboriginal population in Western Australia. But the policy of removing children with a white parent or grandparent continued in all Australian states until the 1970s.

The continuing popularity of the term was demonstrated when US President Obama accused his Republican opponent, Mitt Romney, of 'supporting "thinly veiled social Darwinism" in backing a budget which sharply reduces taxes for millionaires while cutting public spending on education, justice and medical research' (Guardian April 2012). An implicit Social Darwinism is often displayed when the dysfunction and poverty of former colonies is attributed to 'cultural weakness' rather than the depredations of colonialism.[1]

Further Reading: Bannister 1989; Darwin 1871; Dickens 2000; Hofstadter 1955; McGreal 2012; Riggenbach 2011; Viser 2012; Zalums and Stafford 1980.

SPECIESISM

'Speciesism' is the term coined by animal rights philosopher and activist Peter Singer, to designate the belief of most human cultures that they are superior to and very different from other animals. This belief enables humans to justify their killing, eating, abuse, enslavement and experimentation on non-human animals. Peter Singer uses the comparison with human racism to explain the concept:

> Racists violate the principle of equality by giving greater weight to the interests of members of their own race where there is a clash between their interests and the interests of those of another race. Racists of European descent typically have not accepted that pain matters as much when it is felt by Africans, for example, as when it is felt by Europeans. Human speciesists do not accept that pain is as bad when it is felt by pigs or mice as when it is felt by humans.

(Singer 2003: 34)

Though Singer coined the term, he was by no means the first to make such a comparison. Jeremy Bentham, writing at a time when human slavery was still condoned or accepted by most Europeans wrote:

> The day may come when the rest of the animal creation may acquire those rights which never could have been witholden from them but by the hand of Tyranny. The French have already discovered that the blackness of the skin is no reason why a human should be abandoned without redress to the caprice of a tormentor.
>
> (quoted in Singer: 33)

It is important to note, however, that speciesism and racism are not mere analogues. As Jacques Derrida and others have pointed out, racism is actually predicated on speciesism, species being the philosophical and instrumental premise of racism. Citing Jacques Derrida and Georges Bataille, Cary Wolfe explains why: 'Our humanist concept of subjectivity is inseparable from the discourse and institution of "speciesism" since the "human" is by definition the not animal or "animalistic"'. This in turn makes possible a symbolic economy in which we can engage in 'a non-criminal putting to death', as Derrida phrases it, not only of animals, but of other humans as well by marking them as animals (Wolfe? 40). It is (and was) by marking 'others' (of whatever sort) as 'animal' that conquest and colonization (as well as other forms of domination) have been, and continue to be justified and prosecuted – on other peoples as well as on non-human animals themselves.

Thus, the interrogation of the history, concept and uses of the 'species boundary' is an urgent task for the dismantling of racism as well as speciesism.

Further Reading: Crosby 1986; Singer 2003; Wolfe 2003

SUBALTERN

Subaltern, meaning 'of inferior rank', is a term adopted by Antonio Gramsci to refer to those groups in society who are subject to the **hegemony** of the ruling classes. Subaltern classes may include peasants, workers and other groups denied access to 'hegemonic' power. Since the history of the ruling classes is realized in the state, history being the history of states and dominant groups, Gramsci was interested in the historiography of the subaltern classes. In 'Notes on Italian history'

(1934–1935) he outlined a six-point plan for studying the history of the subaltern classes which included: (1) their objective formation; (2) their active or passive affiliation to the dominant political formations; (3) the birth of new parties and dominant groups; (4) the formations that the subaltern groups produce to press their claims; (5) new formations within the old framework that assert the autonomy of the subaltern classes; and other points referring to trade unions and political parties (Gramsci 1971: 52).

Gramsci claimed that the history of the subaltern classes was just as complex as the history of the dominant classes (52), although the history of the latter is usually that which is accepted as 'official' history. For him, the history of subaltern social groups is necessarily fragmented and episodic (54), since they are always subject to the activity of ruling groups, even when they rebel. Clearly, they have less access to the means by which they may control their own representation, and less access to cultural and social institutions. Only 'permanent' victory (that is, a revolutionary class adjustment) can break that pattern of subordination, and even that does not occur immediately.

The term has been adapted to postcolonial studies from the work of the Subaltern Studies group of historians, who aimed to promote a systematic discussion of subaltern themes in South Asian Studies. It is used in Subaltern Studies 'as a name for the general attribute of subordination in South Asian society whether this is expressed in terms of class, caste, age, gender and office or in any other way' (Guha 1982: vii). The group – formed by Ranajit Guha, and initially including Shahid Amin, David Arnold, Partha Chatterjee, David Hardiman and Gyan Pandey – has produced five volumes of Subaltern Studies: essays relating to the history, politics, economics and sociology of subalterneity 'as well as the attitudes, ideologies and belief systems – in short, the culture informing that condition' (vii).

The purpose of the Subaltern Studies project was to redress the imbalance created in academic work by a tendency to focus on élites and élite culture in South Asian historiography. Recognizing that subordination cannot be understood except in a binary relationship with dominance, the group aimed to examine the subaltern 'as an objective assessment of the role of the élite and as a critique of élitist interpretations of that role' (vii). The goals of the group stemmed from the belief that the historiography of Indian nationalism, for instance, had long been dominated by élitism – colonialist élitism and bourgeois-nationalist élitism – both the consequences of British colonialism. Such historiography suggested that the development of a nationalist consciousness was an exclusively élite achievement either of colonial administrators, policy or culture, or of élite Indian personalities, institutions or ideas. Consequently, asserts Guha, such writing cannot acknowledge or interpret the contribution made by people on their own, that is, independently of the élite. What is clearly left out by the class outlook of such historiography is a 'politics of the people' (4), which, he claims, is an autonomous domain that continued to operate when the élite politics became outmoded.

One clear demonstration of the difference between the élite and the subaltern lies in the nature of political mobilization: élite mobilization was achieved vertically through adaptation of British parliamentary institutions, while the subaltern relied on the traditional organization of kinship and territoriality or class associations. Popular mobilization in the colonial period took the form of peasant uprisings, and the contention is that this remains a primary locus of political action, despite the change in political structure (6). This is very different from the claims of élite historiography that Indian nationalism was primarily an idealist venture in which the indigenous élite led the people from subjugation to freedom.

Despite the great diversity of subaltern groups, the one invariant feature was a notion of resistance to élite domination. The failure of the bourgeoisie to speak for the nation meant that the nation of India failed 'to come into its own', and for Guha, 'it is the study of this failure which constitutes the central problematic of Indian historiography' (7). Clearly the concept of the subaltern is meant to cut across several kinds of political and cultural binaries, such as colonialism vs. nationalism, or imperialism vs. indigenous cultural expression, in favour of a more general distinction between subaltern and élite, because, suggests Guha, this subaltern group is invariably overlooked in studies of political and cultural change.

The notion of the subaltern became an issue in postcolonial theory when Gayatri Spivak critiqued the assumptions of the Subaltern Studies group in the essay 'Can the subaltern speak?' This question, she claims, is one that the group must ask. Her first criticism is directed at the Gramscian claim for the autonomy of the subaltern group, which, she says, no amount of qualification by Guha – who concedes the diversity, heterogeneity and overlapping nature of subaltern groups – can save from its fundamentally essentialist premise. Second, no methodology for determining who or what might constitute this group can avoid this essentialism. The 'people' or the 'subaltern' is a group defined by its difference from the élite.

To guard against essentialist views of subalterneity, Guha suggests that there is a further distinction to be made between the subaltern and dominant indigenous groups at the regional and local levels. However, Guha's attempt to guard against essentialism, by specifying the range of subaltern groups, serves only, according to Spivak, to problematize the idea of the subaltern itself still further. 'The task of research is to investigate, identify and measure the specific nature of the degree of deviation of [the dominant indigenous groups at the regional and local level] from the ideal [the subaltern] and situate it historically' (Spivak 1985b: 27). But, asks Spivak, 'what taxonomy can fix such a space?' For the 'true' subaltern group, she says, whose identity is its difference, there is no unrepresentable subaltern subject that can know and speak itself. One cannot construct a category of the subaltern that has an effective voice clearly and unproblematically identifiable as such, a voice that does not at the same time occupy many other possible speaking positions.

Spivak goes on to elaborate the problems of the category of the subaltern by looking at the situation of gendered subjects and of Indian women in particular, for 'both as an object of colonialist historiography and as a subject of insurgency, the ideological construction of gender keeps the male dominant' (28). For if 'in the context of colonial production, the subaltern has no history and cannot speak, the subaltern as female is even more deeply in shadow' (28). Spivak examines the position of Indian women through an analysis of a particular case, and concludes with the declaration that 'the subaltern cannot speak'. This has sometimes been interpreted to mean that there is no way in which oppressed or politically marginalized groups can voice their resistance, or that the subaltern only has a dominant language or a dominant voice in which to be heard. But Spivak's target is the concept of an unproblematically constituted subaltern identity, rather than the subaltern subject's ability to give voice to political concerns. Her point is that no act of dissent or resistance occurs on behalf of an essential subaltern subject entirely separate from the dominant discourse that provides the language and the conceptual categories with which the subaltern voice speaks. Clearly, the existence of postcolonial discourse itself is an example of such speaking, and in most cases, the dominant language or mode of representation is **appropriated** so that the **marginal** voice can be heard.

Further Reading: Beverley 1999, 2004b; Chakrabarty and Bhabha 2002; Coronil 1999; Davis and Gross 1994; Gopal 2004; Gramsci 1971; Guha 1982, 1997, 2001; Guha and Spivak 1988; Koshy 2005; Mignolo 1994, 2000a, 2000b; Moraña and Hallstead 2004; Prakash et al. 1999; Spivak 1985b, 2003.

SUBJECT/SUBJECTIVITY

The question of the subject and subjectivity directly affects colonized peoples' perceptions of their identities and their capacities to resist the conditions of their domination, their 'subjection'. The status of the human individual was one of the key features of Enlightenment philosophy. Descartes' declaration that 'I think, therefore I am' confirmed the centrality of the autonomous human individual, a founding precept of humanism, a precept that effectively separated the subject from the object, thought from reality, or the self from the other. The individual, autonomous 'I' was one that operated in the world according to this separation and was no longer to be seen as merely operated upon by divine will or cosmic forces. The individual self was separate from the world and could employ intellect and imagination in understanding and representing the world. The autonomous human consciousness was seen to be the source of action and meaning rather than their product. This is a position referred to as 'Cartesian individualism', one that tended to overlook or downplay the significance of social relations or the role of language in forming the self.

Although debate about subject–object relations continued in European philosophy throughout the nineteenth century, with the critique of subject-centred reason culminating in Nietzsche's philosophy, the most influential contemporary shift in this Enlightenment position began in the thinking of Freud and Marx. Freud's theories of the unconscious dimensions of the self, revealed that there were aspects of the individual's formation that were not accessible to thought, and which thus blurred the distinction between the subject and object. Marx, in assessing the importance of the economic structure of society to the lives of individual workers, made the famous claim that 'It is not the consciousness of men that determines their being, but, on the contrary, their social being that determines their consciousness'. The combined effect of these two thinkers upon twentieth-century thought was radically to disturb the notion of the integrity and autonomy of the human individual, the theory of subjectivity becoming more formally elaborated by their followers.

The concept of subjectivity problematizes the simple relationship between the individual and language, replacing human nature with the concept of the production of the human subject through ideology, discourse or language. These are seen as determining factors in the construction of individual identity, which itself becomes an effect rather than a cause of such factors. The overlap between theories of ideology, psychoanalysis and post-structuralism has amounted to a considerable attack upon the Enlightenment assertion of individual autonomy, and continuing debate centres on the capacity of the subject so formed by these broad social and cultural forces either to disrupt or to undermine them.

Ideology

The most influential development of Marx's notion of 'social being' was Louis Althusser's theory of the subject's construction by ideology. Ideology is the system of ideas that explains, or makes sense of, a society, and according to Marx is the mechanism by which unequal social relations are reproduced. The ruling classes not only rule; they rule as thinkers and producers of ideas so that they determine how the society sees itself (hegemony). This 'misrepresentation' of meaning and social relations is referred to by Marx as 'false consciousness', or a false view of one's 'true' social condition, something that has a coercive power over the subordinate classes. But for Althusser, ideology is not just a case of the powerful imposing their ideas on the weak: subjects are 'born into' ideology, they find subjectivity within the expectations of their parents and their society, and they endorse it because it provides a sense of iden-tity and security through structures such as language, social codes and conventions. In ideology, the subjects also represent to themselves 'their relation to those conditions of existence which is represented to them there' (Althusser 1984: 37). That is, subjects collude with ideology by allowing it to provide social meaning.

Ideology is perpetuated, according to Althusser, by ideological state apparatuses such as church, education, police, which **interpellate** subjects, that is, apparatuses that 'call people forth' as subjects, and which provide the conditions by which, and the contexts in which, they obtain subjectivity. Interpellation has been explained in the following way: when a policeman hails you with the call 'Hey you!', the moment you turn round to acknowledge that you are the object of his attention, you have been interpellated in a particular way, as a particular kind of sub-ject. Ideological State Apparatuses interpellate subjects in this way. For Althusser, the subject is the individual's self-consciousness as constructed by those institutions. Despite what many critics have seen as the extreme functionalism of this view of subjectivity, the concept of interpellation is still useful for describing how the 'subject' is located and constructed by specific ideological and discursive operations, particularly formations such as **colonial discourse**. Although ideology serves the interests of the ruling classes, it is not static or unchangeable, and its materiality has certain important consequences. For while ideology is dominant, it is also contradictory, fragmentary and inconsistent and does not necessarily or inevitably blindfold the 'interpellated' subject to a perception of its operations.

Psychoanalysis

Perhaps the most influential development of Freud's theories of the unconscious was made by Jacques Lacan's combination of psychoanalysis and structuralist analysis of language. He contended that Freud's major insight was not that the unconscious exists, but that it has a structure – the 'unconscious is structured like a language', but it is a 'language which escapes the subject in its operation and effects'. The similarity to the structure of language was crucial to Lacan because the subject itself is produced through language in the same way that language produces meaning.

The subject is formed through a series of stages. In an initial stage, the infant exists as a dependent and uncoordinated complex of limbs and sounds that can form no distinction between self and other. In the second stage, the 'mirror stage', the infant begins to distinguish itself from the other by perceiving a split between the 'I' that looks, and the 'I' that is reflected in the mirror. While this need not refer to an actual mirror, the 'other' who is perceived as separate from the self appears to have the unity and control of itself that the perceiving 'I' lacks. Although such control is imaginary, the infant nevertheless desires that which it lacks and sees it in the image of the other. Because the child is held up to the mirror by the mother, or sees itself 'reflected', so to speak, in the gaze of the mother, it also sees its similarity to, and difference from, the mother, who becomes the first love object, the first locus of desire. The final stage is an entry into language, a passing from the imaginary phase to the symbolic order in which the subject comes to discover that the locus of power is now located in the 'phallus'. This principle is also called the Law of the Father, and Lacan's theory asserts that the subject obtains an understanding of its gender at the same time as it enters into language. Entering this stage, the subject is both produced in language and subjected to the laws of the symbolic that pre-exist it. The laws of language are themselves metonymic of the cultural complex of laws and rules and conventions into which the subject moves and through which it obtains identity.

Though the subject may speak, it does so only in terms that the laws of language allow. Just as Saussure had argued that the signs that make up a language do not name a pre-existing reality but produce it through a system of differences, so Lacan argues that the position of the 'I' within language, the subject, does not simply represent the presence of a subject that pre-exists it, but produces it by a system of differentiations between the 'I' and that which is not 'I'. This distinction is not static but continuous, the subject being in a continual process of development.

Such a process forms a basis for Derrida's rejection of the concept of 'presence'. Both subjectivity and the language that produces it constitute a process in which meaning is never fully present in any utterance but is continually deferred.

Lacan's theory of the development of the subject has given rise to other approaches, notably those of feminist critics, such as Kristeva, Cixous and Irigary, who concede the importance of language to subjectivity but who contest Lacan's privileging of the phallus, despite its imaginary status. These theorists emphasize the 'feminine' or androgynous aspects of pre-Oedipal language and its potential for development outside the confines of the patriarchally dominated symbolic order.

Discourse

The construction of subjectivity within certain historical, social and cultural systems of knowledge in a society has been elaborated in the work of Michel Foucault. Just as the subject, in psychoanalytical terms, is produced by, and must operate within, the laws of language, so discourse produces a subject equally dependent upon the rules of the system of knowledge that produces it. In this respect, discourse is both wider and more varied than either ideology or language, different subjects being produced by different discourses, but the processes by which the subject is produced is the same. An example of Foucault's approach to subjectivity was his rejection of the author as an originator of meaning. In the essay 'What is an author?' he argues that 'it is a matter of depriving the subject (or its substitute) of its role as originator, and as analysing the subject as a variable and complex function of discourse' (1979: 209). In regard to the authors of texts, we now need to understand how the author function is situated in discourse. 'The author function is therefore characteristic of the mode of existence, circulation, and functioning of certain discourses within the society' (202).

Similarly, other subjects are constructed by the circulation of certain systems of knowledge. Foucault provides detailed analyses of the ways in which power is exercised to produce and control (to 'subject') individual subjects through systems of knowledge about the 'criminal', the 'pervert' and the 'lunatic' within the discourses of criminality, sexuality and psychiatry. Within any historical period, various discourses compete for control of subjectivity, but these discourses are always a function of the power of those who control the discourse to determine knowledge and truth. Thus, while a person may be the subject of various discourses, subjectivity will be produced by the discourse that dominates at the time.

Post-Structuralism

In structuralist and post-structuralist thought, then, the subject could be thought of as a 'site' rather than a 'centre' or a 'presence', something where things happen, or upon which things happen, rather than something that made things happen. Culler, for example, suggests that as the self is broken down into component systems and is deprived of its status as a source and master of meaning, it comes to seem more and more like a construct. 'Even the idea of personal identity emerges through the discourse of a culture: the "I" is not something given but comes to exist as that which is addressed by and related to others' (1981: 33).

Derrida's critique of logo-centrism and the metaphysics of presence has led to perhaps the most radical view of the subject: the claim that any 'concept of a (conscious or unconscious) subject necessarily refers to the concept of substance — and thus of presence — out of which it was born' (Smith 1988: 46). So there can be no concept at all of subjectivity without a partaking in the same metaphysics of presence that underlies the notion of the autonomous individual. In this sense, Derrida appears to be aiming to undermine not only the Cartesian notion of individuality but any notion of a fixed subject. Paul Smith has indicated the great contradiction this produces in Derrida's own work when we begin to think of the position of the deconstructive critic: 'The supposed agent of deconstructive practice is then, paradoxical insofar as it acts, has effects, produces texts, and so on; but still its role is passively to encounter forces which do not depend on it' (50).

The problems inherent in a view of subjectivity as produced by broader social forces focus at precisely this point. For, if the subject is produced by ideology, discourse or language, is it trapped in this subjectivity beyond the power of choice, recognition or resistance? Frantz Fanon refers to a version of the process by which subjects are produced by ideology or discourse when he says that 'Colonialism is fighting . . . to maintain the identity of the image it has of the Algerian and the depreciated image that the Algerian has of himself' (Fanon 1959: 30). Colonial discourse constructs a particular kind of subject with which the subject itself can and often does concur because of its powerlessness. The fact that a statement such as Fanon's can be made suggests that the process of subject construction by discourse can be recognized and therefore contested. Whether the subject can do so in isolation from the social construction and political organization of resistance is a matter of debate. Fanon was the first to examine the psychology of colonialism and its effects on the colonized, and in the conclusion to *Black Skin: White Masks,* he rhetorically proclaims an almost Cartesian **agency** for the colonized subject: 'I am my own foundation. And it is by going beyond the historical, instrumental hypothesis that I will initiate the cycle of my freedom' (Fanon 1952: 231). And again, 'It is through the effort to recapture the self and to scrutinize the self, it is through the lasting tension of their freedom that men will be able to create the ideal conditions of existence for a human world' (232).

Further Reading: Ashcroft 2000; Bhabha 1994; Bhatt 2002; Buchholtz 2004; Easthope and McGowan 1992; Fanon 1952, 1959; Foster 1999; Green et al. 1996; Michel 1995; P.K. Mishra 2000; Ray 1999; Smith 1988; Varadharajan 1995; Werbner and Stoller 2002.

SUSTAINABILITY

Sustainability, literally meaning 'the ability to endure' is usually employed in modern contexts to mean practices that facilitate the survival of the human race into the future in the face of diminishing planetary resources and increasing human populations. Ideals of sustainability frequently preference the local (in terms of production and consumption) over globalized patterns of economic exchange and supply which had their foundations in European imperial/colonial practice. Most sustainability advocacy also stresses minimization of collective and individual human consumption in order to preserve finite resources, and it sponsors alternative modes of production of energy, food and resource use.

Although sustainability thus necessarily involves conserving the earth, its plants, animals and minerals, the notion of sustainability tends to remain an **anthropocentric** conception, since its interest in the conservation of biological and geological resources is primarily to assist human populations to survive an uncertain future.

SURVEILLANCE

One of the most powerful strategies of imperial dominance is that of surveillance, or observation, because it implies a viewer with an elevated vantage point, it suggests the power to process and understand that which is seen, and it objectifies and **interpellates** the colonized subject in a way that fixes its identity in relation to the surveyor. The importance of the gaze has been emphasized by Lacan, since the gaze of the mother in the mirror phase is the initial process by which identity is achieved (see **subject/subjectivity**; **Other/other**; **Othering**). This gaze corresponds to the 'gaze of the grande-autre' within which the identification, objectification and subjection of the subject are simultaneously enacted: the imperial gaze defines the identity of the subject, objectifies it within the identifying system of power relations and confirms its subalterneity and powerlessness.

Foucault in his *Discipline and Punish* describes the profound importance of the introduction of surveillance into the prison system by means of the 'panopticon' – Jeremy Bentham's eighteenth-century design for a circular prison divided into individual cells, all of which could be observed from a single vantage point. This was a form of prison architecture in which guards could maintain constant vigil over the imprisoned. Such surveillance revolutionized the effectiveness of incarceration because its power came from the assumption of the incarcerated that they were always under surveillance and therefore must always act as if they were. For the observer, sight confers power; for the observed, visibility is powerlessness. Clearly, the discipline instilled by the panopticon, and its imposition of 'constant' surveillance, provides a powerful metaphor for the 'disciplinary' operation of dominant discourse of all kinds.

The panopticon remains a powerful metaphor for the surveillance of inmates in all 'total institutions' such as mental asylums, whatever their physical architecture. One consequence of such surveillance is termed 'conversion' by Erving Goffman. This is the process whereby 'the inmate appears to take over the official or staff view of himself and tries to act out the role of the perfect inmate . . . presenting himself as someone whose institutional enthusiasm is always at the disposal of the staff' (1961: 63). In this case, the 'official view' is directly connected to the power exerted by the institution over the inmate's actions. The process of conversion in colonization is far more subtle but just as potent. Whereas imperial power over the colonized subject may not be necessarily as direct and physical as it is in a 'total' institution, power over the subject may be exerted in myriad ways, enforced by the threat of subtle kinds of cultural and moral disapproval and exclusion. The colonized subject may accept the imperial view, including the array of values, assumptions and cultural expectations on which this is based, and order his or her behaviour accordingly. This will produce colonial subjects who are 'more English than the English', those whom V.S. Naipaul called 'The Mimic Men' in the novel of that name. More often, such conversion will be ambivalent, attenuated, intermittent and diffused by feelings of resistance to imperial power, leading to what Homi Bhabha calls 'mimicry', a 'conversion' that always teeters on the edge of menace.

Surveillance of colonial space is a regular feature of **exploration and travel** writing. The emergence of 'landscape' and the concomitant desire for a commanding view that could provide a sweeping visual mastery of the scene was an important feature of eighteenth- and nineteenth-century poetry and fiction. It became a significant method by which European explorers and travellers could obtain a position of panoramic observation, itself a representation of knowledge and power over colonial space. The desire for a literal position of visual command is metaphoric of the 'panoptic' operation of the imperial gaze in which the observed find themselves constituted. When a writer takes this position, as occurs time and again in **Orientalist** discourse, the invulnerable position of the observer affirms the political order and the binary structure of power that made that position possible. As in the panopticon, the writer 'is placed either above or at the centre of things, yet apart from them so that the organization and classification of things takes place according to the writer's own system of value' (Spurr 1993: 16).

The writing of explorers and travellers in the nineteenth century who adopted the motif of 'monarch of all I survey' gives clearest evidence of the panoramic nature of the imperial gaze, but it may be found also in the description of interiors or in accounts of the surveillance of the body itself. David Spurr gives this account of a passage from the explorer Stanley's journal:

> She is of light brown complexion, with broad round face, large eyes and small but full lips. She had a quiet modest demeanour, though her dress was but a narrow fork clout of bark cloth.

> . . . I notice when her arms are held against the light, a
> whitey-brown fell on them. Her skin has not the silky smoothness
> of touch common to the Zanzibaris, but altogether she is a very
> pleasing little creature.
>
> (Spurr 1993: 23)

'The eye treats the body as a landscape: it proceeds systematically from
part to part, quantifying and spatializing, noting colour and texture, and
finally passing an aesthetic judgement which stressed the body's role as
object to be viewed' (23). The woman has been captured during a skir-
mish, a reminder that the freedom of the gaze depends on the security
of the position from which it is being directed.

This concept of the gaze becomes important for postcolonial discourse
because such surveillance, which corresponds to and confirms the gaze
of colonial authority, may be reversed. This is, in Bhabha's formulation, a
particularly potent aspect of the menace in **mimicry**: the displacing gaze
of the disciplined, where the observer becomes the observed and 'partial'
representation rearticulates the whole notion of identity and alienates it
from its essence. The metaphoric displacing and returning of the imperial
gaze is a fundamental operation of the **appropriation** of imperial technologies, discourses and cultural forms. The colonized subject not only
alters these to local needs but uses them to direct the gaze upon the colonizer and thus reverse the orientation of power in the relationship.

Further Reading: Foucault 1977; Johnston 2002; Roy 1995; Spurr 1993.

SYNCRETISM

A term sometimes used to avoid the problems some critics have associated
with the idea of **hybridity** in identifying the fusion of two distinct traditions
to produce a new and distinctive whole (see **synergy**). The term is often
used in religious studies, but it has also found favour in theatre criticism
with references to a syncretic performance tradition or a syncretic ritual.

SYNERGY

A term used to emphasize that postcolonial cultures are the product
of a number of forces variously contributing to a new and complex

cultural formation. Synergy, referring to the product of two (or more) forces that are reduceable to neither is perhaps a way of escaping from some of the less-fortunate aspects of the term **hybridity**, which, as critics such as Robert Young have shown, has a complex and limiting history in nineteenth-century colonial usage (Young 1995). Other terms such as syncretic have occasionally been essayed to avoid the problem some critics perceive to exist with the term hybridity. But the widespread usage of the term syncretic in religious and theological texts has also tended to make its usage limited by its strong associations with these specialist fields. Synergy seems to offer some advantages, as it emphasizes the positive and energetic aspects of the process of **transculturation** and the equal but different elements that the various historical periods and forces have contributed in forming the modern postcolonial condition.

TERRA NULLIUS

The expression *terra nullius*, literally 'land belonging to nobody' comes from the Latin *terra* for earth or land, and *nullius* being no one or nobody. However, the expression is used in two ways: (1) A land where there is no sovereign (law, social order), and (2) A land where there is no recognizable tenure in land (either property rights or cultivation). Although the legal doctrine of *terra nullius* did not make its appearance in Australia until long after early settlement, around the beginning of the twentieth century, it defines the underlying assumptions of early contact.

Terra nullius is used commonly in discussions of the attitudes of colonists in the colonization of Australia. But it is so commonly used in these discussions that it has become misunderstood as a formal policy of early colonial administration. It is significant that explicit references to terra nullius are in fact absent from the historical record of debates about colonial sovereignty. Most historians agree that while the term *res nullius* was used in the eighteenth century, *terra nullius* was coined much later, and colonial officials used neither *res nullius* or *terra nullius* to justify the Crown's assumption of property rights in land. As Benton and Strauman assert that

> res nullius was a concept with a firm foundation in Roman legal sources, but terra nullius was merely derived from the Roman concept of res nullius by analogy. It turns out also to be somewhat

misleading to describe either concept as constituting a "doctrine
of a legal vacuum" or to conflate either term with rationales for
imperial claims based on vacuum *domicilium* (vacancy)

(Benton and Strauman 2010: 2)

In fact, some early legal judgements implied a form of Aboriginal sovereignty. Several judgements determined that the native inhabitants
were only subject to English law where the incident concerned both
natives and settlers, thus implying that Aboriginal tribal groups already
operated under their own legal systems.[2] An example of the ambiguity
of the concept is the proclamation by Governor Bourke in 1835 that
Indigenous Australians could not sell or assign land nor could an individual person acquire it, other than through distribution by the Crown.
While this may be seen to imply the doctrine of *terra nullius*, it may
also be seen to be an act of *expropriation* by the Crown, thus implicitly
acknowledging Indigenous ownership.

In a controversial book, *The Invention of Terra Nullius* (2005), Michael
Connor claimed that the term was a late invention employed erroneously by contemporary historians to rewrite history. But despite the
polemic intention of the book, he acknowledges that 'the argument that
Terra Nullius is an error does not hide or disguise Aboriginal dispossession' (165). He makes the further point that 'The Aborigines were
dispossessed not by the law of the land, but by administrative practices
which developed and expanded' (322). In this respect, the term is similar
to others (such as **Social Darwinism**), which came into use much later
than the practices they described. While *terra nullius* was not used as a
formal legal justification for dispossession, it is now commonly used to
describe the attitudes towards Aboriginal property rights that underpinned the actions of individual colonists and local administrations in
various colonies.

Why the indigenous people's claim to a densely humanized and
carefully husbanded space could be so summarily dismissed has several
answers. Quite apart from the radical othering of a nomadic society
that in and of itself justified invasion, the absence of agriculture meant
that European consciousness was unable to comprehend the owner's
relationship with the land. The assertions concerning property made
by John Locke in *Two Treatises of Government* published in 1690, were
that a man's property is that which he 'removes out of a state of nature'
land that he 'hath mixed his Labour with. . . and thereby makes it his
property' (Locke 1960: 328–329). Consequently, from the eighteenth

century, the words '**place**' and 'property' became subtly but inextricably tangled.

The concept of *terra nullius* was deployed differently in different colonies. Stuart Banner emphasizes the diversity of ways in which *terra nullius* fit within land acquisition schemes across the Anglo-American Pacific. According to him, Australia opted for 'terra nullius by design', California 'ended up as terra nullius' after treaty ratifications failed, and British Columbia 'switched to terra nullius' after a period of land purchases (2007: 3). The diversity of interpretations and the language they employ suggest that the term *terra nullius* may be standing in for not a single doctrine but a legal orientation and a diverse set of practices.

In summary, the doctrine of *terra nullius* may be seen to identify colonization as a continuation of the millennia-old invasion and overwhelming of hunter-gatherer societies by agricultural societies. Despite the arguments about its origin and use, and the ambiguity of formal legal justifications, *terra nullius* was not a formal colonial policy but describes the attitudes to indigenous ownership that underpinned the behaviour of colonial administrators and colonial societies in general. Any land that was neither fenced nor farmed was deemed to be 'unoccupied,' 'un-owned' and hence available to any claimant endorsed by the Crown.

Further Reading: Banner 2005a, 2005b, 2007; Benton and Strauman 2010; Connor 2005; Locke 1960; Ritter 2007; Secher 2007

TESTIMONIO

A testimonio is a novel or novella-length narrative, told in the first person by a narrator who is also the actual protagonist or witness of the events she or he recounts. The unit of narration is usually a life or a significant life episode, such as the experience of being a prisoner. Since in many cases the narrator is someone who is either functionally illiterate, or, if literate, not a professional writer or intellectual, the production of a testimonio generally involves the recording, transcription and editing of an oral account by an interlocutor who is a journalist, writer or social activist (Beverley and Zimmerman 1990: 173). It is a particular and effective example of a form of writing that **appropriates** dominant forms of imperial discourse to create powerful **subaltern** voices.

The aspects of its production, its **oral** nature, its mediation through an intermediary, usually a First World interlocutor, are the source of most of the theoretical issues raised by this genre, particularly the question of **authenticity** and the effect of the interlocutor on the text, because 'the contradictions of sex, class, race, age that frame the narrative's production can also reproduce themselves in the relation of the narrator to this direct interlocutor' (176).

Generally associated with Latin America, testimonio coalesces as a clearly defined genre around the decision in 1970 of Cuba's cultural centre, Casa de las Américas, to begin awarding a prize in this category in their annual literary contest (173). However, Testimonio-like texts have existed for a long time (though without that name) at the margins of literature in many postcolonial cultures, representing in particular those subjects – the child, the 'native', the woman, the insane, the criminal, the proletarian – excluded from authorized representation when it was a question of speaking or writing for themselves. For example, missionary tracts dealing with native life or with the stories of ex-slaves who have converted are frequently cast in the form of such accounts of native life as 'told to' or as 'transcribed by' the missionary author.

The word testimony suggests the act of testifying or bearing witness in a legal or religious sense, distinguishing it from simple recorded participant narrative. In René Jara's phrase, it is a 'narración de urgencia' – a story that needs to be told – involving a problem of repression, poverty, subalterneity, exploitation or simply struggle for survival, which is implicated in the act of narration itself (Vidal and Jara 1986: 3). The existence of the genre at the margins of literature, its occupation of a zone of indeterminacy between speaking and writing, between literature and history, between autobiography and communal record, between the personal and the political statement, makes it most interesting for comparison with other postcolonial interventions into imperial discourse.

The most compelling achievement of *testimonio* is its representation in history of the unhistoricized, the 'voiceless', its capacity to enable the **subaltern** to speak. For Jameson, it is this disruption of history 'in the return to storytelling and a literature of wishes and daily life, and in the experience of history "anonymously" rather than under the aegis of great men, great names, world-historical "heroes"' – which articulates the 'intersection as well as the radical differences between First World postmodernism and the cultures of the various Third Worlds' (Jameson 1991: 27).

More recently the relations of texts produced by interlocutors have been developed into broader ways of considering the complex role of

oral testimony and narratives in establishing the **agency** of the indigenous voice in other postcolonial **contact zones** where societies were characterized by orality e.g. Africa. Although the term testimonio has not usually been applied to these texts, they represent a similar stage in the process of relations between postcolonial subjects and the texts in which they are voiced. Although the earliest life stories and personal accounts of such societies and their people were produced under the controlling **patronage** of First World interlocutors (e.g. **missionaries**), recent accounts have stressed that even under these most unpromising of conditions, these texts can reveal the hidden subjects of the text, uncovering the controlling inscriptive practices of the interlocutor and revealing the occluded voice of the indigenous subject (see Griffiths 2000, 2004, 2005).

Further Reading: Bartow 2005; Behr 2004; Beverley 1989, 2004a; Beverley and Zimmerman 1990; De Costa 2002; Denegri 2003; Dulfano 2004; Gugelberger 1996; Gugelberger and Kearney 1991; Liano 2003; Nance 2006.

THIRD WORLD (FIRST, SECOND, FOURTH)

The term 'Third World' was first used in 1952 during the so-called Cold War period, by the politician and economist Alfred Sauvy, to designate those countries aligned with neither the United States nor the Soviet Union. The term 'First World' was used widely at the time to designate the dominant economic powers of the West, while the term 'Second World' was employed to refer to the Soviet Union and its satellites, thus distinguishing them from the First World. The wider political and economic base of the concept was established when the First World was sometimes used also to refer to economically successful ex-colonies such as Canada, Australia and, less frequently, South Africa, all of which were linked to a First World network of global capitalism and Euro-American defence alliances.

Very quickly, 'Third World images' became a journalistic cliché invoking ideas of poverty, disease and war and usually featuring pictures of emaciated African or Asian figures, emphasizing the increasing racialization of the concept in its popular (Western) usage. The term was, however, also used as a general metaphor for any underdeveloped society or social condition anywhere: 'Third World conditions', 'Third World educational standards', etc., reinforcing the pejorative stereotyping of approximately two-thirds of the member nations of the United Nations who were usually classified as Third World countries. As obvious economic differentials began to emerge within this group, with economic developments in the various regions, notably Asia, the term 'Fourth World' was introduced by some economists to designate the lowest group of nations on their economic scale.

Recent postcolonial usage differs markedly from this classic use in economics and development studies, with the term 'Third World' being less and less in evidence in the discourse. This has been defended by some postcolonial critics on the grounds that the term is essentially pejorative. But in the United States, in particular, the increasing tendency to avoid the term in postcolonial commentary, as well as the decline in the use of terms such as anti-colonial in course descriptions and in academic texts, has sometimes been criticized as leading to a de-politicization of the decolonizing project. The term 'Second World' has been employed also in recent postcolonial criticism by some **settler colony** critics to designate settler colonies such as Australia and Canada (Lawson 1991, 1994; Slemon 1990) to emphasize their difference from colonies of occupation. The term 'Fourth World' is also now more commonly employed to designate those groups such as pre-settler **indigenous peoples** whose economic status and oppressed condition, it is argued, place them in an even more marginalized position in the social and political hierarchy than other postcolonial peoples (Brotherston 1992).

Further Reading: Brotherston 1992; Deena 1997; Dirlik 1996; Harris 1992; Hasseler 1997; Katrak 2006; Larsen 1997; Lazarus 2004; Prasad 1997; R.S. Rajan 1997; San Juan 1995a; Sauvy 1952; Shohat 1997.

TRAFFICKING

Trafficking refers to the illegal movement of goods or people from one country to another for the purpose of profit. There are two principal uses of the term: drug trafficking and human trafficking, and the one of most relevance to postcolonial studies is human trafficking, the illegal trade of human beings for the purposes of reproductive slavery, prostitution or forced labour. The *Trafficking Protocol* (the Protocol to Prevent, Suppress and Punish Trafficking in Persons, especially Women and Children) was adopted by the United Nations in Palermo, Italy in 2000. The Protocol is the first global, legally binding instrument on trafficking in over half a century and the only one that sets out an agreed definition of trafficking in persons. The Trafficking Protocol defines human trafficking as:

> [. . .] the recruitment, transportation, transfer, harbouring or receipt of persons, by means of the threat or use of force or other forms of coercion, of abduction, of fraud, of deception, of the abuse of power or of a position of vulnerability or of the giving or receiving of payments or benefits to achieve the consent of a person having control over another person, for the purpose of exploitation. Exploitation shall include, at a minimum, the exploitation of the prostitution of others or other forms of sexual exploitation, forced labour or services, slavery or practices similar to slavery, servitude or the removal of organs.

Trafficking has been deeply entrenched in the history of colonialism. While **slavery** has existed for millennia, the industrial-level slavery required by sugar plantations established a model for plantation crops throughout the Americas. When indigenous peoples in the Americas had been decimated, the more robust Africans were transported across the Middle Passage – trafficked for the purpose of profit. The system of **indenture**, by which workers – principally South Asian – were transported to the Caribbean and the Pacific to work on colonial plantations, was a traffic in human beings whose labour was regarded as a commodity. Although ostensibly voluntary, and paid for their labour, indentured workers could very rarely save enough money for the passage home and were effectively exiled.

Today, human trafficking remains important to postcolonial studies because the trafficking in former colonies is rife. Human trafficking for prostitution is a world-wide phenomenon with particularly intense activity from regions of the former Soviet Union and Eastern Europe to Western European countries. However, trafficking in Africa is extensive and of two kinds: the trafficking of individuals from poorer African communities to the richer in the south, or from country to city; and the trafficking of African women to Europe, principally to work as prostitutes.

Siddharth Kara's *Sex Trafficking: Inside the Business of Modern Slavery* (2009) argues

> profit numbers. . . indicate that trafficked sex slaves are by far the most lucrative slaves in the world. Only 4.2 percent of the world's slaves are trafficked sex slaves, but they generate 39.1

percent of slaveholders' profits. . . By comparison, Google's net profit margin in 2006 was 29.0 percent, and it is one of the most profitable companies in the United States. The same figure for Microsoft was 28.5 percent; for Intel, 14.3 percent. General Electric posted 12.8 percent profit margin; AT&T, 11.7 percent; and Exxon Mobil, 10.8 percent. It may seem like a stretch to make direct comparisons between multinational corporations and ramshackle brothel, but the superficial point should be clear: Slave labor makes profits soar.

(19–22)

David Batstone reveals that 'in the 1970s traffickers targeted girls from Southeast Asia. . . After ten years or so of mining in Asia, traffickers shifted their focus to Africa – girls from Nigeria, Uganda, and Ghana flooded in the international bazaars' (2007: 172). While trafficking to Europe from former states of the U.S.S.R has been rife, the combination of poverty, powerlessness and social marginalization has meant that the former colonies have become increasingly the target of sex traffickers. So widespread has the phenomenon of sex trafficking become that it is the subject of several African novels, such as Akachi Ezeigbo's *Trafficked* (2008), Abidemi Sanusi's *Eyo* (2009) and Chika Unigwe's *On Black Sister's Street* (2009).

A new development of trafficking has accompanied the rise of the illegal drug trade. Drugs from South and Central America make their way to Africa via Moroccan drug cartels. Young African boys are conscripted to sell the drugs in Europe and suffer extensive abuse and death at the hands of the traffickers if they don't sell enough. As well as a recent mode of trafficking, it is also a pernicious form of **slavery** (Guardian 11 June 2024). As Mark Townsend explains,

> Child protection agencies warned that cocaine gangs, which are exploiting the "unlimited" supply of vulnerable African children at their disposal, are using brutal means to control their victims, including torture and rape if they fail to sell enough drugs.

This combination of human and drug trafficking is an ominous extension of both forms of illegal movement.

Further Reading: Batstone 2007; Ezeigbop 2008; Kara 2009; Sanusi 2009; Unigwe 2009

TRANSCULTURATION

This term refers to the reciprocal influences of modes of representation and cultural practices of various kinds in colonies and metropoles, and is thus 'a phenomenon of the contact zone', as Mary Louise
Pratt puts it. The term has been used by ethnographers to describe
how subordinated or marginal groups select and invent from materials
transmitted to them by a dominant or metropolitan culture (e.g.
Taussig 1993). The word was coined in the 1940s by Cuban sociologist Fernando Ortiz (1978) in relation to Afro-Cuban culture.
Uraguayan critic Angel Rama incorporated the term into literary
studies in the 1970s. Ortiz proposed the term to replace the paired
concepts of acculturation and deculturation that described the transference of culture in reductive fashion, one imagined from within the
interests of the metropoles (Pratt 1992: 228). Though such influences
may be 'reciprocal', Pratt is careful to note that 'contact zones' are
social spaces where 'disparate cultures meet, clash and grapple with
each other, often in highly asymmetrical relations of dominance and
subordination – like colonialism, slavery or their aftermaths as they are
lived out across the globe today' (4).

The concept raises several sets of questions, according to Pratt: How
are metropolitan modes of representation received and appropriated at
the periphery? How does one speak of transculturation from the colonies
to the metropolis? How have Europe's constructions of subordinated
others been shaped by those others? How have those constructions been
shaped by the constructions of themselves and their habitats that they
presented to the Europeans?

> While the imperial metropolis tends to understand itself as
> determining the periphery (in the emanating glow of the civ-
> ilizing mission or the cash flow of development), it habitually
> blinds itself to the ways in which the periphery determines the
> metropolis, beginning, perhaps with the latter's obsessive need
> to present and represent its peripheries and its others continually
> to itself.
>
> (Pratt 1992: 6)

Further Reading: Cornejo Polar and Dennis 2004a, 2004b; Fitz 2001;
García 2006; Kokotovic 2005; Medeiros-Lichem 2004; Mignolo 2003;
Monasterios 2004; Ortiz 1978; Pratt 1992; Rama 1982; Spitta 1995;
Taylor 2003.

TRANSLECTS

This is a term coined by Chantal Zabus and Samir Kumar Das in a discussion of transgender subjects – hijras in India and Sangomas in South Africa. They derive the term from 'genderlect', a style of speech used by a particular gender. Since speech is always assumed to be masculine, a genderlect, by default, refers to feminine speech. Elaine Showalter had lamented that, 'unlike Welsh, Breton, Swahili or Amharic, that is, languages of minority or colonized groups, there is no mother tongue, no genderlect spoken by the female population in a society, which differs significantly from the dominant language' (1991: 192). The authors use the term 'translects' to address

> the way hijras and sangomas as 'transgender individuals' cultivating a culture-specific gender liminality have used words to refer to themselves, their body parts, sexual orientation, societal rituals and practices, usually not in the dominant or standard language and often in a language form intelligible only to them.

While these words were pushed out of history, their reappearance trace a process of linguistic decolonization.

Further Reading: Zabus and Das (2020), Showalter (1991)

TRANSLOCAL

This term accounts for the connection between communities below the levels of nation or region and has become more relevant with the rapid increase of global mobility. 'Translocal' may often be used to overlap terms such as **'diaspora'**, **'borderland'**, 'immigration', **'migrancy'**, 'tourism', 'pilgrimage' or even **'exile'**. But in simple terms, the translocal is a connection between localities made by various forms of movement, whether spatially, historically, linguistically or technologically. While the **transnational** is determined by effects such as nation and citizenship, and explicitly invokes the crossing of national borders, the translocal is a connection between locations determined by the range of factors that create a locality and may operate without reference to the nation-state. Like the concept of **place**, a locality is more than geographical but is actively created by an interaction of language, history, culture, religion and environment. Thus, translocality is created, lived and experienced by millions of people in everyday life. Even remote places are affected by global dynamics that expand a place beyond its immediate locality, and forming a mobile connection of the various dimensions of cultural identity.

The most obvious example of translocal connection is that between communities in a **diaspora** and those same communities in the place of origin. However, translocal relations are formed not only by spatial movement but by various modes of exchange. The transaction between these communities may occur traditionally through travel, mail and landline phone, but in contemporary times, it occurs more often by technological means such as mobile phone, internet – including email and social media – or community radio. It may include an exchange of goods, commodities and money (including trade or remittances) or an exchange of information, ideas and identities, email, phone calls, social media. The possible consequence of such transaction is to confirm a sense of cultural identity and increase **cultural diversity** in **migrant populations**. The exchange of ideas, knowledge, practices, materials and resources across places is a resource that enables local social movements to resist or challenge development paths or change them in their favour. As Weintarub argues 'living in transition, between cultures we are discovering who we are. Home may not be within a family or even a single culture, but between cultures and communities and constantly on the move' (Peth 2018).

The translocal can operate within the borders of the **nation–state**. An example of this distinction between the translocal and the transnational can be found in the postcolonial city. The critical feature of postcolonial cities is that they are the first stage, and the microcosm, of the mobility and cultural intermixing that colonialism sets in motion. It is tempting to see the movement of colonized peoples to Imperial Metropolitan cities as a simple extension of the centuries-old movement from country to city. 'Country', according to Raymond Williams, comes from contra, meaning 'against' or 'opposite' and 'City' from *civitas* or 'community', with the broader connotation of 'citizenship' (Williams 1973: 1). The colonial extension of this sees the 'rural/primitive/ colonials moving to the urban/civilized/ metropolis at the centre of the web of empire, the centre of 'civil society'. The myth of the country as the natural way of life (and the *characteristic* way of life of the nation) as opposed to the city as the place of worldliness and ambition, lies at the foundation of a prejudice that has made the postcolonial city invisible, merely a stage on the way to the metropolis. Nevertheless, the city, wherever located may be the site of a diasporic, 'local' community. As Ramamurthy observes, the urban experience remains inextricably entangled with the rural for millions of poor migrants to cities in the global South who labour in informal economies (2020: 86)

Consequently, in this global/local polarity, we tend to think of the mobility of populations in terms of international **diasporas**. The circulation of imperial power, and its strategies of enforced mobilization such as **indenture** and **slavery**, produced a reciprocal movement in colonized peoples, a movement back to the imperial metropolises and across those national boundaries established by colonial administrations. The spread of empire resulted in the spread of the colonized – an acceleration of migration and a rapid increase in diasporic populations around the world over the last half-century. We can now quite legitimately read these major 'diaspora magnets' – imperial centres such as London, New York, Paris or Berlin – as postcolonial, or at least in postcolonial terms, as John McLeod has demonstrated with *Postcolonial London*.

One fascinating example of the translocal as it has benefitted from the development of internet connections is community radio (Chimbiu 2014). New media technologies open up new spaces for community radio that go beyond the geographical and community of interest to embrace translocal and diasporic communities. For example, Bush Radio in Capetown and Radio Islam in Johannesburg reconceive the nature of community in the digital age. The significance of Radio Islam is that it reconceives the local as connected globally. Such widespread digital connection may compel us to retheorize the concept of community, since with technological advances community radio may reach audiences around the world. In the case of Radio Islam, religion frames the 'local' community and its connecting discourse.

The significance of the translocal to diaspora is that it dispenses with the cliches of absence and loss and confirms the continued connection between source and arrival locations. This is particularly so given the development of communication and travel in the contemporary world.

Further Reading: Chiumbu (2014), Greiner and Sakdopolrak (2013), Peth (2014), Ramamurthy (2020), Robson (2019)

TRANSNATION

This term refers to the capacity of national populations to circulate around the structures and 'bordering practices' of the state. While this may include the movement of people beyond state borders, it refers to much more than 'the international', or 'the **transnational**', which might more properly be conceived as a relation between states, a crossing of borders or a cultural or political interplay between national cultures. Transnation is the fluid, migrating *outside* of the state that begins *within* the nation (Ashcroft 2008). This 'outside' is geographical, cultural and conceptual, a way of talking about subjects in their ordinary lives, subjects who traverse the various categories by which subjectivity is normally constituted, who live 'in-between'. The transnation occupies the space we might refer to as the 'nation', distinct from the political structure of the state, which interpellates subjects as citizens. These subjects may indeed identify themselves as national, particularly in sport and war, but the transnation describes the excess of subject positions swirling within, around and beyond the state. A significant antecedent to the concept is Michel de Certeau's *The Practice of Everyday Life* (1984) which demonstrates how the ordinary spatial practices of people walking in the city create a discourse that weaves in and around the apparently impermeable structures of the built environment. David Pinder develops this by discussing the ways in which the 'everyday utopianism' of citizens' occupation of the city undermines the various utopian projects for town planning from people such as Le Corbusier which wanted to do away with the street (2005, 2010)

This distinction is nicely captured by Deleuze and Guattari's comparison between smooth and striated space, which they explain by contrasting woven textile and felt. A textile fabric is composed of interwoven vertical and horizontal components, warp and woof, a delimited and organized structure that Plato used as a paradigm for 'royal science': 'the art of governing people or operating the state's apparatus' (2004: 475). Felt, on the other hand is a supple solid, more like an 'anti-fabric'. It is an entanglement of fibres rather than a weave, one obtained by rolling the block of fibres back and forth, entangling, rather than weaving them. It is 'smooth' without being 'homogeneous'.

Smooth space, for Deleuze and Guattari, in contrast to "striated space" or ordered space,

> It is a space of affects, more than one of properties. It is haptic rather than optical perception. Whereas in the striated [space] forms organize a matter, in the smooth [space] materials signal forces and serve as symptoms for them. It is an intensive rather than extensive space, one of distances, not of measures and properties. Intense instead of Extensio.
>
> (Deleuze and Guattari 2004: 528)

Yet, smooth space is not separate from striated space. Smooth space takes form when the striated space of government institutions, fixed concepts and essentialized peoples are broken into their composing forces, caught up in a swirling whirlpool that is capable of mixing these forces in new ways to produce monsters that may *defy* the categorizing machines of the institutions of striated space. The smooth space of the transnation operates in, between, around and through the structures of the state. But it is the possibility for the emergence of new and different kinds of subjects and spaces that makes smooth space a space of potentiality, a space where a people and a nation yet to be known may emerge. Smooth space indeed expresses a great intensity or depth that is beyond the measures of governed divisions, like the division of labour between thinking and acting, theory and practice.

If the archive of the nation is national history, the archive of the transnation – that proliferation of in-between subjects – is cultural memory. Various forms of cultural memory, and various relationships with cultural memory distinguish the transnation from any identification with national history. This is because such memory, although it may overlap historical memory, operates in a very different space from that striated space described as 'national culture', which relies on the order provided by typification. Cultural memory is very often connected to particular visions of the future, a future that transforms the present, a future that exists beyond any notion of national destiny. Different literary representations in national literatures: indigenous, settler sacred, diasporic, gendered and artistic, all committed to some revision of place, demonstrate the energy that exists in the smooth space of the transnation. But the most intriguing aspect of this is the utopianism they all share. Unlike pre-independence nationalist utopias, the utopianism of the transnation is a vision of the future grounded in memories that exist outside the memory – some might say the institutionalized forgetting – of history.

Further Reading: Ashcroft (2011, 2017, 2019), De Certeau (1984), Deleuze and Guattari (2004), Pinder (2005, 2010)

TRANSNATIONAL LITERATURES

A term that is rapidly increasing in use in response to deficiencies observed in the terms 'postcolonial literatures' and 'diasporic literatures' in referring to cross-cultural literary writing. In general, the term refers to literature written by people who have immigrated or in some other way travelled from a homeland; to literatures written in a second language; or to literatures with a cross-cultural theme. These literatures may be produced in situations that are neither a direct consequence of colonialism, nor comply with the major features of diaspora. For example, literatures written by South Asians or South-East Asians in America, although written in a language that has resulted from a history of colonialism, cannot be said to be 'postcolonial' in the same way as literatures written in those locations. But neither are they 'diasporic' in the ways in which that term is usually understood – as subjects who are fundamentally 'absent' from their home nation. Although their themes may revolve around similar issues of dislocation, ambivalence, cultural clash and loss, this is not necessarily always the case. Such literatures are produced by writers who are generally more affluent, more mobile than populations regarded as diasporic, who may feel 'at home' in several locations rather than 'exiled' from home and who spend time travelling, and even living in two or more locations. In this respect, the term takes better account of the increasing fluidity of global populations. Furthermore, transnational literatures generally have better access to major metropolitan publishing houses and authors who are more attuned to global issues. It is probably true, however, that the term continues to refer to the same constituencies as postcolonial and diasporic writing. Although equally applicable, the term is less likely to be used with regard to an Italian writing in Russia than to a Sri Lankan writing in America.

Further Reading: Jackson, Crang and Dwyer (2004), Lionnet and Shu-mei (2005), Levitt and Waters (2002)

TRANSLATION

The interpretation of the meaning of a text in one language (the 'source text') and the production, in another language, of an equivalent text (the 'target text', or 'translation'), which ostensibly communicates the same message. Translation has long been a contentious area of literary study and questions of felicity or faithfulness to the original versus beauty, or the adequate transference of aesthetic form have received increased and especially nuanced attention in postcolonial theory. The process of translation must take into account a number of factors, including context, the rules of grammar of both languages, their writing conventions and the cultural nuances of the translated text. An accepted convention of translation studies is that a translation is always more effective if undertaken by a translator in the target language into which the text is being translated. In postcolonial situations, however (such as in India), many translators may be equally fluent in both source and target languages.

Translation has become an issue of growing importance in post-colonial studies, particularly with regard to the translation of literary texts from local languages to world languages such as English. It has emerged as a contentious issue in response to the tendency of postcolonial literary studies to concentrate on writing in English. Postcolonial studies themselves emerged from Anglophone literature departments and apart from the tension this has caused amongst Francophone and Latin American theorists, the ignoring of local literatures has led to the vigorous entry of translation into the post-colonial theoretical landscape. As a result, the principle of translating indigenous and local literatures has become an important issue in the debate about the dominance of English. For some writers and critics in postcolonial societies, the dominance of English texts in postcolonial theory has led to a negative characterization of postcolonial theory. This is especially so in regions where vigorous traditions of writing in the pre-colonial languages continued to exist before and after colonization, e.g. India and South-East Asia. In parts of Africa where oral traditions were very developed and where these led to writing in local languages during and after the colonial period a similar response has occurred (see Barber 1995; Barber and Furniss 2006; Ngugi 1981a). These writers argue that postcolonial critics with a Euro-American orientation in their work have acted to focus attention on English texts and so divert attention from texts in local languages. They contend that this continues to reflect the power relations of colonizer and colonized and the patronage systems for the publication and distribution of texts this engendered. Thus translation is also seen as problematic in so far as it continues to privilege English texts over those in local languages with a flow-on effect for the status of those languages within their own communities. This is underpinned by the fact that English (or another colonial language) tends to be the language used by the post-colonial élite and secures them in power (Ngugi 1981b, 1986). Local language groups see the production of literatures in their languages as a precious, vast and untapped cultural resource. Nevertheless, others have argued that in postcolonial terms, the translation of a large number of indigenous novels into English opens up a potentially huge readership both in the postcolonial countries themselves, e.g. India and the world. Such a cultural resource becomes, through translation, a vehicle of cultural communication and perhaps a mode of cultural survival.

Further Reading: Barber 1995; Barber and Furniss 2006; Bassnett 2002; Bassnett and Trivedi; Munday 2001; Rahmen 2002; Robinson 2000; Venuti 2004.

TRAUMA

In psychology, trauma refers to a psychic injury, especially one caused by emotional shock the memory of which is repressed and remains unhealed (OED). Psychological trauma first emerged in a postcolonial context in Frantz Fanon's *Black Skin, White Masks* (1952), which exposes the 'massive psychoexistential complex' created by colonization. 'White civilisation and European culture have forced an existential deviation on the Negro', says Fanon, so that 'what is often called the black soul is a white man's artifact' (14). Fanon's own experience of being called 'A Negro!' by a fearful child (1952: 93), his sudden sense of alienation from his own skin, and his ensuing impossible attempts at defence, epitomized the trauma of colonialism for himself and for other colonized peoples. Such trauma ensures that the Negro 'lives an ambiguity that is extraordinarily neurotic' (192):

> The Antillean has recognised himself as a Negro, but, by virtue of an ethical transit, he also feels (the collective unconscious) that one is a Negro to the degree that one is wicked, sloppy, malicious, instinctual. Everything that is the opposite of these Negro modes of behaviour is white. This must be recognised as the source of Negrophobia in the Antillean. In the collective unconscious, black = ugliness, sin, darkness, immorality. In other words, he is Negro who is immoral.
>
> (192)

As Bhabha points out, for Fanon, psychic trauma results when the colonized subject realizes that he can never attain the whiteness he has been taught to desire, or shed the blackness he has been taught to devalue (1994: 117). This amounts to the 'permanent psychic injury' that remains repressed and unhealed. Such an injury can have an historic and social dimension when trauma affects a colonized or formerly colonized society. It has particular relevance in indigenous societies of settler colonies where the expropriation of traditional lands, displacement of indigenous populations and child removal (the 'stolen generations') so traumatizes the society that social dysfunction results.

UNIVERSALISM/UNIVERSALITY

The assumption that there are irreducible features of human life and experience that exist beyond the constitutive effects of local cultural conditions. Universalism offers a **hegemonic** view of existence by which the experiences, values and expectations of a dominant culture are held to be true for all humanity. For this reason, it is a crucial feature of imperial hegemony, because its assumption (or assertion) of a common humanity – its failure to acknowledge or value cultural difference – underlies the promulgation of imperial discourse for the 'advancement' or 'improvement' of the colonized, goals that thus mask the extensive and multifaceted exploitation of the colony.

One of the most persistent examples of this phenomenon occurs in English literature, where the value or 'greatness' of a writer's work is proven by the extent to which it depicts the 'universal human condition'. By this means, the link between the universal and the Eurocentric, and in particular the link between universality and the canon of texts that represents English literature, remains intact as an implicit feature of the discourse wherever it is taught. It was the power of this discourse to present the English subject as both attractive and universal that rendered it such an effective tool of socio-political control in India in the nineteenth century and in other colonies in the nineteenth and twentieth centuries, and it is the resilience of this notion of the universal that has maintained a cultural hegemony long after independence throughout the postcolonial world (Viswanathan 1989).

As Homi Bhabha points out, the effects of universalism upon reading are not only that some immanent, universal meaning is produced in the text but that it constructs the reader as someone in whom all conflict is resolved, a reading subject who cannot see how it might itself be ideologically implicated in the historical conflicts it sees in the text:

> Universalism does not merely end with a view of immanent 'spiritual' meaning produced in the text. It also interpellates, for its reading, a subject positioned at the point where conflict and difference resolves and all ideology ends. It is not that the Transcendental subject cannot see historical conflict or colonial difference as

mimetic structures or themes in the text. What it cannot conceive is how it is itself structured ideologically and discursively in relation to those processes of signification which do not then allow for the possibility of whole or universal meanings.

(Bhabha 1984a: 104)

Therefore, not only is the subject of English literature the universal human subject, but the reader is the universal ('cultured') reader, removed from any consideration of the material conditions of the local and present experience of colonization and exploitation.

Charles Larson gives an account of his teaching a Thomas Hardy novel to African students, and recounts the ways in which his initial universalist cultural assumptions were exposed by local experience. Larson was stunned when asked the question 'What is a kiss?' What is natural in one society is not 'natural' at all, he discovered, but cultural.

'How was one to read a Thomas Hardy novel with all those frustrated kisses,' he asks, 'without ever having been kissed?'

One of the more intriguing examples of universalism is indicated by Alan Bishop, who points out that the apparently culture-free discourse of mathematics, whose universal truths appear indisputable, is actually a very culturally determined mode of imperialist discourse. Certainly, Bishop argues, wherever you are in the world, the degrees in a triangle add up to 180; but, he asks,

Where do degrees come from? Why is the total 180? Why not 200, or 100? Indeed, why are we interested in triangles and their properties at all? The answer to all of these questions is, essentially, 'because some people determined it should be that way'. Mathematical ideas, like my other ideas, are humanly constructed. They have a cultural history.

(Bishop 1990: 52)

Not only are there many different forms of mathematics, but the mathematics that are now held to be universal are constituted by certain cultural modes of thought such as rationalism, atomism and objectism, which are particularly characteristic of the philosophical traditions of European societies. One of the most interesting things about universalism is its pervasiveness and the subtlety with which it re-emerges, even in those sensitive to cultural differences and strongly disposed to radical analysis. David Suzuki's study, for instance, which attempts to draw epistemological parallels between Native American cosmology and Western science, fails to question why such a comparison should be desirable or necessary. Such parallelism becomes, in its unreflexive nature, a mode of universalism that cannot escape holding Western science as a 'real' ground of comparison, or assuming that the Native American and Western worlds are the same.

Further Reading: Achebe 1988; Anderson 1998; Assiter 2003; Bishop 1990; Browning 2006; Chakrabarty 2000; Larson 1973; Lawson 2006; Lazarus et al. 1995; Lionnet 1998; Lott 2000; Newman 2000; Palumbo-Liu 1995; Rasmussen 1990; Richter 2004; Robotham 2005; Schulze-Engler 1996; Szegedy-Maszák 1996.

WASHINGTON CONSENSUS

This is a term coined in 1990 to describe the general agreement among economists and Wall Street bankers about the best means to procure global economic growth. It was called the 'Washington Consensus' because Washington is the headquarters of most global financial institutions. The foundation was laid in 1990 by a World Bank economist, John Williamson, who compiled a list of the most widely recommended market-oriented policies: (1) Fiscal discipline; (2) A redirection of public expenditure priorities towards fields offering both high economic returns and the potential to improve income distribution, such as primary health care, primary education and infrastructure; (3) Tax reform (to lower marginal rates and broaden the tax base); (4) Interest rate liberalization; (5) A competitive exchange rate; (6) Trade liberalization; (7) Liberalization of inflows of foreign direct investment; (8) Privatization; (9) Deregulation (to abolish barriers to entry and exit; (10) Secure property rights.

The language of this list spans the philosophical terrain of **neo-liberalism**, with its insistence on the unfettered operation of the market. Although the principles would be unremarkable to many economists, they encompass a programme that many critics have argued is designed to both obfuscate and cement the power of the West. The term 'Washington Consensus' provides a useful description of World Bank and International Monetary Fund (IMF) 'one size fits all' prescriptive economic policies. It is of interest to postcolonial studies first, because it summarizes neoliberal economic policy which itself has its origins in imperial expansion, and second, because it demonstrates the way in which neo-imperial power is maintained by a persuasive ideological language, working in tandem with powerful global institutions.

Williamson originally compiled this list as a reflection of the thinking at Washington-based international financial institutions about the policies needed to reduce Latin America's chronic debt. But even he was surprised to see his list being applied globally in the 1990s in places as diverse as Indonesia and Kazakhstan. His reply to criticisms was that 'the "consensus" should not be taken on as an ideology' (2002) a defence that many critics rejected on the basis that the list summarized the ideology of neo-liberalism quite comprehensively. One critic declared that the list of measures 'was a perfect guide to making an economy attractive to foreign capital' (Ramo 2004). The model not only failed basic tests of suitability for most countries, but often proved socially and economically disastrous, most notably (in the short term at least), for Russia.

The Washington Consensus, which explains the behaviour of the IMF and World Bank in the latter half of the twentieth century, also explains why economic globalization is so often confused with U.S. imperialism. The United States is the largest contributor to the IMF and the only member with an effective veto. In many cases, the effects of structural adjustments in small economies do more for Wall Street bankers than for poor farmers. The response of the IMF to the Asian Financial Crisis for instance was to impose 'cookie cutter' SAPs (Structural Adjustment Packages), which forced debtor nations to behave in exactly the opposite way that the United States behaved when it entered recession in 2001. Michel Chossudovsky in *The Globalization of Poverty* shows that World Bank and IMF programmes create economic strait-jackets that do more to impoverish the recipients and cast them in the yoke of international division of labour than to promote economic growth. Meant to balance national budgets, rectify market imbalances and make the economy more competitive, the unexpected effect of these policies has often been to impoverish the working and middle classes and cause economies to plunge into a serious economic depression due to shrinking internal demand.

Further Reading: Chossudovsky 1997; Ramo 2004; Stiglitz 2002; Williamson 2002.

WHITENESS

Although **race** has been a dominant feature of social construction since the late eighteenth century, it is significant that whiteness as a defining racial category has only recently emerged in the range of **chromatic** ideas of human difference. Since European and later American races occupied the dominant pole in the binaries of race in the post-slavery era and African, Asian and Amerindian peoples were the majority constituents of the subaltern pole, the category white was effectively occluded, naturalized as an always already-given category against which other races could be distinguished and so not needing to be constituted in a specific way as a separate race grouping. In fact, of course, like all chromatic typologies, the terms employed in these racist discourses: black, brown, red, yellow and so forth were designed to homogenize the complexities of difference which exist within the single human species. But the category of white has a special force, since it is un-stated, set apart by its force as the normative. Recent critical accounts have sought to expose this false naturalizing of the category by investigating the different ways whiteness has been employed as a social discriminator. These vary greatly in different places and times, though all seek to construct a unified grouping to oppose against those others which the 'whites' seek to exclude and control. Mike Hill has summarized this 'first wave of work on the topic [as an attempt] to break what Frantz Fanon referred to as the 'ontogenic' seal of white normativity'. The most formal modern recognitions of the category include the use of the term white within the discriminatory legislation associated with **apartheid**. But US scholarship has also pointed to the growth of the term in multicultural societies such as the United States, where racialist groups defending the possibility of 'whites' becoming a minority swamped by racial admixture have employed the term whiteness as a rallying call. Early commentators on this phenomenon, such as Roederer and Hill himself, have always been cautious of the term 'whiteness studies', feeling that 'a critical rush to whiteness would be symptomatic of the very problem of **hegemony** [such studies] sought to demolish' (Hill 2004a). For this reason, Hill, for example, has emphasized that the task is to uncover the power of the term in a world where official and unofficial typologies of racial and ethnic identity are moving rapidly to a position where isolated racial categories are being dismantled, for example in crucial instruments where social control and self-ascription collide, such as the National Census. While this may seem to be a development progressive thinkers might applaud, Hill shows how in practice it can lead to the diminishing of the power of such racial groups as African Americans or Latinos as effective social forces and political lobbyists. Beyond these practical issues lie the more crucial epistemological issues which haunt all such categories. As Hill has summarized this:

The ambivalent prospect of an end to whiteness haunts progressive scholarship on race as much as it haunts the paranoid visions of white-collar racists on the other side of the ethnographic looking-glass. For both groups, ironically, whiteness is both gone and still very much here. And if such a body of discourse called whiteness studies actually exists, there is a sense that the blind proliferation of this work creeps towards an ugly metamorphosis that will keep it from progressive goals.

(Hill 2004a: 9)

Hill concludes, 'Perhaps whiteness studies might better be dubbed after whiteness studies, thus keeping the temporary irony of its absent presence at the forefront and in play' (Hill 2004a: 9).

It's a manner of inquiry I find revealing, one that secretly knows that critical knowledge sustains the phantasmagoric form of the very thing it wants to deconstruct. That we feel shame about such knowledge and try to hide rather than mobilize its contradictions, and that folks exploit such shame across the political spectrum, is the worse part of the whiteness studies game. What people who continue to write on whiteness tend not to realize is that they too are writing from a position that's inherently self-effacing, since their object of study disappears the moment they start working, then comes back, but in ways that are unwanted or unexpected. It's that ghostly encounter with absence I alluded to before. Rather than just scary or impolitic, I find in this hour of ruin a little bit of hope. That white folk are at last in an epistemologically fatal position goes to the very root of the concept of potential.

(Hill 2004b)

In this respect, whiteness studies face a problem similar to that which haunts many contemporary academic fields, including **postcolonial** studies itself, that is that its existence as a field of study preserves the very concept (**colonialism**) it seeks to dismantle.

Although whiteness is a category which is grounded in racist discourses and practices, it also impinges on discourses of **class** and gender (see **feminism** and **postcolonialism** and **transcultural feminism**). Whiteness has frequently been employed in territories as diverse as South Africa, Australia and the United States as a means of recruiting the economically disadvantaged segments of the so-called white population to support national or social programmes which are to their disadvantage in that they divert their attention from the actual causes of their poverty in the broader economic practices of capital.

Parties which emphasize 'family values' and thus the need to protect the 'traditional' roles of the genders have also embraced racist discourses which emphasize the threat changes to gender patterns pose to so-called 'core national values', which values they identify with those of the cultural groupings which have embraced the signifier of 'whiteness', e.g. the emergence of just such an alliance of practices in groupings such as One Nation in Australia, which enjoyed a brief electoral success in many areas in the late 1990s. In the United States, the recently emerged fundamentalist Christian groups, while asserting their lack of political or racial bias ('It's not a black thing, or a white thing, it's a Jesus thing') have often been racially discriminatory as well as politically conservative in their actual practice. They have often shown little regard for the alleviation of minority-group poverty, manifested in their overt opposition to 'welfare' or support for programmes of reform of the ongoing effects of racial bias in educational and training opportunities, employment patterns, etc. In this regard, they have moved away from earlier Christian traditions of anti-slavery advocacy and social reformism. **Religion** has re-emerged in recent times as a force which may create new forms of discrimination against groups such as Muslims, though these are often masked as attacks only on fundamentalist minorities. The identification of 'white' national values with Christianity by those who peddle these simplistic models of religion and its role in the formation of national cultural identities poses a threat of further social divisions along lines which collapse religion and race into new discriminatory signifiers of difference.

Further Reading: Brewster 2010; Dyer 1987; Hill 1997; Hill 2004a, 2004b; Mohanram 2007; Roediger 2002; Young 1990.

WORLD BANK

The World Bank was established in the Bretton Woods Conference of 1944, along with five other institutions, including the IMF. The function of the bank is to provide loans to fund **development** programmes and its official goal is the reduction of poverty. According to the World Bank's Articles of Agreement (as amended effective 16 February 1989), all of its decisions must be guided by a commitment to promote foreign investment, international trade and capital investment. The World Bank comprises two institutions: the International Bank for Reconstruction and (IBRD) and the International Development Association (IDA), which offers what has been called a 'third window' in which the poorer developing countries can receive highly concessional terms for development loans.

Postcolonial criticism of the World Bank and the IMF has centred on their commitment to a linear **development** in which poorer (usually formerly colonized) countries are forced to follow a Western model of economic growth. Despite the huge sums allocated to developing nations, it is the nature of 'development' and the conditions placed on recipients that has been at issue. Both the World Bank and the IMF have been dominant in shaping the development discourse through their research, training and publishing activities. As they are regarded as experts in the field of financial regulation and economic development, their views and prescriptions may undermine or eliminate alternative perspectives on development.

The social and economic impact of the conditions placed on World Bank loans, now widely referred to as 'austerity' measures, have often been socially and economically detrimental. The World Bank and the IMF attach loan conditions based on the **Washington Consensus**, focusing on liberalization – of trade, investment and the financial sector – deregulation and privatization of nationalized industries. These conditions are often attached without due regard for the borrower countries' individual circumstances and the prescriptive recommendations of both institutions often fail to resolve the economic problems within the countries.

IMF conditions may even impinge on national sovereignty when states lose the authority to govern their own economy, as national economic policies are predetermined under IMF packages. The shift in the regulation of national economies from state governments to a Washington-based financial institution in which most developing countries hold little voting power can be regarded as a form of **neo-colonialism**. Nkrumah refers specifically to this kind of financial control when he observes: 'It is possible that neo-colonial control may be exercised by a consortium of financial interests which are not specifically identifiable with any particular State' (1965: 3). Such control may be detected in the bank's undemocratic governance structure – which is dominated by industrialized countries and its privileging of the private sector. Decisions are made and policies implemented by leading industrialized countries – the G7 – because they represent the largest donors without much consultation with poor and developing countries.

The bias towards the private sector has led to concerns that the World Bank, working in partnership with private corporations (including financial intermediaries such as private equity funds and funding of companies associated with tax havens) has threatened to undermine the role of the state as the primary provider of essential goods and services, such as healthcare and education, resulting in the shortfall of such services in countries badly in need of them. Indeed, IMF packages have often been associated with negative social outcomes such as reduced investment in public health and education. Further concerns attach to the kinds of development projects funded. World Bank-funded construction of hydroelectric dams in various countries has resulted in the **displacement** of indigenous peoples of the area.

One of the most trenchant criticisms of the World Bank and IMF comes from Michel Chossudovsky, who asserts, in *The Globalization of Poverty: Impacts of IMF and World Bank Reforms* that Bank and Fund loan programmes create economic strait jackets, which do more to impoverish the recipients and cast them in the yoke of international division of labour than to promote economic growth. Meant to balance national budgets, rectify market imbalances and make the economy more competitive, the real effect of these policies, according to Chossudovsky, is to impoverish the working and middle classes and cause the economy to plunge into a serious economic depression due to shrinking internal demand.

In summary, despite the admirable goal of the World Bank to reduce poverty, the Western-centred notion of **development** it espouses, the conditions placed on the loans, the impact upon indigenous societies of bank-funded programmes, the reduction of state control of essential goods and services, the imbalanced governance of the bank and neoliberal preference for the private sector have often had the opposite impact on postcolonial societies from the one intended.

Further Reading: Chossudovsky 1977; Rotberg 1994; Mosley, Harrigan and Toye 1991; Toussaint 1998; Benjamin 2007.

WORLD ENGLISHES

The proliferation of varieties of English developing around the world in the wake of British imperialism has led to a field of sociolinguistics referred to as World Englishes. The journal *World Englishes* has been published since 1984 and in the past three decades, the study of the

formal and functional implications of the global spread of English, especially in terms of its range of functions and the degree of global penetration, has received considerable attention among scholars of English
language, linguistics and literature, prompting one linguist to remark:
'English is the great laboratory of today's sociolinguist' (Kahane 1986:
495). There is now a growing consensus among scholars that there is not
one English language anymore (if there ever was): rather there are many.

The **appropriation** of English with the simultaneous **abrogation**
of its centrality and standardization has been a classic feature of postcolonial societies. The spread of postcolonial literatures and the diversity of forms of colonial contact has meant that a variety of Englishes,
of varying degrees of difference from received standard and yet com-
prehensible to all English speakers has become the object of intense
scrutiny. The spread and diversification of Englishes is itself a phenomenon of both the plasticity of the language and the spread of the
language through colonization. The subsequent growth of English in
the twentieth century owes as much to the political dominance of the
United States as to the widespread use of English in former colonies.

World Englishes has replaced the older term 'New Englishes' although
some questions have arisen about the term since it tends not to include
British English in its purview. Nevertheless, it corresponds generally
to postcolonial language use as a sign of the remarkable adaptability of
colonized societies in appropriating in transforming a language that was
in many cases forced upon them. Mesthrie and Bhatt (2008: 3–8) propose a number of categories that in some cases run across different postcolonial societies. *Metropolitan Standard* has meant, historically, British
Received Standard English but with the rise of the United States may be
better identified by two metropolitan standards based on the radio and
television networks from London, New York and Los Angeles. *Colonial
Standard* is supposedly the language of Australia, Canada, New Zealand,
South Africa and the former Rhodesia. *Regional Dialects* may be characteristic of a particular regional area, and tend to be more distinctive the
longer the settlement. *Social Dialects* emerge when variations within a
region based on class and ethnicity occur. While such categories suggest
the social variety of forms of English, the concept of categorization
itself, in which, for instance, Australian and Canadian English are placed
together as a 'colonial standard' demonstrate the difficulties in providing
a taxonomy of World Englishes.

Other varieties of English occur with varying levels of distance from
received standard: *Pidgin Englishes* which are rudimentary languages that
have no native speakers and arose commonly in colonial contact; *Creole*

Englishes which are fully developed speech forms although often, as in the Caribbean, placed along a creole continuum rather than operating as discrete isolects; *English as a second language (ESL)* in former colonies where English is taught at school, where national élites are bilingual and where English remains the language of government and commerce; *English as a foreign language (EFL)* in countries such as European countries or those outside the British Empire where the influence of the language has been external; *Immigrant Englishes* which develop as variations spoken by immigrants in English-speaking countries; *Language Shift Englishes* which develop when English replaces the erstwhile primary language of a community, as in Ireland; *Jargon Englishes* which are pidgins with well-defined norms and a widespread use, such as *Tok Pisin* in Papua New Guinea; *Hybrid Englishes* which occur through the development of code mixing.

Questions may arise as to whether jargons, pidgins, creoles or hybrids belong in a list of World Englishes, or whether they are entirely discrete usages. But in a postcolonial context, it is clear that all these operate as widespread languages of communication and are routinely represented in postcolonial literatures. From the point of view of postcolonial literary criticism, such forms are critical elements in the cultural transformation of English that attests to the agency of postcolonial societies. The question might be asked to what extent these forms are accessible to speakers of various standard Englishes, and it is clear that their inclusion in postcolonial literatures has had a twofold effect: establishing the language variance as metonymic of cultural difference (see **metonymic gap**); and providing a context in which such forms are made accessible to a wider audience. Most of these varieties, not only creoles, will be found to overlap in some part of the world or other, so that while a term such as 'World English' fails to convey the great variety of English usage, World Englishes might also suggest that varieties of English are more discrete than they actually are in practice. However, proponents of stratification theory argue that English exists as a polydialectical continuum passing through three concentric circles, corresponding roughly to the United Kingdom and dominions; colonized and formerly colonized societies and an expanding circle of developed and developing nations (Bhatt 2001: 530)

Like postcolonial studies, the field of World Englishes addresses the question of whether the continuing spread of English is a matter of linguistic imperialism or language pragmatics, and the conclusion is that it remains a combination of both. Colonial education was the most important instrument of cultural capital in the colonies, and in South Asia and West Africa, the only source. English provided both the substance and means of cultural capital, which was quickly appropriated by colonial élites, often provoking resistance to the use of indigenous languages as English became the global *lingua franca*. The importance of postcolonial literatures lay in the fact that such cultural capital enabled writers to interpolate global systems of publishing, distribution and readership, and thus take command of the representation of their cultures to a world audience.

Further Reading: Bhatt 2001; Kachru 1986; Kahane 1992; Mexsthrie and Batt 2008; *World Englishes*

WORLD LITERATURE

World literature emerges, ostensibly, in Goethe's ideal of *Weltliteratur* – the dream of 'a common world literature transcending national limits' "I am more and more convinced," Goethe remarked,

> that poetry is the **universal** possession of mankind, revealing itself everywhere and at all times in hundreds and hundreds of men . . . I therefore like to look about me in foreign nations, and advise everyone to do the same. National literature is now a rather unmeaning term; the epoch of world literature is at hand, and everyone must strive to hasten its approach.

Speaking to his young disciple Johann Peter Eckermann in January 1827, the 77-year-old Goethe used his newly minted term *Weltliteratur*, which passed into common currency after Eckermann published his *Gespräche mit Goethe in den letzten Jahren seines Lebens* in 1835, three years after the poet's death. The term crystallized both a literary perspective and a new cultural awareness, a sense of an arising global modernity, whose epoch, as Goethe predicted, we now inhabit.

The most important works in the contemporary establishment of world literature have been Franco Moretti's *Signs Taken for Wonders* (1983) and *The Way of the World* (1987) and a two-volume English edition of *The Encyclopaedia of the Novel* (2006) and Pascal Casanova's *The World Republic of Letters* (2004). A very useful introductory text is David Damrosch's *What is World Literature?* Damrosch takes world literature

> to encompass all literary works that circulate beyond their culture of origin, . . . a work only has an effective life as world literature

whenever, and wherever, it is actively present within a literary system beyond that of its original culture.

(Damrosch 2003: 4)

Yet the term has also been extraordinarily elusive, from the moment of its formulation onwards: What does it really mean to speak of a "world literature"? Which literature, whose world? What relation to the national literatures whose production continued unabated even after Goethe announced their obsolescence? What new relations between Western Europe and the rest of the globe, between antiquity and modernity, between the nascent mass culture and elite productions?

The world of world literature as Goethe practised it was less a set of works than a network, and it is this network that has underpinned most approaches to the field in recent times. Fritz Strich observes that this network has a fundamentally economic character "a traffic in ideas between peoples, a literary market to which the nations bring their intellectual treasures for exchange" (Strich 2010: 13). Marx and Engels adopted Goethe's term in 1847 precisely in the context of newly global trade relations:

> The bourgeoisie has through its exploitation of the world market given a cosmopolitan character to production and consumption in every country. To the great chagrin of reactionaries it has drawn from under the feet of industry the national ground on which it stood. All old-established national industries have been destroyed or are daily being destroyed.
>
> (Communist Manifesto. Cited Damrosch 20003: 3–4)

This relation between an economy of ideas and an economic system has led to the prominence of Wallerstein's world system theory in approaches to the field such as Moretti's and underpins the move towards world literature by Marxist theorists such as Benita Parry and Neil Lazarus.

Further Reading: Casanova 2004; Damrosch 2003; Moretti 1983, 1987; Strich 2010.

WORLD SYSTEM THEORY

A theory of the operation of the world economic, social and political system, formulated by Immanuel Wallerstein (1974a, 1974b). The chief assertion of this theory is that the capitalist system has been the world economic system since the sixteenth century and that one cannot talk about economies in terms of the nation-state, nor of 'society' in the abstract, nor of 'stages' of development, because each society is affected by, indeed is a part of, the capitalist world economy.

> It was only with the emergence of the modern world economy in sixteenth-century Europe that we saw the full development and economic predominance of market trade. This was the system called capitalism. Capitalism and world economy (that is, a single division of labour, but multiple polities and cultures) are obverse sides of the same coin. One does not cause the other.
>
> (Wallerstein 1974b: 391)

World system theory emerged as a refutation of modernization theory, which tended to (a) concentrate on the nation-state, (b) assume that all countries follow a similar path of growth, (c) disregard transnational structures and (d) base explanations on ahistorical ideal types. The proposition of a one-world capitalist system in operation since the sixteenth century radically affects how we view not only world economics but also national politics, class, ethnicity and international relations in general. For instance, the theory rejects the concept of a 'society' as a unit of analysis in favour of two systems of production: 'mini-systems' that are localized and of short duration, and the world system itself (Wallerstein 1976).

A demonstration of how this theory works can be seen in its approach to the feudal-like economies of Latin America. One traditional Marxist view of economic development sees all economies as passing through a series of stages, so it would regard these economies as existing at a pre-bourgeois, pre-industrialized stage of development. But world system theory holds that these economies are already a part of the capitalist world system. They are not an earlier stage of a transition to industrialization, but are undeveloped because they are 'peripheral, raw-material producing' areas, on the margins of, and exploited by, the industrialized world and hence in a state of **dependency**. Such societies may, or may not, develop an industrial base. But whether they do or not depends upon how well they resist dominant states and **appropriate** the capitalist world system (or, as Wallerstein would contend, purely as a result of structural changes in the system) rather than any inevitable process of development. Industrialization can thus be seen as, above all, a political phenomenon.

The world system is primarily a political system, rather than one determined by 'neutral' economic factors, and in this sense overlaps theories of **neo-colonialism** and **decolonization**. The capitalist world system emerged at the same time as the modern European imperial dominance of the world. This had two major consequences: the establishment of the world as a spatio-temporal site of imperial power, and the perpetuation of the imperial **binarism** between colonizing and colonized countries. Although Wallerstein does not develop the link between the capitalist world system and imperialism (since he regards individual world empires as subsidiary to the capitalist world system), it is clear that the world system is intimately tied up with European expansion and that the history of colonization has a great deal of bearing upon which countries are industrialized today, and which are maintained as resource-producing areas (see **globalization**).

According to Wallerstein, the three structural positions in the world economy – core, periphery and semi-periphery – had become stabilized by about 1640. Northwest Europe was the core, specializing its agriculture and adding industries such as textiles, ship building and metal production; Eastern Europe and the Western hemisphere were the periphery, providing exports of grain, bullion, wood, cotton and sugar; and Mediterranean Europe was the semi-peripheral region specializing in high-cost industrial products. Capitalism was from the beginning an affair of the world economy and not of nation-states. The particular geographical location of these structural positions may change, but not their basic function in the system.

Clearly, although Wallerstein sees the capitalist world system as one that overrides any other world system, such as imperialism, the imperial expansion of Europe, its cultural and political, as well as economic dominance, in short, the emergence of **modernity** itself, are inextricable from the rise and dominance of a world economic system. Dominant core states may change, but the structure of the world system, and the dynamics of capital accumulation on which it rests, remain in place. The theory does not explain, nor is it interested in, human subjectivity, the politics of colonization, the continued dominance of certain discursive forms of imperial rhetoric, nor the particular and abiding material consequences of colonialism in individual societies. It offers no place for individual political agency, nor is it concerned with the local dynamics of cultural change, nor even with the operation of 'societies', all these things being subsidiary to the broad structural forces of the world system.

More recently (1991), Wallerstein has addressed the relationship of culture to the world system, contending that culture, both as that which creates distinctions within groups ('Culture'), and that which distinguishes between groups such as nations ('cultures'), are actually 'the consequence of the historical development of [the world] system and reflect its guiding logic' (1991: 32). Both forms of culture serve to mystify people about the world system and thus keep it in place. In this scheme of things, even 'anti-systemic' movements are a product of the world system.

This attachment of the world system to culture has made it an important feature of **decoloniality** with some caveats outlined by Ramon Grosfuguel

> To call 'capitalist' the present world-system is, to say the least, misleading. Given the hegemonic Eurocentric 'common sense', the moment we use the word 'capitalism' people immediately think that we are talking about the 'economy'. However, 'capitalism' is only one of the multiple entangled constellations of colonial power matrix of the 'European modern/colonial capitalist/patriarchal world-system'. It is an important one, but not the sole one. Given its entanglement with other power relations, destroying the capitalist aspects of the world-system would not be enough to destroy the present world-system. To transform this world-system it is crucial to destroy the historical-structural heterogenous totality called the 'colonial power matrix' of the 'worldsystem'
>
> (Grosfuguel 2007: 218–219)

Further Reading: De Santillana 1955; Hopkins 1982; Lane 2006; Lawson 2006; Moretti 2006; Robertson 1992; Spivak 2006; Wallerstein 1974a, 1974b, 1976, 1980, 1991.

WORLDING

A term coined by Gayatri Spivak to describe the way in which colonized space is brought into the 'world', that is, made to exist as part of a world essentially constructed by **Euro-centrism**:

> If . . . we concentrated on documenting and theorizing the itinerary of the consolidation of Europe as sovereign subject, indeed sovereign and subject, then we would produce an alternative

historical narrative of the 'worlding' of what is today called 'the Third World.'

(Spivak 1985a: 128)

Alluding to Heidegger's essay 'The Origin of the Work of Art', Spivak describes the process as the 'worlding of the world on uninscribed earth', which may be described in other terms as the 'inscribing' of imperial discourse upon the colonized 'space'. This kind of inscription is most obviously carried out by activities such as mapping, both by putting the colony on the map of the world and by mapping it internally so as to name it, and by naming it to know it, and hence, control it. But the process of 'worlding' also occurs in much more subtle ways: Spivak offers examples of the ways in which imperialism works to overwrite the colonized place by simply being there, pointing to the example of the solitary British soldier walking across the countryside of India in the early nineteenth century:

> He is actually engaged in consolidating the self of Europe by obliging the native to cathect the space of the Other on his home ground [that is, he is obliging the native to experience his home ground as imperial space]. He is worlding their own world, which is far from mere uninscribed earth. . . . [He is effectively and violently sliding one discourse under another.]

(Spivak 1985a: 133)

This is one of the many different processes of **othering**, which characterize colonial contact. The point Spivak is making here is that the imperial project itself is far from monolithic, that its 'class composition and social positionality are necessarily heterogeneous' (133). This 'cartographic transformation' was not only achieved by the policy makers, but also, and more importantly, by the little people like the solitary soldier – and the thousands of colonists who followed people like him to places that are colonized by an imperial society.

Further Reading: Spivak 1985a.

ZOOCRITICISM

Zoocriticism is 'the cultural study of animals' (O'Brien 2009), a pursuit that draws on both humanistic and scientific studies. Like **ecocriticism**, its focus is on the extra-human, or on animal–human relations. Unlike ecocriticism, however, zoocriticism is exclusively concerned with animals and with animals as individuals as well as species; with the wild as well as the domesticated. Both ecocriticism and zoocriticism attempt to move away from purely **anthropocentric** considerations, in some cases offering modern equivalents of traditional biospheric ontologies swept away by colonialism and its aftermath.

Zoocriticism is of particular importance to postcolonial studies in its detailed exegeses of the convoluted animal/human divide, where racism and speciesism are intrinsically interwoven. As Jacques Derrida and Marjorie Spiegal, amongst others, have pointed out, the category of 'the animal' and the conception of the animalistic offer convenient symbolic depositories where ill-treatment and what Derrida has described as 'a non-criminal putting to death' are mode possible. As Carey Wolfe, citing Derrida puts it

> The humanist concept of subjectivity is inseparable from the discourse and institution of a Speciesism which relies on the tacit acceptance that the full transcendence of the human requires the sacrifice of the animal and the animalistic, which in turn makes possible a symbolic economy in which we can engage in a 'non-criminal putting to death,' as Derrida phrases it, not only of animals, but of humans as well, by marking them as animals.
>
> (1998: 39)

What is 'human' is most frequently defined against 'animal', and the relegation to the status of 'animal' facilitated slavery and continues to underpin the animalization of enemies.

Further Reading: Nichols 2011; O'Brien 2009; Spiegal 1988; Wolfe 1998

NOTES

1 Perhaps the most extraordinary example of this was Republican Presidential contender Mitt Romney's assertion that the reason for the difference in the prosperity of Israel and Palestine was the difference in culture (Viser 2012).
2 *R v Tommy* (Monitor, 28 November 1827), *R v Boatman or Jackass and Bulleyes* (Sydney Gazette, 25 February 1832) and *R v Ballard* (Sydney Gazette, 23 April 1829).

BIBLIOGRAPHY

Abernethy, D. B. (2000) *The Dynamics of Global Dominance: European Overseas Empires, 1415–1980*, New Haven, CT: Yale University Press.

Achebe, C. (1988) *Hopes and Impediments*, London and New York: Doubleday.

Ackerman, J. R. (2017) *Decolonizing the Map: Cartography from Colony to Nation*, Chicago and London: University of Chicago Press.

Adam, I. (1996) 'Oracy and Literacy: A Postcolonial Dilemma?' *The Journal of Commonwealth Literature* 31(1): 97–109.

Adams, W. and Mulligan, M. (2003) *Decolonizing Nature: Strategies for Conservation in a Postcolonial Era*, London and Sterling, VA: Earthscan Publications.

Adeeko, A. (2002) 'Bound to Violence?: Achille Mbembe's on the Postcolony', *West Africa Review* 3: 2.

Agamben, G. (1998) *Homo Sacer: Sovereign Power and Bare Life*, Stanford, CA: Stanford University Press.

Ahluwalia, P. (2001) *Politics and Postcolonial Theory: African Inflections*, London and New York: Routledge.

Ahmad, A. (1992) *In Theory: Classes, Nations, Literatures*, London: Verso.

Ahmad, A. (1995a) 'Jameson's Rhetoric of Otherness and the "National Allegory"', in B. Ashcroft, G. Griffiths and H. Tiffin (eds) *The Post-Colonial Studies Reader*, London: Routledge.

Ahmad, A. (1995b) 'The Politics of Literary Postcoloniality', *Race and Class* 36(3): 1–20.

Ahmad, D. (2009) *Landscapes of Hope: Anti-Colonial Utopianism in America*, Oxford: Oxford University Press.

Albrow, M. (1994) *Globalization: Myths and Realities, Inaugural Lecture*, London: Roehampton Institute.

Albrow, M. and King, E. (1990) (eds) *Globalization, Knowledge and Society*, London: Sage In association with the International Sociological Association.

Alcalá, R. (2022) 'Assimilation', *The Critical Quarterly* 64(93): 59–60.

Alegría, C. (1981) 'Literatura y liberación nacional en El Salvador', *Casa de las Americas* 21(126): 12–16.

Alexander, F. (1969) *Moving Frontiers: An American Theme and Its Application to Australian History*, Port Washington, NY: Kennikat Press.

Alexander, M. J. and Mohanty, C. T. (1997) (eds) *Feminist Genealogies, Colonial Legacies, Democratic Futures*, New York and London: Routledge.

Alexander, N. (1990) *Education and the Struggle for National Liberation in South Africa: Essays and Speeches*, Braamfontein: Skotaville, Educational Division.

Alexander, T. (1996) *Unravelling Global Apartheid: An Overview of World Politics*, Cambridge, MA: Polity Press.

Alexis, J. S. (1956) 'Of the Magical Realism of the Haitians', *Presence Africaine* 8–10: 245–271.

Alkire, S. (2010) *Human Development: Definitions, Critiques and Related Concepts*, Research Paper, United Nations Development Programme.

Alleyne, M. C. (1980) 'Theoretical Orientations in Creole Studies', in A. Valdman and A. Highfield (eds) *Theoretical Orientations in Creole Studies*, New York: Academic Press.

Alonso, A. M. (2004) 'Conforming Disconformity: "Mestizaje", Hybridity, and the Aesthetics of Mexican Nationalism', *Cultural Anthropology* 19(4): 459–490.

Altbach, P. G. (1975) 'Literary Colonialism: Books in the Third World', *Harvard Educational Review* 15(2) (May).

Althusser, L. (1984) *Essays on Ideology*, London: Verso.

Amnesty International (2010) 'Indigenous Peoples Struggle to Survive in Columbia' (23 February) https://www.amnesty.org/en/news-and-updates/report/indigenous-peoples-struggle-survive-colombia-2010-02-23

Amur, G. S. et al. (1985) *Indian Readings in Commonwealth Literature*, New York: Apt.

Amuta, C. (1995) 'Fanon, Cabral and Ngugi on National Liberation', in B. Ashcroft, G. Griffiths and H. Tiffin (eds) *The Postcolonial Studies Reader*, London: Routledge: 158–163.

Anderson, A. (1991) *Race Against Time: The Early Maori-Pakeha Families and the Development of the Mixed-Race Population in Southern New Zealand*, Dunedin, NZ: Hocken Library, University of Otago.

Anderson, A. (1998) 'Cosmopolitanism, Universalism, and the Divided Legacies of Modernity', in P. Cheah and B. Robbins (eds) *Cosmopolitics: Thinking and Feeling beyond the Nation*, Minneapolis: University of Minnesota Press: 265–289.

Anderson, B. (1983) *Imagined Communities: Reflections on the Origin and Spread of Nationalism*, London: Verso.

Anderson, D. and Broch-Due, V. (1999) (eds) *The Poor Are Not Us: Pastoralism and Poverty in East Africa*, Athens: Ohio University Press.

Anderson, V. de J. (2004) *Creatures of Empire: How Domestic Animals Transformed Early America*, New York: Oxford University Press.

Anderson, W. (2000) 'The Possession of Kuru: Medical Science and Biocolonial Exchange', *Comparative Studies in Society and History* 42: 713–744.

Anderson, W. and Adams, V. (2007) 'Pramoedyas's Chickens: Postcolonial Studies of Technoscience', in E. J. Hackett, O. Amsterdamska, M. E. Lynch and J. Wajcman (eds) *The Handbook of Science and Technology Studies*, Cambridge, MA: MIT Press: 181–202.

Angel, M. (2005) 'Brainfood: Rationality, Aesthetics, and Economies of Affect', *Textual Practice* 19(Summer): 323–348.

Ansari, S. (2005) *Life after Partition: Migration, Community and Strife in Sindh: 1947–1962*, Oxford: Oxford University Press.

Ansell-Pearson, K. et al. (1997) (eds) *Cultural Readings of Imperialism: Edward Said and the Gravity of History*, New York: St. Martin's.

Anzaldua, G. (1987) *Borderlands/La Frontera: The New Mestiza*, San Francisco, CA: Aunt Lute.

Appadurai, A. (1986a) (ed.) *'Commodities and the Politics of Value' The Social Life of Things*, Cambridge: Cambridge University Press.

Appadurai, A. (1986b) *The Social Life of Things: Commodities in Cultural Perspective*, Cambridge: Cambridge University Press.

Appadurai, A. (1990) 'Topographies of the Self: Praise and Emotion in Hindu India', in C. Lutz and L. Abu-Lughod (eds), *Language and the Politics of Emotion*, Cambridge: Cambridge University Press.

Appadurai, A. (1991) 'Global Ethnoscapes: Notes and Queries for a Transnational Anthropology', in R. G. Fox (ed.) *Recapturing Anthropology: Working in the Present*, Santa Fe, NM: School of American Research Press: 191–210.

Appadurai, A. (1996) *Modernity at Large: Cultural Dimensions of Globalization*, Minneapolis: University of Minnesota Press.

Appadurai, A. (2003) 'Sovereignty without Territoriality: Notes for a Postnational Geography', in S. M. Low and D. Lawrence Zúniga (eds) *The Anthropology of Space and Place*, Oxford: Blackwell: 337–350.

Appiah, K. A. (1992) *In My Father's House: Africa in the Philosophy of Culture*, London: Methuen.

Appiah, K. A. (2007) *Cosmopolitanism: Ethics in a World of Strangers*, New York: Norton.

Appiah, K. A. and Gates, H. L. (1995) (eds) *Identities*, Chicago: University of Chicago Press.

Arac, J. and Ritvo, H. (1995) (eds) *Macropolitics of Nineteenth-Century Literature: Nationalism, Exoticism, Imperialism*, Durham, NC: Duke University Press.

Armitage, A. (1995) *Comparing the Policy of Aboriginal Assimilation*, Australia, Canada and New Zealand, Vancouver: UBC Press.

Armstrong, C. I. and Hestertun, A. (2006) *Postcolonial Dislocations: Travel, History and the Ironies of Narrative*, Oslo, Norway: Novus Press.

Armstrong, K. (2000) *The Battle for God: Fundamentalism in Judaism, Christianity and Islam*, London: Harper Collins.

Armstrong, K. (2006) *The Great Transformation: The World in the Time of Buddha, Socrates, Confucius and Jeremiah*, London: Atlantic Books.

Arnold, A. J. (2003) 'Perilous Symmetry: Exoticism and the Geography of Colonial and Postcolonial Culture', in F. G. Henry and J. Garane (eds) *Geo/Graphies: Mapping the Imagination in French and Francophone Literature and Film*, Amsterdam, Netherlands: Rodopi: 1–28.

Asad, T. (1973) (ed.) *Anthropology and the Colonial Encounter*, London: Ithaca.

Ashcroft, B. (1994) 'Interpolation and Postcolonial Agency', *New Literatures Review* 28–29: 176–189.

Ashcroft, B. (1996) 'On the Hyphen in Postcolonial', *New Literatures Review* 32: 23–32.

Ashcroft, B. (1998) 'Constructing the Postcolonial Male Body', in L. Dale and S. Ryan (eds) *The Body in the Library*, Amsterdam, Netherlands: Rodopi: 207–223.

Ashcroft, B. (1999) 'The Rhizome of Post-colonial Discourse', in R. Luckhurst and P. Marks (eds) *Literature and the Contemporary: Fictions and Theories of the Present*, London: Longman: 111–125.

Ashcroft, B. (2000) 'Primitive and Wingless: The Colonial Subject as Child', in W. S. Jacobson (ed.) *Dickens and the Children of Empire*, New York: Palgrave.

Ashcroft, B. (2001a) *Postcolonial Transformation*, London: Routledge.

Ashcroft, B. (2001b) *On Postcolonial Futures: Transformations of Colonial Culture*, London: Continuum.

Ashcroft, B. (2003) 'Language and Race', in R. Harris and B. Rampton (eds) *The Language, Ethnicity and Race Reader*, London: Routledge: 37–53.

Ashcroft, B. (2005) 'Modernity's First Born: Latin America and Postcolonial Transformation', in P. McCallum and W. Faith (eds) *Linked Histories: Postcolonial Studies in Globalized World*, Calgary, AB: University of Calgary Press: 189–207.

Ashcroft, B. (2011) 'Australian Transnation', *Special Issue: Modern Mobilities' Australian-Transnational Writing Southerly* 71(1): 18–40.

Ashcroft, B. (2012) 'Introduction: A Convivial Critical Democracy – Postcolonial Studies in the Twenty-First Century', in B. Ashcroft, R. Mendis, J. McGonegal and A. Mukherjee (eds) *Literature for Our Times: Post-Colonial Studies in the Twenty-First Century*, Amsterdam, Netherlands and New York: Rodopi: xv–xxxv.

Ashcroft, B. (2017a) 'Transnation and the Postcolonial City', *Australian Humanities Review* 62: 46–64.

Ashcroft, B. (2017b) 'A Climate of Hope', *Le Simplegadi, University of Udine, Italy* 17(11): 19–34.

Ashcroft, B. (2019) 'Borders, Bordering and the Transnation', *English Academy Review: Southern African Journal of English Studies* 36(1): 5–19.

Ashcroft, B. (2023) 'Transculturality and the Contingency of Belonging', *Textual Practice* 27(8): 1–17.

Ashcroft, B., Devlin-Glass, F. and McCredden, L. (2009) *Intimate Horizons: The Postcolonial Sacred in Australian Literature*, Adelaide: ATF Press.

Ashcroft, B., Griffiths, G. and Tiffin, H. (1989) *The Empire Writes Back: Theory and Practice in Postcolonial Literatures*, London: Routledge.

Ashcroft, B., Griffiths, G. and Tiffin, H. (1995) *The Postcolonial Studies Reader*, London: Routledge.

Ashcroft, B., Griffiths, G. and Tiffin, H. (2002) *The Empire Writes Back: Theory and Practice in Postcolonial Literatures*, 2nd edition, London: Routledge.

Ashcroft, B., Mendis, R., McGonegal, J. and Mukherjee, A. (2012) *Literature for Our Times: Postcolonial Studies in the Twenty First Century*, Amsterdam, Netherlands: Rodopi.

Ashcroft, B. et al. (2024) 'Diaspora, Refugees and Migration', in *Postcolonial Studies Reader*, 4th edition, London: Routledge: 490–527.

Ashcroft, W. D. (1989a) 'Intersecting Marginalities: Postcolonialism and Feminism', *Kunapipi* 11: 23–43.

Ashcroft, W. D. (1989b) 'Is That the Congo? Language as Metonymy in the Postcolonial Text', *World Literature Written in English* 29(2) (Autumn): 3–10.

Ashcroft, W. D., Cotter, M., Docker, J. and Nandan, S. (1977) 'Postcolonial Literature', *New Literature Review* (special issue): 2.

Asher, N. (2008) 'Listening to Hyphenated Americans: Hybrid Identities of Youth from Immigrant Families', *Theory into Practice* 47(1): 12–19.

Assiter, A. (2003) *Revisiting Universalism*, New York: Palgrave Macmillan.

Attwood, B. (1996) 'Mabo, Australia and the End of History', in *The Age of Mabo: History, Aborigines and Australia*, St. Leonards, Sydney: Allen & Unwin: 100–116.

Auguste, E. et al. (2023) 'La Lutte Continue: Louis Mars and the Genesis of Ethnopsychiatry', *American Psychologist* 78(4): 469–483.

Baber, Z. (2002) 'Orientalism, Occidentalism, Nativism: The Culturalist Quest for Indigenous Science and Knowledge', *European Legacy: Toward New Paradigms* 7(6): 747–758.

Bahri, D. (2004) 'Feminism In/and Postcolonialism', in N. Lazarus (ed.) *The Cambridge Companion to Postcolonial Literary Studies*, Cambridge: Cambridge University Press: 199–220.

Baishya, A. R. and Kumar, P. (2022) 'Ends of Worlds or the Continuation of the Planet? Postcolonial Theory, the Anthropocene, and the Nonhuman', *Postcolonial Studies* 25(3): 305–320. https://doi.org/10.1080/13688790.2022.2071724

Baker, A. G. and Worby, G. (2007) 'Aboriginality Since Mabo: Writing, Politics, and Art', in N. Birns and R. McNeer (eds) *A Companion to Australian Literature Since 1900*, Rochester: Camden House: 17–40.

Baker, G. (1996) *Trade Winds on the Niger: The Saga of the Royal Niger Company 1830–1971*, London: The Radcliff Press.

Baker, H. A. et al. (1996) (eds) *Black British Cultural Studies: A Reader*, Chicago: University of Chicago Press.

Baker, S. (1991) 'Magic Realism as a Postcolonial Strategy: The Kadaitcha Sung', *SPAN: Journal of the South Pacific Association for Commonwealth Literature and Language Studies* 32: 55–63.

Bakhtin, M. (1981) *The Dialogic Imagination: Four Essays*, edited by Michael Holquist; translated by Caryl Emerson and Michael Holquist, Austin: University of Texas Press.

Bakhtin, M. (1984) *Rabelais and His World*, translated by Helene Iswolsky, Bloomington: Indiana University Press, [1941].

Bakhtin, M. (1994) *The Bakhtin Reader: Selected Writings of Bakhtin, Medvedev and Voloshinov*, edited by Pam Morris; with a glossary compiled by Graham Roberts, London: Edward Arnold.

Balcárcel, J. L. (1981) 'Literatura y liberaci by Graham Roberts', *London: Casa de las Americas* 21(126): 17–25.

Ball, J. C. (2004) *Imagining London: Postcolonial Fiction and the Transnational Metropolis*, Toronto, ON: University of Toronto Press.

Ballantyne, T. (2001) *Orientalism, Racial Theory and British Colonialism: An Aryan Empire*, Basingstoke: Palgrave.

Bamyah, M. A. (2000) *The Ends of Globalization*, Minneapolis: University of Minnesota Press.

Banner, S. (2005a) 'Why Terra Nullius? Anthropology and Property Law in Early Australia', *Law and History Review* 23(1): 95–131.

Banner, S. (2005b) *How the Indians Lost Their Land: Law and Power on the Frontier*, Cambridge, MA: Harvard University Press.

Banner, S. (2007) *Possessing the Pacific: Land, Settlers, and Indigenous People from Australia to Alaska*, Cambridge, MA: Harvard University Press.

Bannister, R. C. (1989) *Social Darwinism: Science and Myth in Anglo-American Social Thought*, Philadelphia, PA: Temple University Press.

Barber, B. R. (1992) 'Jihad vs. McWorld', *The Atlantic* 269(3): 53–65.

Barber, K. (1991) *I Could Speak until Tomorrow: Oriki, Women and the Past in a Yoruba Town*, Edinburgh: Edinburgh University Press for the International African Institute.

Barber, K. (1995) 'African-Language Literature and Postcolonial Criticism', *Research in African Literatures* 26(4): 3.

Barber, K. and De Moraes-Farias, P. F. (1989) (eds) *Discourse and Its Disguises: The Interpretation of African Oral Texts*, Birmingham: University of Birmingham, Centre of West African Studies.

Barber, K. and Furniss, G. (Fall 2006) 'African Language Writing', *Research in African Literatures* 37(3): 1–14.

Barkan, E. and Bush, R. (1995) (eds) *Prehistories of the Future: The Primitivist Project and the Culture of Modernism*, Stanford, CA: Stanford University Press.

Barkan, E. and Shelton, M. D. (1998) (eds) *Borders, Exiles, Diasporas*, Stanford, CA: Stanford University Press.

Barker, F., Hulme, P. et al. (1985) (eds) *Europe and Its Others: Proceedings of the Essex Conference on the Sociology of Literature*, Colchester: University of Essex.

Barker, F. et al. (1994) *Colonial Discourse, Postcolonial Theory*, Manchester: Manchester University Press.

Barker, M. (1981) *The New Racism: Conservatives and the Ideology of the Tribes*, London: Junction Books.

Barker, M. (1982) *The New Racism: Conservatives and the Ideology of the Tribe*, Frederick, MD: Aletheia Books.

Barlow, T. E. (2005) 'Eugenic Woman, Semicolonialism, and Colonial Modernity as Problems for Postcolonial Theory', in A. Loomba, S. Kaul,

M. Bunzl, A. Burton and J. Esty (eds) *Postcolonial Studies and Beyond*, Durham, NC: Duke University Press: 359–384.

Barnosky, A. D. et al. (2011) 'Has the Earth's Sixth Mass Extinction Already Arrived?' *Nature* 471: 51–57.

Barrett, L. E. (1977) *The Rastafarians: The Dreadlocks of Jamaica*, Kingston, Jamaica: Sangster's Book Store.

Barrett, L. E. (1988) *The Rastafarians: Sounds of Cultural Dissonance*, Boston: Beacon Press.

Barringer, T. J. and Flynn, T. (1998) (eds) *Colonialism and the Object: Empire, Material Culture, and the Museum*, London: Routledge.

Barrington, L. W. (2006) (ed.) *After Independence: Making and Protecting the Nation in Postcolonial and Postcommunist States*, Ann Arbor: University of Michigan Press.

Barrios de Chungara, D. (1977) *Let Me Speak: Testimony of Domatila, a Woman of the Bolivian Mines*, translated by Victoria Ortiz, London: Monthly Review Press.

Bartolome, L. J., de Wet, C., Mander, H. and Nagraj, V. K. (2000) 'Displacement, Restettlement, Rehabilitation, Reparation and Development', Thematic Review I.3 prepared as an input to the World Commission on Dams, Cape Town, *Dams.org* accessed Feb 2012.

Bartolovich, C. and Lazarus, N. (2002) (eds) *Marxism, Modernity, and Postcolonial Studies*, Cambridge: Cambridge University Press.

Bartow, J. R. (2005) *Subject to Change: The Lessons of Latin American Women's Testimonio for Truth, Fiction, and Theory*, Chapel Hill: University of North Carolina Press.

Basch, L. G. (1994) *Nations Unbound: Transnational Projects, Postcolonial Predicaments, and Deterritorialized Nation-States*, New York: Gordon and Breach.

Bassnett, S. (2002) *Translation Studies*, London: Routledge.

Bassnett, S. and Trivedi, H. (1999) (eds) *Postcolonial Translation*, London: Routledge.

Batstone, D. (2007) *Not for Sale: The Return of the Global Slave Trade — and How We Can Fight It*, New York: Harper.

Battiste, M. and Barman, J. (1995) (eds) *First Nations Education in Canada*, Vancouver: UBC Press.

Baucom, I. (1999) *Out of Place: Englishness, Empire, and the Locations of Identity*, Princeton, NJ: Princeton University Press.

Baugh, E. (2000) 'Postcolonial/Commonwealth Studies in the Caribbean: Points of Difference', in R. Smith (ed.) *Postcolonizing the Commonwealth: Studies in Literature and Culture*, Waterloo, ON: Wilfrid Laurier University Press.

Bauman, E. (1998) 'Re-Dreaming Colonial Discourse: Postcolonial Theory and the Humanist Project', *Critical Quarterly* 40(3): 79–89.

Bauman, Z. (1998) *Globalization: The Human Consequences*, New York: Columbia University Press.

Baumgart, W. (1982) *Imperialism: The Idea and Reality of British and French Colonial Expansion 1880–1914*, translated by Ben V. Mast, Oxford: Oxford University Press.

Baxter, P. and Sansom, B. (1972) *Race and Social Difference: Selected Readings*, Harmondsworth: Penguin.

Behdad, A. (2005) 'On Globalization, Again!' in A. Loomba, S. Kaul, M. Bunzl, A. Burton and J. Esty (eds) *Postcolonial Studies and Beyond*, Durham, NC: Duke University Press.

Behr, M. (2004) 'Postcolonial Transformations in Canadian Inuit Testimonio', in A. A. Lunsford and L. Ouzgane (eds) *Crossing Borderlands: Composition and Postcolonial Studies*, Pittsburgh, PA: University of Pittsburgh Press.

Benjamin, B. (2007) *Invested Interests: Capital, Culture and the World Bank*, Minneapolis: University of Minnesota Press.

Bennett, B. (2003) *Resistance and Reconciliation: Writing in the Commonwealth*, Canberra: ACLALS in association with The School of Language, Literature and Communication, University of New South Wales at ADFA.

Benton, L. and Strauman, B. (2010) 'Acquiring Empire by Law: From Roman Doctrine to Early Modern European Practice', *Law and History Review* 28(1): 1–38.

Berend, I. T. (2002) 'Clash of Civilizations?' *European Review* 10(4): 423–428.

Berglund, J. (2006) *Cannibal Fictions: American Explorations of Colonialism, Race, Gender and Sexuality*, Madison: University of Wisconsin Press.

Berkhofer, R. F. (1978) *The White Man's Indian: Images of the American Indian from Columbus to the Present*, New York: Knopf.

Berlin, I. (2004) *American Slavery in History and Memory*, by I. Berlin, Melbourne: La Trobe University History Programme.

Berman, C. V. (2006) *Creole Crossings: Domestic Fiction and the Reform of Colonial Slavery*, Ithaca, NY: Cornell University Press.

Bernasconi, R. (2002) 'The Assumption of Negritude: Aimé Césaire, Frantz Fanon, and the Vicious Circle of Racial Politics', *Parallax* 8(2 [23]): 69–83.

Bery, A. et al. (2000) *Comparing Postcolonial Literatures: Dislocations*, Basingstoke: Macmillan.

Besteman, C. (2020) *Militarized Global Apartheid*, Durham, NC: Duke University Press.

Betts, R. F. (2004) *Decolonization*, New York: Routledge.

Beverley, J. (Spring 1989) 'The Margin at the Center: On testimonio (Testimonial Narrative)', *Modern Fiction Studies* 35(1): 11–28.

Beverley, J. (1999) 'On the Subject of "Studies": Subaltern, Cultural, Women's, Ethnic, etc.' *Journal of Iberian and Latin American Studies* 5(2): 45–63.

Beverley, J. (2003) 'Adiós: A National Allegory (Some Reflections on Latin American Cultural Studies)', in S. Hart and R. Young (eds) *Contemporary Latin American Cultural Studies*, London: Arnold: 48–60.

Beverley, J. (2004a) *Testimonio: On the Politics of Truth*, Minneapolis: University of Minnesota Press.

Beverley, J. (2004b) 'Writing in Reverse: On the Project of the Latin American Subaltern Studies Group', in A. Del Sarto, A. Ríos and A. Trigo (eds) *The Latin American Cultural Studies Reader*, Durham, NC: Duke University Press.

Beverley, J. and Zimmerman, M. (1990) *Literature and Politics in the Central American Revolutions*, Austin: University of Texas Press.

Bhabha, H. K. (1983) 'Difference, Discrimination and the Discourse of Colonialism', in F. Barker, P. Hulme, M. Iverson and D. Loxley (eds) *The Politics of Theory*, Colchester: University of Essex.

Bhabha, H. K. (1984a) 'Of Mimicry and Man: The Ambivalence of Colonial Discourse', October 28 (Spring) (reprinted as Ch. 4 of Bhabha 1994).

Bhabha, H. K. (1984b) 'Representation and the Colonial Text: A Critical Exploration of Some Forms of Mimeticism', in F. Glover Smith (ed.) *The Theory of Reading*, Brighton: Harvester.

Bhabha, H. K. (Autumn 1985) 'Signs Taken for Wonders: Questions of Ambivalence and Authority under a Tree Outside Delhi, May 1817', *Critical Inquiry* 12(1) (reprinted as Ch. 6 of Bhabha 1994).

Bhabha, H. K. (1988) 'The Commitment to Theory', *New Formations* 5: 5–23 (also appears in an altered form in J. Pines and P. Willemen (eds) Questions of Third Cinema, British Film Institute, 1989 and subsequently reprinted as Ch. 1 of Bhabha 1994).

Bhabha, H. K. (1990) (ed.) *Nation and Narration*, London and New York: Routledge.

Bhabha, H. K. (1994) *The Location of Culture*, London: Routledge.

Bhabha, H. K. (1996a) 'The Other Question: Difference, Discrimination, and the Discourse of Colonialism', in H. A. Baker, Jr, M. Diawara, R. H. Lindeborg and S. Best (eds) *Black British Cultural Studies: A Reader*, Chicago, IL: University of Chicago Press.

Bhabha, H. K. (1996b) (ed.) *Nation and Narration*, London: Routledge.

Bhabha, H. K. (2004) *The Location of Culture*. New edition with preface by author, London and New York: Routledge.

Bhabha, J. (1998) '"Get Back to Where You Once Belonged": Identity, Citizenship and Exclusion in Europe', *Human Rights Quarterly* 20(3): 592–627.

Bharucha, N. E. (1997) 'Bombay to Mumbai: Postcolonial Repossessions and Hegemonies', *SPAN: Journal of the South Pacific Association for Commonwealth Literature and Language Studies* 45: 13–36.

Bhatt, C. (2002) 'Primordial Being: Enlightenment and the Indian Subject of Postcolonial Theory', in P. Osborne and S. Sandford (eds) *Philosophies of Race and Ethnicity*, London: Continuum.

Bhatt, R. M. (2001) 'World Englishes', *Annual Review of Anthropology* 30: 527–550.

Biddiss, M. D. (1970) *Father of Racist Ideology: The Social and Political Thought of Count Gobineau*, London: Weidenfeld & Nicholson.

Billington, R. A. (1966) (ed.) *The Frontier Thesis: Valid Interpretation of American History?*, New York: Holt, Rinehart.

Bishop, A. (1990) 'Western Mathematics: The Secret Weapon of Cultural Imperialism', *Race and Class* 32(2): 199.

Blackburn, R. (1988) *The Overthrow of Colonial Slavery, 1776–1848*, London and New York: Verso.

Blake, R. (1996) 'Barbadian Creole English: Insights into Linguistic and Social Identity', *Journal of Commonwealth and Postcolonial Studies* 4(1): 37–54.

Blassingame, J. W. (1971) (ed.) *New Perspectives on Black Studies*, Urbana: University of Illinois Press.

Blaut, J. M. (1987) *The National Question: Decolonizing the Theory of Nationalism*, preface by Juan Mari Bras, London: Zed Books.

Blaut, J. M. (1993) *The Colonizer's Model of the World: Geographical Diffusionism and Eurocentric History*, New York: Guilford Press.

Blomstrom, M. and Hettne, B. (1984) *Development Theory in Transition: The Dependency Debate and Beyond: Third World Responses*, London: Zed Books.

Blundell, V. (2000) *Changing Perspectives in the Anthropology of Art*, Ottawa: Golden Dog Press.

Blundell, V. and Woolagoodja, D. (2005) *Keeping the Wanjinas Fresh: Sam Woolagoodja and the Enduring Power of Lalai*, Fremantle: Fremantle Arts Centre Press.

Blunt, A. and McEwan, C. (2002) *Postcolonial Geographies*, New York: Continuum.

Bochner, S. (1982) (ed.) *Cultures in Contact: Studies in Cross-Cultural Interaction*, Oxford and New York: Pergamon Press.

Boehmer, E. (1991) '*Stories of Women and Mothers: Gender and Nationalism in the Early Fiction of Flora Nwapa*' in Susheila Nasta Motherlands, London: Women's Press.

Boehmer, E. (1995) *Colonial and Postcolonial Literature: Migrant Metaphors*, Oxford: Oxford University Press.

Boehmer, E. (1998) *Empire Writing: An Anthology of Colonial Literature, 1870–1918*, Oxford: Oxford University Press.

Boehmer, E. (2005) *Stories of Women: Gender and Narrative in the Postcolonial Nation*, Manchester: Manchester University Press.

Boer, I. E. (1994) 'This Is Not the Orient: Theory and Postcolonial Practice', in M. Bal, I. E. Boer and J. Culler (eds) *The Point of Theory: Practices of Cultural Analysis*, New York: Continuum: 211–219.

Bongie, C. (1998) *Islands and Exiles: The Creole Identities of Post/Colonial Literature*, Stanford, CA: Stanford University Press.

Boon, J. A. (1982) *Other Tribes, Other Scribes: Symbolic Anthropology in the Comparative Study of Cultures, Histories, Religions, and Texts*, Cambridge: Cambridge University Press.

Boons-Grafé, M.-C. (1992) 'Other/Other', (translated by Margaret Whitford) in E. Wright (ed.) *Feminism and Psychoanalysis: A Critical Dictionary*, Oxford: Blackwell.

Bose, M. (2006) *Bollywood: A History*, Stroude: Tempus.

Bracey, E. N. (2003) *On Racism: Essays on Black Popular Culture, African American Politics, and the New Black Aesthetics*, Lanham: University Press of America.

Brah, A. (1996) *Cartographies of Diaspora: Contesting Identities*, London: Routledge.

Brahms, F. (1995) 'Entering Our Own Ignorance: Subject-Object Relations in Commonwealth Literature', in B. Ashcroft, G. Griffiths and H. Tiffin (eds) *The Postcolonial Studies Reader*, London: Routledge.

Brathwaite, E. K. (1971) *The Development of Creole Society in Jamaica, 1770–1820*, Oxford: Oxford University Press.

Brathwaite, E. K. (1974) *Contradictory Omens: Cultural Diversity and Integration in the Caribbean*, Mona, Jamaica: Savacou Publications.

Brathwaite, E. K. (1981) 'English in the Caribbean: Notes on Nation Language and Poetry: An Electronic Lecture', in L. A. Fiedler and H. A. Baker, Jr (eds) *English Literature: Opening Up the Canon*, Baltimore: Johns Hopkins University Press: 15–53.

Brathwaite, E. K. (1984) *History of the Voice: The Development of Nation Language in Anglophone Caribbean Poetry*, London: New Beacon Books. Cited in Ashcroft et al. (1995): 309–313.

Brathwaite, E. K. (1995a) 'Creolization in Jamaica', in B. Ashcroft, G. Griffiths and H. Tiffin (eds) *The Postcolonial Studies Reader*, London: Routledge: 202–205.

Brathwaite, E. K. (1995b) 'Nation Language', in B. Ashcroft, G. Griffiths and H. Tiffin (eds) *The Postcolonial Studies Reader*, London: Routledge: 309–313.

Bray, T. and Middleton, R. (1979) *Contemporary Modernism*, Milton Keynes: Open University Press.

Braziel, J. E. and Mannur, A. (2003) (eds) *Theorizing Diaspora: A Reader*, Malden, MA: Blackwell.

Breckenridge, C. A., Bhabha, H. K. and Pollock, S. (eds) (2002) *Cosmopolitanism*, London and Durham, NC: Duke University Press.

Breckenridge, C. A. and Veer, P. V. D. (1993) (eds) *Orientalism and the Postcolonial Predicament: Perspectives on South Asia*, Philadelphia: University of Pennsylvania Press.

Breen, K. and O'Neill, S. (2010) (eds) *After the Nation? Critical Reflections on Nationalism and Postnationalism*, London: Palgrave Macmillan.

Bremen, J. (1990) (ed.) *Imperial Monkey Business: Racial Supremacy in Social Darwinist Theory and Colonial Practice, CASA Monographs 3*, Amsterdam: VU University Press.

Brennan, E. (2024) 'Necropolitics and Surplus Life: Mbembe and Beyond', *Theory, Culture and Society* 41(3): 3–19.

Brennan, T. (1989) *Salman Rushdie and the Third World: Myths of the Nation*, London: Macmillan.

Brennan, T. (2004a) 'From Development to Globalization: Postcolonial Studies and Globalization Theory', in N. Lazarus (ed.) *The Cambridge Companion to Postcolonial Literary Studies*, Cambridge: Cambridge University Press.

Brennan, T. (2004b) *The Transmission of Affect*, Ithaca, NY: Cornell University Press.

Brennan, T. (2005) 'The Economic Image-Function of the Periphery', in A. Loomba, S. Kaul, M. Bunzl, A. Burton and J. Esty (eds) *Postcolonial Studies and Beyond*, Durham, NC: Duke University Press.

Brewster, A. (2010) 'Critical Whiteness Studies and Australian Indigenous Literature', in D. Carter and W. Guanglin (eds) *Modern Australian Criticism and Theory*, Qingdao: China Ocean University Press: 190–205.

Brock, P., Etherington, N., Griffiths, G. and Van Gent, J. (2015) *Indigenous Evangelists and Questions of Authority in the British Empire*, Leiden and Boston: Brill.

Brooks, L. (2008) *The Common Pot: The Recovery of Native Space in the Northeast*, Minneapolis: University of Minnesota Press.

Brotherston, G. (1992) *Book of the Fourth World: Reading the Native Americas through Their Literature*, Cambridge: Cambridge University Press.

Brown, R. H. and Coelho, G. V. (1987) (eds) *Migration and Modernization: The Indian Diaspora in Comparative Perspective*, Williamsburg, VA: Department of Anthropology, College of William and Mary.

Browning, D. S. (2006) (ed.) *Universalism vs. Relativism: Making Moral Judgments in a Changing, Pluralistic, and Threatening World*, Plymouth: Rowman & Littlefield.

Brunner, C. (2021) 'Conceptualizing Epistemic Violence: An Interdisciplinary Assemblage', *International Political Review* 9: 193–212.

Bryan, J. (2011) 'Walking the Line: Participatory Mapping, Indigenous Rights, and Neo-Liberalism', *Geoforum* 42(1): 40–50.

Brydon, D. (Winter 1984) 'Re-writing The Tempest', *World Literature Written in English* 23(1).

Brydon, D. (1991) 'The White Inuit Speaks: Contamination as Literary Strategy', in I. Adam and H. Tiffin (eds) *Past the Last Post: Theorising Postcolonialism and Post-Modernism*, New York and London: Harvester Wheatsheaf.

Brydon, D. (2000) (ed.) *Postcolonialism: Critical Concepts in Literary and Cultural Studies*, London: Routledge.

Brydon, D. (2001a) 'Global Designs, Postcolonial Critiques: Rethinking Canada in Dialogue with Diaspora', *Ilha do Desterro: A Journal of Language and Literature* 40: 61–84.

Brydon, D. (2001b) 'Mobilizing Globalization's Undertow', *Ilha do Desterro: A Journal of Language and Literature* 40: 125–126.

Brydon, D. and Tiffin, H. (1993) *Decolonising Fictions*, Aarhus: Dangaroo.

Buchanan, I. (2003) 'National Allegory Today: A Return to Jameson', *New Formations: A Journal of Culture/Theory/Politics* 51: 66–79.

Buchholtz, M. (2004) *Postcolonial Subjects: Canadian and Australian Perspectives*, Torun, Poland: Wydawnictwo Uniwersytetu Mikolaja Kopernika.

Buell, L. (1995) *The Environmental Imagination: Thoreau, Nature Writing, and the Formation of American Culture*, Cambridge, MA: Harvard University Press.

Buell, L. (2005) *The Future of Environmental Criticism*, Malden MA: Blackwell.

Bulbeck, C. (1998) *Re-orienting Western Feminisms: Women's Diversity in a Postcolonial World*, Cambridge: Cambridge University Press.

Burton, A. M. (2003) (ed.) *After the Imperial Turn: Thinking with and Through the Nation*, Durham, NC: Duke University Press.

Burton, G. C. (2004) *Ambivalence and the Postcolonial Subject: The Strategic Alliance of Juan Francisco Manzano and Richard Robert Madden*, New York: Peter Lang.

Butali, U. (2018) *The Other Side of Silence: Voices from the Partition of India*, Durham, NC: Duke University Press.

Butler, J. (1997) 'Gender Is Burning: Questions of Appropriation and Subversion', in A. McClintock, A. Mufti and E. Shohat (eds) *Dangerous Liaisons: Gender, Nation, and Postcolonial Perspectives*, Minneapolis: University of Minnesota Press.

Butler, J. (2020) *Precarious Life: The Powers of Mourning and Violence*, New York: Verso.

Butler, J. E. (1981) *Black Studies – Pedagogy and Revolution: A Study of Afro-American Studies and the Liberal Arts Tradition Through the Discipline of Afro-American Literature*, Washington, DC: University Press of America.

Cabral, A. (1973) *Return to the Sources: Selected Speeches*, New York and London: Monthly Review Press.

Caglar, A. (2022) 'Transnational Migration', in A. Triandafyllidou (ed.) *Routledge Handbook of Immigration and Refugee Studies*, London: Routledge: 34–43.

Cahill, D. (2017) *Neoliberalism*, Konings: Martjin.

Caldwell, R. C., Jr (2003) 'For a Theory of the Creole City: Texaco and the Postcolonial Postmodern', in M. Gallagher (ed.) *Ici-Lá: Place and Displacement in Caribbean Writing in French*, Amsterdam, Netherlands: Rodopi: 25–39.

Callicott, J. B. (1980) 'Animal Liberation: A Triangular Affair', *Environmental Ethics* 2(4): 311–338.

Callicott, J. B. (1989) 'Animal Liberation and Environmental Ethics: Back Together Again', in *Defence of the Land*, Albany, NY: SUNY Press.

Cameron, E. (2011) 'Copper Stories: Imaginative Geographies and Material Orderings of the Central Canadian Arctic', in A. Baldwin, L. Cameron and A. Kobayashi (eds) *Rethinking the Great White North*, Vancouver: UBC Press.

Campbell, H. (1985) *Rasta and Resistance: from Marcus Garvey to Walter Rodney*, Dar es Salaam: Tanzania Publishing House.

Campbell, K. O. S. (2006) *Literature and Culture in the Black Atlantic*, New York: Palgrave/Macmillan.

Campbell-Praed, P. Mrs (1881) *Policy and Passion*, London: Richard Bentley and Sons.

Caquard, S. (2013) 'Cartography: Mapping Narrative Cartography', *Progress in Human Geography* 37(February): 135–144.

Carby, H. (1982) '*White woman listen! Black feminism and the boundaries of sisterhood*' in *The Empire Strikes Back: Race and Racism in 70s Britain, Centre for Contemporary Cultural Studies, University of Birmingham*, London: Hutchinson.

Carlson, A. and Truscello, M. (2003) 'Technocratic Fiction, Indigenous Sovereignty and Counter-Insurgent Infrastructure', *Critique Bolingbroke Society*: 1–12.

Caroppo, E., Muscelli, C., Brogna, P., Paci, M., Camerino, C. and Bria, P. (2009) 'Relating with Migrants: Ethnopsychiatry and Psychotherapy', *Annale dell Istitutio superior di sanita* 45(3): 331–340.

Carothers, J. C. (1953) *The African Mind in Health and Disease: A Study in Ethnopsychiatry*, Geneva: World Health Organization.

Carruthers, J. (2006) 'Contesting Cultural Landscapes in South Africa and Australia', in D. Trigger and G. Griffiths (eds) *Disputed Territories: Land, Culture and Identity in Settler Societies*, Hong Kong: Hong Kong University Press.

Carter, E., Donald, J. and Squires, J. (1993) (eds) *Space and Power: Theories of Identity and Location*, London: Lawrence & Wishart.

Carter, M. (1996) *Voices from Indenture: Experiences of Indian Migrants in the British Empire*, New York: Leicester University Press.

Carter, P. (1987) *Road to Botany Bay: An Essay in Spatial History*, London: Faber and Faber.

Carter, P. (1992) *Living in a New Country: History, Traveling and Language*, London: Faber and Faber.

Carter, P. (1996) *The Lie of the Land*, London: Faber & Faber.

Casanova, P. (2004) *The World Republic of Letters*, translated by M. B. DeBevoise, Cambridge, MA: Harvard University Press [2007].

Casas, M. D. L. C. (1998) 'Orality and Literacy in a Postcolonial World', *Social Semiotics* 8(1): 5–24.

Cashmore, E. (1979) *Rastaman: The Rastafarian Movement in England*, London: Unwin Paperbacks.

Cashmore, E. (1983) *Rastaman: The Rastafarian Movement in England*, London and Boston: Unwin.

Castello, C. (2015) '"Luso-Tropicalism" and Portuguese Late Colonialism', Buala, https://www.buala.org/en/to-read/luso-tropicalism-and-portuguese-late-colonialism.

Castillo, D. A. (1999) 'Border Theory and the Canon', in D. L. Madsen (ed.) *Postcolonial Literatures: Expanding the Canon*, London: Pluto.

Castle, G. (2001) (ed.) *Postcolonial Discourses: An Anthology*, Malden, MA: Blackwell.

Castles, S. (2011) 'Migration, Crisis, and the Global Labor Market', *Globalizations* 8(3): 311–324.

Castro-Klarén, S. (1999) 'Mimicry Revisited: Latin America, Postcolonial Theory and the Location of Knowledge', in A. D. Toro and F. D. Toro (eds) *El debate de la postcolonialidad en Latinoamérica: Una postmodernidad periférica o cambio de paradigma en el pensamiento latinoamericano*, Madrid: Iberoamericana: 137–164.

Célestin, R. (1996) *From Cannibals to Radicals: Figures and Limits of Exoticism*, Minneapolis and London: University of Minnesota Press.

Chakrabarty, D. (2000a) 'Universalism and Belonging in the Logic of Capital', *Public Culture* 12(3): 653–678.

Chakrabarty, D. (2000b) *Provincializing Europe: Postcolonial Thought and Historical Difference*, Princeton, NJ: Princeton University Press.

Chakrabarty, D. (2009) 'The Climate of History: Four Theses', *Critical Inquiry* 35(2): 197–222.

Chakrabarty, D. (2012) 'Postcolonial Studies and the Challenge of Climate Change', *New Literary History* 43(1): 1–18.

Chakrabarty, D. and Bhabha, H. K. (2002) *Habitations of Modernity: Essays in the Wake of Subaltern Studies*, Chicago, IL: University of Chicago Press.

Chamberlain, M. E. (1999) *Decolonization: The Fall of the European Empires*, Malden, MA: Blackwell Publishers.

Chambers, I. and Curti, L. (1996) (eds) *The Postcolonial Question: Common Skies, Divided Horizons*, London: Routledge.

Chanady, A. (1995) 'The Formation of National Consciousness in Latin America: Mestizaje and Monolithic Cultural Paradigms', in M. E. D. Valdés, M. Valdés and R. A. Young (eds) *Latin America and Its Literature*, Whitestone, NY: Council on National Literatures: 170–180.

Chanady, A. (2003) 'Identity, Politics and Mestizaje', in S. Hart and R. Young (eds) *Contemporary Latin American Cultural Studies*, London: Arnold: 192–202.

Chang, E. K. (2001) 'Last Past the Post: Theory, Futurity, Feminism', in M. Dekoven (ed.) *Feminist Locations: Global and Local, Theory and Practice*, New Brunswick, NJ: Rutgers University Press: 60–74.

Chao, S. (2022) *In the Shadow of the Palms: More-Than-Human Becomings in West Papua*, Raleigh, NC: Duke University Press.

Chapin, M., Lamb, Z. and Threlkeld, B. (2005) 'Mapping Indigenous Lands', *Annual Review of Anthropology* 34: 619–638.

Chatterjee, P. (1986) *Nationalist Thought and the Colonial World: A Derivative Discourse*, London: Zed Books.

Chatterjee, P. (1993) *The Nation and Its Fragments: Colonial and Postcolonial Histories*, Princeton, NJ: Princeton University Press.

Cheah, P. (1999) 'Spectral Nationality: The Living on [sur-vie] of the Postcolonial Nation in Neocolonial Globalization', *boundary 2* 26(3): 225–252.

Cheah, P. (2003) *Spectral Nationality: Passages of Freedom from Kant to Postcolonial Literatures of Liberation*, New York, NY: Columbia University Press.

Chevannes, B. (1997) (ed.) *Rastafari and Other African-Caribbean Worldviews*, New Brunswick, NJ: Rutgers University Press.

Childs, P. et al. (2006) *Postcolonial Theory and Literatures: African, Caribbean and South Asian*, Trier, Germany: Wissenschaftlicher.

Childs, P. and Williams, P. (1997) *An Introduction to Postcolonial Theory*, London and New York: Prentice Hall/Harvester Wheatsheaf.

Chin, T. (2006) 'Transnationalism, Diaspora, Politics and the Caribbean Postcolonial', *Small Axe: A Caribbean Journal of Criticism* 19: 189–197.

Chiumbu, S. H. (2014) '"The World Is Our Community": Rethinking Community Radio in the Digital Age', *Journal of African Media Studies* 6(3): 249–264.

Chossudovsky, M. (1997) *The Globalization of Poverty: Impacts of IMF and World Bank Reforms*, London and New Jersey: Zed Books.

Chow, R. (1993) *Writing Diaspora: Tactics of Intervention in Contemporary Cultural Studies*, Bloomington: Indiana University Press.

Chrisman, L. (1998) 'Imperial Space, Imperial Place: Theories of Empire and Culture in Frederic Jameson, Edward Said and Gayatri Spivak', *New Formations: A Journal of Culture/Theory/Politics* 34: 53–69.

Chrisman, L. (2000) 'Rethinking Black Atlanticism', *Black Scholar: Journal of Black Studies and Research* 30(3–4): 12–17.

Chrisman, L. (2002) 'Rethinking Race and Nation', *New Formations: A Journal of Culture/Theory/Politics* 47: 67–143.

Chrisman, L. (2003) *Postcolonial Contraventions: Cultural Readings of Race, Imperialism, and Transnationalism*, Manchester: Manchester University Press.

Chrisman, L. (2004) 'Nationalism and Postcolonial Studies', in N. Lazarus (ed.) *The Cambridge Companion to Postcolonial Literary Studies*, Cambridge: Cambridge University Press: 183–198.

Chrisman, L. (2005) 'Beyond Black Atlantic and Postcolonial Studies: The South African Differences of Sol Plaatje and Peter Abrahams', in A. Loomba et al. (eds) *Postcolonial Studies and Beyond*, Durham, NC: Duke University Press.

Chrisman, L. and Williams, P. (1993) (eds) *Colonial Discourse and Postcolonial Theory: A Reader*, Hemel Hempstead: Harvester Wheatsheaf.

Christian, J. M. and Dowler, L. (2019) 'Slow and Fast Violence: A Feminist Critique of Binaries', *ACME: An International E-Journal for Critical Geographies* 18(5): 1066.

Clark, B. and Foster, J. B. (2009) 'Ecological Imperialism and the Global Metabolic Rift', *International Journal of Comparative Sociology* 50(3–4): 311–334.

Clark, S. (1999) (ed.) *Travel Writing and Empire: Postcolonial Theory in Transit*, London: Zed.

Clark, T. (2011) *The Cambridge Introduction to Literature and the Environment*, Cambridge: Cambridge University Press.

Clarke, S. (2000) 'Dreams of Home: Rastafari's Imagining Community for the African Diaspora', *BMA: The Sonia Sanchez Literary Review* 6(1): 91–108.

Clavin, P. (2005) 'Defining Transnationalism', *Contemporary European History* 14(4): 421–439.

Clayton, D. and Gregory, D. (1996) (eds) *Colonialism, Postcolonialism and the Production of Space*, Oxford: Blackwell.

Clifford, J. (1986) (ed.) *Writing Culture: The Poetics and Politics of Ethnography. A School of American Research Advanced Seminar*, Berkeley: University of California Press.

Clifford, J. (1988) *The Predicament of Culture*, Cambridge, MA: Harvard University Press.

Clifford, J. (1997) *Routes: Travel and Translation in the Late Twentieth Century*, Cambridge, MA: Harvard University Press.

Clough, P. T. and Halley, J. (2007) (eds) *The Affective Turn: Theorizing the Social*, Durham, NC: Duke University Press.

Codell, J. F. and Macleod, D. S. (1998) (eds) *Orientalism Transposed: The Impact of the Colonies on British Culture*, Aldershot: Ashgate.

Coetzee, J. M. (1974) *Dusklands*, Harmondsworth: Penguin.

Coetzee, J. M. (1980) *Waiting for the Barbarians*, Harmondsworth: Penguin.

Coetzee, J. M. (1989) *White Writing: The Culture of Letters in South Africa*, New Haven, CT: Yale University Press.

Colás, S. (1995) 'Of Creole Symptoms, Cuban Fantasies, and Other Latin American Postcolonial Ideologies', *PMLA: Publications of the Modern Language Association of America* 110(3): 382–396.

Colás, S. (2001) 'From Caliban to Cronus: A Critique of Cannibalism as Metaphor for Cuban Revolutionary Culture', in K. Guest and M. Kilgour (eds) *Eating Their Words: Cannibalism and the Boundaries of Cultural Identity*, New York: State University of New York Press.

Coleman, D. (2019) 'Digital Colonialism: The 21st Century Scramble for Africa through the Extraction and Control of User Data and the Limitations of Data Protection Laws', *Michigan Journal of Race and Law* 24: 417–439.

Collett, A. (2002) 'South Africa Post-Apartheid', *Kunapipi: Journal of Post-Colonial Writing* 24(1–2): 1–300.

Collins, F. and Davis, T. (2004) *Australian Cinema After Mabo*, Cambridge: Cambridge University Press.

Collins, L. (2000) 'Daughters of Jah: The Impact of Rastafarian Womanhood in the Caribbean, the United States, Britain, and Canada', in H. Gossai and N. S. Murrell (eds) *Religion, Culture, and Tradition in the Caribbean*, New York: St. Martin's.

Colwill, E. (2023) 'Creole Against Creolization', *Theory and Event* 26(2): 283–317.

Comaroff, J. (2006) *Law and Disorder in the Postcolony*, Chicago: University of Chicago Press.

Comaroff, J. and Comaroff, J. (1993) *Modernity and Its Malcontents: Ritual and Power in Postcolonial Africa*, Chicago, IL: University of Chicago Press.

Connor, M. (2005) *The Invention of Terra Nullius: Historical and Legal Fictions on the Foundation of Australia*, Sydney: Macleay Press.

Connor, W. (1984) *The National Question in Marxist-Leninist Theory and Strategy*, Princeton, NJ: Princeton University Press.

Consentino, D. A. (2000) 'Under the Shadow of God: Roots of Primitivism in Early Colonial Mexico', in E. Camayd-Freixas and J. E. González (eds) *Primitivism and Identity in Latin America: Essays on Art, Literature, and Culture*, Tucson, AZ: University of Arizona Press: 41–52.

Coombes, A. E. (1994) *Reinventing Africa: Museums, Material Culture and Popular Imagination*, New Haven, CT and London: Yale University Press.

Coombes, A. E. (2003) *History After Apartheid: Visual Culture and Public Memory in a Democratic South Africa*, Durham, NC: Duke University Press.

Cooppan, V. (1999) 'W(h)ither Postcolonial Studies? Towards the Trans-national Study of Race and Nation', in L. Chrisman and B. Parry (eds) *Postcolonial Theory and Criticism*, Cambridge: Brewer: 1–35.

Cornejo Polar, A. (1997) 'Mestizaje e hibridez: Los riesgos de las metáforas: Apuntes', *Revista Iberoamericana* 63(180): 341–344.

Cornejo Polar, A. and Dennis, C. (2004a) 'Mestizaje and Hybridity: The Risks of Metaphors-Notes', in A. Del Sarto, A. Ríos and A. Trigo (eds) *The Latin American Cultural Studies Reader*, Durham, NC: Duke University Press: 760–764.

Cornejo Polar, A. and Dennis, C. (2004b) 'Mestizaje, Transculturation, Heterogeneity', in A. Del Sarto, A. Ríos and A. Trigo (eds) *The Latin American Cultural Studies Reader*, Durham, NC: Duke University Press: 116–119.

Coronil, F. (1999) 'Listening to the Subaltern: Postcolonial Studies and the Neocolonial Poetics of Subaltern States', in L. Chrisman and B. Parry (eds) *Postcolonial Theory and Criticism*, Cambridge: Brewer.

Coutinho, E. F. (1992) 'El discurso crítico-teórico latinoamericano y la cuestión de la descolonización cultural', *Casa de las Americas* 32(187): 61–79.

Crane, R. and Mohanram, R. (1996) 'The Postcolonial Body', *SPAN: Journal of the South Pacific Association for Commonwealth Literature and Language Studies* 42–43: 1–173.

Crawford, N. (2002) *Argument and Change in World Politics: Ethics, Decolonization, and Humanitarian Intervention*, Cambridge: Cambridge University Press.

Crenshaw, K. (1991) 'Mapping the Margins: Intersectionality, Identity Politics, and Violence Against Women of Color', *Stanford Law Review* 43(6): 1241–1299.

Croizier, R. C. et al. (2002) (eds) *Colonialism and the Modern World: Selected Studies*, Armonk, New York: M.E. Sharpe.

Crosby, A. W. (1985) *Ecological Imperialism: The Biological Expansion of Europe 900–1900*, Cambridge: Cambridge University Press.

Crosby, A. W. (1986) *Ecological Imperialism: The Biological Expansion of Europe, 900–1900*, Cambridge: Cambridge University Press.

Crosby, A. W. (2003) *The Columbian Exchange: Biological and Cultural Consequences of 1492*, Westport, CT: Praeger.

Crutzen, P. J. and Stoermer, E. F. (2000) 'The "Anthropocene"', *Global Change Newsletter* 41: 17–18.

Cudjoe, S. R. (1980) *Resistance and Caribbean Literature*, Athens and London: Ohio University Press.

Culler, J. (1981) *The Pursuit of Signs: Semiotics, Literature, Deconstruction*, London: Routledge.

D'Andrade, R. G. (1995) *The Development of Cognitive Anthropology*, Cambridge and New York: Cambridge University Press.

D'Cruz, C. (2001) '"What Matter Who's Speaking?": Authenticity and Identity in Discourses of Aboriginality in Australia', *Jouvert: A Journal of Postcolonial Studies* 5(3): 1–15.

da Silva, F. C. and Villaverde Cabral, M. (2020) 'The Politics of the Essay: Lusotropicalism as Ideology and Theory', *American Sociologist* 51: 381–397.

Dale, L. and Ryan, S. (1998) (eds) *The Body in the Library*, Amsterdam, Netherlands: Rodopi.

Dallmayr, F. R. (1996) *Beyond Orientalism: Essays on Cross-Cultural Encounter*, Albany: State University of New York Press.

Dalziell, T. (2004) *Settler Romances and the Australian Girl*, Fremantle, WA: UWA Press.

Damrosch, D. (2003) *What Is World Literature?* Princeton, NJ: Princeton University Press.

Dangaremba, T. (1988) *Nervous Conditons*, London: The Women's Press.

Darby, P. (1997) (ed.) *At the Edge of International Relations: Postcolonialism, Gender, and Dependency*, London: Pinter.

Darby, P. (1998) *The Fiction of Imperialism: Reading Between International Relations and Postcolonialism*, London: Cassell.

Darian-Smith, K., Gunner, L. and Nuttall, S. (1996) (eds) *Text, Theory, Space: Land, Literature and History in South Africa and Australia*, London: Routledge.

Darias Beautell, E. (2000) 'Writing Back and Beyond: Postcoloniality, Multiculturalism, and Ethnicity in the Canadian Context', in R. G. Davis and R. Baena (eds) *Tricks with a Glass: Writing Ethnicity in Canada*, Amsterdam, Netherlands: Rodopi: 19–35.

Darwin, C. (1871) *The Descent of Man*, 1st edition, London: John Murray: 168–169.

Dash, J. M. (1992) *Discours Antillais: Caribbean Discourse: Selected Essays* by Edouard Glissant, translated and with an introduction by J. Michael Dash, Charlottesville: University Press of Virginia.

Dash, J. M. (1995) *Edouard Glissant*, Cambridge and New York: Cambridge University Press.

Dash, J. M. (2003) 'Postcolonial Caribbean Identities', in F. A. Irele and S. Gikandi (eds) *The Cambridge History of African and Caribbean Literature*, Cambridge: Cambridge University Press.

Davidson, B. (1992) *The Black Man's Burden: Africa and the Curse of the Nation-state*, London: James Currey.

Davidson, B. (1994) *The Search for Africa, History, Culture, Politics,* New York: Random House.

Davies, T. (2019) 'Slow Violence and Toxic Geographies: 'Out of Sight' To Whom?' *Environment and Planning C: Politics and Space* 40(2): 409–427.

Davis, G. V. and Maes-Jelinek, H. (1990) *Crisis and Creativity in the New Literatures in English: Cross/Cultures*, Amsterdam, Netherlands: Rodopi.

Davis, J. and Hodge, B. (1985) (eds) *Aboriginal Writing Today*, Canberra: Australian Institute of Aboriginal Studies.

Davis, R. C. and Gross, D. S. (1994) 'Gayatri Chakravorty Spivak and the Ethos of the Subaltern', in J. S. Baumlin and T. F. Baumlin (eds) *Ethos: New Essays in Rhetorical and Critical Theory*, Dallas: Southern Methodist University Press.

De Certeau, M. (1984) *The Practice of Everyday Life*, translated by S. Rendall, Berkeley: University of California Press.

De Costa, E. (2002) 'Voices of Conscience: The Power of Language in the Latin American Testimonio', in I. M. F. Blayer and M. Sanchez (eds) *Story-telling: Interdisciplinary and Intercultural Perspectives*, New York: Peter Lang.

de Moraes-Farias, P. F. and Barber, K. (1990) *Self-Assertion and Brokerage: Early Cultural Nationalism in West Africa*, University of Birmingham African Studies Series 2, Birmingham: Centre of West African Studies.

De Santillana, G. (1955) *Dialogue on the Great World Systems*, Chicago, IL: University of Chicago Press.

De Wet, C. (2010) (ed.) *Development-Induced Displacement: Problems, Policies and People*, Providence, RI: Berghan Books.

De Zwart, P. (2016) *Globalization and the Colonial Origins of the Great Divergence: Intercontinental Trade and Living Standards in the Dutch East India Company's Commercial Empire 1600–1800,* Leiden and Biston: Brill.

DeCamp, D. (1977) 'The Development of Pidgin and Creole Studies', in A. Valman (ed.) *Pidgin and Creole Linguistics*, Bloomington: Indiana University Press.

Deena, S. (1997) 'Colonial and Canonical Control over Third World Writers', in R. K. Dhawan (ed.) *Postcolonial Discourse: A Study of Contemporary Literature*, New Delhi, India: Prestige.

DeFoigny, G. (1995) *The Southern Land, Known*, translated by D. Fausett, Syracuse, NY: Syracuse University Press.

Deleuze, G. and Guattari, F. (1972) *Anti-Oedipus: Capitalism and Schizophrenia*, translated by R. Hurley, M. Seem and H. R. Lane, New York: Viking; reprinted Minneapolis: University of Minnesota Press, 1987.

Deleuze, G. and Guattari, F. (1980) *A Thousand Plateaus: Capitalism and Schizophrenia*, translated and foreword by Brian Massumi, London: Athlone Press.

Deleuze, G. and Guattari, F. (1987) *A Thousand Plateaus: Capitalism and Schizophrenia*, translated by B. Massumi, Minneapolis: University of Minnesota Press.

Deleuze, G. and Guattari, F. (2004) *A Thousand Plateaus – Capitalism and Schizophrenia*, translated by B. Massumi, London and New York: Continuum Books.

Denegri, F. (2003) 'Testimonio and Its Discontents', in S. Hart and R. Young (eds) *Contemporary Latin American Cultural Studies*, London: Arnold.

Denning, M. (2004) *Culture in the Age of Three Worlds*, London: Verso.

Denoon, D. (1979) 'Understanding Settler Societies', *Historical Studies* 18: 511–527.

Denoon, D. (1983) *Settler Capitalism: The Dynamics of Dependent Development in the Southern Hemisphere*, Oxford: Clarendon.

Derrida, J. (1986) 'Racism's Last Word' (Le Dernier mot du Racisme) translated by Peggy Kamuf in Henry Louis Gates (ed.) *'Race,' Writing and Difference*, Chicago: University of Chicago Press.

Desai, G. and Nair, S. (2005) *Postcolonialisms: An Anthology of Cultural Theory and Criticism*, New Brunswick, NJ: Rutgers University Press.

Desmet, K., Ortuño-Ortín, I. and Wacziarg, R. (2017) 'Culture, Ethnicity, and Diversity', *The American Economic Review* 107(9): 2479–2513.

Devy, G. N. (1992) *After Amnesia: Tradition and Change in Indian Literary Criticism*, Hyderabad: Orient Longman and Sangam Books.

Di Chiro, G. (2021) 'Making Ecofeminism(S) Matter…Again', *Women's Studies* 59(8): 820–828.

Dickens, P. (2000) *Social Darwinism: Linking Evolutionary Thought to Social Theory*, Philadelphia: Open University Press.

Dimitriadis, G. (2001) *Reading and Teaching the Postcolonial: From Baldwin to Basquiat and Beyond*, New York: Teachers College Press.

Dirlik, A. (1996) 'The Postcolonial Aura: Third World Criticism in the Age of Global Capitalism', in P. Mongia (ed.) *Contemporary Postcolonial Theory: A Reader*, London: Arnold.

Dirlik, A. (1999) 'Is There History after Eurocentrism? Globalism, Postcolonialism, and the Disavowal of History', *Cultural Critique* 42(0): 1–34.

Dirlik, A. (2005) 'The End of Colonialism? The Colonial Modern in the Making of Global Modernity', *Boundary 2: An International Journal of Literature and Culture* 32(1): 1–31.

Dissanayake, W. and Wickramagamage, C. (1993) *Self and Colonial Desire: Travel Writings of V.S. Naipaul,* New York: Peter Lang.

Dixon, C. J. and Heffernan, M. J. (1991) *Colonialism and Development in the Contemporary World*, London: Mansell.

Dixon, R. (1997) 'Prosthetic Gods: The Australian Colonial Body and Melanesia, 1930–1950', *Southern Review: Literary and Interdisciplinary Essays* 30(2): 130–145.

Docker, J. (1978) 'The Neo-Colonial Assumption in University Teaching of English', in C. Tiffin (ed.) *South Pacific Images, St Lucia, Queensland: Journal of the South Pacific Association for Commonwealth Literature and Language Studies.*

Docker, J. (1992) *Dilemmas of Identity: The Desire for the Other in Colonial and Postcololonial Cultural History*, London: Sir Robert Menzies Centre for Australian Studies, Institute of Commonwealth Studies, University of London.

Donaldson, L. (1993) *Decolonizing Feminisms*, London and New York: Routledge.

Donaldson, L. and Pui-Lan, K. (2002) (eds) *Postcolonialism, Feminism and Religious Discourse*, London and New York: Routledge.

Döring, T. (2002) *Caribbean-English Passages: Intertextuality in a Postcolonial Tradition*, New York: Routledge.

Dotson, K. (2011) 'Tracking Epistemic Violence, Tracking Practices of Silencing', *Hypatia* 26(2): 236–257.

Douglas, M. (1991) *Purity and Danger: An Analysis of the Concepts of Pollution and Taboo*, London: Routledge.

Drescher, S. (1987) *Capitalism and Antislavery: British Mobilisation in Comparative Perspective*, Oxford: Oxford University Press.

Drew, J. (1999) 'Cultural Composition: Stuart Hall on Ethnicity and the Discursive Turn', in G. A. Olson and L. Worsham (eds) *Race, Rhetoric, and the Postcolonial*, Albany: State University of New York Press: 205–239.

Duara, P. (2003) (ed.) *Decolonization: Perspectives from Now and Then*, New York: Routledge.

DuCille, A. (1996) *Skin Trade*, Cambridge, MA: Harvard University Press.

Dulfano, I. (2004) 'Testimonio: Present Predicaments and Future Forays', in L. S. Maier and I. Dulfano (eds) *Woman as Witness: Essays on Testimonial Literature by Latin American Women*, New York: Peter Lang.

Dunn, R. S. (1973) *Sugar and Slaves: The Rise of the Planter Class in the English West Indies 1624–1713*, New York: Norton.

During, S. (1994) 'Rousseau's Patrimony: Primitivism, Romance and Becoming Other', in F. Barker, P. Hulme and M. Iversen (eds) *Colonial Discourse/ Postcolonial Theory*, Manchester: Manchester University Press: 47–71.

Durix, J.-P. (1998) *Mimesis, Genres, and Postcolonial Discourse: Deconstructing Magic Realism*, Basingstoke: Macmillan.

Durrant, S. (2003) *Postcolonial Narrative and the Work of Mourning: J. M. Coetzee, Wilson Harris, and Toni Morrison*, Albany: State University of New York Press.

Dussel, E. (1993) 'Eurocentrism and Modernity (Introduction to the Frankfurt Lectures)', *Boundary 2: An International Journal of Literature and Culture* 20(3): 65–76.

Dussel, E. and Mendieta, E. (1998) 'Beyond Eurocentrism: The World-System and the Limits of Modernity', in F. Jameson and M. Miyoshi (eds) *The Cultures of Globalization*, Durham, NC: Duke University Press: 3–31.

Dyer, R. (1988) 'White', *Screen* 29: 45–64.

Eagleton, T. (1990) *Nationalism, Colonialism, and Literature*, Minneapolis: University of Minnesota Press.

Easthope, A. and McGowan, K. (1992) *A Critical and Cultural Theory Reader*, Sydney: Allen & Unwin.

Easton, S. C. (1964) *The Rise and Fall of Western Colonialism: A Historical Survey from the Early Nineteenth Century to the Present*, New York: Praeger.

Ebner, N. (2023) 'A Borderland Analytic: Thinking Uneven Development from the US-Mexico Borderlands', *Environment and Planning A: Economy and Space* 55(4). https://doi.org/10.1177/0308518X231172201

Echeverría, I. (1998) 'Los rastros de un mestizaje', *Cuadernos Hispanoamericanos* 579: 7–15.

Eddy, J. and Schreuder, D. (1988) (eds) *The Rise of Colonial Nationalism: Australia, New Zealand, Canada and South Africa First Assert Their Nationalities 1880–1914*, Sydney: Allen & Unwin.

Elder, G., Wolch, J. and Emel, J. (1998) 'Race, Place and the Bounds of Humanity', *Society and Animals* 6(2): 183–202.

Ellis, D. (2019) 'Apartheid', *Israel Studies* 24(2): 63–72.

Emberley, J. (1993) *Thresholds of Difference: Feminist Critique, Native Women's Writings, Postcolonial Theory*, Toronto: University of Toronto Press.

Esty, J. (2004) *A Shrinking Island: Modernism and National Culture in England*, Princeton, NJ: Princeton University Press.

Etherington, N. (2005) *Missions and Imperialism, Companion Volume, Oxford History of the British Empire*, Oxford: Oxford University Press.

Evans, J. (2003) (ed.) *Equal Subjects, Unequal Rights: Indigenous Peoples in British Settler Colonies, 1830–1910*, Manchester: Manchester University Press.

Eysteinsson, A. (1990) *The Concept of Modernism*, Ithaca: Cornell University Press.

Ezeigbo, T. A. (2008) *Trafficked*, Lagos: Lantern Books.

Ezzaher, L. E. (2003) *Writing and Cultural Influence: Studies in Rhetorical History, Orientalist Discourse, and Postcolonial Criticism*, New York: Peter Lang.

Faist, T. (2010) *Diaspora and Transnationalism: Concepts, Theories and Methods*, Amsterdam: Amsterdam University Press.

Fanon, F. (1952) *Black Skin: White Masks*, translated by Charles Lam Markmann, London: MacGibbon and Kee (1968).

Fanon, F. (1959) *Studies in a Dying Colonialism*, translated by Haakon Chevalier, New York: Grove (1965, reissued 1970).

Fanon, F. (1961) *The Wretched of the Earth*, translated by Constance Farrington, New York: Grove. Cited in Ashcroft et al. (1995).

Fanon, F. (1964) *Towards the African Revolution*, translated by Haakon Chevalier, Harmondsworth: Penguin (1967).

Fardon, R. (1990) (ed.) *Localizing Strategies: Regional Traditions of Ethnographic Writing*, Edinburgh: Scottish Academic Press.

Faris, W. B. (2004) *Ordinary Enchantments: Magical Realism and the Remystification of Narrative*, Nashville: Vanderbilt University Press.

Farmer, P. (2003) *Pathologies of Power: Health, Human Rights, and the New War on the Poor*, Berkeley: University of California Press.

Fazzini, M. (2004) *Resisting Alterities: Wilson Harris and Other Avatars of Otherness*, Amsterdam, Netherlands: Rodopi.

Featherstone, M. (1990) (ed.) *Global Culture: Nationalism, Globalization and Modernity*, London: Sage.

Featherstone, M., Lash, S. and Robertson, R. (1995) (eds) *Global Modernities*, London: Sage.

Fee, M. (1989) 'Why C. K. Stead Didn't Like Keri Hulme's the Bone People: Who Can Write as Other?', *Australian and New Zealand Studies in Canada* 1.

Fehér, F. (1994) *Biopolitics,* Aldershot: Avebury.

Fenton, S. (2017) *Ethnicity*, 2nd edition, Cambridge and Malden, MA: Polity Press.

Fenwick, M. (2000) 'A Vision of Unity: Braithwaite, Ngugi, Rushdie and the Quest for Authenticity', in R. Smith (ed.) *Postcolonizing the Commonwealth: Studies in Literature and Culture*, Waterloo, ON: Wilfrid Laurier University Press.

Ferguson, J. (2005) 'Decomposing Modernity: History and Hierarchy after Development', in A. Loomba, S. Kaul, M. Bunzl, A. Burton and J. Esty (eds) *Postcolonial Studies and Beyond*, Durham, NC: Duke University Press: 166–181.

Ferguson, M. (1993a) 'The Myth about Globalization', *European Journal of Communication* 7: 69–93.

Ferguson, M. (1993b) *Colonialism and Gender Relations from Mary Wollstonecraft to Jamaica Kincaid: East Caribbean Connections*, New York: Columbia University Press.

Ferguson, R. et al. (1990) (eds) *Out There: Marginalization and Contemporary Cultures*, foreword by M. Tucker, images selected by F. Gonzalez-Torres, New York: New Museum of Contemporary Art, Cambridge, MA: MIT Press.

Fernandes, F. (1970) [1965] *The Negro in Brazilian Society*, New York and London: Columbia University Press.

Ferro, M. (1997) *Colonization: A Global History*, London and New York: Routledge.

Fieldhouse, D. K. (1981) *Colonialism 1870–1945: An Introduction*, London: Weidenfeld & Nicolson.

Fine, R. (2007) *Cosmopolitanism*, London: Routledge.

Fishman, J. A. (1985) *The Rise and Fall of the Ethnic Revival: Perspectives on Language and Ethnicity*, Berlin and New York: Mouton.

Fitz, E. E. (2002) 'From Blood to Culture: Miscegenation as Metaphor for the Americas', in M. Kaup and D. J. Rosenthal (eds) *Mixing Race, Mixing Culture: Inter-American Literary Dialogues*, Austin: University of Texas Press: 243–272.

Fitz, K. (2001) *Negotiating History and Culture: Transculturation in Contemporary Native American Fiction*, Frankfurt, Germany: Peter Lang.

Flint, H. (2006) 'Toni Morrison's Paradise: Black Cultural Citizenship in the American Empire', *American Literature, Duke University Press* 78: 585–612.

Fokkema, D. W. (1984) *Literary History, Modernism, and Postmodernism*, Amsterdam and Philadelphia: John Benjamins.

Forsdick, C. (2001) 'Travelling Concepts: Postcolonial Approaches to Exoticism', *Paragraph: A Journal of Modern Critical Theory* 24(3): 12–29.

Foster, G. A. (1999) *Captive Bodies: Postcolonial Subjectivity in Cinema*, Albany: State University of New York Press.

Foster, J. B., Holleman, H. and Clark, B. (2019) 'Imperialism in the Anthropocen', *Monthly Review, New York* 71(3): 70–88.

Foucault, M. (1971) 'Orders of Discourse: Inaugural Lecture Delivered at the Collège de France', *Social Science Information* 10(2): 7–30.

Foucault, M. (1977) *Discipline and Punish: The Birth of the Prison*, translated by Alan Sheridan, New York: Vintage.

Foucault, M. (1978) *The History of Sexuality, vol. 1: The Will to Knowledge*, London: Penguin.

Foucault, M. (1979) 'What Is an Author?', translated by J. Harari, in David Lodge (ed.) *Modern Criticism and Theory: A Reader*, London and New York: Longman.

Foucault, M. (1980) *Power/Knowledge: Selected Interviews and Other Writings 1972–1977*, New York: Pantheon.

Foucault, M. (1990) *The History of Sexuality*, translated by R. Hurley, New York: Vintage.

Foucault, M. (2002) *Society Must be Defended: Lectures at the College de France, 1975–76*, New York: Picador.

Fox, R. G. (1990) (ed.) *Nationalist Ideologies and the Production of National Cultures*, Washington, DC: American Anthropological Association.

Frame, M. L. (2023) *Ecological Imperialism, Development, and the Capitalist World-System: Cases from Africa And Asia*, London and New York: Routledge.

Franco, J. (1975) 'Dependency Theory and Literary History: The Case of Latin America', *Minnesota Review* 5: 65–80.

Franco, J. (1997) 'The Nation as Imagined Community', in A. McClintock, A. Mufti and E. Shohat (eds) *Dangerous Liaisons: Gender, Nation, and Postcolonial Perspectives*, Minneapolis: University of Minnesota Press.

Frank, A. G. (1979) *Capitalism and Underdevelopment in Latin America*, Harmondsworth: Penguin.

Frankenberg, R. and Mani, L. (2001) 'Crosscurrents, Crosstalk: Race, "Post-Coloniality" and the Politics of Location', in K.-K. Bhavnani (ed.) *Feminism and Race*, Oxford: Oxford University Press: 479–491.

Fraser Taylor, D. R. (2021) 'Mapping with Indigenous Peoples in Canada', in J. B. Hess (ed.) *Digital Mapping and Indigenous America*, New York and Abingdon, Oxon: Routledge: 93–108.

Freeman, E. A. (1898) *The Growth of the English Constitution from the Earliest Times to the Present*, London: Macmillan.

French, J. L. (2005) *Nature, Neo-Colonialism, and the Spanish American Regional Writers*, Re-Encounters with Colonialism series, Hanover, NH: Dartmouth College Press/University Press of New England.

Freyre, G. (1946) [1933] *The Masters and the Slaves*, New York, NY: Knopf.

Freyre, G. (1963) [1936] *The Mansions and the Shanties*, London: Weidenfeld and Nicolson.

Freyre, G. (1970) [1959] *Order and Progress*, Westport, CT: Greenwood Press.

Friedman, S. S. (2006) 'Periodizing Modernism: Postcolonial Modernities and the Space/Time Borders of Modernist Studies', *Modernism/Modernity* 13(3): 425–443.

Friel, B. (1981) *Translations*, London and Boston: Faber & Faber (First performed in September 1980).

Frost, C. (2006) 'Internet Galaxy Meets Postnational Constellation: Prospects for Political Solidarity after the Internet', *Information Society* 22: 45–49.

Fuchs, J. (2000) 'Postcolonial Mock-Epic: Abrogation and Appropriation', *Studies in the Literary Imagination* 33(2): 23–43.

Fuss, D. (1994) 'Interior Colonies: Frantz Fanon and the Politics of Identification', *Diacritics* 24(2–3) (Summer/Fall): 20–42.

Gaard, G. (2010) *Ecofeminism*, Philadelphia: Temple University Press.

Gaard, G. (2017) *Critical Ecofeminism*, Lanham: Lexington Books.

Gaastra, F. S. and Daniels, P. (2003) *The Dutch East India Company: Expansion and Decline*, Zutphen: Walburg.

Galeano, E. (1997) *Open Veins of Latin America*, New York: Monthly Review Press.

Gallien, C. (2018) 'Forcing Displacement: The Postcolonial Interventions of Refugee Literature and Arts', *Journal of Postcolonial Writing* 54(6): 735–750.

Galtung, J. (1969) 'Violence, Peace and Peace Research', *Journal of Peace Research* 6(3): 167–191.

Gamal, A. (2013) 'The Global and the Postcolonial in Post-Migratory Literature', *Journal of Postcolonial Writing* 49(5): 506–608.

Gammage, B. (2011) *The Biggest Estate on Earth: How Aborigines Made Australia*, Sydney: Allen & Unwin.

Gandhi, L. (1998) *Postcolonial Theory: A Critical Introduction*, New York: Columbia University Press.

Gandhi, L. (2006) *Affective Communities: Anticolonial Thought, Fin-de-Siècle Radicalism, and the Politics of Friendship*, Durham, NC: Duke University Press.

Gane, M. (2008) 'Foucault on Governmentality and Liberalism', *Theory, Culture & Society* 25(7–8): 353–363.

Ganguly, K. (2002) 'Adorno, Authenticity, Critique', in C. Bartolovich and N. Lazarus (eds) *Marxism, Modernity, and Postcolonial Studies*, Cambridge: Cambridge University Press.

García, O. (2006) 'Lost in Transculturation: The Case of Bilingual Education in New York City', in M. Pütz, J. A. Fishman, J. Neff-van Aertselaer and C. Baker (eds) *'Along the Routes to Power': Explorations of Empowerment through Language*, Berlin, Germany: Mouton de Gruyter: 157–177.

Gardiner, M. (2001) 'Postcolonial Theory, Modernity and Scottish Cultural Identity', in A. Blake and J. Nyman (eds) *Text and Nation: Essays on Post-Colonial Cultural Politics*, Joensuu, Finland: Faculty of Humanities, University of Joensuu: 73–86.

Garrard, G. (2023) *Ecocriticism*, New York: Routledge.

Gates, H. L., Jr (1986) *'Race', Writing and Difference*, Chicago and London: University of Chicago Press.

Gates, H. L., Jr (1991) 'Critical Fanonism', *Critical Inquiry* 17(Spring): 457–470.

Gaupp, L. and Pelillo-Hestermeyer, G. (2021) (eds) *Diversity and Otherness: Transcultural Insights into Norms, Practices, Negotiations,* Berlin and Boston: De Gruyter.

Gelderblom, O., de Jong, A. and Jonker, J. (2013) 'The Formative Years of the Modern Corporation: The Dutch East India Company, VOC, 1602–1623', *The Journal of Economic History* 73(4): 1050–1076.

Gellner, E. (2006) *Nations and Nationalism*, Oxford: Blackwell.

George, O. (2003) *Relocating Agency: Modernity and African Letters*, Albany: State University of New York Press.

Gérard, A. (1990) 'Literature, Language, Nation and the Commonwealth', in G. V. Davis and H. Maes-Jelinek (eds) *Crisis and Creativity in the New Literatures in English: Cross/Cultures*, Amsterdam, Netherlands: Rodopi: 93–101.

Gerring, J. et al. (2011) 'An Institutional Theory of Direct and Indirect Rule', *World Politics* 63(3): 377–433.

Gerritsen, R. (2008) *Australia and the Origins of Agriculture*, Oxford: Archeopress.

Ghosh, A. (2004) *The Hungry Tide*, New York: Penguin.

Ghosh, B. N. (2000) *Dependency Theory Revisited*, Aldershot: Ashgate.

Gibson, R. (1992) *South of the West: Postcolonialism and the Narrative Construction of Australia*, Bloomington: Indiana University Press.

Giddens, A. (1990) *The Consequences of Modernity*, Cambridge: Polity Press.

Gikandi, S. (1992) 'The Politics and Poetics of National Formation: Recent African Writing', in A. Rutherford (ed.) *From Commonwealth to Post- Colonial*, Aarhus and Sydney: Dangaroo Press.

Gikandi, S. (2000) 'Reading the Referent: Postcolonialism and the Writing of Modernity', in S. Nasta (ed.) *Reading the "New" Literatures in a Postcolonial Era*, Cambridge: Brewer: 87–104.

Gikandi, S. (2001) 'Globalization and the Claims of Postcoloniality', *South Atlantic Quarterly* 100(3): 627–658.

Gikandi, S. (2004) 'Poststructuralism and Postcolonial Discourse', in N. Lazarus (ed.) *The Cambridge Companion to Postcolonial Literary Studies*, Cambridge: Cambridge University Press: 97–119.

Gikandi, S. (2006) 'Postcolonial Theory and the Specter of Nationalism', *CLIO: A Journal of Literature, History, and the Philosophy of History* 36(1): 69–84.

Gilbert, H. (1993) 'Postcolonial Grotesques: Re-Membering the Body in Louis Nowra's Visions and The Golden Age', *SPAN: Journal of the South Pacific Association for Commonwealth Literature and Language Studies* 36: 618–633.

Gilbert, H. (2020) 'Indigenous Festivals in the Pacific: Cultural Renewal, Decolonisation and Nation-Building', *Pacific and American Studies Journal* 20: 41–56.

Gillet, F. and Cornet, A. (2010) *Congo-Belgique 1955–65: Entre Propagande et Réalité*, Brussels: Renaissance du livre.

Gilman, C. (1985) *Pidgin Languages: Form Selection or Simplification?* Bloomington: Indiana University Linguistics Club.

Gilman, S. L. (1985) 'Black Bodies, White Bodies: Toward an Iconography of Female Sexuality in Nineteenth-Century Art, Medicine, and Literature', in H. L. Gates (ed.) *'Race', Writing, and Difference*, Chicago and London: University of Chicago Press.

Gilroy, P. (1987) *There Ain't No Black in the Union Jack: The Cultural Politics of Race and Nation*, London: Hutchinson.

Gilroy, P. (1993) *The Black Atlantic, Modernity and Modern Consciousness*, New York: Verso.

Gilroy, P. (1996) '"The Whisper Wakes, the Shudder Plays": "Race," Nation and Ethnic Absolutism', in P. Mongia (ed.) *Contemporary Postcolonial Theory: A Reader*, London: Arnold: 248–274.

Gilroy, P. (2002) 'The End of Antiracism', in P. Essed and D. T. Goldberg (eds) *Race Critical Theories: Text and Context*, Malden, MA and Oxford: Blackwell: 249–264.

Gilroy, P. (2004) *After Empire: Melancholia or Convivial Culture?*, Abingdon, Oxon: Routledge.

Glissant, E. (1989) *Caribbean Discourse: Selected Essays*, translated by J. Michael Dash, Charlottesville: University Press of Virginia (French version, Paris: Editions Seuill 1981).

Gobineau, J. A., comte de (1853–1855) *Essai sur l'inégalité des Races humaines* (4 vols.), Paris: Firmin Didot.

Gobineau, J. A., comte de (1856) *The Moral and Intellectual Diversity of Races (Essai sur l'inégalité des Races Humaines)*, New York: Garland 1984 (originally published Philadelphia: Lippincott 1856).

Goffinan, E. (1961) *Asylums: Essays on the Social Situation of Mental Patients and Other Inmates*, Harmondsworth: Penguin.

Gòkè-Paríolá, A. (1996) 'African American Vernacular English in Colonial and Postcolonial Perspectives: The Linguistic Paradox', *Journal of Commonwealth and Postcolonial Studies* 4(1): 14–23.

Gokulsing, K. M. and Dissanayake, W. (2004) *Indian Popular Cinema: A Narrative of Cultural Change*, Trentham Books: Stoke on Trent 17.

Goldberg, D. T. and Quayson, A. (2002) *Relocating Postcolonialism*, Malden, MA: Blackwell Publishers.

Gollin, M. (2008) *The Thief at the End of the World: Rubber, Power and the Seeds of Empire*, New York: Viking.

Goodman, J. and James, P. (2007) *Nationalism and Global Solidarities: Alternative Projections to Neoliberal Globalization*, London: Routledge.

Goodwin, K. (1992) 'Studying Commonwealth Literature', *College Literature* 19–20(3–1 [Double issue]): 142–151.

Gooptu, S. (July 2002) 'Reviewed Work(s): *The Cinemas of India* (1896–2000) by Yves Thoraval', *Economic and Political Weekly* 37(29): 3023–3024.

Gopal, P. (2004) 'Reading Subaltern Histor', in N. Lazarus (ed.) *The Cambridge Companion to Postcolonial Literary Studies*, Cambridge: Cambridge University Press.

Gossai, H. and Murrell, N. S. (2000) *Religion, Culture, and Tradition in the Caribbean*, New York: St. Martin's.

Goswami, M. (2005) 'Autonomy and Comparability: Notes on the Anticolonial and the Postcolonial', *Boundary 2: An International Journal of Literature and Culture* 32(2): 201–225.

Gowda, H. H. A. (1983) *The Colonial and the Neo-Colonial Encounters in Commonwealth Literature*, Mysore: Prasaragana University.

Gramsci, A. (1971) *Selections from the Prison Notebooks*, edited and translated by Q. Hoare and G. Nowell Smith, London: Lawrence & Wishart.

Gramsci, A. (1988) *A Gramsci Reader: Selected Writings 1916–1935*, edited by D. Forgacs, London: Lawrence & Wishart.

Gramsci, A. (1991) *Prison Notebooks*, New York: Columbia University Press.

Green, M. J. et al. (1996) (eds) *Postcolonial Subjects: Francophone Women Writers*, Minneapolis: University of Minnesota Press.

Greiner, C. and Sakdapolrak, P. (2013) 'Translocality: Concepts, Applications and Emerging Research Perspectives', *Geography Compass* 7(5): 373–384.

Griffiths, G. (1994) 'The Myth of Authenticity', in C. Tiffin and A. Lawson (eds) *De-scribing Empire: Postcolonialism and Textuality*, London: Routledge.

Griffiths, G. (1997) 'Writing, Literacy and History in Africa', in M.-H. Msiske and P. Hyland (eds) *Writing and Africa*, London: Longman.

Griffiths, G. (2000) *African Literatures in English (East and West)*, London: Longman.

Griffiths, G. (2001) 'Appropriation, Patronage and Control: The Role of the Missionary Text', in G. Stiulz (ed.) *Colonies-Missions-Cultures in the English-Speaking World, General and Comparative Studies*, Stuttgart: Stauffenberg Verlag.

Griffiths, G. (2003) '"Anglophonic" Culture in the New Milllennium: Inteer-Cultural Words and Images in the Cyberage in the Asian Region', in R. Ahrens et al. (eds) *Anglophone Cultures in Southeast Asia*, Heidelberg: Universitätsverlag Winter.

Griffiths, G. (2005) '"Trained to Tell the Truth": Missionaries, Converts and Narration', in N. Etherington (ed.) *Missions and Imperialism, Companion Volume, Oxford History of the British Empire*, Oxford: Oxford University Press.

Griffiths, G. (2007) 'Sites of Purchase: Slavery, Missions and Tourism on Two Tanzanian Sites', in L. Dale and H. Gilbert (eds) *Economies of Representation, 1790–2000: Colonialism and Commerce*, Burlington, VT: Ashgate.

Griffiths, G. (2009) 'Open Spaces, Contested Places: Writing and the Fundamentalist Inscription of Territory', A. Stähler and K. Stierstorfer (eds) *Writing Fundamentalism*, Newcastle upon Tyne: Cambridge Scholars.

Griffiths, G. (2011) '"Saving Africa": Narrative Persistence, Missions, Development and the 'Freeing' of Sub-Saharan Africa', in A. O. Shaul Bassa (ed.) *Experiences of Freedom in Postcolonial Literatures and Cultures,* New York: Routledge.

Griffiths, G. (2012a) 'Narrative, Identity and Social Practice in Tanzania: Abdulrazak Gurnah's Ironic Paradise', in G. Collier et al. (eds) *Engaging with Literature of Commitment* (Vol 1 Africa in the World), Cross Cultures Series 148, Amsterdam, Netherlands and New York: Rodopi.

Griffiths, G. (2012b) 'Postcolonialism and Travel Writing', in *The Cambridge History of Postcolonial Literature*, Vol 1, Cambridge: Cambridge University Press.

Griffiths, G. (2013) 'Resistance or Collusion? Christian Mission, Individualisation and Modernity from the Post-Colonial Perspective', in K. Koschorke and J. Meier (eds) *Individualisierung durch christliche Mission?* "Studien zur außereuropäischen Christentumsgeschichte", Wiesbaden: Verlag Harrassowitz.

Griffiths, G. (2013) 'Conversion, Identity and Resistance in Colonial and Postcolonial Spaces: The Writing of Tiyo Soga 1829-1871', in C. Zabus (ed.) *The Future of Postcolonial Studies*, London: Routledge.

Griffiths, G. (2015) 'Resistance or Collusion? Christian Mission, Individualization and Modernity from the Post-Colonial Perspective', in M. Fuchs, A. Linkenbach and W. Reinhardt (eds) *Individualisierung Durch Christliche Mission?* Wiesbaden: Harrassowitz Verlag: 112–122.

Griffiths, G. and Mead, P. (2018) (eds) *The Social Work of Narrative: Human Rights and the Cultural Imaginary*, Stuttgart: Ibidem Verlag.

Griffiths, G. and Scott, J. S. (2005) (eds) *Mixed Messages: Materiality, Textuality, Missions*, New York: Palgrave.

Griffiths, G. and Singler, J. V. (2004) (eds) *Guanya Pau: The Story of an African Princess (1891)*, Peterborough, ON: Broadview Editions, Broadview Press.

Griffiths, G. and Trigger, D. (2003) (eds) *Disputed Territories: Land, Culture and Identity in Settler Societies*, Hong Kong: Hong Kong University Press.

Griffiths, M. R. (2016) *Biopolitics and Memory in Postcolonial Literature and Culture*, London: Ashgate.

Griffiths, T. and Robin, L. (2011) *Ecology and Empire: Environmental History of Settler Societies*, Edinburgh: Keele University Press.

Grosfoguel, R. (2007) 'The Epistemic Decolonial Turn', *Cultural Studies* 21 (2–3): 211–223.

Grove, R. (1994) *Green Imperialism*, Cambridge: Cambridge University Press.

Gruesser, J. C. (2005) *Confluences: Postcolonialism, African American Literary Studies and the Black Atlantic*, Athens, GA: University of Georgia Press.

Gualtieri, C. (1996) 'The Colonial Exotic Deconstructed: A Suggested Reading Paradigm for Postcolonial Texts', in W. Zach and K. L. Goodwin (eds) *Nationalism vs. Internationalism: (Inter)National Dimensions of Literatures in English*, Tübingen, Germany: Stauffenburg: 47–53.

Guardian (2012) "India blackouts leave 700 million without power," 31st July.

Gugelberger, G. (1996) *The Real Thing*, Durham and London: Duke University Press.

Gugelberger, G. and Kearney, M. (1991) 'Voices for the Voiceless: Testimonial Literature in Latin America', *Latin American Perspectives* 18(3): 3–14.

Guha, R. (1997) (ed.) *A Subaltern Studies Reader, 1986–1995*, Minneapolis: University of Minnesota Press.

Guha, R. (2001) 'Subaltern Studies: Projects for Our Time and Their Convergence', in I. Rodríguez (ed.) *The Latin American Subaltern Studies Reader*, Durham, NC: Duke University Press.

Guha, R. and Martinez-Alier, J. (1997) *Varieties of Environmentalism*, London and Sterlin, VA: Earthscan.

Guha, R. and Spivak, G. C. (1988) (eds) *Selected Subaltern Studies*, New York: Oxford University Press.

Gunew, S. (1994) *Framing Marginality: Multicultural Literary Studies*, Carlton, VIC: Melbourne University Press.

Gunew, S. (1997) 'Postcolonialism and Multiculturalism: Between Race and Ethnicity', *Yearbook of English Studies* 27: 22–39.

Gunew, S. (2004) *Haunted Nations: The Colonial Dimensions of Multiculturalisms*, London: Routledge.

Gunew, S. (2009) 'Subaltern Empathy: Beyond European Categories in Affect Theory', *Concentri: Literary and Cultural Studies* 35(1): 11–30.

Gunner, E. (1994) *Politics and Performance*, Johannesburg: Wits University Press.

Gunner, E. (2004) 'Chapter 1: Africa and Orality', in A. Irele and S. Gikandi (eds) *The Cambridge History of African and Caribbean Literature Vol 1*, Cambridge: Cambridge University Press: 1–18.

Gunner, E. and Furniss, G. (1995) *Power, Marginality and African Oral Literature*, Cambridge and New York: Cambridge University Press.

Gunner, E. and Gwala, M. (1991) (trans. and eds) *Musho! Zulu Popular Praises*, East Lansing: Michigan State University Press.

Gurnah, A. (2000) 'Imagining the Postcolonial Writer', in S. Nasta (ed.) *Reading the 'New' Literatures in a Postcolonial Era*, Cambridge: Brewer: 73–86.

Gurr, A. (1981) *Writers in Exile: The Identity of Home in Modern Literature*, Brighton: Harvester.

Habermas, J. (1981) 'Modernity versus Postmodernity', *New German Critique* 22: 3–14.

Habermas, J. (1987) *The Philosophical Discourse of Modernity*, Cambridge: Polity.

Habib, S. (2021) 'Our Hyphenated Identities: My Story', Amherst: Commonwealth Honors College. https://www.umass.edu/honors/news/our-hyphenated-identities-my-story

Hackett, J., Corbett, J., Olsen, R. and DeRoy, S. (2020) 'Indigenous Mapping', in A. Kobayashi (ed.) *International Encyclopedia of Human Geography*, 2nd edition, Amsterdam: Elsevier: 217–221. https://search.credoreference.com/articles/Qm9va0FydGljbGU6NTg4MTU=?aid=257394

Haddour, A. (2005) 'Sartre and Fanon: On Negritude and Political Participation', *Sartre Studies International: An Interdisciplinary Journal of Existentialism and Contemporary Culture* 11(1–2): 286–301.

Hadiz, V. R. (2006) *Empire and Neoliberalism in Asia*, London: Routledge.

Hadjor, K. B. (1992) *Dictionary of Third World Terms*, Harmondsworth: Penguin.

Hage, G. (1988) *White Nation: Fantasies of White Supremacy in a Multicultural Society*, Annandale, NSW: Pluto Press.

Hage, G. (2000) *White Nation; Fantasies of White Supremacy in a Multicultural Society*, New York: Routledge.

Hage, G. (2003) *Against Paranoid Nationalism: Searching for Hope in a Shrinking Society*, Annandale, NSW: Pluto Press.

Hall, R. A., Jr (1988) *Pidgin and Creole Languages*, London and New York: Longman Linguistics Library.

Hall, C. M. and Tucker, H. (2004) *Tourism and Postcolonialism: Contested Discourses, Identities and Representations*, London: Routledge.

Hall, S. (1989) '*New Ethnicities*' in *Black Film, British Cinema, ICA Documents* 7, London: Institute of Contemporary Arts.

Hall, S. (1991) 'The Local and the Global: Globalisation and Ethnicity', in A. King (ed.) *Culture Globalization and the World System*, London: Macmillan.

Hall, S. (1996) 'Cultural Identity and Diaspora', in P. Mongia (ed.) *Contemporary Postcolonial Theory: A Reader*, London: Arnold: 110–121.

Hammersley, M. and Atkinson, P. (1983) *Ethnography: Principles in Practice*, London and New York: Tavistock.

Hanchard, M. (1997) 'Identity, Meaning, and the African-American', in A. McClintock, A. Mufti and E. Shohat (eds) *Dangerous Liaisons: Gender, Nation, and Postcolonial Perspectives*, Minneapolis: University of Minnesota Press.

Handlarski, D. (2010) 'Pro-Creation-Haraway's "Regeneration" and the Postcolonial Cyborg Body', *Women's Studies* 39(2): 73–99.

Hannerz, U. (1996) *Transnational Connections: Culture, People, Places,* New York: Routledge.

Hansen, R. (2009) 'The Poverty of Postnationalism: Citizenship, Immigration, and The New Europe', *Theory and Society* 38(1): 1–24.

Hanson, E. O. (2006) *Religion and Politics in the International System Today,* Cambridge: Cambridge University Press.

Haraway, D. (2015) 'Anthropocene, Capitalocene, Plantationocene, Chthulucene: Making Kin', *Environmental Humanities* 6(1): 159–165.

Harding, S. (2011) *The Postcolonial Science and Technology Reader,* Durham and London: Duke University Press.

Harding, S. G. and Narayan, U. (2000) (eds) *Decentering the Center: Philosophy for a Multicultural, Postcolonial, and Feminist World,* Bloomington: Indiana University Press.

Hardt, M. and Negri, A. (2001) *Empire,* Cambridge, MA and London: Harvard University Press.

Hardt, M. and Negri, A. (2004) *Multitude: War and Democracy in the Age of Empire,* New York: Penguin Press.

Harlow, B. (1987) *Resistance Literature,* New York: Methuen.

Harlow, B. and Carter, M. (1999) (eds) *Imperialism and Orientalism: A Documentary Sourcebook,* Malden, MA: Blackwell Publishers.

Harris, M. (1992) *Outsiders & Insiders: Perspectives of Third World Culture in British and Postcolonial Fiction,* New York: Peter Lang.

Harris, W. (1970) *Ascent to Omai,* London: Faber.

Harris, W. (1981) *Explorations: A Selection of Talks and Articles 1966–1981,* edited by Hena Maes-Jelinek, Aarhus, Denmark: Dangaroo.

Harris, W. (1983) *The Womb of Space: The Cross-Cultural Imagination,* Westport, CT: Greenwood.

Harris, W. (2004) 'Resistances to Alterities', in M. Fazzini (ed.) *Resisting Alterities: Wilson Harris and Other Avatars of Otherness,* Amsterdam, Netherlands: Rodopi.

Harrison, C., Frascina, F. and Perry, G. (1993) *Primitivism, Cubism, Abstraction: The Early Twentieth Century,* New Haven, CT: Yale University Press, in association with the Open University.

Harrison, N. (2003) *Postcolonial Criticism: History, Theory and the Work of Fiction,* Cambridge: Polity Press, in association with Blackwell Publishers.

Harry, D. (2001) 'Biopiracy and Globalisation: Indigenous Peoples Face a New Wave of Colonialism', *Splice* 7(2 & 3) (January–April 2001). https://www.Geneticsforum.org.uk

Hart, J. (1997) 'Translating and Resisting Empire: Cultural Appropriation and Postcolonial Studies', in B. Ziff and P. V. Rao (eds) *Borrowed Power: Essays on Cultural Appropriation,* New Brunswick, NJ: Rutgers University Press.

Hart, J. (2003) *Comparing Empires: European Colonialism from Portuguese Expansion to the Spanish-American War,* New York: Palgrave Macmillan.

Harvey, D. (2005) *A Brief History of Neoliberalism,* Oxford and New York: Oxford University Press.

Hasseler, T. A. (1997) 'Articulating Feminist Causes and Democratic Futures in Western and Third World Feminism', *ARIEL: A Review of International English Literature* 28(4): 154–168.

Havinden, M. and Meredith, D. (1993) *Colonialism and Development: Britain and Its Tropical Colonies, 1850–1960,* London: Routledge.

Hawes, C. (2003) 'Periodizing Johnson: Anticolonial Modernity as Crux and Critique', in A. Burton (ed.) *After the Imperial Turn: Thinking with and Through the Nation,* Durham, NC: Duke University Press.

Hawley, J. C. (1996) *Writing the Nation: Self and Country in the Postcolonial Imagination,* Amsterdam, Netherlands: Rodopi.

Hawley, J. C. (2001) *Encyclopedia of Postcolonial Studies,* Westport, CT: Greenwood.

Hayes Edwards, B. (2003) *The Practice of Diaspora: Literature, Translation, and the Rise of Black Internationalism,* Cambridge, MA: Harvard University Press.

Head, D. (1999) 'The (im)possibility of Ecocriticism', in R. Kerridge and N. Sammells (eds) *Writing the Environment: Ecocriticism and Literature,* London: Zed Books.

Head, D. (2006) *The Cambridge Guide to Literature in English,* Cambridge: Cambridge University Press.

Healy, C. (1997) *From the Ruins of Colonialism: History as Social Memory,* Cambridge: Cambridge University Press.

Healy, J. J. (1979) *Literature and the Aborigine in Australia,* 2nd edition, St Lucia: University of Queensland Press (1989).

Hennessy, R. with Martha Ojeda (2007) *NAFTA from Below: Maquiladora Workers, Campesinos, and Indigenous Communities Speak Back,* San Antonio, TX: The Coalition for Justice in the Maquiladoras.

Herk, A. V. (1996) 'Pioneers and Settlers', in B. King (ed.) *New National and Postcolonial Literatures: An Introduction,* Oxford: Clarendon.

Hewa, S. (1995) *Colonialism, Tropical Disease and Medicine: Rockefeller Philanthropy in Sri Lanka,* Lanham, MD: University Press of America.

Hiatt, A. (2005) 'Mapping the Ends of Empire', in A. J. Kabir and D. Williams (eds) *Postcolonial Approaches to the European Middle Ages: Translating Cultures,* Cambridge: Cambridge University Press.

Higman, B. W. (1984) *Slave Populations in the British Caribbean 1807–1834,* London and Baltimore: Johns Hopkins University Press.

Hildebrant, M. (1992) 'Mestizaje lingüístico en un vocabulario del siglo XVII', *Boletín de la Academia Argentina de Letras* 57(223–224): 9–30.

Hill, M. (1997) *Whiteness: A Critical Reader,* New York: New York University Press.

Hill, M. (2004a) *After Whiteness: Unmaking an American Majority,* New York: New York University Press.

Hill, M. (2004b) 'Interview with Damien W. Riggs', *Borderlands-ejournal* 3.

Hiller, S. (1991) (ed.) *The Myth of Primitivism: Perspectives on Art,* London and New York: Routledge.

Hobsbawm, E. J. (1968) *Industry and Empire: An Economic History of Britain Since 1750*, London: Weidenfeld & Nicolson.

Hobsbawm, E. J. (1990) *Nations and Nationalism Since 1780*, Cambridge: Canto (Cambridge University Press).

Hobson, J. A. (1902) *Imperialism*, Ann Arbor: University of Michigan Press.

Hochschild, A. (1988) *King Leopold's Ghost: A Story of Greed, Terror and Heroism in Colonial Africa*, London: Houghton Mifflin.

Hodge, B. and Mishra, V. (1990) *The Dark Side of the Dream: Australian Literature and the Postcolonial Mind*, Sydney: Allen & Unwin.

Hodges, H. (2000) 'The Far Eye: Rastafarian Historicism in West Indian Literature', *Process: A Journal of African American and African Diasporan Literature and Culture* 2: 114–136.

Hoeller, C. (2002) 'Africa in Motion' (interview with Achille Mbembe) Springerin, No. 3.

Hofmeyr, I. (1993) *We Spend Our Years as a Tale That Is Told: Oral Historical Narrative in a South African Chiefdom*, Johannesburg: Witwatersrand University Press; New Haven: Heinemann.

Hofmeyr, I. (2004) *The Portable Bunyan: A Transnational History of 'The Pilgrims Progress'*, Princeton, NJ: Princeton University Press.

Hofstadter, R. (1955) *Social Darwinism in American Thought*, Philadelphia: University Pennsylvania Press.

Hogan, P. C. (2000) *Colonialism and Cultural Identity: Crises of Tradition in the Anglophone Literatures of India, Africa, and the Caribbean*, New York: State University of New York Press.

Holm, J. A. (1988) *Pidgins and Creoles: Theory and Structure, Vol. I, Cambridge Language Surveys*, Cambridge: Cambridge University Press: 1–12.

Holm, J. A. (1989) *Pidgins and Creoles*, Cambridge: Cambridge University Press.

Holquist, M. (1984) *'Introduction' to Mikhail Bakhtin Rabelais and His World*, translated by Hélène Iswolsky, Bloomington: Indiana University Press.

Holst-Petersen, K. and Rutherford, A. (1985) *A Double Colonization: Colonial and Postcolonial Womens' Writing*, Aarhus, Denmark: Dangaroo.

Hoogvelt, A. M. M. (2001) *Globalization and the Postcolonial World: The New Political Economy of Development*, Basingstoke: Palgrave.

Hook, D. (2005) 'A Critical Psychology of the Postcolonial', *Theory and Psychology* 15(4): 475–503.

hooks, b. (1997) 'Sisterhood: Political Solidarity between Women', in A. McClintock, A. Mufti and E. Shohat (eds) *Dangerous Liaisons: Gender, Nation, and Postcolonial Perspectives*, Minneapolis: University of Minnesota Press: 396–411.

Hopkins, T. K. (1982) *World-Systems Analysis: Theory and Methodology*, Beverly Hills, CA: Sage Publications.

Horton, J. O. (2004) *Slavery and the Making of America*, New York: Oxford University Press.

Horton, R. (1971) 'African Conversion', *Africa: Journal of the International African Institute* 41(2): 85–108.

Huggan, G. (1989) 'Decolonizing the Map: Postcolonialism, Post-Structuralism and the Cartographic Connection', *Ariel* 20(4): 115–131.

Huggan, G. (1994) 'A Tale of Two Parrots: Walcott, Rhys, and the Uses of Colonial Mimicry', *Contemporary Literature* 35(4): 643–660.

Huggan, G. (1997) '(Post)Colonialism, Anthropology, and the Magic of Mimesis', *Cultural Critique* 38(0): 91–106.

Huggan, G. (2000) 'Counter-Travel Writing and Postcoloniality', in L. Glage (ed.) *Being/s in Transit: Travelling, Migration, Dislocation*, Amsterdam, Netherlands: Rodopi: 37–59.

Huggan, G. (2001) *The Postcolonial Exotic: Marketing the Margins*, London: Routledge.

Huggan, G. (2004) 'Postcolonialism, Globalization, and the Rise of (Trans) Cultural Studies', in G. V. Davis, P. H. Marsden, B. Ledent and M. Delrez (eds) *Towards a Transcultural Future: Literature and Society in a 'Post'-Colonial World*, Amsterdam, Netherlands: Rodopi.

Huggan, G. (2017) 'Unsettled Settlers: Postcolonialism, Travelling Theory and the New Migrant Aesthetics', In G. Huggan (ed.) *Interdisciplinary Measures: Literature and the Future of Postcolonial Studies*, Liverpool: Liverpool University Press.

Huggan, G. (2020) 'Re-Evaluating the Postcolonial Exotic', *Interventions* 22(7): 808–824.

Huggan, G. and Tiffin, H. (2010) *Postcolonial Ecocriticism: Literature, Animals, Environment*, London: Routledge.

Hulme, P. (1986) *Colonial Encounters: Europe and the Native Caribbean 1492–1797*, London: Methuen (reissued Routledge 1992).

Hulme, P. (1989) 'Subversive Archipelagos: Colonial Discourse and the Break-Up of Continental Theory', *Disposition: American Journal of Cultural Histories and Theories* 14(36–38): 1–23.

Hulme, P. (2000) *Remnants of Conquest: The Island Caribs and Their Visitors 1877–1998*, Oxford: Oxford University Press.

Hulme, P. (2005) 'Beyond the Straits: Postcolonial Allegories of the Globe', in A. Loomba et al. (eds) *Postcolonial Studies and Beyond*, Durham, NC: Duke University Press.

Hunt, D. and Stevenson, S. A. (2017) 'Decolonizing Geographies of Power: Indigenous Digital Counter-Mapping Practices on Turtle Island', *Settler Colonial Studies* 7(3): 372–392.

Huntington, S. (1992) 'The Clash of Civilizations?' *Foreign Affairs* 72(3), Summer 1993: 22–49.

Huntington, S. (1996) *The Clash of Civilizations and the Remaking of World Order*, New York: Simon and Schuster.

Husband, C. (1994) *'Race' and Nation: The British Experience*, Perth, WA: Paradigm.

Hyam, R. (1990) *Empire and Sexuality: The British Experience*, Manchester and New York: Manchester University Press.

iDMC (2003) Development Induced Displacement. www.internal-displacement.org

Ingold, T. (1996) (ed.) *Key Debates in Anthropology*, London and New York: Routledge.

Institute of Commonwealth Studies (1982) *The Diaspora of the British*, London: University of London (Institute of Commonwealth Studies).

Irele, F. A. (2003) 'The Harlem Renaissance and the Negritude Movement', in F. A. Irele and S. Gikandi (eds) *The Cambridge History of African and Caribbean Literature*, Cambridge: Cambridge University Press: 759–784.

Isajaw, W. W. (1974) 'Definitions of Ethnicity', *Ethnicity* 1(2): 111–174.

Isitt, M. H. (2020) *Globalization, Amenia*, New York: Grey House Publishing.

Jack, B. E. (1996) *Negritude and Literary Criticism: The History and Theory of 'Negro-African' Literature in French*, Westport, CT: Greenwood Press.

Jackson, P., Crang, P. and Dwyer, C. (2004) (eds) *Transnational Spaces*, London: Routledge.

Jacobs, J. (2004) 'Writing Reconciliation: South African Fiction after Apartheid', in M. Fazzini (ed.) *Resisting Alterities: Wilson Harris and Other Avatars of Otherness,* Amsterdam, Netherlands: Rodopi.

Jahoda, G. (1999) *Images of Savages: Ancients [sic] Roots of Modern Prejudice in Western Culture*, London: Routledge.

Jameson, F. (1986) 'Third World Literature in the Era of Multinational Capitalism', *Social Text* 15(Fall).

Jameson, F. (1991) 'On Literary and Cultural Import-substitution in the Third World: The Case of the Testimonio' unpublished. Cited in George Gugelberger and Michael Kearney, 'Voices for the Voiceless: Testimonial Literature in Latin America', *Latin American Perspectives* 18(3): 3–14.

Janiewski, D. E. (1998) '"Confusion of Mind": Colonial and Postcolonial Discourses about Frontier Encounters', *Journal of American Studies* 32(1): 81–103.

JanMohammed, A. R. (1983) *Manichean Aesthetics: The Politics of Literature in Colonial Africa*, Amherst: University of Massachusetts Press.

JanMohammed, A. R. (1985) 'The Economy of Manichean Allegory: The Function of Racial Difference in Colonialist Literature', *Critical Inquiry* 12(1). In Ashcroft et al. (1995): 18–23.

Janz, B. (2002) Review of Achille Mbembe's on the Postcolony, H-Africa Net, March. https://www.h-net.org/reviews/showrev.cgi?path=122821016818245.

Jarratt, S. C. (2004) 'Beside Ourselves: Rhetoric and Representation in Postcolonial Feminist Writing', in A. A. Lunsford and L. Ouzgane (eds) *Crossing Borderlands: Composition and Postcolonial Studies*, Pittsburgh, PA: University of Pittsburgh Press: 110–128.

Jaspers, K. (1953) *The Origin and Goal of History*, London: Routledge Kegan and Paul.

Jayaprakash, N. D. (June 5, 2005) 'India and the Bandung Conference of 1955', *People's Democracy - Weekly Organ of the Communist Party of India (Marxist)* XXIX(23).

Johnson, G. A. and Smith, M. B. (1990) (eds) *Ontology and Alterity in Merleau-Ponty,* Evanston, IL: Northwestern.

Johnston, A. (2002) 'Tahiti, "the Desire of Our Eyes": Missionary Travel Narratives and Imperial Surveillance', in H. Gilbert and A. Johnston (eds) *Transit: Travel, Text, Empire,* New York: Peter Lang.

Jones, J. (1965) *Terranglia: The Case for English as World Literature,* New York: Twayne.

Jordan, G. and Weedon, C. (1995) *Cultural Politics: Class, Gender, Race, and the Postmodern World,* Oxford and Cambridge, MA: Blackwell.

Joyce, J. A. (2005) *Black Studies as Human Studies: Critical Essays and Interviews,* Albany: State University of New York Press.

Jules-Rosette, B. (2002) 'Afro-Pessimism's Many Guises', *Public Culture* 14(3).

Jurak, M. (1992) 'The Role of New Literatures in the Framework of English Studies', in M. Jurak (ed.) *Literature, Culture and Ethnicity: Studies on Medieval, Renaissance and Modern Literatures,* Ljubljana: Author: 45–49.

Kachru, B. (1986) *The Alchemy of English: The Spread, Fucntions and Models of Non-Native English,* Oxford: Pergamon.

Kahane, R. (1992) 'American English: From a Colonial Substandard to Prestige Language', in B. Kachru (ed.) *The Other Tongue: English Across Cultures,* Urbana: University of Illinois: 211–219.

Kanafani, G. (1987) *Literature of Resistance in Occupied Palestine: 1948–1966,* Beirut: Institute for Arabic Research (in Arabic).

Kanneh, K. (1995) *The Difficult Politics of Wigs and Veils: Feminism and the Colonial Body* (paper presented at the Conference on Gender and Colonialism, U. C. Galway, May 1992, In Ashcroft et al. (1995)).

Kant, I. (1795) *Perpetual Peace: A Philosophical Sketch.* Online. https://www.mtholyoke.edu/acad/intrel/kant/kant1.htm (accessed 2012).

Kanth, R. K. (2005) *Against Eurocentrism: A Transcendent Critique of Modernist Science, Society, and Morals: A Discursus on Human Emancipation: Purporting to be a Speculative Critique and Resolution of the Malaise of Modernism,* New York: Palgrave Macmillan.

Kara, S. (2009) *Sex Trafficking: The Inside Business of Modern Slavery,* New York: Columbia University Press.

Kasmir, S. (2023) [2018] 'Precarity', in F. Stein (ed.) *The Open Encyclopedia of Anthropology, Facsimile of the first edition in The Cambridge Encyclopedia of Anthropology.* Online: https://doi.org/10.29164/18precarity

Katrak, K. H. (1996) 'Postcolonial Women Writers and Feminisms', in B. King (ed.) *New National and Postcolonial Literatures: An Introduction,* Oxford: Clarendon: 230–244.

Katrak, K. H. (2006) *Politics of the Female Body: Postcolonial Women Writers of the Third World,* New Brunswick, NJ: Rutgers University Press.

Kaul, S. (1996) 'Colonial Figures and Postcolonial Reading', *Diacritics: A Review of Contemporary Criticism* 26(1): 74–89.

Kaur, R. and Sinha, A. (2005) *Bollyworld: Popular Indian Cinema through aTransnational Lens,* London and New Delhi: Sage.

Keay, J. (1991) *The Honourable Company: A History of the English East India Company,* London: HarperCollins.

Keita, L. (2006) Review 'On the Postcolony (Mbembe)', *Transforming Anthropology* 13(1): 67–68.

Kemedjio, C. (1999) *De la négritude á la créolité: Edouard Glissant, Maryse Condé et la malédiction de la théorie*, Hamburg, Germany: LIT.

Kennedy, E. C. (1975) (ed. and introd.) *The Negritude Poets: An Anthology of Translations from the French*, New York: Viking.

Kent, J. (1992) *The Internationalization of Colonialism: Britain, France, and Black Africa, 1939–1956*, Oxford: Clarendon Press.

Keown, M. (2005) *Postcolonial Pacific Writing: Representations of the Body*, London: Routledge.

Khan, Y. (2007) *The Great Partition: The Making of India and Pakistan*, New Haven, CT and London: Yale University Press.

Khorana, S. (2018) 'Balancing the Quotidian and the Political: Beyond Empathy in Australian Multi-platform Refugee Narratives', in G. Griffiths and P. Mead (eds) *The Social Work of Narrative: Human Rights and the Cultural Imaginary*, Ibidem: Stuttgart: 301–318.

Kilgour, M. (1993) *From Communion to Cannibalism: An Anatomy of Metaphors of Incorporation*, Princeton, NJ: Princeton University Press.

Kincaid, J. (1985) *Annie John*, London: Picador.

Kincaid, J. (1988) *A Small Place*, London: Virago.

King, A. D. (1991) (ed.) *Culture Globalization and the World System*, London: Macmillan.

King, B. (1974) (ed.) *Literatures of the World in English*, London: Routledge.

King, B. (1980) *The New Literatures in English*, London: Macmillan.

King, B. (1983) 'Nationalism, Internationalism, Periodisation and Common-Wealth Literature', in D. Riemenschneider (ed.) *The History and Historiography of Commonwealth Literature*, Tübingen: Narr.

King, B. (1996) (ed.) *New National and Postcolonial Literatures: An Introduction*, Oxford: Clarendon.

King, R. (1999) *Orientalism and Religion: Postcolonial Theory, India and 'The Mystic East'*, London and New York: Routledge.

King, S. and Jensen, R. J. (1995) 'Bob Marley's "Redemption Song": The Rhetoric of Reggae and Rastafari', *Journal of Popular Culture* 29(3): 17–36.

King, S. A. et al. (2003) (eds) *Reggae, Rastafari, and the Rhetoric of Social Control*, Jackson: University Press of Mississippi.

Kipling, R. (1889) *'The Ballad of East and West' in Rudyard Kipling's Verse: The Definitive Edition*, London: Hodder & Stoughton (1940).

Kipling, R. (1897) *'Recessional' in Rudyard Kipling's Verse: The Definitive Edition*, London: Hodder & Stoughton (1940).

Kipling, R. (1899) *'The White Man's Burden: The United States and the Philippine Islands' in Rudyard Kipling's Verse: The Definitive Edition*, London: Hodder & Stoughton (1940).

Klein, M. A. and Miers, S. (1999) (eds) *Slavery and Colonial Rule in Africa*, Portland, OR: Frank Cass.

Klor de Alva, J. J. (1995) 'The Postcolonization of the (Latin) American Experience: A Reconsideration of "Colonialism," "Postcolonialism," and "Mestizaje"', in G. Prakash (ed.) *After Colonialism: Imperial Histories and Postcolonial Displacements*, Princeton, NJ: Princeton University Press: NP.

Koebner, R. (1961) *Empire,* Cambridge: Cambridge University Press.

Koebner, R. and Schmidt, H. D. (1964) *Imperialism: The Story and Significance of a Political Word, 1840–1960*, Cambridge: Cambridge University Press.

Kofman, E. and Youngs, G. (1996) *Globalization: Theory and Practice*, London: Pinter.

Kokotovic, M. (2005) *The Colonial Divide in Peruvian Narrative: Social Conflict and Transculturation*, Brighton: Sussex Academic.

Köngeter, S. (2011) 'Transnationalism', *Social Work & Society* 8(1).

Korte, B. (2001) 'Exploring without a Mission? Postcolonial Travel in a Global World', in G. Stilz (ed.) *Colonies, Missions, Cultures in the English Speaking World: General and Comparative Studies*, Tübingen, Germany: Stauffenburg: 383–395.

Korte, B. and Matthias, C. (2000) *English Travel Writing from Pilgrimages to Postcolonial Explorations*, Basingstoke: Macmillan.

Koshy, S. (2005) 'The Postmodern Subaltern: Globalization Theory and the Subject of Ethnic, Area, and Postcolonial Studies', in F. Lionnet and S.-M. Shih (eds) *Minor Transnationalism*, Durham, NC: Duke University Press.

Koundoura, M. (2002) 'Reoccupying the Space of Culture: Greece and the Postcolonial Critique of Modernity', *Journal x: A Journal in Culture and Criticism* 6(2): 127–140.

Kraniauskas, J. (2004) 'Hybridity in a Transnational Frame: Latin Americanist and Postcolonial Perspectives on Cultural Studies', in A. Del Sarto, A. Ríos and A. Trigo (eds) *The Latin American Cultural Studies Reader*, Durham, NC: Duke University Press.

Krishna, S. (2009) *Globalization and Postcolonialism: Hegemony and Resistance in the Twenty-First Century*, London: Rowman & Littlefield.

Kroestch, R. (1974) 'Unhiding the Hidden: Recent Canadian Fiction', *Journal of Canadian Fiction* 3. Cited in Ashcroft et al. (1995): 394–396.

Kumar, A. (2003) (ed.) *World Bank Literature*, Minneapolis: University of Minnesota.

Kureishi, H. (2005) *The Word and the Bomb*, London: Faber and Faber.

Kwet, M. (2021) Digital Colonialism: The Evolution of US Empire, https://longreads.tni.org/digital-colonialism-the-evolution-of-us-empire

Lacan, J. (1966) *Ecrits*, Paris: Editions du Seuil.

Lacan, J. (1968) *The Language of the Self: The Function of Language in Psychoanalysis*, translated with notes and commentary, by Anthony Wilden, Baltimore, MD: Johns Hopkins University Press.

Lacan, J. (1977) *Ecrits: A Selection*, translated by Alan Sheridan, London: Tavistock.

Lane, J.-E. (2006) *Globalization and Politics: Promises and Dangers*, Aldershot: Ashgate.

Lang, G. (2000) *Entwisted Tongues: Comparative Creole Literatures*, Amsterdam, Netherlands: Rodopi.

Lapping, B. (1987) *Apartheid: A History*, London: Paladin.

Larsen, N. (1997) 'Poverties of Nation: The Ends of the Earth, "Monetary Subjects without Money," and Postcolonial Theory', *Cultural Logic: An Electronic Journal of Marxist Theory and Practice* 1(1).

Larson, C. (1973) 'Heroic Ethnocentrism: The Idea of Universality in Literature', *The American Scholar* 42(3) (Summer): 463–475.

Lawson, A. (1991) 'A Cultural Paradigm for the Second World', *Australian–Canadian Studies* 9(1–2): 67–78.

Lawson, A. (1994) 'Un/settling Colonies: The Ambivalent Place of Discursive Resistance', in C. Worth et al. (eds) *Literature and Opposition*, Clayton, VIC: Centre for Comparative and Cultural Studies, Monash University.

Lawson, A. (1995) 'Postcolonial Theory and the "Settler" Subject', *Essays on Canadian Writing* 56(Fall): 20–36.

Lawson, P. (2013) *The East India Company: A History*, London and New York: Routledge.

Lawson, S. (2006) *Culture and Context in World Politics*, New York: Palgrave Macmillan.

Lazarus, N. (1993) 'Disavowing Decolonization: Fanon, Nationalism, and the Problematic of Representation in Current Theories of Colonial Discourse', *Research in African Literatures* 24(4): 69–98.

Lazarus, N. (1994) 'National Consciousness and the Specificity of (Post) Colonial Intellectualism', in F. Barker, P. Hulme and M. Iversen (eds) *Colonial Discourse/Postcolonial Theory*, Manchester: Manchester University Press: 197–220.

Lazarus, N. (1999) *Nationalism and Cultural Practice in the Postcolonial World*, Cambridge: Cambridge University Press.

Lazarus, N. (2002) 'The Fetish of "the West" in Postcolonial Theory', in C. Bartolovich and N. Lazarus (eds) *Marxism, Modernity, and Postcolonial Studies*, Cambridge: Cambridge University Press: 43–64.

Lazarus, N. (2004) 'Fredric Jameson on "Third-World Literature": A Qualified Defense', in D. Kellner and S. Homer (eds) *Fredric Jameson: A Critical Reader*, Basingstoke: Palgrave Macmillan.

Lazarus, N. (2005) 'The Politics of Postcolonial Modernism', in A. Loomba, S. Kaul, M. Bunzl, A. Burton and J. Esty (eds) *Postcolonial Studies and Beyond*, Durham, NC: Duke University Press: 423–438.

Lazarus, N. (2016) 'Vivek Chibber and the Spectre of Postcolonial Theory', *Race and Class* 57(3): 88–106. https://doi.org/10.1177/0306396815611853

Lazarus, N. et al. (1995) 'The Necessity of Universalism', *Differences: A Journal of Feminist Cultural Studies* 7(1): 75–145.

Lee, D. (1974) 'Cadence, Country, Silence: Writing in Colonial Space', *Boundary 2* 3(1) (Fall). Cited in Ashcroft et al. (1995): 397–401.

Leer, M. (1992) 'Europe, the Orient and the New World: Conceptual Geography and Historical Cosmology 1492–1992', *Kunapipi* 14(2): 22–34.

Lefevere, A. (1983) 'Interface: Some Thoughts on the Historiography of African Literature Written in English', in D. Riemenschneider (ed.) *The History and Historiography of Commonwealth Literature*, Tübingen: Gunter Narr Verlag.

Lemire, E. (2002) '*Miscegenation*': *Making Race in America*, Philadelphia: University of Pennsylvania Press.

Lemke, T. (2001) 'The Birth of Bio-politics': Michel Foucault's Lecture at the Collège de France on Neo-liberal Governmentality', *Economy and Society* 30(2): 190–207.

Lenin, V. I. (1916) 'Imperialism, the Highest Stage of Capitalism', in *Collected Works of V.I.*, Lenin, Moscow: Foreign Language House, 1960–1969.

Lennon, J. (2004) *Irish Orientalism: A Literary and Intellectual History*, Syracuse, NY: Syracuse University Press.

Leonard, P. (2005) *Nationality between Poststructuralism and Postcolonial Theory: A New Cosmopolitanism*, New York: Palgrave Macmillan.

Leonie, A. et al. (2022) *Rethinking Orality: Codification, Transcodification and Transmission of Cultural Messages*, Berlin, Boston: De Gruyter.

Leoussi, A. S. and Grosby, S. (1988) *Nationalism and Ethnosymbolism: History, Culture and Ethnicity in the Formation of Nations*, Edinburgh: Edinburgh University Press.

Levinas, E. (1969) *Totality and Infinity: An Essay on Exteriority*, translated by A. Lingis, Pittsburgh: Duquesne University Press.

Levitt, P. and Waters, M. C. (2002) (eds) *The Changing Face of Home: The Transnational Lives of the Second Generation*, New York: Russell Sage Foundation.

Levy, D. (2022) 'Patriarchy' Blackwell Encyclopaedia of Sociology Online. https://doi.org/10.1002/9781405165518.wbeosp010.pub2

Lewis, R. (1996) *Gendering Orientalism: Race, Femininity, and Representation*, New York: Routledge.

Leys, R. (2011) 'The Turn to Affect: A Critique', *Critical Inquiry* 37(3) (Spring 2011): 434–447.

Liano, D. (2003) 'Sobre el testimonio y la literatura', in P. Collard, R. D. Maeseneer and R. Vázquez Díaz (eds) *Murales, figuras, fronteras: Narrativa e historia en el Caribe y Centroamérica*, Madrid: Iberoamericana.

Lichteim, G. (1971) *Imperialism*, London: Allen Lane.

Liesen, L. T. and Walsh, M. B. (2012) 'The Competing Meanings of 'Biopolitics' in Political Science: Biological and Postmodern Approaches to Politics', *Politics and the Life Sciences* 31(1/2): 2–15.

Lim, S. G.-L. (2002) 'New Literatures in English and Postcolonial Writers in the Age of Globalization', in G. Collier and F. Schulze-Engler (eds) *Crabtracks: Progress and Process in Teaching the New Literatures in English*, Amsterdam, Netherlands: Rodopi: 141–152.

Lionnet, F. (1995) *Postcolonial Representations: Women, Literature, Identity*, Ithaca, NY: Cornell University Press.

Lionnet, F. (1998) 'Performative Universalism and Cultural Diversity: French Thought and American Contexts', in J.-J. Goux and P. R. Wood (eds) *Terror and Consensus: Vicissitudes of French Thought*, Stanford, CA: Stanford University Press: 119–132.

Lionnet, F. and Shih, S. (2005) (eds) *Minor Transnationalism*, Durham, NC: Duke University Press.

Lloyd, D. (2003) 'Ireland's Modernities', *Interventions: International Journal of Postcolonial Studies* 5(3): 317–474.

Lloyd, D. (2023) 'The Art of Orality: How the Absence of Writing Shapes the Character of Tribal, "primitive" Art', *World Art* 13(3): 303–324.

Locke, J. (1960) *Two Treatises of Government*, introduced by Peter Laslet, Cambridge: Cambridge University Press.

Lockman, Z. (2004) *Contending Visions of the Middle East: The History and Politics of Orientalism*, Cambridge: Cambridge University Press.

Lodge, T. (1986) (ed.) *Resistance and Ideology in Settler Societies*, Johannesburg: Ravan Press.

Longley, K. (1997) 'Places of Refuge: Postcolonial Spaces', *Journal of the South Pacific Association for Commonwealth Literature and Language Studies* 44: 8–21.

Loomba, A. (2005) (ed.) *Colonialism-Postcolonialism*, New York: Routledge.

Loomba, A. et al. (2005) (eds) *Postcolonial Studies and Beyond*, Durham: Duke University Press.

Lott, E. (2000) 'After Identity, Politics: The Return of Universalism', *New Literary History: A Journal of Theory and Interpretation* 31(4): 665–680.

Low, G. C.-L. (1996) *White Skins, Black Masks: Representation and Colonialism*, London: Routledge.

Lucassen, J. (2004) 'A Multinational and Its Labor Force: The Dutch East India Company, 1595–1795', *International Labor and Working Class History* 66: 12–39.

Lugard, F. D. [1922] (1965) '*Introd*', Margery Perham, *The Dual Mandate in British Tropical Africa*, London: Cass.

Mabo and Others v Queensland (No. 2) (1992) 107 ALR 1.

Mackenthun, G. (2000) 'Postcolonial Masquerade: Antebellum Sea Fiction and the Transatlantic Slave Trade', in K. H. Schmidt and F. Fleischman (eds) *Early America Re-Explored: New Readings in Colonial, Early National, and Antebellum Culture*, New York: Peter Lang.

Mackenzie, J. M. (1989) *The Empire of Nature: Hunting, Conservation and British Imperialism*, Manchester: Manchester University Press.

MacKenzie, J. M. (1995) *Orientalism: History, Theory, and the Arts*, Manchester: Manchester University Press.

Maes-Jelinek, H. (1996) 'Another Future for Postcolonial Studies? Wilson Harris' Postcolonial Philosophy and the "Savage Mind"', *Wasafiri: Journal of Caribbean, African, Asian and Associated Literatures and Film* 24: 3–8.

Mains, S. et al. (2013) 'Commentary, Postcolonial Migrations', *Social and Cultural Geography* 14(2): 131–144.

Malik, K. (1996) *The Meaning of Race: Race, History and Culture in Western Society*, New York: New York University Press.

Mamdani, M. (2001) *When Victims Become Killers: Colonialism, Nativism and the Genocide in Rwanda*, Oxford: James Currey.

Mann, H. S. (1995) 'Women's Rights versus Feminism? Postcolonial Perspectives', in G. Rajan and R. Mohanram (eds) *Postcolonial Discourse and Changing Cultural Contexts: Theory and Criticism*, Westport, CT: Greenwood: 69–88.

Manning, P. (1990) *Slavery and African Life: Occidental, Oriental and African Slave Trades*, Cambridge: Cambridge University Press.

Maolain, C. O. (1985) (ed.) *Latin American Political Movements*, Harlow: Longman.

Marriott, D. (2000) 'Border Anxieties: Race and Psychoanalysis', in A. Bery, P. Murray and W. Harris (eds) *Comparing Postcolonial Literatures: Dislocations*, Basingstoke: Macmillan.

Marsden, G. (2022) *Fundamentalism and American Culture*, 3rd edition, New York: Oxford University Press.

Marshall, P. (1968) *The Chosen Place, the Timeless People*, New York: Vintage (1984).

Marty, M. E. and Scott Appleby, R. (1991–1995) *The Fundamentalism Project*, Vols 1–5, Chicago: University of Chicago Press.

Massad, J. (2000) 'The "Postcolonial" Colony: Time, Space, and Bodies in Palestine/Israel', in F. Afzal-Khan and K. Seshadri-Crooks (eds) *The Pre-Occupation of Postcolonial Studies*, Durham, NC: Duke University Press: 311–346.

Massumi, B. (2002) *Parables for the Virtual: Movement, Affect, Sensation*, Durham, NC: Duke University Press.

Mathews, F. (2012) 'The Anguish of Wildlife Ethics', *New Formations* 76: 114–131.

Matthews, J. P. (1962) *Tradition in Exile*, Toronto: University of Toronto Press.

Maxwell, A. (1994) 'Revisionist Histories and Settler Colonial Societies', *Southern Review: Literary and Interdisciplinary Essays* 27(4): 383–402.

Maxwell, A. (1998) *Colonial Photography and Exhibitions*, London: Cassell.

Mayer, R. (2000) '"Africa as an Alien Future": The Middle Passage, Afro-futurism, and Postcolonial Waterworlds', *Amerikastudien/American Studies* 45(4): 555–566.

Mba, N. E. (1982) *Nigerian Women Mobilised: Women's Political Activity in Southern Nigeria 1900–1965*, Berkeley, Institute of International Studies, University of California.

Mbembe, A. (2001) *On the Postcolony*, Berkeley and Los Angeles: University of California Press.

Mbembe, A. (2003) 'Necropolitics', *Public Culture* 15(1): 11–40.

Mbembe, A. (2019) *Necropolitics*, Durham, NC: Duke University Press.

McCallum, P. and Faith, W. (2005) *Linked Histories: Postcolonial Studies in Globalized World*, Calgary, AB: University of Calgary Press.

McClintock, A. (1995) *Imperial Leather: Race, Gender, and Sexuality in the Colonial Contest*, New York: Routledge.

McClintock, A. et al. (1997) *Dangerous Liaisons: Gender, Nation, and Postcolonial Perspectives*, Minneapolis: University of Minnesota Press.

McCormack, D. P. (2007) 'Molecular Affects in Human Geographies', *Environment and Planning* 39(2): 359–377.

McCracken, J. (2008) 'British Central Africa', *The Cambridge History of Africa* 7(1905–1940) Published online by Cambridge University Press, March, 2008.

McDougall, R. (1998) 'Walter Roth, Wilson Harris, and a Caribbean/Postcolonial Theory of Modernism', *University of Toronto Quarterly: A Canadian Journal of the Humanities* 67(2): 567–591.

McDowell, C. (1996) *Understanding Impoverishment: The Consequences of Developpment Induced Displacement*, Providence, RI: Berghan Books.

McGee, P. (1992) *Telling the Other: The Question of Value in Modern and Postcolonial Writing*, Ithaca: Cornell University Press.

McGreal, C. (2012) 'Obama Accuses Republicans of "Social Darwinism" over Paul Ryan Budget', *The Guardian* (Tuesday 3rd April 2012).

McHoul, A. and Grace, W. (1993) *A Foucault Primer: Discourse, Power and the Subject*, Melbourne: Melbourne University Press.

McInturff, K. (2000) 'Disciplining Race: Crossing Intellectual Borders in African American and Postcolonial Studies', *Canadian Review of American Studies* 30(1): 73.

McLaren, J. (1993) *New Pacific Literatures: Culture and Environment in the European Pacific*, New York: Garland Publishers.

McLeod, J. (2004) *Postcolonial London: Rewriting the Metropolis*, London: Routledge.

McLeod, J. (2016) 'Introduction: Postcolonial Environments', *Journal of Commonwealth Literature* 51(2): 192–195 (Special Issue: Postcolonial Environmentalism).

McNeill, W. H. (1983) *The Great Frontier: Freedom and Hierarchy in Modern Times*, Princeton, NJ: Princeton University Press.

McQuillan, M. (2002) 'Irish Eagleton: Of Ontological Imperialism and Colonial Mimicry', *Irish Studies Review* 10(1): 29–38.

Mead, P. (2018) 'Sovereignty of the Mind', in G. Griffiths and P. Mead (eds) *The Social Work of Narrative: Human Rights and the Cultural Imaginary*, Stuttgart: Ibidem.

Medeiros-Lichem, M. T. (2004) 'Amerindian Rhythms in Polylogues: From Transculturation to the Global Presence of Hybrid Cultures', *Trans: Internet-Zeitschrift fur Kulturwissenschaften* 15.

Meeker, J. (1972) *The Comedy of Survival: Studies in Literary Ecology*, New York: Scribner's.

Mehan, U. S. (2001) 'Transgressing Bodies in Postcolonial Fiction', *Journal of Comparative Literature and Aesthetics* 24(1–2): 1–13.

Memmi, A. (1965) *The Colonizer and the Colonized*, translated by H. Greenfield, Boston: Beacon Press.

Menkhaus, K. (2001) 'Review of *The Poor are Not Us*', *Africa Today* 48(1) (Spring): 145–147.

Menon, N. (2005) 'Between the Burqa and the Beauty Parlor? Globalization, Cultural Nationalism, and Feminist Politics', in A. Loomba, S. Kaul, M. Bunzl, A. Burton and J. Esty (eds) *Postcolonial Studies and Beyond*, Durham, NC: Duke University Press: 206–229.

Mercer, K. (1994) *Welcome to the Jungle: New Positions in Black Cultural Studies*, New York: Routledge.

Mesthrie, R. and Bhatt, R. M. (2008) *World Englishes: The Study of New Linguistic Varieties*, Cambridge: Cambridge University Press.

Meyer, S. (1996) *Imperialism at Home: Race and Victorian Womens' Fiction*, Ithaca and London: Cornell University Press.

Mezvinsky, N. and Shahak, I. (1999) *Jewish Fundamentalism in Israel*, London: Pluto Press.

Michaels, W. B. (1995) *Our America: Nativism, Modernism, and Pluralism*, Durham, NC: Duke University Press.

Michel, M. (1995) 'Positioning the Subject: Locating Postcolonial Studies', *Ariel: A Review of International English Literature* 26(1): 83–99.

Middleton, R. (1979) *The Meaning of Modernism*, Milton Keynes: Open University Press.

Mies, M. and Shiva, V. (1993) *Ecofeminism*, Melbourne: Spinifex.

Mies, M. and Shiva, V. (2014) *Ecofeminism*, 2nd edition, London and New York: Zed Books.

Mignolo, W. D. (1994) 'Are Subaltern Studies Postmodern or Postcolonial? The Politics and Sensibilities of Geo-Cultural Locations', *Disposition: American Journal of Cultural Histories and Theories* 19(46): 45–73.

Mignolo, W. D. (1995a) *The Darker Side of the Renaissance: Literacy, Territoriality, and Colonization*, Ann Arbor: University of Michigan Press.

Mignolo, W. D. (1995b) 'La razón postcolonial: Herencias coloniales y teorías postcoloniales', *Revista Chilena de Literatura* 47: 91–114.

Mignolo, W. D. (1995c) 'Afterword: Human Understanding and (Latin) American Interests: The Politics and Sensibilities of Geocultural Locations', *Poetics Today* 16(1): 171–214.

Mignolo, W. D. (2000a) *Local Histories/Global Designs: Coloniality, Subaltern Knowledges, and Border Thinking*, Princeton, NJ: Princeton University Press.

Mignolo, W. D. (2000b) '(Post)Occidentalism, (Post)Coloniality, and (Post)-Subaltern Rationality', in F. Afzal-Khan and K. Seshadri-Crooks (eds) *The Pre-Occupation of Postcolonial Studies*, Durham, NC: Duke University Press.

Mignolo, W. D. (2001) 'Coloniality at Large: The Western Hemisphere in the Colonial Horizon of Modernity', *CR: The New Centennial Review* 1(2): 19–54.

Mignolo, W. D. (2003) 'Double Translation: Transculturation and the Colonial Difference', in F. Schiwy, T. Maranhao and B. Streck (eds) *Translation and Ethnography: The Anthropological Challenge of Intercultural Understanding*, Tucson, AZ: University of Arizona Press: 3–29.

Mignolo, W. D. (2017) 'Coloniality Is Far from Over, and So Must Be Decoloniality', *Afterall: A Journal of Art, Context and Enquiry* 43(1): 38–45.

Mignolo, W. D. and Schiwy, F. (2003) 'Double Translation: Transculturation and the Colonial Difference', in T. Maranhao and B. Streck (eds) *Translation and Ethnography: The Anthropological Challenge of Intercultural Understanding*, Tucson, AZ: University of Arizona Press: 3–29.

Milbourne, P. and Mason, K. (2017) 'Environmental Injustice and Post-Colonial Environmentalism: Opencast Coal Mining, Landscape and Place', *Environmentalism and Planning A* 49(1): 29–46.

Miles, R. (1978) *Between Two Cultures?: The Case of Rastafarianism*, Bristol: S.S.R.C. Research Unit on Ethnic Relations, University of Bristol.

Miller, M. G. (2004) *Rise and Fall of the Cosmic Race: The Cult of Mestizaje in Latin America*, Austin: University of Texas Press.

Miller, N. and Aya, R. (1971) (eds) *Introduction by Eric R. Wolf, National Liberation: Revolution in the Third World*, New York: Free Press.

Mills, C. (2018) *Biopolitics*, Abingdon, Oxon: Routledge.

Mills, S. (1991) *Discourses of Difference: An Analysis of Women's Travel Writing and Colonialism*, London: Routledge.

Mills, S. and Lewis, R. (2003) (eds) *Feminist Postcolonial Theory: A Reader*, New York, NY: Routledge.

Minh-ha, T. T. (1995) 'Writing Postcoloniality and Feminism', in B. Ashcroft, G. Griffiths and H. Tiffin (eds) *The Postcolonial Studies Reader*, London: Routledge: 264–268.

Mishra, P. K. (2000) 'English Language, Postcolonial Subjectivity, and Globalization in India', *Ariel: A Review of International English Literature* 31 (1–2): 383–410.

Mishra, S. (1993) 'Haunted Lines: Postcolonial Theory and the Genealogy of Racial Formations in Fiji', *Meanjin* 52(4): 623–634.

Mishra, S. (1996) 'Frantz Fanon, Aimé Césaire, Roberto Retamar: Estranged and Estranging Bodies; or, Gazing on Caliban: An Essay against Hybridity', *UTS Review: Cultural Studies and New Writing* 2(2): 108–128.

Mishra, S. (2006) *Diaspora Criticism*, Edinburgh: Edinburgh University Press.

Mishra, V. (1996a) 'The Diasporic Imaginary: Theorising the Indian Diaspora', *Textual Practice* 10: 421–427.

Mishra, V. (1996b) '(B)ordering Naipaul: Indenture History and Diasporic Poetics', *Diaspora* 5(2) Fall: 189–237.

Mitchell, D. T. and Hearn, M. (1999) 'Colonial Savages and Heroic Tricksters: Native Americans in the American Tradition', *Journal of Popular Culture* 32(4): 101–117.

Mitchell, W. J. T. (1992) 'Postcolonial Culture, Postimperial Criticism', *Transition* 56. Cited in Ashcroft et al. (1995): 475–480.

Mitchell, W. J. T. (1994) *Landscape and Power*, Chicago and London: Chicago University Press.

Mohan, R. (1995) 'Multiculturalism in the Nineties: Pitfalls and Possibilities', in C. Newfield and R. Strickland (eds) *After Political Correctness: The Humanities and Society in the 1990s*, Boulder: Westview Press: 372–388.

Mohanram, R. (1999) *Black Body: Women, Colonialism and Space*, Minneapolis: University of Minnesota Press (Public World Series).

Mohanram, R. (2007) *Imperial White: Race, Diaspora and the British Empire*, Minneapolis: University of Minnesota Press.

Mohanram, R. and Rajan, G. (1996) *English Postcoloniality: Literatures from Around the World*, Westport, CT: Greenwood Press.

Mohanty, C. T. (1984) 'Under Western Eyes: Feminist Scholarship and Colonial Discourse', *Boundary 2* (Spring/Fall): 71–92.

Mohanty, C. T. (1995) 'Under Western Eyes: Feminist Scholarship and Colonial Discourses', in B. Ashcroft, G. Griffiths and H. Tiffin (eds) *The Postcolonial Studies Reader*, London: Routledge: 259–263.

Mohanty, C. T., Russo, A. and Torres, L. (1991) (eds) *Third World Women and the Politics of Feminism*, Bloomington: Indiana University Press.

Moikabu, J. M. (1981) *Blood and Flesh: Black American and African Identifications*, Westport, CT: Greenwood Press.

Molloy, S. (2005) 'Postcolonial Latin America and the Magic Realist Imperative: A Report to an Academy', in S. Bermann and M. Wood (eds) *Nation, Language, and the Ethics of Translation*, Princeton, NJ: Princeton University Press.

Monasterios, E. (2004) 'Rethinking Transculturation and Hybridity: An Andean Perspective', in I. M. F. Blayer and M. C. Anderson (eds) *Latin American Narratives and Cultural Identity: Selected Readings*, New York: Peter Lang: 94–110.

Mongia, P. (1996) (ed.) *Contemporary Postcolonial Theory: A Reader*, London: Arnold.

Moodie, S. (1852) *Roughing It in the Bush*, Toronto: McLelland and Stewart (1962).

Moore, H. and Sanders, T. (2001) *Magical Interpretations, Material Realities: Modernity, Witchcraft and the Occult in Postcolonial Africa*, London: Routledge.

Moore, S. (2000) '"Anglo-Irish" Hybridity: Problems in Miscegenation, Representation, and Postcolonialism in Irish Studies', *Journal of Common-Wealth and Postcolonial Studies* 7(1): 75–110.

Moore-Gilbert, B. (1996) 'Beyond Orientalism? Culture, Imperialism and Humanism', *Wasafiri: Journal of Caribbean, African, Asian and Associated Literatures and Film* 23: 8–13.

Moran, D. (2006) *Wars of National Liberation*, London: Cassell/Collins.

Moraña, M. (2002) 'De metáforas y metonimias: Antonio Cornejo Polar en la encrucijada del latinoamericanismo internacional', in M. Moraña and J. Beverley (eds) *Nuevas perspectivas desde/sobre América Latina: El desafío de los estudios culturales*, Pittsburgh, PA: Instituto Internacional de Literatura Iberoamericana, University of Pittsburgh: 261–270.

Moraña, M. and Hallstead, S. (2004) 'The Boom of the Subaltern', in A. Del Sarto, A. Ríos and A. Trigo (eds) *The Latin American Cultural Studies Reader*, Durham, NC: Duke University Press.

Moreiras, A. (2004) 'On Infinite Decolonization', *English Studies in Canada* 30(2): 21–28.

Moreton-Robinson, A. (2007) *Sovereign Subjects: Indigenous Sovereignty Matters*, Sydney: Allen and Unwin.

Moreton-Robinson, A. (2015) *The White Possessive: Property, Power and Indigenous Sovereignty*, Minneapolis and London: University of Minnesota Press.

Moretti, F. (1983) *Signs Taken for Wonders: On the Sociology of Literary Forms*, London: Verso [2005].

Moretti, F. (1987) *The Way of the World: The Bildungsroman in European Culture*, London: Verso [2000].

Moretti, F. (2006) 'Evolution, World-Systems, Weltliteratur', in G. Lindberg-Wada (ed.) *Studying Transcultural Literary History*, Berlin, Germany: de Gruyter: 113–121.

Morgan, R. (2016) 'Native', *Appalachian Journal* 44(1/2): 148–148.

Morgan, S. (2006) *The Feminist History Reader*, London: Routledge.

Moses, A. D. (2004) (ed.) *Genocide and Settler Society: Frontier Violence and Stolen Indigenous Children in Australian History*, New York: Berghahn Books.

Mosley, A. G. (1995) (ed.) *African Philosophy: Selected Readings*, Englewood Cliffs, NJ: Prentice Hall.

Mosley, P., Harrigan, J. and Toye, J. (1991) *Aid and Power: The World Bank and Policy-Based Lending*, London: Routledge.

Mostern, K. (2000) 'Postcolonialism after W. E. B. Du Bois', in A. Singh and P. Schmidt (eds) *Postcolonial Theory and the United States: Race, Ethnicity, and Literature*, Jackson: University Press of Mississippi.

Mostert, T. and Clulow, A. (2018) (eds) *The Dutch and English East India Companies: Diplomacy, Trade and Violence in Early Modern Asia*, Amsterdam: Amsterdam University Press.

Motohashi, T. (1999) 'The Discourse of Cannibalism in Early Modern Travel Writing', in S. Clark (ed.) *Travel Writing and Empire: Postcolonial Theory in Transit*, London: Zed.

Moyland, B. (2019) 'Decolonising Historical Maps', National Library of Australia, https://nla.gov.au/stories/blog/decolonising-historical-maps

Msiska, M.-H. and Hyland, P. (1997) (eds) *Writing and Africa*, London: Longman.

Muckle, R. J. (1998) *The First Nations of British Columbia: An Anthropological Survey*, Vancouver: UBC Press.

Mudimbe, V. Y. (1992) (ed.) *The Surreptitious Speech: Presence Africaine and the Politics of Otherness, 1947–1987*, Chicago: University of Chicago Press.

Mudimbe, V. Y. (1994) *The Idea of Africa*, Bloomington: Indiana University Press; London: James Currey.

Mudrooroo (1990) *Writing from the Fringe: A Study of Modern Aboriginal Writing*, South Yarra, VIC: Hyland House.

Muffett, D. J. M. (1978) *Empire Builder Extraordinary, Sir. George Goldie: His Philosophy of Government and Empire*, Douglas: Shearwater Press.

Mukherjee, A. (1990) 'Whose Postcolonialism and Whose Post-Modernism?', *WLWE* 30(2): 1–9.

Mulhausler, P. (1986) *Pidgin and Creole Linguistics*, Oxford: Blackwell.

Munday, J. (2001) *Introducing Translation Studies: Theories and Applications*, London and New York: Routledge.

Munro, M. (2004) 'Can't Stand Up for Falling Down: Haiti, Its Revolutions, and Twentieth-Century Negritudes', *Research in African Literatures* 35(2): 1–17.

Murdoch, H. A. (1999) 'Exploring the Margin: Models of Cultural Identity in the Postcolonial French Caribbean', *Journal of Commonwealth and Postcolonial Studies* 6(1): 153–184.

Murray, P. (2000) 'The Trickster at the Border: Cross-Cultural Dialogues in the Caribbean', in A. Bery, P. Murray and W. Harris (eds) *Comparing Postcolonial Literatures: Dislocations*, Basingstoke: Macmillan.

Murray, S. (1997a) 'Postcoloniality/Modernity: Wilson Harris and Postcolonial Theory', *Review of Contemporary Fiction* 17(2): 53–58.

Murray, S. (1997b) (ed.) *Not on Any Map: Essays on Postcoloniality and Cultural Nationalism*, Exeter: Exeter University Press.

Murrell, N., et al. (1998) (eds) *Chanting Down, Babylon: The Rastafari Reader*; Philadelphia, PA: Temple University Press.

Muysken, P. and Smith, N. (1995) 'The Study of Pidgin and Creole Languages', in J. Arends, P. Muysken and N. Smith (eds) *Pidgins & Creoles: An Introduction*, Amsterdam and Philadelphia: John Benjamins: 3–14.

Naipaul, V. S. (1967) *The Mimic Men*, London: André Deustch.

Nance, K. A. (2006) *Can Literature Promote Justice? Trauma Narrative and Social Action in Latin American Testimonio*, Nashville, TN: Vanderbilt University Press.

Nandy, A. (1983) *The Intimate Enemy: Loss and Recovery of Self under Colonialism*, Delhi: Oxford University Press.

Nasta, S. (2000) *Reading the 'New' Literatures in a Postcolonial Era*, Cambridge: Brewer.

Ndhlovu-Gatseni, S. J. (2013) *Empire, Global Coloniality and African Subjectivity*, New York: Berghahn Books.

Nederveen Pieterse, J. (1992) *White on Black: Images of Africa and Blacks in Western Popular Culture*, New Haven, CT and London: Yale University Press.

Nederveen Pieterse, J. (1995) *The Development of Development Theory Towards Critical Globalism*, Working Paper Series, The Hague: Institute of Social Studies.

Nederveen Pieterse, J. and Parekh, B. C. (1995) (eds) *The Decolonization of Imagination: Culture, Knowledge and Power*, London: Zed Books.

Nelson, E. S. (1993) (ed.) *Writers of the Indian Diaspora: A Bio-bibliographical Critical Sourcebook*, Westport, CT: Greenwood Press.

New, W. H. (1975) *Among Worlds*, Erin, Ontario: Press Porcepic.

Newman, S. (2000) 'Universalism/Particularism: Towards a Poststructuralist Politics of Universality.' *New Formations: A Journal of Culture/Theory/Politics* 41: 95–108.

Newsom, D. D. (2001) *The Imperial Mantle: The United States, Decolonization, and the Third World*, Bloomington: Indiana University Press.

Ngugi, wa T. (1981a) *De-Colonising the Mind: The Politics of Language in African Literature*, London: James Currey.

Ngugi, wa T. (1981b) *Writers in Politics*, London: Heinemann.

Ngugi, wa T. (1983) *Barrel of a Pen: Resistance to Repression in Neo-colonial Kenya*, London: New Beacon Books.

Ngugi, wa T. (1986) *Writing against Neocolonialism*, Wembley: Vita Books.

Ngugi, wa T. (1993) *Moving the Centre: The Struggle for Cultural Freedoms*, London: James Currey; Portsmouth, NH: Heinemann.

Nichols, M. (2011) 'Review of Huggan and Tiffin (2010)', *Critical Quarterly* 523(1) (April): 100–105.

Nightingale, P. (1986) (ed.) *A Sense of Place in the New Literatures in English*, St. Lucia, QLD: University of Queensland Press.

Nixon, R. (2011) *Slow Violence and the Environmentalism of the Poor*, Cambridge, MA: Harvard University Press.

Nkosi, L. (2005) 'Negritude: New and Old Perspectives', in L. Stiebel and L. Gunner (eds) *Still Beating the Drum: Critical Perspectives on Lewis Nkosi*, New York: Rodopi: 267–290.

Nkrumah, K. (1965) *Neo-colonialism: The Last Stage of Imperialism*, London: Nelson.

Nunes, Z. (1994) 'Anthropology and Race in Brazilian Modernism', in F. Barker, P. Hulme and M. Iversen (eds) *Colonial Discourse/Postcolonial Theory*, Manchester: Manchester University Press: 115–125.

O'Brien, S. (2009) 'Ecocriticism and the Postcolony', *Postcolonial Text* 5: 4.

Obeyesekere, G. (1992) 'British Cannibals: Contemplation of an Event in the Death and Resurrection of James Cook, Explorer', *Critical Inquiry* 18 (Summer).

Oglesby, C. (1969) 'Vietnamism has Failed ... The Revolution Can Only Be Mauled, Not Defeated', *Commonweal* 90.

Okonkwo, C. (1999) *Decolonization Agonistics in Postcolonial Fiction*, New York: St. Martin's.

Olaniyan, T. (1992) 'The Poetics and Politics of "Othering": Contemporary African, African-American, and Caribbean Drama and the Invention of Cultural Identities', *Cultural Critique* 34(0): 2922A.

Olson, G. A. and Worsham, L. (1999) (eds) *Race, Rhetoric, and the Postcolonial*, Albany: State University of New York Press.

Ong, W. J. (1982) *Orality and Literacy: The Technologizing of the Word*, London and New York: Methuen.

Oosthuizen, G. C. (1993) 'The Rastafarian Movement and Its Appearance in South Africa', *Syzygy: Journal of Alternative Religion and Culture* 2(3–4): 243–266.

Orgun, G. (2000) 'Marginality, Cosmopolitanism and Postcoloniality', *Commonwealth Essays and Studies* 23(1): 111–124.

Ortiz, F. (1978) *Contrapunto Cubano (1947–1963)*, Caracas: Biblioteca Ayacucho.

Ostby, M. (2018) 'Cosmopolitanism', *New Literary Review* 49(2): 261–266.

Owens, J. D. (1976) *The Rastafarians of Jamaica*, London: Heinemann.

Oyewùmí, O. (1997) *The Invention of Women: Making an African Sense of Western Gender Discourses*, Minneapolis: University of Minnesota Press.

Pain, R. and Cahill, C. (2021) 'Critical Political Geographies of Slow Violence and Resistance', *Politics and Space* 40(2): 359–372.

Palumbo-Liu, D. (1995) 'Universalisms and Minority Culture', *Differences: A Journal of Feminist Cultural Studies* 7(1): 188–208.

Papastergiadis, N. (1996) 'Ambivalence in Cultural Theory: Reading Homi Bhabha's Dissemi-Nation', in J. C. Hawley (ed.) *Writing the Nation: Self and Country in the Postcolonial Imagination*, Amsterdam, Netherlands: Rodopi.

Paranjape, M. (1998) 'Theorising Postcolonial Difference: Culture, Nation, Civilization', *Journal of the South Pacific Association for Commonwealth Literature and Language Studies* 47: 1–17.

Paret, M. and Gleeson, S. (2016) 'Precarity and Agency Through a Migration Lens', *Citizenship Studies* 20(3–4): 277–294.

Parker, A., Russo, M., Sommer, D. and Yaeger, P. (1992) *Nationalism and Sexuality*, London and New York: Routledge.

Parkinson, L. and Faris, W. B. (1995) (eds) *Magical Realism: Theory, History, Community,* Durham, NC: Duke University Press.

Parry, B. (1987) 'Problems in Current Discourse Theory', *Oxford Literary Review* 9: 27–58.

Parry, B. (1994) 'Resistance Theory/Theorising Resistance: Two Cheers for Nativism', in F. Barker, P. Hulme and M. Iversen (eds) *Colonial Discourse/ Postcolonial Theory*, Manchester and New York: Manchester University Press.

Parry, B. (1995) 'Problems in Current Theories of Colonial Discourse', in B. Ashcroft, G. Griffiths and H. Tiffin (eds) *The Postcolonial Studies Reader*, London: Routledge.

Parry, B. (2002a) 'Liberation Theory: Variations on Themes of Marxism and Modernity', in C. Bartolovich and N. Lazarus (eds) *Marxism, Modernity, and Postcolonial Studies*, Cambridge: Cambridge University Press: 125–149.

Parry, B. (2002b) 'Fanon and the Trauma of Modernity', *New Formations: A Journal of Culture/Theory/Politics* 47: 24–29.

Parry, B. (2004) *Postcolonial Studies: A Materialist Critique*, London and New York: Routledge.

Pasco, B. (2018) *Dark Emu: Aboriginal Australia and the Birth of Agriculture*, Perth: Magabala Books.

Patrick, S. and Huggins, A. (2023) 'The Term 'Global South' Is Surging. It Should Be Retired', Carnegie Endowment for International Peace. August 15 Commentary, https://carnegieendowment.org/2023/08/15/term-global-south-is-surging.-it-should-be-retired-pub-90376

Patterson, O. (1967) *The Sociology of Slavery: An Analysis of the Origins, Development and Structure of Negro Slave Society in Jamaica*, London: MacGibbon and Kee.

Peah, C. and Robbins, B. (1998) *Cosmopolitics: Thinking and Feeling Beyond the Nation*, Minneapolis: University of Minnesota Press.

Pearson, D. (2001) *The Politics of Ethnicity in Settler Societies: States of Unease*, Basingstoke: Palgrave.

Pease, D. (1997) 'National Narratives, Postnational Narration', *Modern Fiction Studies* 43(1): 1–23.

Pechey, G. (1994) 'Post-Apartheid Narratives', in F. Barker, P. Hulme and M. Iversen (eds) *Colonial Discourse/Postcolonial Theory*, Manchester: Manchester University Press.

Peel, R. (2023) 'On Defining Fundamentalism', *Religious Studies* 59(4): 729–747.

Peires, J. (2003) *The Dead will Arise: Nongawuse and the Great Xhosa Cattle Killing of 1856-7*, Capetown: Ball.

Pennycook, A. (1998) *English and the Discourses of Colonialism*, London: Routledge.

Pennycook, A. (2002) 'Ruptures, Departures and Appropriations: Post-colonial Challenges to Language Development', in C. D. Villareal, L. R. R. Tope and P. M. B. Jurilla (eds) *Ruptures and Departures: Language and Culture in Southeast Asia*, Quezon City: University of the Philippines Press.

Perera, N. (1998) *Society and Space: Colonialism, Nationalism and Postcolonial Identity in Sri Lanka*, Boulder, CO: Westview Press.

Peretti, B. W. (1995) 'Plantation Cafés: Jazz, Postcolonial Theory, and Modernism', in G. Rajan and R. Mohanram (eds) *Postcolonial Discourse and Changing Cultural Contexts: Theory and Criticism*, Westport, CT: Greenwood: 89–99.

Pérez-Torres, R. (2006) *Mestizaje: Critical Uses of Race in Chicano Culture*, Minneapolis: University of Minnesota Press.

Perham, M. (1956) *Lugard*, London: Collins.

Pesso-Miquel, C. and Stierstorfer, K. (2006) (eds) *Fundamentalism and Literature*, New York: Palgrave Macmillan.

Peth, S. A. (2014) 'What Is Translocality? A Refined Understanding of Place and Space in a Globalized World', https://doi.org/10.34834/2019.0007

Phillips, A. A. (1958) *The Australian Tradition: Studies in a Colonial Culture*, Melbourne: F.W. Cheshire.

Phillips, A. A. (1979) *Responses: Selected Writings*, introduction and checklist by Brian Kiernan, Kew, VIC: Australia International Press & Publications.

Phillips, A. and Sharman, J. C. (2020) *Outsourcing Empire: How Company States Made the Modern World*, Princeton, NJ: Princeton University Press.

Phillips, D. (2003) *The Truth of Ecology: Nature, Culture, and Literature in America*, Oxford: Oxford University Press.

Phillips, M. (2016) 'Postcolonial Endgame', *Journal of Postcolonial Writing* 52(1): 6–12.

Phillips, M. and Rumens, N. (2015) *Contemporary Perspectives on Ecofeminism*, London: Routledge.

Philp, K. R. (1986) (ed.) *Indian Self-Rule: First-Hand Accounts of Indian–White Relations from Roosevelt to Reagan*, Salt Lake City, Utah: Howe Bros.

Philp, K. R. and West, E. (1976) (eds) *Essays on Walter Prescott Webb*, Austin: University of Texas Press.

Pidd, M. (2004) (ed.) *Systems Modelling: Theory and Practice*, Chichester: John Wiley & Sons.

Pinder, D. (2005) *Visions of The City: Utopianism, Power and Politics in Twentieth-Century Urbanism*, Edinburgh: Edinburgh University Press.

Pinder, D. (2010) 'The Breath of the Possible: Everyday Utopianism and the Street in Modernist Urbanism', in M. Gordin, H. Tilley and G. Prakash (eds) *Utopia/Dystopia: Conditions of Historical Possibility*, Princeton, NJ: Princeton University Press: 203–230.

Plasa, C. and Ring, B. J. (1994) (eds) *The Discourse of Slavery: Aphra Behn to Toni Morrison*, London and New York: Routledge.

Plumwood, V. (1993) *Feminism and the Mastery of Nature*, London and New York: Routledge.

Plumwood, V. (2002) *Environmental Culture: The Ecological Crisis of Reason*, London and New York: Routledge.

Pollard, V. and Nettleford, R. (2000) *Dread Talk: The Language of Rastafari*, Kingston, Jamaica and Montreal, QC: Canoe; McGill-Queen's University Press.

Pomeroy, W. J. (1970) *American Neo-Colonialism: Its Emergence in the Philippines and Asia*, New York: International Publishers.

Power, M. (2003) *Rethinking Development Geographies*, New York: Routledge.

Prakash, G. (1995) *After Colonialism: Imperial Histories and Postcolonial Displacements*, Princeton, NJ: Princeton University Press.

Prakash, G. (1997) 'Postcolonial Criticism and Indian Historiography', in A. McClintock, A. Mufti and E. Shohat (eds) *Dangerous Liaisons: Gender, Nation, and Postcolonial Perspectives*, Minneapolis: University of Minnesota Press.

Prakash, G. et al. (1999) (eds) *Subaltern Studies X: Writings on South Asian History and Society*, New Delhi: Oxford University Press.

Prasad, M. (1997) 'On the Question of a Theory of (Third) World Literature', in A. McClintock, A. Mufti and E. Shohat (eds) *Dangerous Liaisons: Gender, Nation, and Postcolonial Perspectives*, Minneapolis: University of Minnesota Press.

Pratt, M. L. (1985) 'Scratches on the Face of the Country; Or, What Mr Barrow Saw in the Land of the Bushmen', *Critical Inquiry* 12(1) Autumn: 138–162. Reprinted in Gates 1986.

Pratt, M. L. (1991) 'Arts of the Contact Zone', in D. Bartholomae and A. Petroksky (eds) *Ways of Reading*, 5th edition, New York: Bedford/ St. Martin's.

Pratt, M. L. (1992) *Imperial Eyes: Travel Writing and Transculturation*, London: Routledge.

Pratt, M. L. (2004) 'The Anticolonial Past', *Modern Language Quarterly: A Journal of Literary History* 65(3): 443–456.

Premnath, G. (2002) 'The Afterlife of National Liberation: Fanon Today', *New Formations: A Journal of Culture/Theory/Politics* 47: 43–45.

Premnath, G. (2003) 'The Weak Sovereignty of the Postcolonial Nation-State', in A. Kumar, J. Berger and B. Robbins (eds) *World Bank Literature*, Minneapolis: University of Minnesota Press: 253–264.

Prentice, C. (1991) 'The Interplay of Place and Placelessness in the Subject of Postcolonial Fiction', *SPAN: Journal of the South Pacific Association for Commonwealth Literature and Language Studies* 31: 63–80.

Prentice, C. (1994) 'Some Problems of Response to Empire in Settler Post-Colonial Societies', in C. Tiffin and A. Lawson (eds) *De-Scribing Empire: Postcolonialism and Textuality,* London: Routledge.

Press, J. (1965) (ed.) *Commonwealth: Unity and Diversity within Common Culture*, London: Heinemann.

Price, R. (2017) 'Créolisation, Creolization, and Créolité', *Small Axe: A Journal of Criticism* 21(1) (52): 211–219.

Price, R. and Rosberg, C. G. (1980) *The Apartheid Regime*, Berkeley: University of California Press.

Punter, D. (2000) *Postcolonial Imaginings: Fictions of a New World Order*, Edinburgh: Edinburgh University Press.

Puri, S. (2004) *The Caribbean Postcolonial: Social Equality, Post-Nationalism, and Cultural Hybridity*, New York: Palgrave Macmillan.

Quayson, A. (2000) *Postcolonialism: Theory, Practice or Process?*, Cambridge: Polity.

Quijano, A. (2007) 'Coloniality and Modernity/Rationality', *Cultural Studies* 21(2–3): 168–178.

Rabasa, J. (1993) *Inventing A-M-E-R-I-C-A: Spanish Historiography and the Formation of Eurocentrism*, Norman, OK and London: University of Oklahoma Press. Cited in Ashcroft et al. (1995): 358–364.

Rabinow, P. and Rose, N. (2006) 'Biopower Today', *Biosocieties* 1: 195–217.

Radford, D. (1982) *Edouard Glissant*, Paris: Seghers.

Radhakrishnan, R. (2000) 'Adjudicating Hybridity, Co-ordinating Betweenness', *Jouvert: A Journal of Postcolonial Studies* 5(1).

Raheja, G. G. (2002) 'The Erasure of Everyday Life in Colonial Ethnography', in D. P. Mines and S. Lamb (eds) *Everyday Life in South Asia*, Bloomington: Indiana University Press: 199–213.

Rahmen, A. (2002) *Translation: Poetics and Practice*, New Delhi: Creative Books.

Raj, K. (2013) 'Beyond Postcolonialism...and Postpositivism: Circulation and the Global History of Science', *Isis* 104: 337–347.

Rajadhyaksha, A. (1998) 'Realism, Modernism, and Postcolonial Theory', in J. Hill, P. C. Gibson, R. Dyer, E. A. Kaplan and P. Willemen (eds) *The Oxford Guide to Film Studies*, New York, NY: Oxford University Press Modernism: 413–425.

Rajan, G. and Mohanram, R. (1995) (eds) *Postcolonial Discourse and Changing Cultural Contexts: Theory and Criticism*, Westport, CT: Greenwood Press.

Rajan, R. S. (1993) *Real and Imagined Women: Gender, Culture and Post-colonialism*, London and New York: Routledge.

Rajan, R. S. (1997) 'The Third World Academic in Other Places: Or, the Postcolonial Intellectual Revisited', *Critical Inquiry* 23(3): 596–616.

Rajen, H. (1997) *Twentieth Century Imperialism: Shifting Contours and Changing Conceptions*, New Delhi: Sage Publications.

Rama, A. (1982) *Transculturacion Narrativa en America Latin*, Mexico City: Siglo: 21.

Ramamurthy, P. (2020) 'Translocal Householding', *Comparative Studies of South Asia, Africa and the Middle East* 40(1): 86–93.

Ramazani, J. (2001) *The Hybrid Muse: Postcolonial Poetry in English*, Chicago: University of Chicago Press.

Ramazani, J. (2006) 'Modernist Bricolage, Postcolonial Hybridity', *Modernism/Modernity* 13(3): 445–463.

Ramo, J. C. (2004) *The Beijing Consensus*, London: Foeign Policy Centre.

Ramraj, V. J. (1996) 'Diasporas and Multiculturalism', in B. King (ed.) *New National and Postcolonial Literatures: An Introduction*, Oxford: Clarendon: 214–229.

Rasmussen, D. M. (1990) (ed.) *Universalism vs. Communitarianism: Contem-Porary Debates in Ethics.* Cambridge, MA: MIT Press.

Ratele, K. et al. (2018) 'Some Basic Questions About (A) Decolonizing Africa (N) - Centred Psychology Considered', *South African Journal of Psychology* 48(3): 331–342.

Rath, S. P. (2000) 'Home(s) Abroad: Diasporic Identities in Third Spaces', *Jouvert: A Journal of Postcolonial Studies* 4(3).

Ray, S. (1999) 'The Postcolonial Critic: Shifting Subjects, Changing Paradigms', in C. Hendricks and K. Oliver (eds) *Language and Liberation: Feminism, Philosophy, and Language*, Albany: State University of New York Press.

Ray, S. (2000) *En-gendering India: Woman and Nation in Colonial and Postcolonial Narratives*, Durham, NC: Duke University Press.

Reddy, W. (2001) *The Navigation of Feeling: A Framework for the History of Emotions*, Cambridge: Cambridge University Press.

Reed, J. and Wake, C. (1965) (eds) *Senghor: Prose and Poetry*, London: Heinemann Educational (reissued 1976).

Reid, W. V. (1993) *Biodiversity Prospecting: Using Genetic Resources for Sustainable Development*, Washington: World Resources Institute.

Reiss, T. J. (2004) 'Mapping Identities: Literature, Nationalism, Colonialism', in C. Prendergast (ed.) *Debating World Literature*, London: Verso.

Revelle, R. and Suess, H. E. (1957) 'Carbon Dioxide Exchange Between Atmosphere and Ocean and the Question of an Increase in Atmospheric CO_2 During the Past Decades', *Tellus* 9: 18–27.

Reynolds, H. (1982) *The Other Side of the Frontier: Aboriginal Resistance to the European Invasion of Australia*, Ringwood, VIC: Penguin.

Reynolds, H. (2007) 'The Judges Judged: Mabo and the Disaffected Historians', *Legal History* 11(2): 231–242.

Rhodes, C. (1994) *Primitivism and Modern Art*, London: Thames & Hudson.

Rice, L. (2003) 'Of Heterotopias and Ethnoscapes: The Production of Space in Postcolonial North Africa', *Critical Matrix: The Princeton Journal of Women, Gender, and Culture* 14: 36–75.

Rich, P. B. (1986) *Race and Empire in British Politics*, Cambridge and New York: Cambridge University Press.

Richards, D. (2000) '"Canvas of Blood": Okigbo's African Modernism', in A. Bery, P. Murray and W. Harris (eds) *Comparing Postcolonial Literatures: Dislocations*, Basingstoke: Macmillan: 229–239.

Richardson, H. H. (1917) *The Fortunes of Richard Mahony*, London: Heinemann.

Richmond, A. H. (1994) *Global Apartheid: Refugees, Racism, and the New World Order*, New York: Oxford University Press.

Richter, V. (2004) 'A New Desire for the Grands Récits? Propositions for a Critical Universalism', in G. V. Davis et al. (eds) *Towards a Transcultural Future: Literature and Society in a "Post"-Colonial World*, Amsterdam, Netherlands: Rodopi: 93–104.

Riemenschneider, D. (1983) (ed.) *The History and Historiography of Commonwealth Literature*, Tübingen: Narr.

Riggenbach, J. (2011) 'The Real William Graham Sumner', *Mises Daily* (Friday April 22, 2011).

Rikap, C. (2021) *Capitalism Power and Innovation: Intellectual Monopoly Capitalism Uncovered*, London: Routledge.

Ritter, D. (2007) 'Myths, Truths and Arguments: Some Recent Writings on Aboriginal History', *Australian Journal of Politics and History* 52(1): 138–148.

Robbins, B. (1992) 'Comparative Cosmopolitanism', *Social Text* 31/32, *Third World and Postcolonial Issues:* 169–86.

Robertson, R. (1992) *Globalization: Social Theory and Global Culture*, London: Sage.

Robertson, R. (1995) 'Glocalization', in M. Featherstone, S. Lash and R. Robertson (eds) *Global Modernities*, London: Sage: 25–44.

Robins, N. (2012) *The Corporation that Changed the World: How the East India Company Shaped the Modern Multinational*, London: Pluto Press.

Robinson, D. (2000) *What Is Translation?*, Kent, OH: Kent Sate University Press.

Robinson, D. F. (2010a) 'Locating Biopiracy: Geographically and Culturally Situated Knowledges', *Environmental Planning A* 42: 38–56.

Robinson, D. F. (2010b) *Confronting Biopiracy*, Abingdon: Earthscan.

Robinson, R. and Gallagher, J. (1981) *Africa and the Victorians: The Official Mind of Imperialism, with Alice Denny*, 2nd edition, London: Macmillan.

Robotham, D. (2005) 'Cosmopolitanism and Planetary Humanism: The Strategic Universalism of Paul Gilroy', *South Atlantic Quarterly* 104(3): 561–582.

Robson, J. P. (2019) 'Indigenous Communities, Migrant Organizations, and the Ephemeral Nature of Translocality', *Latin American Review* 54(1): 103–112.

Rodoreda, G. (2018) 'Introduction', in G. Rodoreda and E. Bischoff (eds) *The Mabo Turn in Australian Fiction*, Oxford: Peter Lang.

Rodrigues, Á. L. (2004) 'Beyond Nativism: An Interview with Ngugi wa Thiong'o', *Research in African Literatures* 35(3): 161–167.

Roediger, D. (2002) *Colored White: Transcending the Racial Past*, Berkeley: University of California.

Romaine, S. (1988) *Pidgin and Creole Languages*, London and New York: Longman.

Rose, D. (1992) *Dingo Makes Us Human*, Cambridge: Cambridge University Press.

Ross, R. (1982) (ed.) *Racism and Colonialism*, Leyden: Martinus Nijhoff.

Rotberg, E. (1994) 'Financial Operations of the World Bank', in Bretton Woods Commission (ed.) *Bretton Woods: Looking to the Future*, Washington, DC: Bretton Woods Commission.

Rotberg, R. with Miles Shore (1988) *The Founder: Cecil Rhodes and the Pursuit of Power*, Johannesburg: Southern Book Publishers.

Rothermund, D. (2006) *The Routledge Companion to Decolonization*, London: Routledge.

Rotter, A. J. (2000) 'Saidism without Said: Orientalism and U.S. Diplomatic History', *American Historical Review* 105(4): 1205–1217.

Rousseau, J. J. (1755) *A Discourse on Inequality*, translated by M. Cranston, London: Penguin (1988).

Rowse, T. (1993) *After Mabo: Interpreting Indigenous Traditions,* Carlton, VIC: Melbourne University Press.

Rowse, T. and Nile, R. (2005) *Contesting Assimilation*, Perth, WA: API Network.

Roy, A. (1995) 'Postcoloniality and the Politics of Identity in the Diaspora: Figuring "Home," Locating Histories', in G. Rajan and R. Mohanram (eds) *Postcolonial Discourse and Changing Cultural Contexts: Theory and Criticism*, Westport, CT: Greenwood: 101–115.

Roy, A. (2001) *The Algebra of Infinite Justice*, London: Flamingo.

Roy, A. (2002) *The God of Small Things*, London: Harper-Collins.

Roy, T. (1995) 'Disciplining the Printed Text: Colonial and Nationalist Surveillance of Bengali Literature', in P. Chatterjee (ed.) *Texts of Power: Emerging Disciplines in Colonial Bengal*, Minneapolis: University of Minnesota Press.

Rubin, W. (1984) (ed.) *Primitivism in 20th-Century Art: Affinity of the Tribal and the Modern*, New York: Museum of Modern Art.

Rueckert, W. (1996) 'Literature and Ecology: An Experiment in Ecocriticism', in C. Glotfelty and H. Fromm (eds) *The Ecocriticism Reader: Landmarks in Literary Ecology*, Athens, GA: University of Georgia Press: 105–123.

Rushdie, S. (1991) *Imaginary Homelands,* London: Granta.

Russell, L. (2001) *Colonial Frontiers: Indigenous-European Encounters in Settler Societies*, Manchester: Manchester University Press.

Russell, L. (2006) (ed.) *Boundary Writing: An Exploration of Race, Culture, and Gender Binaries in Contemporary Australia*, Honolulu: University of Hawaii Press.

Rutherford, A., Holst Petersen, K. and Maes Jelinek, H. (1992) (eds) *From Commonwealth to Postcolonial*, Aarhus and Sydney: Dangaroo.

Ruthven, K. K. (1968) 'Yeats, Lawrence and the Savage God', *Critical Quarterly* 10(1 and 2) (Spring/Summer).

Ryan, S. (1994) 'Inscribing the Emptiness: Cartography, Exploration and the Construction of Australia', in C. Tiffin and A. Lawson (eds) *De-Scribing Empire: Postcolonialism and Textuality,* London: Routledge: 115–130.

Said, E. (1978) *Orientalism: Western Conceptions of the Orient*, London: Penguin (1991).

Said, E. (1983) *The World, the Text, and the Critic*, Cambridge, MA: Harvard University Press.

Said, E. (1984) 'The Mind of Winter: Reflections on Life in Exile', *Harper's* 269: 49–55.

Said, E. (1993) *Culture and Imperialism*, London: Chatto & Windus.

Said, E. (1994) *Representations of the Intellectual*, New York: Pantheon.

Said, E. W. (1999) *Out of Place: A Memoir*, New York: Knopf.

Said, E. W. (2001) 'The Clash of Ignorance', *The Nation* October 22: 1–5.

Saini, M. K. (1981) *Politics of Multinationals: A Pattern in Neo-Colonialism*, foreword by Rasheeduddin Khan, New Delhi: Gitanjali Prakashan.

Salman, M. (2011) 'Clash of Civilizations Thesis: A Critical Evaluation', *Pakistan Journal of International Relations* 2(1): 1–7.

San Juan, E., Jr (1991a) *Writing and National Liberation: Essays in Critical Practice*, Quezon City: University of the Philippines Press.

San Juan, E. (1991b) 'Philippine Writing in English: Postcolonial Syncreticism versus a Textual Practice of National Liberation', *Ariel: A Review of International English Literature* 22(4): 69–88.

San Juan, E., Jr (1995a) 'On the Limits of "Postcolonial" Theory: Trespassing Letters from the "Third World"', *Ariel: A Review of International English Literature* 26(3): 89–115.

San Juan, E. (1995b) *Hegemony and Strategies of Transgression: Essays in Cultural Studies and Comparative Literature*, Albany: State University of New York Press.

San Juan, E., Jr (1996) 'From Postcolonial to Alter/Native National Allegory: Dialectics of Nation/People and World-System in Philippine Writing', in W. Zach and K. L. Goodwin (eds) *Nationalism vs. Internationalism: (Inter)National Dimensions of Literatures in English*, Tübingen, Germany: Stauffenburg.

San Juan, E., Jr (1998) *Beyond Postcolonial Theory*, New York: St. Martin's.

Sanborn, G. (1998) *The Sign of the Cannibal: Melville and the Making of a Postcolonial Reader*, Durham, NC: Duke University Press.

Sanday, P. R. (1986) *Divine Hunger: Cannibalism as a Cultural System*, Cambridge: Cambridge University Press.

Sandiford, K. A. (2000) *The Cultural Politics of Sugar: Caribbean Slavery and Narratives of Colonialism*, Cambridge: Cambridge University Press.

Sanusi, A. (2009) *Eyo*. Nairobi: Word Alive Publishers Limited.

Sardar, Z. (1999) *Orientalism*, Buckingham: Open University Press.

Sarkowsky, K. (2002) 'Beyond Margins and Centres: First Nations Literature and the Challenge to Postcolonial Theory', in G. Collier and F. Schulze-Engler (eds) *Crabtracks: Progress and Process in Teaching the New Literatures in English*, Amsterdam, Netherlands: Rodopi.

Sartre, J.-P. (1957) *Being and Nothingness: An Essay on Phenomenological Ontology*, translated by H. E. Barnes, London: Methuen.

Sassen, S. (1996) *Losing Control? Sovereiugnity in an Age of Globalisation*, New York: Columbia University Press.

Satchidanandan, K. (2002) 'Orientalism Revisited', *Indian Literature* 46(3 [209]): 8–12.

Sauvy, A. (1952) *General Theory of Population*, translated by C. Campos, London: Methuen.

Savishinsky, N. J. (1999) 'Transnational Popular Culture and the Global Spread of the Jamaican Rastafarian Movement', in M. Klass and M. Weisgrau (eds) *Across the Boundaries of Belief: Contemporary Issues in the Anthropology of Religion*, Boulder, CO: Westview.

Sawyer, M. (2003) 'The Noble Savage as Hegelian Hero: Dialectic Process and Postcolonial Theory', *Hispanic Journal* 24(1–2): 65–74.

Schaffer, K. (1989) *Women and the Bush: Forces of Desire in the Colonial Cultural Tradition*, Cambridge: Cambridge University Press.

Schaffer, K. (1995) *In the Wake of First Contact: The Eliza Fraser Stories*, Cambridge: Cambridge University Press.

Schayegh, C. and Di-Capua, Y. (2020) 'Why Decolonization', *International Journal of Middle East Studies* 5(1): 137–145.

Schermerhorn, R. A. (1970) *Comparative Ethnic Relations: A Framework for Theory and Research*, New York: Random House.

Schermerhorn, R. A. (1974) 'Ethnicity in the Perspective of the Sociology of Knowledge', *Ethnicity* 1(1) (April).

Schiller, H. (1975) *Communication and Cultural Domination*, New York: International Arts and Sciences Press.

Schleck, J. and Sen, A. (2017) 'Introduction: Alternative Histories of the East India Company', *Journal for Early Modern Cultural Studies* 17(3): 1–9.

Schmidt, F. (2000) 'Literaturas heterogéneas y alegorías nacionales: ¿Paradigmas para las literaturas poscoloniales?', *Revista Iberoamericana* 66(190): 175–185.

Schoene-Harwood, B. (1998) '"Emerging as the Others of Our Selves": Scottish Multiculturalism and the Challenge of the Body in Postcolonial Representation', *Scottish Literary Journal* 25(1): 54–72.

Scholte, J. A. (1996) 'Beyond the Buzzword: Towards a Critical Theory of Globalization', in E. Kofman and G. Youngs (eds) *Globalisation: Theory and Practice*, London: Pinter.

Scholte, J. A. (2005) *The Sources of Neoliberal Globalization*, Geneva: United Nations Research Institute for Social Development.

Schueller, M. J. (2003) 'Articulations of African-Americanism in South Asian Postcolonial Theory: Globalism, Localism, and the Question of Race', *Cultural Critique* 55: 35–62.

Schulze-Engler, F. (1996) 'Universalism with a Difference: The Politics of Postcolonial Theory', in W. Zach and K. Goodwin (eds) *Nationalism vs. Internationalism: (Inter)National Dimensions of Literatures in English*, Tübingen, Germany: Stauffenburg: 41–46.

Scott, D. (1995) 'Colonial Governmentality', *Social Text* 43: 191–220.

Scott, D. (1996) 'The Aftermaths of Sovereignty: Postcolonial Criticism and the Claims of Political Modernity', *Social Text* 48: 1–26.

Scott, H. (2002) 'Was There a Time before Race? Capitalist Modernity and the Origins of Racism', in C. Bartolovich and N. Lazarus (eds) *Marxism, Modernity, and Postcolonial Studies*, Cambridge: Cambridge University Press: 167–182.

Scott, J. S. and Griffiths, G. (2005) (eds) *Mixed Messages: Materiality, Textuality, Missions*, New York: Palgrave/Macmillan.

Scott, J. S. and Simpson-Housley, P. (2001) *Mapping the Sacred: Religion, Geography and Postcolonial Literatures*, Amsterdam, Netherlands: Rodopi.

Secher, U. (2007) 'The High Court Recognition of Native Title: Distinguishing Between the Doctrines of Terra Nulliu and "Desert and Uncultivated"', *University of Western Sydney Law Review* 11: 1–27.

Seeley, J. R. (1890) *The Expansion of England: Two Courses of Lectures*, London: Macmillan.

Seers, D. (1981) *Dependency Theory: A Critical Re-assessment*, London: Pinter.

Segal, U. A. (2019) 'Globalization, Migration, and Ethnicity', *Public Health* 172: 135–142.

Senghor, L. S. (1964) *'Négritude et humanisme', Ch. 1, Liberté 1*, Paris: Seuil.

Seth, S. (2017) 'Colonial History and Postcolonial Science Studies', *Radical History Review* 127: 63–86.

Seymour-Smith, C. (1986) *Dictionary of Anthropology*, Boston, MA: G.K. Hall.

Sharpe, J. (2000) 'Is the United States Postcolonial? Transnationalism, Immigration, and Race', in C. R. King (ed.) *Postcolonial America*, Urbana: University of Illinois Press: 103–121.

Sharpe, J. (2005) 'Gender, Nation, and Globalization in Monsoon Wedding and Dilwale Dulhania Le Jayenge', *Meridians: Feminism, Race, Transnationalism* 6(1): 58–81 [60 & 75].

Sharrad, P. (2012) 'Frailty and Feeling: Literature for our Times', In Ashcroft et al. (2012).

Shaw, R. (2001) 'Cannibal Transformations: Colonialism and Commodification in the Sierra Leone Hinterland', in H. Moore and T. Sanders (eds) *Magical Interpretations, Material Realities: Modernity, Witchcraft and the Occult in Postcolonial Africa*, London: Routledge.

Shepherd, R. J. (2002) 'Commodification, Culture and Tourism', *Tourist Studies* 2(2): 183–201.

Sheridan, J. (2001) '"When First unto This Country a Stranger I Came": Grey Owl, Indigenous Lessons of Place, and Postcolonial Theory', in J. S. Scott and P. Simpson-Housley (eds) *Mapping the Sacred: Religion, Geography and Postcolonial Literatures*, Amsterdam, Netherlands: Rodopi: 419–439.

Shi-xu, M. K. et al. (2005) (eds) *Read the Cultural Other: Forms of Otherness in the Discourses of Hong Kong's Decolonization*, Berlin, Germany: Mouton de Gruyter.

Shoemaker, A. (1989) *Black Words, White Page: Aboriginal Literature 1929–1988*, St. Lucia, QLD: University of Queensland Press.

Shoemaker, A. (1990) *Swimming in the Mainstream: Australian Aboriginal and Canadian Indian Drama*, London: Sir Robert Menzies Centre for Australian Studies, Institute of Commonwealth Studies, University of London.

Shohat, E. (1994) *Unthinking Eurocentrism: Multiculturalism and the Media*, London and New York: Routledge.

Shohat, E. (1997) 'Framing Post-Third-Worldist Culture: Gender and Nation in Middle Eastern/North African Film', *Jouvert: A Journal of Postcolonial Studies* 1(1).

Shouse, E. (2005) 'Feeling, Emotion, Affect', *M/C Journal* 8.

Showalter, E. (1991) 'Feminist Criticism in the Wilderness', *Critical Inquiry* 8: 190–205.

Shrinkhal, R. (2021) 'Indigenous Sovereignty' and Right to Self-Determination in International Law: A Critical Appraisal', *Alternative: An International Journal of Indigenous Peoples* 17(1): 71–82.

Simmons-McDonald, H. (2003) 'Decolonizing English: The Caribbean Counter-Thrust', in C. Mair (ed.) *The Politics of English as a World Language: New Horizons in Postcolonial Cultural Studies*, Amsterdam, Netherlands: Rodopi: 179–201.

Simpson, L. R. (2004) 'Anticolonial Strategies for the Recovery and Maintenance of Indigenous Knowledge', *American Indian Quarterly* 28(3–4): 373–384.

Simpson, M. (2020) 'The Anthropocene as Colonial Discourse', *Environment and Planning D: Society and Space* 38(1) Special issue on Race and the Anthropocene, eds. Andrew Baldwin and Bruce Erickson.

Singer, E. (2002) *Moving Beyond Nativism: Eine Betrachtung des irischen Gegenwartsromans aus dem Blickwinkel postkolonialer Theorien*, Frankfurt, Germany: Peter Lang.

Singer, P. (2003) 'Practical Ethics', in S. Armstrong and R. Botzler (eds) *The Animal Ethics Reader*, London and New York: Routledge.

Singh, A. and Schmidt, P. (2000) *Postcolonial Theory and the United States: Race, Ethnicity, and Literature*, Jackson: University Press of Mississippi.

Singh, I. (2000) *Pidgins and Creoles: An Introduction*, London: Arnold.

Singh, K. (1956) *Train to Pakistan*, London: Chatto and Windus.

Singler, J. V. (1990) *Pidgin and Creole Tense-Mood-Aspect Systems*, Amsterdam and Philadelphia: John Benjamins.

Sivanandan, T. (2004) 'Anticolonialism, National Liberation, and Postcolonial Nation Formation', in N. Lazarus (ed.) *The Cambridge Companion to Postcolonial Literary Studies*, Cambridge: Cambridge University Press: 41–65.

Sivramkrishna, S. (2014) 'From Merchant to Merchant-Ruler: A Structure-Conduct-Performance Perspective of The East India Company's History, 1600–1765', *Business History* 56(5): 789–815.

Skotnes, P. (1996) *Miscast: Negotiating the Presence of the Bushman*, Cape Town: University of Cape Town Press.

Slemon, S. (1987a) 'Monuments of Empire: Allegory/Counter-Discourse/ Postcolonial Writing', *Kunapipi* 9(3): 16.

Slemon, S. (1987b) 'Cultural Alterity and Colonial Discourse', *Southern Review* 20(March).

Slemon, S. (1988a) 'Magical Realism as Postcolonial Discourse', *Canadian Literature* 116 (Spring).

Slemon, S. (1988b) 'Carnival and the Canon', *Ariel* 19(3) (July).

Slemon, S. (1990) 'Unsettling the Empire: Resistance Theory for the Second World', *World Literature Written in English* 30(2): 30–41.

Slemon, S. (1992) 'Bones of Contention: Postcolonial Writing and the "Cannibal Question"', in A. Purdy (ed.) *Literature and the Body*, Amsterdam, Netherlands: Rodopi.

Slemon, S. (1994) 'The Scramble for Postcolonialism', in C. Tiffin and A. Lawson (eds) *De-scribing Empire: Postcolonialism and Textuality,* London: Routledge.

Slemon, S. (1995) 'Magic Realism as Postcolonial Discourse', in L. P. Zamora and W. B. Faris (eds) *Magical Realism: Theory, History, Community,* Durham, NC: Duke University Press.

Smith, A. (1776) *An Inquiry into the Nature and Causes of the Wealth of Nations*, edited by E. Cannan, New York: Modern Library (1994).

Smith, A. (2004) 'Migrancy, Hybridity, and Postcolonial Literary Studies', in N. Lazarus (ed.) *The Cambridge Companion to Postcolonial Literary Studies*, Cambridge: Cambridge University Press.

Smith, A. (2009) *Ethno-symbolism and Nationalism: A Cultural Approach*, Abingdon, Oxon: Routledge.

Smith, B. (1992) Modernism and Post-modernism: A Neo-colonial Viewpoint, London: Sir Robert Menzies Centre for Australian Studies, Institute of Commonwealth Studies, University of London.

Smith, B. C. (2003) *Understanding Third World Politics: Theories of Political Change and Development*, Basingstoke: Palgrave Macmillan.

Smith, J. D. (1993) (ed.) *Racial Determinism and the Fear of Miscegenation, Post-1900,* New York: Garland Publishing.

Smith, M. P. and Eduardo, G. L. (1998) (eds) *Transnationalism from Below,* New Brunswick, NJ: Transaction Publishers.

Smith, P. (1988) *Discerning the Subject*, Minneapolis: University of Minnesota Press.

Smyth, G. (2000) 'The Politics of Hybridity: Some Problems with Crossing the Border', in A. Bery, P. Murray and W. Harris (eds) *Comparing Postcolonial Literatures: Dislocations*, Basingstoke: Macmillan.

Sollors, W. (1986) *Beyond Ethnicity: Consent and Descent in American Culture*, Oxford and New York: Oxford University Press.

Sollors, W. (1996) (ed.) *Theories of Ethnicity: A Classical Reader*, New York: New York University Press.

Solomon, R. C. (1995) 'The Cross-Cultural Comparison of Emotion', in J. Marks and R. T. Ames (eds) *Emotions in Asian Thought: A Dialogue in Comparative Philosophy*, New York: SUNY Press: 253–294.

Somerson, W. (1999) 'Becoming Rasta: Recentering White Masculinity in the Era of Transnationalism', *Comparatist: Journal of the Southern Comparative Literature Association* 23: 128–140.

Somerville, M. and Perkins, T. (2003) 'Border Work in the Contact Zone: Thinking Indigenous/Non-Indigenous Collaboration Spatially', *International Journal of Intercultural Studies* 24(3).

Sondarjee, M. and Andrews, N. (2022) 'Decolonizing International Relations and Development Studies: What's in a Buzzword?', *International Journal* 77(4): 551–571.

Sono, T. (1999) *Race Relations in Post-Apartheid South Africa*, Johannesburg: South African Institute of Race Relations.

Spears, A. K. and Winford, D. (1997) *The Structure and Status of Pidgins and Creoles: Including Selected Papers from the Meetings of the Society for Pidgin and Creole Linguistics*, Amsterdam: John Benjamins.

Spengler, O. (1926) *The Decline of the West*, translated by C. Francis Atkinson, London: Allen & Unwin.

Spiegal, M. (1988) *The Dreaded Comparison: Human and Animal Slavery*, New York: Mirror.

Spitta, S. (1995) *Between Two Waters: Narratives of Transculturation in Latin America*, Houston, TX: Rice University Press.

Spivak, G. C. (1984–1985) 'Criticism, Feminism and the Institution', interview with Elizabeth Gross, Thesis Eleven 10/11 (November/March): 175–187.

Spivak, G. C. (1985a) 'The Rani of Simur', in F. Barker et al. (eds) *Europe and Its Others Vol. 1 Proceedings of the Essex Conference on the Sociology of Literature*, Colchester: University of Essex.

Spivak, G. C. (1985b) 'Can the Subaltern Speak? Speculations on Widow Sacrifice', *Wedge* 7(8) (Winter/Spring). Cited in Ashcroft et al. (1995).

Spivak, G. C. (1985c) 'Three Women's Texts and a Critique of Imperialism', *Critical Inquiry* 18(4) (Summer): 756–769.

Spivak, G. C. (1987) *In Other Worlds: Essays in Cultural Politics*, New York: Methuen.

Spivak, G. C. (1988) 'Can the Subaltern Speak?', in C. Nelson and L. Grossberg (eds) *Marxism and the Interpretation of Culture*, Chicago: University of Illinois Press.

Spivak, G. C. (1990) *The Postcolonial Critic: Interviews, Strategies, Dialogues*, edited by S. Harasym, New York: Routledge.

Spivak, G. C. (1991) 'Identity and Alterity: An Interview' (with Nikos Papastergiadis) *Arena* 97: 65–76.

Spivak, G. C. (1993) 'The Burden of English', in C. A. Breckenridge and P. van der Veer (eds) *Orientalism and the Postcolonial Predicament: Perspectives on South Asia*, Philadelphia: University of Pennsylvania Press: 134–157.

Spivak, G. C. (1996) 'Poststructuralism, Marginality, Postcoloniality and Value', in P. Mongia (ed.) *Contemporary Postcolonial Theory: A Reader*, London: Arnold.

Spivak, G. C. (1999) *A Critique of Postcolonial Reason: Toward a History of the Vanishing Present*, Cambridge: Harvard University Press.

Spivak, G. C. (2000) 'Translation as Culture', *Parallax* 6(1 [14]): 13–24.

Spivak, G. C. (2003) 'Subaltern Studies: Deconstructing Historiography', in J. Culler (ed.) *Deconstruction: Critical Concepts in Literary and Cultural Studies*, Volume 4, New York: Routledge.

Spivak, G. C. (2005) 'Commonwealth Literature and Comparative Literature', in S. Duangsamosorn (ed.) *Re-Imagining Language and Literature for the 21st Century*, Amsterdam, Netherlands: Rodopi.

Spivak, G. C. (2006) 'World Systems and the Creole', *Narrative* 14(1): 102–112.

Springhall, J. (2001) *Decolonization Since 1945: The Collapse of European Overseas Empires*, Houndmills: Palgrave.

Spurr, D. (1993) *The Rhetoric of Empire: Colonial Discourse in Journalism, Travel Writing and Imperial Administration*, Durham and London: Duke University Press.

Spybey, T. (1996) *Globalization and World Society*, Cambridge: Polity.

Stähler, A. and Stierstorfer, K. (2009) (eds) *Writing and Fundamentalism*, Newcastle-on-Tyne: Cambridge Scholars Publications.

Stallybrass, P. and White, A. (1986) *The Politics and Poetics of Transgression*, London: Methuen.

Standing, G. (2011) *The Precariat: The New Dangerous Class*, London: Bloomsbury Academic.

Stasiulis, D. K. and Yuval-Davis, N. (1995) (ed.) *Unsettling Settler Societies: Articulations of Gender, Race, Ethnicity and Class*, London: Sage.

Steffen, W., Crutzen, P. J. and McNeill, J. R. (2007) 'The Anthropocene: Are Humans Now Overwhelming the Great Forces of Nature?' *Ambio* 36.

Stepputat, F. and Hansen, T. B. (2001) *States of Imagination: Ethnographic Explorations of the Postcolonial State*, Durham, NC: Duke University Press.

Stiglitz, J. (2002) *Globalization and Its Discontents*, New York: Norton.

Stocking, G. W. (1983) (ed.) *Observers Observed: Essays on Ethnographic Fieldwork*, Madison: University of Wisconsin Press.

Stoneham, G. (2000) '"It's a Free Country": Visions of Hybridity in the Metropolis', in A. Bery, P. Murray and W. Harris (eds) *Comparing Postcolonial Literatures: Dislocations*, Basingstoke: Macmillan.

Stratton, F. (1994) *African Literature and the Politics of Gender*, London and New York: Routledge.

Strelein, L. (2009) *Compromised Jurisprudence: Native Title Cases Since Mabo*, Canberra: Aboriginal Studies Press.

Strich, F. (2010) *Goethe and World Literature*, Whitefish: Kessinger Press,

Strongman, L. (2014) 'Postcolonialism and International Development Studies: A Dialectical Exchange?', *Third World Quarterly* 35(8): 1343–1354.

Sugirtharajah, R. S. (2001) *The Bible in the Third World: Precolonial, Colonial, Postcolonial Encounter*, Cambridge: Cambridge University Press.

Sugirtharajah, R. S. (2002) *Postcolonial Criticism and Biblical Interpretation*, Oxford: Oxford University Press.

Sugirtharajah, R. S. (2005) *Bible and Empire: Postcolonial Explorations*, Cambridge: Cambridge University Press.

Suleri, S. (1992) 'Woman Skin Deep: Feminism and the Postcolonial Condition', *Critical Inquiry* 18(4) (Summer): 756–769.

Supriya, K. E. (2004) *Remembering Empire: Power, Memory, and Place in Postcolonial India*, New York: Peter Lang.

Swearingen, C. J. (2004) 'The New Literacy/Orality Debates: Ebonics and the Redefinition of Literacy in Multicultural Settings', in A. A. Lunsford and L. Ouzgane (eds) *Crossing Borderlands: Composition and Postcolonial Studies*, Pittsburgh, PA: University of Pittsburgh Press: 238–254.

Sylvester, C. (1999) 'Development Studies and Postcolonial Studies: Disparate Tales of the "Third World"', *Third World Quarterly* 20: 703–721.

Szegedy-Maszák, M. (1996) 'Universalism and Cultural Relativism', in H. Hendrix, J. Kloek, S. Levie and W. V. Peer (eds) *The Search for a New Alphabet: Literary Studies in a Changing World*, Amsterdam: John Benjamins: 239–244.

Szeman, I. (2001) 'Who's Afraid of National Allegory? Jameson, Literary Criticism, Globalization', *South Atlantic Quarterly* 100(3): 803–827.

Szeman, I. (2003) *Zones of Instability: Literature, Postcolonialism, and the Nation*, Baltimore, MD: Johns Hopkins University Press.

Szeman, I. (2006) 'Who's Afraid of National Allegory? Jameson, Literary Criticisim, Globalization', in C. Irr and I. Buchanan (eds) *On Jameson: From Postmodernism to Globalization*, Albany: State University of New York Press.

Szwed, J. F. (1975) 'Race and the Embodiment of Culture', *Ethnicity* 2: 19–33.

Talib, I. S. (2002) *The Language of Postcolonial Literatures: An Introduction*, London: Routledge.

Tate, S. A. (2023) *Creolization/Créolité*, Oxford: Oxford University Press.

Taussig, M. (1993) *Mimesis and Alterity*, New York: Routledge.

Taylor, D. (2003) *The Archive and the Repertoire: Performing Cultural Memory in the Americas*, Durham, NC: Duke University Press.

Taylor, G. R. (1971) (ed.) *The Turner Thesis: Concerning the Role of the Frontier in American History*, Lexington, MA: Heath.

Taylor, P. (1995) 'Rereading Fanon, Rewriting Caribbean History', in G. Rajan and R. Mohanram (eds) *Postcolonial Discourse and Changing Cultural Contexts: Theory and Criticism*, Westport, CT: Greenwood.

Terdiman, R. (1985) *Discourse/Counter-Discourse: The Theory and Practice of Symbolic Resistance in Nineteenth-Century France*, Ithaca and London: Cornell University Press.

Thakkar, H. (2009) 'Critical Issue in Steamlining Environmental Management of Hydel Projects in India', in K. Prasad and R. S. Goel (eds) *Environmental Management in Hydro Electric Projects*. New Delhi: Concept.

Thayer, C. A. (1989) *War by Other Means: National Liberation and Revolution in Vietnam 1954–60*, Sydney: Allen & Unwin.

Thieme, J. (1996) *The Arnold Anthology of Postcolonial Literatures in English*, London: Arnold.

Thobani, S. (2015) 'Living History, Performing Coloniality: Towards a Postcolonial Ethnography', *Anthropology in Action* 22(3): 43–51.

Thomas, N. (1994) *Colonialism's Culture: Anthropology, Travel and Government*, Oxford: Polity Press.

Thomas, S. (ed.) 'Decolonising Bodies', *Special Issue New Literatures Review* 30 (Winter).

Thompson, V. B. (1987) *The Making of the African Diaspora in the Americas, 1441–1900*, Harlow, Essex and New York: Longman.

Thorpe, B. (1996) *Colonial Queensland: Perspectives on a Frontier Society*, St Lucia, QLD: University of Queensland Press.

Thrift, N. (2004) 'Intensities of Feeling: Towards a Spatial Politics of Affect', *Geografiska Annaler* 86B(1): 57–78.

Tiffin, H. (1983) 'Commonwealth Literature: Comparison and Judgement', in D. Riemenschneider (ed.) *The History and Historiography of Commonwealth Literature*, Tübingen: Narr.

Tiffin, H. (1984) 'Commonwealth Literature and Comparative Methodology', *World Literature Written in English* 23(1): 26–30.

Tiffin, H. (1987) 'Comparative Literature and Postcolonial Counter-Discourse', *Kunapipi* 9(3).

Tiffin, H. (1995) 'Postcolonial Literatures and Counter-Discourse', in B. Ashcroft, G. Griffiths and H. Tiffin (eds) *The Postcolonial Studies Reader*, London: Routledge: 95–98.

Todaro, M. P. and Smith, S. C. (2009) *Economic Development*, 10th edition, Harlow: Addison Wesley.

Todd, L. (1984) *Modern Englishes: Pidgins and Creoles*, Oxford: Basil Blackwell.

Todorov, T. (1984) *Mikhail Bakhtin: The Dialogical Principle*, Minneapolis: University of Minnesota.

Torgovnick, M. (1990) *Gone Primitive: Savage Intellects, Modern Lives*, Chicago: Chicago University Press.

Toussaint, E. (1998) *Your Money or Your Life! The Tyranny of Global Finance*, London: Pluto Press.

Treat, J. (1996) (ed.) *Native and Christian: Indigenous Voices on Religious History in the United States and Canada*, New York: Routledge.

Trees, K. (1997) 'The Politics of Postcolonial Reading Practices as They Relate to the Work of Aboriginal Writers', in A. Collett, L. Jensen, A. Rutherford and B. Thogersen (eds) *Teaching Postcolonialism and Post-Colonial Literatures, Aarhus*, Denmark: Aarhus University Press: 155–159.

Trigger, D. S. (1992) *Whitefella Comin': Aboriginal Responses to Colonialism in Northern Australia*, Cambridge and Sydney: Cambridge University Press.

Trigger, D. S. and Asche, W. (2010) 'Christianity, Cultural Change and the Negotiation of Rights in Land and Sea', *The Australian Journal of Anthropology* 21: 90–109.

Turner, B. S. (1990) (ed.) *Theories of Modernity and Postmodernity*, London: Sage.

Turner, B. S. (1994) *Orientalism, Postmodernism, and Globalism*, London: Routledge.

Turner, F. J. (1961) *Frontier and Section: Selected Essays of Frederick Jackson Turner*, Englewood Cliffs, NJ: Prentice-Hall.

Turner, F. J. (1962) *The Frontier in American History*, with a foreword by R. Allen Billington, New York: Holt, Rinehart.

Turner, L. and Neville, H. A. (2020) (eds) *Frantz Fanon's Psychotherapeutic Approaches to Clinical Work: Practicing Internationally with Marginalized Communities*, London and New York: Routledge.

Ukai, S. and Harrington, L. E. (2005) 'Colonialism and Modernity', in R. F. Calichman (ed.) *Contemporary Japanese Thought*, New York: Columbia University Press.

Unigwe, C. (2009) *On Black Sisters' Street*, London: Jonathan Cape.

Van der Veer, P. (2005) 'Global Conversions', in J. S. Scott, and G. Griffiths (eds) *Mixed Messages: Materiality, Textuality Missions,* New York: Palgrave/ Macmillan.

Van Meersbergen, G. (2017) 'Writing East India Company History after the Cultural Turn: Interdisciplinary Perspectives on the Seventeenth-Century East India Company and Verenigde Oostindische Compagnie', *Journal for Early Modern Cultural Studies* 17(3): 10–36.

Vandergeest, P. (2003) 'Land to Some Tillers: Development-Induced Displacement in Laos', *International Social Science Journal* 55(175) (March).

Varadharajan, A. (1995) *Exotic Parodies: Subjectivity in Adorno, Said, and Spivak*, Minneapolis: University of Minnesota Press.

Veer, P. V. D. (1995) (ed.) *Nation and Migration: The Politics of Space in the South Asian Diaspora*, Philadelphia: University of Pennsylvania Press.

Venn, C. (2006) *The Postcolonial Challenge: Towards Alternative Worlds*, London: Sage.

Venuti, L. (2004) *The Translation Studies Reader*, London: Routledge.

Verdesio, G. (2002) 'The Original Sin Behind the Creation of a New Europe: Economic and Ecological Imperialism in the River Plate', in S. Arias and M. Meléndez (eds) *Mapping Colonial Spanish America: Places and Commonplaces of Identity, Culture, and Experience*, Lewisburg, PA: Bucknell University Press: 137–158.

Vidal, H. and Jara, R. (1986) (eds) *Testimonio y Literatura*, Minneapolis: Institute for the Study of Ideologies and Literature.

Vilanova, M. (1977) 'Mestizaje y marginación: El laberinto de la identidad en la America latina', *Cuadernos Hispanoamericanos: Revista Mensual de Cultura Hispanica* 320–321: 285–299.

Viser, M. (2012) 'Romney's World View Tied to Culture Remark', *Boston.com* (August 3, 2012).

Viswanathan, G. (1987) 'The Beginnings of English Literary Study in India', *Oxford Literary Review* 9(1 and 2).

Viswanathan, G. (1989) *Masks of Conquest: Literary Study and British Rule in India*, New York: Columbia University Press.

Viswanathan, G. (1998) *Outside the Fold: Conversion, Modernity and Belief*, Princeton, NJ: Princeton University Press.

Waite, L. (2009) 'A Place and Space for a Critical Geography of Precarity?' *Geography Compass* 3(1): 412–433.

Walcott, D. (1974) 'The Muse of History', in O. Coombes (ed.) *Is Massa Day Dead? Black Moods in the Caribbean*, New York: Doubleday.

Walder, D. (2000) 'The Necessity of Error: Memory and Representation in the New Literatures', in S. Nasta (ed.) *Reading the 'New' Literatures in a Postcolonial Era*, Cambridge: Brewer: 149–170.

Waldron, J. (2001) 'What Is Cosmopolitan?' *Journal of Political Philosophy* 8(2): 227–243.

Wallerstein, I. (1974a) *The Modern World System: Capitalist Agriculture and the Origin of the European World-Economy in the Sixteenth Century*, New York: Academic Press.

Wallerstein, I. (1974b) 'The Rise and Future Demise of the World Capitalist System: Concepts for Comparative Analysis', *Comparative Studies in Society and History* 16(3): 387–415.

Wallerstein, I. (1976) 'A World-System Perspective on the Social Sciences', *British Journal of Sociology* 27(3): 343–352.

Wallerstein, I. (1980) *The Capitalist World Economy,* Cambridge: Cambridge University Press.

Wallerstein, I. (1991) *Geopolitics and Geoculture: Essays on the Changing World System*, Cambridge: Cambridge University Press.

Walsh, C. (2012) '"Other" Knowledges, "Other" Critiques: Reflections on the Politics and Practices of Philosophy and Decoloniality in the "Other" America', *Transmodernity: Journal of Peripheral Cultural Production of the Luso-Hispanic World* 1(3): 11–27.

Walvin, J. (1992) *Black Ivory: A History of British Slavery*, London: Harper Collins.

Walvin, J. (1996) *Questioning Slavery*, London: Routledge.

Walzer, B. (2023) 'A Rhetoric of Everyday Violence: Embodied Slow Violence', *Philosophy and Rhetoric* 56: 3–4.

Ward, P. (2002) *Exile, Emigration, and Irish Writing*, Dublin: Irish Academic Press.

Ware, V. (1993) *Beyond the Pale: White Women, Racism and History*, London: Verso.

Warren, K. J. (2000) *Ecofeminist Philosophy: A Western Perspective on What It Is and Why It Matters*, Lanham, MD: Rowman and Littlefield.

Wasserman, R. (1984) 'Re-inventing the New World: Cooper and Alencar', *Comparative Literature* 36(2) (Spring).

Wasserman, R. (1994) *Exotic Nations: Literature and Cultural Identity in the United States and Brazil, 1830–1930*, Ithaca: Cornell University Press.

Watt, I. (1957) *The Rise of the Novel*, London: Chatto & Windus.

Weber, D. J. and Rausch, J. M. (1994) (eds) *Where Cultures Meet: Frontiers in Latin American History*, Wilmington, DE: SR Books.

Weber, M. (1968a) *Max Weber on Charisma and Institution Building: Selected Papers*, edited with introduction by S. N. Eisenstadt, Chicago: University of Chicago Press.

Weber, M. (1968b) *Economy and Society*, Vol. 1, New York: Bedminster Press.

Weber, M. (1970) *Max Weber: The Interpretation of Social Reality*, edited with an introduction by J. E. T. Eldridge, London: Joseph.

Weber, M. (1983) *Max Weber on Capitalism, Bureaucracy, and Religion: A Selection of Texts*, edited and in part newly translated by S. Andreski, London and Boston: Allen & Unwin.

Weedon, C. (1999) *Feminism, Theory, and the Politics of Difference*, Malden, MA: Blackwell Publishers.

Weisbord, R. G. (1973) *Ebony Kinship: Africa, Africans, and the Afro-American*, Westport, CT: Greenwood Press.

Werbner, P. (2006) 'Vernacular Cosmopolitanism', *Theory, Culture, Society* 23(2–3): 496–498.

Werbner, R. P. and Stoller, P. (2002) (ed.) *Postcolonial Subjectivities in Africa*, New York: Zed Books.

Wesseling, H. L. (1997) *Imperialism and Colonialism: Essays on the History of European Expansion*, Westport, CT: Greenwood Press.

West-Pavlov, R. (2005) *Transcultural Graffiti: Diasporic Writing and the Teaching of Literary Studies*, Amsterdam, Netherlands: Rodopi.

West-Pavlov, R. (2010) *Spaces of Fiction, Fictions of Space: Postcolonial Place and Literary DeiXis*, Basingstoke: Palgrave Macmillan.

Weston, R. (1996) *Modernism*, London: Phaidon.

White, J. (1985) *Black Leadership in America, 1895–1968*, London and New York: Longman.

Whitlock, G. (1995) *Outlaws of the Text: Women's Bodies and the Organisation of Gender in Imperial Space*. Paper presented at the Australia/Canada: Postcolonialism and Women's Texts research seminar, Calgary Institute for the Humanities, February, 1992; reproduced in Ashcroft et al. (1995).

Whitlock, G. (2018) 'Bringing Literature to Rights: Asylum Seekers as Subjects of English', in G. Griffiths and P. Mead (eds) *The Social Work of Narrative: Human Rights and the Cultural Imaginary*, Stuttgart: Ibidem: 161–182.

Willey, A. (2016) 'A World of Materialisms: Postcolonial Feminist Science Studies and the New Natural', *Science, Technology and Human Values* 41(6): 991–1014.

Williams, D. W. (1969) *Image and Idea in the Arts of Guyana*, Georgetown, Guyana: Edgar Mittelholzer Memorial Lectures, National History and Arts Council, Ministry of Information.

Williams, E. (1964) *Capitalism and Slavery*, London: André Deutsch.

Williams, E. (1966) *British Historians and the West Indies*, London: André Deutsch.

Williamson, J. (2002) 'Did the Washington Consensus Fail?', Centre for Strategic and International Studies. Washington, DC, https://www.iie.com/publications/papers/paper.cfm?ResearchID=488.

Wilson, B., Burnston, A., Calderon, C. and Csordas, T. J. (2023) '"Letting Die" by Design: Asylum Seekers' Lived Experience of Postcolonial Necropolitics', *Social Science and Medicine*. https://doi.org/10.1016/j.socscimed.2023.115714.

Wilson, E. (2004) *Psychosomatic: Feminism and the Neurological Body*, Durham, NC: Duke University Press.

Wise, C. (1995) 'The Dialectics of Négritude: Or, The (Post)Colonial Subject in Contemporary African-American Literature', in G. Rajan and R. Mohanram (eds) *Postcolonial Discourse and Changing Cultural Contexts: Theory and Criticism*, Westport, CT: Greenwood.

Wisker, G. (2000) *Postcolonial and African American Women's Writing: A Critical Introduction*, Basingstoke: Macmillan.

Wisker, G. (2007) *Key Concepts in Postcolonial Literature*, Basingstoke: Palgrave Macmillan.

Wittgenstein, L. (1958) *The Blue and Brown Books*, Oxford: Blackwell (1975).

Woddis, J. (1967) *Introduction to Neo-colonialism*, New York: International Publishers (1972).

Wolch, J. and Emel, J. (1998) (eds) *Animal Geographies Place Politics and Identity: The Nature-Culture Borderlands*, London: Verso.

Wolfe, C. (1998) 'Old Orders for New: Ecology, Animal Rights and the Poverty of Humanism', *Diacritics* 28(2): 28–40.

Wolfe, C. (2003) *Animal Rites: American Culture, the Discourse of Species and Posthumanist Theory*, Chicago and London: University of Chicago Press.

Wolfe, P. (1999) *Settler Colonialism and the Transformation of Anthropology: The Politics and Poetics of an Ethnographic Event*, London: Cassell.

Wolpert, S. (2006) *Shameful Flight: The Last Years of the British Empire in India*, Oxford and New York: Oxford University Press.

Woods, D. (1986) *Apartheid: A Graphic Guide*, illustrated by M. Bostock, London: Camden Press.

Wright, C. (2002) 'Centrifugal Logics: Eagleton and Spivak on the Place of "Place" in Postcolonial Theory', *Culture, Theory, and Critique* 43(1): 67–82.

Wright, R. (1994 [1956]) *The Color Curtain*, Jackson, MS: University of Mississippi Press.

Wynter, S. (1990) 'Beyond Miranda's Meanings', in C. B. Davies and E. S. Fido (eds) *Out of the Kumbla: Caribbean Women and Literature*, Trenton, NJ: Africa World Press. Reprinted in A. Donnell and S. L. Welsh (1996) (eds) *The Routledge Reader in Caribbean Literature*, London and New York: Routledge.

Wynter, S. (2003) 'Unsettling the Coloniality of Being/Power/Truth/Freedom: Towards the Human, After Man, Its Overrepresentation – An Argument', *The New Centennial Review* 3(3): 257–337.

Wynter, S. (2015) 'Unparalleled Catastrophe for Our Specie? Or to Give Humanness a Different Future Conversations', in K. McKittrick (ed.) *Sylvia Wynter: On Being Human as Praxis*, Durham, NC: Duke University Press: 20.

Yee, J. (2016) 'Exoticism and Colonialism', in J. D. Lyons (ed.) *The Cambridge Companion to French Literature*, Cambridge: Cambridge University Press.

Young, R. J. C. (1990) *White Mythologies: Writing History and the West*, London: Routledge.

Young, R. J. C. (1995) *Colonial Desire: Hybridity in Theory, Culture and Race*, London: Routledge.

Young, R. J. C. (1998) 'The Overwritten Unwritten: Nationalism and Its Doubles in Postcolonial Theory', in T. D'haen (ed.) *(Un)Writing Empire,* Amsterdam, Netherlands: Rodopi: 15–34.

Young, R. J. C. (2001) *Postcolonialism: An Historical Introduction,* Oxford: Blackwell.

Young, R. J. C. (2003) *Postcolonialism: A Very Short Introduction,* Oxford: Oxford University Press.

Zabus, C. and Das, S. K. (2020) 'Hijras, Sangomas and Their Translects: Trans(lat)ing India and South Africa', *Interventions* 23(6): 1–24.

Zajonc, R. B. (1980) 'Feeling and Thinking: Preferences Need No Inferences', *American Psychologist* 35: 151–175.

Zalasiewicz, J., Williams, M., Haywood, A. and Ellis, M. (2011) 'The Anthropocene: A New Epoch of Geological Time?' *Philosophical Transactions of the Royal Society*: 835–841.

Zalums, E (Elmar) and Stafford, H. (1980) *A Bibliography of Western Australian Royal Commissions, Select Committees of Parliament and Boards of Inquiry, 1870–1979,* Adelaide: Blackwood.

Zambare, A. V. (2003) 'The Orality of Information Culture: An Interface between Hypertextual and Postcolonial Narrative', *Journal of Commonwealth and Postcolonial Studies* 10(2): 55–71.

Zamora, L. P. and Faris, W. B. (eds) *Magical Realism: Theory, History,* Durham, NC: Duke University Press.

Zavala, I. M. (1992) *Colonialism and Culture: Hispanic Modernisms and the Social Imaginary,* Bloomington: Indiana University Press.

Zeigler, M. B. (1996) 'Postcolonial Contexts of African American Vernacular English', *Journal of Commonwealth and Postcolonial Studies* 4(1).

Zeigler, M. H. and Osinubi, V. (2012) 'Theorizing the Poskoloniality of African American English', *Journal of Black Studies* 32(5): 588.

Ziff, B. H. and Rao, P. V. (1997) (eds) *Borrowed Power: Essays on Cultural Appropriation,* New Brunswick, NJ: Rutgers University Press.

NAME INDEX

Achebe, Chinua 23, 303
Adams, Vincanne 272
Adeeko, Adeleke 279
Ahmad, Aijaz 11, 31, 107, 137, 181,
    229, 266, 268–269, 294
Albrow, Martin 171–172
Alexis, Jacques Stephen 200–201,
    236
Althusser, Louis 6, 10, 69, 204, 256,
    257, 319–320
Amin, Shahid 315
Amnesty International 122
Anderson, Virginia DeJohn 177
Anderson, Benedict 19, 149
Anderson, Warwick 272
Anzaldua, Gloria 46
Appadurai, Arjun 7, 148, 175–176, 195
Appiah, Kwame Anthony 9, 93–94,
    108, 291
Ardrey, Robert 290
Arnold, David 315
Asad, Talal 143
Ashcroft, Bill 103, 160, 207, 256,
    266, 300, 339
Atkinson, Paul 143

Bakhtin, Mikhail 179, 181, 278
Baldwin, James 23
Banner, Stuart 329
Barber, Karin 9, 106, 152, 195,
    243, 342
Barker, Francis 247

Barrett, Leonard E. 225
Barrios de Chungara, Domatila, *Let
    Me Speak* 160
Bataille, Georges 314
Batstone, David 334
Bauman, Zygmunt 174
Baumgart, Winfried 184, 261
Baxter, Paul 291
Benegal, Shyam 43
Bennelong 153
Bentham, Jeremy 314
Berkhofer, Robert F. 165
Beverley, John 329
Bhabha, Homi K. 7, 10, 13–15,
    70–72, 95, 98–100, 175–180, 194,
    212, 214, 232, 265, 266, 325, 343,
    344; *Location of Culture* 95
Biddiss, Michael D. 66
Birch, Geoffrey 248
Bishop, Alan 272
Blundell, Valda 101
Blyden, Edward Wilmot 19, 45, 236
Boehmer, Elleke D. 182
Boons-Grafé, M.-C. 247
Bose, Mihir 41, 43, 44
Brathwaite, Edward Kamau 68, 80,
    97–98, 222–223, 244
Breckenridge, Carol, *Cosmopolitanism* 95
Breen, Keith 281, 282
Brennan, Timothy 224, 227
Brodber, Erna 244
Brydon, Diana 306

Buell, Lawrence 128, 134
Buxton, Thomas Fowell 261

Cabral, Amilcar 20–21, 83, 138,
    157–158, 230, 297, 298
Caesar Augustus 185
Camden, William 289
Campbell, Kofi Omoniyi Sylvanus 40
Carby, Hazel 160; "White Woman
    Listen" 160
Carlyle, Thomas, *Occasional Discourse
    on the Nigger Question* 290
Carruthers, Jane 101
Carter, Paul 90, 121; *The Road to
    Botany Bay* 250
Césaire, Aimé 74, 235
Charles V 307
Chatterjee, Partha 19, 68, 315
Cheah, Pheng and Robbins, Bruce,
    Cosmopolitics 93, 281, 282
Chossudovsky, Michel, *The
    Globalization of Poverty* 352
Cixous, Hélène 321
Clark, Marcus 120
Clifford, James 145, 146
Clive, Robert (Clive of India) 53, 56,
    126, 127
Coetzee, J.M., *Dusklands* 299;
    Waiting for the Barbarians 11, 249
Columbus, Christopher 47–48,
    305, 307
Comaroff, Jean 219
Connor, Michael, *The Invention of
    Terra Nullius* 328
Connor, Walker 230
Conrad, Joseph 34, 82; *Heart of
    Darkness* 27, 34, 176, 217, 303
Coombes, Annie E. 264
Crosby, Alfred W. 92, 94–95, 133
Crummell, Alexander 9, 45
Crutzen, Paul J. 15
Cudjoe, Selwyn, *Resistance and
    Caribbean Literature* 298–299
Culler, Jonathan 322
Cuvier, Georges 287

Damrosch, David 355
Darwin, Charles 312–313; *The Origin
    of Species* 288
Das, Samir, Kumar 336
Davidson, Basil 82, 169, 228,
    286, 308
Deleuze, Gilles 204, 300, 339, 340
Derrida, Jacques 22, 69, 99, 136, 243,
    266, 271, 314, 322, 361
Descartes, René 12, 318
Diop, Cheik Anta 177
Dirlik, Arif 68, 175
Donaldson, Laura 295
Douglas, Frederic 44
Du Bois, W.E.B. 44, 169, 236
DuCille, Ann 8
Dunbar, William 286

Eckermann, Johann Peter 355
El-Khader, Abd 296
Eysenck, Hans, *Race, Intelligence and
    Education* 291
Ezeigbo, Akachi *Trafficked* 334

Fanon, Frantz 9, 20, 45, 74, 100,
    138, 147, 157–158, 230, 263, 273,
    282, 291, 323, 343, 348; *Black
    Skin, White Masks* 157, 343; *The
    Wretched of the Earth* 157
Featherstone, Mike 173–174
Ferguson, Marjorie 171
Field, Barron 120
Fishman, Joshua A. 141
Forster, E.M. 212, 266
Foucault, Michel 37, 69, 72, 76, 118,
    135, 136, 196, 234, 321–322, 324;
    Discipline and Punish 324
Frank, André Gunder 110
Fraser, Eliza 153
Freud, Sigmund 318
Friel, Brian, *Translations* 49
Furniss, Graham 342

Galeano, Eduardo 117
Gallagher, John 186–187

Galton, Francis 290, 311
Garvey, Marcus 44, 236, 292
Geertz, Clifford 143
Gerima, Haile 43
Ghosh, Amitav, *The Hungry Tide* 134
Giddens, Anthony 218–219. 258
Gikandi, Simon 75–76, 177
Gilman, Sander 258
Gilroy, Paul 39–41, 45; *After Empire:
    Melancholia or Convivial Culture* 40;
    Ain't No Black in the Union Jack! 40
Giroux, Henry 221
Glissant, Edouard 46, 121, 207, 263
Gobineau, J.A. Count de 66,
    157–158, 214
Goethe, Johann Wolfgang von 355–356
Gramsci, Antonio 178–179, 314–315
Grant, Charles 14
Griffiths, Gareth 76, 78, 102, 156,
    169, 216, 245, 302
Griffiths, Michael, R. 39
Grosfuguel, Ramon 104, 359
Grove, Richard 132, 134, 177
Guattari, Félix 204, 300, 339
Guevara, Ernest Ché 230
Guha, Ranajit 68–69, 315–216
Gunew, Sneja 7, 221
Gunner, Elizabeth 344
Gurr, Andrew 151

Habermas, Jürgen 217, 219
Hall, Stuart 45, 172, 174, 257
Hammersley, Martyn 143
Hardiman, David 315
Hardt, Michael 132, 222
Hardy, Thomas 269
Harris, Wilson, *Ascent to Omai* 35,
    121, 244, 250–251, 263
Hastings, Marquess of 248
Hastings, Warwick 127, 188–189
Hill, Mike 46, 348–349
Ho Chi Minh 230
Hobsbawm, Eric, *Industry and Empire*
    186
Hobson, John, A., *Imperialism* 185

Hodge, Bob 268, 306
Hoeller, Christian 278
Hofstadter, Richard 311–312
Horton, James Africanus 19
Howarth, R.G. 85
Howell, Leonard Percival 292
Hulme, Keri, *The Bone People* 201
Hulme, Peter 47–48, 82, 'Subversive
    Archipelagoes' 86–87
Huntington, Samuel P., *The Clash of
    Civilizations* 63–64

Irigary, Luce 321
Isajaw, W.W. 138–140

James, C.L.R. 138, 157
Jameson, Frederic 10, 229–230
JanMohammed, Abdul 201–202
Jinnah, Mahammad Ali 252
Jones, Joseph, *Terranglia: The Case for
    English as a World Literature* 85

Kanafani, Ghassan, *Literature of
    Resistance in Occupied Palestine:
    1948–1966* 297–298
Kant, Immanuel: *Observations on the
    Feeling of the Beautiful and Sublime*
    287–288; *Perpetual Peace* 93–94
Kara, Siddharth, *Sex Trafficking: Inside
    the Business of Modern Slavery* 333
Keynes, John Maynard 240
Khorana, Sukhmani 211
King, Richard 167
Kipling, Rudyard 80, 82, 166, 212,
    232; 'White Man's Burden' 80
Knox, Robert, *The Races of Man* 287
Koebner, Richard 185
Kristeva, Julia 321
Kroestch, Robert 261

Lacan, Jacques 136, 202, 246–247,
    266, 320–321, 324
Lamming, George, *Natives of My
    Person* 11
Larson, Charles 345

Las Casas, Bishop 307
Lawson, Alan 237, 261
Lazarus, Neil 68–69
Lee, Dennis 261, 262
Lefevere, André 78
Lenin, Vladimir 230
Levinas, Emmanuel, *Totality and Infinity* 94
Livingstone, David 304
Locke, John, *Second Treatise of Government* 260, 328
L'Ouverture, Toussaint 308
Lugard, Frederick 57, 75
Lugones, Maria 102, 103

Macaulay, Thomas Babington, *Minute to Parliament* 61–62, 212
McLeod, A.L., *The Commonwealth Pen* 85
Malinowski, Bronislav 271
Marley, Bob 243, 293
Marquez, Gabriel Garcia 200
Marx, Karl 67–68, 93, 318–319
Massumi, Brian 5
Mathews, Freya 28–29
Maxwell, Anne 264
Maxwell, D.E.S., 'Landscape and Theme' 86
Mba, Nina Emma 233
Mbembe, Achille 31, 233–235; *On the Postcolony* 275
Mercator, Gerardus 149, 203–204, 262
Mies, Maria 129, 130
Mignolo, Walter, D. 93, 103–105
Mishra, Vijay 268, 306
Mohanty, Chandra Talpade 124, 160–161, 181, 269
Moraes-Farias, P.F. de 9, 74, 110, 184
Morris, Desmond 223
Moses, Anna Mary 'Granma' 217
Mountbatten, Louis (Lord) 192–193
Mudimbe, V.Y. 75, 177
Mukherjee, Arun P. 237
Muysken, Pieter 196

Naipaul, V. S. 154, 155; *The Mimic Men* 156, 254
Nandy, Ashish 84
Napoleon III, 184
Negri, Antonio 132–133, 222, 237
Neto, Agostinho 230
Neville, A.O. Aboriginal Protector 1936–1940 313
Ngugi wa Thiong'o 23–24, 107
Nkrumah, Kwame 103, 106, 230, 236–237; *Neo-Colonialism: The Last Stage of Imperialism* 351

Okri, Ben 242; *The Famished Road* 149
Omai 35, 153
Ortiz, Fernando 335
Orwell, George 212
Oyewùmí, Oyerónké 256

Pandey, Gyan 315
Parry, Benita 68, 137, 181, 232, 269, 356
Phillips, A.A. 109
Picasso, Pablo 217, 285
Plumwood, Val 129–130
Polo, Marco 154
Pratt, Mary Louise 248–249, 335
Protagoras 18, 92

Quijano, Anibal 79, 102–105

Rabasa, José 149, 203, 262
Radcliffe, Sir Cyril 252–253
Rama, Angel 335
Renan, Ernest 223–224, 227
Rhodes, Cecil 58
Rhys, Jean, *Wide Sargasso Sea* 271
Rich, Paul B. 289, 290
Richardson, Henry Handel, *The Fortunes of Richard Mahony* 151
Rimbaud, Arthur 217
Robbins, Bruce 93–95, 124, 174–175, 196
Robinson, Ronald 36, 186

Roederer, Romaine, S. 348

Rousseau, Henri 284

Rousseau, Jean-Jacques: *A Discourse on Inequality* 303–304; *Essay on the Origin of Languages* 34

Roy, Arundhati 123, 129, 310

Rushdie, Salman 26, 108, 253; *Midnight's Children* 149, 193–194

Rutherford, Anna 89

Said, Edward 10, 20, 64–65, 69, 71, 79, 90, 138, 156, 157, 162–163, 184, 187, 282; *Culture and Imperialism* 157; *Orientalism* 119, 244–246

Saro Wiwa, Ken 134

Sartre, Jean Paul 235; *Being and Nothingness* 246

Saussure, Ferdinand de 25, 71, 250

Sauvy, Alfred 331

Schermerhorn, Richard A. 138, 141

Schiller, Herbert 116

Scholte, Jan A. 172

Senghor, Leopold Sédar 235–236

Sestiere, Maurice 42

Shiva, Vandara 129, 130

Showalter, Elaine 336

Singer, Peter 313–314

Slemon, Stephen 11, 267–268, 299, 332

Smith, Adam 185, 240

Smith, Anthony 148–149

Smith, Charles Hamilton, *The Natural History of the Human Species* 220

Smith, Michael 243

Smith, Paul 322

Somerville, Margaret 90

Spears, David 291

Spencer, Herbert 311

Spencer, Stanley 284

Spengler, Oswald 208

Spenser, Edmund 289

Spivak, Gayatri 10, 13, 51, 68, 69, 135, 137, 161, 175, 232, 248, 265, 266, 316–317, 359–360

Spurr, David 23, 34, 325

Spybey, Tony 173

Stalin, Joseph 225, 230

Stallybrass, Peter 214

Strich, Fritz 356

Suleri, Sara 160

Tafari, Ras 292

Taussig, Michael 335

Terdiman, Richard 95–96, 299

Thrift, Nigel 5, 6

Tilak, Bal Gangadhar 91, 293

Todorov, Tzvetan 13

Touré, Sekou 230

Turner, Bryan S. 161

Turner, Frederick Jackson 165–166

Viswanathan, Gauri 61, 90–91

Vivekananda, Sri 293

Wake, Clive 177

Walcott, Derek 244

Wallerstein, Immanuel 104, 280, 356–359

Washington, Booker T. 44

Wasserman, Renata 153

Whitlock, Gillian 161, 264

Williams, Denis 51–52, 62, 121

Williams, Eric, *British Historians and the West Indies* 271

Williamson, John 346, 347

Winthrop, John 38

Wolch, Jennifer 95, 134

Wolfe, Cary 314, 361

Woolagoodja, Donny 101

Wright, Richard, *The Color Curtain* 31

Wynter, Sylvia 17

Yeats, William Butler, *Savage God* 217

Young, Robert 70–71, 98, 181–182, 214–215, 269–270, 327

Zabus, Chantal 336

Zajonc, R.B. 5

Zamora, Lois P. 200

Zimmerman, Marc 329

SUBJECT INDEX

Aboriginal peoples 3, 12, 18, 25, 29, 38–39, 45, 51, 82, 133, 135, 164, 192–193, 199, 200, 217, 231, 260, 264, 285, 312–313, 328; *see also* Australian Aboriginal
abrogation 3–4, 207, 365
acculturation 25, 97, 98, 335
affect 6–7
affiliation 162–163, 208, 315
Africa: and charter companies 57–58; cultural imperialism in 25, 61–62, 75–76, 116, 153, 188, 208; decolonization of 104, 106, 107; diaspora 9, 152; independence 188; mapping of 49, 190; National Liberation Movements in 237; nationalism 228, 230; as postcolony 275–278; and religion 91, 215, 294–295; scramble for vii, 60, 184, 215–216, 304–305; and slavery 39, 114, 307, 333–334; transportation of peoples 333–334
African–American studies 8–10, 43, 169
African National Congress 296
agency 10, 137, 172, 174–175, 196, 203, 268, 273, 292, 323, 331, 354, 358
Algeria 169, 230, 282, 306
allegory 10–12, 202
alterity 12–13, 202
ambivalence 13–15, 33–34, 99, 166, 169, 180, 182–183, 212, 214, 232, 247, 260, 341

American literature 85, 86
American Studies 165, 206
Anthropocentrism 18–19, 133, 272, 361
Anthropological Institute 289
anthropology 133, 143–146, 150, 206, 243, 273
anti-colonial 91, 157
anti-colonialism 19–21, 27, 181, 189, 301
Antilles 47
apartheid 21–23, 82, 214, 296, 306, 348
appropriation 19, 23–24, 36, 51, 84, 91, 102, 112, 149, 159, 173, 194, 197, 294, 299, 326, 353
Argentina 131, 239, 305
Atavism 26–27
Australia: colonial policies 113, 257–258; dislocation in 86, 121, 139, 151; and epistemic violence 135–136; and the exotic 101, 111, 153, 203; independence 81; maps of 49; metropolitan aspect 142; as Neo-Europe ecology 92, 131; settler society 70, 80, 90, 236, 261
Australian Aboriginal 3, 12, 18, 29, 231; and art 285; and biopolitics 38; and black consciousness 45; and Dreaming traditions 12, 29, 260; and First Nations 164; and restitution 264;

and sovereignty 191–193; and stolen generations 312
authentic, authenticity 24, 27–28, 84, 102, 159; and feminism 150, 233
axial/deontic 28–29
Azores 154

Bandung Conference 29–32
Berlin Congo Conference (1885) 184
binarism 32–35, 66, 208, 358
biogenetic law 26
biopolitics/biopower 37–39, 76, 234
bioprospectors 36
black African 40, 206, 235, 286–287
Black Atlantic 39–41, 45, 235
black consciousness 44–45, 158
Black is Beautiful movement 110
Black studies 44–45; the body 161
Bollywood 41–44
borderlands 46, 89
Borneo 3
Brazil 40, 73, 97, 113, 198, 307
Brazza-Moroko, Treaty of (1882) 184
Bretton Woods Conference 31, 238, 350
Britain 40, 55, 57, 70, 80, 81, 85, 86, 97, 115, 125, 127, 141, 158, 184, 186, 208, 209, 256, 289, 290, 308
British Empire 31, 42, 58, 85, 139, 153, 186, 208, 240, 354

Canada: borderland 46; First Nations in 84, 164; First World etc 331–332; independence 81; and indigenous sovereignty 192; and mapping 190; and migrants 209; Neo-Europes 131, 239; as Neo-Europe 92; religion in 295; settler colony 80, 139, 305; World Englishes 353
Canaries 154
cannibal 47–50, 307
capitalism 11, 16, 59, 92, 93, 103, 106, 109, 111, 128, 134, 170, 173,
185–186, 209, 225, 229–230, 236–237, 239–240, 283–284, 305, 331, 357–359
Caribbean 40, 45, 48–49, 74, 97, 98, 121, 132, 154, 170, 189, 206, 233, 235, 236, 251, 271, 292, 293, 296, 298, 305, 307–309, 333; and Magic Realism 200
Caribbean English 45, 96–97, 222–223, 257, 354
cartography 49–51, 53, 150, 154, 165, 190–191, 203–205, 218, 259
catachresis 51, 164
catalysis 51–53, 251
catalytic cultures 121
centre/margin (periphery) 33, 53–54, 115, 300
Charter Companies 54–59, 73
Chicano studies 9
Chimerican Age 237, 299
China 59, 60, 64, 114, 154, 224, 237, 238, 240, 280
chromatism 60–61, 263
civilizations, clash of 63–66
civilizing mission 25, 34, 38, 53, 61–63, 74, 135, 187, 219, 240, 293, 304, 311, 335; see also missions/missionaries
colonial discourse 10, 13–15, 33, 47, 61, 69, 71–73, 86–88, 118, 136, 143, 181, 188, 194, 202–204, 206, 207, 211–213, 218, 231, 232, 247, 248, 251, 265–266, 269, 270, 300, 305, 320, 323
Colonial Educational Systems 77
colonial governance 19, 57, 62, 73–75
Colonial Literature Bureau 77
Colonial patronage 77–78
Colonialism 79–83
Commonwealth 85
Commonwealth literature 85–88, 241, 266
comprador 24, 88–89, 100, 106, 107, 157, 189

contact zone 46, 89–90, 179, 335
contrapuntal reading 90, 163,
    209, 271
conversion 25, 63, 90–92, 168, 300,
    324–325
conviviality 41, 277
cosmopolitanism 92–95, 183, 282
counter-discourse 10, 11, 95–96, 257
Creole/Pidgins 45, 96–97, 179, 206,
    257–258, 353–354
creolization 53, 97–98
critical globalism 171
critical nationalism 157
critical whiteness studies 221
Cuba/Cuban 230, 296, 307, 335
cultural capital 174, 208, 354–355
cultural change 97, 194, 316, 358
cultural decolonization 204
cultural difference/diversity 83,
    98–100, 102, 157, 180, 220, 222,
    228, 232, 337
cultural disruption 260
cultural gap 207
cultural tourism 100–102

decoloniality 17, 21, 102–105,
    208, 359
decolonization 17, 27, 59, 103,
    105–109, 111, 115, 128, 157, 172,
    181, 209, 232, 233, 296, 336, 358
dependency theory 109–110, 112
deracinate 110
desire, colonial 70–71
development/development studies
    50, 111–113, 332
diaspora 39, 45, 95, 114–115, 142,
    148, 185, 233, 280, 336–338, 341
dislocation 129–122, 218, 234, 252,
    255, 258, 341
displacement 136, 147, 152, 211, 225,
    302, 311; and indigenous societies
    344, 352; and place 258–261
double colonization 124, 161, 205,
    256, 263, 296
double vision 212

dreaming (aboriginal) 12, 29
Dutch East Indies 54

East India Company 54–58, 124–127
ecofeminism 128–130
ecological imperialism 114, 131–133,
    239, 262
Egypt 30, 58, 166, 184, 224, 292
Empire 7, 8, 11, 27, 31, 33, 40, 42,
    48, 53, 55, 58, 61, 62, 72, 81,
    109, 117, 119, 124–126, 132–133,
    139, 153, 161, 163, 166, 170, 178,
    184–186, 208, 227, 237, 238, 240,
    247–249, 256, 266, 289, 337, 338,
    354; as term in Hardt and Negri
    85–87, 215   .
environmentalism 59, 128, 133–136
essentialism 28, 136–138, 232,
    316, 317
ethnicity 34, 41, 45, 70, 138–142, 151,
    183, 221, 228, 291, 292, 353, 357
ethno-psychiatry/psychology
    146–147
ethnography 50, 142–146, 278
Eurocentrism 18, 50, 68, 69, 149–150,
    218
exile 9, 67, 151–153, 281, 292, 306, 336
exotic, exoticism 99, 143, 153–154,
    156, 166, 232, 264, 302
expatriation 151
exploration 23, 35, 92, 150, 154–157,
    187, 202, 203, 217, 218, 227,
    262, 325

Fanonism 157–169
Far East 55, 125, 154, 245
feminism 80, 124, 129; and
    postcolonialism 159–161, 256, 257
festivals 83
Fiji 114, 233, 309
filiation 162–163
First Nations 3, 64, 164, 190,
    192–193
First Nations Development Institute
    164

First World 36, 171, 229, 330, 331
Fourth World 332
France 55, 74, 115, 125, 184, 208, 227, 296, 299, 304, 308
FRELIMO 297
French Creoles 9, 96–97
frontier 46, 164–166, 172, 260
fundamentalism 166–169, 241, 295

Ghana 236, 274, 334
global culture 22, 171, 173–174, 196–197, 229, 232
globalization 173–176, 189, 195, 222, 225, 237, 239–241, 272, 279, 281–282, 284, 295, 310, 347, 358
glocalization 174–176, 196
going native 27, 71, 176, 232
Gold Coast 274
Green Postcolonialism 177–178
Guinea-Bissau 230, 297

hegemony 6, 21, 24, 163, 173, 178–179, 188, 213, 215, 244–245, 300, 314, 319, 344, 348
Hottentot Venus 153, 161
hybridity 15, 34, 74, 89, 98–99, 115, 179–183, 194, 221, 326–327

imperialism vii, 8, 14, 33–35, 49, 57, 60, 66, 69, 72, 79–83, 87, 90, 102–103, 106, 111, 114, 116, 119, 123, 124, 127, 132–133, 157, 159, 162, 171–173, 175, 184–188, 205, 210, 212, 215, 219, 226, 227, 236–238, 248, 256–257, 262, 266, 269, 286, 289, 292–293, 297, 300, 316, 347, 352, 358, 360
indentured labour 84, 114, 309; *see also* slave, slavery
independence 9, 19, 30–31, 42, 53, 56, 73, 78, 80–83, 88, 89, 100, 106, 107, 109, 111, 123, 124, 126, 129, 158, 186, 188–189, 206, 209, 236, 237, 251–254, 274–275, 282, 283, 293, 294, 296, 299, 308, 344

India 75, 82, 85, 91, 95, 106, 107, 112–114, 123, 132, 152, 168, 169, 179, 183, 208, 211, 231, 241, 251, 252, 255, 293, 305, 316, 336, 342, 344, 360; and partition 252–254, 274–275; and religion 293, 295
indigenous mapping 190–191
indigenous people 3, 9, 16, 21, 25, 36, 73, 79, 82, 84, 105, 109, 131, 133, 155, 164, 255, 305, 312, 332, 333; and displacement 122, 255, 302, 352; and mapping 190–191, 204; and missions 215, 301; and sovereignty 192
Indonesia 30, 58, 60, 73, 114, 347
Industrial Revolution 15, 16, 35, 185–186
International Bank for Economic Cooperation 237
International Health Exhibition (1884) 290
International Monetary Fund (IMF) 31, 238, 239, 278, 279, 346–347, 350–352
International Women's Year Tribunal (1974) 160
interpellation 178, 194, 319; *see also* subject, subjectivity
Inuit 9, 164, 190, 192, 217
Ireland 49, 85, 166, 251, 271, 289, 306, 311, 354

Kenya 57, 147, 169, 296, 306

language appropriation 4, 23–24, 152–153
Liminality 194–195, 336
literary universality 86, 150
local 195–197

Mabo 190, 192
McWorld 195
magic realism 200–201
Malaya 58, 114, 189, 309
Malaysia 3, 189, 233

Manicheanism 201–202
Maori 45, 192, 231, 296
maps/mapping 49–51, 60, 165; *see also* cartography; indigenous mapping
margins/marginality 205–206, 256, 300; centre/margin 33, 53–54, 115, 300; colonial margins 120, 187, 223, 275; and dependency 357; and development studies 112; literary margins 330; and postcolonialism 66
Mauritius 114
Mestizo etc 46, 73, 206–207, 220
metonymic gap 207
Metropolis 33, 187, 207–208, 265, 335, 337
metropolitan 24, 45, 62, 75, 76, 78, 79, 82, 110, 114–115, 131, 146, 150, 151, 184, 207–208, 235, 269, 270, 306, 335, 337, 341, 353
Middle East 65, 245
Middle Passage 39, 79, 307, 333; *see also* slave, slavery
migrants (and refugees) 26, 95, 147, 152, 183, 209–211, 220, 234, 283, 338
mimicry 14, 33, 71, 180, 211–213, 232, 325, 326
miscegenation 22, 52, 73, 97, 187, 206, 214–215, 220, 232
mission 62, 74, 150, 215–216, 286, 288, 299, 335; and missionaries 49, 155, 185, 215, 216, 238, 331; *see also* civilizing mission
modernism 216–217, 271
modernity 217–220, 231, 234, 258, 259, 272, 273, 294; and world literature 355–357; and world system theory 358
modernization 43, 61, 78, 84, 110, 216, 219, 273, 357; and development theory 111–112; and displacement 123

Mother India 43
Mountbatten Plan 252
Mozambique 73, 198, 230, 298, 306
Mughal Empire 55, 125, 126
mulatto 206, 220
multiculturalism 26, 41, 100, 180, 183, 220–222, 228; and critical multiculturalism 221, 222
multitude 133, 222

naming 18, 49, 190, 203, 250, 262, 360
nation/nationalism 223–229
nation language 183, 222–223
national allegory 11, 229
National Liberation Movements 20, 137, 230–231, 237
nationalism and anti-colonialism 19, 20
native 231–232
Native Americans 3, 8, 9, 164
nativism 115, 158, 232–233, 280
négritude 8, 19, 45, 74, 87, 235–236
neo-colonialism 30, 83, 88, 100, 101, 103, 137, 158, 177, 228, 236–239, 267, 275, 276, 301, 351, 358
Neo-Europes 92, 95
neo-imperialism 96, 236–239
neo-liberalism 40, 238–241, 346, 347
New Englishes 353
New Imperialism 81, 116, 304
New literatures 241–242, 266
New World 31, 47, 51–54, 63, 97, 103, 121, 124, 177, 204, 217, 226; *see also* catalysis
New Zealand 45, 52, 84, 131, 134, 139, 170, 192, 231, 239, 296, 353
Nigeria 57, 58, 75, 78, 112, 146, 169, 258, 274, 308, 334
Noble Savage 303
Non-Aligned Movement 30
Norwegian Refugee Council 123

One Nation 350
orality 77, 107, 242–244, 251, 331

orient/orientalism 10, 65, 69, 71, 86, 119, 144, 150, 165, 244–246, 265, 286
orientalist 65, 223, 244, 245
orientalist discourse 325
O/other 105, 148, 202, 214, 246–247; and cosmopolitanism 93, 94; and epistemic violence 135; and worlding 360
O/othering 13, 48, 166, 247–249, 251, 285, 328, 360
otherness 34, 154, 161; and alterity 12, 13

Pakistan 30, 64, 65, 169, 189, 208, 274, 275; and partition 252–254
palimpsest 203, 249–251, 262
Papua New Guinea 216, 258, 354
Partition 251–254, 274
Pastoralism 255
patriarchy 105, 124, 159, 205, 255–257, 268
patronage 216, 279, 331, 342; see also colonial patronage 77–78
Philippines 80, 114, 169
Place 3, 39, 49, 121, 128, 130, 133, 139, 141, 166, 191, 256–263, 360; and exile 151–152; and local(ity) 336–337; and mapping 203–204, 250; and settlers 305–306; and terra nullius 251, 329
postcolonial: body 263–265; reading 270–271; science 17, 271–274; state 108, 138, 158, 189, 228, 233, 265, 267, 274–275
postcolonialism 47–49, 265–270
postcolony 41, 69, 235, 275–279, 295
post-nationalism 279–282
post-structuralism 99, 319, 322–323
precarity 282–283
primitive societies 27, 311
primitivism 34, 47, 48, 176, 246, 284–285

race: binary 34, 43, 51, 60, 61, 66, 69, 70, 72, 76, 79–82, 103, 110, 136, 138, 140, 142, 147, 151, 161, 176, 179, 182, 187, 189, 198, 199, 209, 214, 227, 228, 235, 251, 256, 261, 263, 271, 285–292, 312, 313, 323, 330, 347–350; hierarchy 22
racism 40, 41, 63, 66, 73, 74, 79, 157, 181, 198, 221, 273, 308, 309, 311, 313, 314, 361
Radcliffe Line 252
RAFI Rural Advancement Foundation 36
Rastafarianism 9, 292–293
religion 14, 25, 26, 65, 91, 140, 142, 155, 166–168, 183, 185, 189, 215–216, 292–296, 336, 338, 350
res nullius 327
resistance 12, 14, 19–21, 24, 28, 31, 34, 38, 68, 87, 92, 95, 106, 119, 159, 177, 182, 189, 205, 207, 210, 212, 228, 230, 261, 264, 266, 267, 273, 277, 292, 294, 296–301, 316, 317, 323, 325, 355
rhizome 300–301
Roman Empire 227

sacred 84, 101, 167–168, 293, 301–302, 306
savage 27, 47, 48, 53, 74, 166, 176, 214, 216, 231, 240, 260, 271, 285, 302–303, 307
Second World 16, 331–332
self 7, 80, 165, 166, 202, 246, 248, 291, 303, 318, 320, 322, 323, 360
settler 3; settler colonies 21, 70, 80, 81, 106, 109, 131, 139, 149, 151, 155, 161, 165, 166, 170, 177, 199, 214, 215, 220, 231, 239, 255, 261, 305–306, 312, 332; settler cultures 82, 87, 90, 133, 305; settler sacred 340; settler societies 242
Six Nations 164

slave, slavery 39, 79, 84, 97, 110, 114, 188, 209, 214, 220, 292, 296, 298, 307–309; black consciousness 44–45; blackbirding 104; Middle Passage 39, 79, 307

Social Darwinism 27, 261, 288, 289, 311–313, 328

South Africa 21–23, 58, 59, 83, 91, 101, 114, 153, 186, 244, 306, 331, 336, 349, 353

South Pacific 114, 209, 216, 231, 271

sovereignty 30, 134, 184; indigenous sovereignty 191–193, 234, 235, 279, 282, 327, 328, 351

Soviet Union 30, 225, 237, 331, 333

speciesism 28, 29, 313–314, 361

strategic essentialism 136–138, 232

subaltern 51, 137, 314–317, 348

subject, subjectivity 10, 11, 13, 14, 17, 28, 51, 63, 73, 76, 79, 89, 94, 124, 135, 136, 143–145, 158, 159, 163, 173, 178, 183, 194, 196, 211–213, 246, 250, 256, 259, 266, 267, 273, 276–278, 299, 302, 314, 317–323, 339, 358, 361; *see also* interpellation

surveillance 7, 116, 117, 145, 214, 278, 324–326

sustainability 112, 177, 323–324

syncretism 202, 326

synergy 180, 326–327

taboo 32–34

terra nullius 49, 155, 193, 203, 251, 327–329

testimonio 329–331

Third Space of enunciation 99, 180

Third World 11, 44, 109–112, 160, 170, 171, 224, 229, 230, 237, 267, 331–332, 360

Tiger economies 110

tourism 84–85; cultural tourism 100–102, 156, 336

trafficking 332–334

transcultural 35, 40, 46, 89, 92, 172, 173, 175, 179, 194, 196, 349

transculturation 53, 89, 180, 206, 327, 335

translation 24, 341–343

transnational literatures 340–341

trauma 343–344

travel 94, 154–157, 203, 249, 262, 325, 337, 338

UNESCO 101, 102, 238, 290

United Nations 30, 93, 111, 192, 279, 280, 332

United States 8, 9, 30, 31, 40, 44, 65, 84–86, 107, 110, 117, 130–132, 134, 138, 139, 164, 165, 167, 168, 172, 209, 220, 236–239, 278, 280, 307, 308, 311, 331, 332, 334, 347–350, 353; African American studies 8; borderland 46; First Nations in 84, 121–122, 164; frontier experience 122; and globalization 225; indigenous sovereignty 192; national parks in 95; Settler colony 305

Universal Races Congress (1911) 290

universalism, universality 280, 285, 344–346

Vietnam 169, 170, 230

Washington Consensus 240, 346–347, 351

Weltliteratur 355

West Africa 76, 78, 96, 114, 152, 176, 184, 274, 354

West Indian 9, 48, 90, 235, 242

West Indies 39, 55, 68, 73, 74, 82, 183, 184, 209

Western modernity 17, 18, 112

whiteness 41, 194, 221, 222, 343, 347–350

World Bank 31, 123, 238, 239, 278, 279, 346, 347, 350–352

World Englishes 352–355
World Literature 11, 85, 356–357
world system 69, 77, 79, 103, 104,
    112, 172, 305, 309
world system theory 79, 102, 103,
    109, 170, 355–356

World Trade Centre 41, 46
worlding 359–360

Zimbabwe (Rhodesia) 58, 147,
    274, 296
Zoocriticism 360–361